Lecture Notes in Computer Science **13971**

Founding Editors

Gerhard Goos
Juris Hartmanis

Editorial Board Members

Elisa Bertino, *Purdue University, West Lafayette, IN, USA*
Wen Gao, *Peking University, Beijing, China*
Bernhard Steffen, *TU Dortmund University, Dortmund, Germany*
Moti Yung, *Columbia University, New York, NY, USA*

The series Lecture Notes in Computer Science (LNCS), including its subseries Lecture Notes in Artificial Intelligence (LNAI) and Lecture Notes in Bioinformatics (LNBI), has established itself as a medium for the publication of new developments in computer science and information technology research, teaching, and education.

LNCS enjoys close cooperation with the computer science R & D community, the series counts many renowned academics among its volume editors and paper authors, and collaborates with prestigious societies. Its mission is to serve this international community by providing an invaluable service, mainly focused on the publication of conference and workshop proceedings and postproceedings. LNCS commenced publication in 1973.

Editors
Isaac Sserwanga
iSchool Organization
Berlin, Germany

Anne Goulding
Victoria University of Wellington
Wellington, New Zealand

Heather Moulaison-Sandy
University of Missouri
Chicago, IL, USA

Jia Tina Du
University of South Australia
Adelaide, SA, Australia

António Lucas Soares
University of Porto
Porto, Portugal

Viviane Hessami
Monash University
Clayton, VIC, Australia

Rebecca D. Frank
University of Tennessee at Knoxville
Knoxville, TN, USA

ISSN 0302-9743 ISSN 1611-3349 (electronic)
Lecture Notes in Computer Science
ISBN 978-3-031-28034-4 ISBN 978-3-031-28035-1 (eBook)
https://doi.org/10.1007/978-3-031-28035-1

© The Editor(s) (if applicable) and The Author(s), under exclusive license
to Springer Nature Switzerland AG 2023
This work is subject to copyright. All rights are reserved by the Publisher, whether the whole or part of the material is concerned, specifically the rights of translation, reprinting, reuse of illustrations, recitation, broadcasting, reproduction on microfilms or in any other physical way, and transmission or information storage and retrieval, electronic adaptation, computer software, or by similar or dissimilar methodology now known or hereafter developed.
The use of general descriptive names, registered names, trademarks, service marks, etc. in this publication does not imply, even in the absence of a specific statement, that such names are exempt from the relevant protective laws and regulations and therefore free for general use.
The publisher, the authors, and the editors are safe to assume that the advice and information in this book are believed to be true and accurate at the date of publication. Neither the publisher nor the authors or the editors give a warranty, expressed or implied, with respect to the material contained herein or for any errors or omissions that may have been made. The publisher remains neutral with regard to jurisdictional claims in published maps and institutional affiliations.

This Springer imprint is published by the registered company Springer Nature Switzerland AG
The registered company address is: Gewerbestrasse 11, 6330 Cham, Switzerland

Isaac Sserwanga · Anne Goulding ·
Heather Moulaison-Sandy · Jia Tina Du ·
António Lucas Soares · Viviane Hessami ·
Rebecca D. Frank
Editors

Information for a Better World: Normality, Virtuality, Physicality, Inclusivity

18th International Conference, iConference 2023
Virtual Event, March 13–17, 2023
Proceedings, Part I

Preface

The first wave of COVID-19 disrupted normality and changed the course of the last two years. People became more restricted to their homes. These became times of reflection with the positive effect of more scientific research and more contributions in diverse fields. The Information Sciences played a pivotal role in sustaining our engagement. Working from home became the new normal. Over time, hybrid work became preferable to in-office work as restrictions were eased. The waves of COVID-19 led to new variants, which caused more specific restrictions, but effective vaccine rollouts reduced the threat until once again borders were opened for business.

The existing and demand-driven platforms opened diverse networking opportunities. This brings us to the hybrid iConference 2023 and its virtual and physical components.

As the academic world still explored the virtual, the organizers of the 18th iConference used remote networking to complement outreach and participation globally. This was inherent in the theme of *Normality, Virtuality, Physicality, and Inclusivity.*

The virtual iConference 2023 took place 10 days before the physical conference in Barcelona, Spain. Its hosts included the Universitat Oberta de Catalunya, Monash University, and University of Illinois at Urbana-Champaign. Physical meetings took place at Casa Convalescència on the historical site of the Hospital de la Santa Creu i Sant Pau.

The conference theme attracted a total of 197 submissions with 98 Full Research Papers, 96 Short Research Papers and 3 Information Sustainability Research Papers.

In a double-blind review process by 346 internationally renowned experts, 85 entries were approved, including 36 Full Research Papers and 46 Short Research Papers. The approval rate was 37% for the Full Research Papers and 48% for the Short Research Papers. Additional submissions were selected for the Workshops and Panels, the Doctoral Colloquium, the Early Career Colloquium, the Student Symposium, the Poster session, and the Spanish-Portuguese and Chinese language paper sessions.

The Full, Short and Information Sustainability Research papers are published for the eighth time in Springer's *Lecture Notes in Computer Science* (LNCS). These proceedings are sorted into the following fourteen categories, reflecting the diversity of the information research areas: Archives and Records, Behavioral Research, Information Governance and Ethics, AI and Machine Learning, Data Science, Information and Digital Literacy, Cultural Perspectives, Knowledge Management and Intellectual Capital, Social Media and Digital Networks, Libraries, Human-Computer Interaction and Technology, Information Retrieval, Community Informatics, and Digital Information Infrastructure.

We greatly appreciate the reviewers for their expertise and valuable review work and the track chairs for their relentless effort and vast expert knowledge. We wish to extend our gratitude to the chairs and volume editors; Full Research Papers chairs, Anne Goulding from Victoria University of Wellington, and Heather Moulaison-Sandy from University of Missouri; Short Research Paper chairs, Jia Tina Du from University of

South Australia, and António Lucas Soares from Universidade do Porto; and Information Sustainability Papers chairs, Viviane Hessami from Monash University and Rebecca D. Frank from University of Tennessee.

The iConference lived up to its global representation of iSchools to harness the synergy of research and teaching in the field of information and complementary areas of sustainability.

January 2023

Isaac Sserwanga
Anne Goulding
Heather Moulaison-Sandy
Jia Tina Du
António Lucas Soares
Viviane Hessami
Rebecca D. Frank

Organization

Organizer

Universitat Oberta de Catalunya, Spain

Conference Chairs

Josep Cobarsí Morales	Universitat Oberta de Catalunya, Spain
Gillian Oliver	Monash University, Australia
J. Stephen Downie	University of Illinois at Urbana-Champaign, USA

Program Chairs

Local Arrangements Chair

Jordi Conesa	Universitat Oberta de Catalunya, Spain

Proceedings Chair

Isaac Sserwanga	Humboldt-Universität zu Berlin (iSchools.Inc), Germany

Full Research Paper Chairs

Anne Goulding	Victoria University of Wellington, New Zealand
Heather Moulaison-Sandy	University of Missouri, USA

Short Research Paper Chairs

Jia Tina Du	University of South Australia, Australia
António Lucas Soares	Universidade do Porto, Portugal

Poster Chairs

Caddie Gao	Monash University, Australia
Fredrik Hanell	Linnaeus University, Sweden

Information Sustainability Chairs

Viviane Hessami	Monash University, Australia
Rebecca D. Frank	University of Tennessee, USA

Spanish - Portuguese Papers Chairs

Sara Martínez Cardama	Universidad Carlos III de Madrid, Spain
Marta Ligia Pomim Valentim	Universidade Estadual Paulista, Brazil
Diana Lucio Arias	Pontificia Universidad Javeriana, Colombia

Chinese Paper Chairs

Lihong Zhou	Wuhan University, China
Lei Pei	Nanjing University, China
Hui Yan	Renmin University of China, China

Chinese Event Co-chairs

Di Wang	Wuhan University, China
Yuehua Zhao	Nanjing University, China
Zekun Yang	Renmin University of China, China

Workshops and Panel Chairs

Misita Anwar	Monash University, Australia
Antoni Pérez-Navarro	Universitat Oberta de Catalunya, Spain
Virginia Ortíz-Repiso	Universidad Carlos III de Madrid, Spain

Student Symposium Chairs

Emi Ishita	Kyushu University, Japan
Peter Organisciak	University of Denver, USA
Romain Herault	Linnaeus University, Sweden

Early Career Colloquium Chairs

Mary Grace Golfo-Barcelona	University of the Philippines, The Philippines
Stefanie Havelka	University College Dublin, Ireland
Kate McDowell	University of Illinois at Urbana-Champaign, USA
J. Stephen Downie	University of Illinois at Urbana-Champaign, USA

Doctoral Colloquium Chairs

Joanne Evans	Monash University, Australia
Peter Darch	University of Illinois at Urbana-Champaign, USA
Kirsten Schlebbe	Humboldt-Universität zu Berlin, Germany

Doctoral Dissertation Award Chair

Sandy Hirsh	San José State University, USA

Conference Coordinators

Michael Seadle	iSchools Organization
Slava Sterzer	iSchools Organization
Katharina Gudat	iSchools Organization

Reviewers Full and Short Papers iConference 2023 (346)

Jacob Abbott
Waseem Afzal
Noa Aharony
Shameem Ahmed
Isola Ajiferuke
Bader Albahlal
Nicole D. Alemanne
Daniel Alemneh
Hamed Alhoori
Lilach Alon
Xiaomi An
Karen Ann Subin
Misita Anwar
Muhamammad Naveed
Tatjana Aparac-Jelusic
Rhea Rowena Ubana
Hanimm Maria Astuti
Alex Ball
Jessica Kristen Barfield
Sarah Barriage
Zoe Bartliff
Gabrielle Baumert
John Robert Bautista
Nanyi Bi
Bradley Wade Bishop
Monisa Biswas
Maria Bonn
Christine L. Borgman
Theo J. D. Bothma
Guillaume Boutard
Leane Bowler
Sarah Bratt
Paulina Bressel
Jenny Bronstein

Jo Ann Brooks
Sarah A. Buchanan
Julia Bullard
Mimi Byun
Jennifer Campbell-Meier
Yu Cao
Zhe Cao
Sunandan Chakraborty
Wayland Chang
Yu-Wei Chang
Yun-Chi Chang
Tiffany Chao
Catherine Chavula
Hadyn Chen
Hsin-liang Chen
Hsuanwei Chen
Hui Chen
Jiangping Chen
Minghong Chen
Xiaoyu Chen
Chola Chhetri
Alfred Chikomba
Inkyung Choi
Wonchan Choi
Yunseon Choi
Steven Siu Fung Chong
Anthony Shong-yu Chow
Alton Y. K. Chua
Eunkyung Chung
Mónica Colón-Aguirre
Andrea Copeland
Chris Coward
Andrew Cox
Peter Cruickshank
Sally Jo Cunningham
Amber L. Cushing
Mats Dahlstrom
Gabriel David
Rebecca Davis
Mozhden Dehghani
Shengli Deng
Tom Denison
Brian Dobreski
Güleda Doğan
Karsten Donnay
Caifan Du
Yunfei Du
Yiran Duan
Kedma Duarte
Avsalom Elmalech
Aems Emswiler
Kristin Eschenfelder
Tao Fan
Bruce Ferwerda
Rachek Fleming-May
Fred Fonseca
Ina Fourie
Rebecca D. Frank
Darin Freeburg
Hengyi Fu
Yaming Fu
Maria Gäde
Abdullah Gadi
Chunmei Gan
Zheng Gao
Emmanouel Garoufallou
Yegin Genc
Diane Gill
Dion Goh
Melissa Gross
Michael Gryk
Ece Gumusel
Qiuyan Guo
Kailash Gupta
Neslihan Gurol
Ayse Gursoy
Hazel Hall
Ariel Hammond
Ruohua Han
Kun Hang
Yue Hao
Bruce Hartpence
Stefanie Havelka
Suliman Hawamdeh
Anisah Herdiyanti
Viviane Hessami
Alison Hicks
Simon Hodson
Darra Lynn Hofman
Chris Holstrom

Liang Hong
Lingzi Hong
Md Khalid Hossain
Wenjun Hou
Tsung-Ming Hsiao
Yuerong Hu
Liuyu Huang
Qian Huang
Ruhua Huang
Yun Huang
Yuting Huang
Isto Huvila
Charles Inskip
Yvette Iribe Ramirez
Vanessa Irvin
Emi Ishita
Jonathan Isip
Hiroyoshi Ito
Fariha Tasmin Jaigirdar
Sabrina Olivia Jeffcoat
Wei Jeng
Michael Jones
Heidi Julien
Jaap Kamps
Jai Kang
Ijay Kaz-Onyeakazi
Mat Kelly
Rebecca Kelly
Heikki Keskustalo
Jigya Khabar
Saurabh Khanna
Mahmood Khosrowjerdi
Jeonghyun Kim
Soo Hyeon Kim
Vanessa Kitzie
Bart Knijnenburg
Kyungwon Koh
Masanori Koizumi
Rebecca Koskela
Adam Kriesberg
Mucahid Kutlu
Sara Lafia
Sucheta Lahiri
Deborah Lee
Jian-Sin Lee
Jin Ha Lee
Jou Lee
Kijung Lee
Lo Lee
Alyssa Lees
Guangjian Li
Ying Li
Yingya Li
Lizhen Liang
Louise Limberg
Chi-Shiou Lin
Chiao Min Lin
Jenny Lindberg
Henry Linger
Zack Lischer-Katz
Ping Liu
Yuyang Liu
Jean D. Louis
Kun Lu
Ana Lucic
Xiao Luo
Lai Ma
Rongqian Ma
Kate Marek
Shutian Ma
Simon Mahony
Krista-Lee Meghan Malone
Jin Mao
Kathryn Masten
Machdel Catharina Matthee
Matthew S. Mayernik
Kate McDowell
Claire McGuinness
Pamela Ann McKinney
David McMenemy
Humphrey Mensah
Shuyuan Metcalfe
Selina Meyer
Shawne Miksa
J. Elizabeth Mills
Stasa Milojevic
Marina Milosheva
Chao Min
Yue Ming
Lorri Mon

Jennifer Moore
Atsuyuki Morishima
Lidia Morris
Angela Murillo
Karim Nader
Jessica Navedo
Leila Nemati-Anaraki
David M. Nichols
Melissa G. Ocepek
Lydia Ladi Ogbadu-Oladapo
Erezi Ruth Ogbo
Gillian Oliver
Peter Organisciak
Felipe Ortega
Abraham Oshni Alvandi
Giulia Osti
Guiyan Ou
Yohanan Ouaknine
Murat Ozer
Kathleen Padova
Shreya Paithankar
Velian Pandeliev
Hyoungjoo Park
Min Sook Park
SoHyun Park
Olivia Pestana
Bobby Phuritsabam
Mary Pietrowicz
Ola Pilerot
Alex Poole
Xin Qian
Redoan Rahman
Diane Rasmussen Pennington
Christopher B. Rauch
Alexandria Rayburn
Ariel Rosenfeld
Vassilis Routsis
Alan Rubel
Sarah Elizabeth Ryan
Jumana Salem
Rachel Salzano
Madelyn Rose Sanfilippo
Vitor Santos
Moritz Schubotz
Charles Senteio
Elizabeth Shaffer
Kalpana Shankar
Ryan Shaw
Kristina Shiroma
T. S. Paumunmuang Simte
Luanne Sinnamon
Stephen Slota
Alexander Smith
Catharine Smith
Sheetal Sonawane
Shijie Song
Clay Spinuzzi
Beth St. Jean
Gretchen Renee Stahlman
Hrvoje Stancic
Owen Stewart-Robertson
Caroline Stratton
Jacob Striebel
Besiki Stvilia
Shigeo Sugimoto
Ran Sun
Sebastian Sünkler
Tanja Svarre
Sue Yeon Syn
Andrea Karoline Thomer
Janet Toland
Chunhua Tsai
Tien-I Tsai
Alissa Tudor
Pertti Vakkari
Lulian Vamanu
Frans van der Sluis
Martie van Deventer
Nicholas Vanderschantz
Nitin Verma
Travis Wagner
Jan Philip Wahle
Di Wang
Hao Wang
Jieyu Wang
Lin Wang
Shengang Wang
Yanyan Wang
Ian Robert Watson
Seren Elisabeth Wendelken

Muhamad Prabu Wibowo
Rachel D. Williams
Steven John Wright
Dan Wu
I-Chin Wu
Peng Wu
Ting Xiao
Jian Xu
Lifang Xu
Shenmeng Xu
Xiao Xue
Hui Yan
Lijun Yang
Yu-Ju Yang
Ayoung Yoon
JungWon Yoon
Sarah Young
Bei Yu
Fei Yu
Xiaojun Yuan
Xianjin Zha
Yujia Zhai
Bin Zhang
Chengzhi Zhang
Chenwei Zhang
Pengyi Zhang
Xiaojuan Zhang
Xinyu Zhang
Ziming Zhang
Yiming Zhao
Yuxiang (Chris) Zhao
Jing Zhou
Lihong Zhou
Qinghua Zhu
Han Zhuang

Contents – Part I

Contents – Part II

Knowledge Management and Intellectual Capital

Social Media and Digital Networks

Libraries

Human-Computer Interaction and Technology

Information Retrieval

Community Informatics

Digital Information Infrastructures

Archives and Records

Are We Missing the Cybersecurity Factors in Recordkeeping?

Fariha Tasmin Jaigirdar[1(✉)], Ozhan Saglik[2], Carsten Rudolph[1], and Joanne Evans[1]

[1] Monash University, Melbourne, Australia
{fariha.jaigirdar,carsten.rudolph,joanne.evans}@monash.edu
[2] Bursa Uludag University, Bursa, Turkey
ozhan.saglik@uludag.edu.tr

Abstract. When creating, storing, and maintaining sensitive records, such as government data or records that reflect citizen rights or represent their health data, those records need to be trustworthy and secure. Since organizations are creating huge digital records, security in recordkeeping grows in complexity, and the relationship between the cybersecurity and recordkeeping domains is also expanding. While integrity and appraisal of records have always been considered important for records, existing standards and security discussions are missing some essential perspectives. Thus, research is needed to understand cybersecurity factors (different cybersecurity standards, techniques, protocols, etc.) for recordkeeping and the potential consequences of ignoring factors. With this goal, we explore two core standards, International Organization for Standardization ISO 15489 and ISO 27001, and selected relevant recent literature. This study makes a case for a universal standard for these cross-domain aspects of recordkeeping and cybersecurity by considering the existing standards and identifying the missing cybersecurity factors in recordkeeping. It also discusses relevant challenges and future research directions.

Keywords: Cybersecurity · Recordkeeping · Archives

1 Introduction

Security has always been considered important for records and archives. Researchers discuss confirming audit processes [29], information governance, policies and safety rules [4,11] approach achieving cybersecurity by imposing different standards [5] and suggest blockchain-based trusted systems [7,8]. Despite these various approaches, reports show different cybersecurity vulnerabilities and threats in record management [1], which urges the need for further study between these different domains [2].

© The Author(s), under exclusive license to Springer Nature Switzerland AG 2023
I. Sserwanga et al. (Eds.): iConference 2023, LNCS 13971, pp. 3–13, 2023.
https://doi.org/10.1007/978-3-031-28035-1_1

Records have characteristic features like integrity, authenticity, reliability, and usability that are required for records to be regarded as trustworthy. Integrity is mainly related to the preservation of the records, meaning they are unaltered and not subject to unauthorized modifications. Authenticity is more focused on the records' provenance, i.e., that the record has been created from an authentic source, by an authentic person, or another authentic entity. The suitability of a person in the record to have the authenticity to sign the record and make transactions and relevant activities combined with trusting the systems involved, can be used to explain reliability [31]. A usable record is one that can be located, retrieved, presented, and interpreted by connecting it to the business process [13].

Records management can be defined as the efficient and systematic control of records [13]. It includes the processes for records to be the representatives of transactions so that records have an evidential and informational value [32]. Malicious activities can potentially threaten all phases of record management. Cybersecurity has the techniques and methods for preserving the integrity, authenticity, and usability of the records [14]. Although cybersecurity mechanisms analyze how the qualities of the data can be protected and offer solutions, it is argued that there is not enough attention [2,12] to maintain the security of complete digital record lifespan from creation to appraisal. Therefore, it is anticipated that cybersecurity approaches can be applied to create and maintain reliable records.

Interestingly, recent discussions on trusted recordkeeping mostly cover the area of blockchain and how blockchain technology can be used as a method for trusted repositories. It is particularly focused on *preserving* records and maintaining authenticity rather than protecting the complete process. It seems that large parts of recordkeeping and record management processes are not covered in the current discussion, and in particular, the relevance of cybersecurity for record authenticity is underrepresented. While blockchain technology can potentially support secure record management after the record has been created and added to the chain, we focus on investigating cybersecurity for the complete data chain leading to the creation and potential future adaption of the record. To explore this area and identify further research opportunities, in this paper, we address the following research question.

- **Research Question (RQ)**: Does the current approach to cybersecurity in recordkeeping consider all relevant factors?

This paper aims to demonstrate what we currently have in recordkeeping in terms of cybersecurity and to identify missing cybersecurity factors in the complete lifespan of record creation to record adoption. Additionally, it poses new research questions that both subject-matter specialists need to address.

2 Research Approach

To address the research question, we follow a two-way approach. First, identifying and analyzing the related standards, and second, investigating closely related literature in these two domains. The authors of this paper are well-balanced experts in these domains: two of them are cybersecurity experts, one is a recordkeeping expert, and the other one is a scholar in these two interdisciplinary areas.

This paper analyses standards and draws from recent academic research. For the first one, standards that are core have been selected: ISO 15489 [13] for recordkeeping and ISO 27001 [14] for cybersecurity. This study can potentially be extended in the future through covering other standards for recordkeeping such as ISO 22428 [23], 18829 [18], 15801 [16], 14641 [20], and 17068 [17] and cybersecurity such as ISO 27002 [24], 27003 [19], 27005 [21], 27035 [15], and 27050-1 [22]. However, none of these standards is focused on cybersecurity and recordkeeping. Therefore, for this first step in the research we analyse the core requirements provided in the two core standards. For the second segment, we search for closely relevant literature exclusively in this two domains by specific keywords: "cybersecurity AND recordkeeping (records management)" and "cybersecurity AND archives". From our search results, we explored news articles, research reports/articles, investigation reports, conceptual papers and identified the key approaches/ideas used, whether there were any comments for future research/challenges. Further, we discussed the suitability of the articles among the authors and identified ten articles from 2016 to 2022 that were closely related to the research scope.

3 Findings on Correlated Areas: Cybersecurity and Recordkeeping

Since organizations are adopting more and more digitized processes, they need to have a 'reliable' and 'trustworthy' recordkeeping system to demonstrate the records are produced following their business processes and are authentic. Thus, cybersecurity techniques and approaches are obvious for the success of reliable recordkeeping. In this section, we first discuss two core standards in two domains and then illustrate ten relevant articles. We discuss our findings that show the connections between these domains, pertinent challenges, and potential future research directions.

3.1 Core Standards for Recordkeeping and Information Cybersecurity

There are various ISO standards for cybersecurity and recordkeeping like 27002 [24], 18829 [18], 27035 [15] and 14641 [20]. However, given that the underlying concepts of these standards are applicable to cybersecurity and recordkeeping, and taking into account the size of the study, we concentrate on two fundamental criteria: "ISO 15489: Records Management" and "ISO 27001: Information Security Management Systems". To explain their acceptability, "ISO 15489 establishes the core concepts and principles for the creation, capture, and management of records. It sits at the heart of a number of International Standards and Technical Reports that provide further guidance and instruction on the concepts, techniques, and practices for creating, capturing and managing records" [13]. For ISO 27001, "this standard has been prepared to provide requirements for establishing, implementing, maintaining and continually improving an information security management system" [14].

While records management is about current records, archiving examines the non-current records. However, the qualifications of the records that will be archival material are determined in the process of records management. Principles regarding records management also apply to archiving. Thus, there is no self-contained standard for archive management as a part of ISO 15489. Since the cybersecurity process naturally does not distinguish between current and non-current records, records management and archiving are interpreted together in this study which examines the relationship between cybersecurity and record-keeping.

ISO 15489 defines records management as the "field of management responsible for the efficient and systematic control of the creation, receipt, maintenance, use and disposition of records, including processes for capturing and maintaining evidence of and information about business activities and transactions in the form of records" [13]. Therefore "records should possess the characteristics of authenticity, reliability, integrity, and usability to be considered authoritative evidence of business events or transactions" [13]. It is understood that authenticity, reliability, integrity, and usability are the key requirements of the records.

A similar approach has been seen in the ISO 27001 Information Security Management Systems. According to the standard, "the information security management system preserves the confidentiality, integrity, and availability of information by applying a risk management process and gives confidence to interested parties that risks are adequately managed" [14]. Therefore, it can be said that ISO 27001 and ISO 15489 cover overlapping security requirements for data but have a different focuses. We further analyze these two standards with ten common requirements: policy and procedures, integrity, authenticity, reliability, usability, classification, access control, security, documentation, and disposition. We cite the quotes in the standards, ISO 15489 and 27001, then discuss challenges or/and directions for future research in Table 1.

Table 1. Overlapping of ISO 15489 and ISO 27001 with comments

Require ments	ISO 15489	ISO 27001	Comments for future research/challenges
Policy and procedures	Policies on the management of records should be developed, documented, and implemented	Information security incidents shall be responded to in accordance with the documented procedures	Do the records management policies/procedures of organizations include documenting cybersecurity incidents?
Integrity	A record that has integrity is complete and unaltered	Records shall be protected from loss, destruction, falsification, unauthorized access, and release, following legislation, regulatory, contractual, and business requirements	Integrity is a rather weak requirement. ISO 27001 is more precise and requires protection from falsification. Semantic integrity and tamper evidence is needed to check if the context is preserved, which is not satisfied by using integrity measures, such as hash values and checksums
Authenti city	Records creators should be authorized and identified	Assets associated with information and information processing facilities shall be identified and an inventory of these assets shall be drawn up and maintained	Standards state what should be done, but practitioners need how they should be carried out. Therefore the question of the organizations has a framework or concept about authenticity comes to mind
Relia bility	A reliable record is one whose contents can be trusted as a full and accurate representation of the activities	Event logs recording user activities, exceptions, faults, and information security events shall be produced, kept, and regularly reviewed	Do the current logs enough to assess the reliability of the records? What additional cybersecurity factors would be helpful?
Usability	A usable record should be connected to the business process or transaction that produced it	All relevant legislative statutory, regulatory, contractual requirements and the organization's approach to meet these requirements shall be explicitly identified, documented and kept up to date for each information system and the organization	How are the records linked to the business processes to document cybersecurity requirements?
Classification	Development of business classification schemes that are applicable to records should be based on an analysis of functions, activities and work processes	Information shall be classified in terms of legal requirements, value, criticality and sensitivity to unauthorised disclosure or modification. An appropriate set of procedures for information labeling shall be developed and implemented in accordance with the information classification scheme adopted by the organization	Do organizations identify cybersecurity risks and interrelate them to the business functions? How?
Access control	Access to records should be managed using authorized processes	An access control policy shall be established, documented and reviewed based on business and information security requirements	Do organisations' access control processes include cybersecurity requirements? If yes, are secure processes implemented and are events logged? What additional factors would be helpful?
Security	The measures should be put in place to ensure the following: routine protection and monitoring of physical and information security	Large segments of ISO 27001 are relevant for this requirement	Which security measures for digital records need to be applied to satisfy the ISO 15489 requirement? What is there and what is missing?
Documentation	Records requirements and decisions on how to fulfill them should be documented	Operating procedures shall be documented and made available to all users who need them	Can the requirements of ISO 27001 be adopted for the documentation of the complete lifespan of digital records?
Disposition	Disposition processes should be carried out in conformance with rules in authorized and current disposition authorities	Media shall be disposed of securely when no longer required, using formal procedures	How is the disposition of the digital records carried out by adopting cybersecurity requirements? Do the organizations fulfill General Data Protection Rules (GDPR) requirements?

The review of ISO 15489 and ISO 27001 shows how closely cybersecurity and recordkeeping are intertwined with each other. Organizations that want good records management should base their systems on good cybersecurity techniques. The guidelines for using these techniques need to be part of record management tenets. Otherwise, if the records management principles do not adopt cybersecurity for the provenance, appraisal, storage and maintenance of records, there is a substantial risk that the core requirements for recordkeeping cannot be achieved.

Considering all of these, we note several challenges. For example, various cybersecurity factors are missing for recordkeeping while describing policy and procedures, integrity, reliability, and access control policies in Table 1. Other open questions include whether organizations include cybersecurity techniques (different cybersecurity factors) in their records management policy, or are records management principles based on their cybersecurity procedures? What is missing in logs and audit trails from the cybersecurity and recordkeeping perspective? Do organizations assess the risks related to records by applying cybersecurity viewpoints? These aspects should support future research directions on cybersecurity and reliable records management systems.

3.2 Recordkeeping And/or Archival Studies and Cybersecurity

In this section, we discuss selected relevant literature to illustrate scholarly knowledge/understanding of the relation between cybersecurity and recordkeeping. Table 2 illustrates ten relevant research publications in this context along with key approaches used in these articles and comments for future research.

Table 2. Relevant literature in recordkeeping and cybersecurity with comments

Research area/content	Key approach/ideas	Comments for future research/challenges
Risk in trustworthy digital repository certification [10]	Discussion on risks involved in digital preservation from the social phenomenon, which authors organized into five categories: financial, legal, organizational governance, repository processes, and technical infrastructure	Future research should focus on the cybersecurity perspectives of the risks involved to handle real-life digital record vulnerabilities
Compliance with the NSW cyber security policy (CSP) [2]	Discussion on why CSP is not achieving the objectives of improved cyber governance controls and cultures	Recommendation on prioritizing improvements to cybersecurity resilience as a matter of urgency. The next challenges to be considered are: a) How to work on cybersecurity resilience? b) What should be the next step to include resilience in the record life span?

(continued)

Table 2. (*continued*)

Research area/content	Key approach/ideas	Comments for future research/challenges
Professional and ethical balance in digital record management [12]	Discussion on maintaining and promoting professional and ethical balance in the records management system and provide a theoretical framework	Further research strives to include cybersecurity factors with ethical discussion
Attacks in record handling in service NSW [1]	Discussion on phishing emails targeting service NSW employees from a spoofed domain. Call for multi-factor authentication to be added on email	Future research needs to add cybersecurity factors (for example, information on service providers, software version details, and protocol used)
Evaluation of email records management and cybersecurity issues [6]	Discussion on how archivists, record managers, and cyber security experts issued impossible-to-follow guidance for electronic records and emails	Motivation for further research in designing acceptable guidance for cross-domains
A meta-model for recordkeeping metadata [30]	Discussion on possibilities for participatory recordkeeping that embraces multiple participants, a diversity of perspectives, and inclusiveness of engagement. Access control is discussed in the paper with authentication, authorization, reproduction rights management, tracing, and audit	Further investigation is needed to explore the issues of trust and the role of authoritative sources in a semantic network. For example, how should end-users locate, identify and evaluate the veracity of sources of recordkeeping documentation?
Integrity in nation's records [26]	Discussion what integrity means for records and why it is important to maintain integrity	Further discussion is needed for born-digital and digitized records to maintain integrity.
Trust in digital record [9]	Discussion on the importance of transparency to achieve trust in records. Transparency, accountability, accessibility, choice, integrity, and preservation are discussed as issues that are critical to trust of online records	Cybersecurity in the cloud received little debate. But the cloud just tells a portion of the tale; what about a data record's entire lifespan?
Trust in records [27]	Discussion on trusted digital recordkeeping (focusing on long-term management and preservation of trusted digital records). Implications of relying on blockchain technology for the long-term management and preservation of trusted digital records	Discussion on several limitations and challenges in implying blockchain for record preservation. What can be done regarding authenticity, reliability, and risks in digital records? could be a future research focus
Contents of born-digital records [3]	Born digital records pose many challenges for government departments, including high volumes of records and a lack of structure. There are broader information management and security concerns for born-digital record collections.	Further research strives to design an acceptable model for cross-domains

While the literature clearly identifies a number of challenges, the analysis shown in Table 2 identifies several additional questions: For trusted records, is the overall lifespan of a record considered? Who needs to check whether the source of the record is secured? Do we have any list of cybersecurity requirements/factors that need to be checked for resilience? What are the missing cybersecurity factors? Who needs to check whether record processing steps are secured and how?

4 Discussion and Conclusion

This study explores evidence that shows the current understanding of cybersecurity factors in recordkeeping. The prominence of digital archives and record management increases the urgency of establishing trustworthy systems not only for archives or storage, but across the complete record management systems and including documenting security of the systems that generate data for record appraisal. One main problem is that cyber attacks can be stealthy, and any traces of the attack can be removed after records have been manipulated. Thus, data can potentially be corrupted, deleted, or additional data added via an attacked system without creating any evidence of the change. Furthermore, even strong security mechanisms, such as digital signatures, can be exploited to create a false sense of security if a malicious actor gets access to the private keys used to digitally sign. As a result, for reliable recordkeeping, cybersecurity measures and documenting cybersecurity-relevant aspects are essential.

This study makes the case for a universal standard for these cross-domain aspects of recordkeeping and cybersecurity by considering the existing standards and identifying the missing cybersecurity factors in recordkeeping. ISO 15489 and ISO 27001 are created by different technical committees. 27001 belongs to the committee of "Information security, cybersecurity and privacy protection", and 15489 is owned by the "Archives/records management" committee. Even though it is usual that standards take different approaches to trustworthiness, when discussing digital records, requirements for cybersecurity are similar to requirements identified in generic cybersecurity standards. These include authenticity, reliability, access control, and disposition. Therefore, it is important to consider cybersecurity and digital records management together. In this study, missing cybersecurity factors in recordkeeping are demonstrated. However, the inverse is needed to be researched as well. In particular, the question of recordkeeping principles are ignored in cybersecurity processes.

While existing standards provide generic guidance for metadata of records to show that actions taken on records are properly defined and managed, the metadata may not include cybersecurity factors like risk assessment, event history, or access trails which provides information on the risk of attacks to the systems involved or the communication links used to transfer data. Current provenance mechanisms in archival science and records management collect data history that provides evidence of the creator's and project data lineage by indicating the entities, activities (workflows), and users involved in producing data and data flows. This provenance information should be extended to enable users to achieve better situational awareness and to empower them to adequate risk assessment.

The trustworthiness of digital records and repositories in existing standards is not sufficient to derive information on records' cybersecurity properties across the complete lifespan. It is essential to associate cybersecurity techniques with organisational policies and procedures, information governance approaches, records metadata, and archival legislation for securing trustworthy records. Besides, records are composed of various data. This data should come from a trusted source and should not been changed or manipulated between data processing and aggregation. Data provenance, for example, following the PROV standard by the W3C [28] defines what kind of information needs to be collected in a data flow to describe who is responsible for data creation or related activities and when. Also the effects to modern concepts of recordkeeping, for example following the records continuum perspectives [30], need to be investigated. Cybersecurity metadata is not part of existing standards, and fundamental cybersecurity issues remain to be resolved.

This study also discusses opportunities for future research by incorporating cybersecurity factors as security evidence in digital recordkeeping. Recent research [25] has shown that extending provenance by cybersecurity metadata can provide substantial insight into the risks of manipulations. Identifying potential sources of corruption, misuse, or manipulation of data and consequences of mined, mapped, compiled, implied or inferred records will become an essential task for record management systems to achieve high resilience against cybersecurity attacks. A transparent system with an indication of the risks involved also provides an opportunity for better decision-making. This is in principle applicable to all types of digital data with a risk of being manipulated. Examples include health records, where manipulations can have dramatic consequences, financial records, business analytics, stock markets, political records, or digital evidence. Thus, extending metadata in recordkeeping with cybersecurity evidence is highly significant for digital archives and records management. Further, it builds on current research on cybersecurity-aware provenance and provides innovative extensions to the developing field of continuous recordkeeping for digital data.

References

1. Attacks in record handling in service NSW. https://www.itnews.com.au/news/service-nsw-told-to-urgently-improve-data-handling-after-cyber-attack-559244
2. Compliance with the NSW cyber security policy (CSP). https://www.audit.nsw.gov.au/our-work/reports/compliance-with-the-nsw-cyber-security-policy
3. The application of technology-assisted review to born-digital records transfer, inquiries and beyond. Technical report, The National Archives UK (2016)
4. Allegrezza, S., et al.: Policies for recordkeeping and digital preservation. Recommendations for analysis and assessment services-code 04. Project report (2017)
5. Bak, G.: Trusted by whom? TDRs, standards culture and the nature of trust. Arch. Sci. **16**(4), 373–402 (2016)
6. Bearman, D.: Office of the secretary: evaluation of email records management and cybersecurity requirements, ESP-16-03. Am. Arch. **80**(2), 459–462 (2017)
7. Bralić, V., Stančić, H., Stengård, M.: A blockchain approach to digital archiving: digital signature certification chain preservation. Rec. Manag. J. **30**(3), 345–362 (2020)
8. Bui, T., et al.: Archangel: tamper-proofing video archives using temporal content hashes on the blockchain. In: Proceedings of the IEEE/CVF Conference on Computer Vision and Pattern Recognition Workshops (2019)

9. Duranti, L., Rogers, C.: Trust in records and data online. In: Integrity in Government through Records Management, pp. 227–238. Routledge (2016)
10. Frank, R.D.: Risk in trustworthy digital repository audit and certification. Arch. Sci. **22**(1), 43–73 (2022)
11. Hofman, D., Lemieux, V.L., Joo, A., Batista, D.A.: The margin between the edge of the world and infinite possibility: blockchain, GDPR and information governance. Rec. Manag. J. **29**, 240–257 (2019)
12. Huda, M.: Empowering professional and ethical balance in digital record management. Organ. Cybersecur. J. Pract. Process People **2**(1), 60–73 (2021)
13. International Organization for Standardization (ISO): 15489 information and documentation - records management - Part 1: concepts and principles. Standard, ISO, Cenevre (2016)
14. ISO: 27001 information technology - security techniques - information security management systems - requirements. Standard, ISO, Cenevre (2013)
15. ISO: 27035 information technology - security techniques - information security incident management - Part 1: principles of incident management. Standard, ISO, Cenevre (2016)
16. ISO: 15801 document management - electronically stored information - recommendations for trustworthiness and reliability. Standard, ISO, Cenevre (2017)
17. ISO: 17068 information and documentation - trusted third party repository for digital records. Standard, ISO, Cenevre (2017)
18. ISO: 18829 document management - assessing ECM/EDRM implementations - trustworthiness. Standard, ISO, Cenevre (2017)
19. ISO: 27003 information technology - security techniques - information security management systems - guidance. Standard, ISO, Cenevre (2017)
20. ISO: 14641 electronic document management - design and operation of an information system for the preservation of electronic documents - specifications. Standard, ISO, Cenevre (2018)
21. ISO: 27005 information technology - security techniques - information security risk management. Standard, ISO, Cenevre (2018)
22. ISO: 27050-1 information technology - electronic discovery - Part 1: overview and concepts. Standard, ISO, Cenevre (2019)
23. ISO: 22428 managing records in cloud computing environments - Part 1: issues and concerns. Standard, ISO, Cenevre (2020)
24. ISO: 27002 information security, cybersecurity and privacy protection - information security controls. Standard, ISO, Cenevre (2022)
25. Jaigirdar, F.T., Rudolph, C., Bain, C.: Prov-IoT: a security-aware IoT provenance model. In: 2020 IEEE 19th International Conference on Trust, Security and Privacy in Computing and Communications (TrustCom), pp. 1360–1367. IEEE (2020)
26. Larsen, D.: Integrity and keeping the nation's records. Public Sector **42**(2), 23–24 (2019)
27. Lemieux, V.L.: Trusting records: is blockchain technology the answer? Rec. Manag. J. (2016)
28. Moreau, L., et al.: The open provenance model core specification (v1.1). Future Gener. Comput. Syst. **27**(6), 743–756 (2011)
29. Mosweu, O., Ngoepe, M.: Trustworthiness of digital records in government accounting system to support the audit process in Botswana. Rec. Manag. J. **31**(1), 89–108 (2021)
30. Rolan, G.: Towards interoperable recordkeeping systems: a meta-model for recordkeeping metadata. Rec. Manag. J. **27**(2), 125–148 (2017)

31. SAĞLIK, Ö.: Arşivlenen elektronik belgelerin güvenilirliğini tehdit eden riskler: Teknolojik koşullar açısından bir inceleme. Bilgi Ve Belge Araştırmaları (16), 29–47
32. Yeo, G.: Records, information and data: exploring the role of record-keeping in an information culture. Facet Publishing London (2018)

Recovering and Reusing Historical Data for Science: Retrospective Curation Practices Across Disciplines

Amanda H. Sorensen(✉), Camila Escobar-Vredevoogd, Travis L. Wagner, and Katrina Fenlon

University of Maryland, College Park, MD 20742, USA
asorens1@umd.edu

Abstract. While data curation research and practice have provided a growing body of guidance for and tools to support the curation, sharing, and reuse of recent and future scientific data, attention to retrospective data curation has been limited. The Recovering and Reusing Archival Data for Science project draws on semi-structured interviews with scientists and data curators to investigate data recovery and reuse efforts focused on historical data, or data drawn from legacy research materials, across a wide range of institutional, disciplinary, and research contexts. This paper describes selected findings related to (1) the perceived value of historical data for current and future scientific research; (2) challenges particular to recovering historical data; and (3) ethical quandaries that arise in historical data recovery and reuse. These findings shed light on the potential impact of historical data recovery and implications for retrospective data curation practices in support of active scientific research across disciplines.

Keywords: Scientific data · Data recovery and reuse · Legacy data · Data curation · Data sharing

1 Introduction

Masses of potentially useful scientific data are hiding in the unprocessed, accumulated collections of scientific research institutions, repositories, and archives—in historical research records, in the papers of retired scientists, on hard drives of data from concluded projects, in boxes of historical publications, in working files and field notes. These sources hold data that may be keys to advancing research in the sciences and beyond. Yet, these data and documents often remain hidden, at risk of being lost or destroyed by technical obsolescence or gradual obscurity. Despite increasing recognition within various scientific disciplines of the potential value of data in archival records or in historical research materials, research and practice in data curation have focused on saving current and future data for reuse. Increasing scientific research relying on legacy data highlights the need for study on primarily retrospective data curation, focused on recovering reusable data from the historical record or defunct research materials.

© The Author(s), under exclusive license to Springer Nature Switzerland AG 2023
I. Sserwanga et al. (Eds.): iConference 2023, LNCS 13971, pp. 14–28, 2023.
https://doi.org/10.1007/978-3-031-28035-1_2

The "Recovering and Reusing Archival Data for Science" project (RRAD-S) addresses the question: What opportunities and challenges confront the recovery and reuse of historical or defunct data for active scientific research across disciplines and organizational contexts? The impetus for this project began in case studies of recovering useful data from historical data collections at the National Agricultural Library. Having developed tools to assist memory institutions with data rescue [1], our research turned to a systematic study of the wider landscape of historical data recovery, through a semi-structured interview study with scientists and data curators. This research builds upon prior work on recovering or rescuing data at risk of loss, including from the Research Data Alliance Data Rescue Interest Group and the CODATA Data-at-Risk Task Group [2, 3]. We aim to build upon their progress with an empirical study of scientific and curatorial practices across a range of disciplines, organizations, and research contexts.

This paper discusses selected outcomes of this research pertaining to (1) the perceived value of historical data for current and future scientific research; (2) challenges particular to recovering data from historical sources; and (3) ethical quandaries that arise in historical data recovery and reuse. Our findings shed light on practices that have been ongoing for decades across disciplines, both within specific scientific projects and in the daily professional work of archivists and curators, but which have remained largely invisible to the wider body of literature in data curation. These practices have long been obscured by our focus—within the domain of data curation research and practice—on current and future scientific data, as opposed to data from archival settings or from long-defunct or historical research projects. In addition, scientists from wide-ranging disciplines have undertaken data recovery efforts but do not always publish on their recovery and curation practices (preferring to publish, instead, on the scientific outcomes of their analyses of recovered data). Where they do publish about their recovery practices, their efforts tend to remain siloed within a single discipline despite the relevance of their approach and insights to recovery efforts in other domains. There remains, too, a disconnect between archivists' and other professional curators' work on data recovery—which often focuses on recovery to support open-ended reuse of data—and the data recovery work of scientists who are undertaking the effort to support research on a specific question.

2 Prior Work

Data recovery is the process of enabling the sustained use and reuse of data that would otherwise go unused [4]. What data recovery looks like in practice tends to vary widely in different contexts. In general, data targeted by recovery efforts is salvaged from digital or analog sources that have been compromised by time, technological decay, or the gradual creep of obscurity. This includes data that reside on defunct hardware or inaccessible storage media, websites or digital publications no longer being maintained, databases forgotten on unplugged hard drives, data tables lurking among the unsorted papers of retired scientists, unprocessed boxes of photographs in deep storage, or in spaces and platforms—in the cloud and on the ground—affected by natural disasters, war and conflict, political shifts, etc.

The term *data recovery* marks a distinctive area within the wider landscape of data curation, defined as the ongoing management of research data through its lifecycle of interest and usefulness [5]. Data curation broadly encompasses practices such as data appraisal, description, transformation, and preservation measures necessary to keep data useful over time [6, 7]. Within this landscape, data recovery emphasizes aspects of curation applied to data that are no longer in use: data at risk of being lost or corrupted, and data from the past. Mayernik et al. [8] offer a matrix for understanding the risk factors that compromise the availability and usefulness of research data, including (but not limited to) losses of funding, losses of contextual knowledge, catastrophes, changes in legal status or ownership, and cybersecurity breaches. The challenges facing the preservation of scientific data are numerous, even for "healthy" data currently embedded in preservation systems or surrounded by users, funding, and supportive tools. Historical or otherwise defunct data face the same challenges and more, compounded by the passage of time, divorce from their original contexts, the inaccessibility of data creators, and technological deterioration and obsolescence.

Prior work from major professional organizations focused on data curation, including the Research Data Alliance Data Rescue Interest Group and the CODATA Data-at-Risk Task Group, have illuminated the need for cross-sector collaboration to build networks of support for preserving historical scientific data and supporting its reuse across disciplines [2, 3]. Yet, much of the on-the-groundwork of data recovery done in the sciences remains disconnected from parallel work in other scientific disciplines, and from the professional domain of data curation.

The most well-known data recovery initiatives stem from large-scale "community science," "citizen science," or crowdsourcing projects. But the long tail of data recovery efforts is largely invisible, going unpublished and unfunded, often serving the localized purposes of a single project or lab. Many varieties of recovery projects are ongoing every day across scientific domains, including documented efforts in climatology, astronomy, geology, pharmacology, oceanography, agriculture, etc. These efforts may leverage the work of crowds of volunteers, of automated approaches, or may rely on the manual labor of solo curators. Some fields prefer the term "data rescue", but in information science that term tends to have a narrower denotation of distributed, grassroots, and politically-motivated efforts such as those of the "Data Refuge" initiative, a widespread effort to save climate change data from administrative turnover after the 2016 U.S. presidential election [9].

"Data rescue" provides an alternative framing for recovery. Like recovery, rescue highlights the abundance of data, scientific or otherwise, in need of retrieval from dire, curatorial circumstances. However, rescue also advocates for the reevaluation of existing data, the identification of unacknowledged data sets, and, generally speaking, a more communal and crowdsourced approach to data curation [9]. In the context of archival practice, this includes a focused attempt to identify data often overlooked within commercial, proprietary curation software, and data produced within rather than outside of archives [10]. Such work also requires deliberate and adaptive cross-institutional collaboration, much of which necessitates building proactive preservation plans into data creation, curation, and management [11]. Further, since data rescue work often occurs in response to larger systemic issues of data value, it tends to be inherently activist, responding to perceived threats relative to shifts in governmental administrations, funding, and public support for scientific endeavors [12].

Regardless of the specific impetus or disciplinary context, all data recovery efforts, at base, aim to enable the possibilities of new knowledge from extant evidence. While data recovery encompasses a potentially vast range of tools, techniques, and strategies, depending on the data and the context for recovery, most documented recovery projects entail two basic stages: identifying potentially useful data, and performing systematic conversions of data or sources into more sustainable, useful formats [13, 14]. These efforts are invariably resource-intensive [15, 16]. Recovery efforts may serve myriad specific research purposes, but all those purposes can be understood within the frame of *reuse*. Data recovery supports the reuse of scientific data to serve contemporary, ongoing, or future scientific research. Recovered data can, in parallel, support historical research and social studies of science. Data may be recovered in pursuit of a specific research objective, which is often the case when recovery is done by scientists, or to support open-ended possibilities of reuse, which tends to be the case when recovery is led by data curation professionals within knowledge or memory organizations, such as a libraries, archives, or data repositories. Historical data has been shown to support longitudinal and meta-analyses, computational modeling, and cross-disciplinary research in various domains. Pasquetto et al. [17] offer distinctions among different kinds of data reuse: reuse to serve the reproducibility or replication of scientific research; independent reuse, in which data are deployed to answer novel questions; and integrative reuse, in which data are combined with other data in order to serve comparisons, new models, or new research questions altogether.

Most of the rich literature of theory and practice on data sharing and reuse focuses on data from current and future science: on data sharing practices among scientists, on data repositories and open infrastructures to support data sharing, and on standards, practices, and tools that allow curation professionals and scientists themselves to capture adequate contextual information about data to support reuse [17–19]. This literature has focused largely on the increasingly professionalized roles of data curators, and on scientific practices at their intersections with institutions like repositories.

In contrast, data recovery is distinguished by focusing on data that may never have been shared as such. It focuses on data that predate or have otherwise slipped through the growing infrastructures and best practices supporting open science. These data were not necessarily created with open-ended futures of broad access and reuse in mind. As a result, they exist in forms that are not readily accessible, whether by people or machines. Such data tend to arise from grassroots efforts, both within and independent of curation institutions. Relative to data curation more broadly, data recovery is poorly studied. There is a distinct need for cross-disciplinary, empirical research on facilitating the reuse of data that are not already amenable to use *as data*.

In addition, we need to understand the potential ethical hazards and sociotechnical implications of data recovery and reuse in different contexts. Like the shift from data recovery to data rescue, questions of ethical data reuse must navigate complexities around consent and beneficence, both for relevant communities of origin and original data curators. As a clear-cut example, data in health sciences often raise questions around benefits to both individual patients and broader advances within medicine [20]. In addition, shifts towards transparent models of data reuse and economic benefit continue to emerge in response to discussions both within academic and popular spaces on the use of data from historically marginalized populations, through practices such as biobanking [21]. Beyond health information—and the privacy and exploitation risks so visible in that context—documented ethical concerns in data recovery and reuse pertain to data sovereignty, community ownership and beneficence, creator intent, and ethics of access, e.g. [22, 23].

Ethical data reuse also necessarily factors in the role that scientific data transparency plays in the advancement of global knowledge [24]. Of course, this framing ignores broader sociocultural issues latent in the open sharing of scientific data, most prominently questions tied to data ownership and authorship within academic publication settings [24]. Scientific competition and ideologies around citation metrics and mantras of "publish or perish" dissuade scientists from sharing data out of legitimate fears of poaching [25]. To alleviate some of these concerns, models for identifying otherwise defunct data imagine new venues of data reuse, colloquially referred to as "data thrifting" [26]. This project offers a start on addressing these gaps in our knowledge.

3 Methods

This study comprised 23 semi-structured interviews with practitioners engaged in recovering and reusing historical, scientific data in a wide range of disciplinary, organizational, and research contexts. Our interview participants included research scientists, science librarians, curators, archivists, and volunteers working with crowdsourcing platforms, digital humanities centers, museum collections, scientific libraries, universities, academic organizations, and within many other contexts. Some of these participants are professionally trained data curators with academic backgrounds in library and information science. However, other participants, including research scientists, were not formally trained in digital curation methods.

The goal of interviews was to capture a broad range of data curation practices specific to historical data recovery and reuse. This phase of the research builds upon prior case studies of historical data collections at the United States Department of Agriculture's National Agricultural Library (NAL). In these forerunning case studies, reported in Shiue et al. [1], the research team undertook the curation of historical data from three diverse NAL special collections, including analog data, such as handwritten field notes, and tabular data on paper from early 20th-century collections of high scientific impact, and born-digital data from the donated papers of a recently retired scientist, much of which existed in obsolete and proprietary file formats. As we observed the myriad challenges that arose in these original case studies of data recovery and reuse and encountered the various communities in different sub-disciplines of agriculture doing related work largely without sharing their processes or outcomes, we identified a need for a broader overview of the landscape of historical data recovery and curation work across scientific fields, and the range of people, roles, and approaches involved.

Our interviews broached questions about participants' objectives for and experiences with scientific data recovery and reuse, how they identify data worthy of recovery, how they went about data recovery, and what challenges they encountered. Interviews took roughly one hour to complete and were audio-recorded with the permission of participants. All audio recordings were transcribed using Otter.ai and recordings were deleted upon completion of transcription. The interviews were then subject to qualitative content analysis.

The research team collaboratively built a codebook emically focusing on themes and key concepts as they emerged from participant discussions [27]. The codebook included 15 codes related to themes, including institutional practices, policies, curation practices, and data value to name a few. For the purposes of this paper, the team randomly selected a sample of 10 interviews to begin preliminary analysis. We coded these transcripts with qualitative coding software *NVivo*. To assure validity and intercoder reliability, the research team engaged in the constant comparative method and discussed discrepancies in coding [28]. When emergent codes or themes arose, the team would discuss new codes and reapply coding as necessary. Table 1 below represents a sample of codes, their definitions, and relevant quotes from participants. When writing, interview quotations were selected based on how they summarize key themes and perspectives succinctly. To assure participant anonymity, potentially identifying information in some quotations has been removed and replaced with a relevant descriptor, given in square brackets. Each interview participant has also been assigned an identifier (e.g., "P01"), which serves as their pseudonym to ensure their anonymity, as promised in our participation consent forms.

Table 1. Sample of codebook used in analysis

Code	Brief definition	Sample quote(s)
Data sharing challenges	Specific obstacles or barriers to data sharing, data exchange, or data transfer in any setting – whether in an institutional setting, between users and repositories, etc.	P01: "researchers hate sharing their data, they hate the public access policy, because it requires new work from them"
Formats	Particular formats, file formats, documentation practices or policies, metadata standards (formal or informal), or other facets of representation and description	P01: "Yeah, we have Microsoft Excel spreadsheets. We have CSVs, we have database files, some created in Access, some created in SQL, some created in other languages"
Evaluation	How participants gauge success or completion, how they evaluate their outcomes, indicators of success, completion, or impact	P02: "To make it more reproducible and more useful to more people if I finally get all the data extracted from these journals, these conference proceedings that I've set out for myself, that would be good"

4 Preliminary Findings

This research surfaced numerous challenges and opportunities for historical data recovery and reuse. Many of the findings parallel familiar challenges from data curation more broadly, including the labor-intensiveness of preparing data for reuse, whether of migrating data to new formats or documenting them sufficiently. In this section we focus on a set of themes that are specific to the curation and reuse of *historical* data to support current and future science. While these themes echo some in the literature on the curation of contemporary scientific data, there are nuanced distinctions specific to retrospective data curation. Specifically, we will examine what our study revealed about (1) the perceived value of historical data for current and future scientific research and related projects; (2) challenges particular to recovering data from historical sources; and (3) ethical quandaries that arise in historical data recovery and reuse.

4.1 Data Value

The immediately evident value of historical data to contemporary science is supporting longitudinal analysis, such as complex modeling of natural systems over time. Our findings confirm this value, but also shed light on the nuances of the value of recovered data for different kinds of reuse: not only for longitudinal reuse within a domain, but longitudinal reuse across domains, for serving newly enabled research questions or methodologies, and for addressing social or infrastructural problems in public domains outside of academia. In summary, the cues to the value of historical data that we have identified so far stem from a wide variety of kinds of reuse by diverse communities:

- Reuse by researchers in the same domain, to support the study of novel research questions in light of new methodological opportunities or the advancement of contextual scientific understanding;
- Reuse in new, tangentially-related disciplines to study novel questions;
- Reuse to support meta-analysis, such as the historical study of science, or the evaluation of metrics or standards;
- Reuse by professional practitioners for decision-making, to inform policy and practice, and improve infrastructure or social conditions;
- Reuse by public communities to guide local decision-making or action.

We describe each of these varieties of reuse, which indicate different facets of the value of historical data, below.

Participants described needing long-term, observational data to make conclusions about scientific phenomena that require sweeping evidence, such as changes in biodiversity or climate conditions. For example, P17 describes the enduring value of observational data in ocean science:

> one of my main interests in data rescue and the reason that I do this work is that as an oceanographer, I was always data limited. Always. Right. There is not enough money in the world to get you out to sea often enough, in enough places, for long enough to get all the observational data that you want to have in order to describe an ecosystem, or even a place.

Informed by these data limitations, P17 wants to make historical ocean data available for researchers across multiple disciplines to enable longitudinal analysis and interdisciplinary modeling: "And in order to make an assessment of change in the ocean, you need time series data, and whether that's biology or chemistry or meteorology, or what. And as you know, you can't go back and re-collect the data. I mean, that's why we do data rescue."

Some participants described reusing archival data to address questions or test hypotheses newly enabled by technological developments or the progression of scientific knowledge and theory in certain domains. For example, P07, an assistant professor, described a recovery initiative "to understand how fish populations have changed in [one U.S. state] over time." P07's team is recovering historical fish survey records generated by a state agency to ask novel questions, such as, "can we use this data to accurately model the conditions that happened and therefore accurately model how things might happen in the future?", and to test other ecological hypotheses related to species biodiversity and climate change. These are questions which were impossible to broach with these data in their original incarnation. Original lake inventories were done to support fishery management and to assess the success of fish stocking programs. The new questions being asked of these data are enabled by methodological advancement—particularly the development of computational and modeling techniques—but also by the advance of scientific theory in relevant ecological domains.

The same participant, speaking about a totally separate recovery initiative, described two further uses of the data: both to support pragmatic planning in the home collecting institution, and to support meta-analysis of scientific practice and standards. P07, speaking about the reuse of historical, paleontological data, describes how museum professionals plan to study "backlog fossils that are sitting in bags that have not been prepared…And they need to plan for a new building, and they want to use this data to better estimate the size of things for the new building." This participant also has meta-analytic questions about the history of science and standardization, addressed through the paleontological data: "I'm interested in standards and how those change over time. I want to look at how the measurement system has changed over time".

Our interviews show how recovered data are not only enabling new scientific inquiry but are being leveraged to address problems with immediate impact on professional practice, infrastructure, or public communities. One participant described their recovery and rescue work with agricultural data. P06, a data curator, discussed how "the history of the development of the crop varieties that we now use, is actually pretty valuable, especially as [person] says, under climate change, because …We're going to have to develop new varieties to handle these conditions." In this case, the recovered agricultural data are valuable because they can facilitate innovative crop production in the face of climate change.

In another case, a participant described pivoting the use of historical transportation data away from the original research motivation related to transportation *efficiency*, and toward consideration of transportation *equity*, reframing the data toward a newly perceived ethical imperative. P01, who is a data curator, detailed their experience working with transportation data, focusing on how data collected for one purpose can support another goal: "people weren't thinking about it as equity. Even though it was a data set about transit in lower income neighborhoods in the United States, they weren't thinking about equitable access to transportation. We want to bring that out." Speaking further about this data, P01 discusses their intentions for the future use of this transportation data: "I want that work to have a positive impact on peoples' lives on peoples' health and decisions that get made about transportation in the future. It's much less about just saving the data to save the data. It's saving the data so it can be used to make people's lives better."

Other participants discussed not only reframing data toward novel, socially centered uses, but also reframing recovery initiatives themselves to center community needs that emerged during the initiative. P10 discussed their engagement with museums, associated Native American Graves Protection and Repatriation Act (NAGPRA) contacts, and plant legacy data, specifically describing the guidelines they assisted in creating, which outline access to collections based on Tribal protocols:

> But I worked with a NAGPRA person and the [museum] to determine the best home for some of the plant specimens, the photographs, because they're representative of multiple Tribal communities in the region, and things like that. But we also are working with them to open up access to the papers and then restrict it again and make it so that you need to talk to Tribal review boards to have access to it, because this would be considered sacred knowledge, where some of these plant locations are and things like that.

These procedures put Indigenous nations in control of who can access certain knowledge as based on Tribal sovereignty.

Another participant described refocusing a data rescue initiative to support the emergent, pragmatic needs of the data's originary community, in this case an Indigenous nation. P12, a librarian at an academic institution, described how a collaboration that started to address issues around archival descriptions, specifically the use of Native place names, became refocused on recovering data related to water usage in order to support an Indigenous nation's water claims. When it became clear to P12 that "some of the concerns that I thought that we would talk about, like Native place names, ...that was not really a huge deal", P12 and their collaborators refocused their work on providing platforms to support this community: "They want the history, but they're also involved in legislation trying to get their water back. Making these materials discoverable, findable, having those conversations really focused us on the data related to the water history documents." P12's perspectives indicate a potential for pivoting data recovery work to be responsive to originary community needs. In this case, the effort was refocused on supporting Indigenous sovereignty at the intersection of data recovery and reuse. As discussed earlier, data recovery efforts can provide the long-term data needed to make broad conclusions about scientific phenomena, but they can also surface legacy data which may be valuable to vulnerable peoples and places, and their collaborators, furthering efforts that support Indigenous sovereignty and water claims.

Finally, data may be reused outside of research science to guide public and community action. P11, an associate professor, detailed how crowdsourced data collected to support research can be reused by people interested in maintaining their yards around the needs of local bird populations: "...the casual uses that people make – they use zebra [finch] data for things like deciding when to trim their trees, so they won't disturb breeding birds, right? Like very small scale homeownery, kind of landowner uses, those are also legit." People who are not scientists or researchers can also make use of scientific data as they care for their gardens.

4.2 Challenges Associated with Historical Data Recovery

It is well documented that scientists are reluctant to undertake data sharing and deposit even for their current data collections due to the difficulty and labor-intensiveness of data remediation, and the fact that the incentives at play in systems of scientific evaluation and credit make the publication of findings significantly more rewarding than the publication of data [29]. Historical data and data with differing original creators only compound this challenge. Our participants described prioritizing the curation and sharing of recent or current data, leaving no resources for the curation of older data. Given the priority that scientific research, funding, publishing, and evaluation place on novelty and innovation, there are also few incentives in the sciences for investigators to publish data that are not novel, or which originated from a different scientific author or investigator. Many participants working in positions and institutions dedicated to curation (rather than original scientific research) described a parallel conundrum. They expressed that it is difficult to justify digitization work to institutional leaders and funding agencies as work on legacy data, even when it is known to have high research value, is seen as in competition with work on more current data, which is considered burdensome enough on its own. Justification often comes from the data being desired for research, but the invisibility of legacy data leads to a perception that it is irrelevant. P20, a metadata manager, described this problem: "sometimes it's a matter of does, is someone wanting this data now? And then I can go to the powers that be and say, someone wants this data, can we have resources for it? But if nobody, it's a catch 22: If no one knows it's there, no one's going to ask for it."

Even when the funding and time are available for the recovery of historical data, the data itself is often difficult to extract: legacy data is saved in file types or formats that no longer exist, or are inaccessible to modern tools used for data curation and management. P01 described a specific scenario wherein data had to be manually scraped from webpages:

> …they've asked us to go back and preserve the legacy data and help pull it off the webpage, because all these files are attached to HTML pages. And some of them aren't actually saved anywhere in a drive that we can find. So, the only file available is an attachment to an HTML page. And we all know that that's a nightmare waiting to happen. So, we're often scraping hand, scraping links from web pages and downloading stuff.

These factors together mean that recovery of data from historical sources is often time- and labor-intensive and is often an additional or marginal side project for curators rather than the central focus of any dedicated position. Necessarily, shortcuts are sometimes taken, resulting in suboptimal or "good-enough" recovery efforts. P01 states:

> And oftentimes, what we would like to make that into a time series or something else, we don't have the time for that so it's: save each survey as we can, pull up documentation off of the web page, and then preserve it and make it public, with the caveat that the public presents us with a request and a good use case, we will do more work. But oftentimes, it's how do we make the most efficient use of our time to make this public in at least an open format.

4.3 Ethics of Data Recovery

Alongside larger challenges of data reuse, participants also observed ethical concerns related to data recovery. Ethical questions emerged in two strands. The first considered questions around how data condenses from a larger relationship to historical inequities in naming choices and in research practice. The second category of ethical concern reflected questions of researcher knowledge production and the intent behind data reutilization. Participants expressed concerns about using data collected from vulnerable or marginalized populations, particularly where those populations do not justly or equitably benefit from the outcomes of the research, or where the same communities do not have control over how data are ultimately used. P06 stated:

> …it's also a priority for [organization], because it's a priority for this president, to make sure that we're doing things equitably. And so, to my mind, that means not just — are we serving those populations with our programs fairly? But are we making sure that if we're collecting data from those populations, on their farming practices, or on their use of nutritional benefits, for example, is the data being used fairly? And do they have some say in how their data is going to be used?

For the latter concern, P05 tied the impact of data recovery to a larger exploration of artificial intelligence (AI) research and ethics. Expressing concern that scientists working with AI techniques are frequently guilty of "introducing bias into algorithms," P05 suggested that the availability of data for recovery and reuse should not equate to free, unregulated use. Highlighting the value of information professionals and librarians in ethical AI, P05 asserted that ethical recovery and reuse of data should include funded "training" and methods for identifying "expertise" within data curation work. In notable divergence, P11 argued that this type of credentialing raises its own ethical concerns given what they see as chronic acts of dismissing community-based science and the use of data by non-experts as irrelevant to the advancement of knowledge. Overall, these ethical quandaries probe issues surrounding who benefits from the use of recovered data and how academia understands recovered data as a method of knowledge production.

5 Discussion and Future Work

This research illuminates new aspects of the value of historical data recovery and reuse. We have offered a very preliminary framework of kinds of reuse, organized around diverse reuse communities—including domain scientists and researchers in new disciplines to support the study of new research questions in light of new methodological opportunities or the advancement of scientific understanding, or for cross-disciplinary analysis; by researchers in different disciplines doing meta-analysis, including social and historical studies of science; by professional practitioners, working in professional domains or knowledge institutions; and by public communities, to guide decision-making or local action. There are valuable prior frameworks of scientific data reuse [17], and separate frameworks related to the value and impact of archival data [30]. Prior work on data reuse has mainly considered contemporary scientific data (rather than historical data). Prior work on archival impact has largely omitted the scientific applications of archival or cultural data. Because we developed our preliminary framework through inductive coding, we have not yet aligned our findings with prior frameworks, but we believe our findings will round out prior frameworks with an emphasis on historical data and data across disciplines.

Historical data recovery poses myriad challenges. Many of them echo factors from the extensive prior literature on scientific data curation, data sharing, and data reuse. For example, as has been widely documented in prior work on scientists' data practices [31], many researchers who recover and recreate historical datasets are reluctant to openly share data after its recovery, due to concerns about how others will perceive the data's quality, the additional labor of preparing data for sharing (e.g., of providing adequate documentation to support independent understandability of the data), or the necessity of retaining competitive research advantages. Even the familiar challenges, however, are compounded by the fact that data stemming from recovery initiatives are divorced from their original creators and contexts. They may never have been shared originally *as data*, since these datasets have often been manually reconstructed from analog or digital sources in fundamentally different formats: from narrative text of field notes, from the coded fields of ships logs, from the captions or labels of images or graphs, or from tabular data in different units of measurement. Because they are often being repurposed and recontextualized, these data require a certain level of expertise to be constructed in the first place without introducing errors of historical misinterpretation. In fact, these data may never have been purposefully shared *at all*, having been recovered and disseminated after a scientist's retirement or decades after the work was done, without the data creators' knowledge or consent.

In addition, many historical datasets were collected under paradigms of scientific observation and data collection that do not meet contemporary ethical standards of research—in terms of how they exploit historical or current communities and their resources, or how they represent or identify entities within the data in offensive or outmoded ways. For this reason, data being recovered and reused to support new scientific research have much in common with data leveraged in humanistic, historical, and anthropological research, derived directly from historical primary sources and gathered from archival collections built through exploitative or colonial collecting practices. They also share characteristics with qualitative and social scientific data, which are notoriously fraught with potential risks to the privacy, confidentiality, and wellbeing of human-subjects research participants. These branches of data curation research—across the sciences, social sciences, and humanities—rarely intersect. Future work aims to identify opportunities for more well-established practices and discourse around data reuse across the humanities and social sciences to inform scientific data recovery. There is also a need to bring research on archival data recovery into conversation with the theory and practice related to collections-as-data [32, 33] and ethical implications in archives, and library and information science. Mapping our findings to extant frameworks of data curation activities [34] as part of this future work will also help identify gaps in current data curation training and practice relative to retrospective curation.

Finally, future work on this research will aim to produce and disseminate guidance for archivists, librarians, and data curators who work with and preserve historical materials, to support the extraction and reuse of useful scientific data as part of broader digital curation processes, or to support individual scientists' efforts. This work is situated in a broader need to explore the distinctions between how research scientists go about data recovery, to find answers to specific questions, and how professional curators approach data recovery to support open-ended possibilities of reuse. Our future work, looking at data curation across a broader spectrum of disciplines, aims to shed light on this question and the convergence of curatorial roles.

References

1. Shiue, H.S.Y., Clarke, C.T., Shaw, M., Hoffman, K.M., Fenlon, K.: Assessing legacy collections for scientific data rescue. In: Toeppe, K., Yan, H., Chu, S.K.W. (eds.) iConference 2021. LNCS, vol. 12646, pp. 308–318. Springer, Cham (2021). https://doi.org/10.1007/978-3-030-71305-8_25
2. Choudhury, S.: Data at risk and research libraries. In: AGU Fall Meeting Abstracts, IN21E-01 (2017)
3. Mayernik, M.S., et al.: Stronger together: the case for cross-sector collaboration in identifying and preserving at-risk data. Figshare, 1 (2017). https://doi.org/10.6084/m9.figshare.4816474.v1
4. Downs, R.R., Chen, R.S.: Curation of scientific data at risk of loss: data rescue and dissemination. Columbia University Academic Commons (2017). https://doi.org/10.7916/D8W09BMQ
5. Cragin, M.H., Heidorn, P.B., Palmer, C.L., Smith, L.C.: An educational program on data curation. Poster Presentation. American Library Association, Washington, D.C., 25 June 2007. https://hdl.handle.net/2142/3493
6. Higgins, S.: The DCC curation lifecycle model. Int. J. Digit. Curation **3**(1), 134–140 (2008). https://doi.org/10.2218/ijdc.v3i1.48
7. Vearncombe, J., Riganti, A., Isles, D., Bright, S.: Data upcycling. Ore Geol. Rev. **89**, 887–893 (2017). https://doi.org/10.1016/j.oregeorev.2017.07.009
8. Mayernik, M.S., Breseman, K., Downs, R.R., Duerr, R., Garretson, A., Hou, C.-Y.: Risk assessment for scientific data. Data Sci. J. **19** (2020). https://doi.org/10.5334/dsj-2020-010
9. Janz, M.M.: Maintaining access to public data: lessons from data refuge, 5 March 2018. https://doi.org/10.31229/osf.io/yavzh
10. McGovern, N.Y.: Data Rescue. ACM SIGCAS Comput. Soc. **47**(2), 19–26 (2017). https://doi.org/10.1145/3112644.3112648
11. Allen, L., Stewart, C., Wright, S.: Strategic open data preservation: roles and opportunities for broader engagement by librarians and the public. Coll. Res. Libr. News **78**(9) (2017). https://doi.org/10.5860/crln.78.9.482

12. Walker, D., Nost, E., Lemelin, A., Lave, R., Dillon, L.: Practicing environmental data justice: from DataRescue to data together. Geo Geogr. Environ. **5**(2) (2018). https://doi.org/10.1002/geo2.61
13. Brunet, M., Jones, P.: Data Rescue Initiatives: bringing historical climate data into the 21st century. Climate Res. **47**(1), 29–40 (2011). https://doi.org/10.3354/cr00960
14. Wyborn, L., Hsu, L., Lehnert, K., Parsons, M.A.: Guest editorial: special issue rescuing legacy data for future science. GeoResJ **6**, 106–107 (2015). https://doi.org/10.1016/j.grj.2015.02.017
15. Fallas, K.M., MacNaughton, R.B., Sommers, M.J.: Maximizing the value of historical bedrock field observations: an example from Northwest Canada. GeoResJ **6**, 30–43 (2015). https://doi.org/10.1016/j.grj.2015.01.004
16. Specht, A., Bolton, M., Kingsford, B., Specht, R., Belbin, L.: A story of data won, data lost and data re-found: the realities of ecological data preservation. Biodivers. Data J. **6** (2018). https://doi.org/10.3897/bdj.6.e28073
17. Pasquetto, I.V., Randles, B.M., Borgman, C.L.: On the reuse of scientific data. Data Sci. J. **16**(8), 1–9 (2017). https://doi.org/10.5334/dsj-2017-008
18. Borgman, C.L.: Big Data, Little Data, No Data: Scholarship in the Networked World. MIT Press, Cambridge (2015)
19. Palmer, C.L., Weber, N.M., Cragin, M.H.: The analytic potential of scientific data: understanding re-use value. Proc. Am. Soc. Inf. Sci. Technol. **48**(1), 10 (2011). https://doi.org/10.1002/meet.2011.14504801174
20. Meystre, S.M., Lovis, C., Bürkle, T., Tognola, G., Budrionis, A., Lehmann, C.U.: Clinical data reuse or secondary use: current status and potential future progress. Yearb. Med. Inform. **26**(01), 38–52 (2017)
21. Wolinetz, C.D., Collins, F.S.: Recognition of research participants' need for autonomy: remembering the legacy of Henrietta Lacks. JAMA **324**(11), 1027–1028 (2020)
22. Marsh, D.E., Punzalan, R.L., Johnston, J.A.: Preserving anthropology's digital record: CoPAR in the age of electronic fieldnotes, data curation, and community sovereignty. Am. Arch. **82**(2), 268–302 (2019). https://doi.org/10.17723/aarc-82-02-01
23. Mannheimer, S.: Data curation implications of qualitative data reuse and big social research. J. eSci. Librariansh. **10**(4), 5 (2021). https://doi.org/10.7191/jeslib.2021.1218
24. Duke, C.S., Porter, J.H.: The ethics of data sharing and reuse in biology. Bioscience **63**(6), 483–489 (2013)
25. Voytek, B.: The virtuous cycle of a data ecosystem. PLoS Comput. Biol. **12**(8), e1005037 (2016)
26. Curty, R.G.: Beyond "data thrifting": an investigation of factors influencing research data reuse in the social sciences. Doctoral dissertation, Syracuse University (2015)
27. Guba, E.G., Lincoln, Y.S.: Competing paradigms in qualitative research. In: Handbook of Qualitative Research, vol. 2, no. 163–194, p. 105 (1994)
28. Boeije, H.: A purposeful approach to the constant comparative method in the analysis of qualitative interviews. Qual. Quant. **36**(4), 391–409 (2002)
29. Acord, S.K., Harley, D.: Credit, time, and personality: the human challenges to sharing scholarly work using Web 2.0. New Media Soc. **15**(3), 379–397 (2013)
30. Marsh, D.E., Punzalan, R.L.: Studying and mobilizing the impacts of anthropological data in archives. In: Crowder, J.W., Fortun, M., Besara, R., Poirier, L. (eds.) Anthropological Data in the Digital Age, pp. 163–183. Springer, Cham (2020). https://doi.org/10.1007/978-3-030-24925-0_8
31. Fecher, B., Friesike, S., Hebing, M.: What drives academic data sharing. PLoS ONE **10**(2), e0118053 (2015). https://doi.org/10.1371/journal.pone.0118053

32. Padilla, T., Allen, L., Frost, H., Potvin, S., Roke, E.R., Varner, S.: Always already computational: collections as data: final report. University of Nebraska Digital Commons. University of Nebraska, Lincoln (2019). https://digitalcommons.unl.edu/scholcom/181/. Accessed 18 Sept 2022
33. Coleman, C.N.: Managing bias when library collections become data. Int. J. Librariansh. **5**(1) (2020). https://doi.org/10.23974/ijol.2020.vol5.1.162
34. Lafia, S., Thomer, A., Bleckley D., Akmon, D., Hemphill, L.: Leveraging machine learning to detect data curation activities. In: 2021 IEEE 17th International Conference on eScience (eScience), pp. 149–158 (2021). https://doi.org/10.1109/eScience51609.2021.00025

#Receipts: A Case Study of the Sonja Ahlers Archive as Platform Feminism

Jennifer Douglas[1(✉)] and Alexandra Alisauskas[2]

[1] University of British Columbia, Vancouver V6T 1Z1, Canada
jen.douglas@ubc.ca
[2] University of Calgary, Calgary T2N 1N4, Canada

Abstract. This paper reports on the early findings of a case study of artist Sonja Ahlers' recordkeeping to position archives as a kind of discursive feminist platform, predating the rise of digital feminist platforms but aligned in motive and function with them. This short paper represents an early phase in a project exploring archives as platforms; it aims to ground the study within a theoretical framework drawn from digital feminist platform studies, and to suggest some of the ways digital feminist studies can inform theories about records and archives, and vice versa.

Keywords: Archival studies · Archives · Platforms · Feminist archives · Digital feminism

1 Introduction: Archives and Platform Feminisms

In their recent book on digital feminist activism, Mendes, Ringrose and Keller explore how digital platforms such as Twitter, Facebook and Instagram provide feminists (and emerging feminists) with innovative ways to "dialogue, network and organize [in order] to challenge contemporary sexism, misogyny and rape culture" [1]. Mendes, Ringrose and Keller credit these digital media platforms with affordances that not only permit innovation, but also increase the visibility of feminist activist initiatives. Social media platforms, they argue, "have produced new spaces for debates over feminism, opportunities for feminist 'awakenings' and spaces to challenge rape cultures;" social media sites "offer women a platform where they can communicate, form communities of support, engage in consciousness-raising, organize direct action, disrupt the male gaze, and collectively call out and challenge injustice and misogyny through discursive, cultural, and political activism" [2].

In these arguments about social media platforms as spaces where diverse feminisms can be explored and enacted, Mendes, Ringrose and Keller, along with other scholars of digital feminism, tend to emphasize the *newness* of this type of space. This focus on the newness of digital platforms for feminist organizing and consciousness raising runs the risk of obscuring, even if not intentionally, the existence of earlier platforms that have permitted similar types of reflection and activity. In this paper, we report on the early findings of a case study of artist Sonja Ahlers' archives. We aim to position archives as a

© The Author(s), under exclusive license to Springer Nature Switzerland AG 2023
I. Sserwanga et al. (Eds.): iConference 2023, LNCS 13971, pp. 29–35, 2023.
https://doi.org/10.1007/978-3-031-28035-1_3

kind of discursive feminist platform, predating the rise of digital feminist platforms but aligned in motive and function with them. This short paper represents an early phase in a project exploring archives as platforms, which is to ground the study within a theoretical framework drawn from digital feminist platform studies, and to suggest some of the ways digital feminist studies can inform theories about records and archives.

1.1 Platform Feminism: A Brief Literature Review

Writing about digital platforms, Rentschler and Thrift explain that "social media platforms foster different ways of doing feminism" [3] because of the platforms' particular technological and discursive affordances. Gibbs et al. define what they call "platform vernaculars": "unique combinations of styles, grammars, and logics, genres of communication that emerge from the affordances of particular social media platforms and the ways they are appropriated and performed in practice." As Gibbs et al. note, affordances that are "built into" a platform's hardware and software "delimit particular modes of expression or action," influencing what gets communicated in different spaces and how [4].

One affordance of digital platforms facilitating feminist activism is ease of access and use; because platforms like Twitter and Instagram present relatively low barriers to participation, they shift the ability to produce and share feminist content to a wide array of creators. Clark notes how "digital media have provided feminists of color and feminists working outside of formal organizations with a new, effective means of exposing their work and connection with others." As Clark explains, large organizations and initiatives (e.g., NOW, the National Organization for Women) "no longer [necessarily] structure communication within the feminist movement; rather, communication itself, from blog posts to Twitter hashtags, has become an important organizational structure for movement" [5]. Clark's comments emphasize the role of platforms in communicating within feminist movements and show how the ubiquity and accessibility of digital platforms can facilitate feminist communication outside of established and institutionalized channels and discourses. As Baer notes, these new digital platforms offer "great potential for broadly disseminating feminist ideas, shaping new modes of discourse about gender and sexism, connecting to different constituencies, and allowing creative modes of protest to emerge" [6]. Digital platforms, Mendes, Ringrose and Keller conclude, provide communities – and maybe especially "marginalized communities" – with "new means through which to 'posit counter-discourses in a way that can spread widely'" [7].

The use of hashtags on social media posts is an example of this kind of counter-discourse circulation, facilitated by the affordances of particular platforms. Scholars who study "hashtag feminism" [8] explain how the ability within social media platforms to aggregate posts (e.g. tweets) about the same topic or event creates a critical mass of experience and commentary that if not brought together this way, can be more easily dismissed as the experience or opinion of a few (complaining) feminists. In this way, a hashtag can acquire "significance in its own right as a memetic disruption of dominant discourses;" for example, a hashtag like #YesAllWomen denies the "misogynist violence" inherent in assumptions that violence against those who identify as women is rare and isolated [9]. Gibbs et al. discuss how hashtags are used "across a wide variety of online platforms," showing how "the affordances and performances that constitute a vernacular are not necessarily specific to a [single] platform;" however, they also assert that "every platform has a vernacular *specific to it* that has developed over time, through design, appropriation, and use" [10]. In our emerging work on archives as platforms, we are interested in exploring how archives function as platforms, the kinds of platform vernaculars that are specific to archives, and how archival creators perform these vernaculars for particular – and particularly, feminist – discursive and communicative purposes.

1.2 Archives and/as Platforms

Despite their insistence on the importance of the context of an archives' creation, its relationship to its creator's activities, and its authenticity and reliability as evidence of past facts and acts, archivists have paid scant attention to the ways an archive as a whole might perform a communicative function. Exceptions to this include MacNeil's exploration of archives as a particular kind of *text*, which by virtue of the particular processes by which archives are compiled, organized and re-organized, function and should be read as "embodied arguments" [11, 12]. In this view, archives are not just randomly collected together at the end of a creator's life or the time of donation to a repository, but are assembled together as the result of deliberate decisions and actions and for particular purposes. In a similar vein, Douglas and MacNeil consider the ways that archival collections function as lifewriting texts. Douglas and MacNeil argue that by making decisions about what materials to include (or not) in their archives, how to organize them, and what stories to tell about them, archival creators are engaging in autobiographical acts, using the archives to tell a particular story [13].

In her work on the archival turn in feminism, Eichorn discusses how "feminist scholars, cultural workers, librarians and archivists born during and after the rise of the second wave feminist movement" have begun to understand "the archive as an apparatus to legitimize new forms of knowledge and cultural production" [14]. Eichorn's view of the archive as legitimizing apparatus and the emphasis on archives as texts seen in works by Douglas and MacNeil direct attention to the ways archives – like the digital platforms examined by Ringrose, Keller, Mendes and others – function as a particular means of making arguments and communicating them across time and space. In the next section, we explore this type of function in the context of a specific archival case study.

2 A Case Study: Sonja Ahlers

Sonja Ahlers is a visual artist and poet from Victoria, B.C., whose art practice and works are difficult to categorize. In the 1990s, Ahlers was a key figure in feminist zine networks and is best known for her artist books, including *Temper Temper* (1998), *Fatal Distraction* (2004), and *The Selves* (2010). Her latest book, *Swan Song,* was published in 2021. These books fuse collage and text with a zine aesthetic and diaristic sensibility in a style that has been referred to as graphic poetry. To compile these texts, Ahlers has drawn extensively on the significant archive she has amassed as a lifelong collector. Brought together and arranged within the pages of each book, these archival materials perform a particular kind of feminist, social analysis. In conversations with us, Ahlers described being deeply influenced by the *idea* embodied in the title of Alice Munro's prototypical feminist novel, *The Lives of Girls and Women*: in her art practice and in her archives, Ahlers attempts to document how girls' and women's lives are defined and documented for them in mainstream culture. Both her art and her archives are ways of talking back to that dominant culture.

Ahlers' archives include a large body of her own collage and poetry work, files of collected source materials, drafts, and binders of project documentation. The archive also includes personal materials such as journals, family records, correspondence and materials sent to her from a significant number of friends and penpals. Like many artists' archives, Ahlers' archive is both part of her art practice – a space she draws from and works with to create new works – and the documentation of that practice, the material evidence of her work, and also of her personal life and relationships. She is currently in the process of working with the archives as part of a planned retrospective exhibition at the same time as she is preparing materials for potential donation to an archival repository.

Traditional archival theory posits archives as aggregations that accrue through the unselfconscious actions of their creators; in contrast, Ahlers' work creating, sorting, pulling from, using, re-using and preserving her archives is an example of an archives as a site of creative activity and deliberate self-fashioning. In previous work, we introduce the concept of "records work" to describe the "active roles" creators play in compiling their archives; the term "considers how people work with records as well as how records themselves work (i.e. what work they perform and what they accomplish or do)" [15]. In the next two sections, we explore two types of records work performed by the Sonja Ahlers archives that help us to also position Ahlers' archives – and archives more generally – as a particular type of communicative platform.

2.1 The Archives as 'Crime Scene'

In an interview with curator Godfre Leung and the second author, Ahlers discussed the function of her archives in her life. "My identity is wrapped up in my archives," she explained. "The archive is evidence I exist." Ahlers describes a "forensic" process by which she investigates her own archives, uncovering and recovering materials that help her make sense of her "fractured" past selves and provide source material for her work. "The archive is evidence to me," she reiterates. "I can't not do something with it, because it exists. It gives me source material that I can't deny." The archive is "like a crime scene," and by going back to it in her forensic manner, Ahlers finds ways to "connect more dots," to "see things in a whole new light" [16]. In an interview with the first author, Ahlers explained how by looking through her archives she can see harmful patterns in relationships that she did not understand at the time they were unfolding. The archive provides evidence of how she was being groomed, gaslighted and 'negged,' terms that did not exist (or were not commonly used) in the 1990s and early 2000s to describe the experiences of those who identify as girls and women. A piece in Ahlers' upcoming exhibition titled "Men Explained Things to Me" mines the archives to refigure these relationships that felt like flattery but in fact were "grooming and predatory" [17]. In these examples, we see how Ahlers works with and through the archives to both affirm and understand past relationships and to reconfigure them in ways that allow her to take control of the narrative.

2.2 The Archive as Feminist Platform

Ringrose, Keller and Mendes discuss digital feminist activism in the context of #metoo and rape culture. Citing Alcoff's work, they consider how within rape culture, women are "denied presumptive credibility," required always to plead their case in a context of "structural disbelief" [18]. In the parlance of hashtag feminism, those who identify as women and girls need to keep #receipts. In some keyways, Ahlers' archives are also #receipts. As described in the previous section, Ahlers has characterized her archives both as documentation of the lives of girls and women in particular socio-cultural contexts as well as a "crime scene." As such, the archive provides evidence – the #receipts – of how she experienced life as a girl and woman. As "source material [she] can't deny," her personal archives provide her with a discursive space in which she can gather, create, preserve and make public evidence of the lives of girls and women in ways that both foreground and talk back to how that evidence is disregarded in other spaces. Ahlers worked for several years as a page at the Yukon Archives in Whitehorse, Canada, and, like the feminist activist archivists Eichorn talks to, understands how archives are discursively aligned with evidence, valued for their evidentiary qualities, and treated as spaces to preserve, uncover and publicize the 'true' history of an individual, organization or event.

Eichorn's analysis of how feminists use archives as a legitimizing apparatus acknowledges the role archives can play – and the use feminists can make of them – in shaping discourse. Creating archives is an agential act in the shaping of particular narratives, stories and histories that have a specific relationship to legitimacy and authority. In her art practice and in the preparations, she is making for archival donation, Ahlers seems aware of the legitimating and evidentiary affordances of archives. Eichorn argues that "rather than simply reflecting a desire to understand the past, the current archival turn [in feminism] reflects a desire to *take control* of the present through a *reorientation* to the past" (emphasis added) [19]. If we consider archives as platforms, with vernaculars specific to them, we can see how Ahlers and the feminists interviewed and studied by Eichorn take advantage of the particular affordances of archives – their association with evidence and legitimacy – not only to tell stories about their pasts, but also to preserve and present the #receipts necessary for a feminist retelling of the lives of (those who identify as) girls and women.

3 Archives as Platform: Building Theory of What Archives Do

Our research in this area is in its early stages, and we continue to explore Ahlers' archives as well as other archives we have identified that function similarly (i.e., where their creators are active agents using archival creation as a mode of feminist communication and activism) to further develop this theory of archives as (feminist) platforms. While archives are commonly described as preserving the past, this is not their only, or even their most important role [20]. Thinking about the discursive affordances of archives as platforms invites us to think about how personal archives are assembled and deployed for particular communicative aims, as well as how feminists have found means to assert agency and publicize #receipts prior to the ubiquity of new social media platforms. Interpreting archives through the lens of digital feminist studies – trying to understand archives as feminist platforms – requires a shift in thinking about what archives *are*, to what archives *do*. This shift could prove productive for thinking about what archives are for, more broadly, and has implications related to what, why and how we preserve. Positioning archives as feminist platforms may also prove productive for scholars of gender studies, rhetoric, communication and/or media studies, when there is an emphasis on archives not simply as accumulations of source material, but as MacNeil argues, rhetorical texts in their own rights.

While their focus is entirely on digital platforms Mendes, Ringrose and Keller advise that "digital feminist activism can only be comprehensively understood via affective, material, technological and cultural lenses." Digital feminism, they argue, "should not be merely understood via digital artifacts, but through social and cultural processes and their entanglement with technologies" [21]. In our work, we take this argument seriously by focusing on the social and cultural processes of archives creation, and the archive as a feminist technology and platform. As we continue to develop this research, we hope our work will contribute to a broader understanding of the technologies, including archives, digital or not, by which personal, political and activist discourses are created, preserved and circulated, as well of the cultural and affective contexts in which these activities occur.

In his analysis of queer uses and effect on Tumblr [22], Cho shows how the "particularities of Tumblr's sociotechnical affordances" create "distinctive affective registers that are an integral part of the Tumblr experience" [23]. While both archives and digital platforms provide opportunities for feminists to protest and raise consciousness through increased visibility and publicity, a particular sociotechnical feature of archives as platforms relates to their unusual status as theoretically publicly accessible but in practice also cloistered in archival reference spaces, whether physical or online. Eichorn highlights this aspect of archives, explaining, for example, how in the Riot Grrrl collections at the Fales Library in New York, the capacity for materials to be public but *"within limits"* (emphasis in original) was appealing to the grown up grrrls who contributed their records [24]. Keenan and Darms further explicate this appeal with an analysis of Fales' reference rooms as a "safe space" [25]. For Ahlers, the archive is a safe space that affords her a unique genre of communication; it is a means of safekeeping *and* of sharing stories, which, when she was younger either could not be told or were not heard, so that they can speak in other ways. With its associations with evidence, truth, permanence and legitimacy the archives as platform becomes an affectively powerful staging ground for a particular kind of calling to account in the lives of girls and women, one that provides opportunities to talk back to "structural disbelief." Archives provide another, different way of *doing feminism.* As we continue to explore the idea of archives as feminist platforms we expect to deepen understanding of these sociotechnical and affective affordances of archives, to be able to characterize the *platform vernacular* of archives, and to strengthen the case that archives matter not only for what they contain, but for what they are and do in the world.

References

1. Mendes, K., Ringrose, J., Keller, J.: Digital Feminist Activism: Girls and Women Fight Back Against Rape Culture, p. 2. Oxford University Press, Oxford (2019)

2. Mendes, K., Ringrose, J., Keller, J.: Digital Feminist Activism: Girls and Women Fight Back Against Rape Culture, pp. 12–16. Oxford University Press, Oxford (2019)
3. Rentschler, C.A., Thrift, S.C.: Doing feminism: event, archive, techné. Fem. Theory **16**(3), 239–249 (2015). Qtd in Mendes, Ringrose, Keller, p. 32
4. Gibbs, M., Meese, J., Arnold, M., Nansen, B., Carter, M.: #Funeral and Instagram: death, social media and platform vernacular. Inf. Commun. Soc. **18**(3), 257 (2015)
5. Clark, R.: 'Hope in a hashtag': the discursive activism of #WhyIStayed. Fem. Media Stud. **16**(5), 789 (2016)
6. Baer, H.: Redoing feminism: digital activism, body politics, and neoliberalism. Fem. Media Stud. **16**(1), 18 (2016)
7. Mendes, K., Ringrose, J., Keller, J.: Digital Feminist Activism: Girls and Women Fight Back Against Rape Culture, p. 7. Oxford University Press, Oxford (2019)
8. Clark, R.: #NotBuyingIt: hashtag feminists expand the commercial media conversation. Fem. Media Stud. **14**(6), 1108–1110 (2014)
9. Thrift, S.: #YesAllWomen as feminist meme event. Fem. Media Stud. **14**(6), 1090–1092 (2014)
10. Gibbs, M., Meese, J., Arnold, M., Nansen, B., Carter, M.: #Funeral and Instagram: death,social media and platform vernacular. Inf. Commun. Soc. **18**(3), 257 (2015)
11. MacNeil, H.: Archivalterity: rethinking original order. Archivaria **66**(1), 17 (2008)
12. MacNeil, H.: Deciphering and interpreting an archival fonds and its parts. In: Gilliland, A.J., McKemmish, S., Lau, A.J. (eds.) Research in the Archival Multiverse, pp. 161–197. Monash University Publishing, Monash AU (2017)
13. Douglas, J., MacNeil, H.: Arranging the self: literary and archival perspectives on writers' archives. Archivaria **67**(1), 25–39 (2009). See also MacNeil, H.: Understanding the archival fonds as autobiographical text through three discourses. Italian Journal of Library and Information Science 10 (3), pp. 47–58 (2019) and Douglas, J.: The archiving 'I': A closer look in the archives of writers. Archivaria 79, pp. 53–89 (2015)
14. Eichorn, K.: The Archival Turn in Feminism: Outrage in Order, p. 4. Temple University Press, Philadelphia (2013)
15. Douglas, J., Alisauskas, A., Mordell, D.: 'Treat them with the reverence of archivists': records work, grief work and relationship work in the archives. Archivaria **88**(2), 101 (2019)
16. Ahlers, S., Alisauskas, A., Leung, G.: The archive is evidence I exist: a conversation with Sonja Ahlers. Reissue. https://reissue.pub/articles/the-archive-is-evidence-i-exist-a-conversation-with-sonja-ahlers/. Accessed 28 Aug 2022
17. Interview with Douglas, 10 September 2021
18. Alcoff, L.: Finally heard. The Indypendent, 22 December 2017. Quoted in Mendes, Ringrose and Keller, p. 7. Accessed 28 Aug 2022. https://indypendent.org/2017/12/finally-heard/
19. Eichorn, K.: The Archival Turn in Feminism: Outrage in Order, p. 7. Temple University Press, Philadelphia (2013)
20. Mendes, K., Ringrose, J., Keller, J.: Digital Feminist Activism: Girls and Women Fight Back Against Rape Culture, p. 6. Oxford University Press, Oxford (2019)
21. Caswell, M.: Urgent Archives: Enacting Liberatory Memory Work. Routledge, Abingdon (2021)
22. Cho, A.: Queer reverb: Tumblr, affect and time. In: Hillis, K., Paasonen, S., Petit, M. (eds.) Networked Affect. MIT Press, Cambridge (2015)
23. Mendes, K., Ringrose, J., Keller, J.: Digital Feminist Activism: Girls and Women Fight Back Against Rape Culture, p. 32. Oxford University Press, Oxford (2019)
24. Eichorn, K.: The Archival Turn in Feminism: Outrage in Order, p. 105. Temple University Press, Philadelphia (2013)
25. Keenan, E.K., Darms, L.: Safe space: the Riot Grrrl collection. Archivaria **76**(2), 55–74 (2013)

Standing on the Outside Looking in: Testing the Concept of Societal Embeddedness from a User and Pluralising Perspective

Erica Hellmer(✉)

Department of Information Systems and Technology (IST), Mid Sweden University, Sundsvall, Sweden
Erica.hellmer@miun.se

Abstract. The fourth dimension of the Records Continuum Model, pluralize, is often characterized as the link to understanding records' function in the societal and collective memory. Recently, Frings-Hessami (2021) presented the concept of societal embeddedness as an enhanced understanding of the fourth dimension. The concept is proposed to be used as a tool to interpret and analyse pluralization processes, and Frings-Hessami argues that pluralization does not just involve sharing in the future—but also societal expectations in both records and recordkeeping. The purpose of this paper is, from a user perspective, to test the concept of societal embeddedness as an analytical tool in a specific recordkeeping story, and to reflect on the societal contexts of records to enhance sustainable recordkeeping of digital information. The paper is based on a research project in the context of the Swedish private sector and digital recordkeeping of company bankruptcies. The results strongly suggest that the concept of societal embeddedness can contribute to an enhanced understanding to why records are created, used, and consequently, understanding user need. Overall, analyses show that the fourth dimension affects all other dimensions and societal embeddedness can be used as a tool to understand the actions taking place in them.

Keywords: Recordkeeping · Records continuum model · Fourth dimension · Societal embeddedness · User

1 Introduction

In 2021, Frings-Hessami presented the concept of societal embeddedness. Based on the records continuum model, Frings-Hessami [1] proposes using the concept to interpret and analyse pluralisation processes. The concept was created as an extension of Hans Hofman's Dutch translation of the fourth dimension "maatschappelijk inbedden", which translated into English means "to embed in the society" [1]. The concept of societal embeddedness is presented as a way to illustrate and explain the perspective of pluralization, by highlighting that pluralization does not just involve sharing in the future but also regards societal expectations in both records and recordkeeping. Different contexts and different societies have laws, regulations, and expectations that affect and explain

© The Author(s), under exclusive license to Springer Nature Switzerland AG 2023
I. Sserwanga et al. (Eds.): iConference 2023, LNCS 13971, pp. 36–48, 2023.
https://doi.org/10.1007/978-3-031-28035-1_4

the creation of records as well as the use of them. The purpose of records creation is thus to meet the societal expectations – records are therefore "captured, managed, accessed, shared, and used in ways that meet those expectations" [1]. Frings-Hessami has used the records continuum model as a teaching tool and argues that the model's multidimensional essence has often been misunderstood, especially the fourth dimension. Difficulty in interpreting the literature and the lack of examples of how to practice the model are described as two reasons for the misunderstandings. The purpose of the article was to contribute to an enhanced understanding of pluralisation and to engage archival researchers, practitioners, as well as students to reflect on the societal contexts of records [1].

The fourth dimension of the records continuum model is often described as connected to the representation of the records' function as a collective memory beyond the boundaries of the organization where the record was first created [2, 3]. Figuratively, with a pluralize perspective, "we're on the 'outside' looking in" [4]. From this perspective, a record can be used and interpreted through spacetime outside of its original context and is "always in a process of becoming" [5]. Or as Cumming describes a record in a continuum perspective: "it operates through time, not in time" [6]. An inward reading of the records continuum model is described as emanating from social and cultural contexts that are represented by the fourth dimension [7]. Thus, with a records continuum perspective, records can have multiple lives depending on the use of them, and they can be reused outside of the context where they were originally created. However, all dimensions are present in the records continuum theory. Even though organizational recordkeeping foremost focuses on perspectives regarding the first, second, and third dimension, the organizational recordkeeping is still connected to and informed by concerns derived from the fourth dimension [7]. Or as Reed argues: "recordkeeping does not occur in a social, cultural or political void" [8] – societal expectations and social influences reverberate through all dimensions and affect records creation, capture, and organization [7, 9]. Social requirements may be different depending on both context and time, and the fourth dimension represents the broader social environment as well as the "capacity of a record to exist beyond the boundaries of a single entity" [8]. The concept of societal embeddedness that Frings-Hessami proposes is described to enhance the understanding of the fourth dimension, from records creation to use and reuse in different contexts [1].

But, can the concept be used as a tool to explain and understand societal expectations and pluralisation in any recordkeeping story regardless of context? In the article Frings-Hessami [1] presents how a record moves between all dimensions using a wedding photo as an example. A wedding photo by itself represents several societal embedded contexts of when the photo first was created. The existence of the photo mirrors the expectations from society and "[...] is a reflection of the importance attached to weddings as symbolic events deemed important to capture in that society at that particular time" [1]. How can the concept of societal embeddedness be used to explain pluralisation processes in the context of digital recordkeeping and reuse of information and records of company bankruptcies?

The purpose of this paper is to test the concept of societal embeddedness as an analytical tool to reflect on the societal contexts of records. This paper focuses on the digital recordkeeping process of the investigation of bankruptcies and the incorporation of societal expectations in this specific context.

2 Research Context

This paper is based on a research project in the context of the Swedish private sector and company bankruptcies. The research project aims to create a digital service to increase the capacity to manage digital records to support business needs as well as preservation needs. Involved in the project are the creators of this digital service, the users of the service, and participants representing the Mid Sweden University. The creators are employees of a Swedish information company that specializes on creating digital solutions for long-term information management for both public and private sector. The users of the digital service are official receivers. The purpose of the University's participation was to observe the working process when creating the service, as part of the present study. The discipline of the official receivers has traditionally focused on analogue, physical information and documents, and not on digital information within the companies' different digital systems. A common scenario when a company has been declared bankrupt is that official receivers are assigned to manage the company's entire assets. According to the Bankruptcy Act [10] the official receivers then collects an inventory of the company's assets and debts based on assessed values. These assets are all property that belonged to the debtor at the time of the bankruptcy and the official receivers aim to extract money or other assets to the creditors. The official receivers need to preserve the material for at least seven years after the time of bankruptcy [10]. After these seven years, the preserved material is usually thrown away. The life cycle usually ends here. However, a transition towards digital management would increase the availability and the possibility to reuse records and to increase the ability to detect shortcomings in an effective way.

3 Research Approach

This paper is based on empirical data from one abductive action case study, an approach that originates from information systems research. An action case study is a mix of a case study approach and action research approach which involves an interpretative as well as an interventive stance [11]. Here, the researcher observed and actively participated in project meetings. Such an interventive approach affects to different degrees and it is possible that the researcher influences project members in the creation of the digital service. The empirical data were collected in Sweden from January to October 2021. The data collection methods consisted of participation observation in forty-five hours of project meetings, four semi-structured interviews with creators and users, one semi-structured group interview with both creators and users of the digital service, and document studies of project documentation by the creators. Notes were taken during each project meeting, which were then used as guidelines when developing interview questions. The project meetings as well as the semi-structured interviews were conducted via a video-conferencing tool. The transcriptions of interviews and notes from the participation observation of project meetings were analysed using the reading of the model by Frings-Hessami [1] as an analytical guiding tool.

The recordkeeping story presented by the users of the service was analysed from a fourth-dimension perspective and consisted of an inward and an outward reading of the records continuum model. In the article Frings-Hessami [1] presents how a record moves between all dimensions using a wedding photo as an example. By using the example of a wedding photo, Frings-Hessami [1] discusses the importance of metadata as well as possible reuses. A wedding photo by itself could represent several societal embedded contexts of when the photo first was created. Although, with added metadata such as who, time, and place, the possibility of reusing of the photograph could increase.

4 Theoretical Framework

"Models are ways of seeing things" [12], and the records continuum model has been used as an analytical and teaching tool which enables different perspectives of recordkeeping. The model was created by Upward [2, 13], together with McKemmish and Iacovino, and is based on postmodern thinking and structuration theory. It was created "[...] for recordkeeping in an age when accessibility of records was more important than their location" [14]. In contrast to the North American life cycle model with its linear lifeline perspective of records, the records continuum model "[...] questions the need for, and even the existence of, boundaries within and between recordkeeping processes and roles" [15]. The model enables action-structure within different recordkeeping contexts and specialisations such as contemporary recordkeeping, regulatory recordkeeping, and historical recordkeeping [13]. It can also be an analytical tool in contexts where there is no conscious records continuum frame of reference [3].

The model consists of four interrelated axes (Identity, Evidentiality, Transactionality, and Recordkeeping containers) and four overlapping dimensions that describe the recordkeeping process (Create, Capture, Organize, and Pluralize). The model (see Fig. 2) can be read from different perspectives depending on the contexts and purposes of the reading. Documents are created in the first dimension (create) which is described as "the locus of all action" [8]. The trace of action is further captured as trace of record which is evidence of an activity in the second dimension (capture). In the second dimension, metadata is added and the record is communicated and connected to context in personal and organizational recordkeeping systems [8]. In the third dimension (organise), records are organised and aggregated with other records as a corporate and individual memory. The fourth dimension (pluralize), represents the records' function as a collective memory beyond the organisational boundaries that first created the record [2, 3]. As described by McKemmish, a record is "always in a process of becoming", and from a pluralize perspective this means that a record is not fixed (unlike its content and structure) and can be interpreted through spacetime outside of its original context [5]. Or as Frings-Hessami [16] has argued, there is no end stage from a records continuum model perspective. After being pluralized, records "[...] are susceptible to be reused, recreated, recaptured, reorganised and repluralised" [16]. Records can have multiple lives depending on the use of them, and they can be reused outside of the context where they were originally created. Interpretation and re-presentation of records depends on the context of use and can therefore change [17] (Fig. 1).

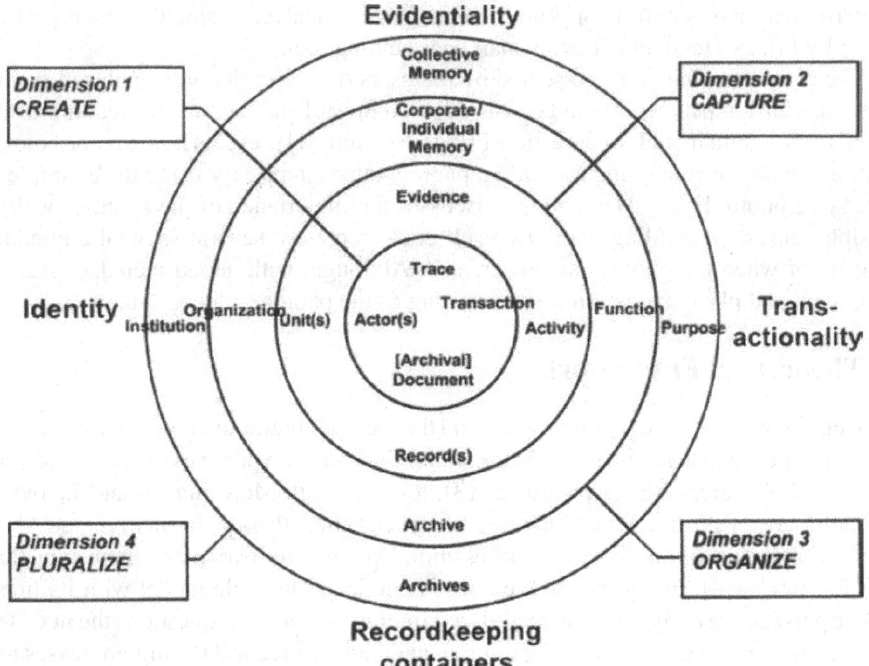

Fig. 1. The records continuum model © Frank Upward.

The concept of societal embeddedness that Frings-Hessami proposes is described as enhancing the understanding of the fourth dimension, from a records' creation to use and reuse in different contexts, by elucidating societal expectations in both records and recordkeeping [1]. As the fourth dimension is described to elucidate sharing beyond organizational contexts connected to collective memory [13], the concept of societal embeddedness aims to enhance the dimension further [1]. A records continuum perspective can also be used to analyse records that have been kept secret and not made public outside of the organisation that created them. The reasons for keeping them secret derives from concerns from the fourth dimension and could be reasons such as "[…] the need to preserve national security or to conform to privacy legislation" [18].

In the following part of the article, the concept of societal embeddedness has been used in the analytical process in the study to further analyse the recordkeeping story of the process of investigation of bankruptcies.

5 Results and Discussion

This section presents the result of the action case study and begins with an introduction of the different roles of the creators and the users in the creation of the digital service. It continues with the creators and users view on how they value information. This is followed by a presentation of the process of investigation of bankruptcies with a reading of the records continuum model based on the concept of societal embeddedness.

5.1 Roles of Users and Creators

The users in this study are official receivers (OR). The role of these users in the project is to contribute with their perspectives on what and how much information they need to fulfil their duty as OR. They also contribute to the structure, design, and testing of the digital service. In an interview, a user described that they do not usually extract digital information from different digital systems since they do not possess that kind of knowledge. Their expectation on this service is to be able to identify assets that may be hidden in different systems and that the digital service could be a part of their routine as official receivers.

The creators are employees at Swedish information company that specializes in creating digital solutions for long-term information management for both the public and the private sector. They describe themselves as a company that strives for a proactive information management where the information is viewed as something that has continuing value and can be used for other reasons and in different contexts. According to the creators, the users and their needs is what they focus on, and what the user values may change over time and depends on who the user is. Traditional archival records management is described as something that is more static and reactive rather than proactive. The creators of the digital service focus on the digital information that is not being used today. They aim to be able to refine and redefine values in information and to capitalise information. Value is described as something that is non-fixed and that can always be expanded, something that is based on the ability to track information, to find, retrieve, and sort information. The creators base their structure on the explicit need of these specific users. Their role is to retrieve the information from the different systems, to structure and classify the information and further preserve the information in an archival system and make it searchable for further use.

5.2 Valuing Information

In interviews with the creators of the service, a concept that reoccurred was the concept of value. Value of information was described as something that is connected to subjective understandings and needs. Information value was described as the value that a person ascribes to the information and as something that can change over time.

> "We can identify who the information is valuable for, here and now, but it can also be valuable in other ways than we can see here, in this moment. The value of information is determined by the beholder and the user, or the one that has the need for the information"
>
> (Interview with creator)

The creators argue that the value lies in the eye of the beholder. They also emphasise that value is connected to use, meaning that value is connected to whether information can be useful and accessible. According to the creators, there is also a possibility that aggregation of data and information of bankruptcies could have continuing value for society as a whole. The creators argue that even though bankruptcies may be described as events that most people would like to forget, this type of aggregation could paint a picture of entrepreneurship and its life cycle in a society. The creators also add that aggregation of data and information of bankruptcies could give a broader picture of bankruptcies, processes behind the bankruptcies, economic structures, how companies run their organisations, and facilitate discovering connections between them et cetera.

According to the users of the digital service, the value of information is connected to the main goal of the profession: to retrieve as much information as possible that can contribute to discovering more and other assets and therefore fulfil their commitments as OR. One commitment is to detect shortcomings and conscious or unconscious errors that they are obliged to report to the Swedish Economic Crime Authority.

5.3 A Recordkeeping Story – The Process of Investigating Bankruptcy

The following part of the article presents the process of investigation of bankruptcies, interpreted as a recordkeeping story. An outward and inward reading of the records continuum model is based on interviews with users (official receivers) of the service, on notes from project meetings, and notes from the participation observation of the testing of the service. An inward reading of the record continuum model in this specific context will start from the societal and cultural context of the official receivers' point of view, in the fourth dimension. The records that are created from this perspective are determined by the purposes and need of use by the OR.

According to the OR, several different information assets are important to consider in their process of investigation of bankruptcies. These information assets could be bookkeeping, contracts, and emails. The different information assets can also be represented by physical items such as different vehicles owned by the bankruptcy company. The ORs described three main factors that regulate their process of bankruptcy: 1) comply with laws and regulations, 2) resolve creditors, 3) maintain an organised society. The OR has legal demands to manage the bankruptcy and dismantle the company in a structured way. The Swedish Enforcement Authority monitors the process of bankruptcies, ensuring that the OR complies with the Bankruptcy Act [10]. A debtor is a company or a person in bankruptcy that has debts to the creditors. The OR is obliged to make sure that the process of debts to the creditors can be solved [10]. The factors presented above are factors described by the OR and impacts the creation of records from a pluralized perspective. In this specific study, the ORs are the proposed users of the service being created. The service is based on the need of these users and they contribute with knowledge regarding what and how much information they need to fulfil their duties as ORs. Thus, they are active users and described in an interview with creators as "the most important link in order to extract value in information". Consequently, the value of information is connected to the need and the need is bound to specific contexts and users. It could be agreed that different users' equal different needs. Sundqvist [19] describes that within archival theory users are described as equal to records creators. According to research in design and development of recordkeeping systems, users should be more involved in the creation process of records systems. These systems should be based on the needs and perspectives of the users [20].

When the ORs carry out the process of investigation they also do an outward reading of the records continuum model seeing the creation of records from the perspective of the company that first created them. The company has, as the OR, factors that regulate how and why they carry out their business processes. In an example of contracts where the OR searches for evidence of documents that reveal what the contract is for, who or whom it considers, determining when it was created and when it expired, the OR needs to go back to the Create dimension. The contract is a trace of an agreement between presumably two actors, but in contrast to the example with the wedding photo, metadata is already added and therefore it exists in both the Create and Capture dimensions. According to the OR, a contract usually reveals information (or metadata) regarding time, actors involved, what the contract is for, and payment. As the OR argued, contracts are often captured in different systems such as bookkeeping systems together with other documents that connects other companies, other actors, or transactions to the contract, which takes place in the Organise dimension. It can also be assumed that the contract has been sent by email to the other party of the contract and therefore shared outside the company, which has created a new and separate recordkeeping trail (Pluralize dimension). Thus, the inward reading from the perspective of the OR starts with an outward reading from the perspective of the company.

Since the ORs are not a part of the company they are investigating or involved with the records that were created by the company, their analytical process begins from the fourth dimension perspective. From this perspective the ORs investigate what systems they have access to and how records have been managed (Organise dimension). According to an interview with an OR, a common system is a digital bookkeeping system that often contains captured and organized evidence that verifies activities such as different material of agreements, contracts, receipts, or other documents (Capture dimension). These are often scanned or photographed and connected to different bookkeeping actions. The OR searches for the traces of the creation of the different documents which is located in the first dimension; an agreement that has been created by an actor has presumably been sent to another actor or actors (Create dimension). According to the OR this is most often done by email. An email can be regarded as a record and when sent it is seen as "a deliberate act of communication and represents an action designed to evoke reaction" [8]. The email is created in the first dimension and moves outwards to the second dimension when sent with intent. The ORs creates a new recordkeeping trail when they capture a contract in their own recordkeeping system. Together with traces of transactions, bookkeeping, or emails, these documents are then organised and managed in the recordkeeping system.

The role of the users was also to test the service after the digital information had been gathered and sorted by the creators. In the testing the OR searched for expenses that could be verified by invoices or receipts. In their search they found several documents that contained invoices that had been photographed. The photos had been taken with the invoices placed on a sofa (see Fig. 3). The invoice verified the transaction the OR was searching for. It contained metadata such as: date, invoice number, actors (salesperson and buyer), address, a specification of the specific service, terms of payment, total amount, value-added tax, et cetera. It looked like typical Swedish invoices of today, the contents of which are regulated by the Value Added Tax Act [21]. Using the concept of societal embeddedness as an analytical tool it is possible to explain and understand why and what determines the creation of the invoice. It is regulated by laws of today (fourth dimension), it is organised and captured within a digital system of the company, a technical solution that is at hand today (third dimension and second), and it is created as a trace of action. So, how can the photograph of the invoice be reused? As mentioned, the creators of the service have argued that aggregation of data and information of bankruptcies could have continuing value for society as a whole. The creators have argued that it could be reused to conduct research when exploring the processes behind bankruptcies, how companies run their organizations, or exploring economic structures. When looking at this specific photograph of the invoice and with the analytical tool of societal embeddedness at hand, the photograph mirrors a society of flexibility and digitalization. The photograph was presumably taken at someone's home, maybe with a mobile phone. A possible reuse of the photograph, that the creator could not have predicted, is perhaps a cultural anthropological research study exploring different work environments. The photograph does not mirror a typical office landscape but a rather a picture of working from home in a time when the lines between being at home and being at the office are blurred and diffused. Another interpretation could be that it is not a large business with regulated recordkeeping routines but rather a smaller business with a more flexible work environment.

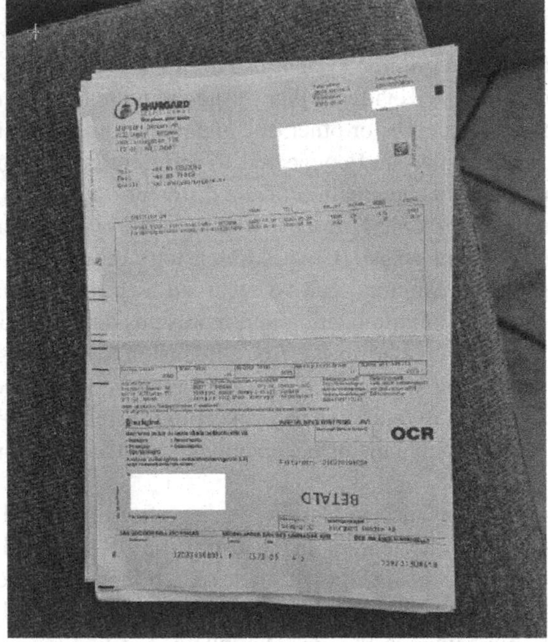

Fig. 2. The photograph of the invoice.

As Frings-Hessami [1] emphasises, an inward reading of the records continuum model takes its starting point "[…] from the cultural contexts and the mandates for the creation of records in the Pluralise dimension" [1]. As presented above, the ORs has three different factors of concern to consider to fulfil their duties: 1) comply with laws and regulations, 2) resolve creditors, and 3) maintain an organised society. These three factors constitute why and how they conduct their business affairs, which dictates the records they need to create. In other words, these three factors constitute the user need, in this case, which are also the three factors of concern to fulfil their duties. Why records are created, in the first dimension, derives from the need in the fourth dimension, how they are captured and organised also derives from the need in the fourth dimension. The records these users need to create are based on the laws, regulations, and the societal expectations of establishing an organised society that mirrors a democratic society. The third factor, maintain an organised society, is connected to their role in society as a whole, and the expectations that are needed for a society to function. A parallel can be drawn to the broader purpose of archives where records can be preserved for a variety of reasons. Seen from a democratic point of view, "[…] archives are meant to enable accountability by providing access that can empower citizens against potential maladministration, corruption and autocracy" [22]. The third factor that aims to dismantle companies in a structured way is a factor for a just society. The question is, as Cunningham emphasised, how "[…] archival institutions balance the often-competing demands of public and private interests?" [22]. New initiatives of reuse that derive from the need of contemporary users flourishes and create new grounds for continuing use and reuse of records. When analysing the process of investigation of bankruptcies from a user perspective (fourth dimension) and with the perspective of societal embeddedness as an analytical lens, all dimensions are present. This could be visualised as shown in Fig. 3.

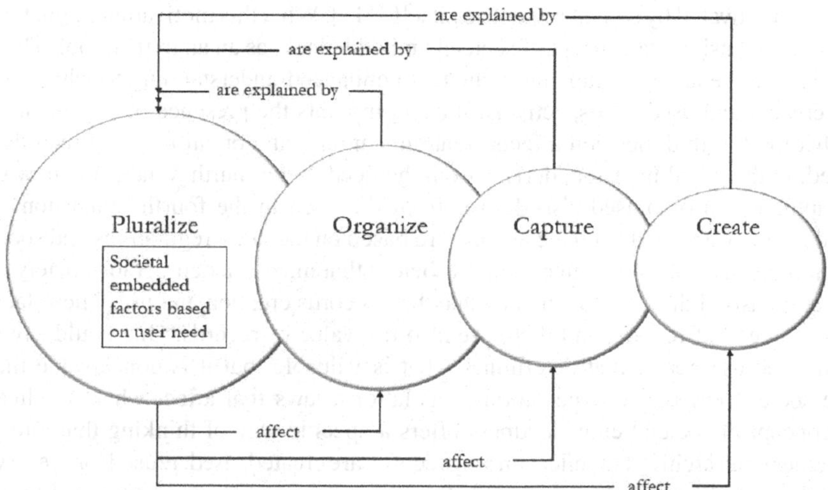

Fig. 3. Outward and inward reading of the records continuum model from a pluralize perspective.

Figure 3 represents both an outward and an inward reading of the records continuum model and both readings are seen from a pluralize perspective where the created, captured, organised, and pluralized records are affected by the societal embedded factors that derive from the user need. In the process of valuing information of bankruptcies, the ORs start with a retrospective perspective and pursue their work by exploring actions, events, and participants before a company is declared bankrupt. They search for evidence and trace for the creation that may confirm traces of events and actions, and they usually look for traces such as documents, transactions, bank statements, agreements, et cetera. These different information sources are then aggregated and become a narrative of the company. The reasons for the recreation of records, why they capture and organise and pluralize these records is then explained by the societal embedded factors that are derived from the needs of the OR.

6 Conclusion

Frings-Hessami [1] proposed the use of the concept of societal embeddedness to interpret and analyse pluralisation processes. A pluralisation process is described as involving not just sharing outside of the organisations but also involving societal expectations in both records and recordkeeping. With a pluralise perspective we are standing on the outside looking in [4], based on our specific societal and cultural contexts. These contexts are different depending on when and who is looking in. The purpose of this paper was to test the concept of societal embeddedness as an analytical tool in a specific recordkeeping story. It further aimed to reflect on the societal contexts of records to enhance sustainable recordkeeping of digital information.

The creators based their creation of the service on the explicit needs of the user. As Sundqvist has emphasised, "records are used because they are needed, and the need for records is motivated by something outside itself" [19]. What this motivation might be can be interpreted using the concept of societal embeddedness as an analytical tool. The use of societal embeddedness can contribute to an enhanced understanding to why records were created and used retrospectively. It also pinpoints the presence of all dimensions and that the fourth dimension affects creation, capture, and organize. Why records are created; in the first dimension, derives from the need in the fourth dimension, how they are captured and organised also derives from the need in the fourth dimension. The records these users need to create and use are based on the laws, regulations and societal expectations of establishing an organised society that mirrors a democratic society. The users emphasised three factors that dictate their records creation and use. These factors affect the need of records and therefore also the value of records. One could say that it is not the use per se that determines what is valuable, but it is conceivable that it is the societal embedded expectations, regulations, laws that affect what is valuable. The concept of societal embeddedness offers a specific way of thinking that allows a researcher or an archivist to reflect on why records are created, used, reused, or preserved.

In this specific case, after a company has gone bankrupt, a new continuous life starts where the information and records created by the company live on with new values assessed by new users based on their specific social and cultural contexts.

References

1. Frings-Hessami, V.: The societal embeddedness of records: teaching the meaning of the fourth dimension of the Records Continuum Model in different cultural contexts. Arch. Sci. **21**(2), 139–154 (2020). https://doi.org/10.1007/s10502-020-09349-6

2. Upward, F.: Structuring the records continuum (Series of two parts) Part 1: post custodial principles and properties. Arch. Manuscr. **24**(2), 268–285 (1996). https://search.informit.org/doi/10.3316/ielapa.970505406
3. McKemmish, S.: Placing records continuum theory and practice. Arch. Sci. **1**(4), 333–359 (2001). https://doi.org/10.1007/BF02438901
4. McKemmish, S.: Yesterday, today and tomorrow: a continuum of responsibility. In: Proceedings of the Records Management Association of Australia 14th National Convention, RMAA, Perth (1997)
5. McKemmish, S.: (2016). Recordkeeping in the continuum: an Australian tradition. In: Gilliland, A., McKemmish, S., Lau, A. (eds.) Research in the Archival Multiverse, pp. 122–160. Monash University Publishing, Melbourne (2016)
6. Cumming, K.: Ways of seeing: contextualising the continuum. Rec. Manag. J. **20**(1), 41–52 (2010). https://doi.org/10.1108/09565691011036224
7. Reed, B.: Beyond perceived boundaries: imagining the potential of pluralised recordkeeping. Arch. Manuscr. **33**(1), 176–198 (2005). https://search.informit.org/doi/10.3316/ielapa.200601143
8. Reed, B.: Reading the records continuum: interpretations and explorations. Arch. Manuscr. **33**(1), 18–43 (2005). https://search.informit.org/doi/10.3316/ielapa.200601137
9. Upward, F.: The records continuum and the concept of an end product [Reply to Macpherson, Paul. Theory, Standards and Implicit Assumptions: Public Access to Post-current Government Records; in v. 30, May 2002.]. Arch. Manuscr. **32**(1), 40–62 (2004). https://search.informit.org/doi/10.3316/ielapa.200407661
10. SFS, 1987:672: Konkurslag. Ändrad t.o.m. SFS 2022:979 [Bankruptcy Act 1987:672, updated by SFS 2022:979] (1987). https://www.riksdagen.se/sv/dokument-lagar/dokument/svensk-forfattningssamling/konkurslag-1987672_sfs-1987-672
11. Halecker, B.: Action case study—a research strategy based on abduction for relevant and rigorous management research. Int. J. Bus. Res. **15**(4), 23–32 (2015). https://doi.org/10.18374/IJBR-15-4.3
12. Upward, F.: Modelling the continuum as paradigm shift in recordkeeping and archiving processes, and beyond - a personal reflection. Rec. Manag. J. **10**(3), 115–139 (2000). https://doi.org/10.1108/EUM0000000007259
13. Upward, F.: Structuring the records continuum (Series of two parts) Part 2: structuration theory and recordkeeping. Arch. Manuscr. **25**(1), 10–35 (1997). https://search.informit.org/doi/10.3316/ielapa.980100005
14. Oliver, G.: Managing records in current recordkeeping environments. In: MacNeil, H., Eastwood, T. (eds.) Currents of Archival Thinking, 2nd edn., pp. 83–106. Libraries Unlimited, Santa Barbara (2017)
15. Dingwall, G.: Life cycle and continuum: a view of recordkeeping models from the postwar era. In: Currents of Archival Thinking. Libraries Unlimited, ABC-CLIO, Santa Barbara (2011)
16. Frings-Hessami, V.: Continuum, continuity, continuum actions: reflection on the meaning of a continuum perspective and on its compatibility with a life cycle framework. Arch. Sci. **22**(1), 113–128 (2021). https://doi.org/10.1007/s10502-021-09371-2
17. Lewellen, M.J.: The impact of the perceived value of records on the use of electronic recordkeeping systems (2015). http://hdl.handle.net/10063/4144
18. Frings-Hessami, V.: The flexibility of the records continuum model: a response to Michael Karabinos' "in the shadow of the continuum." Arch. Sci. **20**(1), 51–64 (2019). https://doi.org/10.1007/s10502-019-09316-w
19. Sundqvist, A.: Conceptualisations of the use of records. Tidsskriftet Arkiv **6** (2015). https://doi.org/10.7577/ta.1358
20. Engvall, T.: User participation: what can be learned from the information systems domain? Rec. Manag. J. **29**(3), 320–332 (2019). https://doi.org/10.1108/RMJ-04-2018-0008

21. SFS, 1994:200: Mervärdesskattelag. Ändrad t.o.m. SFS 2022:413, omtryckt SFS 2000:500 [Value Added Tax Act 1994:200, updated by SFS 2022:413 and reprinted as SFS 2000:500] (1994). https://www.riksdagen.se/sv/dokument-lagar/dokument/svensk-forfattningssamling/mervardesskattelag-1994200_sfs-1994-200
22. Cunningham, A.: Archives as a place. In: MacNeil, H., Eastwood, T. (eds.) Currents of Archival Thinking, 2nd edn. ABC-CLIO, Santa Barbara (2017)

Plus ça change, plus c'est la même chose – The Australian Records Management Case

Sherry L. Xie[1,2,3,4], Yubao Gao[1], and Linqing Ma[1,2,3,4](✉)

[1] School of Information Resource Management, Renmin University of China, Beijing 100872, China
malinqing2010@126.com

[2] Center for Digital Records Management Research, Renmin University of China, Beijing 100872, China

[3] Key Laboratory of Data Engineering and Data Knowledge of the Ministry of Education of China, Beijing 100872, China

[4] Center for Archival Undertakings, Renmin University of China, Beijing 100872, China

Abstract. Intrigued by the information management replacing records management phenomenon, this study aimed at shedding light on it. Relying on preserved websites, the study examined relevant contents from 2007 to early 2022. It discovered the battle between records and information, and later on information asset. This battle incurred dazzling changes in managerial considerations, yet the challenges to management – either towards records, information, information and records, or information asset – remained the same. So were the unsatisfactory outcomes. A case seemed perfect to tell the plus ça change, plus c'est la même chose story. It is our hope that future studies can gather mighty strengthen and thus settle down the records-information battle once for all.

Keywords: Records management · Information management · Information asset

1 Introduction

Records management (RM) is not native to Australia but the Australian RM has developed into a leading position internationally. It is the first country that had a national RM standard (i.e., AS 4390 – 1996 Records Management) and it contributed directly to the publication of the first international RM standard (i.e., ISO: 15489 – 2001 Information and documentation–Records management). Today, the Australian RM voice remains strong in the ISO setting and its domestic RM policies are frequently consulted by RM practitioners and researchers worldwide. Representing this Australian RM force is the National Archives of Australia (NAA), which shoulders the responsibility of "overseeing Commonwealth record-keeping" as stipulated in the Archives Act 1983 [1]. Crafting record-keeping policies and standards has been the most typical way of fulfilling that responsibility. The term record-keeping in the Archives Act does not have a designated meaning but it functions in this context as an equivalent to records management. To use the most recent version of RM definition, RM refers to the field of management

© The Author(s), under exclusive license to Springer Nature Switzerland AG 2023
I. Sserwanga et al. (Eds.): iConference 2023, LNCS 13971, pp. 49–65, 2023.
https://doi.org/10.1007/978-3-031-28035-1_5

"responsible for the efficient and systematic control of the creation, receipt, maintenance, use and disposition of records, including processes for capturing and maintaining evidence of and information about business activities and transactions in the form of records" [2]. Not an intuitive one, the definition nevertheless points out 1) the goal of RM (i.e., efficient and systematic control) and 2) the series of activities that are needed for managing records (i.e., the rest of the definition). In searching for NAA policies on artificial intelligence (AI), the emerging RM related technology and also the current focus of the InterPARES Trust Artificial Intelligence (ITrustAI) project (2021–2026), it was discovered that there were drastic changes on the NAA website relating to RM: the RM space is now an Information Management (IM) space, in which only two out of the total thirteen menu items are record(s) related, i.e., "Records authorities" and "Building trust in the public record". The term space here refers to the aggregation of webpages that are devoted to RM or IM, and devotion here is defined by 1) the existence of an entrance page that is clearly marked by the phrase Records Management or Information Management and 2) a menu that organizes contents. A quick going-back to the Archives Act 1983 did not, however, find any principal updates on RM matters and there were no traces of information management in it. So, why this IM-replacing-RM makeover on the NAA website? Is it because that RM has changed into IM in practice yet the Archives Act has not followed up in time (which is common and understandable)? If yes, then what are the fundamental differences between RM and IM in practice, and what provided for the replacement? A study was conceived to look into these questions as a literature search for answers to them did not yield any results. It was rationalized as a component inquiry of the RM & AI study of the ITrustAI project [3], which has equally two focuses of RM and AI. The inquiry utilized a method of historical examination, taking advantage of the historical data that were made possible by digital preservation sites. This paper reports on the findings of the study.

2 Historical Examination

The historical examination undertaken by the study refers to the locating and analyzing of the relevant NAA webpages retrieved from the Internet Archive. The determination of relevance is rather straightforward as all webpages/contents are located within the clearly bordered RM or IM space. The locating process followed the menu items, including their orders, which we considered reflections of the NAA focuses on policies and work. The retrieval precision, i.e., the earliest page and the last page of a certain time period, cannot be guaranteed as the Internet Archive chiefly relies on auto-crawling for its collections, and any auto means has gaps. The timelines emerging from the retrievals, expressed in specific dates, are thus not absolute – despite they may give that impression. Nonetheless, as these specific dates were results of one-by-one clicking on all captures, they are largely reliable for aiding the analysis of the retrieved contents. The analysis followed the path of 1) identifying the RM contents, 2) identifying the IM contents, and 3) comparing RM and IM. The contents identifying processes paid particular attention to changes and the times of changing within the respect RM and IM time periods and the comparison looked into the entire RM to IM time period. Content-wise, the comparison consists of three aspects: 3.1) concepts of record(s) and information, i.e., the object of the management, 3.2) managerial considerations, and 3.3) performance, i.e., the results of the considerations.

3 The Contents and the Changes

The contents-and-changes identifying process included the parts of RM contents and changes, IM contents and changes, From RM to IM, and The entire process.

3.1 RM Contents and Changes

By the first retrievable RM page and the last retrievable RM page, we established the RM time period as from 2007-08-30 to 2016-10-18. The RM space changed its appearance around 2011-10-16, we did not, however, consider this change warranting further compartmentation. The change was only about color schemes and the arrangement of contents remained the same. In particular, the central message, i.e., the text at the center of the first page of the RM space that answered the question "Why records matter" remained unchanged. By analyzing menu items, a series of changes were discerned. On the first (retrievable) RM page, five menu items were presented: Check-up, Records authorities, Normal administrative practice, Training, and Where to get help. As the Archives Act requires NAA to provide assistance to the Australian Commonwealth institutions regarding RM matters (i.e., S5(2)(c)), we distinguished the menu items into the categories of NAA core assistance (naa-CA) and NAA supplementary assistance (naa-SA). As naa-CA items correspond to representative RM activities (i.e., what RM does and how it's been doing), we used their NAA-given titles in our analysis to indicate their core assistance nature, e.g., Records authorities, and did not individually label them as also naa-CA to avoid repetition. Conversely, we used the naa-SA label for items of a more general nature and grouped them mostly prima facie, e.g., naa-SA (Training; Where to get help). In our analytical tables (Tables 1, 2 and 3), we used symbols in addition to table column titles for analysis demonstration: '+' indicates a new item that is added to a previous label, e.g., naa-SA (+ Publication) and '→' indicates a newer version, an expansion, or a reduction regarding a previous item, e.g., (Check-up) → Check-up 2.0. Table 1 summarizes the times of changing after the first RM page and the changes.

Table 1. RM contents and changes

{2007-08-30, the 1st RM page:
naa-CA: Check-up; Records authorities; Normal administrative practice
naa-SA: Training, where to get help}

Time	The updated	New item	Removed item	The same
2007-10-11	• naa-SA (+ Publication)	• Create, capture & describe • Keep, destroy, or transfer • Secure, store & preserve • Access	• Records authorities • Normal administrative practices	• Check-up
2008-04-13	• None	• Information management framework • IT systems	• None	• All 2007-10-11 items
2011-03-11	• → Check-up 2.0 • naa-SA (+ Glossary + Register for updates)	• None	• None	• All other 2008-04-13 items
2011-10-06	• naa-SA (→ Training and events; → Publication and tools)	• Strategic information and records management • Managing your agency records	• All other 2011-03-11 items	• Check-up 2.0 • naa-SA (Where to go for help; GAIN Australia)
2012-05-27	• None	• Digital transition policy	• None	• All other 2011-10-06 items
2014-06-25	• → Check-up Digital [4] • Naa-SA (→ Training, events, and development)	• naa-SA (A–Z of information and records management)	• None	• naa-SA (Publications and tools; Where to go for help; GAIN Australia) • All other 2012-05-27 items
2014-12-17	• → Digital transition and digital continuity	• None	• None	• All other 2014-06-25 items
2016-03-02 (till 2016-10-18)	• → Digital Continuity 2020	• Information governance • RM agency survey	• None	• All other 2014-12-17 items

From Table 1, we observed that, during this period, eight times of changing had taken place and the changes occurred with both the NAA core and supplementary assistances. The degrees of change, however, are significantly different. For clarity, we further labeled the two parts of NAA core assistance into managerial considerations (i.e., what RM should do; naa-CA-mc) and performance (how RM has been doing; naa-CA-p). We observed that naa-SA and naa-CA-p were both rather steady and naa-CA-mc was the main part of change. While individual items were updated, replaced, or added, naa-SA had always concentrated on providing general information on the core assistance and offering customized help when needed for both institutions and individual RM professionals. Like the supplementary assistance, naa-CA-p, representatively the Check-up tool developed by NAA for agencies' self-assessment of RM matters, had been in existence from the first page to the last page and only advanced in versions (i.e., from Check-up to Check-up 2.0 to Check-up Digital). In 2016, another performance tool occurred on the menu, i.e., the RM agency survey, which was devised to gather more information from agencies on RM matters. According to NAA, the RM agency survey was of a "whole-of-government" nature, focusing on NAA's understanding of issues "common to agencies across the Australian Government" [5].

The changes to naa-CA-mc are clearly indicated by the new and removed items and we described them generally as 'jumping between records and information'. By considering 1) whether or not "records" is in the name of item and 2) the order between records and information when they both occur (i.e., "records and information" or "information and records"), we identified the following changes in terms of (dis/re) appearance:

- 2007-10-11: records disappeared with Records authorities.
- 2008-04-13: information appeared (in the new "Information management framework" and "I(nformation) T(echnology) systems");
- 2011-10-06:
  - information and records appeared (in the new "Strategic information and records management";
  - records reappeared (in the new "Managing your agency records");
- 2016-03-02: information appeared (in the new "Information governance").

From these (dis/re) appearances, it is clear that changes happened and happened to both the object of management (i.e., from records to information and records) and management itself (i.e., from management to management and governance).

3.2 IM Contents and Changes

By the first retrievable IM page, we established the beginning of the IM space as at 2016-11-13. As the IM space is still current, we used the end of our data collection time as the end of the IM space for the purpose of our study, which is 2022-01-30. Like the RM space, the IM space went through one site change; unlike the RM space, however, this site change went through not only colors but also the way of displaying contents. In addition to a drop-down menu, there were three boxes under the central message that were used to highlight three menu items. Moreover, the central message was changed. As such, we deemed this change worth compartmentation and accordingly divided the IM space into two phases: the first, from 2016-11-13 to 2019-01-29 and the second, from 2019-10-31 to 2021-01-16. Table 2 below lists, for the first IM phase, the times of changing and the changes, following the column titles of Table 1.

For the first IM phase, five times of changing occurred after the first IM page. Similar to the RM space, naa-SA and naa-CA-p remained steady, with the former appearing in a more consolidated manner and the latter advanced into the version of Check-up PLUS. For naa-CA-mc, the 'jumping between records and information' ceased and two trends emerged: 1) records (in "Records authorities") remained steady (i.e., from the first page to the last page), and 2) items relating to information were continuously being

Table 2. IM contents and changes of the first phase

{2016-11-13, the 1st page of the IM first phase:
naa-CA: Digital Continuity 2020; Information governance; Check-up Digital Records authorities; Managing information
naa-SA: Training and events; Support}

Time	The updated	New item	Removed item	The same
2017-01-01	• naa-SA (→ Support and professional development)	• None	• None	• naa-SA (Training and events) • All other 2016-11-13 items)
2017-1-21	• None	• None	• naa-SA (Training and events)	• All other 2017-01-01 items
2017-05-09	• None	• Information Management standard	• None	• All other 2017-01-21 items
2018-05-29	• → Check-up PLUS (2018)	• None	• •None	• All other 2017-05-09 items
2019-01-29	• None	• Building interoperability	• None	• All other 2018-05-29 items

added (e.g., Information Management standard), including sometimes items that did not have the term information in their names, e.g., Building interoperability. Building interoperability aimed at making "information, systems and processes to be interoperable" or "information and data between different systems" exchangeable [6]. During this time period, the object of management appeared to be completely information yet management and governance were both still present.

Table 3 lists the times of changing and the changes for the second phase following mostly the column titles of Table 1, but not all of them: the column Removed Item was eliminated as there was only one item that belonged to this category (i.e., Digital Continuity 2020, which is attached to the The Same column) and the column The Highlighted was added to reflect the changed way of content display, which the study considered reflections of policy emphases.

For the second phase of the IM space, five times of changing occurred after the first page but four of them are related to one subject, i.e., the Building trust in the public record policy. Of the naa-CA-mc category, this policy and its developing process were highlighted on the IM space home page, which became the other record occurrence of the two record(s) occurrences for this time period. Records authorities continued its persistence, appearing from the first page to the last page and occupying one of the highlighted areas. The trend of adding information-related item also continued, here

Table 3. IM contents and changes of the second phase

{2019-10-31, the 1st page of the second IM phase:
• naa-CA: Digital Continuity 2020; Information Management standards
Information governance; Building interoperability; Check-up PLUS 2019; Records authorities; Information management legislation; Information management policies; Types of information and systems
• naa-SA: Agency Service Centre; GAIN Australia
• The Highlighted (from left to right): Introduction to the Digital Continuity 2020 Policy; Check-up PLUS 2019; Records authorities}

Time	The updated	New item	The same	The highlighted
2020-08-01	• None	• None	• All other 2019-10-31 items	• Same (Introduction to the Digital Continuity 2020 Policy) • Have your say on our next policy for government; • Same (Records authorities)
2020-09-20	• None	• None	• All other 2020-08-01 items	• Same • Our next policy for government (from 2021) • Same
2020-10-31	• → Check-up PLUS (2021) [7]	• None	• All other 2020-09-20 items	• Same • Building trust in the public record policy (from 2021) • Same
2021-01-16	• None	• Building trust in the public record	• All other 2020-10-31 items except Digital Continuity 2020	• Building trust in the public record • Same (Records authorities) • Check-up PLUS (2021) [8]
2021-04-01 (till 2022-01-04)	• None	• Information management and data capabilities	• All other 2021-01-16 items	• Same

with the Information management and data capabilities. For the naa-CA-p, Check-up PLUS is now at its 2021 version and the naa-SA remained exactly the same throughout.

3.3 From RM to IM

As the above tables sort out changes within the established time periods respectively, there are gaps between RM and the first IM phase as well as the first IM phase and the second IM phase. Between 2016-10-18 the last RM page and 2016-11-13 the first page of the IM first phase, items were both removed and added:

- Removed: Strategic information and records management; Managing your agency records; naa-SA (Publications and tools; Where to go for help; GAIN Australia; A-Z of information and records management);
- Added: Records authorities; Managing information; naa-SA (Support)

Between 2019-10-08 the last page of the first IM phase and 2019-10-31 the first page of the second IM phase, items were as well both removed and added:

- Removed: Managing information; naa-SA (Support and professional development)
- Added: Information management legislation; Information management policies; Types of information and systems; naa-SA (Agency Service Centre; GAIN Australia)

By combining these moved and added items, we identified 1) the time when Records authorities was added to the IM space (i.e., 2016-11-13) and 2) the time when the less formal expression Managing information was replaced by formal ones such as Information management legislation and Information management policies (i.e., 2019-10-31).

3.4 The Entire Process

For the entire process, we observed that:

- The object of management changed from records, information and records, to information.
- The managerial considerations changed accordingly from centering on records to more and more on information.

  1. Information governance emerged alongside information management (standards, legislation, and policies);
  2. The only survival records item is Records authorities, which was removed from menu during the initial emergence of information management within the RM time period and added back during the first phase of IM;

- Performance information had been collected throughout.

4 The Comparison

Following the above observations, we compared relevant specifics for furthering understanding.

4.1 Object of Management

As the object of management, either record(s) or information should have a formal definition. The situation, however, is not that simple. First, record(s) has a formal definition, yet information does not have any; second, record(s) has more than one formal definitions; and third, information is used to explain record(s). Both the Archives Act and the AS ISO 15489 RM standard formally define records, with the former stipulating a record as "a document, or an object, in any form (including any electronic form) that is, or has been, kept by reason of: (a) any information or matter that it contains or that can be obtained from it; or (b) its connection with any event, person, circumstance or thing" (s3) [1] and the latter characterizes record(s) as "information created, received and maintained as evidence and as an asset by an organization or person, in pursuit of legal obligations or in the transaction of business" [2]. Neither the wordings nor the meanings are compatible with each other entirely. For our analysis, we recognized that in comparison with information (which, again, does not have a definition in either the Archives Act or the RM standard), record(s) 1) has a more concrete and sometimes physical format and 2) record(s) contains/carries information.

NAA's approach towards the meanings of records and information was to put out a central message, conveying also the significance and affordance of their management. The central message of the RM space explained records by the following points:

- (RM-1) Records are an essential tool of good business and efficient administration. For government agencies, records document what is done and why. They provide information for planning and decision-making and evidence of government accountability;
- (RM-2) In the long term, some of the records your agency makes will be retained as national archives and so become part of Australia's documentary heritage;
- (RM-3) They are often subject to specific legal requirements [9].

The central message of the first phase of the IM space (IMI) made the following points:

- (IMI-1) Information and records are important government assets. They support planning and service delivery.
- (IMI-2) Good information and records will help reduce risks for your agency;
- (IMI-3) Managing and storing information and records in the right place means they will be protected and easily found;
- (IMI-4) All information created, sent and received as part of your work for the Australian Government is a record;
- (IMI-5) In the long term, some of the records your agency creates will be retained as national archives and become part of Australia's documentary history.

The central message of the second phase of the IM space (IMII) made the following points:

- (IMII-1) Managing and storing information, data and records in the right place and the right way means they will be protected and easily found; and
- (IMII-2) At the National Archives of Australia, we provide advice and support to help everyone working in government to achieve this goal.

From RM to IMI to IMII, the clarity of these messages progressively declined. The RM central message made clear what records could offer (RM-1 and RM-2) and how records were controlled (RM-3), yet the IM messages clouded the "offer" part increasingly and retired the "control" part entirely. The IMI message caused confusions by adding information to records without explaining why (IMI-1, IMI-2 and IMI-3) and the IMII message caused further confusions by adding data in between information and records without explaining why (IMII-1). The IMI message was clearer than the IMII one because it defined the relationship between records and information (i.e., IMI-4) and it maintained records' affordance as part of the nation's documentary history (RM-2 and IMI-5) – a noble destination of records. These efforts disappeared in the IMII message; instead, an emphasis on NAA's role appeared (IMII-2), which was unprecedented in this NAA RM-IM history.

These messages seem to reflect also the changed thoughts behind the NAA's approaches. We recognized the following: 1) highlighting legal requirement vs not mentioning it, 2) rationalizing systematically vs concisely, 3) limiting to the present vs including also the future, and 4) focusing on agencies vs individual employees.

4.2 Managerial Considerations

The Pure RM. The item names in the above tables indicated that managerial considerations for records and information are mostly intermingled. For example, Information management framework and Information governance appeared during the RM period (i.e., 2007-08-30–2016–10-17) and the item Records authorities had been in existence throughout the entire IM period (i.e., 2016-11-13–2022-01-04). As such, it seemed that only the beginning of the RM period (i.e., 2007-08-30–2008-04-13) is fully and clearly RM focused: the considerations for creating, capturing, describing, keeping, destroying, transferring, and preserving were all about records [10]. Information, as stipulated by the legal definition of records, remained to be "contained" in records (Archives Act 1983, 2022). The adding of information to the RM space destroyed this clarity as its advent was not accompanied by any explanations – not even a definition of information that could help with some level of comprehension. The adding was literarily to place information next to records, i.e., "information and records" or "records and information" (which is overall rare) [11]. It is clear that there was a battle between information and records in terms of occurrence, which is logically relevant to substance as substance requires occurrence to display it.

Records over Information, or not? On the pages of Information management framework [12] and IT systems [13], records – not records and information, just records – dominated. Information management framework during this time period (i.e., 2007/10/27 – 2011/09/03) was clearly about records, so was IT systems during its existence (i.e., 20071028 – 20110903). Therefore, the term information here appeared as a cover only, under which were indeed managerial considerations for records. Moreover, the pure RM items of the RM beginning time were carried on for this time period.

The next round is Strategic information and records management (20111014–20160730) replacing Information management framework and IT systems. The occurrence of "information and records" largely increased and the term records was moved to the label, making one more "information and records". Managerial considerations towards information and records could not be distinguished as nowhere differences could be discerned when they were together. For example, when requiring that "your agency should have an information and records management strategy", it explained "strategy" as "systematic approach" but offered nothing on how information and records should function respectively or together against the systematic approach [14]. Another example is the part What are information and records management policies and procedures?, a place where one expect to find useful information regarding the differences between RM and IM. Yet, the first sentence beneath it stated only as "Policies and procedures should be approved by the head of agency or other senior management" [14], apparently not answering the "what". On the other hand, records evidently received much more attention than information: 1) Managing your agency records (20111008 – 20160417) co-existed with Strategic information and records management, 2) records occurred frequently alone (e.g., "Linking business to records" and "Set out the principles for managing records") yet information did only once (i.e., Information architecture), 3) under Information architecture, the content was about both information and records (e.g., "An information architecture outlines how information and records are used, described and organized across the whole of your agency") [14], and 4) the section Standards and legislation was entirely about records (e.g., "Records and legislation" and "Records in Evidence") [15].

This records-dominating (in spite of the information presence) situation started to tilt when information governance appeared as a submenu item under Strategic information and records management at 2013/04/11. On the Information governance page, information (e.g., "information assets" and "digital information" in addition to "information governance") dominated. Only a handful records occurred when accountability was being referred to and only one independent occurrence, i.e., records manager [16]. At 2015/11/13[1], Information governance moved up to the RM main menu, explaining Information governance as "an approach to managing information assets across an entire organization to support its business outcomes" [17], same as the one on the 2013/04/11 page. It must be pointed out that one of the two objects of governance, i.e., information asset (the other being digital information) was not defined or explained. Its difference

[1] Note that in Table 1, the date for Information governance's occurrence on the menu is 20160302. The discrepancy is caused by the different tracing URLs. For Table 1, the URL for records management was used and here, the URL for Information governance was used. The rest is all on the Wayback Machine.

with records, therefore, remained unknown (as well). Moreover, records were still being placed next to information, raising the question as to the differences between "information asset" and "information and records". Also, the question about the differences between management and governance emerged. From the above explanation for information governance (i.e., governance is "an approach to managing …"), management seemed to be synonymous to governance. If so, then why were there existences of both information management and information governance?

Despite of all these confusions, we recognized the trend/intention of intensifying the presence of information and information asset over records.

Information over Records, or not? The dividing of the IM space into two phases was due to the way of content display, not the substance of the contents. Both the phases conspicuously focused on information and the second one formalized (or fortified) the intention of the first one in terms of menu item names. Apart from the persistent Information governance, the major information items of the first phase were Information Management Standards and Managing information. The Information Management Standards page excluded any occurrence of records [18]; however, the ideas for both the IM benefits and principles were identical to those for records except the replacement of the term records with the term "business information". For example, both records and business information were stated essential for government accountability [19] and both records and business information were required to be created, described, transferred, etc. [20].

The Building interoperability page followed the suit of the Information Management Standards, i.e., to exclude records altogether. The difference between these two is that the former introduced data into the information focus as building interoperability "means you can exchange information and data between different systems" [21]. Accordingly, Data governance and management appeared, characterized as "an essential component of information governance" [22]. If this characterization tells minimally the relationship between data and information (part of), it does not, however, help with the conceptual understanding of these terms: what are the differences between them? By extension, why are they better than records to be the object of management?

The IM second phase removed the still records-dominating item Managing information and added four more information related items to its menu, i.e., Information management legislation, Information management policies, Types of information and systems, and Information management and data capabilities, which gave rise to the above information-intensified observation. However, these new items did not follow the suit of Information Management Standard and Building interoperability in terms of excluding any occurrence of records in their contents. Under Information management legislation were acts relating to records, i.e., the Archives Act 1983 and the Archives Regulations [23], and the opening sentence for the Types of information and systems stated that "Business systems create and manage digital information and capture information about records" [24]. The Information management policies page featured the Digital Continuity 2020 Policy, which "enables the integration of information governance principles and practices into the work of agencies" [25], exhibiting a tie with Information governance. As we observed above, Information governance did not exclude records but used (while in small quantity) the expression of "information and records". The Information governance in the IM second phase kept still records, but used not only "records and information" but also "records management" [26], which was frequently seen in the pure RM phase but rare subsequently. The Information management and data capabilities "outline[s] the skills and knowledge that employees and their organizations need to create and manage information assets (records, information and data) effectively to meet business and accountability requirements" [27]. As such, it included certainly records. Moreover, the skill and knowledge requirements were devised based on all other information items such as Information legislation and Information governance [28], it therefore would be difficult for it not to include any content relating to records. By putting all these together, we recognized that the intensity of information taking over records was noticeably softened by the contents underneath the item names.

The Policy That Travelled Through RM and IM. As indicated by the above three tables, the Digital Continuity 2020 Policy had been an important policy for a long time, running from 2016-03-02 (in Table 1) to 2021-10-27 (in Table 3), across both the RM and IM periods. It had occupied one of the three boxes of highlight during the second IM phase till its replacement by the Building trust in the public record policy. We examined the following four versions of the policy with the hope to shed light on the records-information-records puzzle: the 2016-03-02 one (DC2020-2016, first time on the RM main), the 20170122 one (DC2020-2017, first time on the menu of the IM first phase), the 2019-10-31 one (DC2020-2019, first time on the menu of the IM second phase), and the 2021-10-21 (DC2020-2021, last time of our data collection period). Also, due to the statement in DC2020-2016 that "The Digital Continuity 2020 policy builds on the Digital Transition Policy" [29], we examined this Digital Transition Policy as well.

The Digital transition policy was first approved in 2011 and remained valid at the time when DC2020 2016 version arrived. The purpose of this policy is "to move Australian Government agencies to digital information and records management for efficiency purposes" [30]. As indicated by this purpose statement, this policy concerned itself with records and "information and records", conforming seamlessly to the "records over information" situation that was evident during the Strategic information management and Managing your agency records time period. The DC2020 2016 version, however, seemed to have created a 50%-50% situation, where information dominated yet records appeared to be the endgame or destination of information. The term information was used for all important places, e.g., "enables the integration of information governance principles and practices into the work of agencies" (purpose), "Agencies will manage their information as an asset" (outcome), and "Information is valued" (principle)). Under the Authority section, the policy stated that by the Archives Act, records "cover all information in digital and non-digital formats that is created, used or received as part of government business" [31], which corresponded to one of the points made by the central message of the first phase of IM (i.e., IMI-4). Which is over which? Challenging to say. We, however, asked this question: why was information needed – in fact, all over the place – when there was a legal concept for record(s)? As the other three versions (i.e., DC2020 2017, DC2020 2019, and DC2020 2021) carried on the content of the DC2020 2016, our "over" judgment remained uncertain, and our question remained unanswered.

The successor of DC2020, i.e., the Building trust in the public record policy 2021, continued the records-information swinging situation. In this policy, information asset – not records, not information – dominated. However, this term "refer to records, information and data collectively", its Terminology section explained [32]. This new term, therefore, made no contribution to the existent situation in terms of clarifying confusions such as those concerning the differences between records and information. Were managerial considerations applicable to information asset equally applicable to records and information? If so, why are records and information still needed? If not, how can them be collectively managed? Moreover, the full title of the policy, i.e., Building trust in the public record: managing information and data for government and community, seemed to suggest that record covered information and data – an idea that was promulgated in DC2020.

4.3 Performance

The Check-up series are online self-assessment tools designed by NAA for agencies, specifically, questionnaires for self-administration. Early assessments, i.e., those by Check-up and Check-up 2.0, are only accessible to agencies. Later on, NAA started to produce summary reports and published them online, which include 2016 Check-up Digital Analysis of 2015 Survey Data and the 2018, 2019, and 2020 Check-up PLUS assessment. As the design of the questions was based on NAA intentions, these reports could not be strictly considered as performance reports. Moreover, as they are self-administered questionnaires, accuracy cannot be guaranteed across the board. Nevertheless, their content would still shed light on the management situation. Our examination of these reports focused on the most problematic areas, or as the 2016 report stated, "areas that require ongoing attention" [33]; or as the PLUS reports stated, areas that were at the "lowest maturity level" [34]. We observed that from the 2015 report to all the PLUS reports, areas relating to retention and disposition (where the item Records authorities is the soul) and later on information governance (one that our study identified as mostly confusing) had persistently remained as the most problematic areas.

5 Conclusions

Our study was triggered by the IM replacing RM phenomenon and we aimed at why. We found out that RM in practice had not changed into IM because the differences between IM and RM had never been clear, from the start to end. In other words, the particularities of managerial considerations towards information could not be discerned. High level justifications or explanations regarding the replacement did not seem to exist either. As such, we could not distill answers for the why question. What we have discovered seemed to be a perfect case of plus ça change, plus c'est la même chose: behind the dazzling changes (i.e., the large number of managerial considerations), the matter (managerial challenges and outcomes) remained the same.

We still hope future studies – by us or anyone interested – can do better in coming up with empirical explanations for the replacement. Given the conceptual confusions here, however, we expect a much more systematic approach: we would need insights from the RM and IM practitioners, from those who led the dazzling changes, from those who implemented (or refused to implement) those changes, and the public who will be much more impacted by government decisions in the artificial intelligence world. A daunting task, but one that needs to be done.

References

1. Attorney-General's Department, Canberra ACT: Archives Act (1983)
2. Online Browsing Platform (OBP) ISO 15489-1:2016(en). https://www.iso.org/obp/ui/#iso:std:iso:15489:-1:ed-2:v1:en. Accessed 21 May 2022
3. ITRUSTAI homepage. https://interparestrustai.org/trust. Accessed 23 June 2022
4. National Archives of Australia Check-up Digital. https://web.archive.org/web/20140625050405/http://naa.gov.au/records-management/check-up/index.aspx. Accessed 9 Mar 2022
5. National Archives of Australia RM agency survey. https://web.archive.org/web/20160317024046/http://www.naa.gov.au/records-management/rm-survey.aspx. Accessed 7 Apr 2022
6. National Archives of Australia Building interoperability. http://web.archive.org/web/20190217051208/http://www.naa.gov.au/information-management/Building-interoperability/index.aspx. Accessed 25 May 2022
7. National Archives of Australia Check-up Plus. http://web.archive.org/web/20201027231442/https://www.naa.gov.au/information-management/check-plus. Accessed 21 Mar 2022
8. National Archives of Australia Check-up Plus. http://web.archive.org/web/20210123040432/https://www.naa.gov.au/information-management/check-plus. Accessed 26 July 2022
9. National Archives of Australia Records management. https://web.archive.org/web/20161018000731/http://www.naa.gov.au/records-management/. Accessed 20 Aug 2022
10. National Archives of Australia Create, capture & describe. https://web.archive.org/web/20071011174401/http://naa.gov.au/records-management/create-capture-describe/index.aspx. Accessed 23 June 2022
11. National Archives of Australia Information management framework. https://web.archive.org/web/20080413071516/http://www.naa.gov.au/records-management/IM-framework/index.aspx. Accessed 11 July 2022
12. National Archives of Australia Information management framework. https://web.archive.org/web/20110311220248/http://www.naa.gov.au/records-management/IM-framework/index.aspx. Accessed 14 Apr 2022
13. National Archives of Australia IT systems,https://web.archive.org/web/20080413071653/http://www.naa.gov.au/records-management/systems/index.aspx. Accessed 25 Mar 2022
14. National Archives of Australia Strategic information and records management. https://web.archive.org/web/20111014095617/http://www.naa.gov.au/records-management/strategic-information/index.aspx. Accessed 12 Apr 2022
15. National Archives of Australia Standards and legislation. https://web.archive.org/web/20111007080252/http://naa.gov.au/records-management/strategic-information/standards/index.aspx. Accessed 23 July 2022
16. National Archives of Australia Information governance. http://web.archive.org/web/20130411101806/http://naa.gov.au/records-management/strategic-information/information-governance/index.aspx. Accessed 8 Mar 2022
17. National Archives of Australia Information governance. http://web.archive.org/web/20151113114034/http://www.naa.gov.au/records-management/information-governance/index.aspx. Accessed 18 Mar 2022

18. National Archives of Australia Information Management Standard. http://web.archive.org/web/20170506060823/http://www.naa.gov.au/information-management/information-management-standard/index.aspx. Accessed 17 May 2022
19. National Archives of Australia Records management. https://web.archive.org/web/20160302110113/http://www.naa.gov.au/records-management/index.aspx. Accessed 1 Apr 2022
20. National Archives of Australia Managing your agency records. https://web.archive.org/web/20160305074902/http://www.naa.gov.au/records-management/agency/index.aspx. Accessed 5 June 2022
21. National Archives of Australia Building interoperability. http://web.archive.org/web/20190217051208/http://www.naa.gov.au/information-management/Building-interoperability/index.aspx. Accessed 9 July 2022
22. National Archives of Australia Data governance and management. http://web.archive.org/web/20190315014342/http://naa.gov.au/information-management/Building-interoperability/interoperabilitydevphases/datagov/index.aspx. Accessed 22 June 2022
23. National Archives of Australia Information management legislation. http://web.archive.org/web/20191031114504/http://www.naa.gov.au/information-management/information-management-legislation. Accessed 24 July 2022
24. National Archives of Australia Types of information and systems. http://web.archive.org/web/20191031114519/https://www.naa.gov.au/information-management/types-information-and-systems. Accessed 11 Aug 2022
25. National Archives of Australia Information management policy. http://web.archive.org/web/20200112023428/https://www.naa.gov.au/information-management/information-management-policies. Accessed 11 Apr 2022
26. National Archives of Australia Responsibilities of the National Archives and Australian Government Agencies. http://web.archive.org/web/20200408181323/https://www.naa.gov.au/information-management/information-governance/responsibilities-national-archives-and-australian-government-agencies. Accessed 14 June 2022
27. National Archives of Australia Information management and data capabilities. http://web.archive.org/web/20210413161120/https://www.naa.gov.au/information-management/information-management-and-data-capabilities. Accessed 11 Aug 2022
28. National Archives of Australia Capabilities for information management professionals. http://web.archive.org/web/20210418074216/https://www.naa.gov.au/information-management/information-management-and-data-capabilities/capabilities-information-management-professionals. Accessed 1 June 2022
29. National Archives of Australia Digital Continuity 2020. http://web.archive.org/web/20160317013330/http://naa.gov.au/records-management/digital-transition-and-digital-continuity/index.aspx. Accessed 11 July 2022
30. National Archives of Australia Digital Transition Policy. http://web.archive.org/web/20160317084719/http://www.naa.gov.au/%2frecords-management%2fdigital-transition-and-digital-continuity%2fdigital-transition-policy%2findex.aspx. Accessed 21 July 2022
31. National Archives of Australia Digital Continuity 2020 Policy. http://web.archive.org/web/20160302113041/http://naa.gov.au/records-management/digital-transition-and-digital-continuity/digital-continuity-2020/index.aspx. Accessed 23 Aug 2022
32. National Archives of Australia Building trust in the public record: managing information and data for government and community. http://web.archive.org/web/20210305145101/https://www.naa.gov.au/information-management/information-management-policies/building-trust-public-record-policy/building-trust-public-record-managing-information-and-data-government-and-community#role-of-naa. Accessed 2 Sept 2022

33. National Archives of Australia Check-up Digital. http://web.archive.org/web/20140530103556/http://naa.gov.au/records-management/check-up/index.aspx. Accessed 28 June 2022
34. National Archives of Australia Check-up plus whole of government report 2019. http://web.archive.org/web/20210308091746/https:/www.naa.gov.au/sites/default/files/2020-02/Check-Up-Plus-Whole-Of-Government-Report-2019.pdf. Accessed 21 Aug 2022

Information Sustainability in Rural Bangladesh: The Use of Analogue and Digital Backups

Viviane Frings-Hessami(✉)

Monash University, Clayton, VIC, Australia
Viviane.Hessami@monash.edu

Abstract. Access to information plays an important role in supporting sustainable development goals. In marginalised communities where people have limited access to information, preservation of information previously accessed can play a crucial role in supporting economic, social, and personal activities and fostering sustainable development. However, little is known about how marginalised rural communities in developing countries preserve information and how digital technologies have impacted on their practices. In order to investigate how individuals in remote rural communities access and preserve the information that they need to support their work and daily activities, the author organised two focus group discussions and ten individual interviews with village men and women in the district of Satkhira in Bangladesh. The findings from the research show that villagers, who have limited access to smartphones and to the internet, are conscious of the fragility of digital technologies and digital data and use paper notebooks as a form of backup for information found on the internet, and that some of them also use digital backups to preserve important information. These findings highlight the importance of ensuring the sustainability of information and of encouraging the use of methods to access and preserve information that are appropriate to the cultural and technological contexts and that meet the needs of the marginalised communities.

Keywords: Information sustainability · Information preservation · Analogue backups · Digital backups · Bangladesh · Sustainable development

1 Introduction

Little is known about how rural communities in developing countries preserve information and how digital technologies have impacted on their practices. Access to information plays an important role in supporting sustainable development [1]. In contexts where continuous access to information cannot be guaranteed, the preservation of previously accessed information can help ensure that individuals will be able to access information when they need it. However, personal information management (PIM) research and digital preservation research have focused on urban contexts in developed countries where individuals have access to large amount of information and can use digital tools to manage the information they wish to preserve [2]. The information landscape is very

© The Author(s), under exclusive license to Springer Nature Switzerland AG 2023
I. Sserwanga et al. (Eds.): iConference 2023, LNCS 13971, pp. 66–78, 2023.
https://doi.org/10.1007/978-3-031-28035-1_6

different in rural areas in developing countries where individuals have limited access to information and to technologies to access and preserve information.

A recent research project conducted in Bangladesh showed that rural women who were involved in an information and communication technology for development (ICT4D) project, the PROTIC project [3], were very conscious of the fragility of digital technologies and used notebooks to transcribe information sent to them by text messages because they thought that paper records would last longer than digital information kept on their phones [2, 4]. After the end of the project, the majority of the women could not afford the cost of a new smartphone and regular data packages, but they continued to use their notebooks to access information that they had received during the project and to write new information because this method of preserving information worked well for them [2, 5]. Women in Bangladesh perform more than half of agricultural activities [6]. However, they often have limited access to information because they face socio-cultural and religious restrictions [7] that make it difficult for them to go to the nearby towns to consult with agriculture extension officers or to bring their animals to the livestock hospital. By providing 300 women in remote villages with smartphones and setting up an information system for them, the PROTIC project had endeavoured to bridge the distance between the women and sources of information. With their smartphones, the women were able to access information that enabled them to start cultivating new crops and to set up small economic ventures [3, 8]. However, no measures had been put in place to ensure that the women would continue to have access to that information after the end of the project. After some of the phones broke down and information was lost, the women themselves took the initiative to write down in notebooks the information they found important and wanted to preserve for future use. Two years after the end of the project, they still used those notebooks to check information and to write new information they wanted to keep because it was a method that was working well for them [2, 5].

In order to determine if the practice of preserving information in notebooks is an innovation brought about by the PROTIC project or is common in rural areas of Bangladesh, the research conducted for this paper investigated how other villagers from the same area, who had not been involved with the PROTIC project, accessed and preserved information and whether they also used notebooks to preserve information. By conducting interviews both with men and women, the author also intended to assess whether the methods used by women to access and preserve information differed significantly from those used by men. Two focus groups, one with men and one with women, and ten individual interviews with five men and five women were organised in April 2022.

The paper starts with a brief literature review and an explanation of the methodology used to conduct the research. Before discussing the methods that the participants used to preserve information, the author presents the findings of the research on the types of phones that the participants owned or had access to, the methods they used to access information and the types of information they accessed. The author compares the methods used by the participants in this research with those used by the PROTIC women, discusses the differences between the practices adopted by men and women, and raises questions for further research. The conclusions highlight the importance of ensuring the sustainability of information and of encouraging the use of methods to access and preserve information that are appropriate to the cultural and technological contexts and that meet the needs of the communities.

2 Literature Review

Access to information plays an important role in supporting sustainable development goals [1, 9]. Agricultural productivity can be improved through access to information on new seeds, fertilisers, medicines and pesticides, and farmers can increase their income through timely information on crop prices in different markets [10–13]. However, people leaving in marginalised communities in developing countries are often unable to access the information they need due to their distance from sources of information [12]. In order to remedy this limitation, ICT4D projects have been designed to help marginalised communities in developing countries to use ICTs to access information. However, ICT4D projects focus on technology to access information rather than on the information itself [14, 15] and do not plan for the preservation of the information accessed during the projects [16]. The research conducted by Frings-Hessami et al. [4] during the PROTIC project was the first study of information preservation practices in an ICT4D project. It showed that the female participants in that ICT4D project started transcribing in notebooks the information that was sent to them via text messages after some of the phones that had been provided to them broke down and they lost data, because they felt that paper notebooks would last longer than phones. Research conducted two years after the end of the project showed that the women were still using those notebooks to access the information they had written in them and that some of them continued to write new information in their notebooks [2]. By then, most of the smartphones provided by the project had broken down and few women had been able to afford the cost of a new smartphone. In those circumstances, the curated, localised information offered by the project was a valuable source of information for women who had limited access to new information.

In marginalised communities where people have limited access to information, preservation of information previously accessed can play a crucial role in supporting economic, social and personal activities. However, the literature review conducted for this paper showed that no previous research had been conducted on information preservation practices by rural communities in a developing country besides the research conducted about the PROTIC project. Personal information management (PIM) research has been conducted in contexts where people have easy access to information and need help to manage the abundance of information [17–19]. The research done in these contexts is of little relevance to people in marginalised communities in developing countries, for whom limited access to information and to technology to access information is a problem. A few studies [e.g. 20, 21] have investigated how individuals manage their personal information through analogue means in everyday activities and leisure activities, but the North American contexts in which those studies were conducted are very different from those in which Bangladesh rural communities live.

Bangladesh is a developing country affected by frequent flooding and cyclones where 61% of the population live in rural areas [22] and 29.5% live in poverty according to the official statistics [23]. Literacy rates have improved considerably in the past decade, with preliminary results from the 2022 census showing that the general literacy rate increased from 51.77% in 2011 to 74.66% in 2022 although substantial differences remain between urban and rural areas and between men and women [24, 25]. The latest figures available for the district of Satkhira in the division of Khulna, where research for this paper was conducted, show that in 2011, 46.61% of rural women and 54.47% of rural men in that district were literate [26].

In recent years, Bangladesh has achieved a rapid development of its mobile phone network. The Bangladeshi government has made it one of its priorities to develop information and communication technologies (ICTs) and to provide government services online [27]. In 2021, there were 171.85 million mobile phone subscriptions [28], or about one phone per person in a country of 165 million people, although many people own more than one phone, while many, particularly women in rural areas, do not have any. Of those phones, 41% are smartphones and the rest are basic phones [29]. According to GSMA's Mobile Gender Gap Report 2021, Bangladeshi women are 42% less likely than men to own a smartphone and 42% less likely to use mobile internet [29]. Recent research has shown that mobile phones are commonly shared within families [30, 31] so that women who do not own a smartphone may have access to the smartphone of a family member. Nevertheless, access to information and services remain restricted for people living in rural areas and particularly for women. Through interviews with men and women in a marginalised community in the South of Bangladesh, the research conducted for this paper gathered some interesting data about the ways men and women use mobile phones to access information and about their use of analogue and digital technologies to preserve information.

3 Methodology

The data for this paper was collected during two focus group discussions (FGD), one with eight men and one with eight women, and ten individual semi-structured interviews with five men and five women organised in April 2022 in the sub-district of Shyamnagar (district of Sahkhira) where previous research had been conducted on the information preservation practices of PROTIC women [2]. The numbers of interviews were relatively small due to time constraints, but the author's aim was to get an idea of practices used in the village before developing a larger study. The interview questions were prepared by the author and the focus group and interviews were conducted by a Bangladeshi team consisting of one research collaborator and two students. Participants were selected among the local community by a local non-governmental organisation (NGO) involved in development projects in the area, which provided logistics support for the project on the ground. The author did not specify any criteria for inclusion in the research, except in the case of women, that they had not been PROTIC participants. The FGD were held in a meeting hall (for the women) and in a school (for the men) and the interviews were organised in places chosen by the interviewees. Questions discussed in the FGD and semi-structured interviews included questions on phone ownership and use, information access and information preservation, and specific questions on the use of notebooks to record and preserve information. The interviews and FGD were audio-recorded with the participants' permission. They were translated by Bangladeshi students, then analysed thematically by the author. In order to preserve their anonymity, in this paper, the interview participants are given the codes of IM1–5 for the men and IF1–5 for the women.

4 Findings

4.1 Phone Ownership and Internet Access

Among the participants, more men than women owned a smartphone. However, there was a difference between the men who participated in the FGD and those who took part in individual interviews. Only two out of the eight men (25%) who participated in the FGD owned a smartphone whereas all the interviewees had one. Three of them (two from the FGD and one interviewee) kept their smartphones at home and also had a basic phone that they took with them when they went out. All of the others only owned a basic phone. For the women, the FGD and interviewees groups were similar. In each group, only one woman owned a smartphone. Three of the interviewees had a basic phone and one did not have any phone. The other seven FGD participants owned a basic phone (see Table 1).

Table 1. Type of phone owned by FGD and interview participants.

Phone owned	Men interviews	Men FGD	Women interviews	Women FGD
Smartphone	4	0	1	1
Basic phone, plus a smartphone kept at home	1	2	0	0
Basic phone	0	6	3	7
No phone	0	0	1	0
Total	5	8	5	8

All the male interviewees who had a smartphone used it regularly to access information. The interviewee (IM2) who owned a button phone and kept a smartphone a home for everyone's use explained that he was not very confident using it to access the internet and that when he needed to get information from the internet, he asked his son to help him. All the male FGD participants who only had a basic phone were able to ask a relative, friend or neighbour to use their smartphone if they needed to access the internet. However, they did not all specify if they could do it themselves or if they needed help to do it.

The two women who had a smartphone used it regularly to access information on the internet. For the other women, not owning a smartphone did not mean that they did not have access to the internet. Smartphones were commonly shared among relatives. For example, IF2 who only had a basic phone used the internet on her husband's phone when she needed it and bought herself data packages for it. The women who did not know how to use the internet asked a relative or a neighbour to do it for them. For example, IF5 asked her husband to look for information for her on his smartphone, and IF4 asked her neighbour's son, who had a smartphone, to look for a solution for her when she encountered a problem. The female interviewee (IF1) who did not own any mobile phone was able to borrow her husband's phone to make calls, but if she needed information from the internet, she asked her husband or her son to search it for her. Five of the seven female FGD participants who did not have a smartphone were able to ask a relative to look for information for them on their smartphone when they needed information, and one of them was able to do it herself with the smartphone that was kept at home for the whole family's use. The last one could only benefit from the internet when her son came for a visit and looked for information for her.

4.2 Access to Information

The ways that the participants used to access information were influenced by their phone ownership. Since more men owned a smartphone, more of them were able to use the internet to access information and felt confident doing it. Four out of the five male interviewees said that their preferred method to access information was the internet, whereas only one female interviewee preferred that method. IM1 commented that he preferred to use the internet to access information because "I do not have to call someone and wait for them to arrive and give solutions, it saves me a lot of time". On the other hand, one male interviewee (IM2) preferred to go and talk to the agriculture extension officers in Shyamnagar because he preferred face-to-face communication. Three of the female interviewees were more comfortable calling the agriculture officers than using the internet even though they could have borrowed a relative's phone to do so. For example, IF4 said that "the internet seems an easier and faster way to get information… but I am more comfortable using my mobile phone and calling officers for help since I do not know how to use the internet".

The men who used the internet read the news, checked the weather forecast and the price of goods in the local market, looked for solutions to problems they encountered in their farming and animal husbandry or to health issues of their family, on Google, Facebook and YouTube. They shared information on Facebook, and communicated with extension officers and vets via Messenger or WhatsApp, sending them pictures of their crops or sick animals so that the extension officers or the vets could diagnose the problem and prescribe a treatment. They also used the internet to get educational resources for their children, to listen to religious podcasts and for entertainment.

The female interviewee who owned a smartphone, IF3, also used Google and YouTube to search for information and sent messages to the vets, doctors and agriculture officers via Messenger. The women who occasionally used the internet browsed Facebook and sent messages through Messenger to the agriculture officers, doctors, or vets.

Although most of the male FGD participants did not own a smartphone, they all concurred that the internet was the most convenient way to access information. However, when asked how they usually got information, all of them said that they used other methods than the internet. One participant said that the first thing they usually did when they had a question on an agricultural matter was to call the agricultural officers or sometimes to go and visit them. Another participant explained that "for agriculture or farming, it is best to call the farming officers; however, if they are not available, searching the internet becomes the best option". A third participant added that they used the internet to send pictures to the agriculture officers so that they could diagnose their problems and prescribe a remedy. The participants also went to the local agricultural supplies shop to ask for information and used books that they had received from the local NGO during agricultural training.

Similarly, all the female FGD participants and the interviewee who did not own a phone thought that the internet was the most convenient way of finding information. However, when asked how they usually looked for information, they said that they asked knowledgeable people in their area, called or visited the farming officers or read books that the local NGO gave them during agricultural training sessions.

The participants who were proficient in using the internet thought that the information they could find online was more detailed than the information they could get from the extension officers because these officers are too busy to spend time explaining the details. On the other hand, participants who were not confident using the internet thought that the information they got from the farming officers was more specific and more relevant to their farming conditions.

Although men and women appreciated the quality of the information they could obtain from the extension officers, two male FGD participants commented that the internet is better because "there is authentic information there" and "because you cannot always trust people and word of mouth from people is always exaggerated". This scepticism was extended to the local shopkeepers, with one participant commenting that in cases where they had to seek advice from the agricultural supplies shop, they cross-checked the names of the medicines on the internet "because there can be a chance that the shopkeeper is deliberately giving and selling us wrong medicines to make money out of us; we cannot always trust them so cross-checking the medicine is important".

4.3 Information Preservation

All the participants made efforts to preserve information. Both men and women wrote down information that they wanted to keep because they were aware of the fragility of digital technologies and digital data and felt that paper documents would last longer than information preserved on their phones. The five male interviewees and all the male FGD participants said that they preferred to write down important information. Several of them stated that they had been using notebooks for a long time. IM1 explained that he preferred to write down information because he thought that it was a more reliable way of keeping information: "I prefer writing [information] down in a notebook because saving information on a mobile phone is unreliable because if I lose my phone by any chance, the information will be lost as well."

IM4 sometimes took screenshots of important information that he found, but he preferred to write information in his notebook because he thought that he "cannot rely on mobile screenshots because they might get deleted accidentally". IM3 concurred:

> *I download a lot of information, but I cannot rely on it much because four to five of my mobile sets have already broken accidentally. So, I note down a lot of information that is important to me. Say, for example, if a come across a video*

about pigeons' health, first I download it, and then I take notes from it; or if I come across information about fishing, crops or anything important, I quickly note the important points. I include the diseases and their treatments and later whenever I need the information, I simply look at those treatments from my notes.

In these cases, the notebooks act as backups of the information saved on their phones. However, some of the participants took the backing up process one step further, creating both analogue and digital backups as explained by IM5:

When I come across any important piece of information on Facebook or YouTube, I take screenshots, then later I write it down and also take pictures of my handwritten notes and save them on my phone. For example, names of medicines for my crop or livestock, or names of fertilisers, I write them down.

Most of the male interviewees also reported taking pictures of their important documents, such as their identity cards, land titles, birth certificates, and medical prescriptions, and keeping them on their phone for backup and easy access. One of the male FGD participant (who only owned a basic phone) had another reason to take pictures of important information on his phone. He commented that "these pictures help to keep evidence". He explained that for example:

when there is any project happening in the village, during the opening ceremony, I take pictures of *the people and the timeline. Later on, if they are delaying the work, I straight away show them the pictures where they promised to finish the work on a specific timeline and directly charge them to finish the work on time.*

The female participants also reported writing important information that they wanted to preserve. Four out of the five female interviewees said that they preferred to write down information that they wanted to keep. For example, IF1 said that she preferred to write information in a notebook "because saving information on a mobile phone is unreliable because the pictures might get deleted accidentally or the mobile phone might get damaged or lost so that the information will be lost as well."

However, one woman (IF3) said that she preferred to save information on her phone even though she also wrote down important information in her notebook and kept books that she got from training sessions. She explained that she took pictures of packets of medicine or fertilisers, downloaded videos and took screenshots to keep information on her phone. In a way similar to IM5 quoted above, she created both analogue and digital backups: "When I come across any important piece of information on Facebook or YouTube, I take screenshots, then later I write it down and also take pictures of my handwritten notes and save them on my phone." She thought that it was safe to keep information on her phone because she had a Google Drive account. She commented that:

I prefer to save information on Google Drive because if I lose my phone, or even if I lose the notebook or paper where I wrote information, the information I have saved on my Google Drive will always be safe and available. I will just have to login through a different device.

It is unclear how she learnt to use Google Drive since she described herself as a housewife, but it is a solution that worked for her. Many female participants reported that they memorised a lot of things and did not feel it necessary to write down much information, but that they wrote down in a notebook important information that they might forget. Two of them commented that with small children at home, who might draw in their notebooks, papers and notebooks easily got damaged or lost. Although some women may be writing less than their male counterparts, men and women write the same type of information in their notebooks: names of medicines, fertilisers and pesticides recommended by the vets or found online, new farming techniques learnt during training sessions, dates of birth and vaccination of their livestock, common diseases and their cures both for their animals and for their family, and important family dates. In addition, both men and women also used their notebooks to keep track of their family expenses and the costs and profits from their farming activities. One of the male interviewees (IM3) recounted that he had been using a notebook since he started working in farming. He had a big notebook in which he was keeping all the information that he found. Before he recently started using the internet, he used to go to Shyamnagar to ask the agriculture and fishing officers for information and to take notes of the advice they gave him. He added that he still wrote it immediately in his notebook when he found important information. Similarly, one woman (IF2) commented that: "basically all sorts of important information I come across, I note it down", while another women (IF3) explained that she wrote in her notebook the names of medicines for her crops and livestock, fertilisers or pesticides, symptoms of common diseases, such as stomach ache, along with their cure, so that if anyone asked her for help when they were sick, she could "open her notebook and advise them".

5 Discussion

It is clear that all the Bangladeshi villagers who took part in this research – men and women – understand the fragility of digital technologies and of information kept in digital formats. All except one prefer to write down information on paper rather than to keep it on their phones because they think that analogue formats are more reliable. Like the PROTIC women in their village [4], they commonly use notebooks to preserve information. They write in them important information that they find and want to keep for future use. Men and women write similar types of information – information related to agriculture, health remedies, expenses, important dates, etc. – although some women are writing less.

Some of the participants, particularly men, also take pictures of important information to keep it on their phones for backup and easy access. It is common for them to keep a picture of their identity cards and other important documents on their phones. In addition, some of them also extend that practice to taking pictures of information written in their notebooks as a further backup. Their risk mitigation strategy therefore includes the creation of both analogue and digital backups. The analogue backups are a precaution against the short lifespan of mobile phones and the digital backups act as a safeguard in case their notebooks would get lost or damaged by water.

The differences between men and women in relation to information access are due to differences in phone ownership and in confidence with using technology. More men than women in the research sample owned a smartphone and, consequently, more men than women used the internet to access information. This reflects general phone ownership statistics in Bangladesh that show that women are less likely than men to use a smartphone and to access the internet [29]. Previous research in the same village [30, 31] showed that mobile phones were commonly shared between family members. The participants in this research reported similar practices. However, the findings also show that most of the participants who did not own a smartphone were not confident using one and relied on relatives to look for information for them, which indicates that there is a correlation between ownership of a smartphone and confidence in using it. The participants who did not own a smartphone might have had access to one, but did not have the opportunity to develop the confidence to use its internet functionalities. As a consequence, they were more confident asking local experts, such as the agriculture extension officers, for information than trying to find it online. Since fewer women than men owned a smartphone, this behaviour was more common among women, but it appears to be related to their phone ownership rather than to their gender. With regards to information preservation, the behaviours of men and women appear to be similar and do not seem to be influenced by their phone ownership. Both men and women found it more reliable to write information in a notebook than to keep it on a phone.

Because of the small sample sizes and of the disparities between the male FGD and interview samples, in-depth interviews with larger samples of participants are needed to further investigate some of the themes that emerged from this research. This will be the next phase in the author's research. Regarding phone ownership and its impact on gendered information practices, the samples were too small to draw conclusions. However, it is clear that all participants, men and women, whatever the phones they owned and whatever their familiarity with technology, understood the fragility of digital technologies and used analogue backups as a risk mitigation strategy. If some women wrote less in their notebooks than men, this could be because they had access to less information or because they had less time to write. More research is needed to understand their writing practices and to determine if there are differences between the practices adopted by women and those espoused by men.

The interviews also raised important questions that require further investigation in relation to what Bangladeshi villagers consider quality information. Several interviewees mentioned that they thought that information found on the internet was more reliable and more detailed than information obtained from local experts, whereas others trusted more the local sources of information. Further research is needed to determine how these differences can be related to the digital information literacy of the villagers and to the quality of information available locally.

6 Conclusions

The research conducted for this paper show that Bangladeshi villagers who were not involved in the PROTIC project share the PROTIC women's understanding of the fragility of digital information and, like them, use backups, including paper notebooks, to preserve information. Therefore, the use of notebooks is not unique to PROTIC women, but common in their area. This is an important finding, which highlights the importance of information sustainability in marginalised communities and the continuing importance of analogue methods of preserving information. Individuals and communities need access to information to support their work and daily activities and if they do not have continuous access to information, it makes sense for them to preserve the information they will need to use again. This paper showed that Bangladeshi villagers have developed ways to preserve information which work well in their context. The findings from this research draw attention on the importance of ensuring the sustainability of information and of encouraging the use of methods to access and preserve information that are appropriate to the cultural and technological contexts and that meet the needs of marginalised communities.

Acknowledgement. The research for this paper was supported by a DECRA Fellowship from the Australian Research Council (DE210100012).

References

1. Chowdhury, G., Koya, K.: Information practices for sustainability: role of iSchools in achieving the UN Sustainable Development Goals (SDGs). J. Assoc. Inf. Sci. Technol. **68**(9), 2128–2138 (2017). https://doi.org/10.1002/asi.23825
2. Frings-Hessami, V., Oliver, G.: Accessing and preserving information: combining ICT4D and archival science to empower marginalized communities. J. Assoc. Inf. Sci. Technol. (2022). https://doi.org/10.1002/asi.24702
3. Stillman, L., Sarrica, M., Anwar, M., Sarker, A., Farinosi, M.: Sociotechnical transformative effects of an ICT project in rural Bangladesh. Am. Behav. Sci. **64**(3), 1871–1888 (2020). https://doi.org/10.1177/0002764220952126
4. Frings-Hessami, V., Sarker, A., Oliver, G., Anwar, M.: Documentation in a community informatics project: the creation and sharing of information by women in Bangladesh. J. Doc. **76**(2), 552–570 (2020). https://doi.org/10.1108/JD-08-2019-0167
5. Frings-Hessami, V., Sarker, A.: Access to information two years after an ICT4D project in Bangladesh: new digital skills and traditional practices. In: Smits, M. (ed.) iConference 2022. LNCS, vol. 13193, pp. 123–135. Springer, Cham (2022). https://doi.org/10.1007/978-3-030-96960-8_9
6. Food and Agriculture Organization: The state of food and agriculture 2010–2011. Women in agriculture: closing the gender gap for development. FAO, Rome (2011). https://reliefweb.int/sites/reliefweb.int/files/resources/12C5112E3B7A2EDFC125784C0038AE91-Full_Report.pdf
7. Lewis, D.: Bangladesh: Politics, Economy and Civil Society. Cambridge University Press, Cambridge (2011)
8. Jannat, F., Chakraborty, T.R., Aktar, P., Stillman, L.: Evaluating a smartphone phone project in Bangladesh through community monthly meeting reports. In: Stillman, L., Anwar, M. (eds.) Proceedings of the 16th CIRN Conference, Prato, Italy, pp. 110–124 (2018)
9. United Nations: Transforming our world: the 2030 agenda for sustainable development (2015). https://sdgs.un.org/2030agenda
10. Hoq, K.M.G.: Role of information for rural development in Bangladesh: a sector-wise review. Inf. Dev. **28**(1), 13–21 (2012). https://doi.org/10.1177/0266666911417642
11. Mahindarathne, M.G.P.P., Min, Q.: Developing a model to explore the information seeking behaviour of farmers. J. Doc. **74**(4), 781–803 (2018). https://doi.org/10.1108/JD-04-2017-0065

12. Phiri, A., Chipeta, G.T., Chawinga, W.D.: Information behaviour of rural smallholder farmers in some selected developing countries: a literature review. Inf. Dev. **35**(5), 831–838 (2019). https://doi.org/10.1177/0266666918804861
13. Naveed, M.A., Hassan, A.: Sustaining agriculture with information: an assessment of rural citrus farmers' information behaviour. Inf. Dev. **37**(3), 496–510 (2021). https://doi.org/10.1177/0266666920932994
14. Unwin, T.: ICT4D: Information and Communication Technology for Development. Cambridge University Press, Cambridge (2009)
15. Walsham, G.: ICT4D research: reflections on history and future agenda. Inf. Technol. Dev. **23**(1), 18–41 (2017). https://doi.org/10.1080/02681102.2016.1246406
16. Anwar, M., Frings-Hessami, V.: Empowering women through access to information: the sustainability of a community informatics project in Bangladesh. In: Sundqvist, A., Berget, G., Nolin, J., Skjerdingstad, K.I. (eds.) iConference 2020. LNCS, vol. 12051, pp. 3–14. Springer, Cham (2020). https://doi.org/10.1007/978-3-030-43687-2_1
17. Bruce, H., Jones, W., Dumais, S.: Information behaviour that keeps found things found. Inf. Res. **10**(1), paper 207 (2004)
18. Kaye, J., Vertesi, J., Avery, S., Dafoe, A., David, S., et al.: To have and to hold: exploring the personal archive. In: Grinter, R., Rodden, T., Aoki, P., Cutrell, E., Jeffries, R., Olson, G. (eds.) CHI 2006 Proceedings of the SIGCHI Conference on the Human Factors in Computing Systems, Montréal, Québec, Canada, 22–27 April 2006, pp. 275–284. Association for Computing Machinery, New York (2006). https://doi.org/10.1145/1124772.1124814
19. Oh, K.E.: Social aspects of personal information organization. J. Doc. **77**(2), 558–575 (2021). https://doi.org/10.1108/JD-06-2020-0104
20. Hartel, J.: Managing documents at home for serious leisure: a case study of the hobby of gourmet cooking. J. Doc. **66**(6), 847–874 (2010). https://doi.org/10.1108/00220411011087841
21. McKenzie, P., Davies, E.: (2012) Genre systems and 'keeping track' in everyday life. Arch. Sci. **12**(4), 437–460 (2012). https://doi.org/10.1007/s10502-012-9174-5
22. World Bank: Indicators (2021). https://data.worldbank.org/indicator/SP.RUR.TOTL.ZS?view=chart
23. Ovi, I.H.: Covid-19 impact: national poverty rate rises to 29.5% as of June. Dhaka Tribune (2020). https://archive.dhakatribune.com/health/coronavirus/2020/08/12/covid-19-impact-national-poverty-rate-rises-to-29-5-as-of-june
24. Census 2022: Literacy rate in Bangladesh up 22.89% (2022). https://www.dhakatribune.com/bangladesh/2022/07/27/census-2022-literacy-rate-in-bangladesh-up-2289
25. Bangladesh literacy rate now 74.66% (2022). https://www.thedailystar.net/youth/education/news/bangladeshs-literacy-rate-now-7466-3080701
26. Bangladesh Bureau of Statistics: Population and housing census 2011: Zila Sathkira. Bangladesh Bureau of Statistics, Statistics and Informatics Division (2015) http://203.112.218.65:8008/WebTestApplication/userfiles/Image/PopCenZilz2011/Zila-Satkhira.pdf
27. Government of Bangladesh: Digital Bangladesh & Vision 2021 (2019). https://investindigitalbd.gov.bd/page/digital-bangladesh-vision-2021
28. Bangladesh Telecommunication Regulatory Commission: Mobile phone subscribers in Bangladesh (2021). http://www.btrc.gov.bd/content/mobile-phone-subscribers-bangladesh-january-2021
29. GSMA: Connected women: The mobile gender gap report 2021 (2021). https://www.gsma.com/r/wp-content/uploads/2021/06/The-Mobile-Gender-Gap-Report-2021.pdf

30. Sarker, A.: ICT for women's empowerment in rural Bangladesh. Ph.D. thesis, Monash University (2020). https://figshare.com/articles/thesis/ICT_for_Women_s_Empowerment_in_Rural_Bangladesh/14538588
31. Anwar, M., Oliver, G., Frings-Hessami, V., Saha, M., Sarker, A.: Collective aspects of information literacy in developing countries: a Bangladeshi case. J. Doc. (2022, ahead of print). https://doi.org/10.1108/JD-09-2021-0185

Participatory Web Archiving: Multifaceted Challenges

Cui Cui[1,3](✉), Stephen Pinfield[1], Andrew Cox[1], and Frank Hopfgartner[2]

[1] Information School, The University of Sheffield, 211 Portobello, Sheffield, UK
{ccui3,s.pinfield,a.m.cox}@sheffield.ac.uk

[2] Institute for Web Science and Technologies (WeST), Universität Koblenz, Koblenz, Germany
hopfgartner@uni-koblenz.de

[3] Bodleian Libraries, University of Oxford, Broad Street, Oxford, UK

Abstract. There has been increasing interest in participatory web archiving in recent years. Indeed, it is widely regarded as a necessary step in the development of web archives. From a theoretical point of view, it has been seen as driven by the "archival turn" in which the origin of archives is critically analysed, and it becomes clear that established power dominates archives while marginalized voices are absent. Web archiving benefits from this "archival turn", not only in addressing limitations inherited from conventional archives, but also in challenging embedded systemic and selection biases when choosing what to archive from the Web. Through a critical literature review, this paper addresses the need to analyse participatory web archiving practices, the mechanisms and power relations within them through political theories of power and participation.

Keywords: Web archives · Web archiving · Participatory · Archival selection · Archival appraisal · Archival turn

1 Context of the Research

Archives are sites where power is exercised and legitimised. Ovenden [1] vividly described how colonial archives were created as parts of the archives of the colonialising power, and were later subjected to deliberate elimination in order to control how history is understood. These long-standing issues in conventional archives continue in the digital world. Web archives are a new form of archival material curated through a process of selecting and preserving websites, web pages or their contents using techniques, tools and platforms with long term preservation and access strategies in place. Major efforts in preserving the Web were first initiated by the Internet Archive. National libraries and archives, government organisations and research institutions have then taken on the role, as evident from surveys conducted from 2010 to 2017 [2–7], and the list of web archiving initiatives globally from Wikipedia[1]. Some national archives, libraries and heritage institutions have a mandate to archive the national web domain arising from legislation

[1] https://en.wikipedia.org/wiki/list_of_web_archiving_initiatives accessed 26/11/2022.

© The Author(s), under exclusive license to Springer Nature Switzerland AG 2023
I. Sserwanga et al. (Eds.): iConference 2023, LNCS 13971, pp. 79–87, 2023.
https://doi.org/10.1007/978-3-031-28035-1_7

or to produce thematic collections of websites/pages supported by heritage preservation traditions. However, web archives have developed as a new paradigm - one that has often stood alone in terms of theoretical development. Yet web archives need to respect conventional archival principles: they are still subject to many of the same practices [8] and face similar challenges in terms of collections.

The issue of *what* to archive has long been debated in traditional archival practice [9] and the Web is no different [10]. In conventional archives, the answer tends to reflect the nature of the archival institutions concerned and the power to choose what is important and so remembered vested in government administrative and bureaucratic hierarchies. Likewise, selection bias in web archives can be just as systemic and as much the consequence of human actions.

The "archival turn", in which the archive itself rather than just its contents becomes a subject of study, arises from a number of critical positions, including post-colonial theory [11, 12]. This "turn" encourages archivists to consider the ways in which vested interests and prevailing power structures shape the collection of materials in conventional archives. Web archives collate and curate a different type of material, but also do so within a particular political, social, and economic context. Institutional control over technologies and the infrastructure facilitating these technologies is forming another force that is decisive in what ends up in web archives. Essentially, the issue is that of "power": who exercises it and the tools at hand to exercise it. This is to a large extent decisive in determining what materials are archived.

In resistance to this tendency, participatory archiving, which involves working in collaboration with different communities to build archives, is increasingly practiced in conventional archives [13]. It has now become one of the main themes of web archive development too [6, 10, 14–19]. Participatory web archiving is an approach deploying established strategies in a new paradigm to tackle inherent limitations rooted in the theory and practice of conventional archiving. Through community participation, it is attempted to redistribute the power to various, networked often interdependent actors/stakeholders that include community partners, content creators and users.

Through a critical literature review, this paper attempts to identify what are key issues in the development of participatory web archiving. They include: the mechanisms involved in participatory approaches; the ways in which the impacts of the mechanism can be measured and evaluated; the nature and composition of participation partners; the extent to which they have gained the power to shape the process and how that power is redistributed; and the extent to which their participation can address the inherent limitations and reduce or mitigate embedded biases.

2 Web Archives as a Different Form of Archive

Web historians and theorists have tried to untangle the complexity of the components that constitute the Web [8, 20, 21]. These components are open to different interpretations, which has fundamental implications on for what and how the Web should be archived and, in fact, what web archives actually are. The Web could be thought of as having three components: content, context and technology. Brügger [22] has argued that the archived web distinguishes itself from other document types. It is the reborn digital version of a constructed unique representation of the online web, which is essentially different from the original. Moreover, it changes during the process of collection and preserving [20, 22, 23]. The archived fragments of the Web often hold significant features of incompleteness, temporal and spatial inconsistency.[8]. It is also difficult, indeed nearly impossible, to capture every single component of a website so that the archived version can be reconstructed as exactly as the original [8]. The contextual environment of the archived individual website or webpage may be cut out from certain points.

Material in web archives therefore does not consist of the original websites/webpages, but a type of new material originated from the live Web and reconstructed with human and technology interventions. When archiving the Web, the aim cannot be either to preserve the original, or totally replicate the original. Instead, it is collecting fragments of the website, parts of content, the design of the developer and the experience of users, technologies to support the system, and contextual links. These characteristics constitute a fundamental difference between archived web materials and conventional archival materials under the care of same archival organisations. Yet web archival practices have grown out of the established practices designed for types of materials that are different. This does not point to a fundamental break from conventional archives, especially when the responsibilities of archiving the Web are in the care of conventional archives [8].

During the early modern period, the legal dimension of archives became apparent. It did so in two respects: the preservation of original legal documents; and the reinforcement and preservation of the social and legal order [24]. Archives also served as the guarantors of political and administrative continuity due to the power of archives to help preserve memory of things [24]. As evidence of legal and business transactions, as well as memories of figures and events that were deemed worthy of celebrating, or memorializing, archives in effect legitimized established power and marginalized those without power [25]. To some extent, power structures are likely to be replicated in web archives in the same way.

It is the very survival of documents that determines what archives are composed of. The context of archive development concerns why some documents were made into archives in the first place, while others were not after "appraisal", and why in some cases archives were purposely destroyed or relocated. Without this knowledge, our understanding of archives is often limited. Understanding these limitations can offer the promise of richer intellectual and emotional approaches in our engagement with the past [26]. These considerations apply to web archives, too. The major theoretical development and shift in archival thinking over the past 20 years offers a better understanding of a much more complex social context of archives. It also provides us with a new perspective when it comes to the future development of archives in respect of both traditional and born-digital materials.

3 Developing Web Archives in the Direction of the "Archival Turn"

The "archival turn" – that is, the re-evaluation of archives, their purpose, and their development by various disciplines – has exerted a significant impact on archival theories [27]. One of these archival turns, grounded in post-colonial studies, points to "a move from archives as *sources* to archives as *epistemological sites* and the *outcome of cultural practices*" [27]. It treats archives themselves as primary documents of history, and re-examines their origins and establishments [11, 12]. In essence, this view arises from the struggle to navigate histories away from the imperial metropole in favour of anticolonial nationalist movements [11].

The development of institutional archives has always been closely associated with legal rights of established power. Thus, archives do not present the point of view and experiences of the whole of society but powerful record creators [28]. The recognition of the silencing of marginalised groups and communities in archives has promoted archival theorists to think about being more inclusive as well as diverse.

It follows that archives can be understood as "dynamic sites within a spectrum of pasts, presents, and futures" rather than being static [29]. Public and historical accountability demands that archives extend the definition of society's memory to offer citizens "a sense of identity, locality, history, culture and personal and collective memory" rather than one limited solely to the documentary residue left over (or chosen) by powerful record creators [28].

In parallel, the purpose of web archiving is to preserve web material deliberately and purposively and must in some degree reflect the specific reasons, such as for research purposes, record keeping, and as evidence. This may be to serve research project, or preserve memories and a nation's culture heritage [23, 30]. Both Ben-David & Amram and Ogden et al., have shown that the knowledge on the Internet Archive Wayback Machine is generated through a series of complex, intertwined socio-technical epistemic processes. They include proactive human curation and intervention, as well as editorial decisions by archival teams, and continuing efforts to repair and maintain, eventually facilitate access [31, 32]. During this process, unavoidably, both human and technology factors introduce embedded systemic and selection bias that in turn reflect wider power structures in societies.

The embedded bias in web archives starts from the digital divide in creating and accessing web content. Unavoidably, this division will be carried over to web archives that negatively affects the representation in web archives [8]. Furthermore, systemic bias in large scale international or national broad crawls are apparent, since popular websites are likely to be found within the scope of archiving strategies, and consequently are most likely to be archived [8]. Moreover, selection bias can be even more prominent within smaller collections as they are often curated by a library, or an archive, or other institutions, which have particular collecting priorities. As technologies play an essential part when archiving the Web, the extent of technological expertise and the establishment of mass infrastructure may centralise decision-making when it comes to the selection of web archives [8].

As the choices made to decide what to archive are embedded in a complex, unsystematic, and less transparent environment [33], web archival practices are facing even greater challenges than conventional archives when coming to select what to archive and define the scope of the archive collections. Content created by least known or smaller organisations are likely to be less visible and influential on the Web and have a smaller chance to be archived. How to identify these marginalised materials can be challenging when the searching algorisms are in place to work in a different direction; various collecting strategies need to be in place purposely to address these problems.

4 Participatory Web Archiving

In the context of the "archival turn", greater focus of what has been understood to be valuable or worth archiving offers us an opportunity to reassess the contextual environment around archival development. Cook [13] summarised paradigm shifts of archival theory as those from "evidence to memory", to identity, and to participatory archiving as a community. Archivists shifted their focus from "truth, evidence, authenticity, and defending the integrity of the record" to consciously "co-creating the archive", to telling stories and narratives, and (Cook envisioned the possible fourth phase of development) to "share that appraisal function with citizens, broadly defined, where we engage our expertise with theirs in a blend of coaching, mentoring, and partnering" [34]. These paradigm shifts should arguably also be influential for web archives.

Participatory practices in the cultural heritage sector are not new. They are not limited to new technologies [35]. The potential benefits for institutions include deepening relationships, enhancing collections, potential cost savings in staff resources [36], promoting engaged access [37, 38], and extending existing user groups [39]. However, they do not necessarily lead to wider representation, due to the observed "long tail" participation pattern, in which the "crowd" is dominated by a small group of active participants [39, 40].

Participatory web archiving has gained increasing attention over the past few years both on practical and theoretical levels. An interview by Geeraert with Bingham [41] touched on some practical challenges for the development of web archives collaborating with wider communities, such as the curation decisions for a website with extreme views on Covid nominated by the "crowd", setting shared collecting standards with collaborating partners, overrepresented materials in English over other languages despite the fact that the collection contains materials in 51 languages. Schafer & Winters [19] have brought participatory web archiving within a "good governance" framework to address the political role of web archives. But less is known about how participation plays its role in this framework. Here we are dealing with an old problem in a new situation: can participatory web archiving tackle inherent limitations rooted in conventional archival theories and practices? And can it address embedded bias that is intensified by the prevailing digital and political environment? If so, how? We need to understand participation within a new paradigm. Political science has the potential to help us answer these questions.

Since it first became a prominent topic in governance in the 1960s, the focus of interest in public participation has changed from debating whether it should be applied in public-policy making to its application and evaluating its impact, practices and methods [42]. As far as application is concerned, studies of participatory development have addressed the ineffectiveness of externally imposed and expert-oriented forms of research and planning that was increasingly evident in the 1980s [43].Participatory approaches emerged as an alternative to donor-driven and outsider-led development approaches. They have been justified in term of their sustainability, relevance and empowerment, making people central to development, allowing marginalised groups to be involved in interventions that affect them, and presenting their perspectives, knowledge, priorities and skills [43].

However, participation is often situated within complex and fluid power relations. As such, its outcomes depend on many factors and are often limited by three sets of participatory development "tyrannies" identified by Cooke and Kothari [43]; "the tyranny of decision-making and control, the tyranny of the group, the tyranny of method". That is the tyranny where facilitators control over the process, when the existing dominating interests are reinforced, and participatory methods become the only legitimate approaches. They raise key points on evaluating the power dimensions in participatory web archiving: actors who have the power of decision making, interests of groups they represent, and the dominance of participatory methods undermining other valid approaches and reinforcing the existing power.

Later more attention was paid to the transformative impact of participation. Cornwall [44] focused on the dynamics of power and difference within invited spaces and analysed participation as a spatial practice that emphasises the transformative possibilities of participation. Similarly, Williams [45] addressed the spatial and temporal aspects of empowerment that participation seeks to achieve. Furthermore, from the evaluation point of view, he [45] offered an alternative way of "examining the effects of participation on political capabilities: how, if at all, do specific instances of participation contribute to processes of political learning, reshape networks of power, and change patterns of political representation?" These studies indicate we could analyse the transformation impact of participatory web archiving on representation through knowledge sharing and learning.

Furthermore, from an analytical point, Foucault's concept of "governmentality"[2], offers us a framework to address the dimensions of power, and how various forms of knowledge and theories clustered under the heading of governance may inform its exercise in political and administrative reforms [46]. This term contains a wider analytical scheme (genealogy) [46]. Within it, "the analytics of government not only concentrates on the mechanisms of the legitimisation of domination or the masking of violence, beyond that it focuses on the knowledge that is part of the practices, the systematisation and 'rationalisation' of a pragmatics of guidance"[47]. "Governmentality" thus offers a potential analytic framework for articulating this hidden power dominance created and legitimised during the process of knowledge creation and sharing in participatory web archiving.

Although the purpose of public participation may differ in various situations, we argue for a need to focus on some key issues, which are drawn from above theoretical frameworks. Firstly, there is a need to understand how participation in web archiving influences the power structure which not only arises from its origins in conventional archiving but is also reshaped when the power is redistributed to multiple networked yet independent stakeholders in a new digital environment. Secondly, it is important to articulate the extent to which participation in web archiving can reduce or mitigate embedded biases during the knowledge creation process. Fundamentally, there are three

[2] The term "governmentality" was introduced in the lecture, given at the Collège de France in February 1978 by Foucault [46].

main themes emerging from this analysis: power relations, knowledge creation, and representation. To collect evidence and make these relationships and power dynamics in web archiving explicit, it is important to revisit and ground the research in the foundation of political science and methodologies.

5 Conclusion

This paper has reviewed the relevant literature on web archives and participation. It links web archives with conventional archives, as well as considering their theoretical and practical connections with each other. It also examines ways in which the "archival turn" has shaped the direction of travel of web archiving, and how participation has gained attention in the field of web archiving. Applying existing approaches in a new paradigm, it stresses the need to ground the analysis of power relations, knowledge creation, and representation in political theories of power and participation. It highlights emerging research needs to seek ways in which power relations in web archiving, and contradictions and conflicts can be articulated and decoupled, so that opportunities of participation can be exploited to advance the practice of web archiving.

References

1. Ovenden, R.: Burning the Books: A History of Knowledge Under Attack. John Murray, London (2020)
2. Gomes, D., Miranda, J., Costa, M.: A survey on web archiving initiatives. In: Gradmann, S., Borri, F., Meghini, C., Schuldt, H. (eds.) TPDL 2011. LNCS, vol. 6966, pp. 408–420. Springer, Heidelberg (2011). https://doi.org/10.1007/978-3-642-24469-8_41
3. Costa, M., Gomes, D., Silva, M.J.: The evolution of web archiving. Int. J. Digit. Libr. **18**(3), 191–205 (2016). https://doi.org/10.1007/s00799-016-0171-9
4. NDSA: National Digital Stewardship Alliance web archiving survey: Report produced by the NDSA content working group (2012)
5. Bailey, J., Hanna, K., Archive, I., Hartman, C., Mccain, E., Taylor, N.: Web archiving in the United States: A 2013 survey (2014)
6. Bailey, J., Grotke, A., McCain, E., Moffatt, C., Taylor, N.: Web archiving in the United States : An NDSA report results of a survey of organizations preserving web content (2017). https://doi.org/10.17605/OSF.IO/R5PQK
7. Farrell, M., McCain, E., Praetzellis, M., Thomas, G., Walker, P.: Web archiving in the United States: A 2017 Survey (2018). https://doi.org/10.17605/OSF.IO/3QH6N4
8. Milligan, I.: History in the age of abundance? : How the web is transforming historical research. McGill-Queen's University Press, Montreal ; London (2019)
9. Cook, T.: Building an archives: Appraisal theory for architectural records. Am. Arch. **59**, 136–143 (1996)
10. Leetaru, K.: Why it's so important to understand what's in our web archives-annotated. https://www.forbes.com/sites/kalevleetaru/2015/11/25/why-its-so-important-to-understand-whats-in-our-web-archives/#6c71e0f73f8c. Accessed 15 May 2021
11. Dirks, N.: Autobiography of an Archive: A Scholar's Passage to India. Columbia University Press, New York, NY (2015)
12. Stoler, A.: Colonial archives and the arts of governance. Arch. Sci. **2**, 87–109 (2002). https://doi.org/10.1007/BF02435632

13. Cook, T.: Evidence, memory, identity, and community: four shifting archival paradigms. Arch. Sci. **13**, 95–120 (2013). https://doi.org/10.1007/s10502-012-9180-7
14. Brügger, N., Schroeder, R.: The Web as History. UCL Press, London (2017)
15. Summers, E., Punzalan, R.: Bots, seeds and people: web archives as infrastructure. In: Proceedings ACM Conference Computer Supported Cooperative Work. CSCW, pp. 821–834 (2017). https://doi.org/10.1145/2998181.2998345
16. Gail, T.: Web Archiving Environmental Scan. Harvard Library Report (2016)
17. Dougherty, M., Meyer, E.T., Madsen, C., van den Heuvel, C., Thomas, A., Wyatt, S.: Researcher engagement with web archives: state of the art. Joint Information Systems Committee Report, London (2010)
18. Bingham, N.: Harnessing the crowd: Coronavirus topical collection at the UK. https://blogs.bl.uk/webarchive/2020/04/harnessing-the-crowd-coronavirus-topical-collection-at-the-uk-web-archive.html. Accessed 15 May 2021
19. Schafer, V., Winters, J.: The values of web archives. International J. Digital Humanities **2**(1–3), 129–144 (2021). https://doi.org/10.1007/s42803-021-00037-0
20. Brügger, N.: The Archived Web: Doing History in the Digital Age. The MIT Press, Cambridge, Massachusetts; London, England (2018)
21. Masanès, J.: Web archiving: Issues and methods. In: Web archiving, pp. 1–54. Springer, Berlin (2006). https://doi.org/10.1007/978-3-540-46332-0_1
22. Brügger, N.: The archived website and website philology: a new type of historical document? Nord. Rev. **29**, 155–175 (2008). https://doi.org/10.1515/nor-2017-0183
23. Brügger, N., Finnemann, N.O.: The Web and digital humanities: theoretical and methodological concerns. J. Broadcast. Electron. Media. **57**, 66–80 (2013). https://doi.org/10.1080/08838151.2012.761699
24. Friedrich, M., Dillon, J.N.: The Birth of the Archive: A History of Knowledge. University of Michigan Press, Ann Arbor, Michigan (2018)
25. Cook, T.: What is past is prologue: a history of archival adeas since 1898, and the future paradigm shift. Archivaria. **43**, 17–63 (1997)
26. Prescott, A.: The textuality of the archive. In: Craven, L. (ed.) What are archives? Cultural and theoretical perspectives: A reader, pp. 31–52. Ashgate, Aldershot (2012)
27. Ketelaar, E.: Archival turns and returns: studies of the archive. In: Gililand, A.J., McKemmish, S., Lau, A.J. (eds.): Research in the archival multiverse. pp. 228–268. Clayton, Victoria (2017)
28. Cook, T.: Archival science and postmodernism: new formulations for old concepts. Arch. Sci. **1**, 3–24 (2001). https://doi.org/10.1007/BF02435636
29. Lee, J.A.: Beyond pillars of evidence: Exploring the shaky ground of queer/ed archives and their methodologies. In: Gililand, A.J., McKemmish, S., Lau, A.J. (eds.): Research in the archival multiverse. , Clayton, Victoria (2017)
30. Brügger, N.: Web archiving: between past, present, and future. In: Consalvo, M., Ess, C. (ed.): The handbook of internet studies. pp. 24–42. Wiley-Blackwell, Malden (2011)
31. Ben-David, A., Amram, A.: The Internet Archive and the socio-technical construction of historical facts. Internet Hist. **2**, 179–201 (2018). https://doi.org/10.1080/24701475.2018.1455412
32. Ogden, J., Halford, S., Carr, L.: Observing web archives: the case for an ethnographic study of web archiving. In: Proceedings of the 2017 ACM on web science conference, pp. 299–308. ACM (2017). https://doi.org/10.1145/3091478.3091506
33. Milligan, I.: Historiography and the web. In: Brügger, N. (ed.): The SAGE handbook of web history. SAGE Publications Ltd, London (2018)
34. Cook, T.: "We are what we keep; we keep what we are": archival appraisal past, present and future. J. Soc. Arch. **32**, 173–189 (2011). https://doi.org/10.1080/00379816.2011.619688

35. Benoit, E., Eveleigh, A.: Defining and framing participatory archives in archival science. In: Benoit, E., Eveleigh, A. (eds.) Participatory archives : theory and practice, pp. 1–12. Cambridge Core, London (2019)
36. Ridge, M.: Crowdsourcing our cultural heritage: introduction. In: Ridge, M. (ed.) Crowdsourcing our cultural heritage, pp. 1–13. Ashgate, Farnham (2014)
37. Carletti, L.: Participatory heritage: scaffolding citizen scholarship. Int. Inf. Libr. Rev. **48**, 196–203 (2016). https://doi.org/10.1080/10572317.2016.1205367
38. Owens, T.: Digital cultural heritage and the crowd. Curator Museum J. **56**, 121–130 (2013). https://doi.org/10.1111/cura.12012
39. Bonacchi, C., Bevan, A., Keinan-Schoonbaert, A., Pett, D., Wexler, J.: Participation in heritage crowdsourcing. Museum Manag. Curatorsh. **34**, 166–182 (2019). https://doi.org/10.1080/09647775.2018.1559080
40. Reinsone, S.: Searching for deeper meanings in cultural heritage crowdsourcing. In: Hetland, P., Pierroux, P., Esborg, L. (eds.): A history of participation in museums and archives : Traversing citizen science and citizen humanities. Routledge, London (2020)
41. Geeraert, F., Bingham, N.: Exploring special web archives collections related to COVID-19: The case of INA, an interview with Nicola Bingham (British Library) conducted by Friedel Geeraert (KBR). WARCnet. (2020)
42. Quick, K.S., Bryson, J.M.: Public participation. In: Ansell, C., Torfing, J. (eds.) Handbook on theories of governance, pp. 158–168. Edward Elgar Publishing, Northampton (2022)
43. Cooke, B., Kothari, U.: The case for participation as tyranny. In: Cooke, B., Kothari, U. (eds.) Participation: The new tyranny?, pp. 1–15. Zed Books, London (2001)
44. Conrwall, A.: Space for transformation? reflections on issues of power and different in participation in development. In: Hickey, S. and Mohan, G. (eds.): Participation: from tyranny to transformation?: Exploring new approaches to participation in development. Zed, London (2004)
45. Williams, G.: Towards a re-politicisation of participatory development: political capabilities and spaces of empowerment. In: Hickey, S., Mohan, G. (eds.) Participation: from tyranny to transformation?: Exploring new approaches to participation in development, pp. 92–107. Zed, London (2004)
46. Triantafillou, P.: Governmentality. In: Ansell, C. and Torfing, J. (eds.) Handbook on theories of governance, pp. 378–388. Edward Elgar Publishing, Northampton (2022)
47. Lemke, T.: Foucault, governmentality, and critique. Rethink. Marx. **14**, 49–64 (2002). https://doi.org/10.1080/089356902101242288
48. Foucault, M.: Governmentality. In: Burchell, G., Gordon, C., and Miller, P. (eds.) The Foucault effect: Studies in governmentality, with two lectures by and an interview with Michel Foucault, pp. 87–104. University of Chicago Press, Chicago (1991)

Behavioural Research

Understanding the Influence of Music on People's Mental Health Through Dynamic Music Engagement Model

Arpita Bhattacharya, Uba Backonja, Anh Le, Ria Antony, Yujia Si, and Jin Ha Lee(✉)

University of Washington, Seattle, WA 98195, USA
arpitab@uci.edu, {backonja,anhle,rantony,yujias6,jinhalee}@uw.edu

Abstract. Research shows that music helps people regulate and process emotions to positively impact their mental health, but there is limited research on how to build music systems or services to support this. We investigated how engagement with music can help the listener support their mental health through a case study of the BTS ARMY fandom. We conducted a survey with 1,190 BTS fans asking about the impact BTS' music has on their mental health and wellbeing. Participants reported that certain songs are appropriate for specific types of mood regulations, attributed largely to lyrics. Reflection, connection, and comfort were the top three experiences listeners shared during and after listening to BTS' music. External factors like knowledge about the context of a song's creation or other fans' reactions to a song also influenced people's feelings toward the music. Our research suggests an expanded view of music's impact on mental health beyond a single-modal experience to a dynamic, multi-factored experience that evolves over time within the interconnected ecosystem of the fandom. We present the Dynamic Music Engagement Model which represents the complex, multifaceted, context-dependent nature of how music influences people's mental health, followed by design suggestions for music information systems and services.

Keywords: Music information systems and services · Mental health · Wellbeing

1 Introduction

The benefits of music on people's mental health and wellbeing have been well-researched in music psychology, neuroscience, psychiatry, and music information retrieval (MIR). There is potential for music to be used in treatment and therapy as it can influence complex neurobiological processes in the brain [26, 31], regulate moods and emotions, and support the overall wellbeing of listeners [32, 33, 41]. Music can lessen anxiety, ease tension and stress, reduce pain, [8, 11, 20, 37, 54], and can provide beneficial intervention for people with mental illness [13, 34]. In their review of 33 studies on the topic, McFerran and colleagues [35] found that young people's perception that music can have a positive impact on their mental health was strong, especially in the voices of adolescents themselves.

© The Author(s), under exclusive license to Springer Nature Switzerland AG 2023
I. Sserwanga et al. (Eds.): iConference 2023, LNCS 13971, pp. 91–108, 2023.
https://doi.org/10.1007/978-3-031-28035-1_8

Research investigating how music and mental health are related typically focus on subjectively or objectively measuring either passive (e.g., listening) or active (e.g., playing an instrument) music engagement [14]. Studies that show how music engagement directly and indirectly contributes to mental health in the real world are limited, particularly, with the increasingly pervasive use of digital media for consuming and sharing music. We aim to examine this engagement with music and its influence on listeners' mental health from the perspective of information science.

The current information ecosystem allows users to have a much more complex engagement with musical content beyond a simple auditory experience. The prevalence of social media, music streaming services, collaborative playlists, music mixing and creation apps, and music games has changed the ways people engage with music [27, 39]. Schedl and Flexer [51] discuss the importance of user-centric MIR approaches. They highlight how in addition to the factors related to the music content (e.g., rhythm, melody), music context (e.g., semantic labels, lyrics) and user context (e.g., mood, activities) influence perception of music. Furthermore, the fans (defined as "individuals who maintain a passionate connection to popular media, assert their identity through their engagement with and mastery over its contents, and experience social affiliation around shared tastes and preferences" [18]) have started playing a much more active and complex role in engaging with music and music related content [15, 28]. Many artists are much more visible to the fans in this information environment and there are more ways for fans to get connected with their favorite artists. This can also influence the fan's perception and thoughts on music. For instance, prior research in fan studies highlight how the relationship between artists and fans and/or fan-to-fan relationships in communities can influence people's mental health and wellbeing [17, 21].

Transmedia storytelling approach, which is becoming increasingly common in pop culture, is discussed as an opportunity where fans take a much more active and participatory role in appreciating and engaging with media content [10, 19, 50]. The development of new apps and virtual environments to stream music and host collective music listening experiences like live concerts and streaming parties continues to change the way people access music and music related information [1, 39] which may impact people's listening behavior. However, when studying how music benefits the listener's mental health and wellbeing, currently there is a lack of consideration for these contextual and social aspects of using information systems and services to access music. Consequently, this limits the design of music information systems to support such beneficial experiences with music and music information.

We aim to study how fans engage with music and relevant content in the real-world situation in their current environment to better understand how music supports people's mental health and wellbeing. Understanding the music fans' behavior is important as the information systems and services which provide access to music and related media are avidly used by fans [28]. This improved understanding helps us derive design implications for music information systems to improve and support people's positive engagement with music and relevant content for their wellbeing.

Through this research, we answered the following research questions:

RQ1. What aspects do we need to consider to comprehensively understand how people engage with music to support their mental health within the current information ecosystem?

1.1. Which aspects of music do people describe as being helpful for supporting their mental health?
1.2. How do listeners describe their experiences with music in terms of supporting their mental health?

RQ2. What are the implications for building MIR systems and services to facilitate people's engagement with music to support their mental health?

We answered these research questions through a case study of the ARMY fandom, a global fan community supporting the Korean music group BTS. We selected this method as it is a useful approach for investigating "a contemporary phenomenon within its real-life context, especially when the boundaries between the phenomenon and context are not clearly evident [56]". We chose the ARMY fandom as a representative case in the current popular music environment as they are considered as one of the largest global music fandoms [2, 28]. Furthermore, several prior studies suggested that the music of BTS is helpful for supporting fans' mental health [7, 29, 47]. Based on an online survey with 1,190 ARMYs on experiences of engaging with music for their wellbeing, we present the Dynamic Music Engagement Model to represent the complex and multifaceted nature of how music influences fans' mental health.

2 Related Work

2.1 Popular Music and Mental Wellbeing

Music positively impacts a listener's mental health, including physiological and emotional changes to manage stress [32, 33, 41, 48]. Music used in a therapy can support recovery and self-development, such as for people coping with a long-term illness [5]. However, there are inconsistencies in the literature regarding different music related behaviors, indicating a need for studies collecting "comprehensive data about the full range of individuals' musical behaviors (active/receptive, preferences, intentions for music use), and correlat[ing] these with health outcomes reported from a variety of perspectives" [36], a gap we aim to address in our research.

An increasing number of studies investigate the connection of popular music and mental health. Teenagers might gravitate towards specific genres and imagery in popular music related to underlying mental health needs [4], such as emotional vulnerability [3], or choose to positively engage with music based on their needs [36]. In certain popular music genres such as rap, there has been a significant increase in references about mental health [22]. Artists who experience mental health challenges have included lyrical content about their struggles, which allows fans to relate to the messages [12]. Popular artists from the United States including Selena Gomez, Lady Gaga, and Kehlani have been outspoken about their own struggles with mental illnesses through their music, and the reach of these popular artists encourages fans to not only become aware of their mental health, but also actively seek help [42].

2.2 Popular Music and Fan Engagement

Fans often engage with artists' music individually through melody and the messages within music. With the pervasive use of social media, fans are also able to engage with artists and music socially. Fans who are not able to attend music concerts in-person can still experience live streaming of the concerts while simultaneously being in the presence of or engaging with other fans online [6]. Rendell [43] discusses how artists who are unable to tour, especially due to the pandemic, use an array of streaming and social media sites such as Twitch livestream, Stageit (a web-based performance venue), and Instagram to connect with their audience. The evolving digital landscape for remote global entertainment in the post-pandemic era provides a timely opportunity to study fan-artist engagement made possible by online information systems.

Fan engagement across multiple digital platforms can be seen in the BTS ARMY fandom. The connection ARMYs feel towards BTS, which is well documented, is primarily through the song lyrics, which highlights each member's artistic talent, the group's authenticity, and their lived experiences [38]. Lee et al. [29] found that fans perceive emotional connection through artists' messaging in their lyrics, and in the knowledge that other fans are listening to the same music. ARMYs also connect with the artists through shared mental health experiences and challenges that BTS members discuss in interviews and media other than music. Some ARMYs take an active participatory role in interpreting and creating content and engaging with the artists and others [28]. BTS expresses care and gratitude for ARMY, such as by dedicating songs and messages ARMY (e.g., *2!3!*, *Magic Shop*) and engaging in reciprocal play [45]. This relationship between BTS and ARMY has led to fans' engagement beyond their music, with individuals and ARMY as a whole, creating a collective that is aiming to transform society and culture at a global scale, exemplified through efforts like #MatchAMillion [40]. Online interactions also lead to offline fan interactions in the form of in-person group meetups, concerts, and meetings [23], further expanding the social network of the fans.

2.3 Technologies for Emotional Connection and Music for Fan Communities

Being part of a fan community and interacting with other fans can have a positive impact on emotional connection and wellbeing. Reysen et al. [44] found that ingroup identification within fan communities was positively associated with wellbeing. Similarly, Laffan [24] found that being a fan of Kpop was a significant predictor of happiness, social connectedness, and self-esteem, speculating that a sense of positive connection with artists is possible due to social media technologies.

Currently, the design of music streaming platforms such as YouTube or Spotify support limited socializing, such as commenting or uploading fan made content. These tools are separate from social media platforms such as Twitter, the latter supporting direct multimedia fandom engagement through dialog, translations, and fanmade content. At the time of writing this paper, BTS uses social media (e.g., Weverse, Instagram, TikTok, and Twitter), streaming platforms for sharing music (e.g., YouTube, Apple Music, Spotify, Soundcloud, Melon, Genie), and multimedia platforms dedicated to BTS ARMY that are run by HYBE, the entertainment company managing BTS (VLIVE and Weverse). Conversations among fans occur within and across these multiple systems based on the preferences and access needs of the fan. In addition to Korean and English, the ARMY fandom brings together people speaking many different languages [2] across these platforms. In this paper, we aim to learn how the fans' connections with music, artists, and other fans are facilitated in this complex digital information ecosystem to influence their mental wellbeing.

3 Study Design and Methods

We asked Twitter users ($\geq$13 years old) across the world who self-identified as listeners of BTS' music to complete a descriptive, mixed-methods survey in February 2021. The study was approved by the institutional review board at the University of Washington.

We developed an online survey using Qualtrics. Using Saarikallio and Erkkilä's [49] framework on seven mood regulation strategies as a guide, we developed 38 questions about: fans' engagement with BTS' musical and non-musical content, BTS-related activities, overall experience in the fandom, and their mental health. The survey also included demographic information regarding gender identity, race, country of residence, and mental health diagnoses.

We distributed the survey via Twitter, which is the most actively used social media in the ARMY fandom [25]. When participants accessed the survey link, they were asked to indicate their consent via Qualtrics before proceeding the survey questions. They could skip any question they did not want to answer or quit the survey at any time. No incentive was given to participate, and we did not collect identifying information. The survey was open for two weeks. We obtained a total of 1,190 valid responses after removing duplicate, incomplete, and spam responses. Table 1 presents the aggregated demographic information.

Table 1. Demographic information of survey participants.

Age (years)	Mean = 26, Min = 13, Max = 71, Standard Deviation = 10.02
Race	Asian = 567, White = 317, Hispanic = 210, Black = 43, Native Hawaiian/Pacific Islander = 7, American Indian/ Alaska Native = 3, Described in own words = 106
Gender	Female = 1105, Non-binary = 29, Male = 15, Described in own words = 26
Country of Residence	USA = 268, Philippines = 155, India = 123, Indonesia = 54, Malaysia = 47, Mexico = 45, South Africa = 38, UK = 32, Germany = 29, Canada = 26

* We only report for countries where 20 or more participants indicated residence

To analyze the open-ended questions, a codebook was developed after rounds of inductive coding with four coders and iteration through consensus [16]. We inductively coded all open-ended responses and then compiled themes through an affinity diagramming exercise where each coder noted themes that emerged through coding. We collaborated to consolidate themes and created a codebook with two main categories: 1) attributed aspects of a BTS song that helped participants experience different mood regulations supporting their mental wellbeing (e.g., vocal/rap, lyrics, melody, rhythm), and 2) participants' experience when engaging with BTS' music (e.g., negative emotions, positive emotions, imagery, remembering). As the analysis progressed, we iterated on the codebook and discussed coding discrepancies with the entire team, ultimately coming to consensus. We used a finalized codebook (Fig. 1) to code the remaining responses using ATLAS.ti.

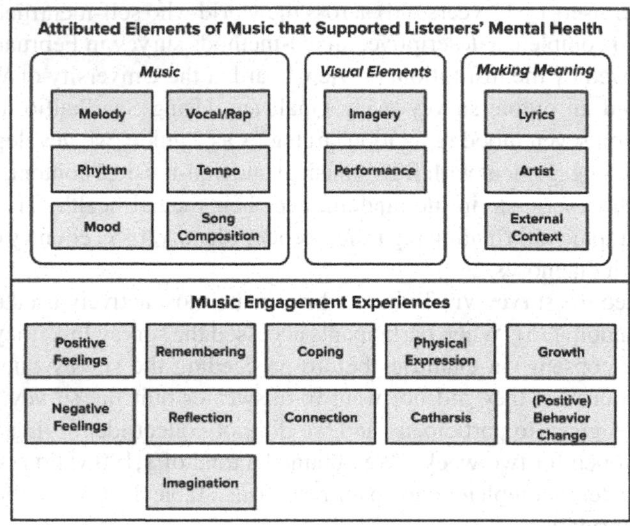

Fig. 1. Codes for helpful music elements and listeners' music engagement experiences.

4 Findings

4.1 Elements of Music Helpful for Mental Health

BTS has a diverse range of songs in their discography spanning over 9 years of releases, incorporating elements from a variety of music genres. We wanted to understand what participants considered as their "go-to" songs for changing their moods and supporting their mental health. In Table 2, we summarize the top songs mentioned by participants in each category of Saarikallio and Erkkilä's [49] framework on seven mood regulation strategies (i.e., entertainment, revival, strong sensation, diversion, discharge, mental work, and solace) and explain how it impacted their mood.

Table 2. Summary of top songs in each category of mood regulation.

Mood regulation	Top song	Elements stated to be helpful	Freq
Expressing negative mood (Discharge)	UGH!	Lyrics, tempo, rhythm: a rap song with high tempo and central lyrical messaging towards a criticism of society with intense audio elements like gunfire	168
Forgetting negative mood (Diversion)	Magic shop	Lyrics, context: song dedicated to ARMY; listeners found hope and comfort during difficult times	93
Feeling understood/comforted (Solace)	Magic shop	Melody, lyrics, imagery: a song that brought warmth, comfort, and feeling like getting a hug and/or being in a safe place where one's worries are removed	167
Reflection (Mental work)	Spring day	Lyrics, context of survivors of Sewol ferry tragedy, and chord progressions stimulating memories, personal/artists' experiences, and creating emotional space to reflect	73
Revised/Relaxed (Revival)	Life goes on	Lyrics and context of accepting the pandemic	92
Maintaining positive mood (Entertainment)	Dynamite	Rhythm, imagery: Upbeat disco-pop song with bright positive imagery in lyrics and music video	148
Feeling thrilled/energized (Strong sensation)	Mic Drop	Lyrics, rhythm, artists' context: A hip hop song with distinctive beats and lyrics about winning despite haters	108

Figure 2 shows the frequency of elements that were mentioned by participants as being helpful for supporting their mental wellness. Among the elements of BTS' songs, **lyrics** were most frequently cited by listeners as the element that helped them experience the seven moods. Lyrics play an important role in the musical experience allowing the listener to directly connect with the artists' words and intentions and depending on how it is used with other stimuli like melody, it can counteract or reinforce different emotions [53]. BTS' expression of their emotions and past experiences in their lyrics was something participants noted as helping them express their own feelings and experiences (elaborated in 4.2).

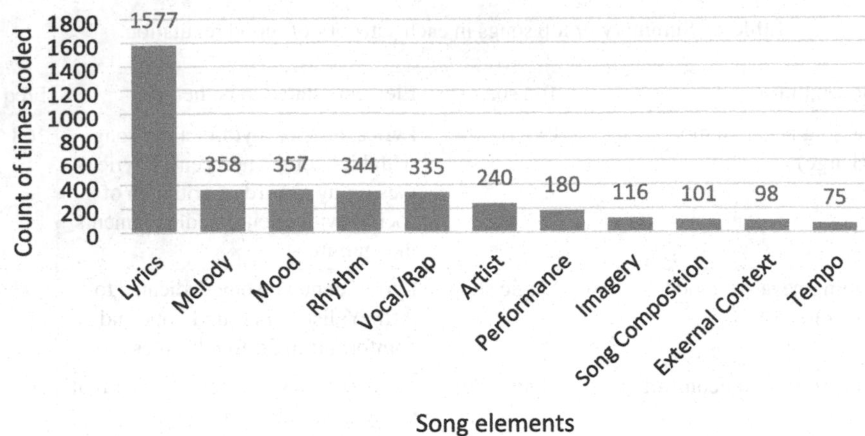

Fig. 2. Attributed helpful elements for supporting music listeners' mental wellbeing.

In addition, listeners mentioned that BTS' songs created the perfect atmosphere for the mood they wanted to experience. This atmosphere was attributed to the rhythm and melody of the song. **Rhythm and melody** often supplement a song's lyrics, increasing the impact the lyrics had on listeners. Listeners who did not know Korean often encountered the non-lyrical elements first. Referencing the song *Butterfly*, P1154 stated, "prior to reading the lyrics I could already feel how the song felt like finally a hand to hold after reaching out for so long. So when I did read the lyrics, it became even more meaningful."

Additionally, many participants brought up the intense energizing experience of **hearing the songs in live concerts** they attended. This experience heightened a sense of connection with the songs because of the memories they evoked afterwards, making them recall the overall concert experience and memories of experiencing specific songs. Live performances of *So What* were most frequently mentioned. P1175 reflected that, "*So What* has and always will be my first choice for feeling thrilled and energized…Being at the concerts, I was my best self. I did not have any worries and I had so much fun." Specific experiences of the live concert brought additional energy for P79: "Whenever I listen to this song, I think of their Speak Yourself concert…I feel really energized every time I think about it."

4.2 Experiences of How BTS' Music Supported Mental Health

Participants' self-reported experiences with the music are presented in Fig. 3. Participants reported feeling an array of emotions, feeling connected to the artists and other fans, as well as changes in their behavior or perspective in some cases.

Participants explained that BTS' lyrical content played an integral role in helping them **feel connected to artists' lived experiences** expressed through their music. BTS members take part in writing these songs and listeners find comfort in knowing that BTS members' feelings and experiences are reflected in their songs so that they are not alone. P658 noted this for *Magic Shop*:

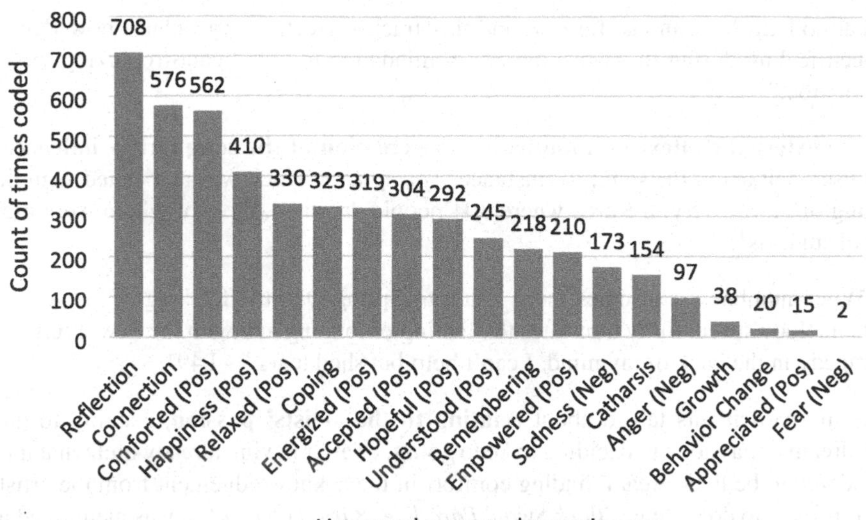

Fig. 3. Listeners' reported music engagement experiences. (Pos: positive feelings; Neg: negative feelings; other experiences can be a mix of positive, neutral, and/or negative)

> "Where many artists' approach to writing is to romanticize troubles and end a song on that note, BTS often consistently provides solutions and advice to their fans through music. This one tells the message of the power within me and my endless ability…It makes me want to show up for myself and be my best self just like I know the boys would want for me."

P624 explained BTS' **authenticity** saying that *Blue & Grey*, *The Truth Untold*, and *Outro: Tear*, among several other BTS songs, "are proof that the boys also experience what we usually experience too, since we are all humans here. They are somewhat saying that it's okay to feel such things, it's normal…" P673 explained a **healing** experience of being understood and remembering their childhood trauma through the lyrics of *Inner Child*: "The song talked to a part of me I forgot I had, and helped me begin to heal, to form a healthy, much needed connection with my own inner child."

Participants related with BTS' regular inclusion of lyrics that discussed **serious issues plaguing current society** and in particular the challenges faced by youth. Their authentic messages transcended time, generations, and geographic locations. They debuted with a single, *No More Dream*, in which they talk about South Korean youth's challenges with the education system and being forced into specific career paths at an early age. BTS' messages through lyrics have evolved since then to include more songs that openly express negative emotions like grief, as described in *Spring Day*'s lyrics. Although written before the pandemic, *Spring Day* resonated with P392 during the pandemic:

> "I don't know how they did it but they made a pandemic song years before the actual pandemic. The lyrics about missing people and not quite being able to reach them are so appropriate for this time in particular. There is always comfort in knowing

that no hardship can last forever, and this track perfectly encapsulates how I've been feeling during the pandemic and reminds me to avoid catastrophizing the situation."

The **external context that motivated the creation of the song** further influenced how users felt about the song; for instance, *Spring Day* which was associated with the sinking of Sewol ferry in Korea where 304 people drowned, most of whom were high school students[1]:

"When numbness consumes me, I listen to Spring Day to "feel" again because the melody successfully translates the feeling of longing and with the Sewol ferry tragedy in the back of my mind, I can't help but shed tears." - P491

Some participants talked about **relating to the artists' passion**, wanting to quit their dream or passion but deciding to keep going, or after having already quit what they considered to be their dream, finding comfort in the acknowledgement from the artists that it is okay to do so (e.g., *Black Swan, Paradise, Burn it*). *Paradise* was mentioned as a form of comfort for those who did not know what their dream or next step was. P472 stated that in *Paradise*, BTS expresses "exactly how I feel about not having a goal and tell me it's okay. That I will figure it out."

BTS' lyrics often complemented music, making listeners **reflect on their own life** and in some cases, **feel powerful**. The music of *Fire* for P428 was an "instant energy booster" and the lyrics also energized them:

"Whenever I hear this line from [the] song, 'Live however you want, it's your life anyway.' It just pumps me up & helps me realise I don't need to follow others to fulfill their expectations. I should just look out for what makes me feel happy."

Some listeners used the inspiration they get from BTS and their songs to channel their **anxieties and worries into creative outlets** such as painting, writing poems, and singing. The lyrics and melodies were used by participants in their writing and when making music ("I like making music myself as a hobby and often make covers of their songs, sample them, or generally take inspiration to write original works." (P668); "If I feel inspired by a song they have done, I will sometimes paint, just to get the feelings out, or if a book is recommended, I will often read it." (P360)). Several participants described BTS songs motivating them to dance along, at times, inspiring intentional movement and at other times making the listener "wanna dance despite myself" (P468). Specific songs that inspired participants to dance included *Fire*, which made P444 "dance like a kid", and *Serendipity*, which S1049 listens to "almost every night…and dance with myself to this song."

Songs also helped participants **engage in existing or make new social connections**, something that can impact mental health and was affected during the COVID-19 pandemic. Participants shared and discussed BTS songs and performances with existing friends, the music catalyzing P284 to "dance and sing and bond with my friends who

---

[1] https://www.reuters.com/article/us-southkorea-ferry-idUSKBN0NJ07R20150428.

aren't ARMY." BTS' music helped forge new friendships in the fandom, with some new bonds impacting mental health in a positive way.

Seeing **how the music affected other fans** also had an impact on some ARMYs. For instance, P1032 shares "Seeing how fans comment on BTS music, has saved them from suicide or getting through worst moments in life was really the start of me asking the question of 'what is it in their music that made fans relate?'" P749 also talked about a specific incident where a comment from another fan led them to helpful music:

> "Once I wrote on weverse in Korean about not feeling well because of a traumatic experience and that it felt like the feeling would never leave. K-armys immediately tried to cheer me up and one of them quoted 지나가 [the song, *everythingoes*] so I went to listen again to the music while reading the translation and it actually helped me a lot moving forward."

Sharing personal reactions to music on social media or streaming services also led to **support from other fans** in certain cases. For instance, P567 shared:

> "I had a breakdown in 2016 after my marriage ended in the summer. During the *Blood Sweat and Tears* comeback I was having a very hard time not attempting suicide (again) and one night when I was streaming the music video, I randomly mentioned it in the comments and loads of ARMYs I didn't know came to give me support."

The comfort and care experienced by our participants shows that the artists' intention with their music is highly important in helping to regulate the listeners' mental health. P1067 shares how BTS' openness to discuss mental health issues help create a culture in the community to value mental health and support each other:

> "Being part of a fandom that values mental health and openly supports anyone who is struggling has lowered the barrier and removed any reservations about sharing struggles to the community."

5 Discussion and Implications

5.1 A Model of Dynamic Music Engagement

Informed by the social-ecological model [9], findings of this study, and additional information about BTS and ARMY, and prior work on music engagement in the context of mental health, we propose a model of "Dynamic Music Engagement" (DME). This model explains the multifaceted interactions of music on the listener's mental health outcomes (Fig. 4). In our survey sample, BTS fans do more than just passively listen to songs; they engage with the music listening experience holistically and within a greater socio-cultural context.

Much of the previous research investigating the connection with music and mental health tends to focus on specific song attributes (e.g., lyrics, melody) or limited musical behaviors (e.g., passive listening, music creation). Furthermore, there is a lack of consideration for how the context of the listeners, artists, the fan community, and the

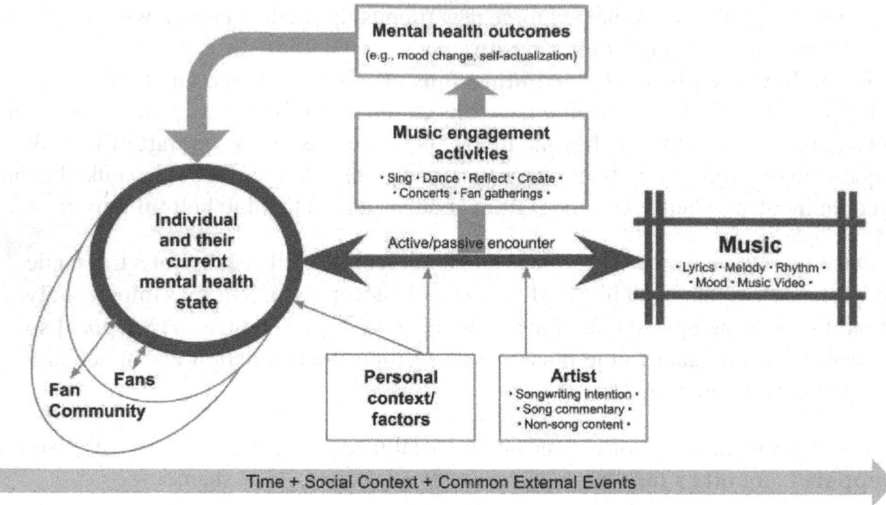

Fig. 4. Dynamic music engagement model.

interactions among them influence the ways people feel about the music. Through a case study of BTS and ARMY, we found that interacting with the lyrics, tempo, melody, among others–both alone and with other fans– impacts how listeners benefit from music with regards to their mental health. This impact on mental health is dynamic, changing over time as listeners discover new aspects of the songs, such as hearing a song and being moved by the melody and then moved again later after reading the lyrics. Listeners' individual situations and common community experiences also impact how the songs impact their moods; this includes experiences they had during BTS concerts and impacts of the COVID-19 pandemic on their lives. Our results provide evidence that passively listening to music can impact a listener's mental health (e.g., listening to *Life Goes On* catalyzing a cathartic response) and a person's mental health can impact what music they are actively seeking or choosing to listen to (e.g., listening to *Spring Day* when feeling nostalgic). Therefore, the nature of the relationship between the individual and their current mental health state with music is bidirectional (Fig. 4).

This research reveals the complex ways in which an artist's discography – and even an individual song – can influence a person's mental health through different modalities, during changing personal and societal contexts, and over time. In the context of BTS and ARMY, authentic and mutual sharing of each other's challenges and motivation is reflected in the artists' lyrics[2], interviews[3], social media posts, concerts and live interactions with fans, award show messages, and the stories they share behind their songs. Our study describes how songs influence mental health in the complex, real-world information ecosystem that listeners find themselves in. Therefore, songs are

[2] https://doolsetbangtan.wordpress.com/2018/06/01/two-three/.

[3] https://www.rollingstone.com/music/music-features/new-bts-song-2021-worlds-biggest-band-1166441/.

more than just pitches and words – they are an intricate, dynamic experience, and rich in its messaging that can positively support listeners' mental health.

5.2 Design Implications

In this section, we use the DME model to suggest several design ideas for music information systems and services to support people's engagement with music for their mental health. These ideas incorporate evolving contexts beyond the music itself, including fan-artist interactions, creative participatory engagement, and interactive collective listening.

Designing for Dynamic Participatory Creative Engagement with Fans and Artists. The DME Model highlights the importance of a fan's engagement with music beyond listening to the song. New media supporting participatory and social experience that nurture the connections between the artist and fans, and among fans, will be increasingly important [28]. Beyond mood regulation or coping, we identified several music engagement activities that involve some creative aspect (e.g., writing songs/poems) that could support the listener's mental health or are a consequence of an improving mental health. Participants shared that listening to music can lead to positive engagement including the **physical expressions** of singing, dancing, reflecting, creating, attending concerts, and gathering at fan meetups. Content creation social media tools such as TikTok and Instagram support such engagement [52, 55]. Participants were actively reflecting on the songs' meaning as well as on their own memories, experiences, fears, and hopes. Moreover, this demonstrates that the impact of music on listeners' mental health lasts longer beyond when actively listening to music, including when discussing it with other fans. Music streaming services can also support creative activities and self-awareness of this change in mental health through using visual markers (e.g., colors representing different moods).

A better integration with other media to foster a sense of connection with artists and other fans can happen through choreo/dance challenge videos. BTS and their company HYBE have encouraged mass participation from fans through TikTok dance challenges and YouTube Shorts (e.g., *Permission to dance* challenge, sharing memories with BTS through *Yet to come* challenge). While these kinds of participation are curated, recorded, and asynchronous, they still foster a sense of belonging and relating with others' experiences. Vizcaíno-Verdú and Abidin [55] argue that music challenges are a mode of storytelling where the TikTokers tell the story about themselves and their feelings about the music as a form of transmedia rather than a competition. With the emergence of ad hoc, one-to-many bidirectional auditory interfaces such as Twitter Spaces (that allows the host and participants to speak), there is a potential for technologies to support participatory synchronous and remote audio engagement. Content that supports singing along (e.g., remote social karaoke among fans), live but remote singing with artists (similar to in-person concert experience), or practicing fan chants (a chant that fans recite in unison during the artists' performances consisting of parts of the lyrics, names of the group/members, or other words) could be beneficial for more active engagement with the song.

Furthermore, the specific context in which music is experienced, affects the users' emotions as they recall that context; for instance, the life experiences the user was going through at the moment (e.g., losing someone close, first year of college) or the place and person associated with that experience (e.g., going to a concert with a friend, dance practices). Participants often shared these memorable experiences which in turn made them feel strong emotional connections with specific songs.

Features that connect the records of the user's music listening behavior with other content created by the user, for instance, showing what songs the user listened to most for specific time periods represented by the photos or videos they also took at that time, could help users recall those connections and experience the emotions. Developing more interactive features in live streamed concerts that augments the listeners' experience without overly distracting them could also be appealing. Recently, HYBE collected audio recordings of ARMYs fan chants, and aggregated and played it at an online concert to help create an atmosphere that is more like a real concert. They also selected fans to show on multi-screened background walls so the artists could see the fans' reactions and other fans could also see the messages fans were holding. These are examples of supporting the interactions that would occur in a real concert in an online environment which would not replace the in-person experience but can still help create a positive experience in a virtual setting.

Designing for Dynamic Meaning Making of the Songs and Lyrics.
In our DME Model, we have identified that individuals' mental health state is both actively and passively influenced by artists' intentions behind a song or the context of creation through lyrical content. However, this kind of information may not be apparent in the lyrics itself. An annotation system where more knowledgeable users can provide such information in the streaming services for music or music-related content for other users can help enrich the listening experiences [29]. Genius (https://genius.com), a platform for crowdsourced annotation of song lyrics, is one example of such a system. Genius relies on users to source the lyrics, annotate the interpretation, and edit it over time [30]. Users can access information about the artists' context (e.g., interview about the song), get links to other relevant media (e.g., performance video), and get answers to various questions they have about the songs. Further including and/or highlighting how the music impacted other fans may help support the user's engagement with the music for positive mental wellbeing. This kind of feature could also be useful for cases of global fandom where people are listening to music that is not in their own language (e.g., a translation note app such as LibL allows Korean fans to explain Korean memes and puns by Kpop artists to non-Korean fans).

Furthermore, the DME Model draws attention to the bidirectional relationship between a fan's current mental state and their engagement with other fans and with the fandom at large. Fans can not only share their reflections on the song's meaning but also on how their mindset has been influenced by the lyrics. This is possible within the music streaming services or through other social media. For instance, social radio services like Stationhead in which users can stream songs and chat together, can incorporate Danmu (a type of video commentary used on the internet that consists of scrolling user/viewer remarks shown on top of the video in real time) into each station allowing users to multitask – sending Danmu to express their thoughts at the main page while listening simultaneously to the same track. The use of Spaces on Twitter to host live discussion sessions or Q&A with the artists is another example to facilitate the collective experience of reflection.

Ultimately, these suggested features are based on the perspective of viewing context, not as static surroundings that impact the user's reception of music, but as a collection of dynamic relationships that are constructed due to the listener's engagement with music [46] and the information systems they use for music. Fans' relationships with the artists and active efforts to interpret music and share it with other fans, and their consequent influence on how other fans engage with music are examples of how music engagement in the digital context is dynamically and constantly shifting.

6 Conclusion and Future Work

With the increase in use of online technologies, engagement with music and related information go beyond an individual, and beyond the moment of listening to the music. Through a case study on the mental health experiences of the ARMY fandom when engaging with BTS' music, we present empirical findings from a survey with 1,190 ARMYs. These findings provide insights into a music fan's complex and multifaceted context in which they engage with music and music related content and informs the various ways such engagement supports the user's mental wellbeing. Based on the temporally changing social context of fans, we derive the Dynamic Music Engagement Model. This model provides a lens to inform the design of future information systems to intentionally support listeners' mental health experiences, particularly building participatory connection with the artists and their fan community. In addition, it can be used to codesign and prototype these systems to understand the real-world applicability and tensions. This research is based on a case study of BTS ARMY fandom, and future research is needed to examine how the model applies in different contexts and cultures where music engagement occurs and investigate whether there are additional aspects to consider extending the model.

References

1. Arditi, D.: Precarious labor in COVID times: the case of musicians. Fast Capitalism **18**(1), 13–25 (2021)
2. ARMY Census. https://www.btsarmycensus.com/2022-results. Accessed 8 Sep 2022
3. Baker, F., Bor, W.: Can music preference indicate mental health status in young people? Australas. Psychiatry **16**(4), 284–288 (2008)
4. Baker, T.D.: The ghost of "emo:" searching for mental health themes in a popular music format. J. School Counseling **11**(8), 35 (2013)
5. Batt-Rawden, K., Tellnes, G.: How music may promote healthy behaviour. Scandinavian J. Public Health **39**(2), 113–120 (2011)
6. Bennett, L.: Patterns of listening through social media: online fan engagement with the live music experience. Soc. Semiot. **22**(5), 545–557 (2012)
7. Blady, S.: Bulletproof to Stigma. Speak Up. https://www.speak-up.co/bulletproof-tostigma. Accessed 2 Sep 2022

8. Chanda, M.L., Levitin, D.J.: The neurochemistry of music. Trends Cogn. Sci. **17**(4), 179–193 (2013)
9. Clinical and Translational Science Awards Consortium Community Engagement Key Function Committee Task Force on the Principles of Community Engagement: Principles of Community Engagement (2011). https://www.atsdr.cdc.gov/communityengagement/pdf/PCE_Report_508_FINAL.pdf. Accessed 7 Dec 2022
10. Davidson, D.: Cross-Media Communications: An Introduction to the Art of Creating Integrated Media Experiences. Carnegie Mellon University (2018).https://doi.org/10.1184/R1/6686735.v1
11. de la Rubia Ortí, J.E., et al.: Does music therapy improve anxiety and depression in alzheimer's patients? The J. Alternative and Complementary Medicine **24**(1), 33–36 (2018)
12. Garringer, J.: How does music connect the artist and fans? Ray Browne Conference on Cultural and Critical Studies (2018). https://scholarworks.bgsu.edu/rbc/2018conference/005/7/. Accessed 8 Sep 2022
13. Grocke, D., Bloch, S., Castle, D.: Is there a role for music therapy in the care of the severely mentally ill? Australas. Psychiatry **16**, 442–445 (2008)
14. Gustavson, D.E., Coleman, P.L., Iversen, J.R., Maes, H.H., Gordon, R.L., Lense, M.D.: Mental health and music engagement: review, framework, and guidelines for future studies. Translational Psychiatry 11(1), 370 (2021). https://www.nature.com/articles/s41398-021-01483-8.pdf
15. Hagen, W.R.: Fandom: Participatory Music Behavior in the Age of Postmodern Media. University of Colorado at Boulder (2010). https://www.proquest.com/docview/507898725
16. Hill, C., Thompson, B., Williams, E.: A guide to conducting consensual qualitative research. Couns. Psychol. **25**(4), 517–572 (1997)
17. Hoffner, C.A., Bond, B.J.: Parasocial relationships, social media, & well-being. Current Opinion in Psychology **45**, 101306 (2022). https://doi.org/10.1016/j.copsyc.2022.101306
18. Jenkins, H.: Fan Studies. Oxford Bibliographies (2012). https://doi.org/10.1093/obo/9780199791286-0027
19. Jenkins, H.: Convergence Culture. Where Old and New Media Collide. New York University Press, New York, NY (2006)
20. Knight, W.E.J., Rickard, N.S.: Relaxing music prevents stress-induced increases in subjective anxiety, systolic blood pressure, and heart rate in healthy males and females. J. Music Ther. **38**(4), 254–272 (2008)
21. Kresovich, A.: The influence of pop songs referencing anxiety, depression, and suicidal ideation on college students' mental health empathy, stigma, and behavioral intentions. Health Commun. **37**(5), 617–627 (2022)
22. Kresovich, A., Collins, M.K.R., Riffe, D., Carpentier, F.R.D.: A content analysis of mental health discourse in popular rap music. JAMA Pediatr. **175**(3), 286–292 (2021)
23. Kusuma, A., Putri Purbantina, A., Nahdiyah, V., Khasanah, U.U.: A virtual ethnography study: fandom and social impact in digital era. ETNOSIA: Jurnal Etnografi Indonesia, pp. 238–251 (2020)
24. Laffan, D.A.: Positive psychosocial outcomes and fanship in K-pop fans: a social identity theory perspective. Psychol. Rep. **124**(5), 2272–2285 (2021)
25. Lee, J.: BTS and ARMY Culture. CommunicationBooks, Seoul, South Korea (2019)
26. Lee, J., Thyer, B.A.: Does music therapy improve mental health in adults? a review. J. Hum. Behav. Soc. Environ. **23**(5), 591–603 (2013)
27. Lee, J.H., Cho, H., Kim, Y.-S.: Users' music information needs and behaviors: design implications for music information retrieval systems. J. Am. Soc. Inf. Sci. **67**(6), 1301–1330 (2016)

28. Lee, J.H., Nguyen, A.T.: How music fans shape commercial music services: a case study of BTS and ARMY. In: Proceedings of the International Society for Music Information Conference, ISMIR, Montréal, Canada, pp. 837845 (2020)
29. Lee, J.H., Bhattacharya, A., Antony, R., Santero, N.K., Le, A.: Finding home: understanding how music supports listener's mental health through a case study of BTS. In: Proceedings of ISMIR, pp. 358–365 (2021)
30. Lim, D., Benson, A.R.: Expertise and dynamics within crowdsourced musical knowledge curation: a case study of the Genius platform. In: ICWSM, pp. 373–384 (2021)
31. Lin, S.-T., et al.: Mental health implications of music: insight from neuroscientific and clinical studies. Harv. Rev. Psychiatry **19**(1), 34–46 (2011)
32. MacDonald, R.A.R.: Music, health, and well-being: a review. International Journal of Qualitative Studies on Health and Well-being **8**(1), 20635 (2013)
33. MacDonald, R., Kreutz, G., Mitchell, L.: Music, Health, and Wellbeing. Oxford University Press (2012)
34. McCaffrey, T., Edwards, J., Fannon, D.: Is there a role for music therapy in the recovery approach in mental health? Arts Psychother. **38**(3), 185–189 (2011)
35. McFerran, K.S., Garrido, S., Saarikallio, S.A.: Critical interpretive synthesis of the literature linking music and adolescent mental health. Youth & Society **48**(4), 521–538 (2016)
36. McFerran, K.S., Saarikallio, S.: Depending on music to feel better: being conscious of responsibility when appropriating the power of music. Arts Psychother. **41**(1), 89–97 (2013)
37. Nilsson, U.: The anxiety- and pain-reducing effects of music interventions: a systematic review. Aorn Journal **87**(4), 780–807 (2008)
38. Parc, J., Kim, Y.: Analyzing the reasons for the global popularity of BTS: a new approach from a business perspective. J. International Business and Economy **21**(1), 15–36 (2020)
39. Park, S.Y., Laplante, A., Lee, J.H., Kaneshiro, B.: Tunes together: Perception and experience of collaborative playlists. In: Proceedings of the International Society for Music Information Conference, ISMIR, Delft, The Netherlands (2019)
40. Park, S.Y., Santero, N., Kaneshiro, B., Lee, J.H.: Armed in ARMY: a case study of how BTS fans successfully collaborated to #MatchAMillion for Black Lives Matter. In: Proceedings of CHI 2021, ACM, New York, NY, USA (2021)
41. Pereira, C.S., Teixeira, J., Figueiredo, P., Xavier, J., Castro, S.L., Brattico, E.: Music and emotions in the brain: familiarity matters. Public Library of Science **6**(11), e27241 (2011)
42. Philip, J., Cherian, V.: Psychiatry and 'pop' culture: millennials for mental health – psychiatry in music. Br. J. Psychiatry **217**(6), 678 (2020)
43. Rendell, J.: Staying in, rocking out: online live music portal shows during the coronavirus pandemic. Convergence: The International Journal of Research into New Media Technologies **27**(4), 1092–1111 (2021)
44. Reysen, S., Plante, C., Chadborn, D.: Better together: social connections mediate the relationship between fandom and well-being. AASCIT Journal of Health **4**(6), 68–73 (2017)
45. Ringland, K.E., Bhattacharya, A., Weatherwax, K., Eagle, T., Wolf, C.T.: ARMY's Magic Shop: understanding the collaborative construction of playful places in online communities. In: Proceedings of the CHI Conference on Human Factors in Computing Systems, pp. 1–19 (2022)
46. Rolvsjord, R., Stige, B.: Concepts of context in music therapy. Nord. J. Music. Ther. **24**(1), 44–66 (2015)
47. Rubin, S.: Strong experiences with music (SEMs) as experienced by ARMY. https://sydneyrubin.com/2021/03/23/strong-experiences-with-bts-music/. Accessed 2 Sep 2022
48. Ruud, E.: Music in therapy: increasing possibilities for action. Music and Arts in Action **1**(1), 46–60 (2008)
49. Saarikallio, S., Erkkilä, J.: The role of music in adolescents' mood regulation. Psychol. Music **35**(1), 88–109 (2007)

50. Scolari, C.: Transmedia storytelling: new ways of communicating in the digital age. AC/E Digital Culture Annual Report. https://www.dosdoce.com/upload/ficheros/noticias/201404/digital_culture_report__english_version.pdf. Accessed 2 Sep 2022
51. Schedl, M., Flexer, A.: Putting the user in the center of music information retrieval. In: Proceedings of ISMIR pp. 385–390 (2012)
52. Shutsko, A.: User-generated short video content in social media. a case study of TikTok. In: International Conference on Human Computer-Interaction, pp. 108–125 (2020)
53. Stratton, V.N., Zalanowski, A.H.: Affective impact of music vs lyrics. Empir. Stud. Arts **12**(2), 173–184 (1994)
54. Thayer, R.E., Newman, R., McClain, T.M.: Self-regulation of mood: strategies for changing a bad mood, raising energy, and reducing tension. J. Pers. Soc. Psychol. **67**(5), 910–925 (1994)
55. Vizcaíno-verdú, A., Abidin, C.: Music challenge memes on TikTok: understanding in-group storytelling videos. Int. J. Commun. **16**, 883–908 (2022)
56. Yin, R.K.: Case Study Research, Design and Methods. 3rd ed. SAGE (2003)

Your Online Favorites are Overwhelming When You're Having Fun: An Investigation of Fear of Missing Out, Social Media Affordances and Digital Hoarding

Dawei Wu[1], Yuxiang Chris Zhao[1(✉)], Xiaolun Wang[2], and Jingwen Lian[3]

[1] Nanjing University of Science and Technology, Nanjing 210094, China
yxzhao@vip.163.com
[2] Nanjing University of Aeronautics and Astronautics, Nanjing 211106, China
[3] Nanjing University, Nanjing 210033, China

Abstract. The symbolic collection technology has greatly simplified information preservation in social media, resulting in an overwhelming amount of users' "favorites" collections. Digital hoarding, a new problematic use in hedonic social media, has gradually appeared as a serious phenomenon nowadays. This study aims to investigate the mechanism underlying digital hoarding in the hedonic context, exploring the causes of digital hoarding and how it is exacerbated in social media. First, we draw on the conceptual lens of Fear of Missing Out (FoMO) to understand the generation mechanism of digital hoarding in social media. Meanwhile, we consider the moderating effect of social media affordances between the relationship of FoMO and digital hoarding from a human-information interaction perspective. Our preliminary study collected 233 valid questionnaires and tested the hypotheses by partial least squares structural equation modeling. The tentative findings show that FoMO has a significant positive effect on digital hoarding, which is strengthened by content sharing affordance. Moreover, information anxiety and attachment anxiety can strongly predict FoMO. Finally, we discuss the potential contributions and future directions of this work.

Keywords: Digital hoarding · Fear of missing out · Affordance · Social media

1 Introduction

With the development of information technology, a new digital problematic use, *digital hoarding*, is emerging. Digital hoarding refers to the massive accumulation of digital materials that leads to a cluttered digital space [1]. Although digital hoarding does not occupy our physical space, it can lead to serious problems such as psychological pressure and cybersecurity threat, thus further impair individuals' normal life and work [1, 2].

Prior research on digital hoarding mainly focuses on the contexts of work and everyday life, including hoarding emails or digital photos [1, 3]. However, few studies have been concerned about digital hoarding in the hedonic context. In UGC-based hedonic

© The Author(s), under exclusive license to Springer Nature Switzerland AG 2023
I. Sserwanga et al. (Eds.): iConference 2023, LNCS 13971, pp. 109–117, 2023.
https://doi.org/10.1007/978-3-031-28035-1_9

social media (such as Twitter, YouTube, or Tik Tok), symbolic collection technology has greatly simplified information preservation. We can add interested content to bookmarks with just "one-click". However, the costless way of storage has resulted in an overwhelming amount of users' favorites collections, which creates a serious digital hoarding phenomenon commonly existed among social media users [4].

Therefore, this study aims to investigate the mechanism underlying digital hoarding in the hedonic context. One on hand, **we adopt the conceptual lens of *Fear of missing out (FoMO)* to explore *why digital hoarding appears in social media*.** Different from the utilization value of e-mails and memorable value of digital photos, the reason of digital hoarding behavior in the hedonic context has been underexplored. FoMO, the "dark side feelings" that emerges from social media use, is defined as the negative emotions such as anxiety or panic when users fail to keep an instant link with social media [5, 6]. Numerous studies investigated the impact of FoMO on multiple social media problematic use such as addiction and phubbing behavior [7, 8], yet the relationship between FOMO and digital hoarding has never been studied. On the other hand, **we also incorporate *social media affordance* to explore *how digital hoarding exacerbates in social media.*** Social media affordance refers to the action possibilities enabled by social media features, which provides a theoretical lens for understanding the effects of system design [9]. Studies have shown that multiple social media affordances provide a convenient channel for information accumulation [10]. This raises a new question that whether social media affordance is always good because it might aggravate digital hoarding phenomenon. Overall, we are among the first to combine FoMO and social media affordance to analyze the reason and accelerator of digital hoarding in social media.

A quantitative study with 233 valid questionnaires was conducted. The results show that FoMO has a significant positive effect on digital hoarding, which is strengthened by content sharing affordance. Moreover, information anxiety and attachment anxiety can strongly predict FoMO. Our research may shed light on the antecedents for users' digital hoarding in hedonic social media and the possible dark side of hedonic interactive elements design.

2 Related Work

2.1 Digital Hoarding

Since van Bennekom et al. [1] presented a typical case of hoarding of digital pictures. Digital hoarding is emerging as a new intersection of psychology and information science [4, 11].

Most of the prior literature attempt to explore dimensions, antecedents, and outcomes of digital hoarding. First, studies have shown that digital hoarding includes at least two dimensions of positive acquisition and negative deletion [4]. Neave et al. [3] has developed the Digital Hoarding Questionnaire (DHQ) based on this consideration, accumulating and difficulty deleting are two core factors in this scale. Second, the antecedent of digital hoarding can involve different aspects. It includes emotional factors such as concerns about future use, emotional attachment to digital content, personal factors such as laziness, as well as technical factors such as convenient cloud storage [2, 12]. Finally, in terms of outcomes, digital hoarding is harmful to users' psychological well-being and cognitive function, possibly causing cyberphobia and avoidance behaviors. Severe digital hoarding may develop into physical hoarding, which can further affect individuals' normal life and interpersonal relationships [1, 2, 4, 13].

In summary, previous research provides a theoretical basis and measurement for digital hoarding. However, few previous studies have conducted quantitative empirical research to explore the relationships between the possible antecedent and digital hoarding, which may provide more credible evidence for the formation of digital hoarding.

2.2 Fear of Missing Out in Social Media

FoMO is a serious problem in social media and may become more prevalent with the emerging of new features [6]. FoMO is considered to be a psychological state arising from insufficient innate needs [5]. Since social media's autonomous features can satisfy users' innate needs [10], any impairment of the connection between users and social media may cause FoMO [6]. However, the emergence of new features has increased the vulnerability of this connection. People may generate new FoMO feelings due to their reliance on new social media features. For example, sharing features can facilitate communication between people, but it may also lead to people checking their phones more frequently for fear of missing content. This inspires us to think about how to avoid the FoMO problems that may come with technological development.

Although FoMO is not explicitly considered a mental illness, it can still pose serious problems. FoMO has received widespread attention for its complex negative psychological and behavioral effects on social media users. On the one hand, FoMO can make social media users develop emotional symptoms such as anxiety, depression, boredom, and fatigue, which may reduce users' life well-being [6, 14, 15]. On the other hand, FoMO as problematic psychology may further induce problematic behavior, such as compulsive use and phubbing [7, 8, 16]. These behaviors may further jeopardize interpersonal relationship satisfaction and even impair mental health (e.g., elicit depression) and physical health [17, 18].

To sum up, FoMO is the antecedent of many "online dark sides", but few studies have explored the effect of FoMO on digital hoarding. By clarifying the impact effect of FoMO on digital hoarding, we can provide insights for social media practitioner to manage digital hoarding at the source.

3 Research Hypothesis and Model

3.1 FoMO and Digital Hoarding

Social media users suffered FoMO need to keep online to relieve their anxiety, which may lead to users' overuse behavior. Studies have shown that users with FoMO may use social media more frequently, and more intensely than the average users [5, 19], even develop into addictive behaviors [7]. Frequent interaction may provide better conditions for users to acquire and accumulate information. Meanwhile, users with FoMO are more likely to develop attachment emotions [20], this attachment emotion may lead FoMO users to value the collected content and could not bear to delete. Hence, we propose the following hypothesis:

H1: FoMO has a positive influence on digital hoarding in social media context.

3.2 Determinants of FoMO

Information Anxiety. Information anxiety is a state of stress in situations of information overload or underload [21]. Currently, information anxiety is a common phenomenon in social media context. Social media users with information anxiety try to combat negative emotions by getting more information. This may make them afraid of missing out on information that is beneficial to them [22]. It has been shown that there is a strong correlation between anxiety and FoMO [23]. Therefore, we propose the following hypothesis:

H2: Information anxiety has a positive influence on FoMO in social media context.

Attachment Anxiety. Attachment anxiety refers to fear and anxiety that arises when people are separated from attachment figures [24]. Users in an attachment anxiety state are used to seeking help from others on social media networks [25] and may fear losing this stable online social support. Studies have shown that attachment anxiety can predict FoMO in general context. Hence, we propose:

H3: Attachment anxiety has a positive influence on FoMO in social media context.

3.3 The Moderating Effects of Social Media Affordances

In this section, we mainly explored the moderating role of social media affordances in the effect of FoMO on digital hoarding. By investigating the functional features of social media, we chose two social media affordances that are closely related to content acquisition for our study, including *recommendation affordance* and *content sharing affordance*. They may exacerbate users hoard digital content.

Recommending Affordance. Recommending affordance refers to the potential for the system to recommend customized information to the user by capturing the user's preferences or interests [10]. Recommended information is more attractive to social media users [26]. Thus, users with FoMO may be more reluctant to miss out on recommended information, which leads to retaining more information and not being willing to delete it. Accordingly, we hypothesized the following:

H4: Recommending affordance strengthens the relationship between FoMO and digital hoarding in social media context.

Content Sharing Affordance. Content sharing affordance refers to the function of "*Users can share and distribute content unrelated to self to others in a social media setting, such as sharing funny video or news item* [9]". This affordance is based on the information interaction between users, which enhances their feelings of social support [27]. High FoMO individuals are very concerned about their community involvement [5]. Thus, they may place more importance on the information shared by others. Hence, we propose:

H5: Content sharing affordance strengthens the relationship between FoMO and digital hoarding in social media context.

Based on the above hypotheses, we constructed the research model (see Fig. 1).

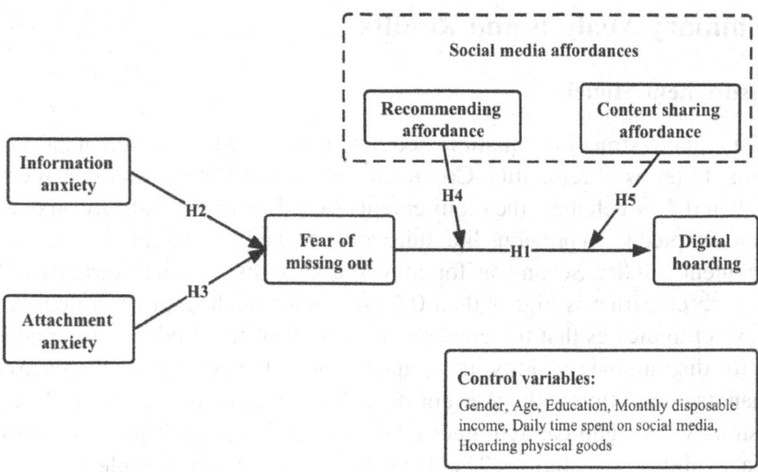

Fig. 1. Research model.

4 Methodology

Our constructs were measured by seven-point Likert-type scale and adapted from previously validated scales. Information anxiety was adapted from the work of Marteau and Bekker [28]. Attachment anxiety was adapted from the classic Experiences in Close Relationships Inventory (ECR) of Brennan et al. [29]. Recommending affordance was measured in keeping with the scale of Song et al. [10]. Content sharing affordance was adapted from Lai and Yang [27] and Mills et al. [30]. FoMO was measured using items adapted from Przybylski et al. [5] and Song et al. [31]. We measured digital hoarding with eight items adapted from Neave et al. [3]. We developed the original items from English to Chinese, and the process was facilitated by two linguistics professors.

Our questionnaire was mainly created in Wenjuanxing (www.wjx.cn), a professional questionnaire survey platform in China. We mainly distribute questionnaires through Baidu Tieba, Douban, Zhihu, and other online communities. Each participant received 5–10 yuan (approximately 1 ~ 2 dollars) as a reward. The survey lasted 15 days from June 10 to June 24, 2022, 387 questionnaires were collected.

Subsequently, we conducted a sample screening. We asked participants to (1) have more than 3 years of social media use; (2) use social media for entertainment activities for at least half an hour a day; (3) have experience in collecting content in social media. Finally, we retained 233 valid questionnaires. In the final sample, male and female participants accounted for 59.23% and 40.77%, respectively. Most respondents were aged 21–30 (106, 45.49%) and have a bachelor's or higher degree (202, 86.70%). 82.40% of them have experience of hoarding physical goods.

5 Preliminary Analysis and Results

5.1 Measurement Model

Partial least-squares structural equation modeling (PLS-SEM) was used in the data analysis process. In terms of reliability, Cronbach's alpha and CR values of each construct is greater than 0.7, which meet the requirements [32]. In terms of validity, first, because all items are adapted from previous literature and checked by multiple experts, the scale has high content validity. Second, as for convergent validity, average variance extracted (AVE) of each construct is higher than 0.5 and factor loading of each item is higher than 0.7, which indicates that the convergent validity of the model is acceptable [32]. Third, as for discriminant validity, the square root of the AVE of each construct was greater than its correlation with other construct [32]; meanwhile, the items loadings of each construct were significantly higher than its cross-loadings. Therefore, our model' discriminant validity was eligible. The detailed data are shown in Table 1.

Table 1. Correlations and psychometric characteristics of constructs.

	1	2	3	4	5	6
1. Information anxiety	**0.889**					
2. Attachment anxiety	0.549	**0.834**				
3. Fear of missing out	0.662	0.724	**0.845**			
4. Recommending affordance	0.482	0.444	0.633	**0.826**		
5. Content sharing affordance	0.314	0.327	0.467	0.717	**0.915**	
6. Digital hoarding	0.422	0.482	0.603	0.702	0.583	**0.796**
Cronbach's Alpha	0.864	0.782	0.867	0.766	0.903	0.904
Composite Reliability	0.918	0.873	0.909	0.865	0.939	0.923
Average Variance Extracted (AVE)	0.790	0.696	0.714	0.682	0.837	0.633

Note: Values on the diagonal represent the square root of average variance extracted (AVE) for each construct.

5.2 Structural Model

We tested the hypotheses, results as illustrated in Fig. 2. First, FoMO ($\beta = 0.316, p < .01$) can strongly predict digital hoarding, which supports H1. Second, the antecedents of, information anxiety ($\beta = 0.372, p < .01$) and attachment anxiety ($\beta = 0.447, p < .01$), all have positive effects on digital hoarding. Therefore, H2 and H3 were tested. Finally, we tested the moderating effects of the two social media affordances. The results show that content sharing affordance ($\beta = 0.084, p < .1$) can strengthen the positive effect of FoMO on digital hoarding. Thus, H5 was supported. However, the moderating effect of recommending affordance was not significant ($\beta = 0.035, n,s$), which meant H4 was not supported. The possible reason is recommending affordance brings the problem of information cocoon, users lose the interest of storing too much homogeneous information. Therefore, recommending affordance does not exacerbate the digital hoarding.

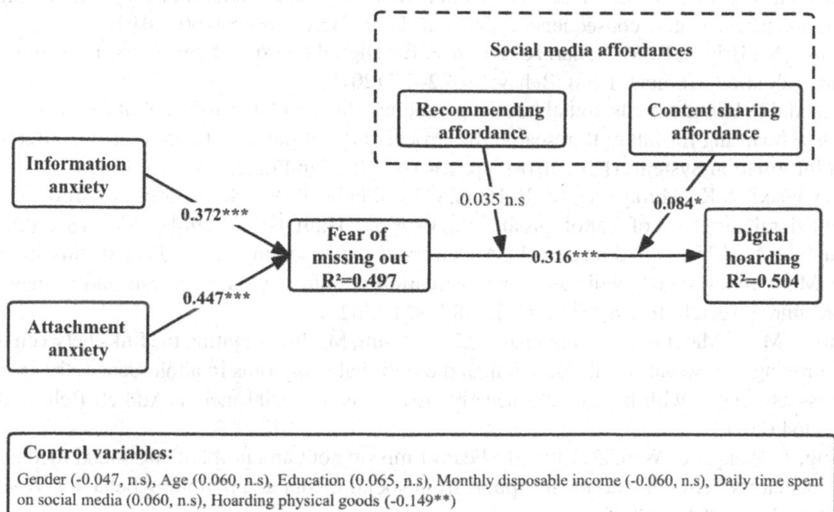

Note: * indicates $p < .1$; ** indicates $p < .05$; *** indicates $p < .01$; n.s.: not significant; one-tailed test.

Fig. 2. Results from the PLS model.

6 Preliminary Contributions

In the preliminary study, we found the positive effect of FoMO on digital hoarding in the hedonic social media context. This is consistent with previous studies in which FoMO generated problematic use of social media [8]. Meanwhile, the content sharing affordance positively moderates the effect of FoMO on digital hoarding, whereas recommending affordance doesn't. Furthermore, the results also show that FoMO is associated with information anxiety and attachment anxiety.

This study has profound theoretical and practical implications. In theory, we are among the first to explore digital hoarding in the hedonic social media context, which can provide contributes to literature for understanding digital hoarding as an emerging problematic use in the new context. Specifically, we propose FoMO as the emotional antecedent of digital hoarding, and social media affordances as the accelerator between FoMO and digital hoarding from system design perspective. In practice, our findings caution social media users to store less in "favorite" collections since it comes from the sick state of FoMO. Besides, social media practitioners should be more careful about designing features that may exacerbate digital hoarding. In the future, we attempt to enhance the study by including more social media affordances, improving the measurement of digital hoarding, and using a larger sample of data.

References

1. van Bennekom, M.J., Blom, R.M., Vulink, N., Denys, D.: A case of digital hoarding. British Medical Journal Case Reports (2015)
2. Sweeten, G., Sillence, E., Neave, N.: Digital hoarding behaviours: underlying motivations and potential negative consequences. Comput. Hum. Behav. **85**, 54–60 (2018)
3. Neave, N., Briggs, P., McKellar, K., Sillence, E.: Digital hoarding behaviours: measurement and evaluation. Comput. Hum. Behav. **96**, 72–77 (2019)
4. Sedera, D., Lokuge, S.: Is digital hoarding a mental disorder? development of a construct for digital hoarding for future IS research. In: Proceedings of the 39th International Conference on Information Systems (ICIS 2018), pp. 13–16. AIS, San Francisco, USA (2018)
5. Przybylski, A.K., Murayama, K., DeHaan, C.R., Gladwell, V.: Motivational, emotional, and behavioral correlates of fear of missing out. Comput. Hum. Behav. **29**(4), 1841–1848 (2013)
6. Tandon, A., Dhir, A., Almugren, I., AlNemer, G.N., Mäntymäki, M.: Fear of missing out (FoMO) among social media users: a systematic literature review, synthesis and framework for future research. Internet Res. **31**(3), 782–821 (2021)
7. Fabris, M.A., Marengo, D., Longobardi, C., Settanni, M.: Investigating the links between fear of missing out, social media addiction, and emotional symptoms in adolescence: the role of stress associated with neglect and negative reactions on social media. Addict. Behav. **106**, 106364 (2020)
8. Fang, J., Wang, X., Wen, Z., Zhou, J.: Fear of missing out and problematic social media use as mediators between emotional support from social media and phubbing behavior. Addict. Behav. **107**, 106430 (2020)
9. Karahanna, E., Xu, S.X., Xu, Y., Zhang, N.A.: The needs–affordances–features perspective for the use of social media. MIS Q. **42**(3), 737–756 (2018)
10. Song, S., Zhao, Y.C., Yao, X., Ba, Z., Zhu, Q.: Short video apps as a health information source: an investigation of affordances, user experience and users' intention to continue the use of TikTok. Internet Res. **31**(6), 2121–2142 (2021)
11. Luxon, A.M., Hamilton, C.E., Bates, S., Chasson, G.S.: Pinning our possessions: associations between digital hoarding and symptoms of hoarding disorder. J. Obsessive-Compulsive and Related Disorders **21**, 60–68 (2019)
12. Vitale, F., Odom, W., McGrenere, J.: Keeping and discarding personal data: exploring a design space. In: Proceedings of the 2019 on designing interactive systems conference, pp. 1463–1477. Association for Computing Machinery, New York, USA (2019)
13. Tolin, D.F., Frost, R.O., Steketee, G., Gray, K.D., Fitch, K.E.: The economic and social burden of compulsive hoarding. Psychiatry Res. **160**(2), 200–211 (2008)
14. Dempsey, A.E., O'Brien, K.D., Tiamiyu, M.F., Elhai, J.D.: Fear of missing out (FoMO) and rumination mediate relations between social anxiety and problematic Facebook use. Addictive Behaviors Reports **9**, 100150 (2019)
15. Bright, L.F., Logan, K.: Is my fear of missing out (FOMO) causing fatigue? advertising, social media fatigue, and the implications for consumers and brands. Internet Res. **28**(5), 1213–1227 (2018)
16. Dhir, A., Yossatorn, Y., Kaur, P., Chen, S.: Online social media fatigue and psychological wellbeing—a study of compulsive use, fear of missing out, fatigue, anxiety and depression. Int. J. Inf. Manage. **40**, 141–152 (2018)
17. Adams, S.K., Murdock, K.K., Daly-Cano, M., Rose, M.: Sleep in the social world of college students: bridging interpersonal stress and fear of missing out with mental health. Behav. Sci. **10**(2), 54 (2020)
18. Roberts, J.A., David, M.E.: My life has become a major distraction from my cell phone: partner phubbing and relationship satisfaction among romantic partners. Comput. Hum. Behav. **54**, 134–141 (2016)

19. Lee, K.H., Lin, C.Y., Tsao, J., Hsieh, L.F.: Cross-sectional study on relationships among FoMO, social influence, positive outcome expectancy, refusal self-efficacy and SNS usage. Int. J. Environ. Res. Public Health **17**(16), 5907 (2020)
20. Holte, A.J., Ferraro, F.R.: Anxious, bored, and (maybe) missing out: evaluation of anxiety attachment, boredom proneness, and fear of missing out (FoMO). Comput. Hum. Behav. **112**, 106465 (2020)
21. Bawden, D., Robinson, L.: The dark side of information: overload, anxiety and other paradoxes and pathologies. J. Inf. Sci. **35**(2), 180–191 (2009)
22. Song, X., Song, S., Zhao, Y.C., Min, H., Zhu, Q.: Fear of missing out (FOMO) toward ict use during public health emergencies: an investigation on predictors and outcomes. J. Database Manage. **32**(2), 20–35 (2021)
23. Elhai, J.D., Gallinari, E.F., Rozgonjuk, D., Yang, H.: Depression, anxiety and fear of missing out as correlates of social, non-social and problematic smartphone use. Addict. Behav. **105**, 106335 (2020)
24. Han, L., Geng, J., Jou, M., Gao, F., Yang, H.: Relationship between shyness and mobile phone addiction in Chinese young adults: mediating roles of self-control and attachment anxiety. Comput. Hum. Behav. **76**, 363–371 (2017)
25. Wei, M., Russell, D.W., Zakalik, R.A.: Adult attachment, social self-efficacy, self-disclosure, loneliness, and subsequent depression for freshman college students: a longitudinal study. J. Couns. Psychol. **52**(4), 602 (2005)
26. Zhang, X., Wu, Y., Liu, S.: Exploring short-form video application addiction: socio-technical and attachment perspectives. Telematics Inform. **42**, 101243 (2019)
27. Lai, C.Y., Yang, H.L.: Determinants of individuals' self-disclosure and instant information sharing behavior in micro-blogging. New Media Soc. **17**(9), 1454–1472 (2015)
28. Marteau, T.M., Bekker, H.: The development of a six-item short-form of the state scale of the Spielberger State—Trait Anxiety Inventory (STAI). Br. J. Clin. Psychol. **31**(3), 301–306 (1992)
29. Brennan, K.A., Clark, C.L., Shaver, P.R.: Self-report measurement of adult attachment: an integrative overview. In Simpson, J.A., Rholes, W.S. (eds.): Attachment theory and close relationships, pp. 46–76. Guilford, New York, USA (1998)
30. Mills, L.A., Knezek, G., Khaddage, F.: Information seeking, information sharing, and going mobile: three bridges to informal learning. Comput. Hum. Behav. **32**, 324–334 (2014)
31. Song, X., Zhang, X., Zhao, Y., Song, S.: Fearing of missing out (FoMO) in mobile social media environment: conceptual development and measurement scale. iConference 2017 Proceedings, pp. 733–738. iSchool, Wuhan, China (2017)
32. Fornell, C., Larcker, D.F.: Evaluating structural equation models with unobservable variables and measurement error. J. Mark. Res. **18**(1), 39–50 (1981)

Extending the PIM-B Concept: An Exploration of How Nonbinary People Maintain Personal Information Over Time

Amber L. Cushing(✉) and Páraic Kerrigan

School of Information and Communication Studies, University College Dublin, Dublin, Ireland
{amber.cushing,paraic.kerrigan}@ucd.ie

Abstract. This paper reports early results from an ongoing study exploring the personal information management of nonbinary people in Ireland. Data collection has been stalled due to an unforeseen issue which is described, and results presented are based on three semi-structured interviews. Cushing [1, 2] and other PIM scholars have found that that personal information is partly maintained because it represents an individual's identity to themselves and others. In the context of inequality, Cushing, and Kerrigan [3] found that PIM can be perceived as a burden, abbreviated as a PIM-B. This study furthers PIM-B work through exploring the lived experiences of nonbinary individuals that must maintain personal information that does not represent their identity in order to engage in society. Nonbinary people often find themselves in the position of maintaining personal information that does not represent their gender identity because of the traditional binarised structure of society more broadly. How does the requirement to maintain this information that is not representative of gender diversity mediate PIM? Using reflexive thematic analysis, our early analysis of 3 interviews suggests that nonbinary people in Ireland perceive both the information use and the exertion of control over distribution of *personal information management as a burden* (PIM-B). This finding can be used to refine the concept of a PIM-B [3] while also using PIM-B as an indicator of the inequalities that gender minorities face.

Keywords: Personal information management · Gender · Qualitative

1 Introduction

Frequently situated between human computer interaction and information behaviour, personal information management (PIM) has generally been defined from two perspectives that differ in how personal information is defined. Jones [4] and Jones and Teevan [5] consider personal information to include unique information, but also information that the individual consumes and information about an individual created and managed by someone else (ex. Medical records created by a doctor, held at a hospital, about an individual patient). Bergman and Whittaker [6] define personal information as only the unique information that the individual creates and as such, this unique information must be carefully curated. Regardless of what personal information includes, both PIM models agree that maintaining information is vital to the practice of PIM. Cushing [1, 2, 7]

© The Author(s), under exclusive license to Springer Nature Switzerland AG 2023
I. Sserwanga et al. (Eds.): iConference 2023, LNCS 13971, pp. 118–125, 2023.
https://doi.org/10.1007/978-3-031-28035-1_10

has explored the maintenance of personal digital information over time, finding that this information often represents the individual's identity to themselves and to others. This paper adopts Jones' [4] definition of PIM as "the practice and the study of the activities a person performs in order to acquire or create, store, organise, maintain, retrieve, use and distribute the information needed to meet life's many goals and to fulfill life's many roles and responsibilities" (p. 5) with focus on the activity of maintaining personal information over time.

If representing one's identity is a vital component of the effort to maintain personal digital information, what happens when individuals must maintain personal information that does not represent them, in order to engage with society more broadly? In particular, how does this manifest when individuals find that their identity is at odds with broader society and that there is no way to represent their identity accurately through personal information? How does this affect how they represent their identity to themselves or others? How can these experiences further our understanding of maintaining personal information over time?

Considering these questions, the main research question guiding this paper is as follows: *how does managing personal information serve as a burden for nonbinary people?* Relying on Cushing and Kerrigan's [3] themes of personal information management as a burden (PIM-B), this paper seeks to address gender diversity and nonbinary identity, specifically noting the ways in which nonbinary individuals must manage their personal information and information infrastructures more broadly. Through interviews with members of this gender diverse community, we sought to explore the ways in which managing personal information can serve as a burden in PIM, when this is not the case for those who identify within the traditional gender binary.

2 Literature Review

One of the most widely cited definitions of PIM is from Jones and Teevan [5], who define PIM as "both the practice and the study of the activities people perform to acquire, organize, maintain, retrieve, use, and control the distribution of information items such as documents (paper-based and digital), Web pages, and email messages for everyday use to complete tasks (work-related and not) and to fulfil a person's various roles (as parent, employee, friend, member of community, etc.)" (p. 3). Since 2007, several authors have expanded the definition of PIM to include "nonwork" personal information, especially in discussions of personal archiving, where the focus is on maintaining personal information over time [7–10]. In a 2019 study of personal information from activity tracker technology, Feng and Agosto [11] found that the PIM activity tended to focus on what Jones' [4] previously labelled as "meta level activities". This included organisation, maintenance, managing privacy, measuring and evaluating and making sense. Bergman and Whittaker [6] believe that curation is the central activity in PIM, which overlaps with the ways in which Jones [4] describes organising and maintaining.

Explorations of personal digital archiving often overlap with PIM activities, but the central focus remains on maintaining the personal information over time. Marshall [12] identified that maintaining and organising personal information over time can take considerable effort on the part of the individual. Cushing [1, 2] found that individuals are more likely to engage in maintaining digital personal information over time if the information is considered a digital possession, which are characterised as providing evidence of the individual, representing the individual's identity, recognised as having value and exhibiting a sense of bounded control.

In contrast, in their study of LGBQ parents attempting to obtain birth certificates and personal identity information for their children in Ireland, Cushing and Kerrigan [3] found that the effort to organise and maintain this personal information is perceived as a burden due to the perception that the PIM activities serve as representations of inequality and lack of recognition for same-sex parenting. Cushing and Kerrigan [3] draw on previous work in information behaviour which explores the concept of invisible information work, marginalisation, and information overload [13–18] to identify 4 themes of a PIM-B: 1) additional PIM tasks, 2) negative affect, 3) lack of self-extension to digital possessions, and 4) additional information seeking.

The experience of nonbinary individuals serves as an example to further explore the concept of PIM and marginalisation. Research pertaining to PIM and nonbinary communities is currently minimal. Emerging research in broader areas is beginning to focus on the ways in which nonbinary people navigate technological infrastructures. To that extent, Spiel's research [19] focused on how these technological infrastructures encode gender as fixed and binarised, which consequently prevented nonbinary people from registering their correct gender identity, even though they may have received legal recognition. This is an instance where varying obstacles emerge around PIM and nonbinary identities. Other studies, such as that by Quinan et al. [20] have examined the implications of potential new measures for inclusion on state documents for nonbinary communities, such as that of an X marker to indicate a nonbinary status. This form of declaring personal gender identity on state documents was considered by Quinan et al. [20] as facilitating state regulation of gender-diverse individuals, noting how individuals grafted their own meanings onto this non-binary marker. In other instances, research has demonstrated how the declaration of personal information on input forms on websites or online services has resulted in many nonbinary individuals not being able to select their correct gender category. As Schuerman et al. [21] note, digital health forms, social media websites and dating apps did not recognise non-binary identities, which was particularly acute for online health forms where this gender information is crucial for healthcare. Schuerman et al. [21] conclude by noting that designers of online gender web forms need to be sensitive to the information needs of non-binary people. This paper speaks to this gap in the literature through attempting to understand the lived experiences of nonbinary individuals and their experiences of PIM.

3 Method

We used semi-structured interviews to gather data from the lived experiences of nonbinary people living in Ireland to understand their experiences of maintaining personal information that does not represent their identities. We developed an initial set of interview questions based on consultation with a PhD student and nonbinary person who is conducting parallel research about information seeking in transgender and nonbinary populations. We also developed questions based on our experience with our PIM-B study [3]. We then pilot tested questions with an individual identifying as nonbinary based outside of Ireland, as a means of not using potential participants from our targeted sample population. Based on the pilot, we revised the questions before official data collection began. We used word of mouth, postings on social media and with permission, solicited participation on several private social media pages with the stated mission of supporting nonbinary people in Ireland. No one was contacted directly based on their gender identity status, we relied on individuals to contact us if they were interested in participating in an interview. Interviews were conducted via Zoom, beginning in early August 2022. One or both authors completed the interview, using the same questions.

Reflexive Thematic Analysis was used to analyse the data [22]. We used a combination of inductive and deductive processes to identify themes using Braun and Clarke's [22] six steps, including: familiarising oneself with the data through reading and rereading transcripts, generating initial codes, collating codes into potential themes, reviewing themes, defining, and naming themes and producing the final analysis report (findings).

4 Early Findings

This project is still in progress; thus far we have conducted three interviews, upon which we base our initial findings discussed below. Our data collection slowed after one month, which could be related to several key news pieces that dominated news headlines in Ireland at this time.[1]

As a result of this cultural climate, we are finding that there is less interest to participate in the research project. We hope that these volatile events for gender minorities will dissipate, but in the meantime, it has led to an (understandable) slowdown in data collection. This experience demonstrates that research which relies upon participants from marginalised communities can be impacted directly by a cultural climate and constructed moral panic being distributed by news headlines and social media.

Based on our three interviews, our initial findings suggest that the concept of maintaining information that does not represent an aspect of one's identity (their gender queer status) was also discussed as being a burden (Table 1).

[1] On 30 August 2022, news broke that a Secondary School had put teacher Enoch Burke on administrative leave because he refused to comply with the school's newly adopted gender affirming policy for students, refusing to refer to a student by their they/them pronouns. Once placed on leave, Burke refused to stay off school grounds, leading the school to obtain a restraining order, which Burke repeatedly ignored. On the last occasion, Burke entered school grounds, confronted the school Principal, and was ultimately arrested for violating the restraining order. Several media outlets have reframed Burke's arrest for violation of a restraining order as a teacher being arrested for refusing to use "they" instead of "he" [23]. The social media accounts of Burke, his family and friends, and his supporters, position him a victim of 'woke culture' gone 'too far'. As this story has continued to make headlines in Ireland, an anonymous nonbinary person who did not want to participate in this study suggested to us that the case had engendered a climate of fear in the nonbinary community in Ireland. This case has not occurred in a vacuum and there has been an ever-increasing amount of media reportage purporting gender critical frames, with gender critical generally describing a belief that an individual's sex is biological and unchanging and cannot be combined with someone's gender identity. For

Table 1. Participant ages

Participant No.	Age
1	42
2	67
3	45

4.1 Furthering the Concept of a Personal Information Burden

Cushing and Kerrigan [3] identified four themes of a PIM-B: personal information associated with 1) additional PIM tasks, 2) negative affect, 3) lack of self-extension to digital possessions, and 4) additional information seeking. The authors use the PIM-B concept to demonstrate how managing personal information over time can vary based on marginalization (such as sexual orientation, which Cushing & Kerrigan investigated), which reinforces feelings of inequality and triggers feelings of burden. Below, we attempt to understand how nonbinary individuals experience inequality via PIM and how this connects with the concept of a PIM-B.

Most participants described that their chosen name that they go by is often not their name on official documents such as passports. The name assigned to the participants at birth, rather than their chosen name, was also present on government benefit information such as social protection, medical information and was also their registered name with An Post, the State-owned provider of postal services in Ireland. As a result, when participants needed to engage with these government entities, their chosen names and nonbinary status was not recognised. Accordingly, the participants frequently requested changes be made to data collection procedures, which often fell on deaf ears. Participant 1 described how "breaking a chain" in personal information collection is more difficult with banks and medical providers who often require "official" identity documents such as a birth certificate or passport, whereas an online shopping company may let you create a shipping address without the need for you to state a gender or use the same name found on an "official" document:

> …my passport is the thing that identifies me for my driving license, and that identifies me for my bank account, and so on. Well, we started with one name, and I don't have any way of breaking that chain" (Participant 1).

The concept of viewing personal information as a chain of information is novel and has the potential to impact the way researchers approach PIM. How does PIM mitigate the ways in which different examples of personal information connect with other examples within a personal information collection? In the context of a PIM-B, addressing the feeling of burden may require modelling personal information as a chain, as a way to understand the root of the burden. If feelings of burden associated with PIM can be isolated, PIM research may be able to be developed to alleviate these feelings

example, the Trans Writers' Union has called for a boycott of *The Irish Times* for "anti-trans rhetoric" and gender critical news articles [24].

experienced during PIM. While the traditional focus of PIM has been efficiency, future PIM research could focus on how to make PIM a more enjoyable experience, or at the least, feeling like less of a burden. However, if the root of feelings of burden stem from the acknowledgement of systemic inequality, it is unlikely technology or methods associated with PIM can "solve" this problem. As such, understanding the role of PIM in policies, specifically government policies that are meant to provide citizens equal access to benefits and services, may address feelings of PIM-B that marginalised individuals' experience.

When asked about official avenues of name change, our participants instead preferred to go by a shortened version of their given name, or the Irish version of their given name. As background, it is not uncommon in Ireland for people to go by the Irish language version of a given English language name. In fact, as Participant 2 notes, they fostered the Irish version of their name as it reduced feelings of dysphoria from the name assigned to them at birth alongside the fact that the name tended not to be gendered more broadly, with the exception on occasion of Irish speakers. Participant 1 similarly notes how abbreviating their name by shortening it reduced their feelings of dysphoria with their gender identity. In managing personal information in this way, participants noted how it led to better wellbeing outcomes for themselves.

In discussing PIM as burden, most participants agreed that there was some level of additional burden associated with personal information and nonbinary status, but participants described this burden differently. For example, Participant 1 spoke of how there is a feeling of *cognitive burden* when faced with a gender drop down box on a web form that list only male or female. Extending from this, the participant noted the difficulties and emotional turmoil of having to think about which gender to select and the ramifications of selecting each gender choice every time personal information is collected, served to be "a cognitive and emotional load:

> It's a cognitive burden because I have to make these choices every time. And I'm sitting there and the doctors, and there's this free text box that was a paper form [previously]. There's a box where I can write it in. It says gender, and I'm there for five minutes. What do I put? And yeah, the majority of people don't have to have that kind of cognitive load, and it is an emotional load as well (Participant 1)

Participant 2 was more severe in their description of burden:

> It's absolutely exhausting, and I guess I have two twin emotions about that. Sadness, that it is that way. It's also anger, or it just pisses me off. But I've learned over a lifetime of using my anger as fuel, you know, to make change and rattle cages (Participant 2)

On follow up, when Participant 2 was asked what it might feel like if the burden was removed, they responded "Oh my God! I think I could breathe." Interestingly, Participant 3 applied less strength in their discussion of burden, describing it as: "an annoyance, it's kind of frustrating, but I don't know if I would call it a burden." This suggests that a range may exist in the experience of a PIM-B. Future research could explore this range of the experience of burden.

5 Discussion

Our early insights into data from three interviews focused on whether our concept of a PIM-B could be applied to a similar, but different population, and if the concept could be further refined. Our early analysis indicates that the concept of a personal information burden (PIM-B) extends to personal information management of our sample of nonbinary people in Ireland. However, the burden is not limited to information seeking or maintaining personal information as with our sample population in Cushing and Kerrigan [3], but the burden extends to the way in which individuals use and control the distribution of personal information, including name and gender identity, to interact with other people and their official data gathering instruments. Cushing and Kerrigan [3] characterised a PIM-B using four themes: 1) additional PIM tasks, 2) negative affect, 3) lack of self-extension to digital possessions, and 4) information seeking. While our research is ongoing, our early data analysis suggests that the concept of a PIM-B may need to be expanded to include information use and the control of the distribution of information. In addition, the concept of a personal information chain will continue to be explored: if it is specific to a PIM-B, or if it is referenced in additional literature in different contexts. We also aim to develop future trajectories for this work, including range of feelings of burden experienced, how to limit the experience of a PIM-B via methods and tools, as well as understanding the role of PIM in government policy.

6 Conclusion

As this study began to recruit participants, the political and cultural climate for the gender-diverse community became extremely volatile and contentious within Ireland, with a number of high profile, ‘gender critical’ incidents occurring that has left much of the community in fear of systems of power, not to mention researchers in academic institutions. While our data collection has currently stalled, we will continue to collect data via semi-structured interviews, to further refine our concept of a PIM-B and develop tools and methods to address the concept of a PIM-B, as well as understand the role of PIM in government policy.

References

1. Cushing, A.L.: Possession and Self Extension in Digital Environments: Implications for Maintaining Personal Information (Doctoral dissertation). University of North Carolina at Chapel Hill, Chapel Hill, NC, USA (2012)
2. Cushing, A.L.: “It’s the stuff that speaks to me”: exploring the characteristics of digital possessions. J. American Society of Information Science Technol. **64**(8), 1723–1734 (2013)
3. Cushing, A.L., Kerrigan, P.: Personal information management burden: a framework for describing nonwork PIM in the context of inequality. J. Society for Inf. Sci. Technol. **73**(11), 15431558 (2022)
4. Jones, W.: Keeping Found Things Found: The Study and Practice of Personal Information Management. Morgan Kaufmann Publishers (2008)
5. Jones, W., Teevan, J. (eds.): Personal Information Management (Vol. 14). University of Washington Press, Seattle (2007)

6. Bergman, O., Whittaker, S.: The Science of Managing Our Digital Stuff. The MIT Press (2016)
7. Cushing, A.L.: The preservation of personal digital information from the perspective of the archives and records management tradition. Library Hi-Tech. **28**(2) (2010)
8. Marshall, C.C., Bly, S., Brun-Cottan, F.: The long term fate of our digitalbelongings: Toward a service model for personal archives. In: Proceedings of Archiving 2006, pp. 25–30. Presented at the Archiving 2006, Ottawa, Canada: Society for Imaging Science and Technology (2006)
9. Marshall, C.: Rethinking personal digital archiving part II: Implications for services, applications and institutions. D-Lib Magazine **14**(3/4), 3 (2008a)
10. Marshall, C.: Rethinking personal digital archiving part I: Four challenges from the field. D-Lib Magazine **14**(3/4), 2 (2008b)
11. Feng, Y., Agosto, D.: Revisiting personal information management through information practices with activity tracking technology. J. Am. Soc. Inf. Sci. **70**(12), 1352–1367 (2019)
12. Marshall, C.C.: How people manage information over a lifetime. In: Personal Information Management, pp. 57–75. University of Washington Press, Seattle, Washington (2007)
13. Ancker, J.S., Witteman, H.O., Hafeez, B., Provencher, T., Van de Graaf, M., Wei, E.: The invisible work of personal health information management among people with multiple chronic conditions: qualitative interview study among patients and providers. J. Med. Internet Res. **17**(6), 1–13 (2015)
14. Bawden, D., Holtham, C., Courtney, N.: Perspectives on information overload. ASLIB Proc. **51**(8), 249–255 (1999)
15. Dalmer, N.K., Huvila, I.: Conceptualizing information work for heath contexts in library and information science. Journal of Documentation **76**(1), 96–108 (2019)
16. Dalmer, N.K.: 'Add info and stir': an institutional ethnographic scoping review of family care-givers' information work. Ageing Soc. **40**, 663–689 (2020)
17. Greyson, D.: Health information practices of young parents. Journal of Documentation **73**(5), 778–802 (2017)
18. Gibson, A.N., Martin, J.D.: Re-situating information poverty: information marginalization and parents of individuals with disabilities. J. Am. Soc. Inf. Sci. **70**(5), 476–487 (2019)
19. Spiel, K.: Why are they all obsessed with Gender?"—(Non) binary navigations through technological infrastructures. In: ACM Designing Interactive Systems Conference 2021, pp. 478–494 (2021)
20. Quinan, C.L., Hunt, M.: Non-binary gender markers: mobility, migration, and media reception in Europe and beyond. European Journal of Women's Studies (2021). https://doi.org/10.1177/13505068211024891
21. Scheuerman, M.K., Jiang, A., Spiel, K., Brubaker, J.R.: Revisiting gendered web forms: an evaluation of gender inputs with (non-) binary people. In: Proceedings of the 2021 CHI Conference on Human Factors in Computing Systems, CHI '21, New York, NY, USA. Association for Computing Machinery (2021)
22. Braun, V., Clarke, V.: Thematic Analysis: A Practical Guide. SAGE (2021)
23. O'Toole, F.: Enoch Burke's Transformation into an Icon of Freedom of Expression is Frankly Hilarious (2022). https://www.irishtimes.com/opinion/2022/09/13/fintan-otoole-enoch-burke-is-no-icon-for-freedom-of-expression/
24. Mak, N.: USI votes to boycott the Irish Times alongside the Trans Writers Union. GCN (2022). https://gcn.ie/usi-votes-boycott-irish-times/

"I Always Asked a Lot of Questions"– The Information Journey of Young Adults with Cancer in Germany

Paulina Bressel(✉)

Berlin School of Library and Information Science, Humboldt-Universität zu Berlin, Berlin, Germany
p.bressel@hu-berlin.com

Abstract. About 19.3 million people are newly diagnosed with cancer each year, but only a small percentage of all diagnoses refers to young adults (18 - 39 years). Therefore, they are often not focused on within the healthcare infrastructure, although they have age-specific information, care and service needs. This results in difficulties that will be examined in this article concerning the information journey of the target group. Based on fourteen semi-structured qualitative interviews, this article describes the use of information sources during the cancer patient journeys of young adults. Furthermore, it describes problems the target group experiences. The data indicate that young adults, regardless of whether they actively seek information or rarely seek information at all, often have to rely on serendipity to obtain helpful information. Furthermore, problems regarding the reliability of information sources have been identified and information relating to non-medical needs must be sought autonomously, which results in overload and uncertainty. For the circumvention of these difficulties, improvements are needed in the provision of information for young adults. The knowledge about validated information sources would support the information journeys during their cancer patient journeys.

Keywords: Health information behavior · Information journey · Young adults with cancer · Information seeking · Patient journey

1 Introduction

Every year about 19.3 million people are newly diagnosed with cancer and according to latest calculations in 2020, 9.96 million people will die because of this disease [26]. In Germany, 16.500 young adults are newly diagnosed with cancer each year [21, 40]. These are only 3.3% of all new diagnoses. Even though the target group gets more attention during the final years, there are still occurring problems and difficulties that need to be addressed.

The German health infrastructure often pairs young adults together with adolescents or older adults, which have both age-specific characteristics that do not match the characteristics of this target group [13]. Especially young adults are going through a transition phase, which includes social, mental and physical aspects. Therefore, a diagnosis of a

© The Author(s), under exclusive license to Springer Nature Switzerland AG 2023
I. Sserwanga et al. (Eds.): iConference 2023, LNCS 13971, pp. 126–143, 2023.
https://doi.org/10.1007/978-3-031-28035-1_11

life-threatening disease as cancer during this phase strongly influences the individual, and results in special information, care and service needs [6, 13, 32, 34, 47]. If those needs are not met, they experience difficulties coping with the disease and its influence on their every-day lives [18, 28]. Further the information seeking behavior of young adults during their cancer patient journey is affected by the lack of available useful information specified for their age-group. This is affecting the accessibility of helpful information during the cancer patient journey [13].

This article is based on the research data of Bressel [12], who conducted 14 semi-structured guided interviews with young cancer patients regarding their information needs. The dataset also contains insights in the information seeking behavior of young adults in Germany during their cancer patient journey, which have not been analyzed before and therefore are part of this article. To understand the information seeking behavior of young adults with cancer during their patient journey and furthermore occurring problems and difficulties, the research questions for this article are the following:

1. Which information sources do young adults with cancer in Germany use during their information journeys at different stages of their cancer patient journey?
2. Which problems and difficulties occur during their information journeys?

Even though the information seeking behavior of young cancer patients is no new research field, this target group is still not treated as a separate patient group in the German health infrastructure. By focusing on used sources and specific stages in which problems regarding information seeking occur, this paper enables insights into specific needed improvements regarding young adults with cancer.

2 Background

2.1 Information Seeking of Young Adults with Cancer

Young adults (YA) are individuals between the age of 18 to 39 [6, 13, 16, 22, 33, 45]. Due to their age, YA are at an unsettled stage of their life, which is dominated by emotional, physical and social changes [5–7, 13, 46].

Especially in this phase, a cancer diagnosis and the subsequent time during treatment and aftercare influences one's identity by taking away crucial elements or changing them through new disease-related circumstances [6, 7, 28]. For YA a cancer diagnosis results in information, service and care needs in ten areas. Those areas include organizational and financial needs, questions regarding the disease itself (diagnosis, prognosis, rehabilitation, and aftercare) and its influence on health practices, fertility, mental health, and the social context [13].

In medical studies, the information seeking of young adults was already researched with focus on specific sources such as the internet, social media and social networking sites [4, 15, 16, 24, 36] or the general preferences of YA and adolescents regarding digital technologies [1]. Boakye et al. [10] moreover compared the health information seeking of adults with and without cancer, where they focused on demographic differences, sources, and topics. Furthermore Germeni et al. [23] identified that research on the information seeking behavior of sick individuals should always include research on information avoidance, because of the correlation of their behaviors in the role of informed patients.

Separate from the target group, research exists about the usage of different channels and sources during a cancer disease [8, 27, 29, 30, 41, 44]. It is known that the use of information sources depends on demographic factors such as age, level of education and income [41].

In addition, individuals with a disease tend to consult interpersonal channels. For medical questions, the first source is family and friends and if the information need is not fulfilled, they consult health professionals [27]. Nevertheless, health professionals, especially doctors, are seen as an authority, depending on the reliability of answers. Regardless, patients tend to seek answers on the internet before consulting health professionals, because it seems to be more credible and able to equalize deficits of doctors in real life [8, 44].

2.2 The Information Journey vs. The Patient Journey Model

In 2005, Adams and Blandford defined the information seeking behavior in the health and academic sector as an information journey. This model consists of three stages: information initiation, information facilitation and information interpretation.

Information initiation is the first stage of the information journey, in which external factors initiate the requirement for information actively throughout a task (e.g., supporting a sick relative) or passively by a person or situation (e.g., receiving a cancer diagnosis). Information facilitation marks the second stage of the information journey, and contains the information retrieval aspects of the information seeking process. The information is sought actively with the help of information systems, or persons relevant to the recognized information need (e.g., consultation by a doctor). The last stage of the original model, the information interpretation, is defined by the process of interpreting the information based on a specific context [2]. Especially in the health context the interpretation process is supported "by someone or some system" to help the following decision-making process (e.g., starting treatment) [3].

Nguyen et al. [39] expanded the information journey in their article about information needs of family carers in collaborative healthcare to another stage of the information journey. Their four-stage journey model consists of three similar stages to the original model (identification, searching, interpretation), and one added stage, the information sharing. This new stage was invented because the sharing process was identified as an important step in a collaborative context, especially if not only the patient but also the carer is involved in the information journey during diseases.

In a non-health-related sector, Du [17] also introduced an information journey. She described the information journey of marketing professionals as determining the work task-generated information need, information seeking, judging, and evaluating the information, sense-making and information use as well as information sharing.

In 2010 a new expanded version of the original information journey by Adams & Blandford [2] was invented. This new version additionally contains the use of the interpreted information as fourth stage (see Fig. 1).

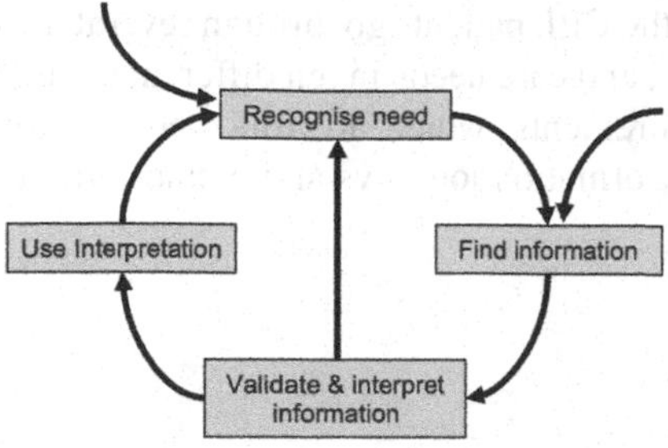

Fig. 1. Extend information journey model by Blandford & Attfield [2]

This fourth stage includes the usage of the previously interpreted information based on the subjective context. Thus, further information journeys can arise if more information is needed or if the information previously interpreted as useful turns out to be unhelpful for the personal context.

Especially papers in the health sector use the term journey as well to describe experiences and processes of individuals affected by a disease. They refer to different stages patients go through during the experience of a disease. Instead of stages related to information processes, which are described in the information journey model, these models describe the behavior of affected individuals during their disease. The concept behind is often referred to as patient journey [11]. In the cancer research field, it was used to analyze unmet information needs of cancer patients of all ages at different stages of their patient journey [25, 31, 35, 37, 43] and information needs of young adults with cancer [13]. It was also used to understand the uncertainty of patients while receiving information during their cancer patient journey [38] and to analyze the information seeking and avoidance behavior of cancer patients [23].

Regarding Bressel [13] the cancer patient journey (CPJ) of YA is divided into two cycles. The main journey, containing the diagnosis stage, treatment stage and aftercare stage and the extended journey containing a longer treatment stage before the aftercare stage is reached (see Fig. 2).

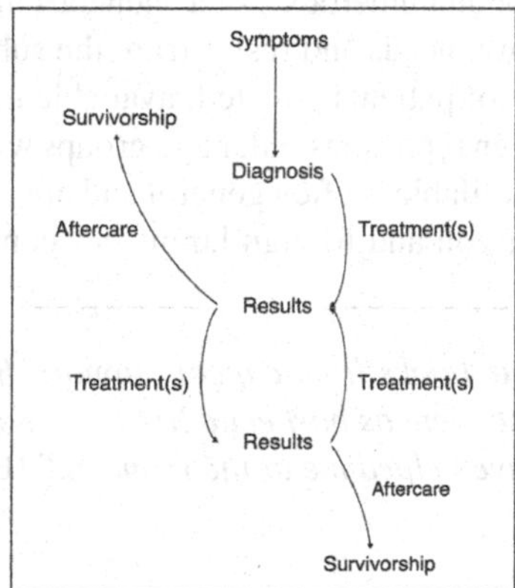

Fig. 2. The cancer patient journey model by Bressel [13]

During each stage of the CPJ, patients go through several information journeys. They have information, service, and care needs in ten different areas [13]. Each of these areas lead to information requirements, which are followed by information journeys. This paper focuses on these information journeys and defines difficulties YA face.

3 Method

3.1 Dataset

The dataset for this study was collected in November and December 2020 for another study to analyze the information needs of YA with cancer in Germany. The dataset contains 14 qualitative semi-structured interview transcripts. The interviewed YA were affected by eight different diagnoses at the end of their treatment, or while already in aftercare (see Table 1). All participants were treated in Germany and the interviews were conducted in German. The transcribed interview data shows clearly that information needs are connected to the information seeking behavior of YA with cancer, and that an analysis of the information seeking behavior based on this dataset would be valuable.

3.2 Analysis

To answer the first research question, the interview transcripts were coded by a deductive approach, based on the identified stages of the CPJ [13] and all infrastructures, sources, and services, named by the participants. For the second research question, the dataset was coded inductively by concentrating on difficulties and problems YA experienced while seeking information at different stages of their CPJ. All quotes were translated from German to English after the analysis.

4 Results

4.1 The Accepting vs. The Active Seeking Behavior

During their CPJ, YA go through numerous, heterogeneous information journeys which correlate with their information needs and result from the subjective context of the YA. Because of the small number of patients affected, available information in sources such as the internet or literature often represents older age groups with different needs. In addition, the information that is available is often general and not adaptable to their situations (P3, P12, P13) or medical jargon and foreign languages complicate the understanding (P4, P5).

> "*I mean, you get your blue books from cancer support. But you can as well put them in the garbage or use them as barbecue lighters. It contains general stories but nothing that would have helped me at the moment.*" (P13)

Table 1. Information about the sample

Age (Diagnosis)	Cancer type	Subtype	Comment
35	Breast cancer	Triple negative mammary carcinomy (genetic)	Pregnant during treatment
34		Specific diagnosis unknown	
28		Specific diagnosis unknown	
22		Specific diagnosis unknown	
35 (1) 38 (2)		Hormone-positive mammary carcinoma (1) Triple negative mammary carcinoma (genetic) (2)	Initial diagnosis (1) Second diagnosis (2)
33		Hormone-positive mammary carcinoma + Liver metastases, Lung metastases	Incurable due to spreading
34	Brain tumor	Glioblastoma	Incurable
40		Anaplastic astrozytoma (sinistral)	
25	Testicular cancer	Testicular carcinoma (unilateral)	
27	Thyroid cancer	Papillary thyroid carcinoma + Metastases + Lymphatic gland	
18	Bone tumor	Ewing's sarcoma (scapula unilateral)	
33	Lymphoma	Hodgkin's lymphoma	
32	Uterus cancer	Endometrium carcinoma	
39	Salivary glands cancer	Mucoepidermoid carcinoma	

Helpful information about YAs information, care or support needs are often hard to discover, which impacts the information interpretation negatively and results in two information behaviors: the accepting behavior vs. the active seeking behavior.

Regarding the data, this distinction especially appears related to diagnosis-, fertility- and prognosis-related questions during the diagnosis stage. While some participants mention that they have no intention to seek information and are satisfied with the information handed to them by health professionals (P1, P2, P3, P6, P8, P9, P14), others seek extensively (P4, P10, P11, P13) as explained by P13:

"Maybe someone who is 60 is more likely to say: Yeah okay, I'm going to do what the doctors say. But I think it's the young people, and I'm one of them, who really have to figure it out for themselves. Looking for something else, like alternatives, right?" (P13)

"Of course, I have asked doctors and nurses a lot, also in the doctor's meetings and with the gynecologist. I always asked a lot of questions. [...] So, I always made sure that I got rid of a lot of questions and actually got lots of answers." (P10)

Primarily the active information seeking process leads to the extension of the patient's state of knowledge, which is needed for meaningful decisions during the interpretation stage. Especially if information needs are answered by different sources and second opinions, the final interpretation remains with the YA, what for some young patients results in overload (P1, P11, P13).

Accepting behavior on the other hand can cause the same result after the initiation stage. Patients don't know how to answer their information needs (P1, P2, P6, P9, P14), feel left alone by their doctors (P4, P5, P7, P8, P9) or can't understand or follow fast explanations of complex medical information (P2, P8, P9, P10, P12, P12, P13, P14). This feeling of overload can further result in information avoidance, as P9 explains:

"It's difficult to keep yourself informed about all the things they tell you and what they do to you. You can't research all of it, and at some point, you just don't want to research it. Yeah, I think you just don't want to." (P9)

In some cases, the seeking behavior of YA changes during the CPJ. For example, the diagnosis stage is characterized by little knowledge about cancer and associated needs. Reaching aftercare, patients gain knowledge through their experiences. For some YA this leads to a shift from accepting behavior to active seeking behavior, because they are finally able to understand the given information better based on their experiences, which simplifies the information interpretation (P4, P6, P7, P8, P9, P14).

4.2 Use of Sources During Information Journeys

The use of sources during information journeys of YA with cancer is connected to the subjective context of the patients. Differences were recognized regarding the motivation to seek information based on identified information needs within the initiation stage, as well as the choice of sources during the facilitation stage.

The lack of motivation to start an information journey can have various reasons concerning the personal context and subjective preferences of YA. The choice for sources to seek information during the facilitation stage is often connected to the topic for which information is required, the YA's state of knowledge, personal preferences, and available resources.

The following tables depict the summary of all sources used by YA with cancer during their cancer patient journeys. The structure inspired by Adams et al. [3] includes three stages: *initiation, facilitation,* and *interpretation* (see Tables 2, 3, 4). The fourth stage *use* was omitted because it only includes the affected YA, but no other sources. The sources are assigned to the information needs of YA with cancer identified by Bressel [13].

Adams et al. [3] identified information facilitation as when "someone or some system facilitates required information retrieval" (p. 114). For this reason, the column *facilitation* does not include sources where YA sought and found needed information but sources which supported the seeking process. The last column *interpretation* includes sources, which supported YA interpreting the information.

The dataset includes total answers from 14 participants. This sample indicates sources which are used during the information journey of YA with cancer. Nevertheless, it is not a statistically proven overview of sources and cannot represent indicators of the frequency of use. For those results, another quantitative study could be carried out based on this study.

Table 2. Sources of the information journeys during the diagnosis stage

Diagnosis stage			
Information, Service and Care Needs	Initiation (active + passive)	Facilitation	Interpretation
Organisation & Financing	Affected YA	Affected YA	Affected YA
	Family & Friends	Family & Friends	
			Insurances (health, financial)
			Laywers
			Tax/Financial advisor
		Foundations	Foundations
		Social service	Social service
			Employment offices
Diagnosis-specific questions, Prognosis & Fertility	Affected YA	Affected YA	Affected YA
	Health professionals (doctors)	Health professionals (doctors, nurses)	Health professionals (doctors, nurses)
	Family & Friends	Family & Friends	
			Affected peers
	Internet (f.e. forums, research articles, foundations)	Internet (search engines, foundations)	Internet (f.e. forums, research articles, foundations)
		Social media	Social media
			Books and other Literature
Social context	Affected YA	Affected YA	Affected YA
	Family & Friends	Family & Friends	
		Health professionals (psychologists, nurses)	
		Internet (f.e. forums, institutions, foundations)	Internet (forums, support groups)
		Social media	
		Information brochure, Flyer & magazines	

As said earlier, the information journeys of YA with cancer are individual and depend on the subjective context of the patients. The tables represent all sources named by the participants, but not all patients have the same possibilities. The interview data clarified that often, except for diagnosis and prognosis-related questions, young cancer patients must depend on themselves.

As seen in the tables above, the number of sources for the facilitation differs regarding needs. Information on organizational and financing needs is distributed over various sources such as insurances, layers, foundations or social service. These information sources can interpret information regarding the individual case of patients, but the YA first need to find these appropriate sources during the facilitation stage. However, this process is often complicated by the fact that patients do not know who to turn to with these

Table 3. Sources of the information journeys during the treatment stage

Treatment stage			
Information, Service and Care Needs	Initiation (active + passive)	Facilitation	Interpretation
Organisation & Financing	Affected YA	Affected YA	Affected YA
	Affected peers	Affected peers	
			Insurances (health & financial)
		Foundations	Foundations
Diagnosis-specific questions	Affected YA	Affected YA	Affected YA
	Health professionals (doctors)	Health professionals (doctors)	Health professionals (doctors)
	Internet (f.e. forums, medical sites, research articles)	Internet (search engines, forums)	Internet (f.e. forums, medical sites, research articles)
Social context	Affected YA	Affected YA	Affected YA
	Affected peers	Affected peers + support groups	
		Family & Friends	
		Health professionals (psychologists, nurses)	
		Internet (search engines, forums)	
		Social media	
		Information brochure, Flyer & magazines	
Health practices	Affected YA	Affected YA	Affected YA
	Health professionals (doctors)	Health professionals (doctors, nutritionists)	Health professionals (doctors, nutritionists)
	Internet (f.e. forums, foundations)	Internet (search engines, forums, institutions, foundations)	Internet (f.e. forums, medical sites, research articles, institutions, foundations)
			Books and other Literature

questions. Unhelpful sources delay receiving useful answers, and can lead to reduced motivation to further seek information. Although this stage is supported by some sources, such as family and friends or sometimes from foundations or social service, in general YA have to handle this situation on their own.

Diagnosis-specific information needs are present during the whole cancer patient journey. The main source at all stages of the information journey is health professionals, who initiate the information journey and support the seeking process by providing and searching for helpful information. Afterwards, they interpret the information and adapt it to the individual cases so that YA can use it. Even though some individuals still seek second opinions (P1, P5, P10) or information elsewhere before trusting the interpretation (P4, P9, P11, P12, P13), most participants are satisfied and pleased with the support of health professionals during their information journey.

The situation is different with the use of the Internet. Some respondents frequently consult the Internet to seek information via forums or support groups (P3, P4, P6, P7, P13). Other respondents generally do not trust the Internet or feel that the information is not appropriate to their own situation. For this reason, they avoid or question this source regarding most information needs (P1, P8, P9, P10, P11, P12). Nevertheless, the Internet was mentioned for almost all needs and thus is frequently used.

In conclusion, there are existing sources which can support the facilitation and interpretation stage of the information journeys of YA with cancer. Different contexts affect the use of sources, which leads to heterogeneous facilitation processes. Likewise, the accessibility of sources, which support the interpretation process is affected (see Tables 2, 3, 4).

Table 4. Sources of the information journeys during the aftercare stage

Aftercare stage			
Information, Service and Care Needs	**Initiation (active + passive)**	**Facilitation**	**Interpretation**
Organisation & Financing	Affected YA		Affected YA
	Affected peers	Affected peers	
			Insurances (health)
		Foundations	Foundations
Prognosis	Affected YA	Affected YA	Affected YA
	Health professionals (doctors)	Health professionals (doctors)	Health professionals (doctors)
	Internet (f.e. forums, medical sites, research articles)		Internet (f.e. forums, medical sites, research articles)
Social context	Affected YA	Affected YA	Affected YA
	Affected peers	Affected peers + Support groups	
		Internet (search engines, forums, institutions, foundations)	
		Social media	
Health practices	Affected YA	Affected YA	Affected YA
	Affected peers	Affected peers	
	Health professionals (doctors)	Health professionals (doctors, nutritionists)	Health professionals (doctors, nutritionists)
	Internet (f.e. forums, foundations)	Internet (search engines, forums, institutions, foundations)	Internet (f.e. forums, research articles, institutions, foundations)
			Books and other Literature
Mental Health	Affected YA	Affected YA	Affected YA
	Affected peers	Affected peers	Support groups
			Health professionals (psychologists)
		Internet (search engine)	
Rehabilitation & Aftercare	Affected YA	Affected YA	Affected YA
	Health professionals (doctors)	Health professionals (doctors)	Health professionals (doctors)
	Affected peers	Affected peers + Support groups	
			Insurances (health & financial)
	Internet (f.e. forums, foundations)	Internet (search engines. forums, foundations)	Internet (f.e. forums, foundations)

4.3 Issues During Information Journeys of YA with Cancer

The analysis of the information seeking behavior of YA with cancer regarding the information journey model has shown that there are potentially sources to help YA during the facilitation and interpretation stage. The main problem however is the knowledge about the existence of information for their needs and about helpful and valid sources (P2, P3, P4, P5, P6, P7, P8, P10, P14). In particular, this affects needs regarding organizational and financial needs, health practices and aftercare. Regarding these topics, YA feel left alone during the facilitation stage and are dependent on themselves to find helpful and reliable information (P3, P4, P5, P6, P7, P8, P10, P11, P12, P13, P14).

> *"I did it all myself. [...] Unfortunately, you are left alone completely."* (P14)

Even infrastructures and services that are supposed to support the facilitation (e.g. social services) often do not fulfill this task, which exacerbates the problem (P4, P6, P7, P8, P12, P13). The only exception is the *German Foundation for young adults with cancer* (P8, P10, P12, P13).

> *"I've also had the experience that the social service in the hospital was a joke. First of all, it was never available. [...]I researched all that on my own. I tried to call the woman ten times to ask her if she could help me. [...] I never spoke to the social worker, because I never reached her."* (P4)

> "*And what I also disliked at that moment was that you had to check out everything individually. […] I also ask myself how people manage that! Well, I had my husband, who intercepted a lot of these material questions. But others, no idea how they manage that.*" (P11)

The consequence of this is a negative influence or even a discontinuation of the information journeys, as some YA are not able to facilitate helpful sources parallel to side effects of their disease and treatments (P1, P7, P14). This difficulty, combined with contradictory information, which further complicate the interpretation stage, results in overload and insecurities (P1, P5, P6, P7, P8, P9, P14). For some patients, this leads to information avoidance during the diagnosis and treatment stage of their CPJ (P1, P2, P7, P9, P14).

> "*And once you start looking, you get endless information that is also completely contradictory. The doctor tells you that you need nutritional supplements for your body to be in good shape. But a film on the internet about breast cancer patients from a senologist says you should be careful with nutritional supplements: they can be life-shortening under certain circumstances. And then you are there as a cancer patient who wants to do everything to survive, asking: What do I do now?*" (P6)

> "*Chemotherapy can also restrict brain abilities, this chemo brain. And then making a selection was sometimes super difficult for me.*" (P8)

Information journeys regarding all CPJ-related information needs are influenced by experiences of YA. The increasing state of knowledge leads to the ability to better understand the information regarding the disease and related needs over time (P1, P2, P6, P8, P9, P14). Further, a subjective trust-building process regarding reliable and helpful information sources develops. In retrospect, this can result in the feeling of disappointment, or the wish for more knowledge from the beginning.

> "*If you have questions, you could ask them. But it just goes on for an hour and then he already looks at the clock, because then he has to go to the next appointment. But you can ask questions and they are also more or less answered. But afterwards, you actually have completely different questions. Or partly completely different questions, right? I could always ask only from surgery to chemo to radiation. My knowledge or my attempted knowledge. And now, in retrospect, I would just ask completely different questions, because it's just clear what's happening.*" (P9)

> "*The bottom line is that I realized I was getting good therapy. […] But in retrospect, with all the experience I've had, I would have arranged the course of therapy differently.*" (P4)

Another aspect that became apparent from the data was the serendipitous reception of information. This concerns the topics of aftercare, social context or organization and finances (P4, P5, P7, P10, P11, P12, P13). In contrast to the information journey by Adams and Blandford [2], in which the starting point is the initiation, information journeys of YA with cancer often start during the information interpretation. They receive information serendipitously or by seeking information for other needs (P1, P4, P5, P7, P8, P10, P11, P12, P13), often through contact with peers (in person, via the internet or social media) (P4, P5, P7, P10, P11, P12).

By interpreting the information based on their subjective context, they recognize the importance for themselves, and they start the fourth stage of the information journey (P7, P9, P10, P13). If the information is not usable, but they recognize an information need based on the information found, a new information journey starts with the information initiation. One difficulty is that especially YA who have no contact with peers in the same situation and who do not receive this serendipitous information, can only act based on their own experiences, which results in limited sources for the interpretation (P1, P2, P7, P14).

Regarding the last stage of the information journey, the information use, some YA expressed the desire to share their experiences and gained knowledge based on their information journeys to help peers during their CPJ or to process their experiences (P3, P4, P8, P12, P13, P14).

5 Discussion

The analysis of the information seeking behavior of YA with cancer in this study indicates a dependence on sources and topics similar to Boakye et al. [10], as well as on the subjective context of this heterogeneous target group. In contrast to Abrol et al. [1], who said that digital resources potentially improve the experience and engagement of patients, this study identified an ambivalence toward the internet and social media. The difference in both studies is the age of the target group. This affects the success of the seeking behavior of patients. While adults in general can find more information online, unless they are diagnosed with rare cancer types, the needs of YA are more specific. Available information online is often too general or poorly adapted to age-related needs and should be adapted more to the information needs of YA, as already mentioned by Mooney et al. [36]. Additionally, health information literacy is not always present in (young) patients, complicating the selection and finding of needed information online [24].

For the information interpretation of medical, organizational and financial needs, YA tend to consult interpersonal sources first. Similar to Tustin [44], Johnson & Case [27] and Bertelsmann Foundation [8], health professionals are the most important and credible source for medical needs during their whole information journey. In contrast to earlier studies, YA seek information from health professionals during the whole CPJ first, before seeking answers on the internet [8, 44]. This is due to the trust in the competence of health professionals and uncertainty regarding the validity of information from the internet regarding medical needs and health practices.

In the information behavior field, Lambert et al. [29] identified understanding and acceptance concerning the amount of their information seeking behavior, explained as "playing my part and taking care of myself" (p.15). This acceptance was identified regardless of diagnosis, sex, education, or seeking behavior. A distinction regarding age is not further analyzed. In contrast, the YA of this study were overwhelmed by the amount of information-linked responsibility on them. For them, their part is often too much and sometimes not manageable, which affects organizational, financial and social during the beginning and end of their CPJ. Medical needs are excluded, because they are already answered sufficiently by doctors and health professionals. This comparison supports the need to distinguish between YA and older patients in healthcare and research.

Based on the data, validating the information and sources is the first main problem, which results in uncertainty and the feeling of overload in terms of organizational and financial needs, health practices and aftercare. The amount of information, which YA must actively seek from various sources, sometimes results in information avoidance. This was also indicated by Chae et al. [14], Germeni et al. [23] and Serçekus et al. [42]. Accordingly, the concept of the informed patient [23] and its impact on sick individuals, in addition to the effects of their treatments, should be further explored to avoid a negative impact on YA's CPJ.

The second main problem of YA is their lack of knowledge about information and information sources for needs they are not aware of. YA often are dependent on getting information serendipitously, instead of any active seeking behavior. This was also explained by Lambert et al. [29], who identified, that sick individuals start the information exchange with other patients in information grounds as waiting and treatment rooms or support groups [20] whereby serendipitous information is received. In terms of YA, the main difference is the dependency on this information exchange, which is further complicated by little contact to peer in the German health infrastructure.

In particular, this affects needs for aftercare, social context or organization and finances. Sometimes information needs are not recognized by YA until they happen to receive helpful information, such as already explained by Bressel [13]. Regarding the information journey, this causes the lack of two stages of the information journey by Blandford and Attfield [9]. Since the interpretation of serendipitous information starts immediately, the information initiation and facilitation stage fail to occur. However, this implies that not all YA with cancer will receive the same helpful information, which affects the satisfaction and experience during their CPJ. Especially if they have no contact with affected peers or do not actively seek.

To overcome these two problems, YA with cancer in Germany need informative support. Already in 2010, Ferrari et al. discussed the ideal support program for YA with cancer [19]. While Australia, Canada, the United States, the United Kingdom and some Scandinavian countries developed specialized programs for YA and adolescents, Germany barely progressed in this area. Only some sources and infrastructures exist for YA. The *German Foundation for young adults with cancer* and the *University Hospital Cologne* are two examples, which meet some wishes for improvement of YA [13]. The foundation website provides guides for all stages of the CPJ and serves as an information platform. The hospital conducts a survey at the diagnosis stage, to identify mental health, organizational and social service needs. Nonetheless, the data implies that YA, who are not treated at advanced hospitals or get provided with information about the foundation at the diagnosis stage, do not benefit from these offers. To overcome this, information sources such as the foundation website should be actively communicated to the YA by a trusted source at the beginning of their CPJs. Ideally, this would be health professionals, who consult with the YA during their diagnostic phase and who are assessed as trustworthy, based on the data, as well as on Tustin [44], Johnson and Case

[27] and Bertelsmann Foundation [8]. Thus, the information journeys of YA with cancer would be supported by simplifying the information facilitation by one reliable source, substantiating the interpretation with age-related information and in the end simplifying the information use.

5.1 Information Sharing Behavior of YA with Cancer

The data indicates prospects about the information sharing behavior of young adults with cancer. As mentioned before, some patients verbalized the desire to share their experiences and knowledge with affected peers, to help them during their CPJ. This implies an extension to the form of information sharing, for the information journey, similar to Ngyuen et al. [39]. The difference with their paper is the integration of information sharing as the fourth stage of the information journey. This is because sharing behavior is fundamental during the information journey of carers for sick individuals. For YA, the sharing behavior includes the desire to share experiences and acquired knowledge after they have gone through their CPJ, as distinguished from the exchange in support groups during aftercare. Accordingly, it remains to be discussed whether this process should be considered part of the information journey at all, or whether it represents a separate information phenomenon.

More research on reasons behind the information sharing of young adults with cancer or other life-threatening diseases, the positive and negative impact or the motivation to help peers could provide interesting results. Especially since this and previous studies have recognized that YA receive helpful information primarily from peers, since they receive only limited official information relevant to them [f.e. 30].

6 Limitations

Even though the dataset was conducted in November and December 2020, the data still represents current experiences and opinions about the German health infrastructure. Since then, few changes have been initiated to the health care system, with the exception of the project-based informational and service-oriented expansion of the *German Foundation for young adults with cancer*.

7 Conclusion

The goal of this study was the analysis of the information seeking behavior of YA with cancer in Germany based on the information journey model by Blandford and Attfield [9]. Two research questions were addressed. First, which information sources do young adults with cancer in Germany use during their information journeys at different stages of their cancer patient journey? Second, which problems and difficulties occur during their information journeys?

YA go through numerous information journeys during their CPJ, for which they consult various sources. A distinction can thereby be made between the accepting behavior and the active seeking behavior. It is impossible to draw a general conclusion about the sources used by all YA, based on this qualitative study approach. The selection depends on a subjective context and the individual access or the availability of sources. Nevertheless, three tables with all named sources consulted by the participants of this study have been created. From these tables, indications of frequently sought sources can be made. The amount of existing sources and the number of sources used, varies depending on the needs. Affected are the information facilitation and interpretation during an information journey.

Concerning the second research question, two main problems were identified, during the information journey of YA with cancer. The first problem relates to the missing stage of information initiation for some needs during an information journey. This results from an unawareness of YA regarding some of their own needs, which are only identified after serendipitous information discovery. This leads partially to a deviation from the information journey invented by Blandford and Attfield [9]. Depending on the awareness of needs, the start of the information journey varies between the information initiation and the information interpretation. The second problem refers to the difficulty in trusting the reliability of information and sources, which complicates the information facilitation and interpretation for YA.

In conclusion, improvements in information provision for YA with cancer in Germany are still needed. Even though helpful information sources are available, their delivery is lacking. By drawing attention to existing validated information sources at the beginning of the CPJ, negative effects such as uncertainty and overload could be circumvented and the experience of YA during their CPJ could be optimized by better supported information journeys. Further, there should be a functioning social service and additionally a guide about the most important organizational first steps, independent of medical treatment, to reduce the dependency on serendipitous information receiving.

References

1. Abrol, E., Groszmann, M., Pitman, A., Hough, R., Taylor, R.M., Aref-Adib, G.: Exploring the digital technology preferences of teenagers and young adults (TYA) with cancer and survivors: a cross-sectional service evaluation questionnaire. J. Cancer Surviv. **11**(6), 670–682 (2017). https://doi.org/10.1007/s11764-017-0618-z
2. Adams, A., Blandford, A.: Digital libraries' support for the user's 'information journey. In: Proceedings of the 5th Acm/Ieee Joint Conference on Digital Libraries, pp. 160–169 (2005). https://doi.org/10.1145/1065385.1065424
3. Adams, A., Blandford, A., Attfield, S.: Implementing digital resources for clinicians and patients varying needs. Medical Informatics and the Internet in Med. **30**(2), 107–122 (2005). https://doi.org/10.1080/14639230500298875
4. Aggarwal, R., et al.: Health-related social media use and preferences of adolescent and young adult cancer patients for virtual programming. Support. Care Cancer **28**(10), 4789–4801 (2020). https://doi.org/10.1007/s00520-019-05265-3
5. Ahmad, S.S., Reinius, M.A.V., Hatcher, H.M., Ajithkumar, T.V.: Anticancer chemotherapy in teenagers and young adults: managing long term side effects. BMJ, 2016(354), i4567 (2016). https://doi.org/10.1136/bmj.i4567
6. Barnett, M., et al.: Psychosocial outcomes and interventions among cancer survivors diagnosed during adolescence and young adulthood (AYA): a systematic review. J. Cancer Surviv. **10**(5), 814–831 (2016). https://doi.org/10.1007/s11764-016-0527-6

7. Bellizzi, K.M., et al.: the Adolescent and Young Adult Health Outcomes and Patient Experience (AYA HOPE) Study Collaborative Group. Positive and negative psychosocial impact of being diagnosed with cancer as an adolescent or young adult. ACS Journals **2012**(118), 5155–5162 (2012). https://doi.org/10.1002/cncr.27512
8. Bertelsmann Stiftung: Gesundheitsinfo. Wer sucht, der findet - Patienten mit Dr. Google zufrieden. Bertelsmann Stiftung. 2018(2) (2018). ISSN Print: 2364–4788, ISSN Online: 2364–5970
9. Blandford, A., Attfield, S.: Interacting with Information. Morgan & Claypool Publishers, San Rafael, CA (2010)
10. Boakye, E.A., et al.: Correlates of health information seeking between adults diagnosed with and without cancer. PLoS ONE **13**(5), e0196446 (2018). https://doi.org/10.1371/journal.pone.0196446
11. Brailsford, S.C., Lattimer, V., Tarnaras, P., Turnbull, J.: Emergency and on-demand health care: modelling a large complex system. Journal of the Operational Research Society **55**(1), 34–42 (2004). https://doi.org/10.1057/palgrave.jors.2601667
12. Bressel, P.: Die übergangenen Patient*innen: Eine qualitative Analyse der Informationsbedarfe von jungen Erwachsenen mit Krebs in Deutschland [master thesis, Humboldt-Universität zu Berlin] (2021). https://doi.org/10.18452/22913
13. Bressel, P.: Information needs of young adults with cancer in Germany. In Proceedings of ISIC: the information behaviour conference, Berlin, 26-29 September, 2022. Information Research, 27(special issue). isic2212. (2022). https://doi.org/10.47989/irisic2212
14. Chae, J., Lee, C., Jensen, J.D.: Correlates of cancer information overload: focusing on individual ability and motivation. Health Commun. **31**(5), 626–634 (2016). https://doi.org/10.1080/10410236.2014.986026
15. Claridy, M.D., et al.: Patterns of Internet-based health information seeking in adult survivors of childhood cancer. Pediatric Blood & Cancer **65**(5), e26954 (2018). https://doi.org/10.1002/pbc.26954
16. Domínguez, M., Sapiña, L.: "Others like me". an approach to the use of the internet and social networks in adolescents and young adults diagnosed with cancer. J. Cancer Educ.: the Official J. American Association for Cancer Educ. **32**(4), 885–891 (2017). https://doi.org/10.1007/s13187-016-1055-9
17. Du, J.T.: The information journey of marketing professionals: incorporating work task-driven information seeking, information judgments, information use, and information sharing. J. Association for Inf. Science and Technol. **65**(9), 1850–1869 (2014). https://doi.org/10.1002/asi.23085
18. Fernandez, C.V., Barr, R.D.: Adolescents and young adults with cancer: an orphaned population. Paediatrics Child Health **11**(2), 103–106 (2006). https://doi.org/10.1093/pch/11.2.103
19. Ferrari, A., et al.: Starting an adolescent and young adult program: some success stories and some obstacles to overcome. J. Clin. Oncol. **2010**(28), 4850–4857 (2010). https://doi.org/10.1200/JCO.2009.23.8097
20. Fisher, K.E.: Information grounds. In: Fisher, K.E., Erdelez, S., McKechnie, L.E.F. (eds): Theories of Information Behavior. Medford, NJ: ASIST Monograph Series 185Y190 (2005)
21. Freund, M.: Studienportal – Nachhaltige Forschung für den Bereich, "Jung & Krebs". German Foundation for young adults with cancer (2022). https://junge-erwachsene-mit-krebs.de/studienportal-nachhaltige-forschung-fuer-den-bereich-jung-krebs/
22. German Foundation for young adults with cancer (2022). Motivation & Goals. https://junge-erwachsene-mit-krebs.de/ueber-uns/motivation-und-ziele/
23. Germeni, E., Schulz, P.J.: Information seeking and avoidance throughout the cancer patient journey: two sides of the same coin? a synthesis of qualitative studies Psycho-Oncology **2014**(23), 1373–1381 (2014). https://https://doi.org/10.1002/pon.3575

24. Grace, J.G., Schweers, L., Anazodo, A., Freyer, D.R.: Evaluating and providing quality health information for adolescents and young adults with cancer.Pediatric Blood & Cancer (2019). https://doi.org/10.1002/pbc.27931
25. Halkett, G.K.B., Kristjanson, L.J., Lobb, E., O'driscoll, C., Taylor, M., Spry, N.: Meeting breast cancer patients' information needs during radiotherapy: what can we do to improve the information and support that is currently provided? European Journal of Cancer Care 2012(19), 538–547 (2010). https://doi.org/10.1111/j.1365-2354.2009.01090.x
26. International Agency for Research in Cancer (2020). Cancer today. In: Data visualization tools for exploring the global cancer burden in 2020. https://gco.iarc.fr/today/data/factsheets/cancers/39-All-cancers-fact-sheet.pdf
27. Johnson, J.D., Case, D.O.: Health Information Seeking. Peter Lang Publishing Inc. (2012)
28. Keegan, T.H.M., et al.: the AYA HOPE Study Collaborative Group. Unmet adolescent and young adult cancer survivors information and service needs: a population-based cancer registry study. Journal of Cancer Survivorship 2012(6), 239–98250 (2012). https://doi.org/10.1007/s11764-012-0219-9
29. Lambert, S.D., Loiselle, C.G., Macdonald, M.E.: An in-depth exploration of information-seeking behavior among individuals with cancer: Part 1: understanding patterns of disinterest and avoidance. Cancer Nursing **32**(1), 11–23 (2009a). https://doi.org/10.1097/01.NCC.0000343372.24517.bd
30. Lambert, S.D., Loiselle, C.G., Macdonald, M.E.: An in-depth exploration of information-seeking behavior among individuals with cancer: Part 2: understanding patterns of disinterest and avoidance. Cancer Nursing **32**(1), 26–36 (2009b). https://doi.org/10.1097/01.NCC.0000343373.01646.91
31. Lea, S., Martins, A. Morgan, S., Cargill, J., Taylor, R.M., Fern, L.A.: Online information and support needs of young people with cancer: a participatory action research study. Adolescent Health, Medicine and Therapeutics 2018(9), 121–135 (2018). https://doi.org/10.2147/AHMT.S173115
32. Lea, S., Martins, A., Fern, L.A.: The support and information needs of adolescents and young adults with cancer when active treatment ends. BMC Cancer **20**(697) (2020). https://doi.org/10.1186/s12885-020-07197-2
33. Leuteritz, K., Friedrich, M., Sender, A., Nowe, E., Stoebel-Richter, Y., Geue, K.: Life satisfaction in young adults with cancer and the role of sociodemographic, medical, and psychosocial factors: Results of a longitudinal study. ACS Journals **124**(22), 4374–4382 (2018). https://doi.org/10.1002/cncr.31659
34. McCarthy, M.C., McNeil, R., Drew, S., Orme, L., Sawyer, S.M.: Information needs of adolescent and young adult cancer patients and their parent-carers. Support. Care Cancer **26**(5), 1655–1664 (2018). https://doi.org/10.1007/s00520-017-3984-1
35. Mistry, S.W., Priestman, T., Damery, S., Haque, M.S.: How do the information needs of cancer patients differ at different stages of the cancer journey? a cross-sectional survey. The Royal Society of Medicine J. **1**(4), 110 (2010). https://doi.org/10.1258/shorts.2010.010032
36. Mooney, R., et al.: Adolescent and young adult cancer survivors' perspectives on their internet use for seeking information on healthy eating and exercise. J. Adolesc. Young Adult Oncol. **6**(2), 367–371 (2017). https://doi.org/10.1089/jayao.2016.0059
37. Mulgund, P., Sharman, R., Purao, S., Thimmanayakanapalya, S.S., Winkelstein, P.: Mapping information needs of patients with sexually transmitted infections using web-based data sources: grounded theory investigation. Journal of Medical Internet Research, **23**(11), e30125 (2021). https://doi.org/10.2196/30125
38. Nanton, V., Docherty, A., Meystre, C., Dale, J.: Finding a pathway: Information and uncertainty along the prostate cancer patient journey. British J. Health Psychology 2009(14), 437–458 (2010). https://doi.org/10.1348/135910708X342890

39. Nguyen, L., Shanks, G., Vetere, F., Howard, S.: Information systems and healthcare XXVIII: the information needs of family carers in collaborative healthcare. Communications Association for Information Syst. **23**, 179–192 (2008). https://doi.org/10.17705/1cais.02310
40. Robert Koch Institut: Krebs in Deutschland für 2015/2016 (12th ed.). Zentrum für Krebsregisterdaten (2019). https://doi.org/10.17886/rkipubl-2016-014
41. Finney Rutten, L.J., et al.: Cancer-related information seeking among cancer survivors: trends over a decade (2003–2013). J. Cancer Educ. **31**(2), 348–357 (2015). https://doi.org/10.1007/s13187-015-0802-7
42. Serçekuş, P., Gencer, H., Özkan, S.: Finding useful cancer information may reduce cancer information overload for internet users. Health Information and Libraries J. **37**(4), 319–328 (2020). https://doi.org/10.1111/hir.12325
43. Tran, Y., Lamprell, K., Easpaig, B.N.G., Arnolda, G., Braithwaite, J.: What information do patients want across their cancer journeys? A network analysis of cancer patients' information needs. Cancer Med. 2019(8), 155–164 (2018). https://doi.org/10.1002/cam4.1915
44. Tustin, C.: The role of patient satisfaction in online health information seeking. J. Health Communication: International Perspectives **15**(1), 3–17 (2010). https://doi.org/10.1080/10810730903465491
45. US National Cancer Institute: Introduction to Adolescent and Young Adult Cancers [Video] (2018). https://www.youtube.com/watch?v=1mIAbOE7Jkg
46. Zebrack, B.: Information and service needs for young adult cancer patients. Support Care Cancer 2008(16)**,** 1353–1360 (2008). https://doi.org/10.1007/s00520-008-0435-z
47. Zebrack, B., Chesler, M.A., Kaplan, S.: To foster healing among adolescents and young adults with cancer: What helps? What hurts? Support Care Cancer 2010(18). 131–135 (2010). https://doi.org/10.1007/s00520-009-0719-y

Using Crossmodal Correspondence Between Colors and Music to Enhance Online Art Exhibition Visitors' Experience

Qian Guo[1] and Tingting Jiang[1,2](✉)

[1] School of Information Management, Wuhan University, Wuhan, Hubei, China
tij@whu.edu.cn
[2] Center for Studies of Information Resources, Wuhan University, Wuhan, Hubei, China

Abstract. Background music has been widely used in online art exhibitions to enhance visitors' art appreciation experience. At present, what music to use is highly dependent on exhibition designers' personal understanding, experience, or even intuition. In fact, it is possible to systematically identify matching music for given artwork due to the crossmodal correspondence between visual and auditory inputs. This paper presents an exploratory study of the crossmodal correspondence between color hues and music tempos and its effects on online art appreciation experience based on two experiments. According to Experiment 1, warm colors were congruent with fast music, whereas cool colors were congruent with slow music. In Experiment 2, congruent and incongruent background music was used in an online exhibition of oil paintings, and several findings were engendered. For warm-colored paintings, congruent (fast) music helped visitors remembered significant more paintings. For cool-colored paintings, visitors collected or shared more paintings when hearing congruent (slow) music but viewed the paintings for longer durations when hearing incongruent (fast) music. The findings not only enrich the understanding of the roles of audio-visual crossmodal correspondence, but also inform online art exhibition designers of how to make background music work in harmony with artwork to better engage visitors.

Keywords: Crossmodal correspondence · Colors · Music tempos · Online art exhibition

1 Introduction

Traditional exhibitions have appealed primarily to just one sense as vision. To further improve public interest in the artifacts displayed, now exhibitions have been integrating and stimulating multiple human senses rather than just a feast for eyes [1]. Many museums and art galleries also provide online access to the contents of their collections for the public to help the collections widespread. Different from physical exhibitions which can integrate the design of visual, auditory, olfactory, and other senses cues to trigger multisensory experiences [2], the sensory design for online exhibitions is restricted due to technical limitations. Visual and auditory stimuli are the most common cues that can

© The Author(s), under exclusive license to Springer Nature Switzerland AG 2023
I. Sserwanga et al. (Eds.): iConference 2023, LNCS 13971, pp. 144–159, 2023.
https://doi.org/10.1007/978-3-031-28035-1_12

be seen in online exhibitions. Besides, it has been affirmed that visual and auditory cues are the most powerful multisensory cues combination that positively affects user experience and behavior on a digital exhibition website [3]. Generally, collections, e.g., paintings, are the typical visual cues and background music is the typical auditory cue in online exhibitions. Existing studies explored the associations between art collections and background music in terms of their semantic or content, e.g., affective meaning [4, 5]. Besides, formal features, which can be defined independently of content [6], have also found can influence human behavior. Color has the effectiveness in attracting attention and influencing consumers' purchase intentions memory. For example, blue is more effective than red in promotion recall of information [7]. Background music tempo also influences user's behavior, for example, fast music can enhance optimal exercising [8].

When humans interact with multisensory environments, their sensory modalities are related to one another and can influence each other, which is called *crossmodal interaction* psychologically. As a particular class of crossmodal interaction, *crossmodal correspondence* is a common phenomenon in humans that refers to the non-arbitrary perceptual associations between different stimulus features [9, 10]. For example, high lightness is associated with high pitch while low lightness is associated with low pitch. The majority of previous studies about crossmodal correspondence are devoted to revealing the associations between stimuli from different sensory modalities [11, 12]. Only a few studies have explored the influence of crossmodal correspondence on attention, perception, and behavior in a specific context [13–15]. Particularly, the congruence between stimulus features is beneficial to information perception, processing, and memory, and such influence has been explored in the context of products package and retailing [14, 16, 17]. In art, olfactory-color crossmodal has attracted researchers' attention [18], incongruent scents and artworks increase arousal relative to congruent scents and artworks [19]. Unfortunately, to the best of our knowledge, despite background music being widely used in exhibitions, there is little work exploring the role of visual-auditory crossmodal correspondence play on user behavior and memory.

Exploring the relationship between crossmodal correspondence and user behavior and memory in digital art exhibitions could help the design of the websites and art communication with visitors, this study aims to verify the association between color and background music and explores the influence of audiovisual crossmodal correspondence on users' user behavior and memory when they view art paintings. The research questions are:

RQ1. How do visual color and music tempo match?
RQ2. Does visual color-music tempo crossmodal correspondence play a role in user behavior and memory?

To answer these questions, two experiments were conducted. First, it is necessary to investigate whether the correspondence between color and music tempo could be identified. Thus, study 1 investigated whether people reliably matched music tempo with color (hue/saturation/lightness) in China. As the perception of color hue is more intuitive than lightness and saturation in a painting, study 2 further explored whether such association between color hue and background music tempo could affect user behavior and memory in an online art exhibition. A2 (background music tempo: fast/slow) *2 (color hue: warm/cool) mixed-subjects design was used in study 2, while the background music was treated as a between-subjects factor and color hue treated as a within-subject factor. User behavior was measured via two physical interactions, dwell time on painting and user actions with the painting (collecting or sharing), while memory a recognition test.

2 Related Work

2.1 The Effects of Background Music

The influences of background music have been explored by researchers in multiple disciplines. It has been found that music can positively affect consumer purchase behavior [20] and promote second language acquisition [21], but it may also distract students during the learning process [22]. In the exhibitions, music can be a catalyst for the exhibit to convey messages in it and influence user experience and behavior. Music affected the emotion and pace of the museum visit, e.g., relaxing music may induce a slower pace of visit [4, 23].

The impact of background music on tasks depends on the semantic congruency and formal congruency between music and the task [24]. The semantic congruency emphasizes the similarity of content between auditory and visual, which helps to communicate the meaning of the content. In the supermarket, French music would guide consumers to buy French wine, while German music would guide consumers to buy German wine [25]. Background music can generate more visual attention, higher cognitive workload, and withdrawal reactions when it is incongruent with advertisement content than when they are congruent [5]. In addition, the formal congruency provides a united perceptual form to auditory and visual information, which can also influence the responses of users [24]. For example, when users are exposed to online advertise or a website with fast music and warm color background, they would feel more aroused and pleasure than those who experienced slow tempo and cool color [26, 27]. The formal congruency is focused on this study.

2.2 Crossmodal Correspondence Between Color and Music Tempo

One important line of previous studies of crossmodal correspondence has devoted to revealing the associations between stimuli from different sensory modalities. Most of them focused on simple properties of elementary stimuli, such as visual color hue and auditory pitch [12, 28]. Complex stimuli that are more common in everyday life have not received much attention. Self-report methods have been adopted to determine the associations. Specifically, the participants were asked to directly select the most/least consistent stimuli for a given stimulus. With respect to visual stimuli, color is the most widely investigated property. Hue, saturation, and lightness are three basic dimensions of color. Colors have all been found to be associated with the auditory stimuli in related studies, including pitch, loudness, timbre of a sound, and mode and tempo of music [12, 29, 30].

The music-to-color associations are mediated by emotional associations [31, 32]. Fast music is considered more arousing and happier than slow one. Warm color can increase arousal while cool color tends to induce calmness and peace. Besides, Palmer et al. [31] found that U.S. and Mexican participants tended to associate red/yellow color (warm color) with fast tempo classic music while blue color (cool color) with slow tempo; High lightness/saturation with fast tempo while low lightness/saturation with slow tempo. Qi et al. [28] found that Chinese undergraduate and graduate students matched higher-pitched sounds from Chinese instruments with red rather than black or gray. However, to the best of our knowledge, how do color and tempo associate in Chinese remains unknown.

2.3 Crossmodal Correspondence and User Responses

The crossmodal correspondence between visual and auditory has been found to affect people's responses. As for visual attention, it is shown that congruency between auditory pitch and visual lightness can influence visual search performance by means of top-down facilitation [16]. High-pitch sounds can cause users to fixate on light objects faster and longer while low-pitch sounds cause users to fixate on dark objects faster and longer, which was observed in undergraduates [14]. Besides, high pitch can guide user attention to a higher location [33]. The congruency effect can also be found in infants: they looked at an object whose height or size is congruent with pitch longer than an object whose height or size is incongruent with pitch [34, 35].

Crossmodal correspondence can also affect users' behavior intention and memory. When exposed to high pitch music in a supermarket, consumers were more likely to purchase products from light decorative shelves, while low pitch music was opposite [14]. Metatla et al. [15] examined the role of crossmodal display in gameplay and found that users had higher engagement levels with the congruent display than incongruent. Their results also indicated that congruent display had a positive performance effect on the memory task. Besides, in the context of art, the association between scent and artworks has an impact on undergraduate visitors' perception: incongruence can enhance the level of attention and increase arousal [19].

3 Study 1: Crossmodal Correspondence Between Music Tempo and Color

Study 1 aims to replicate and extend previous findings of crossmodal correspondence between music tempo and color in Chinese participants. A within-subject design was conducted in a classroom at a Chinese university. All the participants were asked to choose five colors to match or mismatch music in order they were listening to.

3.1 Participants

The participants of this experiment were recruited in a Chinese university. It was required that the participants had no defective color vision and or acoustic impairment. A total of 50 participants (28 females and 22 males, Mage = 20.06 years) meeting both the requirements participant in the study 1. All of them are Chinese students but none of them were professional artists or professional composer/theorist. Among them, 27 participants self-report unfamiliar with music theory, and 23 participants self-report kind familiar with music theory. Each participant signed a consent form before the experiment. This study was approved by the University Research Ethics Committee and strictly followed the general ethical guidelines.

3.2 Materials

Colors. The colors stimuli were chosen based on Palmer et al. [31], which included eight hues (red (R), orange (O), yellow(Y), chartreuse(H), green (G), cyan (C), blue (B), and purple (P)) sampled at four cuts (saturation/lightness levels): saturated (S), light (L), muted (M), and dark (D). Colors were initially sampled from Munsell space, with the highly saturated colors within each hue. Then less-saturated versions of those hues at varying lightness levels were chosen, the M colors being approximately halfway between S colors and neutral gray, the L-colors were approximately halfway between S-colors and white, and the D colors were approximately halfway between S-colors and black. White, black, and three grays whose lightness was approximately the average lightness were also included (see Fig. 1a).

Music. As this study mainly focused on music tempo, the auditory stimuli were two classic music with no Lyrics, chosen from Bach's Brandenburg Concerto, no. 2 and no. 6, both in major mode but different in the tempo: one is fast tempo, and another is slow tempo.

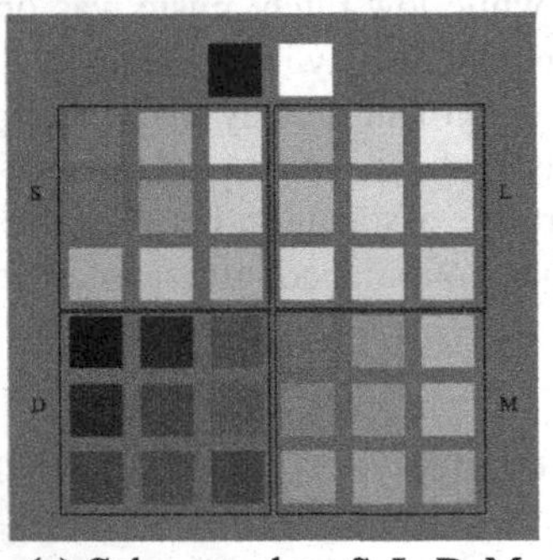

(a) Color samples - S, L, D, M

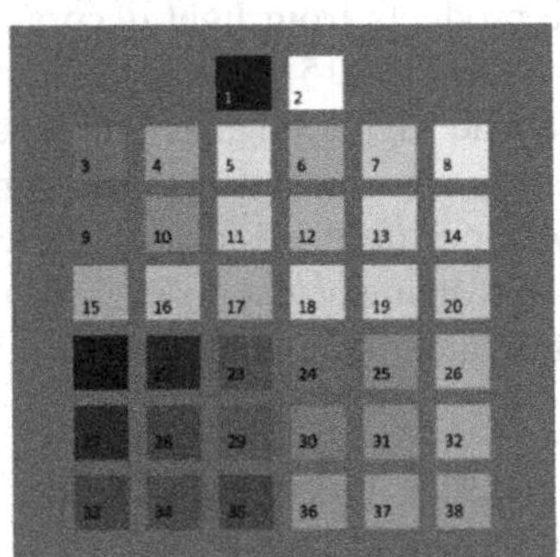

(b) Color card

Fig. 1. The display of 37 colors

3.3 Procedure

The experiment was conducted in a classroom. All participants were concentrated in the classroom and seated in their places. Color cards were presented in front of them with each color numbered (see Fig. 1b). Then they were told to choose the five colors in order that were most consistent with the music, and the five colors in order that were inconsistent with the music they listened. The two pieces of music (lasting 50 s) were both played twice so that the participants had enough time to make choice.

3.4 Results

All of the color were transformed into CIELAB color space and CIELCH color space. The three coordinates of CIELAB represent the lightness of the color, the position between red and green, and the position between yellow and blue, while one coordinate of CIELCH represent saturation of the color. As for the color chosen with music, the four dimensions (D_d represents the value of each dimension and d represents each dimension: Red/Green, Yellow/Blue, Lightness, and Saturation) were calculated by a linearly weighted average of the ratings chosen with the music: the ratings of the five colors chosen as most consistent with the music (C_d) minus an analogous weighted average of the ratings of the five colors chosen to be inconsistent with that music (I_d) [31].

$$C_d = \left(5c_{1,d} + 4\,c_{2,d} + 3c_{3,d} + 2c_{4,d} + 1c_{5,d}\right)/15 \quad (1)$$

$$I_d = \left(5i_{1,d} + 4i_{2,d} + 3\,i_{3,d} + 2\,i_{4,d} + 1i_{5,d}\right)/15 \quad (2)$$

$$D_d = C_d - I_d \quad (3)$$

where C_j represents the value participants picked as the most consistent with music, where j ranges from 1 to 5, and I_j represents the value participants picked as the most inconsistent with music, where j ranges from 1 to 5.

One-way ANOVAs was used to examine the relationship between the music tempo and the four-color dimensions. According to the results (see Fig. 2), faster tempo was associated with lighter ($F(1,98) = 42.303$, $p = 0.000$), more saturated ($F(1,98) = 100.636$, $p = 0.000$), yellower ($F(1,98) = 21.707$, $p = 0.000$), and redder ($F(1,98) = 151.059$, $p = 0.000$) colors. Slower tempo was associated with darker, less saturated, bluer, and greener colors.

4 Study 2: Relationships Between Crossmodal Correspondence and User Responses

The results in study 1 showed the existence of crossmodal correspondence between music tempo and color (hue, lightness, and saturation), which is consistent with existing research [31, 32]. Specifically, fast tempo was more strongly associated with warmer colors (yellower/redder colors) and slow tempo was more associated with cooler colors (bluer/greener colors). As the perception of color hue is more intuitive than lightness and saturation in a painting, study 2 would further test the role of crossmodal correspondence between color hue and music tempo in human responses. Study 2 used a 2 (music tempo: fast/slow) *2 (color: warm/cool) mixed-subjects design, with music tempo treated as a between-subjects factor and color treated as a within-subject factor.

4.1 Participants

A recruitment advertisement that specified the purpose and requirements of the experiment was posted on social media. It was required that the potential participants had

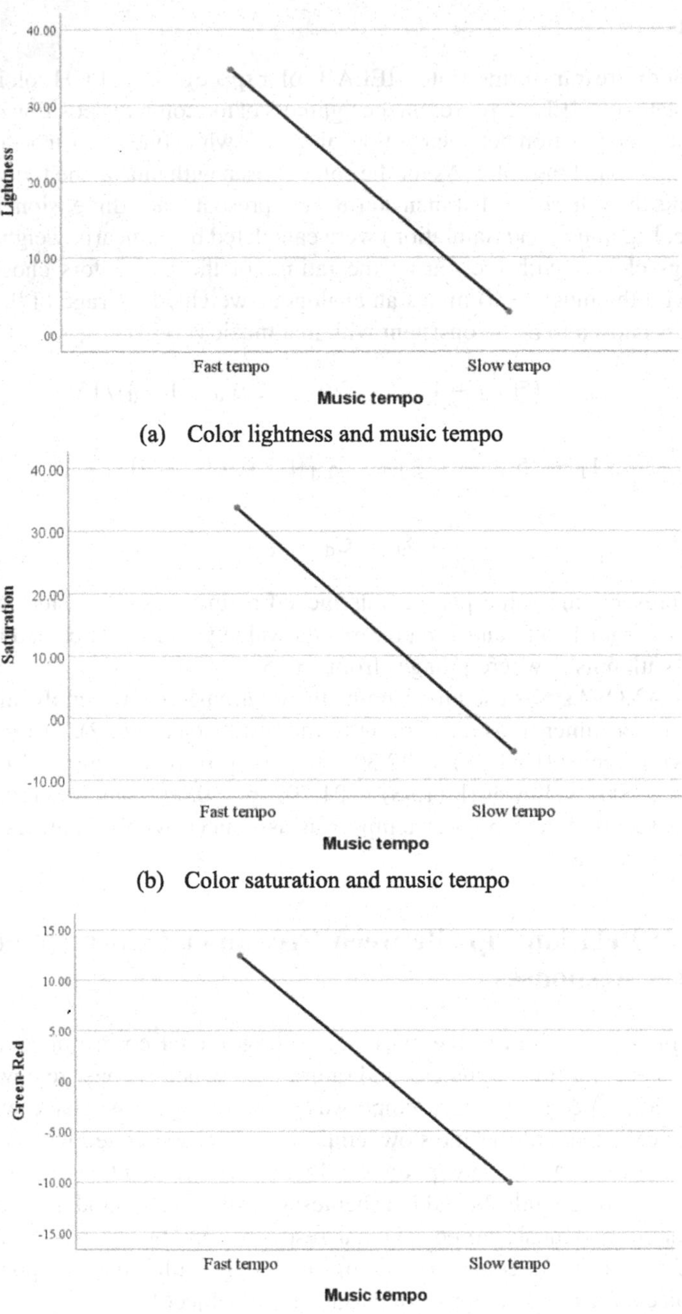

(a) Color lightness and music tempo

(b) Color saturation and music tempo

(c) Red/green and music tempo

Fig. 2. Mean value of color and music tempo

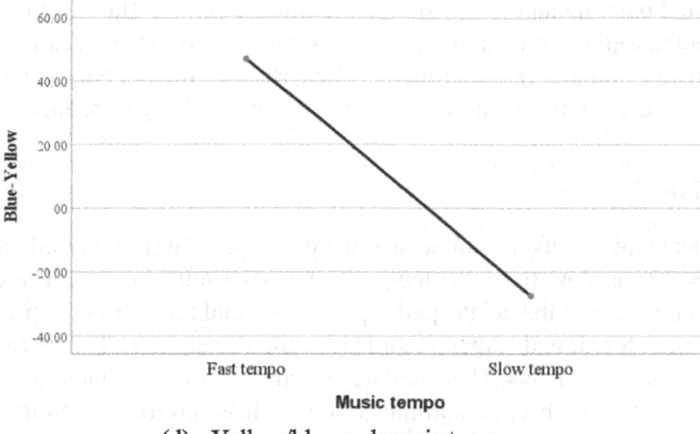

(d) Yellow/blue and music tempo

Fig. 2. (*continued*)

a normal sense of visual and hearing. In addition, music or art professionals were not asked as they may have different than normal experiences when viewing the paintings, which helped minimize possible individual differences. As a result, a total of 39 Chinese participants (29 females, 10 males, Mage = 22.1 years) met these requirements and then participated in the experiment, all aged between 18 and 30. Among them, 35 participants were occasional visitors of art museums/galleries online or offline and 4 never visit. The familiarity with music theory or oil painting was assessed with the question: "Rate how much you are familiar with music theory" and "Rate how much you are familiar with oil paintings" (1-very unfamiliar, 7-very familiar). According to the results, all participants did not have a broad knowledge of music theory (Mean rank = 2.41) or oil paintings (Mean rank = 2.54). All participants signed a consent form before the experiment and received 15 RMB as compensation after it. This study was approved by the University Research Ethics Committee and strictly followed the general ethical guidelines.

4.2 Materials

This study built a mockup online art exhibition using the prototyping tool Axure. The exhibition consisted of 20 landscape oil paintings, with 10 warm-colored ones (dominated by red or yellow colors) and 10 cool-colored ones (dominated by blue or green colors). These paintings were selected by three professional visual designers based on three criteria: (1) lack of distinction; (2) excluding humans and animals; and (3) roughly the same levels of color lightness or saturation. Each painting was displayed at the center of a webpage and accompanied by textual information indicating the title, author, year, and country of the painting. The length of textual information was controlled to the same to avoid potential influence. Besides, two buttons, *collect* and *share*, were placed below the textual information to enable visitors to interact with the painting. Additionally, the *previous* and *next* buttons under the painting helped visitors navigate in the exhibition.

The warm-colored paintings alternated with the cool-colored ones in the exhibition. Two schemes of sequence were created based on a 2 * 2 Latin Square, one starting with a warm-colored painting and the other a cool-colored painting. Background music was embedded in the online art exhibition and auto played upon visitors' arrival. The two pieces of music examined in Experiment 1, i.e., Bach's Brandenburg Concerto No. 2 and No. 6, were used in the exhibition as fast and slow auditory materials, respectively.

4.3 Procedure

The experiment was conducted online, and the participants were randomly allocated to the fast ($n = 20$) or slow ($n = 19$) tempo background music group. The experiment consisted of three parts. First, all the participants were told that the whole process would be remotely monitored, and screen recorded by the researchers. This permission was obtained from the participants. Then they were instructed to see a landscape oil painting exhibition while hearing background music in a website prototype and they can view paintings, collect, and share the paintings just as the way they behave as normal. After viewing each painting, they needed to evaluate the color perception, ranging from 1 as cool color (blue/green) to 7 as warm color (yellow/red). After viewing all the paintings, they needed to evaluate the tempo of the background music ranging from 1 (slow) to 7 (fast), and how much they like the music ranging from 1 (dislike) to 7 (like). The second part was three minutes distractor task, during which they worked on math problems [36]. The third part was a recognition test. Each participant was presented with a total of 40 paintings and asked to recognize from them 20 target paintings that had appeared in the online art exhibition. The remaining 20 paintings were irrelevant to the exhibition and randomly arranged in the 40 paintings as distractors. For each painting, the participants needed to indicate whether they had viewed the painting during art appreciation. They were given three options, i.e., "yes", "no", and "not sure". The entire experiment lasted 20 min on average.

4.4 Results

This study first checked if the color and music tempo was successfully manipulated. The Mann-Whitney U test was adopted to compare subjective ratings between warm and cool colors, fast and slow music, and the liking degree of the music as those data had no specific distribution [37]. The results showed that participants felt warm-colored paintings are yellower/redder and cool paintings are bluer/greener ($Z = -22.896$, $p = 0.000$, Mean rank: warm 568.38 > cool 207.16). The perceived tempo in the fast music group was faster than the slow music group ($Z = -4.818$, $p = 0.000$, Mean rank: fast 28.38 > slow 11.18). The degree of liking of music did not differ between the fast and slow tempo groups ($Z = -1.085$, $p = 0.296$). Those results suggested that the manipulation of the experiment was successful.

Secondly, to assess the differences in dwell time, behavior, and retention between warm-colored and cool-colored paintings, paired t test was conducted while the data satisfied parametric assumptions, and Wilcoxon signed rank test was conducted while the data did not satisfy parametric assumptions [38]. One-way ANOVA was used for assessing the differences between fast and slow tempo groups.

Dwell Time. This study defined dwell time as the time spent viewing a painting, an indicator of the user's involvement in interacting with the painting. The mean dwell time on cool-colored paintings (M = 10.27 s) was longer than warm-colored paintings (M = 10.04 s). The fast tempo group had a longer mean dwell time (M = 10.32 s) than the slow group (M = 9.98 s). However, there existed no significant difference in mean dwell time between warm-colored and cool-colored paintings ($t = -0.622$, $p = 0.537$), as well as fast and slow tempo ($F(1,37) = 0.04$, $P = 0.843$). Results further revealed that mean dwell time on warm-colored paintings in fast tempo group did not differ from slow tempo group ($F(1,37) = 0.010$, $p = 0.919$), either on cool-colored paintings ($F(1,37) = 0.236$, $p = 0.630$).

Next, the congruency effect was analyzed in terms of two tempo groups. As seen in Fig. 3, participants viewed paintings with incongruent color paintings longer than congruent. The difference was significant in fast tempo group ($M_{congruent} = 9.95$ vs. $M_{incongruent} = 10.7$; $t = -2.142$, $p = 0.045 < 0.05$), whereas not in slow tempo group ($t = -0.527$, $p = 0.605$). These results suggested that the crossmodal correspondence between color and music tempo can play a role on users' dwell time. Specifically, when the background music was fast, the participants spent more time on cool-colored paintings than warm-colored paintings.

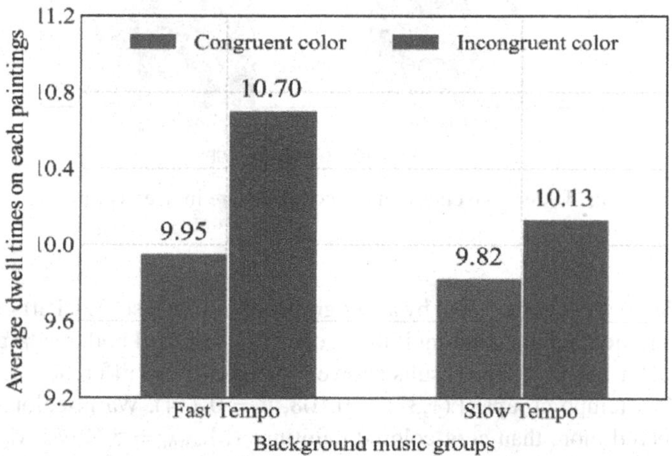

Fig. 3. Average dwell time on each painting

Collecting and Sharing. When viewing the paintings, users may collect or share, indicating that they approach the paintings more intensively. The number of collects or shares by each participant was extracted. No significant differences were found between fast tempo and slow tempo groups ($F(1,37) = 0.480$, $P = 0.493$). Cool-colored paintings attracted more intense approach clicks than warm-colored paintings ($M_{warm} = 2$ vs. $M_{cool} = 2.90$; $Z = -2.310$, $p = 0.021 < 0.05$). Results further revealed that clicks on warm-colored paintings in fast tempo group did not differ from the slow tempo group

(F (1,37) = 0.733, p = 0.397), either on cool-colored paintings (F (1,37) = 0.166, p = 0.686).

The congruency effect was analyzed in terms of two tempo groups. As seen in Fig. 4, participants collected or shared more paintings with incongruent color than congruent with fast tempo condition, while more paintings with congruent color than incongruent in slow tempo condition. The differences were significant in slow tempo group ($M_{congruent} = 2.74$ vs. $M_{incongruent} = 1.8$; $t = 2.150$, $p = 0.045 < 0.05$) but not in fast tempo group ($Z = -1.256$, $p = 0.209$). That is, when the background music was slow, the participants collected or shared more cool-colored paintings than warm-colored paintings.

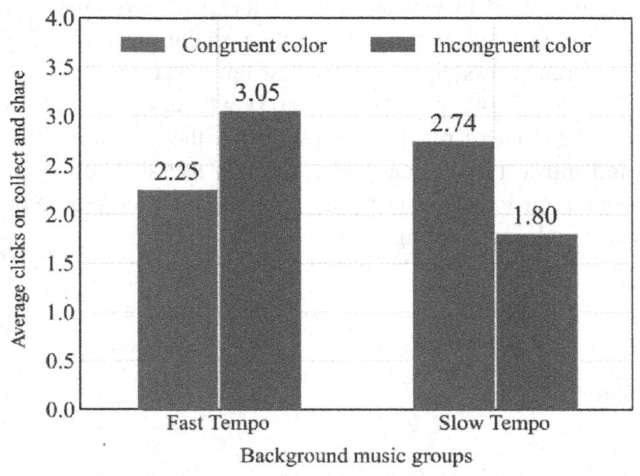

Fig. 4. Average clicks on collect and share in one visiting

Memory. Memory can be revealed by a recognition memory test [39]. Participants were considered to remember the painting if they correctly identified both the target painting and the distractor painting. The results showed no significant differences between fast tempo and slow tempo groups (F(1,37) = 0.108, P = 0.744). Warm-colored paintings were remembered more than cool-colored paintings ($M_{warm} = 5.62$ vs. $M_{cool} = 4.67$; $Z = -2.769$, $p = 0.006 < 0.05$). Results further revealed that the number of memories of warm-colored paintings in the fast tempo group did not differ from the slow tempo group (F(1,37) = 0.344, p = 0.561), either of cool-colored paintings (F(1,37) = 0.003, p = 0.959).

The congruency effect was analyzed in terms of two tempo groups. As seen in Fig. 5, the number of correct memories on paintings with congruent color was more than with incongruent. The difference was significant in fast tempo group ($M_{congruent} = 5.85$ vs. $M_{incongruent} = 4.65$; $t = 2.812$, $p = 0.011$) but not in slow tempo group ($t = -1.556$, $p = 0.137$). That is, when the background music was fast, the participants would remember more warm-colored paintings than cool-colored ones.

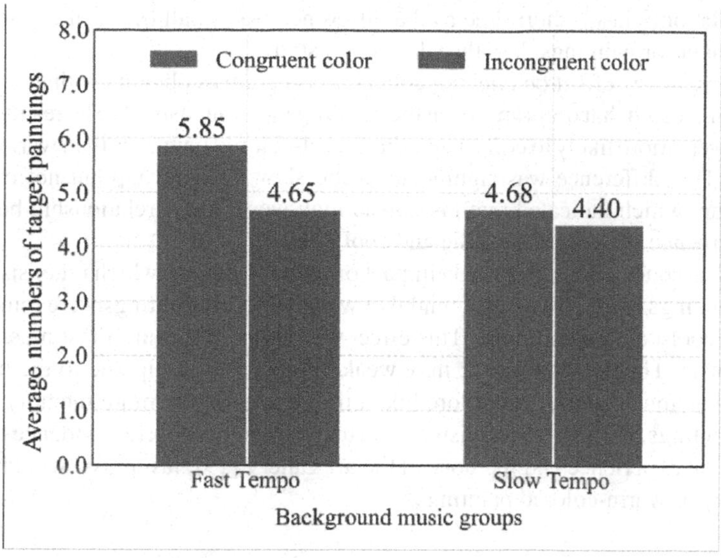

Fig. 5. Average numbers of target paintings recognized

5 Discussion

5.1 Crossmodal Correspondence in Online Art Exhibition

Background music is commonly used in art galleries, museums, and so on. However, how visual-auditory senses are interactively matched, and the consequences of such interaction remain unknown. This study was particularly interested in the crossmodal correspondence between color of paintings and background music and the relationship between them and user responses in an online art exhibition.

Different from the positive congruency effect on viewing times found in [34], this study found that the dwell time was longer on incongruent color paintings than congruent, but only in the fast music environment. When consumers are in online retail stores, warm color is considered to result in high arousal and pleasure than cool color, and fast music is associated with a higher level of arousal and pleasure. The match between warm color and fast music can enhance customers' emotions and create a desired environment [27]. However, the perception of art might be different from the evaluation of objects and it might be more complex than in a retailing setting: consumers' judgment may be influenced mainly by rational factor in retailing setting [40] while art exhibitions is an aesthetic experience [41]. A similar study that focused on visual-olfactory crossmodal correspondence found the negative influence of congruence on attention in an art exhibition because the arousal diminished and incongruence would enhance the level of attention [19].In addition, several studies have shown that faster music can speed up customers' activity [42], this study further found that if the fast music color does not consistent with the painting, users' activity may slow down. Compared to paintings with congruent music, paintings with incongruent music would force users from no conscious control (thinking fast) to conscious control (thinking slow) [43], but this incongruent effect maybe only last a short time as the difference was small between congruent and incongruent color paintings, less than 1 s in this study.

The congruency effect on clicking collect and share was obvious in this study. Both behaviors indicated that users approach the painting more intensively. The results showed that users were more likely to collect and share cool-colored paintings than warm-colored paintings. This difference was significant in the slow music group but not in the fast music group, which indicated that fast music may weaken this relationship because of the incongruence between fast music and cool color.

The congruency effect also has an impact on users' memory, which is consistent with previous findings [44]. This study found that warm-colored paintings were remembered more than cool-colored paintings. This effect was still significant in fast music but not in slow music. That is, slow music may weaken this relationship due to the mismatch between slow music and warm-colored paintings and promote more memory on cool-colored paintings. Different from visual-olfactory crossmodal correspondence that scent destroyed the experience and memory in the art gallery [19], fast music would enhance the memory of warm-colored paintings.

5.2 Implications

This study presents two theoretical contributions to the literature on crossmodal correspondence and the interaction of visual and auditory cues. First, this study confirmed the robustness of crossmodal correspondence between color and music tempo: warm color and fast tempo were crossmodally matched; cool color and slow tempo were crossmodally matched. Second, this study adds understanding in the multisensory in online art exhibitions by examining the role of crossmodal correspondence between the color hue of paintings and music tempo play on users' behavior and memory formation.

The major findings of this study also have practical implications for multisensory design in online art exhibitions. Visual and auditory stimuli are common cues in digital art exhibitions. An effective multisensory design would help the artworks widely spread. The current findings indicate that the creation of a sensory between painting's color hue and background music tempo may enhance user behavior and memory when they visit digital art exhibitions. It is worth noting that the balance between congruence and incongruence needs to be taken into account. For example, if an online art exhibition designer wants users to attend to paintings, cool-colored paintings should be displayed in fast music environment. But if the designer wants users to collect or share more paintings, cool-colored paintings should be displayed in slow background music. In addition, audio-visual technology has been applied in the majority of current VR/AR [45]. Our results also provide implications for Virtual Reality (VR) and Augmented Reality (AR) design to improve user experience. Multisensory stimuli integrated in VR/AR have made it possible to develop an immersive environment [46]. In the future, the crossmodal correspondence between other sensory stimuli can be explored to help further understand users' experience in VR/AR.

6 Conclusions

This study investigated the association between visual color and music tempo and how such sensory correspondence contributes to user behavior and memory. The results in Study 1 showed that warm colors were reliably matched with fast music and cool colors with slow music. In addition, study 1 also found the association between high lightness/saturation and fast tempo, as well as low lightness/saturation and slow tempo. In terms of the relationship between crossmodal correspondence and user responses, several significant results were found in study 2: In the fast music environment, users spend more time on paintings with incongruent color than that with congruent color, but they tend to remember more paintings with congruent color than that with incongruent color. In the slow music environment, users would collect or share more paintings with congruent color than that incongruent color. This research revealed findings that the balance between congruence and incongruence should be considered. This calls for more research towards the potential mediators between crossmodal correspondence and user responses. In addition, our future work will investigate the effects of crossmodal correspondence between other sensory features, such as lightness/saturation and music tempo, on user responses. Besides, some potential mediators, such as subjective experiences, arousal, pleasure, and immersion can also be investigated in future works to further explore the influence mechanism.

Acknowledgement. This research has been made possible through the financial support of the National Social Science Foundation of China under Grant No. 22&ZD325 and the National Natural Science Foundation of China under Grant No. 72074173.

References

1. Vi, C.T., Ablart, D., Gatti, E., et al.: Not just seeing, but also feeling art: mid-air haptic experiences integrated in a multisensory art exhibition. Int. J. Hum Comput Stud. **108**, 1–14 (2017)
2. Spence, C.: Scenting the anosmic cube: on the use of ambient scent in the context of the art gallery or museum. i-Perception **11**(6), 1–26 (2020)
3. Guo, K., Fan, A., Lehto, X., et al.: Immersive digital tourism: the role of multisensory cues in digital museum experiences. J. Hosp. Tour. Res., 1–23 (2021)
4. Chen, C.-L., Tsai, C.-G.: The influence of background music on the visitor museum experience: a case study of the Laiho memorial museum. Taiwan. Visit. Stud. **18**(2), 183–195 (2015)
5. Ausín, J.M., Bigne, E., Marín, J., et al.: The background music-content congruence of TV advertisements: a neurophysiological study. Eur. Res. Manag. Bus. Econ. **27**(2), 100154 (2021)
6. Kim, K.-H., Iwamiya, S.-I.: Formal congruency between telop patterns and sound effects. Music Percept. **25**(5), 429–448 (2008)
7. Yu, C.-E., Xie, S.Y., Wen, J.: Coloring the destination: The role of color psychology on Instagram. Tour. Manag. **80**, 104110 (2020)
8. Edworthy, J., Waring, H.: The effects of music tempo and loudness level on treadmill exercise. Ergonomics **49**(15), 1597–1610 (2006)

9. Spence, C.: Crossmodal correspondences: a tutorial review. Atten. Percept. Psychophys. **73**(4), 971–995 (2011)
10. Lin, A., Scheller, M., Feng, F., et al.: Feeling colours: crossmodal correspondences between tangible 3D objects, colours and emotions. In: Proceedings of the 2021 CHI Conference on Human Factors in Computing Systems (2021)
11. Sun, X., Li, X., Ji, L., et al.: An extended research of crossmodal correspondence between color and sound in psychology and cognitive ergonomics. PeerJ **6**, e4443 (2018)
12. Jonas, C., Spiller, M.J., Hibbard, P.: Summation of visual attributes in auditory–visual crossmodal correspondences. Psychon. Bull. Rev. **24**(4), 1104–1112 (2017). https://doi.org/10.3758/s13423-016-1215-2
13. Motoki, K., Velasco, C.: Taste-shape correspondences in context. Food Qual. Prefer. **88**, 104082 (2021)
14. Hagtvedt, H., Brasel, S.A.: Cross-modal communication: sound frequency influences consumer responses to color lightness. J. Mark. Res. **53**(4), 551–562 (2016)
15. Metatla, O., Correia, N.N., Martin, F., et al.: Tap the shapetones: Exploring the effects of crossmodal congruence in an audio-visual interface. In: Proceedings of the 2016 CHI Conference on Human Factors in Computing Systems, New York, NY. ACM Press (2016)
16. Klapetek, A., Ngo, M.K., Spence, C.: Does crossmodal correspondence modulate the facilitatory effect of auditory cues on visual search? Atten. Percept. Psychophys. **74**(6), 1154–1167 (2012). https://doi.org/10.3758/s13414-012-0317-9
17. Velasco, C., Woods, A.T., Petit, O., et al.: Crossmodal correspondences between taste and shape, and their implications for product packaging: a review. Food Qual. Prefer. **52**, 17–26 (2016)
18. Spence, C.: Olfactory-colour crossmodal correspondences in art, science, and design. Cognit. Res. Princ. Implic. **5**(1), 1–21 (2020). https://doi.org/10.1186/s41235-020-00246-1
19. Cirrincione, A., Estes, Z., Carù, A.: The effect of ambient scent on the experience of art: not as good as it smells. Psychol. Mark. **31**(8), 615–627 (2014)
20. Andersson, P.K., Kristensson, P., Wästlund, E., et al.: Let the music play or not: the influence of background music on consumer behavior. J. Retail. Consum. Serv. **19**(6), 553–560 (2012)
21. Kang, H.J., Williamson, V.J.: Background music can aid second language learning. Psychol. Music **42**(5), 728–747 (2014)
22. Flowers, P.J., O'Neill, A.A.M.: Self-reported distractions of middle school students in listening to music and prose. J. Res. Music Educ. **53**(4), 308–321 (2005)
23. Webb, R.C.: Music, mood, and museums: a review of the consumer literature on background music. Visit. Stud. **8**(2), 15–29 (1996)
24. Tan, S.-L., Cohen, A.J., Lipscomb, S.D., et al.: The Psychology of Music in Multimedia. Oxford University Press, Oxford (2013)
25. North, A.C., Hargreaves, D.J., McKendrick, J.: The influence of in-store music on wine selections. J. Appl. Psychol. **84**(2), 271 (1999)
26. Wu, C.-S., Cheng, F.-F., Yen, D.C.: The atmospheric factors of online storefront environment design: an empirical experiment in Taiwan. Inf. Manag. **45**(7), 493–498 (2008)
27. Cheng, F.-F., Wu, C.-S., Yen, D.C.: The effect of online store atmosphere on consumer's emotional responses–an experimental study of music and colour. Behav. Inf. Technol. **28**(4), 323–334 (2009)
28. Qi, Y., Huang, F., Li, Z., et al.: Crossmodal correspondences in the sounds of Chinese instruments. Perception **49**(1), 81–97 (2020)
29. Anikin, A., Johansson, N.: Implicit associations between individual properties of color and sound. Atten. Percept. Psychophys. **81**(3), 764–777 (2018). https://doi.org/10.3758/s13414-018-01639-7
30. Adeli, M., Rouat, J., Molotchnikoff, S.: Audiovisual correspondence between musical timbre and visual shapes. Front. Hum. Neurosci. **8**, 352 (2014)

31. Palmer, S.E., Schloss, K.B., Xu, Z., et al.: Music–color associations are mediated by emotion. Proc. Natl. Acad. Sci. **110**(22), 8836–8841 (2013)
32. Whiteford, K.L., Schloss, K.B., Helwig, N.E., et al.: Color, music, and emotion: bach to the blues. i-Perception **9**(6), 1–27 (2018)
33. Chiou, R., Rich, A.N.: Cross-modality correspondence between pitch and spatial location modulates attentional orienting. Perception **41**(3), 339–353 (2012)
34. Walker, P., Bremner, J.G., Mason, U., et al.: Preverbal infants' sensitivity to synaesthetic cross-modality correspondences. Psychol. Sci. **21**(1), 21–25 (2010)
35. Fernández-Prieto, I., Navarra, J., Pons, F.: How big is this sound? Crossmodal association between pitch and size in infants. Infant Behav. Dev. **38**, 77–81 (2015)
36. Bookbinder, S., Brainerd, C.: Emotionally negative pictures enhance gist memory. Emotion **17**(1), 102 (2017)
37. McKnight, P.E., Najab, J.: Mann-Whitney U test. The Corsini encyclopedia of psychology, 1 (2010)
38. McCrum-Gardner, E.: Which is the correct statistical test to use? Br. J. Oral Maxillofac. Surg. **46**(1), 38–41 (2008)
39. Wichmann, F.A., Sharpe, L.T., Gegenfurtner, K.R.: The contributions of color to recognition memory for natural scenes. J. Exp. Psychol. Learn. Mem. Cognit. **28**(3), 509 (2002)
40. Lee, K., Joshi, K.: Examining the use of status quo bias perspective in IS research: need for re-conceptualizing and incorporating biases. Inf. Syst. J. **27**(6), 733–752 (2017)
41. Bedford, L.: The Art of Museum Exhibitions: How Story and Imagination Create Aesthetic Experiences. Routledge (2016)
42. North, A.C., Hargreaves, D.J., Krause, A.E.: Music and Consumer Behaviour. Oxford University Press, Oxford (2009)
43. Daniel, K.: Thinking, Fast and Slow. Macmillan, New York (2011)
44. North, A.C., Sheridan, L.P., Areni, C.S.: Music congruity effects on product memory, perception, and choice. J. Retail. **92**(1), 83–95 (2016)
45. Ranasinghe, N., Jain, P., Thi Ngoc Tram, N., et al.: Season traveller: multisensory narration for enhancing the virtual reality experience. In: Proceedings of the 2018 CHI Conference on Human Factors in Computing Systems (2018)
46. Halabi, O., Saleh, M.: Augmented reality flavor: cross-modal mapping across gustation, olfaction, and vision. Multimedia Tools Appl. **80**(30), 36423–36441 (2021). https://doi.org/10.1007/s11042-021-11321-0

Information Governance and Ethics

Research with User-Generated Book Review Data: Legal and Ethical Pitfalls and Contextualized Mitigations

Yuerong Hu(✉), Glen Layne-Worthey, Alaine Martaus, J. Stephen Downie, and Jana Diesner

School of Information Sciences, University of Illinois Urbana-Champaign, Champaign, USA
{yuerong2,gworthey,martaus2,jdownie,jdiesner}@illinois.edu

Abstract. The growing quantity of user-generated book reviews has opened up unprecedented opportunities for empirical research on books, reading, and readership. While there is an abundance of literature addressing the legal and ethical use of user-generated and social media data in general, for user-generated book reviews, such discussions have been mostly absent. From a library and information sciences perspective, user-generated book reviews can pose novel challenges because each book reviewer may simultaneously be (1) a presumably anonymous and safe online user; and, (2) an identifiable reader who can suffer real harm, e.g., cyber doxing and personal attack. This user/reader duality can create conflicting recommendations regarding which legal or ethical guidelines to follow. According to our review, potential legal issues include copyright infringement and violations of terms of service/end-user license agreements and privacy rights, while ethical concerns are centered on users' expectations, informed consent, and institutional reviews. This paper reviews (1) potential legal and ethical pitfalls in leveraging user-generated book reviews; and, (2) professional and scholarly references that might serve as useful guidelines to avoid or manage these pitfalls.

Keywords: Book reviews · Digital humanities · Scholarly communication · User-generated content · Social computing · Responsible data science

1 Background and Introduction

Reading is one of the most ubiquitous activities in our daily lives. We have limited knowledge about historical everyday readers and their reading behavior due to a lack of records left by or collected from them [108]. In the last two decades, the increasing availability of user-generated book reviews from online sources[1]

[1] In the context of this paper, user-generated book reviews include not only actual book reviews but also numerical ratings, crowdsourced tags, user-curated book lists, virtual collections of books, graphic content, etc.

© The Author(s), under exclusive license to Springer Nature Switzerland AG 2023
I. Sserwanga et al. (Eds.): iConference 2023, LNCS 13971, pp. 163–186, 2023.
https://doi.org/10.1007/978-3-031-28035-1_13

has opened up unprecedented opportunities for computational and empirical research on readerships and everyday reading behavior. Scholars from different fields, e.g., library science, digital humanities, communication studies, and natural language processing, have leveraged such data to examine a variety of topics, such as review classification, social network analyses of readers, impact assessment and sales prediction of books [20,64,69,80,85,99,150,152,163]. With the evolution of book review studies, challenges and limitations have also emerged, ranging from disciplinary divergences (such as reader-orientated theories vs. book-centric models [31,66]) to limitations of the scholarly usability of review corpora (such as review credibility and inclusiveness [66,67,70,73,115,118,168]). This paper asks another insufficiently discussed question that has yet to be fully explored in prior empirical and computational studies of user-generated book reviews: How to best use online book reviews for scholarly research from legal, ethical, and compliance perspectives?

This paper is motivated by two factors: First, while the ethical use of user-generated content and social media data for research purposes has been critically discussed [33,34,46,107,168], contextualized investigations of specific genres remain very much in need. As Crawford and Finn have pointed out, "*social and mobile datasets have limitations that, if not sufficiently understood and accounted for, can produce specific kinds of analytical and ethical oversights*" [29]. In their own research on crisis data, they demonstrated the necessity and potential of this research direction by critically examining (1) what crisis data actually represents; and, (2) how these data were used in crisis research [29]. Other studies that focused on specific datasets and use cases have also shed light on specific research challenges and responsibilities by examining ethical issues that stem from work in specific domains or research contexts [22,35,37,48,50,98].

Following these exemplary studies, we propose to scrutinize the challenge of legal, ethical, and compliant research conduct in the context of user-generated book reviews. We argue for a deeper engagement with these datasets because of the dual role that many book reviewers play as (1) social media producers and content consumers; and, (2) readers. When people voluntarily post book reviews, they also reveal aspects of their reading history, whether they are aware of that or not. As a result, user-generated book reviews, like most social media data, may contain directly or indirectly personally identifiable information[2] [10]. At the same time, similar to library patron data, user-generated book reviews record activities and thoughts that are protected as part of people's intellectual freedom and valuable contributions to the diversity of viewpoints in society [8]. For instance, online book reviewers might express opinions, values, and beliefs, which can be vehement, controversial, or even illegal (e.g., acquiring and reading banned books). Reviewers may also share personal experiences, information about their physical and mental health, and their socio-demographic identities. These types of sensitive information lead to concerns about the legitimacy and ethics of using such data in scholarly research.

[2] For example, book reviews may contain user names that overlap with real names, email addresses, identifying parts of addresses, or workplaces.

Second, we examine the usage of book reviews to further minimize potential risks for reviewers and researchers. In order to ensure library patrons' freedom to read, an unfettered exchange of ideas, and equal access to diverse materials and services, library professionals have long protested against policies that would harm the confidentiality of their patrons' data (e.g., search records, book loans, reference interviews) [6–9,77,78,134]. In practice, many libraries regularly remove circulation records and decline to keep certain patron data in order to protect their patron's privacy from "irresistible government requests" [43,90]. For similar reasons, book reviewers' reading records and opinions also need protection because reviews might be subject to censorship and could be used against those reviewers. However, online book reviews have not been protected or managed like library patron data, possibly because they have not been conceptualized in this way, but rather as reviews of consumer goods. This is problematic because censorship, trolling, scams, and harassment targeted at online book reviewers have increased [83,104]. Disliked online book reviews have led to cyber doxing and personal attacks on individual reviewers from book authors, translators, and the public, both online and offline, around the world [17,83,92,116,128]. For instance, in 2014, a teenage girl in the U.K. was tracked down and assaulted by an author because the girl had left a negative review about one of the author's books on Wattpad[3] [17,117]. Although this horrifying incident was an unexpected result of the review posting itself, without any research involved, researchers need to consider the potential for actual harm when designing their studies and reproducing (or even amplifying) potentially harmful content.

At the same time, researchers might be exposed to professional, institutional, and legal consequences of scraping and analyzing user-generated book reviews, such as copyright infringement, violations of policies and end-user license agreements (EULA)/terms of service (TOS),[4] and conflicts of interest with various stakeholders' policies. Most user-generated book reviews are considered copyrighted material and/or material governed by TOS/EULAs. Some platforms that make a profit with their user-generated book reviews have explicitly forbidden unauthorized third-party use of their data via TOS, which means researchers are expected to acknowledge the potential legal hazards that come with their accessing and using of reviews. Also, for research based on copyrighted data that is not subject to fair use, scholarly use of the data for non-commercial purposes or the public good does not serve as an exemption from the possibility of legal consequences. For example, the HathiTrust[5] was sued by The Authors

[3] Wattpad is a storytelling and social reading platform based in Canada [160].

[4] EULA is a contract between the licensor and the licensee, which establishes the licensee's right to use a proprietary product. TOS refers to a contract between a provider and a user which defines the rules that a user should follow in order to use a service. In our research contexts, we consider them interchangeable terms, as both of them specify the permissions and prohibitions for using the book review platforms' service, products, and/or data.

[5] The HathiTrust is a consortium of several hundred academic libraries that have collaborated (with scanning agencies like Google) to create a massive digital library [15,61].

Guild for copyright infringement because of the use of books scanned by Google [15], and the Internet Archive[6] was sued by major book publishers for "grossly" exceeding what libraries were permitted to do by providing "emergency" access to digital teaching materials during the COVID pandemic [57,146]. These cases are reminders that even for public institutions, it is difficult to manage the legal risks associated with their use of data. We conclude that researchers need to understand how they can access and use user-generated book reviews in ways that protect both their human research subjects and themselves from harm and risks.

Therefore, this paper examines the legitimacy and ethics of leveraging user-generated book reviews in scholarly research. We draw upon library standards and practices in addition to existing scholarly discussions to identify potential pitfalls and solutions. Specifically, we investigate (1) relevant laws; (2) platform policies; (3) user rights and expectations; and, (4) existing research on the ethical use of user-generated data at large. Here are the two primary questions we posit and how we analyze them:

1. **Question**: What does prior research say about compliance and ethical conduct of research that uses user-generated book reviews?
   Analysis: We review 100 research articles that feature empirical analyses of user-generated book review datasets and their creators/users. We collected these references as part of our empirical and computational research on book reviews [25,72,73,93,127].[7] The findings are presented in Sect. 2.
2. **Question**: What factors should researchers consider for assessing the appropriateness of their use of data while minimizing potential risks caused by their research?
   Analysis: We analyze a broader range of literature to understand the norms, regulations, and concerns for employing user-generated content (book reviews included) from the perspective of legislation, platform providers, users, and researchers. The analyses are presented in Sect. 3.

Then, in Sect. 4, we discuss the findings and limitations of our investigation. In Sect. 5, we summarize our research contributions and propose topics for future work. Due to variance in legislation, expectations, and norms for ethics and compliance across place, time, and disciplines, this paper does not provide a comprehensive review of prior research on user-generated book reviews, but is consciously situated primarily in a contemporary, U.S.-centric context. We invite readers to extend our approach to their own disciplinary and local contexts.

---

[6] The Internet Archive is a large digital library that preserves and provides digitized content to the public [154].

[7] Due to length constraints of this paper, we only discussed some of the articles that we reviewed for this paper. The full list of references is available at https://github.com/Yuerong2/iConference2023appendix/blob/main/iconference2023referencesAppendix.pdf. Our literature review is limited to empirical research on user-generated book reviews based on computational and/or qualitative methods. We did not consider theoretical work on user-generated book reviews without empirical data involved.

2 Literature Review of Computational and Empirical Studies that Use User-Generated Book Reviews

Existing research on user-generated book reviews has investigated a variety of datasets from different sources around the globe and in a variety of languages [115], such as reviews in Chinese [59,64,111,164,165], Dutch [19,86], and German [40,119]. Among these, book reviews in English obtained from Amazon, Goodreads, and LibraryThing [12,20,68,150,152,162,163][8] are most frequently used. Data leveraged include (1) actual review texts, crowdsourced tags, book ratings, rankings, and lists; (2) reviewers' public profiles and networks; (3) forum discussions and social media posts; and, (4) information about book sales and price [4,12,20,32,60,64,68,69,99,139,150,152,162,163].The scale and granularity of previously compiled and referenced datasets vary drastically, ranging from hundreds to millions of records [4,60,115,124,130,152]. For instance, Wan and colleagues scraped 1,378,033 English book reviews for spoiler detection [152], while Tan and He qualitatively compared 200 book reviews in Chinese and English as part of a multi-method analysis on cross-cultural reception [130].

These book review datasets have enabled computational and empirical research in various disciplines, including library and information sciences (LIS) [162,163], digital humanities and cultural analytics [20,85,150], computer supported cooperative work [12], social network analysis [99], computational linguistics [152], recommender systems and marketing [27,151], decision making [64,68,69], etc. In turn, each discipline has brought topics to the research. For instance, LIS scholars have studied reviews through the lenses of crowd cataloging and social tagging [16,24,97,139,149]; citation index and impact assessment [111,153,166,169]; and readers' social networks and activities [110,136–138,162]. Cultural historians and literary scholars have asked questions about the evolution of literary genres, the formation of literary canons, and reception of literary works [20,39,42,127,150]. Marketing, economics, and system scientists have examined the relationship between book reviews and book sales [27,64,99,129]. Natural language processing scholars and computational linguists have built models for review classification (e.g., fake, spoiler, and most helpful reviews) [50,68,141,152], sentiment analysis and opinion mining [69,96], and extracting narratives and relationships among characters [63,125]. Several taxonomies and conceptual frameworks have been proposed to map and synthesize prior work on user-generated book reviews [89,118].

Despite the differences between previously used datasets in terms of language, source, scale, and research topic, most datasets are collected via web scraping [26,75,150,152], using application programming interfaces (APIs) provided by the hosting platforms (for example, Goodreads used to provide an API, and

[8] Amazon (Amazon.com: Books) is currently the largest online bookseller worldwide. Goodreads is one of the dominant social reading and book review platforms based in the United States, with 90 million registered members as of 2019. LibraryThing is one of the most impactful social cataloging platforms based in the United States, with 2.6 million users as of 2021 [54,73,95,156–159].

Amazon web services (AWS) provides an API for individuals) [69,71,122,153, 169], or a combination of the two [36,99].[9] Robots.txt files are a server-side solution for determining what data can be accessed and how, and can inform web scraping efforts. APIs implement the rules for data collection that providers define for their service, and are therefore a recommendable solution for data gathering. Not all platforms provide APIs, however, because enabling research may not be part of a provider's business model or might conflict with their user agreements. For instance, Goodreads shut down its API for accessing book review data in 2020 and made large-scale data scraping difficult by restricting its webpage content (e.g., sorting reviews with its proprietary algorithms) [36, 150]. Given such implementations, data scraping is broadly adopted for data collection, although it might violate copyright and the EULA/TOS of a platform.

Legal risks and ethical concerns associated with book review scraping and related downstream tasks have been discussed before, but only in small numbers. One of the articles we reviewed mentioned copyright exemptions for research [114]. A few articles have discussed the acquisition of permissions for data collection [162,163] and attempts to request permissions [114] from the provider platforms. Considerations of human subjects research and institutional ethics review are also often absent.[10] Within publications of U.S.-based scholars, we only found two articles where consideration of and exemption from Institutional Review Board (IRB)[11] oversight was explicitly mentioned [12,102]. Relatedly, only a small number of articles explicitly discussed actions taken to protect the identities of the book reviewers, such as (1) removing user names and other user profile information that might reveal a reviewer's real-world identity (e.g., self-reported non-binary gender identities) [4,32,38,88,102,114,120,122,130], paraphrasing quoted reviews [20], and/or (2) not publishing the original data scraped, which might also violate copyright and EULAs [12,131,150]. In contrast, most research did not describe how researchers pre-processed potential personally identifiable information; such information might remain accessible in existing book review datasets [62,103].[12].

In conclusion, our literature review indicates a general absence of (1) informed consent from authors of book reviews; (2) permissions obtained from data sources; or (3) institutional ethics review in existing computational studies of

[9] In some publications, data collection methods are not explicitly specified, and general terms like "got", "collected", "downloaded" and "extracted" are used in lieu of providing more detailed collection method descriptions. [4,27,36,64,139].

[10] Such considerations might not apply to studies on user-generated data. We elaborate on this issue in Sect. 3.4.

[11] In the United States, an Institutional Review Board (IRB) is an administrative unit formally designated to review and monitor research activities using human research subjects. IRBs approve or disapprove research proposals prior to their initiation to ensure the rights and welfare of human research subjects [144].

[12] Due to copyright and perform restrictions, it is recommendable to share only unique key identifiers for collected data items instead of actual datasets such that other researchers can rehydrate the data, which bears the risk of collecting incomplete datasets [32,109].

user-generated book reviews. Discussions of legal and ethical risks associated with such practices were also largely absent. As discussed in the introduction, failure to consider these issues could pose risks to online users/readers, researchers, and academia alike. Therefore, we survey a broader range of literature and guidelines to fill this gap in legal and ethical considerations of the scholarly usage of user-generated book reviews.

3 Analysis and Findings

We analyze (1) relevant laws; (2) platform policies; (3) user rights and expectations; and, (4) researchers' discussion of ethical issues in user-generated data research. We combine our analysis with real-world and research cases, particularly studies on book reviews. Our findings are presented in the following four subsections. The four aspects we consider are not isolated; in practice, they intertwine with each other in complementary or sometimes conflicting ways (as exemplified in the following discussions). For example, some research aspects might be ethical but not legal, e.g., violating TOS to scrape publicly available book information, or legal but not ethical, for example, quoting snippets from identifying public information of vulnerable communities.

3.1 Legal Permissions and Risks

One primary legal risk associated with research based on user-generated book reviews comes from data scraping. Various data-scraping lawsuits have been initiated, claiming violations of TOS, copyright infringements, or unfair competition [15,57]. In this subsection, we consider cases in the U.S. as an example. Researchers from other jurisdictions should refer to the corresponding regulations that apply to their research scenarios. For U.S.-based studies, researchers should first consult the Copyright Law of the United States [143] and the fair use doctrine for risks associated with copyright infringement, and the Computer Fraud and Abuse Act (CFAA) [30] to minimize the risks of being sued. Fair use only conditionally permits unlicensed use of copyright-protected work under certain circumstances[13]. Scholarship and research activities are typically activities protected by the fair use doctrine [143], but a self-assessment of each use case and/or consultation with a copyright specialist can help to make responsible decisions.

For research based on large-scale scraped data [122,152], to reduce legal risks associated with copyrighted content, researchers may consider making

[13] The US copyright law demands consideration of four factors for determining whether fair use is applicable: purpose and character of the use; nature of the copyrighted work; amount and substantiality of the portion used; and the effect of the use upon the potential market for the copyrighted work. For research based on user-generated book reviews, the first two conditions of fair use may be less of a concern, but researchers should pay more attention to the third and fourth conditions.

transformative and non-consumptive use of the data[14], which has been increasingly adopted in computational studies of massive cultural data [79,113,123]. Furthermore, scholarly use of book review data might not fall under the concerns of the CFAA as the usage is non-commercial and for educational/research only [5]. However, it is essential for researchers to understand the CFAA and address other potential conflicts between their intended use of data and the provider platforms' policies (e.g., TOS/EULAs), which are discussed in the following subsections.

Second, researchers need to comply with laws that govern the use of personal data and privacy. In the U.S., applicable laws include privacy laws [3,82], state laws like the California Consumer Privacy Act (CCPA) [23], and state laws protecting the privacy of library records. Library records typically include online search records, circulation records, interlibrary loan records, personally identifiable uses of library materials and services, etc. Although no federal legislation or case law has been established to protect the privacy of library records, forty-eight states and the District of Columbia have established laws regarding the confidentiality of library records [7,90].[15] While accessing and presenting publicly accessible user-generated book reviews obtained from commercial websites is different from disclosing confidential user records held by libraries, both actions might expose individual reviewers' personal data to a third party or the public. Therefore, we advise researchers to check relevant laws on library records to understand legal requirements associated with library patron records and data alike.

Last but not least, researchers should note that user-generated content is often contributed by users from around the globe, regardless of where the platforms are based. For instance, while Goodreads is based in the U.S., its user base is global [122,140]. Therefore, researchers working on data collection from U.S.-based providers should examine international and regional regulations as well, such as The World Intellectual Property Organization (WIPO) Copyright Treaty [161], and Europe's Directive on Copyright in the Digital Single Market [135] and the General Data Protection Regulation (GDPR) [44], and China's Personal Information Protection Law (PIPL) [155]. This recommendation applies to research based in other areas of the world, too.

[14] "Transformative use" of the data alters original content to give it "new expression, meaning or message" [133]. "Non-consumptive use" refers to computer-assisted research, which has been found not to conflict with copyright holders' interests. For instance, in transformative and non-consumptive research, digital humanities scholars can conduct computational text analysis of millions of books (copyrighted books included) without actually reading or re-disseminating (i.e., without human "consumption" of) any expressive content of those books [113].

[15] It should be noted that "these state laws, however, are overridden or trumped by federal laws that allow federal agencies to seek library records" [21,90]. They vary by state, however, they reflect a consensus that library users' data are confidential and should only be disclosed under certain circumstances (e.g., with the user's informed consent, under a court order, etc.).

3.2 Policies and Guidelines Issued by Platforms Provider

Three types of documents from platform providers are most relevant for understanding the permitted use of book review data (any of them, or none, may be available): data access solutions provided by the platform (e.g., APIs, AWS), TOS/EULAs, and "robots.txt" files[16]. These files specify what and how data from these services can or cannot be used, among other things. For instance, the TOS of Goodreads [56][17] severely limit use of data to prevent inappropriate commercial competition, copyright infringement, and violations of user privacy rights. It states that the allowable use of Goodreads data does not include "*any use of data mining, robots, or similar data gathering and extraction tools*" [56] and restrict the data that people can access from their front page via review sorting algorithms and user-interface design [150]. In addition, Goodreads' robots.txt excludes a list of sitemaps and webpages from web scraping even though they are publicly accessible [55], and the site retired their API in 2020 [122]. Given these limitations, the next question for researchers might be: what are the consequences of scraping data from platforms that explicitly or implicitly prohibit scraping?

On one hand, researchers might argue for their use of data scraping or scraped data against the platforms' policies under certain conditions, e.g., when the research's "*benefits to society outweigh the harm of violating terms of service*" [145]. One important aspect in advocating for this position is to consider how "public" the scraped data are: while dominant social media platforms are likely to "*continue to push the boundaries on allowable methods to limit data scraping*", the Supreme Court's decisions on the case of hiQ Labs vs. LinkedIn signaled "*a shift in the way courts may be viewing attempts to restrict data scraping*" [53] in the U.S.[18] While heated debates on the implications of this verdict continue, a widely recognized takeaway for researchers is that scraping data that is publicly accessible without access control, such as passwords, paywalls, physical or technical barriers (e.g., software verification), is not necessarily unlawful, even if such scraping is prohibited by the platform's TOS/EULAs [14,49]. This verdict, to some extent, suggests that researchers are not doomed to be criminalized for scraping publicly accessible data without a platform's permission or against its policies. On the other hand, the legal and ethical consequences of violating TOS/EULAs in data collection for research purposes remain an open

[16] Robots.txt files are developed and used primarily to inform search engines and web scrapers whether data on a webpage is prohibited or permitted for harvesting. They are widely adopted by the websites to regulate scraping, although their prohibitions "*fall into a legal grey area*" [123].

[17] Accessed in August 2022.

[18] In this case, hiQ scraped publicly available user data from LinkedIn's website to supply its own business, in spite of LinkedIn's no-data-scraping policies, letters specifically addressed to hiQ, and technical measures enacted against hiQ. LinkedIn claimed that hiQ's scraping violated the CFAA, the Digital Millennium Copyright Act, and state trespass law, while hiQ denied these claims and asserted its right to scrape publicly accessible data [53].

question [46,145,148], as the feasibility and enforceability of platforms' TOS, particularly their prohibitions, are subject to further examination [5,28]. Existing research on the TOS of over a hundred global social media platforms found that "*though these provisions are very common, they are also ambiguous, inconsistent, and lack context*" and "*may reflect possibly conflicting values*" [3,46]. It is also important to note that platform policies might not align with the best interests of their users or researchers' ethical considerations [3,46].

In short, although there is no clear answer to "*whether researchers should be permitted to violate TOS when collecting data*" [46], a violation of TOS alone does not necessarily criminalize researchers' data scraping. In the U.S., current federal regulation does not enforce researchers to follow EULAs and does not criminalize scraping as a violation of the CFAA (although scraping might still violate copyright and privacy laws and regulations). Researchers whose plans for data scraping do not align with the platform policies are recommended to conduct a careful assessment of their use case. For instance, they should consider if the data to be scraped are publicly accessible, and they should avoid scraping from disallowed webpages/websites that are specified in robots.txt files/EULA/TOS. Finally, even if data collection procedures follow the requirements and guidelines of a platform, researchers also need to consider how to protect users, as EULAs/TOS do not necessarily align with the best interest of users [3,47].

3.3 User Rights and Expectations

Relevant laws and platform policies may fail to protect user rights or meet their privacy expectations: "*Users care about how their content can be used yet lack critical information*" [47]. Therefore researchers should assess how their planned work might conflict with the interests of users. To help with that, based on our literature review, we identified four potential pitfalls and approaches for avoiding them. First, a user's acceptance of TOS is not the same as their "informed consent" to any third-party use of their data. Prior surveys have shown that most users do not read the TOS they accept or consent to due to "*lack of choice, inaptitude, or habituation*" [18,105]. Meanwhile, without prior knowledge or additional information, it is beyond any individual user's capability to predict the third-party use of their data and potential hazards of that use. Therefore, responsible researchers should not assume that their use of user-generated data is within the expectations of the data creators simply due to their acceptance of a platform's TOS.

Second, researchers should not necessarily take publicly accessible data as "data open for use". This false assumption has led to various problems, such as re-identification of users in data shares and violations of user privacy [35,167,168]. There is a fundamental difference between (1) the data is public; and (2) the data has been consciously made public by users. The degree to which user (generated) data is public varies: some data are actively created and shared by users (e.g., book reviews that are set to be visible to all), while other data are passive traces automatically generated by algorithms based on user activities (e.g., location information based on IP addresses, time stamps associated with user activities, etc.) [65]. For the first case, some platforms, such as LibraryThing, allow users to set and alter the level of visibility of their contributed content (e.g., write a review that is public to all or kept to oneself) [94]. If reviewers explicitly choose to make their data public, researchers can assume that users are aware of their choice, even though they might not anticipate use cases beyond the visibility of the given site.[19] Even in this case and moreover in general, users might not be aware that their data is part of passive digital traces or is available for third-party use.

Third, using public user data does not free the researchers from responsibility to avoid accidental or inappropriate use of private information, even though it might have been the users who disclosed their private information in the first place. As mentioned, user-generated book reviews may disclose personally identifiable and other personal information [62,103,122]. Additionally, online book reviews may disclose the identities of people other than the reviewers themselves [94], including vulnerable groups of people who have no knowledge of or control over the existence of a review. For instance, in online book reviews of children's books, ages, gender identities, grades, and first names of children are frequently shared by adult reviewers [106]. Such information, when cross-referenced with reviewer profiles, can put a child's real-world identity at risk. Responsible researchers are advised to remove any personally identifying information from their datasets.

Fourth, ethical research should respect and protect the book reviewers' intellectual freedom and freedom of speech, both of which are particularly pertinent to the missions and values of LIS [112]. Book reviews may contain controversial opinions that may not only frustrate or irritate other readers but also unsettle the public at large [104]. Taking library practices in the U.S. as an example, as long as a review does not break any laws or TOS, a reviewer is entitled to "*write what they think*" and "*dispute ideas and words without limitation*" [94], even though others may oppose them. Such principles are debated among online book reviewers. For example, a group of book reviewers on Goodreads repeatedly gave one-star reviews to LGBTQIA+ books, sometimes even before the release of advanced copies or as part of book campaigns [126]. Many users consider such behavior to be trans- and homophobic actions targeting LGBTQIA+ groups and marginalized authors, and demanded moderation from Goodreads to remove these reviews [126]. However, Goodreads did not remove the ratings as requested because one-star ratings themselves did not directly violate any platform regulations (while personal attacks and hate speech, for example, would violate their guidelines) [41]. In controversial cases, researchers from different disciplines and cultural backgrounds could potentially approach the data in different ways, which may or may not align with the interests and expectations of either the users or the platforms involved. We are not in a position to question anyone's research priorities or personal stances; we simply remind researchers that every reader is entitled to their intellectual freedom

[19] However, in practice, it is difficult for researchers to verify whether the reviewers are indeed aware of the public accessibility of their data. Researchers should not make assumptions about users' awareness.

and freedom of speech, and that library professionals adhere to these principles [84,91]. Responsible researchers should stay alert to any personal biases and feelings toward different groups of reviewers. All users/readers should be equally protected from unexpected and unwanted surveillance, tracking, blaming, and attacks in scholarly research.

3.4 Discussions and Concerns from the Research Community

There have been various case studies, guidelines, and statements for how to conduct compliant, responsible, and ethical research on user-generated data in general and for specific genres [1,2,11,46,52,58,81,87,121,148], as well as more specialized discussions on this topic from LIS perspectives [13,100,101]. Here we zoom in on three topics that have been heatedly discussed: (1) explicit informed consent from human research subjects; (2) institutional/administrative review and approval; and (3) platform restrictions.

As for informed consent and institutional/administrative review, while some researchers argue that such conventional research practices should be applied to research on user-generated data from online sources [46,51,147], others disagree [74,87,147]. The latter group argues that scholarly research of such data may be exempt from informed consent under certain conditions, e.g., when it is almost impossible to obtain "retrospective" informed consent for archival research [87][20]; and when research projects involve "*no more than minimal risk to the subjects*" and "*could not practicably be carried out without the waiver or alteration*" [74]. Other researchers claim that institutional/administrative review and approval, such as IRBs in the U.S., tend to apply "*overly restrictive guidelines developed for biomedical research to lower risk studies*", and sometimes lack "*the expertise to effectively evaluate technical proposals*" [147]. They also argue that tensions between conventional requirements (such as IRBs) and social computing research could actually "*increase risks to participants, delay data collection, or substantively change a research project*" [147]. Furthermore, researchers' attitudes toward platform restrictions also diverge. For example, some researchers insist that the legitimacy and enforceability of TOS are questionable [46,148], which raises concerns about the legal consequences and ethics of either following or violating the TOS. So far, no consensus has been reached on these three topics with regard to the unobtrusive analysis of user-generated content [147], although opinions are converging on other aspects of ethical social computing, such as ensuring participants' access to the research outcomes [148].

Nevertheless, there exists consensus on the holism, contextuality, and complexity of the ethical conduct of research [45,167]. It has been broadly acknowledged that weighing potential harms and intended benefits for all stakeholders (e.g., users, platforms, and society at large) and mitigating different considerations are

[20] Kosinski and colleagues argue that no consent is needed and user-generated online data can be conceptualized as archival data if (1) users consciously made their data public; (2) data collected is anonymized; (3) researchers do not interact with participants; and, (4) no identifiable user information is published. [87].

hard [46,147]. We have consistently found such dilemmas and trade-offs in existing book review studies. For example, some studies de-identified reviewers by removing their original usernames and partial user profiles (e.g., location, gender identities) [4,122]. This makes reviewers less likely to be tracked down, although risks of re-identification remain [122,168]. However, such de-identification deprives the book reviewers of credit for their intellectual contributions and copyrighted work, to which they are entitled as content creators [22]. To overcome this limitation, some researchers choose to seek informed consent from book reviewers they intend to quote in their research publications, particularly as to whether the reviewers want to be quoted verbatim under their scraped usernames [12,150]. However, getting permission from individual reviewers requires personal contact with human research subjects, which means their data collection is no longer unobtrusive. For U.S.-based studies, unless an IRB review is conducted, this strategy would be considered risky and inappropriate[21]. Similar trade-offs have emerged from data publication as well. Some researchers chose to selectively publish their scraped data, or not to publish any of their scraped data at all, in order to protect reviewers' data from inappropriate use [122,150]. However, this raises questions about research reproducibility and transparency [76,132].

4 Discussion and Limitations

When planning responsible research projects, different factors and considerations might not align or conflict with each other in actual practice, leaving researchers with a number of dilemmas to solve and difficult decisions to make. For instance, as book review platforms often neither provide APIs nor permit scraping, researchers need to evaluate the risks associated with violating platform policies or even laws. Researchers are furthermore expected to honor readers' rights and expectations, which are crucial concepts that are not always prioritized by platforms' policies. There are trade-offs and risks associated with many decisions that have to be made by researchers. While researchers might not always be able to resolve them, they should minimize potential harm and make situation-specific decisions to guarantee that the benefits of their research to society outweigh the risks of potential problems. Institutional review and oversight, such as IRBs, share this goal, but they might not apply to working with archival and/or online data, such that researchers need not only to understand these risks, but also have the knowledge and skills to mitigate them. Although our research emphasizes legal risks and ethical problems

[21] Different IRBs might make different decisions on requests for exemption based on specific research proposals. For instance, we learned from our own research experience that analysis of publicly available and de-identified book review data without any interaction with the reviewers is mostly likely to be considered "Not Human Subjects Research" (NHSR) by the IRB at our home institution [142]. In this case, researchers who believe their work does not require IRB review or oversight should submit a request to their institution's IRB for a designation as Not Human Subjects Research. They might also consider asking for an Exempt Status determination, in which case they are performing Human Subjects research but are exempt from regular oversight.

associated with research on user-generated book reviews, by no means do we intend to discourage research with this genre or type of data. We rather hope to critically engage with this research area by contributing LIS perspectives and facilitating future research by flagging potential pitfalls and suggesting potential solutions.

Our investigation is limited in several ways. As we are neither law practitioners nor policymakers, we are not in a position to give legal advice. Besides, given the broad multidisciplinary reach of user-generated data research, discussions about our research questions remain controversial, without a clear consensus or cross-disciplinary norms. Most importantly, scientific research often comes with risks and uncertainties, and decisions should be made based on the specific context of a research problem. As there is no panacea for minimizing research risks or guaranteeing ethical practice, instead of crafting "guidelines for everyone", we synthesized prior relevant literature, case studies, and library practices to understand (1) what researchers should look out for; and (2) what they should leverage to guide and assess their scholarly usage of user-generated book review data. Second, given the breadth and multidisciplinarity of book review research, our scope of analysis was unavoidably yet necessarily narrowed down. For instance, we took a U.S.-centric perspective, and some of that might not apply to other regions of the world. Nevertheless, the U.S. context serves to contextualize and exemplify the complexities of the legal and ethical issues in book review studies, and provides a regional research case. As an overview, our research outlines the primary legal and ethical concerns about scholarly usage of user-generated book reviews, which are not limited to research based in the U.S.

Finally, while we put legal and ethical considerations forward as an insufficiently discussed problem in research practice of user-generated book reviews, these considerations are by no means overlooked in research at large. Instead, as our discussion shows, there exist plenty of generally applicable and insightful papers and guidelines to refer to. Thus, this paper calls for more attention to both (1) the paucity of scholarly discussions about legal and ethical concerns in book review research; and, (2) how researchers can leverage existing resources to address this particular problem.

5 Conclusions and Future Work

This paper presents an overview of legal risks and ethical concerns associated with scholarly usage of user-generated book reviews. Our review was primarily motivated by (1) the lack of attention to this problem in prior computational and empirical studies of user-generated book reviews; and, (2) the dual role of the users and readers who are subject to potential harm caused by scholarly use of their data. We reviewed relevant laws, platform policies, user expectations, and prior research to inform future researchers of potential legal and ethical pitfalls, and offer some suggestions for how to avoid them through practical solutions. We also drew on library practices and guidelines to better understand why and how researchers should protect data generated by users/readers. The pitfalls identified and discussed include copyright infringement, violations of TOS/EULAs, conflicts with user rights and expectations, and the role of informed consent and institutional reviews.

The intended contributions of this paper are threefold. First, given the dual role of online book reviewers as (1)content consumers and producers; and, (2) readers, we emphasized the significance of evaluating and reducing risks associated with scholarly usage of user-generated book reviews. Second, we analyzed legal and ethical concerns that have been under-investigated in the context of user-generated book reviews. We hope these insights help to inform future studies on how to reduce potential risks and better protect the users/readers. Third, under the overarching umbrella of responsible data-driven research, we demonstrated how to assess legal and ethical issues associated with the characteristics, stakeholders, and research contexts of book reviews.

For future work, there are more questions to scrutinize. First, there is a variety of data analyses on user-generated book reviews: some studies annotate individual book reviews word by word while others only map high-level patterns in corpora (e.g., average book ratings). Should different ethical expectations be applied to different use cases depending on the research scale, granularity, and "distance from the readers"? For instance, can researchers consider informed consent inapplicable for de-identified and paraphrased quotations or non-consumptive text mining of book reviews? To answer these questions, we need to examine more prior research to understand the needs and costs (e.g., time and administrative procedures) of different actions taken. There are also open questions from the perspective of libraries, such as the argument that libraries are losing competency as a result of their "hands off user data" practice, which sometimes limits their ability to serve their patrons [43,90]. Are user-generated book review datasets filling the gaps or taking advantage of libraries' "moral absence", and if so, where do researchers stand on this question? To explore this question, qualitative studies, such as interviews with researchers working with user-generated book reviews and/or questionnaires among online book reviewers, might be effective methods for gaining a nuanced understanding of different stakeholders' needs, expectations, and concerns. We also encourage collaborations among researchers from diverse communities and different cultures or regions to cross-examine and broaden our knowledge of this issue.

References

1. ACM Code 2018 Task Force: ACM code of ethics and professional conduct (2018). https://www.acm.org/code-of-ethics
2. ACM Technology Policy Council, ACM Europe Technology Policy Committee and ACM US Technology Policy Council: Statement on principles for responsible algorithmic systems (2022). https://www.acm.org/binaries/content/assets/public-policy/final-joint-ai-statement-update.pdf
3. Acquisti, A., Brandimarte, L., Loewenstein, G.: Privacy and human behavior in the age of information. Science **347**(6221), 509–514 (2015)

4. Albrechtslund, A.M.B.: Negotiating ownership and agency in social media: community reactions to amazon's acquisition of Goodreads. First Monday (2017)
5. American Civil Liberties Union: Federal court rules 'big data' discrimination studies do not violate federal anti-hacking law (2020). https://www.aclu.org/press-releases/federal-court-rules-big-data-discrimination-studies-do-not-violate-federal-anti
6. American Library Association: The USA patriot act (2009). https://www.ala.org/ala/washoff/WOissues/civilliberties/theusapatriotact/usapatriotact.htm
7. American Library Association: Intellectual freedom: issues and resources (2017). https://www.ala.org/advocacy/intfreedom
8. American Library Association: Ala statement on book censorship (2021). https://www.ala.org/advocacy/statement-regarding-censorship
9. American Library Association: State privacy laws regarding library records (2021). https://www.ala.org/advocacy/privacy/statelaws
10. American Library Association Council: Policy concerning confidentiality of personally identifiable information about library users (1991). https://www.ala.org/advocacy/intfreedom/statementspols/otherpolicies/policyconcerning
11. Annette Markham and Elizabeth Buchanan: Ethical decision-making and internet research: recommendations from the AoIR ethics working committee (version 2.0) (2012). https://aoir.org/reports/ethics2.pdf
12. Antoniak, M., Walsh, M., Mimno, D.: Tags, borders, and catalogs: social re-working of genre on librarything. Proc. ACM Hum.-Comput. Interact. **5**(CSCW1), 1–29 (2021)
13. Asher, A., et al.: Ethics in research use of library patron data: glossary and explainer (2018). https://doi.org/10.17605/OSF.IO/XFKZ6
14. Association for Computing Machinery: Scraping by: reconsidering law & technology for online data collection - 19 May 2022 (2022). https://www.acm.org/public-policy/ustpc/hottopics/online-data-collection
15. Band, J.: LCA comments on authors guild v. hathitrust decision (2012). https://www.arl.org/news/lca-comments-on-authors-guild-v-hathitrust-decision/
16. Bartley, P.: Book tagging on LibraryThing: how, why, and what are in the tags? Proc. Am. Soc. Inf. Sci. Technol. **46**(1), 1–22 (2009)
17. BBC News: Author Richard Brittain attacked reviewer with bottle (2015). https://www.bbc.com/news/uk-scotland-edinburgh-east-fife-34775814
18. Böhme, R., Köpsell, S.: Trained to accept? A field experiment on consent dialogs. In: Proceedings of the SIGCHI Conference on Human Factors in Computing Systems, pp. 2403–2406 (2010)
19. Boot, P., Koolen, M.: Captivating, splendid or instructive?: assessing the impact of reading in online book reviews. Sci. Study Lit. **10**(1), 35–63 (2020)
20. Bourrier, K., Thelwall, M.: The social lives of books: reading Victorian literature on goodreads. J. Cult. Anal. **1**(1), 12049 (2020)
21. Bowers, S.L.: Privacy and library records. J. Acad. Librariansh. **32**(4), 377–383 (2006)
22. Bruckman, A.: Studying the amateur artist: a perspective on disguising data collected in human subjects research on the internet. Ethics Inf. Technol. **4**(3), 217–231 (2002)
23. California Legislative Information: Title 1.81.5. California consumer privacy act of 2018 (2018). https://leginfo.legislature.ca.gov/faces/codes_displayText.xhtml?division=3.&part=4.&lawCode=CIV&title=1.81.5

24. Carman, N.: LibraryThing tags and Library of Congress Subject Headings: A comparison of science fiction and fantasy works. School of Information Management at Victoria University of Wellington (2009)
25. Chang, K., et al.: Book reviews and the consolidation of genre. In: DH2020 (ADHO) Proceedings (2020). http://dx.doi.org/10.17613/02q2-1v27
26. Chen, P.Y., Dhanasobhon, S., Smith, M.D.: All reviews are not created equal: the disaggregate impact of reviews and reviewers at amazon.com (2008)
27. Chevalier, J.A., Mayzlin, D.: The effect of word of mouth on sales: online book reviews. J. Mark. Res. **43**(3), 345–354 (2006)
28. Court of Appeal, Second District, Division 3, California.: Long v. Provide Commerce Inc (2016). https://caselaw.findlaw.com/ca-court-of-appeal/1729412.html
29. Crawford, K., Finn, M.: The limits of crisis data: analytical and ethical challenges of using social and mobile data to understand disasters. GeoJournal **80**(4), 491–502 (2015)
30. Computer Crime and Intellectual Property Section Criminal Division: Prosecuting computer crimes manual (2010). https://www.justice.gov/criminal/file/442156/download
31. Dai, L.: From the history of the book to the history of reading: theories and methods for historical studies of reading. Xinxing (2017)
32. De Greve, L., Martens, G.: # bookstagram and beyond: the presence and depiction of the Bachmann literary prize on social media (2007–2017). Digit. Humanit. Benelux J. **3**, 81–102 (2021)
33. Diesner, J., Chin, C.: Seeing the forest for the trees: considering applicable types of regulation for the responsible collection and analysis of human centered data. In: Human-Centered Data Science (HCDS) Workshop at 19th ACM Conference on Computer-Supported Cooperative Work and Social Computing (2016)
34. Diesner, J., Chin, C.L.: Usable ethics: practical considerations for responsibly conducting research with social trace data. In: Proceedings of Beyond IRBs: Ethical Review Processes for Big Data Research (2015)
35. Diesner, J., Chin, C.L.: Gratis, libre, or something else? Regulations and misassumptions related to working with publicly available text data. In: Actes du Workshop on Ethics In Corpus Collection, Annotation & Application (ETHICA2), LREC, Portoroz, Slovénie (2016)
36. Dimitrov, S., Zamal, F., Piper, A., Ruths, D.: Goodreads versus amazon: the effect of decoupling book reviewing and book selling. In: Ninth International AAAI Conference on Web and Social Media (2015)
37. Drew, C.: Data science ethics in government. Philos. Trans. R. Soc. A Math. Phys. Eng. Sci. **374**(2083), 20160119 (2016)
38. Driscoll, B., Rehberg Sedo, D.: Faraway, so close: seeing the intimacy in goodreads reviews. Qual. Inq. **25**(3), 248–259 (2019)
39. Driscoll, B., Rehberg Sedo, D.: The transnational reception of bestselling books between Canada and Australia. Global Media Commun. **16**(2), 243–258 (2020)
40. Ehrmann, T., Schmale, H.: The hitchhiker's guide to the long tail: the influence of online-reviews and product recommendations on book sales-evidence from German online retailing. In: ICIS 2008 Proceedings, p. 157 (2008)
41. Ellis, D.: What charles and anti-charles reveal about goodreads homophobia (2020). https://bookriot.com/goodreads-homophobia/
42. English, J., Ungar, L., Dhakecha, R.H., Scott, E.: Mining goodreads (literary reception studies at scale) (2018). https://pricelab.sas.upenn.edu/projects/goodreads-project

43. Estabrook, L.S.: Sacred trust or competitive opportunity: using patron records. Libr. J. **121**(2), 48–49 (1996)
44. European Union (EU): Complete guide to GDPR (general data protection regulation) compliance (2016). https://gdpr.eu/
45. Fiesler, C.: Ethical considerations for research involving (speculative) public data. Proc. ACM Hum.-Comput. Interact. **3**(GROUP), 1–13 (2019)
46. Fiesler, C., Beard, N., Keegan, B.C.: No robots, spiders, or scrapers: legal and ethical regulation of data collection methods in social media terms of service. In: Proceedings of the International AAAI Conference on Web and Social Media, vol. 14, pp. 187–196 (2020)
47. Fiesler, C., Lampe, C., Bruckman, A.S.: Reality and perception of copyright terms of service for online content creation. In: Proceedings of the 19th ACM Conference on Computer-Supported Cooperative Work & Social Computing, pp. 1450–1461 (2016)
48. Fiesler, C., Proferes, N.: "Participant" perceptions of twitter research ethics. Soc. Media+ Soc. **4**(1), 2056305118763366 (2018)
49. Fiesler, C.: Law & ethics of scraping: what HiQ v Linkedin could mean for researchers violating TOS (2017). https://cfiesler.medium.com/law-ethics-of-scraping-what-hiq-v-linkedin-could-mean-for-researchers-violating-tos-787bd3322540
50. Fornaciari, T., Poesio, M.: Identifying fake amazon reviews as learning from crowds. In: Proceedings of the 14th Conference of the European Chapter of the Association for Computational Linguistics, pp. 279–287. Association for Computational Linguistics (2014)
51. Franzke, A.S., Bechmann, A., Zimmer, M., Ess, C.: Internet research ethics guidelines (IRE 3.0 6.1) (2019). https://aoir.org/reports/ethics3.pdf
52. Gilbert, E., Karahalios, K.: Understanding deja reviewers. In: Proceedings of the 2010 ACM Conference on Computer Supported Cooperative Work, pp. 225–228 (2010)
53. Goldfein, S., Keyte, J.: Big data, web 'scraping' and competition law: the debate continues. New York Law J. **258**(49), 1–3 (2017)
54. Goodreads: About goodreads (2022). https://www.goodreads.com/about/us
55. Goodreads: Goodreads robots.txt file (2022). https://www.goodreads.com/robots.txt
56. Goodreads: Terms of use (2022). https://www.goodreads.com/about/terms
57. Gray, J., Foong, C.: Publishers vs the internet archive: why the world's biggest online library is in court over digital book lending (2022). https://theconversation.com/publishers-vs-the-internet-archive-why-the-worlds-biggest-online-library-is-in-court-over-digital-book-lending-187166
58. Greene, D., Hoffmann, A.L., Stark, L.: Better, nicer, clearer, fairer: a critical assessment of the movement for ethical artificial intelligence and machine learning. In: Proceedings of the Annual Hawaii International Conference on System Sciences, pp. 2122–2131 (2019)
59. Guan, X., Li, Y., Gong, H., Sun, H., Zhou, C.: An improved SVM for book review sentiment polarity analysis. In: 2018 International Conference on Transportation Logistics, Information Communication, Smart City (TLICSC 2018). Atlantis Press (2018)
60. Hajibayova, L.: Investigation of goodreads' reviews: kakutanied, deceived or simply honest? J. Doc. **75**(3), 612–626 (2019)
61. HathiTrust Digital Library: Our digital library (2022). https://www.hathitrust.org/digital_library

62. He, R., McAuley, J.: Ups and downs: modeling the visual evolution of fashion trends with one-class collaborative filtering. In: Proceedings of the 25th International Conference on World Wide Web, pp. 507–517 (2016)
63. Holur, P., Shahsavari, S., Ebrahimzadeh, E., Tangherlini, T.R., Roychowdhury, V.: Modelling social readers: novel tools for addressing reception from online book reviews. Roy. Soc. Open Sci. **8**(12), 210797 (2021)
64. Hong, H., Xu, D., Xu, D., Wang, G.A., Fan, W.: An empirical study on the impact of online word-of-mouth sources on retail sales. Inf. Discov. Deliv. **45**(1), 30–35 (2017)
65. Howison, J., Wiggins, A., Crowston, K.: Validity issues in the use of social network analysis with digital trace data. J. Assoc. Inf. Syst. **12**(12), 2 (2011)
66. Howsam, L.: Old Books and New Histories: An Orientation to Studies in Book and Print Culture. University of Toronto Press, Toronto (2006)
67. Hu, N., Bose, I., Gao, Y., Liu, L.: Manipulation in digital word-of-mouth: a reality check for book reviews. Decis. Support Syst. **50**(3), 627–635 (2011)
68. Hu, N., Bose, I., Koh, N.S., Liu, L.: Manipulation of online reviews: an analysis of ratings, readability, and sentiments. Decis. Support Syst. **52**(3), 674–684 (2012)
69. Hu, N., Koh, N.S., Reddy, S.K.: Ratings lead you to the product, reviews help you clinch it? The mediating role of online review sentiments on product sales. Decis. Support Syst. **57**, 42–53 (2014)
70. Hu, N., Liu, L., Sambamurthy, V.: Fraud detection in online consumer reviews. Decis. Support Syst. **50**(3), 614–626 (2011)
71. Hu, N., Liu, L., Zhang, J.J.: Do online reviews affect product sales? The role of reviewer characteristics and temporal effects. Inf. Technol. Manag. **9**(3), 201–214 (2008)
72. Hu, Y.: Synthesizing digital libraries and digital humanities perspectives for illuminating under-investigated complexities associated with user-generated book reviews. In: Proceedings of the 22nd ACM/IEEE Joint Conference on Digital Libraries, pp. 1–2 (2022)
73. Hu, Y., LeBlanc, Z., Diesner, J., Underwood, T., Layne-Worthey, G., Downie, J.S.: Complexities associated with user-generated book reviews in digital libraries: temporal, cultural, and political case studies. In: Proceedings of the 22nd ACM/IEEE Joint Conference on Digital Libraries, pp. 1–12 (2022)
74. Hudson, J.M., Bruckman, A.: "Go away": participant objections to being studied and the ethics of chatroom research. Inf. Soc. **20**(2), 127–139 (2004)
75. Hui, N.: Content-specific ranking prediction for online reviews-case of douban book reviews. Manag. Rev. **33**(2), 176 (2021)
76. Hutton, L., Henderson, T.: Making social media research reproducible. In: Proceedings of the International AAAI Conference on Web and Social Media, vol. 9, pp. 2–7 (2015)
77. International Federation of Library Associations and Institutions: IFLA code of ethics for librarians and other information workers (full version) (2012). https://www.ifla.org/publications/ifla-code-of-ethics-for-librarians-and-other-information-workers-full-version/
78. International Federation of Library Associations and Institutions: IFLA statement on privacy in the library environment (2015). https://www.ifla.org/publications/ifla-statement-on-privacy-in-the-library-environment/
79. Jett, J., Cole, T., Maden, C., Downie, J.: The hathitrust research center workset ontology: a descriptive framework for non-consumptive research collections. J. Open Humanit. Data **2** (2016)

80. Jiang, M., Diesner, J.: Issue-focused documentaries versus other films: rating and type prediction based on user-authored reviews. In: Proceedings of the 27th ACM Conference on Hypertext and Social Media, pp. 225–230 (2016)
81. Jiang, M., Diesner, J.: Says who...? Identification of expert versus layman critics' reviews of documentary films. In: Proceedings of COLING 2016, the 26th International Conference on Computational Linguistics: Technical Papers, pp. 2122–2132 (2016)
82. Kaminski, M.: A recent renaissance in privacy law. Commun. ACM **63**(9), 24–27 (2020)
83. Kayla: Book chat: Authors being negative towards reviewers (2017). https://gracelingaccountantblog.wordpress.com/2017/12/06/book-chat-authors-being-negative-towards-reviewers/
84. Klinefelter, A.: Reader privacy in digital library collaborations: signs of commitment, opportunities for improvement. ISJLP **13**, 199 (2016)
85. Koolen, M., Neugarten, J., Boot, P.: 'This book makes me happy and sad and i love it'. a rule-based model for extracting reading impact from English book reviews. J. Comput. Literary Stud. **1**(1) (2022)
86. Koolena, M., Bootb, P., van Zundertb, J.J.: Online book reviews and the computational modelling of reading impact. In: Proceedings of Workshop on Computational Humanities Research (CHR), vol. 1613, p. 0073 (2020)
87. Kosinski, M., Matz, S.C., Gosling, S.D., Popov, V., Stillwell, D.: Facebook as a research tool for the social sciences: opportunities, challenges, ethical considerations, and practical guidelines. Am. Psychol. **70**(6), 543 (2015)
88. Kuijpers, M.M.: Bodily involvement in readers' online book reviews: applying text world theory to examine absorption in unprompted reader response. J. Lit. Semant. **51**(2), 111–129 (2022)
89. Kutzner, K., Petzold, K., Knackstedt, R.: Characterising social reading platforms-a taxonomy-based approach to structure the field. In: Proceedings of the 14th International Conference on Wirtschaftsinformatik (2019)
90. Lambert, A.D., Parker, M., Bashir, M.: Library patron privacy in jeopardy an analysis of the privacy policies of digital content vendors. Proc. Assoc. Inf. Sci. Technol. **52**(1), 1–9 (2015)
91. Lamdan, S.S.: Why library cards offer more privacy rights than proof of citizenship: librarian ethics and freedom of information act requestor policies. Gov. Inf. Q. **30**(2), 131–140 (2013)
92. Lanjinger: One-star reviewing bombing started from the truce (the diary of martín santomé) (orginally in Chinese) (2021). https://k.sina.com.cn/article_5617041192_14ecd3f280200135ul.html
93. Lavin, M.J., et al.: Cultural analytics and the book review: models, methods, and corpora. In: DH2020(ADHO) Proceedings (2020). https://dh2020.adho.org/wp-content/uploads/2020/07/516_CulturalAnalyticsandtheBookReviewModelsMethodsandCorpora.html
94. LibraryThing: Privacy policy, community rules, and terms of service (2020). https://www.librarything.com/privacy
95. LibraryThing: About librarything (2022). https://www.librarything.com/about
96. Lin, E., Fang, S., Wang, J.: Mining online book reviews for sentimental clustering. In: 2013 27th International Conference on Advanced Information Networking and Applications Workshops, pp. 179–184. IEEE (2013)
97. Lu, C., Park, J.R., Hu, X.: User tags versus expert-assigned subject terms: a comparison of librarything tags and library of congress subject headings. J. Inf. Sci. **36**(6), 763–779 (2010)

98. Lunnay, B., Borlagdan, J., McNaughton, D., Ward, P.: Ethical use of social media to facilitate qualitative research. Qual. Health Res. **25**(1), 99–109 (2015)
99. Maity, S.K., Panigrahi, A., Mukherjee, A.: Book reading behavior on goodreads can predict the amazon best sellers. In: Proceedings of the 2017 IEEE/ACM International Conference on Advances in Social Networks Analysis and Mining 2017, pp. 451–454 (2017)
100. Mannheimer, S., Pienta, A., Kirilova, D., Elman, C., Wutich, A.: Qualitative data sharing: data repositories and academic libraries as key partners in addressing challenges. Am. Behav. Sci. **63**(5), 643–664 (2019)
101. Mannheimer, S., Young, S.W., Rossmann, D.: On the ethics of social network research in libraries. J. Inf. Commun. Ethics Soc. (2016)
102. Martens, M., Balling, G., Higgason, K.A.: # booktokmademereadit: young adult reading communities across an international, sociotechnical landscape. Inf. Learn. Sci. (ahead-of-print) (2022)
103. McAuley, J., Targett, C., Shi, Q., Van Den Hengel, A.: Image-based recommendations on styles and substitutes. In: Proceedings of the 38th International ACM SIGIR Conference on Research and Development in Information Retrieval, pp. 43–52 (2015)
104. McCluskey, M.: Goodreads' problem with extortion scams and review bombing (2021). https://time.com/6078993/goodreads-review-bombing/
105. McDonald, A.M., Cranor, L.F.: The cost of reading privacy policies. ISJLP **4**, 543 (2008)
106. Mengting, W.: UCSD book graph: Goodreads datasets (2019). https://sites.google.com/eng.ucsd.edu/ucsdbookgraph/home
107. Metcalf, J., Crawford, K.: Where are human subjects in big data research? The emerging ethics divide. Big Data Soc. **3**(1), 2053951716650211 (2016)
108. Milligan, I.: The problem of history in the age of abundance (2016). http://hdl.handle.net/10012/11817
109. Mishra, S., Saini, A., Makki, R., Mehta, S., Haghighi, A., Mollahosseini, A.: Tweetnerd-end to end entity linking benchmark for tweets. arXiv preprint arXiv:2210.08129 (2022)
110. Nakamura, L.: "Words with friends": socially networked reading on goodreads. PMLA/Publ. Mod. Lang. Assoc. Am. **128**(1), 238–243 (2013)
111. Nan, X., Li, M., Shi, J.: Using altmetrics for assessing impact of highly-cited books in Chinese book citation index. Scientometrics **122**(3), 1651–1669 (2020)
112. Oltmann, S.M.: Intellectual freedom and freedom of speech: three theoretical perspectives. Libr. Q. **86**(2), 153–171 (2016)
113. Organisciak, P., Downie, J.S.: Research access to in-copyright texts in the humanities. In: Information and Knowledge Organisation in Digital Humanities, pp. 157–177. Routledge (2021)
114. Pianzola, F., Rebora, S., Lauer, G.: Wattpad as a resource for literary studies. quantitative and qualitative examples of the importance of digital social reading and readers' comments in the margins. PLoS ONE **15**(1), e0226708 (2020)
115. Pianzola, F., et al.: Books' impact in digital social reading: towards a conceptual and methodological framework. In: Digital Humanities 2022 Conference Abstracts, pp. 94–98 (2022). https://dh2022.dhii.asia/dh2022bookofabsts.pdf
116. Pinch, T.: Book reviewing for amazon.com: how socio-technical systems struggle to make less from more. In: Managing Overflow in Affluent Societies, pp. 80–99. Routledge (2012)
117. Reads with Rachel: Author attacks book reviewer |Richard Brittain | authors behaving badly (2022). https://www.youtube.com/watch?v=4Z5iIP8c5qs

118. Rebora, S., et al.: Digital humanities and digital social reading. Digit. Scholarsh. Humanit. **36**(Supplement_2), ii230–ii250 (2021)
119. Rebora, S., Messerli, T., Herrmann, J.B.: Towards a computational study of German book reviews. A comparison between emotion dictionaries and transfer learning in sentiment analysis. 8. Jahrestagung «Digital Humanities im deutschsprachigen Raum»(DhD), Potsdam, D. (2022)
120. Rebora, S., Pianzola, F.: A new research programme for reading research: analysing comments in the margins on wattpad. DigitCult-Sci. J. Digit. Cult. **3**(2), 19–36 (2018)
121. Rezapour, R., Diesner, J.: Classification and detection of micro-level impact of issue-focused documentary films based on reviews. In: Proceedings of the 2017 ACM Conference on Computer Supported Cooperative Work and Social Computing, pp. 1419–1431 (2017)
122. Sabri, N., Weber, I.: A global book reading dataset. Data **6**(8), 83 (2021)
123. Samberg, R.G., Hennesy, C.: Law and literacy in non-consumptive text mining: guiding researchers through the landscape of computational text analysis (2019)
124. Sen, S., Lerman, D.: Why are you telling me this? an examination into negative consumer reviews on the web. J. Interact. Mark. **21**(4), 76–94 (2007)
125. Shahsavari, S., et al.: An automated pipeline for character and relationship extraction from readers literary book reviews on goodreads.com. In: 12th ACM Conference on Web Science, pp. 277–286 (2020)
126. Sharma, R.: Black and LGBTQ+ authors say they're being harassed on goodreads and trolled with one-star book reviews (2021). https://inews.co.uk/culture/books/goodreadsbookreviewsblacklgbtq-authorsharrassedtrolled949179
127. Sharmaa, A., Hu, Y., Wu, P., Shang, W., Singhal, S., Underwood, T.: The rise and fall of genre differentiation in English-language fiction. In: DH2020 (ADHO) Proceedings, vol. 1613, p. 0073 (2020)
128. Sheila (Book Journey): When authors attack... (2011). https://bookjourney.net/2011/12/04/when-authors-attack/
129. Shen, X., Zhang, K.Z., Zhao, S.J.: Understanding information adoption in online review communities: the role of herd factors. In: 2014 47th Hawaii International Conference on System Sciences, pp. 604–613. IEEE (2014)
130. Shenglan, T., Haiqing, H., JIANG, L., Xu, Z., SELMAN, R.L.: Chinese and English reviews of a story about teenagers' struggles: a multi-method analysis of cultural differences in narrative interpretation. Beijing Int. Rev. Educ. **2**(3), 365–387 (2020)
131. Sourati Hassan Zadeh, Z., Sabri, N., Chamani, H., Bahrak, B.: Quantitative analysis of fanfictions' popularity. Soc. Netw. Anal. Mining **12**(1), 1–11 (2022)
132. Srivastava, A.K., Mishra, R.: Analyzing social media research: a data quality and research reproducibility perspective. IIM Kozhikode Soc. Manag. Rev. **12**(1), 39–49 (2021)
133. Supreme Court: Campbell v. acuff-rose music (92-1292), 510 U.S. 569 (1994). https://www.law.cornell.edu/supct/html/92-1292.ZS.html
134. Szkolar, D.: The USA patriot act: should your library have an official policy? (2013). https://ischool.syr.edu/the-usa-patriot-act-should-your-library-have-an-official-policy/
135. The European Parliament and the Council of the European Union: Directive (EU) 2019/790 of the European parliament and of the council of 17 April 2019 on copyright and related rights in the digital single market and amending directives 96/9/EC and 2001/29/EC (2019). https://eur-lex.europa.eu/legal-content/EN/TXT/HTML/?uri=CELEX:32019L0790&from=EN

136. Thelwall, M.: Book genre and author gender: romance > paranormal-romance to autobiography > memoir. J. Assoc. Inf. Sci. Technol. **68**(5), 1212–1223 (2017)
137. Thelwall, M.: Reader and author gender and genre in goodreads. J. Librariansh. Inf. Sci. **51**(2), 403–430 (2019)
138. Thelwall, M., Kousha, K.: Goodreads: a social network site for book readers. J. Am. Soc. Inf. Sci. **68**(4), 972–983 (2017)
139. Thomas, M., Caudle, D.M., Schmitz, C.: Trashy tags: problematic tags in librarything. New Library World (2010)
140. Slee, T.J.: Who is the average goodreads user? You'll be surprised! (2017). https://www.goodreads.com/author_blog_posts/14538341-who-is-the-average-goodreads-user-you-ll-be-surprised
141. Tsur, O., Rappoport, A.: Revrank: a fully unsupervised algorithm for selecting the most helpful book reviews. In: Proceedings of the International AAAI Conference on Web and Social Media, vol. 3 (2009)
142. University of Illinois Office for the Protection of Research Subjects: Decision trees (2022). https://oprs.research.illinois.edu/review-processes-checklists/decision-trees
143. US Copyright Office: Copyright law of the united states (title 17) (2021). https://www.copyright.gov/title17/
144. U.S. Food and Drug Administration: Institutional review boards frequently asked questions (1998). https://www.fda.gov/regulatory-information/search-fda-guidance-documents/institutional-review-boards-frequently-asked-questions
145. Vaccaro, K., Karahalios, K., Sandvig, C., Hamilton, K., Langbort, C.: Agree or cancel? Research and terms of service compliance. In: ACM CSCW Ethics Workshop: Ethics for Studying Sociotechnical Systems in a Big Data World (2015)
146. Verma, P.: The fight between authors and librarians tearing book lovers apart (2022). https://www.washingtonpost.com/technology/2022/07/25/internet-archive-digital-lending-lawsuit/
147. Vitak, J., Proferes, N., Shilton, K., Ashktorab, Z.: Ethics regulation in social computing research: examining the role of institutional review boards. J. Empir. Res. Hum. Res. Ethics **12**(5), 372–382 (2017)
148. Vitak, J., Shilton, K., Ashktorab, Z.: Beyond the belmont principles: ethical challenges, practices, and beliefs in the online data research community. In: Proceedings of the 19th ACM Conference on Computer-Supported Cooperative Work & Social Computing, pp. 941–953 (2016)
149. Voorbij, H.: The value of librarything tags for academic libraries. Online Inf. Rev. **36**(2), 196–217 (2012)
150. Walsh, M., Antoniak, M.: The goodreads 'classics': a computational study of readers, amazon, and crowdsourced amateur criticism. J. Cult. Anal. **4**, 243–287 (2021)
151. Wan, M., McAuley, J.J.: Item recommendation on monotonic behavior chains. In: Pera, S., Ekstrand, M.D., Amatriain, X., O'Donovan, J. (eds.) Proceedings of the 12th ACM Conference on Recommender Systems, RecSys 2018, Vancouver, BC, Canada, 2–7 October 2018, pp. 86–94. ACM (2018). https://doi.org/10.1145/3240323.3240369
152. Wan, M., Misra, R., Nakashole, N., McAuley, J.J.: Fine-grained spoiler detection from large-scale review corpora. In: Korhonen, A., Traum, D.R., Màrquez, L. (eds.) Proceedings of the 57th Conference of the Association for Computational Linguistics, ACL 2019, Florence, Italy, 28 July–2 August 2019, Volume 1: Long Papers, pp. 2605–2610. Association for Computational Linguistics (2019). https://doi.org/10.18653/v1/p19-1248

153. Wang, K., Liu, X., Han, Y.: Exploring goodreads reviews for book impact assessment. J. Informet. **13**(3), 874–886 (2019)
154. Wikipedia contributors: Internet archive. Wikipedia (2022). https://en.wikipedia.org/wiki/Internet_Archive
155. Wikipedia contributors: Personal information protection law of the people' s republic of china (2021). https://en.wikipedia.org/wiki/Personal_Information_Protection_Law_of_the_People%27s_Republic_of_China
156. Wikipedia contributors: Amazon books (2022). https://en.wikipedia.org/wiki/Amazon_Books
157. Wikipedia contributors: Amazon (company) (2022). https://en.wikipedia.org/wiki/Amazon_(company)
158. Wikipedia contributors: Goodreads (2022). https://en.wikipedia.org/wiki/Goodreads
159. Wikipedia contributors: Librarything (2022). https://en.wikipedia.org/wiki/LibraryThing
160. Wikipedia contributors: Wattpad (2022). https://en.wikipedia.org/wiki/Wattpad
161. World Intellectual Property Organization (WIPO): Wipo copyright treaty (1996). https://wipolex.wipo.int/en/text/295166
162. Worrall, A.: "like a real friendship": translation, coherence, and convergence of information values in librarything and goodreads. In: iConference 2015 Proceedings (2015)
163. Worrall, A.: "connections above and beyond": information, translation, and community boundaries in librarything and goodreads. J. Assoc. Inf. Sci. Technol. **70**(7), 742–753 (2019)
164. Zhang, C., Tong, T., Bu, Y.: Examining differences among book reviews from various online platforms. Online Inf. Rev. **43**(7), 1169–1187 (2019)
165. Zhou, Q., Zhang, C.: Relationship between scores and tags for Chinese books-in the case of douban book. J. Data Inf. Sci. **6**(4), 40 (2013)
166. Zhou, Q., Zhang, C., Zhao, S.X., Chen, B.: Measuring book impact based on the multi-granularity online review mining. Scientometrics **107**(3), 1435–1455 (2016). https://doi.org/10.1007/s11192-016-1930-5
167. Zimmer, M.: Addressing conceptual gaps in big data research ethics: an application of contextual integrity. Soc. Media+ Soc. **4**(2), 2056305118768300 (2018)
168. Zimmer, M.: "But the data is already public": on the ethics of research in Facebook. In: The Ethics of Information Technologies, pp. 229–241. Routledge (2020)
169. Zuccala, A.A., Verleysen, F.T., Cornacchia, R., Engels, T.C.: Altmetrics for the humanities: comparing goodreads reader ratings with citations to history books. Aslib J. Inf. Manag. (2015)

The Content Structure of Science Technology and Innovation Policy—Applying Co-word Analysis to Funding Calls in Colombia

Julián D. Cortés[1,2,3,4](✉) and María Catalina Ramírez-Cajiao[2]

[1] School of Management and Business, Universidad del Rosario, Bogotá, Colombia
julian.cortess@urosario.edu.co
[2] Engineering School, Universidad de Los Andes, Bogotá, Colombia
[3] School of Business, Woxsen University, Hyderabad, India
[4] Fudan Development Institute, Fudan University, Shanghai, China

Abstract. STIP (science, technology, and innovation policy/es) affect how rules, methods and practices are designed and applied to develop basic or applied research within national borders. Literature on STIP has been fertile in multiple streams, such as theoretical/conceptual frameworks for improving STIP. This study built on the literature stream by unveiling the underlying structure of STIP expressed in the key areas and research fields explicitly supported for the case of Colombia 2005–2018 via co-word network analysis. We empirically identify the changing STIP priorities between two government administrations. While government-A prioritized Physical Sciences and Life Sciences and gave room for bi-disciplinary field communities, government-B doubled Health Sciences presence and balanced the participation of all areas. Social Sciences and Humanities had transversal participation in research field clusters. There were three fields with the highest weighted degree in both governments: renewable energy, sustainability, and the environment; general agricultural and biological sciences; and general medicine. This study provides a novel view based on well-established techniques to empirically study the structure of STIP and the effect of the government agenda for managing national science, technology, and innovation capacities by providing direction through research-oriented funding and proposal calls.

Keywords: Research policy · Co-word analysis · Text mining · Scientometrics · Colombia

1 Introduction

Every government has its STIP (science-research-technology policy/ies) agenda. However, STIP priorities might change in every government transition. Thus, how to study its changing structure? In this study, we unveil the underlying structure of STIP expressed in the key disciplines/research areas explicitly supported for the case of Colombia 2005–2018 via co-word network analysis and discuss the STIP agenda redirection according to the change of government.

© The Author(s), under exclusive license to Springer Nature Switzerland AG 2023
I. Sserwanga et al. (Eds.): iConference 2023, LNCS 13971, pp. 187–196, 2023.
https://doi.org/10.1007/978-3-031-28035-1_14

STIP are complex processes and procedures within and outside the government that affect how rules, regulations, methods, practices, and guidelines are designed and applied for developing basic or applied research within national borders [33]. STIP, therefore, affects knowledge production [27]. Furthermore, NSTIS (national science, technology, and innovation systems) adapt themselves and their environment to changing socio-technological forces [5, 25, 26, 39]. The literature on STIP has been fertile in multiple streams, such as theoretical/conceptual frameworks for improving evaluation and its impact on NSTIS (and individual actors) performance [4, 19, 20].

For the case of middle-low income countries and Colombia, few specialized studies have explored the growth of China and the crucial role of firms in their NSTIS [21]. For Brazil, Ref. [1] argued that STIP, which incentivizes the acquisition of machinery-equipment, was more effective at stimulating innovation activities. For the concrete case of Colombia [36], recent findings argue—as consistent with the literature—that there is a positive and significant correlation between R&D investment and STI activities (e.g., numbers of national master's and Ph.D. programs, total scholarships, research groups, and the like).

Despite such a fruitful stream, this study addresses four factors that have not been examined with similar interest: i) the evolution of the STIP agenda structure at funding and proposal calls granularity; ii) its (re)direction according to the change of government; iii) in developing countries; iv) via informetrics techniques. Our findings could be of use by practitioners and policymakers in the private and public sectors as a technique to map the structure of the STIP changes and identify the national/regional supports for NSTIS actors and areas and research fields in the context of developing countries. After this introduction, we present the methodology. Then, we display the results, followed by the discussion and conclusion section.

2 Methodology

2.1 Materials

We search for the public archive of funding and proposal research-oriented calls available on the official website of the national institution in charge of '*formulate policies pertaining to their office, direct administrative activity and execute the law.*' [7, 8, 30]. In Colombia, such a role has been led by Colciencias, now: MinCiencias. The repository of funding and proposal calls has stored information since 2005. However, there is no standard metadata storage (e.g., some funding and proposal have specific objectives, disciplines/research areas supported, others do not). Therefore, we hand-curated the key information for each call by looking at the complete terms of reference. We omitted non-research-oriented funding and proposal calls (e.g., tax incentives, national research groups, or scientific journal assessments). In sum, we conducted the following process:

- Terms of reference documents were manually examined in strategic sections. The scanning focused on identifying the explicit mention of areas of research fields to be supported or fostered by the call (e.g., energy, environmental issues).
- Since key terms could be redundant (e.g., energy efficiency, energy transition), we standardized the funding and proposal calls key terms using the ASJC (All Science

Journal Classification) [37]. The ASJC is a standard system designed by Scopus to assign a serial title to single or multiple fields. There are 334 fields in five areas: physical sciences (contains ~31% of the fields), life sciences (~12%), health sciences (~37%), social sciences and humanities (~18%), and multidisciplinary. We standardized each key term by contrasting them with the ASJC (e.g., biotech, bio-inspired technology, was assigned to the ASJC field of *Biotechnology*).

- As expected, there were multiple key terms with no counterpart in the ASJC. For those cases, we searched in Scopus for the most cited/influential article on the key terms in its title and used the ASJC of the journal in which such an article was published. If a journal was assigned to multiple ASJC fields, all of them were considered.
- We excluded funding and proposal calls with less than two ASJC fields identified. Each funding and proposal call reflects at least a triad of fields.
- Due to the project's undergoing stage, we analyzed 2005–2018 period.

2.2 Method

We used co-word network analysis. This technique was initially proposed to visualize the *network structure of problems* [6]. Its uses have expanded to manifold research fields, such as management and strategic planning [11, 16], innovation studies [10, 15], consumer behavior [32], nanotechnology [31], and information sciences [13, 14]. However, to the authors' best knowledge, this approach is so far unexplored to study STIP. Here, we will use this appraisal to assemble an information-based network [40] with the strategic disciplines/research fields explicitly prioritized by the abovementioned funding and proposal calls.

Table 1 displays an example of assembling a co-word network. The column 'Key terms' correspond to the explicit key terms identified in the call document; columns 'ASJC field' to the ASJC field matched; column 'ASJC edge list' to the resulting edge list after processing the co-word of 'ASJC fields.' An edge list is a data structure representing a network as a list of its edges, i.e., links between connected nodes. In the edge list, column 'Weight' shows the frequency of co-occurrence of both nodes 'From' and 'To.' Finally, column 'ASJC co-word network' corresponds to the modeled network based on the edge list. We followed that process for the complete set of funding and proposal calls and their corresponding ASJC fields.

The result is an undirected and weighted network since a pair of ASJC research fields detected denotes a two-way relationship which can be of a higher weight if the pair have a higher frequency of co-occurrence [38]. We computed the weighted degree for each node, i.e., the number of edges of a node (field) pondered with the weight of each edge [2]. We used modularity appraisal for clustering and the ForceAtlas algorithm for network layout [2, 22]. The shape of each node reflects the field's area, bringing a disciplinary intra-composition to each cluster Table 3.

Table 1. ASJC co-word network

Key terms	ASJC field	ASJC edge list			ASJC co-occurrence network
		From	To	Weight	
Cultural processes	Museology History Archeology	Museology	History	1	Archeology Museology History
		Museology	Archeology	1	
		History	Archeology	1	

Source: Bastian et al. [2].

Table 2 displays the government changes timeline 2005–2018, modeled co-word networks according to each government period, and the number of funding and proposal calls analyzed by government and year. Colombian elected government term last four years. Governments A & B were re-elected. Government B suppressed re-election in 2015. Since the government transition takes place in August, we settled the starting period for each government in the following year. In sum, we could analyze six years of funding and proposal calls for government-A and eight for government-B.

Table 2. Timeline of co-word networks modeled according to government periods

Co-word network modeled	Network - 1						Network - 2							
Government periods	Government-A (2002-2010)						Government-B (2011-2018)							
Year	05	06	07	08	09	10	11	12	13	14	15	16	17	18
Colciencias-MinCiencias funding and proposal calls ***(n = 322)*** by government	14	40	34	23	9	13	18	32	15	NA	30	25	33	36
	133						189							

Source: Colciencias-MinCiencias [7, 30].

3 Results

Figures 1 and 2 display the networks modeled. Table 3 presents the network structural properties: # nodes (fields), clusters (% of nodes and color) and intra-cluster ASJC area composition. Government-A expressed 145 fields among its funding and proposal calls. Despite the dominance of Physical Sciences in the government-A funding and proposal calls, there is a diverse composition in the clusters formed. The most crowded cluster has a relatively balanced composition of all five ASJC areas, led by Life Sciences. Also,

Social Sciences and Humanities fields are consistently embedded in all five clusters, followed by Physical Sciences in four.

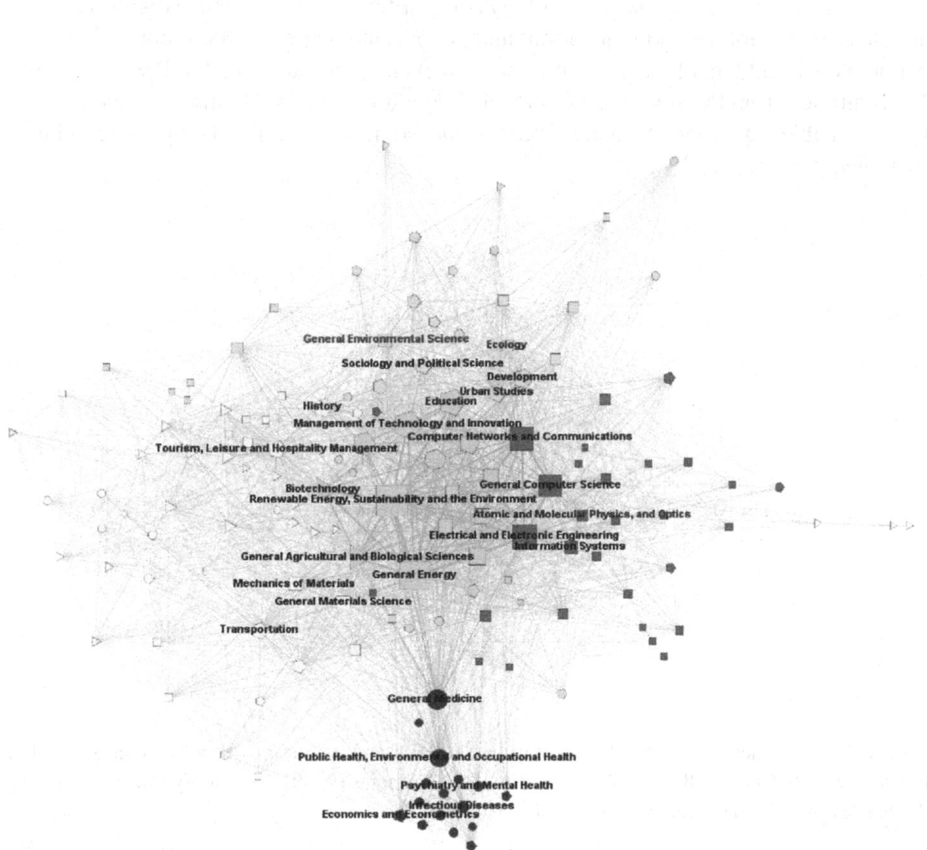

Fig. 1. Co-word network of funding and proposal calls and its composition by areas and fields government-A 2005–2010. Source: Colciencias-MinCiencias [7, 30]. Note: only top-5 nodes with the highest weighted degree by clusters are visible.

In contrast, Health and Life Sciences fields were present in three clusters. It also highlights the formation of two bi-disciplinary clusters: Physical Sciences-Social Sciences and Humanities; and Health Sciences-Social Sciences and Humanities. The nodes with the highest weighted degree by area were general medicine; general agricultural and biological sciences; renewable energy, sustainability, and the environment; and management of technology and innovation.

The co-word network of government-B holds considerable structural differences. First, it expressed 232 fields among its funding and proposal calls, +80 fields than government-A. All nodes were grouped in four instead of five clusters: a higher field community's definition. The composition of Life Sciences and Social Sciences and

Humanities is relatively stable. In contrast, Health Sciences composition almost doubled, while Physical Sciences decreased in ~6%. Also, the disciplinary composition is more balanced, e.g., no bi-disciplinary clusters found. The nodes with the highest weighted degree by area were renewable energy, sustainability, and the environment; general agricultural and biological sciences; sociology and political science—which displaced management of technology and innovation; and general medicine. Government-B deployed a more consistent (smaller dissension/clustering) and field-balanced STIP with a visible re-orientation from Physical Sciences towards Health Sciences. On the other hand, there was no visible sidelining of Social Sciences and Humanities; quite the opposite: it has a sustained presence in all clusters.

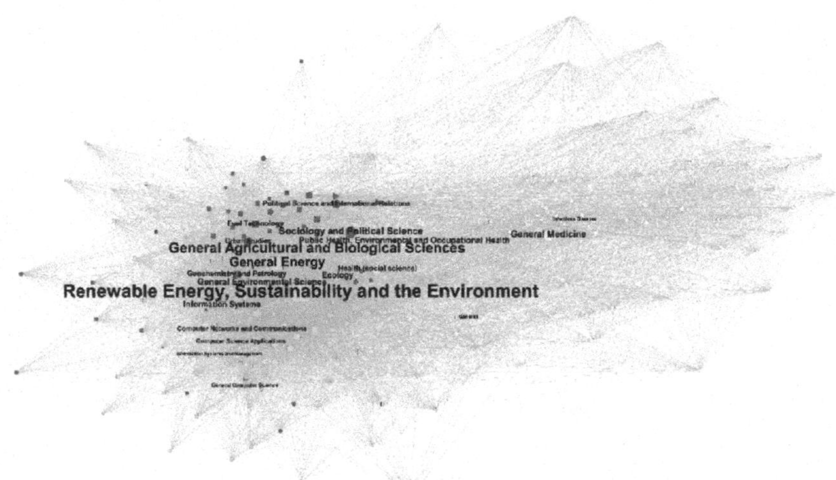

Fig. 2. Co-word network of funding and proposal calls and its composition by areas and fields government-B 2011–2018. Source: Colciencias-MinCiencias [7, 30]. Note: only top-5 nodes with the highest weighted degree by clusters are visible.

4 Discussion and Conclusion

This study provides a novel view based on well-established techniques to empirically study the structure of STIP and the effect of the government agenda for managing national science, technology and innovation capacities by providing direction through research-oriented funding and proposal calls. Our approach enriches the bi-direction of STIP stream on, first, theoretical/conceptual frameworks for improving evaluation and, second, STIP impact on NSTIS (and individual actors) performance [4, 19, 20]. Furthermore, applying co-word network analysis unveils the STIP changing structure and priorities in government transitions, helping policy-makers and the NSTIS actors, in general, to identify strategic fields to focus on and those sidelined.

Our second observation relies on the political spectrum (e.g., left, right) [3] of the two governments analyzed and how it reflected their priorities via STIP funding and

Table 3. Network structural properties.

		Clusters color - % of nodes	Health Sciences - ○	Life Sciences - △	Physical Sciences - □	Social Sciences & Humanities - ⬠	STEM ⬡
Government-A	#	~33%	3,40%	14,50%	9,00%	6,20%	
	nodes	~23%			17,90%	2,80%	
	145	~21%	8,30%			2,80%	
		~12%		1,40%	6,20%	3,40%	0,70%
		~11%	2,10%	1,40%	9,00%	11,00%	
		Total by area	13,80%	17,20%	42,10%	26,20%	0,70%
Government-B	#	~36%	1,30%	6,00%	16,40%	6,90%	0,40%
	nodes	~31%		1,30%	11,60%	5,20%	
	232	~18%	1,30%		6,50%	6,50%	
		~14%	23,70%	8,20%	1,30%	3,00%	
		Total general	26,30%	15,50%	35,80%	21,60%	0,40%

Source: the author based on Colciencias-MinCiencias [7, 30].

proposal calls. Government-A leaned towards right extremism, while government–B leaned towards centrism [18, 24]. Our context-based examination would tend to place a higher weight on Physical-Social Sciences for a right political spectrum government and Physical-Health Sciences for a centrism one. However, we acknowledge that this is undergoing field of work and the evidence provided here is scarce to reach such a conclusion. Just recently, a complete issue of the *ANNALS of the American Academy of Political and Social Science* dedicated a complete issue to the subject: *the politics of science* [28]. Further stages of our project will deal with the subject in more detail and the nascent theoretical framework and evidence.

Our findings also could be discussed in light of the literature on STIP-NSTIS path dependence [9, 17, 34]. Novel elements (e.g., government vision of science) should adapt and interlock with the existing conditions of both STIP-NSTIS. That is part of a self-reinforcing dynamic. For instance, if a new funding or proposal call is open to national institutions, STIP potentially supports current NSTIS capacities instead of a moon-shoot unreachable research endeavor (e.g., a Colombian particle accelerator), considering the current status of the local context. Factors explaining such a self-reinforcing dynamic are: i) the accumulation of experience, ii) the crystallization of expectations, iii) the widening circle of their diffusion, iv) the diffusion of the knowledge thereof, and of v) the actions predicated upon that knowledge. In that way, despite the evident changes in priorities for each government, the most connected fields in both networks did not change significantly. In other words, several features changed at the networks' meso (clusters) level. However, at the micro level, the research fields' path dependence was clear.

Our findings also partially contrast studies on the comparative scientific advantage of countries. Disciplinary specialization due to geographical, historical, and economic factors in Colombia orbits botany; agricultural and food sciences [29]; ecology; internal medicine; and surgery [35]. Such fields are similar to the most connected fields (general agricultural and biological sciences; general medicine). However, there is also a noticeable mismatch regarding other highly connected fields (renewable energy, sustainability, and the environment; sociology and political science) and areas (Physical Sciences). The decisive influence of the post-Millennium Development Goals (MDGs-2000) among the most connected fields could be partly explained by the changing institutional infrastructure modeled by the global development agenda [12].

The following stages of the project could integrate the effect of STIP funding and proposal calls into the (changing) trajectory of knowledge production—scientific articles or patents—and the scientific workforce capacities. Also, more robust network science methods, such as multilayer network analysis to include multiple network layers and aspects in a more comprehensive analytical framework [23], and controlling for other variables—(sub)continental research production by area/field—could enrich the insights here presented.

References

1. Avellar, A.P.M.D., Botelho, M.D.R.A.: Impact of innovation policies on small, medium and large Brazilian firms. Appl. Econ. **50**(55), 5979–5995 (2018). https://doi.org/10.1080/00036846.2018.1489109
2. Bastian, M. et al.: Gephi: an open source software for exploring and manipulating networks. In: International AAAI Conference on Weblogs and Social Media (2009)
3. Blazina, C.: Americans at ends of ideological spectrum are most active in U.S. politics. https://www.pewresearch.org/fact-tank/2022/01/05/americans-at-the-ends-of-the-ideological-spectrum-are-the-most-active-in-national-politics/. Accessed 15 Nov 2022
4. Borrás, S., Laatsit, M.: Towards system oriented innovation policy evaluation? Evidence from EU28 member states. Res. Policy. **48**(1), 312–321 (2019). https://doi.org/10.1016/j.respol.2018.08.020
5. Boswell, C., Smith, K.: Rethinking policy "impact": four models of research-policy relations. Palgrave Commun. **3**, 1 (2017). https://doi.org/10.1057/s41599-017-0042-z
6. Callon, M., et al.: From translations to problematic networks: an introduction to co-word analysis. Soc. Sci. Inf. **22**(2), 191–235 (1983). https://doi.org/10.1177/053901883022002003
7. Colciencias: Convocatorias. https://legadoweb.minciencias.gov.co/convocatorias. Accessed 05 Sept 2022
8. Constitución Política de Colombia: Capítulo 4 del Título 7 De los ministros y directores de los departamentos administrativos, Bogotá (1991)
9. Coombs, R., Hull, R.: Knowledge management practices' and path-dependency in innovation. Res. Policy. **27**(3), 237–253 (1998). https://doi.org/10.1016/S0048-7333(98)00036-5
10. Cortés-Sánchez, J.D.: Patents for all: a content analysis of an open-access dataset of Colombian patents 1930–2000. In: Pardo Martínez, C.I., Cotte Poveda, A., Fletscher Moreno, S.P. (eds.) Analysis of Science, Technology, and Innovation in Emerging Economies, pp. 65–93. Springer, Cham (2019). https://doi.org/10.1007/978-3-030-13578-2_4
11. Cortés, J.D.: Identifying the dissension in management and business research in Latin America and the Caribbean via co-word analysis. Scientometrics (2022). https://doi.org/10.1007/s11192-021-04259-5
12. Cortés, J.D. et al.: Innovation for sustainability in the Global South: bibliometric findings from management & business and STEM (science, technology, engineering and mathematics) fields in developing countries. Heliyon **7**(8), e07809 (2021). https://doi.org/10.1016/j.heliyon.2021.e07809

13. Cortés, J.D.: Journal titles and mission statements: Lexical structure, diversity, and readability in business, management and accounting research. J. Inf. Sci., 016555152110437 (2021). https://doi.org/10.1177/01655515211043707
14. Cortés, J.D.: Top, mid-tier, and predatory alike? The lexical structure of titles and abstracts of six business and management journals. Manag. Rev. Q., 1–20 (2021). https://doi.org/10.1007/s11301-021-00240-x
15. Cortés, J.D.: What is the mission of innovation?—Lexical structure, sentiment analysis, and cosine similarity of mission statements of research-knowledge intensive institutions. PLoS ONE **17**(8), 1–20 (2022). https://doi.org/10.1371/journal.pone.0267454
16. Cortés, J.D., Dueñas, J.: What is the Message of Mission Statements? Acad. Manag. Proc. **1**, 10083 (2022). https://doi.org/10.5465/AMBPP.2022.10083abstract
17. David, P.A.: Why are institutions the 'carriers of history'?: path dependence and the evolution of conventions, organizations and institutions. Struct. Chang. Econ. Dyn. **5**(2), 205–220 (1994). https://doi.org/10.1016/0954-349X(94)90002-7
18. Delaney, N.: "I believe in this generation": Juan Manuel Santos MC/MPA 1981 delivers 2019 HKS graduation address. https://www.hks.harvard.edu/faculty-research/policy-topics/public-leadership-management/i-believe-generation-juan-manuel-santos. Accessed 15 Nov 2022
19. Edler, J., et al.: The practice of evaluation in innovation policy in Europe. Res. Eval. **21**(3), 167–182 (2012). https://doi.org/10.1093/reseval/rvs014
20. Gök, A., Edler, J.: The use of behavioural additionality evaluation in innovation policy making. Res. Eval. **21**(4), 306–318 (2012). https://doi.org/10.1093/reseval/rvs015
21. Ito, A., et al.: Multi-level and multi-route innovation policies in China: a programme evaluation based on firm-level data. Millenn. Asia **8**(1), 78–107 (2017). https://doi.org/10.1177/0976399616686866
22. Jacomy, M., et al.: ForceAtlas2, a continuous graph layout algorithm for handy network visualization designed for the Gephi software. PLoS ONE **9**(6), e98679 (2014). https://doi.org/10.1371/journal.pone.0098679
23. Kivelä, M., et al.: Multilayer networks. J. Complex Netw. **2**(3), 203–271 (2014). https://doi.org/10.1093/comnet/cnu016
24. Kjsiu, B.: Las ideologías y movilizaciones políticas del uribismo y petrismo: dos Colombias distintas. http://unperiodico.unal.edu.co/pages/detail/las-ideologias-y-movilizaciones-politicas-del-uribismo-y-petrismo-dos-colombias-distintas/. Accessed 15 Nov 2022
25. Li, Y., Mao, J., Zhang, L., Wang, D., Shen, S., Huang, Y.: How scientific research incorporates policy: an examination using the case of China's science and technology evaluation system. Scientometrics (2022). https://doi.org/10.1007/s11192-021-04215-3
26. Louder, E., et al.: A synthesis of the frameworks available to guide evaluations of research impact at the interface of environmental science, policy and practice. Environ. Sci. Policy. **116**, 258–265 (2021). https://doi.org/10.1016/j.envsci.2020.12.006
27. Marginson, S.: What drives global science? The four competing narratives. Stud. High. Educ., 1–19 (2021). https://doi.org/10.1080/03075079.2021.1942822
28. Mervis, J.: Politics, science, and public attitudes: What we're learning, and why it matters. https://www.science.org/content/article/politics-science-and-public-attitudes-what-we-re-learning-and-why-it-matters. Accessed 15 Nov 2022
29. Miao, L., et al.: The latent structure of global scientific development. Nat. Hum. Behav. **6**(9), 1206–1217 (2022). https://doi.org/10.1038/s41562-022-01367-x
30. MinCiencias: Convocatorias, https://minciencias.gov.co/convocatorias/todas?page=97. Accessed 05 Sept 2022
31. Muñoz-Écija, T., Vargas-Quesada, B., Chinchilla-Rodríguez, Z.: Identification and visualization of the intellectual structure and the main research lines in nanoscience and nanotechnology at the worldwide level. J. Nanopart. Res. **19**(2), 1–25 (2017). https://doi.org/10.1007/s11051-016-3732-3

32. Muñoz-Leiva, F., et al.: An application of co-word analysis and bibliometric maps for detecting the most highlighting themes in the consumer behaviour research from a longitudinal perspective. Qual. Quant. **46**(4), 1077–1095 (2012). https://doi.org/10.1007/s11135-011-9565-3
33. Neal, H., et al.: Beyond Sputnik - U.S. Science Policy in the Twenty-First Century. University of Michigan Press, Ann Arbor (2008). https://doi.org/10.3998/MPUB.22958
34. North, D.C.: Institutions, Institutional Change and Economic Performance. Cambridge University Press, Cambridge (1990). https://doi.org/10.1017/cbo9780511808678
35. Observatorio Colombiano de Ciencia y Tecnología-OCyT: Atlas del Conocimiento. https://atlasdelconocimiento.ocyt.org.co/general/. Accessed 14 Sept 2022
36. Pardo Martínez, C.I., Cotte Poveda, A.: Science, technology, innovation, theory and evidence: the new institutionality in Colombia. Qual. Quant. **55**(3), 845–876 (2021). https://doi.org/10.1007/S11135-020-01032-3/TABLES/11
37. Scopus: What is the complete list of Scopus Subject Areas and All Science Journal Classification Codes (ASJC)? https://service.elsevier.com/app/answers/detail/a_id/15181/supporthub/scopus/. Accessed 10 Dec 2021
38. Scott, J.: Social Network Analysis - A Handbook. SAGE Publications Ltd., London (2009)
39. Shibayama, S., Baba, Y.: Impact-oriented science policies and scientific publication practices: the case of life sciences in Japan. Res. Policy **44**(4), 936–950 (2015). https://doi.org/10.1016/j.respol.2015.01.012
40. Yan, E., Ding, Y.: Scholarly network similarities: How bibliographic coupling networks, citation networks, cocitation networks, topical networks, coauthorship networks, and coword networks relate to each other. J. Am. Soc. Inf. Sci. Technol. **63**(7), 1313–1326 (2012). https://doi.org/10.1002/asi.22680

Measuring Users' Awareness of Content Recommendation Algorithm: A Survey on Douyin Users in Rural China

Shuyi Wei(✉) and Pu Yan

Department of Information Management, Peking University, Beijing, China
Weishuyi_mail@163.com

Abstract. Algorithms have penetrated into every aspect of our lives. While promoting the development of the digital economy, algorithms have also brought many problems. China is one of the first countries to introduce laws and regulations on recommendation algorithms to safeguard users' rights of independent choice in the digital information environment. In the policy context of algorithmic governance, we need more empirical research on algorithm awareness from the perspective of information users. This study focuses on Chinese rural users' content recommendation algorithm awareness on Douyin, a short-video platform. We triangulated survey and in-depth interviews to explore factors behind different levels of content recommendation algorithm awareness, as well as the link between content recommendation algorithm awareness and user experience, and users' attitude towards turning off the recommendation algorithm function, which has been listed in China's recent algorithm regulation as a required function that digital platforms have to provide to users. In this study, we constructed a multi-dimensional scale on algorithm awareness, and identified two types of factors that account for users' algorithm awareness: External and internal factors. We also proposed suggestions and counter-measures to improve users' algorithm awareness. Findings from this research have implications on the policymaking of algorithm governances in China and beyond, particularly, the research suggests regulatory directions for increasing the transparency of content recommendation algorithms and practical approaches to protect users' rights in shaping what they consume on a daily basis.

Keywords: Algorithm awareness · Content recommendation algorithm awareness · Recommendation algorithm · Digital divides · Douyin · Short-video platform

1 Introduction

1.1 The Rise of Algorithmically Driven Content Recommendation Systems

In recent years, the rapid development of the Internet accelerates the digitalization of various industries in China, and algorithms are becoming an important underlying architecture of Internet platforms. However, algorithms have also brought a series of problems

© The Author(s), under exclusive license to Springer Nature Switzerland AG 2023
I. Sserwanga et al. (Eds.): iConference 2023, LNCS 13971, pp. 197–220, 2023.
https://doi.org/10.1007/978-3-031-28035-1_15

such as algorithmic black boxes, information "filter bubbles", the lack of diverse social values, and the invasions of user privacy. Regulators of digital platforms are aiming to strengthen their research and policymaking on algorithm auditing [1]. As a result, the management and governance of algorithms have received increasing media attention and public scrutiny.

Algorithm governance has become an important issue for various countries and international organizations. The G20 and IEEE released their guidelines on artificial intelligence and algorithm ethics, the European Union also introduced regulatory frameworks such as GDPR (General Data Protection Regulation), DSA (Digital Services Act) and DMA (Digital Markets Act). China took the lead in introducing one of the world's first legislations on recommendation algorithm: the *Regulations on Recommendation algorithm for Internet Information Services*, which is considered as a comprehensive and systematic regulation of algorithm services.

Algorithms are increasingly involved in information users' everyday information seeking, search and sharing processes. Short-video platforms, which recommend personalized short videos to users using automatic personalization algorithms, have become one of the most popular social media platforms among the young generations and are important digital platforms for understanding the social impact of algorithmic recommendation technologies. As of December 2021, China has over 934 million short-video platform users [2]. Douyin is the largest short-video platform in China. As a short video community platform for all ages, users can browse other people's videos or make their own short videos on Douyin. The total number of its users has exceeded 800 million. Douyin users are highly engaging in interacting with the platform. The high engagement levels of users on short-video platforms mean that users have richer and more complex interactions with algorithms than users of other social media platforms. Algorithms are playing a key role in shaping information flows for Douyin users and also having a strong influence on how users engage and interact with algorithmically driven content recommendation systems. This paper addresses the important question of how users perceive algorithms by focusing on Douyin and users' awareness of content recommendation algorithm on Douyin.

1.2 A New Digital Divide?

The changing media environment, which is now increasingly shaped by algorithms as gatekeepers, might have differentiated consequences for various social groups. While the existing divide between the information-rich and information-poor users still exists in how users adopt, adapt and use information technologies, new forms of digital divides are appearing in how users engage and interact with algorithms in everyday contexts.

The concept of digital divide focuses on inequalities in the access, adoption, and use of digital technologies. Secondary and tertiary digital divides (adoption or use divide) shift the focus of digital divide research to the gap in Internet use skills and purposes between different groups [3, 4]. At the digital divide use level, the presence or absence of the awareness of algorithms and the strength of algorithm awareness become important differentiating factors: "People's awareness and understanding of the systems that operate behind-the-scenes to bring content to users" [5] is listed as one of the Internet skills [6].

In this study, we refer to this skill as algorithm awareness, which describes users' level of awareness of the existence, function, and impact of algorithms on a digital platform, and whether or not they are able to interact with algorithms consciously and critically. Existing research suggests that algorithm awareness can improve other Internet skills and overall information skills. However, this digital advantage is distributed differently across the population [7]. Therefore, algorithm awareness can be seen as a new and reinforcing dimension of the secondary and tertiary digital divides [7].

While empirical studies of the Chinese rural Internet have depicted a widening digital divide in China [8–10], it is unclear if the digital divides in the level of algorithm awareness also exist in China. Also missing from the literature is what social-economic or internet use factors could account for the users' variances in their level of algorithm awareness.

This study will combine quantitative and qualitative methods to examine the users' awareness of content recommendation algorithm among rural users of Douyin. Findings from this research will help to understand the dimensions, variances, and factors of algorithm awareness among Chinese short-video users. Three main research questions are raised: What are the factors influencing algorithm awareness? Does algorithm awareness have an impact on users' platform experience? Does algorithm awareness affect users' willingness to turn off features related to personalized recommendation algorithms? More importantly, by answering these research questions, this study can also help regulators, technology companies, researchers to explore how to build a better algorithmically driven media environment for Chinese Internet users and how to create a better future of algorithm governance that benefits both information rich and poor populations.

2 Literature Review and Research Questions

2.1 Algorithm Awareness as an Important Digital Skill

Recent research has begun to focus on people's understanding and adoption of algorithms, and "algorithms" are appearing more often in public discourses and academic research on digital divides. Hargittai et al. highlighted inequalities in Internet use skills and digital literacy. She argues that group differences in Internet use skills are evident in most online activities, from the types of content people seek and consume to the content materials they produce and share [11]. Algorithmic skill can be therefore viewed as an Internet skill [5]. Algorithmic skills are also referred to as algorithm awareness in other empirical studies. Algorithm-based applications are embedded in the daily lives of users, and how users interact with algorithms forms a new form of digital divide in the increasingly complex digital environment [12].

Scholars have also conducted a series of empirical studies to measure and compare users' algorithm awareness and algorithmic attitudes across different digital platforms. Most empirical research have focused on social media and news platforms. Studies have found that, surprisingly, more than half of Facebook users are unaware of the existence of Facebook news streaming algorithms [13]. Some scholars studied users' attitudes and perceptions of algorithmic news in Mainland China and found that 67% of users are aware of recommendation algorithms when using news platforms, but were unaware of the algorithmic rules [14]. This shows that there is a general lack of algorithm awareness and algorithmic knowledge among users of algorithmic platforms. Meanwhile, compared to social media or digital news platform, fewer studies have been conducted on the algorithm awareness of video platform users.

Users' algorithm awareness can be defined and measured, and some empirical studies on algorithmic cognition and attitudes have designed algorithmic attitude scales for users [7, 14], but few studies have systematically measured algorithm awareness. Zarouali et al. developed and validated the Algorithm Media Content Awareness (AMCA) [15], this scale includes four dimensions of algorithm awareness: Content filtering, Automated decision making, Human-algorithm interplay, and Ethical considerations. This scale is a reliable and valid tool for measuring users' algorithm awareness, which is tested on Facebook, YouTube, and Netflix. However, there are many different platforms using algorithms, and there is still much room for discussion on how to measure algorithm awareness.

2.2 Mechanisms for the Formation of Algorithm Awareness

What factors influence people's algorithm awareness? Based on the knowledge gap hypothesis [16] and digital divides theory, we argue that information inequality is associated with socioeconomic disadvantages (e.g., low education and income levels), which implies that more resourceful and more privileged social groups are better prepared to benefit from algorithms [17]. Researchers have found that differences in user attitudes toward algorithms are to some extent caused by the digital divides, with users who spent longer hours online, users with higher education, and higher media literacy levels are also the same group of users who are more aware of algorithmic logics and potential risks with algorithms [14].

While mobile devices are considered as internet leapfrogging technologies for developing countries, users who solely depend on mobile devices as internet access channels might be more disadvantaged than users who also have PCs to access the Internet. Studies have shown that people who use PCs to access the Internet have higher levels of user engagement, content creation, and information search than those who only use mobile devices, implying that the gap in knowledge and skills needed to use the Internet effectively increases with the proportion of people who are "mobile-only" [18]. Thus, the use of Internet access devices may also affect algorithm awareness.

Moreover, the level of "digital literacy", which is a key dimension of the secondary and tertiary digital divides, is found to be related to the capabilities of internet users to utilize digital technologies for capital-enhancing activities [19, 20]. Digital literacy is an important skill for everyday learning and working living in the digital era, and improving digital literacy is the key step to bridging the digital divide in Internet usage. Since algorithmic skills can be used as a new enhanced dimension of Internet skills, this study will add digital literacy to the discussion of factors influencing algorithm awareness.

Based on the above-mentioned empirical studies, this study hopes to describe the current status and influencing factors of algorithm awareness among rural users who use the short-video platform Douyin in China. The study of the factors influencing algorithm awareness will demonstrate user variances in algorithm awareness across different social groups and pinpoint which social groups are more likely to be in a disadvantaged position in terms of algorithm awareness. We propose the following research questions and hypotheses based on existing literature of digital divides and digital literacy.

RQ1: What are the main factors that influence users' algorithm awareness?
H1*: Socio-demographic factors are significantly and positively associated with users' algorithm awareness.*
H2*: Internet device access is related to users' algorithm awareness.*
H3*: Users' digital literacy is significantly and positively related to users' algorithm awareness.*

Researchers have pointed out that algorithms can be more easily understood through the perspective of users [17]. Based on this perspective, we need to focus on users' everyday experience and actual usage of algorithms. In a survey of Facebook users, it was found that after experiencing and being aware of the presence of algorithms, users strengthened their overall sense of control over Facebook's algorithms, and the extent to which users understand and experience algorithms may influence their attitudes toward using the platform [13]. Algorithm awareness guides users to envision, understand, and interact with algorithms [21]. Awareness of the presence of recommendation algorithms on online platforms may make users think more critically about the content they see, and users' algorithm awareness may help them make careful assessments of the platform and decide how to interact with algorithms [15]. An important insight from studies that center around users' everyday experiences with algorithms is that users' awareness of algorithms is a dynamic process, which might change while users interact with the algorithmic platform. Through understanding how users interact with platforms, researchers can also infer the level of user awareness of algorithms. Therefore, we are also interested in exploring the influence of users' daily interactions with algorithms on algorithmic awareness. We propose the following hypotheses that focus on user interactions with algorithms:

H4*: Users' experience and intensity of platform use are significantly and positively related to users' awareness of algorithms.*
H5*: The interaction behavior between users and algorithms is related to users' algorithm awareness.*

2.3 Algorithm Awareness and User Experience

Algorithm awareness can further help users to meet their personal needs in the algorithm society. Studies have shown that the understanding of algorithmic systems can increase users' motivation to use algorithmic platforms and users' trust in algorithms [22]. The level of user understanding of recommendation algorithms positively influences users' trust in and acceptance of the platform [23]. User satisfaction is the metric that is of interest to most digital platforms. Yet studies have found that users' satisfaction increases when the digital platform can explain the recommendation results to the user [24]. Users have a cognitive need for algorithmic recommendation mechanisms, and there is a strong link between user experience and the level of transparency of algorithms used by digital platforms [25]. Therefore, this study also focuses on the link between users' platform usage experience and algorithm awareness by asking a second research question.

RQ2: Does algorithm awareness influence users' experiences of the digital platform?

Nowadays, the collection, use, and storage of users' personal data is a mandatory condition for users to enjoy algorithmic services. Users should have the right to know what private data they give up in return for the services they received and make an informed decision on whether users want to reveal personal data to digital platforms [26]. The permanent retention of data has led to digital surveillance and large-scale collection of sensitive personal data [27], and the legal community has responded to the risk of personal information collection by private companies [26]. "The right to be forgotten" was first introduced in the GDPR to uphold the right of information subjects to demand that information controllers delete their personal information. In algorithmic governance, user rights are an important consideration, and we should also focus on this in algorithm awareness research.

We note that the algorithm regulation in China explicitly requires algorithmic service platforms to provide users with the option to turn off algorithmic recommendation services, and this regulation was originally set up to protect users' rights and interests. Technology companies such as Douyin has added a function that will allow users to turn off personalized content recommendations and personalized ad. This allows users to opt out of the recommendation algorithm service provided by Douyin with one click. However, it is unclear whether or not users are aware of the function or to what extent users feel empowered after using this function. This study hopes to investigate users' attitudes and practices regarding the algorithmic recommendation function from the perspective of their algorithm awareness, and therefore poses the third research question.

RQ3: Does algorithm awareness affect users' willingness to withdrawal from features related to personalized recommendation algorithms?

To date, algorithm awareness research mainly focuses on users' algorithmic cognition and attitude, user-algorithm interaction, and user rights in algorithmic society; previous research has extensively focused on traditional search engines, social networking sites, or news recommendation platforms, leaving popular digital platforms such as TikTok (or Douyin in China) unstudied. Meanwhile, although countries around the world are enhancing algorithmic governance to protect users' rights when engaging with algorithmically shaped content, very few studies have discussed algorithmic governance in the context of algorithm awareness. We believe that the understanding of the level of user awareness of algorithm will significantly contribute to the debate about and discussion of algorithm governance.

Findings from our research will have the following contributions: First, this study focuses on short-video platforms and investigates users' algorithm awareness and its influence mechanism by combining quantitative and qualitative approaches. We will contribute new findings about users' everyday experiences on short-video platforms. Second, we are also interested in exploring factors accounting for the levels of users' awareness of algorithms, including socio-economic factors, internet use, and users' engagement in digital platforms. Understanding the mechanisms of the shaping of algorithm awareness will contribute to the empirical research on digital divides, algorithmic divides, and algorithm literacy. Finally, our research will also test if algorithm awareness is related to users' sense of control in front of platform algorithms.

3 Methods

3.1 Quantitative Research Design

This study built an algorithm awareness framework and a scale to understand users' algorithm awareness. We build the scale of algorithm awareness based on AMCA and applied the new scale in the context of Douyin, an example of short-video platforms. We defined four dimensions of algorithm awareness for Douyin users, including a total of 14 questions (see Table 1).

The first dimension is users' awareness of personalized recommendation algorithms and content filtering. Compared to the AMCA framework, we added the users' independent judgment on the degree of algorithm awareness in this dimension. This dimension refers to users' awareness of the existence of the Douyin algorithm and its personalized recommendation and filtering features. Algorithm awareness should be based on users' knowledge of the algorithm for personalized content filtering, because this knowledge and awareness play an important role in changing users' choice of platform and behavior on the platform.

The second dimension is the awareness of algorithmic automation. Considering the difficulty of understanding, we condensed and simplified the AMCA question items. Algorithms are designed to implement human judgments in an efficient way, hence, user awareness of this automated judgment or decision-making process is an important step in understanding how algorithms shape the network environment [15].

The third dimension is user awareness of the human-algorithm interaction, which we have refined this dimension based on the characteristics of short-video platforms. The algorithm collects user information and presents the content on the platform through logical operations, so the user's behavior, the information provided and the algorithm's logical operations collaborate to produce the push content [28]. We argue that a sense of control, or the feeling that users can influence the algorithm's output through online behaviors is an important part of algorithm awareness. For example, Douyin users' interests may change over time, and if users do not know how to provide feedback or interact with the algorithm, they may not be able to reject receiving content that they are not interested in.

The fourth dimension is whether users are aware of the ethical issues related to the recommendation algorithm. Based on the literature review, we summarize the ethical privacy issues of algorithms into three dimensions, including the possible bias and discrimination of algorithms, algorithmic transparency from the users' perspective, and personal information security issues. As discussed earlier, the policies related to algorithm governance in China required technology companies to provide switch-off bottoms for users to opt out of content recommendation algorithms and protect users' rights to algorithm transparency. Therefore, we add questions about user-initiated privacy function settings as an extension to AMCA.

Table 1. Dimensions and questions of algorithm awareness

Dimensions	Questions
Personalized recommendation algorithms and content filtering	1. I've heard of Douyin algorithmic recommendation mechanism
	2. I understand how to influence Douyin algorithm
	3. The content I see on Douyin is pushed through the algorithm
	4. The Douyin algorithm makes the content seen by each person different
	5. The content recommended by the Douyin algorithm for me will be tailored to personal interests
Algorithmic automation	6. The algorithm automatically decides what content I see on Douyin
	7. When the algorithm decides what content I see on Douyin, no human judgment or intervention is required
Human-algorithm interaction	8. My various actions on Douyin (such as retweeting, liking, commenting, etc.) will affect the content I see on Douyin
	9. The information I provide to Douyin (such as gender, location) and my device information will affect what I see on Douyin
	10. I can adjust the content Douyin pushes by giving feedback to the platform about what I am interested in and what I am not interested in
Ethical privacy issues of the algorithm	11. I think Douyin should be more transparent in introducing the basic principles of its algorithm to users
	12. The algorithm's personalized approach to recommending content can exacerbate social inequality and bias
	13. Douyin's algorithm makes excessive use of personal data (such as age, gender, location, etc.), and I am worried that my personal information will be leaked
	14. I will actively turn off certain permissions that I don't think Douyin should have access to, such as access to location information, contacts, calendar, photo albums, etc.

Scholars have not yet agreed on the definition and measurement of digital literacy. We note that some scholars have categorized and used the type of online activity in the discussion of Internet skills and use in the secondary digital divide [29], and we measured digital literacy in terms of the type and frequency of users' online activities.

To explore users' awareness of the opt-out option required by the new algorithm governance policy in China, we demonstrated to users in the questionnaire that they could turn off the Douyin algorithmic recommendation feature and showed the steps to turn it off to those who were unaware of this feature. This part of survey questions is placed after the measurement of algorithm awareness and platform engagement. We hope to explore if users' awareness of algorithms is associated with the likelihood of opting out of content recommendation algorithms. Table 2 shows the important variables included in the questionnaire.

Table 2. Main variables included in the questionnaire.

Main variables	Type
Algorithm awareness	Likert scale
Digital literacy	Likert scale
Use experience	Continuous variable
Intensity of use	Continuous variable
Douyin feature usage (user interaction with algorithm)	Likert scale
Use experience	Likert scale
Demographic variables	
Gender	Categorical variables
Age	Continuous Variable
Marital status married	Categorical variables
Children	Categorical variables
Annual income	Continuous Variable
Career	Categorical variables
Education	Categorical variables
Permanent residence	Categorical variables
Whether to opt out of content recommendation algorithms	
Turn off the personalized content recommendation function	Categorical variables
Turn off the personalized ad recommendation function	Categorical variables

This study combines surveys and interviews to explore users' awareness of algorithms. The survey method was adopted to collect quantitative data. The sample was residents of X town, Du'an County, Hechi City, Guangxi Province, and the main respondents were residents over 18 years old who grew up or live in this area. Before sending out the survey, we ran a pilot study with a smaller sample of population. We then distributed the final survey questionnaire using a snowballing approach by sharing the questionnaire through two channels: WeChat and QQ. We set filter questions and test questions in the questionnaire, with the filter questions distinguishing between respondents who use Douyin and those who are non-users, and the test questions requiring respondents to select specific Likert scale dimensions to identify invalid responses and ensure the quality of survey data.

3.2 Qualitative Research Design

In order to gain a deeper understanding of the algorithm awareness of rural users of Douyin, this study also designed an interview outline based on the research questions and existing empirical research. The qualitative interview contains three aspects regarding algorithm on Douyin: algorithm awareness, user interaction, and user feedback.

We selected respondents who completed the survey questionnaire to participate in in-depth interviews. In the process of selecting interviewees, we ensured that the demographic backgrounds of respondents were diverse. We selected interviewees based on their levels of algorithmic literacy, experiences in using Douyin, whether or not they choose to turn off the personalized recommendation algorithm function, and whether or not they use Douyin to actively create content online. We invited six interviewees for the qualitative study and transcribed the interviews for in-depth analysis.

4 Results

4.1 Descriptive Analysis

A total of 377 valid questionnaires were collected in this study, and a total of 309 people had used Douyin (82%). The overall Cronbach's α of the questionnaire was 0.898, which was greater than 0.8 and close to 0.9, which indicates a satisfactory level of reliability. The reliability of the subscales ranged from 0.807 to 0.885, indicating high reliability of the questionnaire scale measurements.

4.2 Exploratory Factor Analysis of Algorithm Awareness

To understand the algorithm awareness of Douyin users, respondents were required to assess and score 14 statements about Douyin algorithms. This study examined the feasibility of the scale through Exploratory Factor Analysis and adjusted the scale accordingly. Before conducting the factor analysis, the Kaiser-Meyer-Olkin (KMO) was conducted, and the results showed a KMO of 0.837 and Bartlett's sphericity test of 0.000 for the probability of compatibility, indicating the suitability of the algorithm awareness scale for factor analysis. We selected principal component analysis and performed factor matrix rotation using the variance maximization method. The first four factors had factor eigenvalues greater than 1 and explained 61.348% of variances (see Table 3).

The results of the factor analysis differed somewhat from the expected framework, and we divided the scale of algorithm awareness into four factors (see Fig. 1). These were (1) awareness of the personalized content filtering characteristics of algorithms; (2) awareness of ethical privacy issues posed by algorithms, including concerns about personal data leakage, awareness of limiting algorithm permissions, and awareness that algorithms may exacerbate inequality and bias; (3) hearing about and understanding algorithms, including hearing about the Douyin algorithm and thinking they understand how to influence personalized information. (4) Awareness of the automated nature of the algorithm, is that the algorithm automates the pushing of content without human intervention.

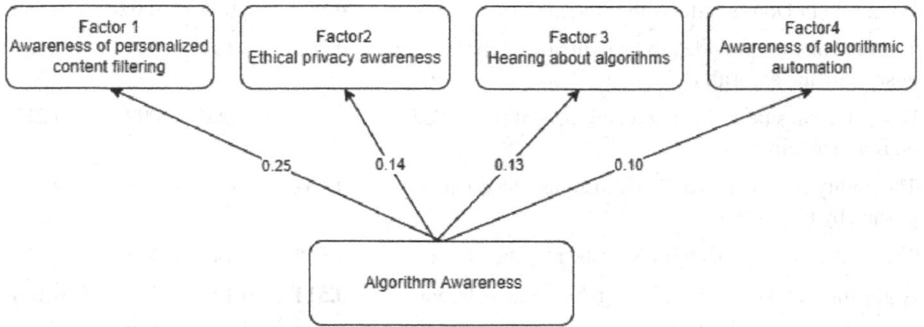

Fig. 1. Four factors of algorithm awareness

The proportion of variance contributions corresponding to each common factor was used as the weight coefficient to calculate and generate the new variable algorithm awareness composite score (AA_Score). The algorithm awareness composite score will be used as the main reference to measure users' algorithm awareness, and the higher the score, the higher the level of algorithm awareness. The formula for calculating the Algorithm awareness Score is as follows.

$$\begin{aligned} \text{AA\_Score} = {} & 25.091 \div 61.348 \times \text{FAC1} + 13.602 \div 61.348 \times \text{FAC1} + 12.552 \\ & \div 61.348 \times \text{FAC3} + 10.102 \div 61.348 \times \text{FAC4} \end{aligned}$$

4.3 Results Analysis

RQ1: What are the Factors Influencing Algorithm Awareness? From the results of the correlation analysis, it can be seen that the socio-demographic variables that are significantly related to users' algorithm awareness are marital status, occupation, education level and age, and H1 holds. H2 considers the influence of users' Internet access, and whether or not they use devices other than cell phones is significantly related to algorithm awareness. H5 considers users' interactive behaviors with algorithms, and it is found that among the 14 interactive behaviors, only the behavior of following Douyin account is related to algorithm awareness. In this regard, we believe that Douyin is a content product, and users shape personalized content by following accounts of interest. "Follow" is a way for users to express their liking of videos or creators and their expectation of similar content, and this participation itself has a strong user initiative.

Table 3. Specific factor loadings for algorithm awareness exploratory factor analysis

Questions	Factor 1	Factor 2	Factor 3	Factor 4
What I do in Douyin affects the content I see	**0.804**	0.069	−0.028	0.165
The information provided to Douyin affects the content pushed by the algorithm	**0.765**	0.194	0.049	−0.104
Douyin pushes personalized recommendations based on individual interests	**0.747**	0.080	0.099	0.217
The ability to provide feedback to adjust the content pushed by the algorithm	**0.654**	0.040	0.098	0.014
The content I see in Douyin is pushed by the algorithm	**0.569**	0.143	0.468	0.112
Algorithms make the content seen by users different	**0.511**	0.138	0.417	0.168
Douyin should be more transparent about the algorithm	**0.492**	0.374	0.257	−0.089
I am worried about personal information leakage	0.243	**0.801**	−0.074	0.073
I will actively restrict Douyin permissions	0.170	**0.752**	−0.024	−0.192
Algorithms exacerbate inequality and bias	−0.104	**0.682**	0.115	0.390
I understand how to influence the Douyin algorithm	−0.073	−0.032	**0.813**	0.049
I have heard of Douyin algorithmic recommendation mechanism	0.275	−0.023	**0.765**	0.031
The algorithm pushes content without human intervention	0.058	0.040	0.081	**0.853**
Content on Douyin is automatically pushed by the algorithm	0.534	−0.014	0.047	**0.596**

To further explore the possible differences in H1, we conducted multiple regressions using the aggregated score of algorithm awareness as the dependent variable and demographic variables as the independent variables (see Table 4). It has been argued that the variable of educational attainment is an important variable explaining variances in algorithm awareness [17]. With the addition of the educational attainment variable in Model 2, income and education remained significant predictors of algorithm awareness, and the increase in R^2 of the model indicated that the variable of educational attainment accounted for a larger variance in algorithm awareness, and that there was a larger educational difference in users' overall algorithm awareness, with users with high school and bachelor's degrees having higher algorithm awareness compared to those with middle school or less education.

Table 4. Linear regression of demographic factors and algorithm awareness composite score

	Model 1		Model 2	
	B	p	B	p
Age	−0.007	0.459	−0.005	.543
Annual income	2.191E−6**	0.009	1.946E−6*	.035
Gender female	0.022	0.736	0.005	.940
Marital status married	−0.196	0.375	−0.079	.720
children yes	−0.007	0.973	0.102	.617
Education				
High school			0.463**	.005
College			0.304	.051
Bachelor			0.569**	.000
Graduate and above			0.335	.175
R^2	0.056 0.040 F (5,303) = 3.583, p = 0.004		0.116 0.089 F (9,299) = 4.364, p = 0.000	
Adjusted R^2				
F Statistic				

*p < 0.05; **p < 0.01.

For the digital literacy factor, the results of factor analysis showed that the digital literacy scale could be downscaled into five factors (see Fig. 2). Finally, we calculated the overall digital literacy score based on the exploratory factor analysis data of digital literacy (see Table 5) to measure the high level of digital literacy of users. The correlation analysis shows that digital literacy is significantly correlated with algorithm awareness. Specifically, except for online sales literacy, all other digital literacy factors are significantly correlated with algorithm awareness, and H3 holds.

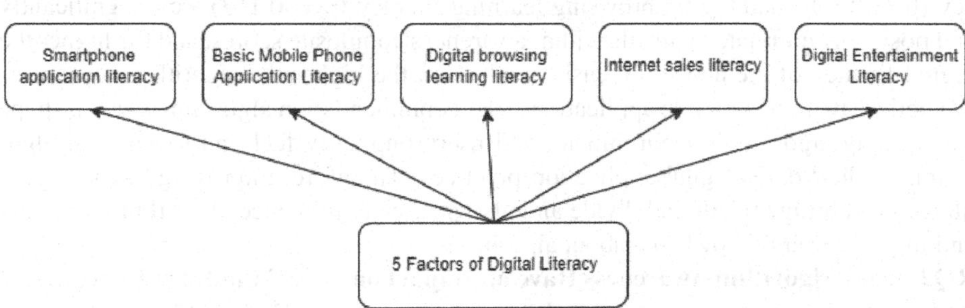

Fig. 2. Five factors of digital literacy

Table 5. Factor loadings for exploratory factor analysis of digital literacy

	Factor 1	Factor 2	Factor 3	Factor 4	Factor 5
Shopping using e-commerce platforms	**0.798**	0.181	−0.044	−0.050	0.174
Using search engines	**0.717**	0.036	0.186	0.276	0.176
Watching online videos, movies, or TV series	**0.615**	0.508	−0.007	0.092	−0.003
Listening to music	**0.536**	−0.072	0.490	0.100	0.012
Using Internet financial tools	0.110	**0.776**	0.085	−0.150	0.135
Browsing online news	0.380	**0.601**	0.192	0.279	0.121
Using social media	−0.211	**0.524**	0.211	0.439	0.151
Receiving and sending text messages or doing text editing	0.343	**0.368**	0.202	0.307	−0.220
Locating or navigating	0.072	−0.003	**0.758**	0.180	0.007
Receiving or making phone calls	0.209	0.134	**0.713**	−0.014	0.029
Receiving or sending emails	−0.174	0.268	**0.668**	0.145	0.173
Make, edit, or share videos	−0.005	0.113	0.003	**0.753**	0.111
Play online games	0.293	−0.196	0.200	**0.606**	0.267
Use e-commerce platforms to sell	0.309	0.134	0.299	**0.520**	−0.080
Watching short-videos	−0.019	−0.007	0.073	0.000	**0.807**
Taking online classes or participating in online training	0.311	0.251	0.065	0.238	**0.653**
Read e-books or online novels	0.277	0.435	0.027	0.218	**0.525**

The regression analysis of each factor of digital literacy and the composite score of algorithm awareness showed (see Table 6) that the addition of each factor variable of digital literacy increased the adjusted R^2, indicating that the variable of digital literacy was more important in algorithm awareness. Specifically, smartphone application literacy ($\beta = 0.330$) and digital browsing learning literacy ($\beta = 0.153$) were significantly and positively correlated with algorithm awareness composite scores, and the higher the digital literacy of the above dimensions of users, the higher the algorithm awareness. We believe that most mobile applications use recommendation algorithms, which shape users' daily algorithmic environment, and users implicitly feel and understand algorithms in their daily digital application practices. Therefore, improving users' digital literacy can bridge the digital divide and also positively influence algorithm awareness and improve users' knowledge about algorithms.

RQ2: Does Algorithm Awareness Have an Impact on Users' Platform Experience? Answering this question requires a downscaling of users' Douyin usage experience scale. According to the results of factor analysis, the nine items of users' Douyin usage experience can be downscaled into two factors. Factor 1 is named video production and social interaction experience, and factor 2 is named content and advertising experience.

Table 6. Linear regression of digital literacy factors and algorithm awareness composite score

	Algorithm awareness composite score		Algorithm awareness composite score	
	B	P	B	P
Age	−0.005	−0.005	−0.005	0.646
Annual income	1.946E−6*	1.946E−6*	1.946E−6*	0.031
Gender female	0.005	0.005	0.005	0.608
Marital status married	−0.079	−0.079	−0.079	0.953
Children yes	0.102	0.102	0.102	0.768
Education				
High school	0.463**	0.463**	0.463**	0.123
College	0.304	0.304	0.304	0.204
Bachelor	0.569**	0.569**	0.569**	0.004
Graduate and above	0.335	0.335	0.335	0.527
Factor 1 - smartphone application literacy				0.000
Factor 2 - basic mobile phone literacy				0.101
Factor 3 - digital browsing and learning literacy				0.004
Factor 4 - online sales literacy				0.508
Factor 5-digital entertainment literacy				0.099
Constant	−0.388	−0.388	−0.388	0.319
R^2	0.116		0.249	
Adjusted R^2	0.089		0.214	
F statistic	F (9,299) = 4.364, p = 0.000		F (14,294) = 6.95, p = 0.000	

*p < 0.05; **p < 0.01.

After correlation tests, it was found that hearing about and understanding the Douyin algorithm and being aware of the automation features of the algorithm were related to user video production and social interaction experience; being aware of the personalized content filtering features of the algorithm and being aware of the ethical privacy issues of the algorithm were significantly related to user content and advertising experience. The results of linear regression showed (Table 7) that Model 2 increased Adjusted R^2 with the addition of variables for the algorithm awareness factor, indicating that algorithm awareness is a significant influencing factor in the experience of using Douyin. Hearing about the algorithm ($\beta = 0.1885$) and being aware of the algorithm as an automated push ($\beta = 0.137$) were positively associated with video creation and social interaction experience, with the former having higher importance on the experience impact; being aware of the algorithm as personalized recommended content ($\beta = 0.351$) and being aware of the algorithm's ethical privacy issues (β = 0.239) were positively associated with the content and advertising experience, with the former having a and ad experience were higher.

Table 7. Linear regression of algorithm awareness factors and users' experience of using Douyin

	Video creation and social interaction experience		Content and ad experience	
	Model 1	Model 2	Model 1	Model 2
Age	0.034* (0.049)	0.039* (0.023)	−0.010 (0.580)	−0.008 (0.617)
Annual income	9.515E−7 (0.587)	3.496E−7 (0.842)	5.251E−7 (0.771)	−7.634E−7 (0.651)
Gender female	0.167 (0.171)	0.230 (0.057)	0.006 (0.961)	−0.037 (0.750)
Marital status married	0.092 (0.826)	0.032 (0.939)	−0.162 (0.706)	−0.059 (0.881)
Children yes	−0.416 (0.284)	−0.517 (0.176)	0.172 (0.667)	0.145 (0.693)
Education				
High school	−0.156 (0.614)	−0.271 (0.378)	0.773* (0.015)	0.436 (0.142)
College	−0.433 (0.144)	−0.409 (0.162)	0.481 (0.114)	0.187 (0.507)
Bachelor	−0.471 (0.067)	−0.533* (0.040)	0.429 (0.104)	−0.053 (0.832)
Graduate and above	0.072 (0.878)	0.086 (0.854)	0.028 (0.954)	−0.310 (0.489)
Factor 1 - Awareness of personalized content filtering		0.018 (0.761)		0.351** (0.000)
Factor 2 - Ethical privacy awareness		−0.033 (0.544)		0.239** (0.000)
Factor 3 - Hearing about algorithms		0.185** (0.001)		0.063 (0.243)
Factor 4-Automated algorithmic push		0.137* (0.013)		0.077 (0.143)
Constant	−0.546 (0.250)	−0.619 (0.188)	−0.175 (0.720)	0.235 (0.604)
R^2	0.090	0.141	0.037	0.203
Adjusted R^2	0.062	0.103	0.008	0.167
F statistic	F (9,299) = 3.274 p = 0.001	F (13,295) = 3.731 p = 0.000	F (9,299) = 1.279 p = 0.248	F (13,295) = 5.765 p = 0.000

*p < 0.05;**p < 0.01.

In our qualitative study, we found that algorithm awareness influenced users' awareness of Douyin's video posting assistance features and rules, which further influenced the experience of using the video posting feature. Douyin users can choose to add a topic in the form of "#+text" when posting videos. Adding a topic enables more users interested in the same topic to see the video and get more traffic. People with low algorithm awareness may have used hashtags but do not understand the recommended features they carry. One interviewee had added a hashtag when posting a video (see Fig. 3), but she said:

> *I don't know what the '#' means, let alone what it does. It seems like this is a quote? I saw it and clicked to add it.*

Fig. 3. Topic tags (marked in red) were used in the video content posted by a respondent.

RQ3: Does Algorithm Awareness Affect Users' Willingness to Turn off Features Related to Personalized Recommendation Algorithms? Among respondents who use Douyin, half of the users think they know how to turn off the personalized content recommendation function. Overall, 1/3 of users chose to turn off personalized content recommendation function, and 2/3 of users chose to turn off personalized advertising recommendation function.

Based on the interviews, we speculate that some respondents were actually unaware of the exact location of the button to turn off algorithmic recommendations. One respondent chose in the questionnaire that he knew how to turn off the personalized content recommendation function, stating:

The relevant buttons for these softwares are normally in the settings, I guess, but I haven't gone through them.

Currently, Douyin does not place the button to turn off the personalized recommendation algorithm function in a conspicuous location, and it takes at least four steps to turn off the button within Douyin (see Fig. 4). Some respondents said that Douyin hides the button to turn off the function too deeply and that it is "too much trouble" to turn off the button.

Fig. 4. Steps to turn off the personalized content recommendation feature in Douyin.

RQ3 focused on the relationship between algorithm awareness and turning off algorithmic recommendations. The results of the analysis showed that the overall score of algorithm awareness was significantly correlated with whether or not users turned off personalized ad display. Whether to turn off the personalized content recommendation function was significantly correlated with Algorithm Awareness Factor 1 and Algorithm Awareness Factor 2, and whether to turn off the personalized ad recommendation function was significantly correlated with Algorithm Awareness Factor 2. Further dichotomous logistic regression results showed that (see Table 8), the more aware and perceptive users are of the algorithm's personalized content, the more likely they are to keep the personalized content recommendation function; the more aware users are of the possible ethical privacy issues of the algorithm, the more likely they are to choose to turn off the personalized content recommendation function.

In the interview, we found that users' acceptance of personalized advertising is also related to the individual's willingness to shop online. In the digital economy, digitalization is the key to connecting buyers and sellers. Douyin often induce users to click and consume by serving advertising videos, and these ads are determined by algorithms. The combination of ads and personalized videos greatly affects user attention, engagement and decision-making. "Prevent myself from shopping online because of ads", "Lessen my desire to consume" are the reasons often cited by respondents who choose to turn off personalized ads displays.

Table 8. Logistic regression of algorithm awareness factors and whether to turn off personalized content recommendations

	Whether to turn off personalized content recommendation (yes = 0, no = 1)			
	Model 1		Model 2	
	B	P	B	P
Age	0.060	0.142	0.061	0.145
Annual income	0.000	0.165	0.000	0.172
Gender female	0.517	0.052	0.515	0.063
Marital status married	−0.621	0.531	−0.453	0.660
Children yes	−1.049	0.270	−0.947	0.342
Education				
High school	0.858	0.285	0.796	0.347
College	−0.609	0.350	−0.648	0.336
Bachelor	−0.362	0.532	−0.336	0.584
Graduate and above	−1.614	0.136	−1.504	0.175
Algorithm awareness factors				
Factor 1 - awareness of personalized content filtering			0.331*	0.025
Factor 2 - ethical privacy awareness			−0.519**	0.000
Factor 3 - hearing about algorithms			−0.148	0.281
Factor 4-automated algorithmic push			0.023	0.861
Constant	−0.672	0.548	−0.705	0.549
Chi-square cardinality	16.171(p = 0.063)		36.674(p = 0.000)	
Predicted overall percentage	67.6		70.2	
R^2	0.071		0.155	

*p < 0.05; **p < 0.01.

5 Conclusion and Discussion

Algorithms have embedded in almost every aspect of our daily lives, and the development of technology often carries two sides. In the context of the hot debate of algorithm criticism and the policy of algorithm governance, more empirical research is needed on algorithm awareness from the users' perspective.

This study contributes to the research of digital divides, algorithm literacy, algorithm governance from the perspective of algorithm awareness. First, this study supplements and extends the digital divide theory and applies it to the digital environment of algorithmic recommendations, contributing to the empirical study of the social impact of algorithms. This study focuses on algorithmic users and chooses the popular short-form video platform, Douyin, to examine content recommendation algorithms. Second, this study contributes important measures of algorithm awareness, and the designed algorithm awareness scale integrates important dimensions such as personalized filtering, automated features, and ethical safety awareness of content recommendation algorithms. This scale shows good reliability and validity in the investigation of content recommendation algorithm awareness for Douyin users. The valid and reliable algorithm awareness scale provides a toolkit for studying the algorithm awareness of Chinese internet users, especially short-video platform users. In the future, we aim to apply the scale of algorithm awareness in other empirical studies of recommendation algorithms, including but not limited to search engines, short-video platforms, and mobile news Apps. Third, this study adds an important qualitative research perspective on users' algorithm usage experience and algorithm choice. We find that users' algorithm awareness affects users' platform usage experience, and together with other factors, influences users' consideration of recommendation algorithm functions, which leads us to start a discussion on platform algorithm governance policy implementation.

5.1 The Mechanisms of User Variances in Algorithm Awareness

Existing literature have emphasized the importance of user awareness of algorithms. We identified several different types of factors explaining variances in user awareness of algorithms. First, the socio-demographic factors. We found that demographic variables such as age, marital status, education level, and occupation are significantly associated with algorithm awareness. Regression analysis showed that income and education were the main significant predictors of algorithm awareness, which is consistent with previous research on socioeconomic status and algorithmic knowledge [17], demonstrating the impact of economic income and education on the digital divide in the new technological environment. People with higher education and income have a higher level of algorithm awareness. This gap may stem from the stratification and inconsistency of various resources brought about by education and income; higher income and education provide users with greater advantages in terms of access to processing relevant information and exposure to algorithmic knowledge, etc. The objective conditions and social experiences of this distinction are unconsciously internalized into the users themselves, which can bring about differences in habits of thinking, feeling, and acting [30, 31], which is also reflected in user algorithm awareness.

Second, we can see a significant relationship between Internet devices that users access and the level of their algorithm awareness. This echoes findings from studies that revealed that mobile devices exacerbate digital inequality, and mobile Internet access cannot fully replace PC Internet access [18]. We can see that in today's highly popular mobile Internet, those who receive poor quality content in mobile algorithmic platforms and overly rely on algorithmic push mechanisms face new challenges in online information seeking [18]. We found that this group is also situated in a disadvantaged position of algorithm awareness, and one way to help these groups improve their algorithm awareness is to conduct digital literacy training and algorithmic education across different network terminals. We verified the correlation between digital literacy and algorithm awareness in our study. The level of algorithm awareness showed a positive correlation with users' Internet skills.

In summary, this study concludes that users' algorithm awareness is influenced by both external and internal factors. The former requires more algorithm knowledge popularization by platforms or education systems, more media coverage and discussion of algorithms, and policies inform users of their choices in algorithmically shaped information environment. Meanwhile, user awareness of algorithms, as we identified in this research, largely stems from the education and resources shaped by the socio-economic variables. This indicates that the improvement of users' awareness of algorithm also require policymakers and technology companies to pay close attention to the structural variances in how users perceive and understand technologies. Existing divides in the access, adoption and usage of digital technology are still reflected in how users engage with algorithms.

Therefore, to raise the level of algorithm awareness and bridge the algorithm gap, we should consider two aspects: First, increase the publicity and discussion of algorithms, prioritizing debates around algorithms as a more prominent social discussions, and create a social environment that focuses on improving algorithm awareness among the public. Second, increase digital literacy training and algorithm education, and emphasize data thinking and risk perception when popularizing algorithm knowledge from the perspective of algorithm users [32] and to improve people's vigilance awareness and critical thinking of algorithms [33].

In addition, we found that information diversity is an important element behind algorithm awareness. Diversity here refers to not only the diversity in platforms, but also diversity in information content users receive on a daily basis. As our findings suggest, an overly simplistic personalization algorithm will have a negative impact on the empowerment of information users, restricting the quality and quantity of information they receive from the platform. Therefore, we argue that as content recommendation algorithm push personalized content to users, technology companies need to consider how to best inform users of a more diversified information diet, and how to educate users of the technological functions available on the digital platforms.

5.2 Strengthen the Transparency of Algorithms and Protect the Subjectivity of Users

The results of RQ2 prove the significant relationship between user satisfaction and platform algorithm transparency. To a certain extent, algorithmic literacy represents users' awareness of the platform and their ability to use it, and the higher the algorithm awareness, the higher users' ability to use the platform to meet their informational needs. Our study found that users' awareness of algorithmic personalized content filtering and awareness of algorithmic ethical privacy issues influenced users' experience of using the platform. In addition, algorithm awareness directly affects users' understanding and use of functions such as platform production and publishing, which further affects their experience of using the platform.

Therefore, improving the level of users' algorithm awareness is a win-win solution for both users and the platform. Platforms that want to enhance positive feedback from users should appropriately increase the transparency of their algorithms, explain their rules in sorting, pushing and retrieval in a simple and clear way, pay attention to algorithm transparency and interpretability to avoid adverse effects on users and prevent disputes and controversies. In the long run, algorithmic transparency is not only one of the ways to improve users' awareness of algorithms, but also an inevitable issue to be discussed in algorithm regulation and algorithm optimization [34]. At the same time, algorithmic transparency should not stop at the design of hidden functions under policy mandates. We found that the steps to turn off the algorithm function in Douyin are cumbersome, and users generally cannot easily find the close button. When the function that empowers users to actively close algorithmic recommendations is hidden behind a heavy user interface design, it essentially violates the principle of transparent and open presentation and does not effectively implement the right of algorithmic users to close algorithmic recommendations.

Algorithm platform should ensure that human intervention and the users' right to independent choice, in the "provisions" in Article 17, in addition to the clear platform to provide the option to close the recommendation algorithm service, but also provides that "the recommendation algorithm service provider should provide the user with the ability to select or delete the user tag for the recommendation algorithm service for their personal characteristics" In view of the purpose of users' use of the platform, the diversity of demands and the differences in users' algorithm awareness, we believe that the platform should also design a functional interface to meet the users' power to manage and delete their own tags when implementing the regulations. Algorithm platforms should further refine industry standards, ethical norms, and software practices for tag management in personalized recommendation algorithms, and actively seek a balance between user empowerment and user experience.

Algorithm awareness research from the users' perspective helps us explore which groups may be at a disadvantage of the digital divide in a digital environment where algorithmic recommendations are popular. And understand whether the closure of algorithmic recommendation interfaces required by the policy is truly accessible to users and whether user rights and interests are truly protected. Currently, much effort is still needed to raise the algorithm awareness of different social groups.

5.3 Limitation

There are still a number of limitations in this study. In terms of data collection, limited by the online questionnaire survey method, there are many samples of undergraduate and people under the age of 25, and the incomplete data has a certain impact on the analysis results. In terms of data analysis, more complex statistical analysis can be performed for some data results. In terms of interview design, there is also a lack of more qualitative interview samples. In follow-up research, a return survey can be conducted to explore the changes and performance of user algorithm awareness.

References

1. Gorwa, R., Binns, R., Katzenbach, C.: Algorithmic content moderation: Technical and political challenges in the automation of platform governance. Big Data Soc. **7**(1), 2053951719897945 (2020)
2. CNNIC: Statistical report on Internet development in China 2022. China Internet Network Information Center (2022)
3. Hargittai, E.: Second-level digital divide: differences in people's online skills. First Monday **7**(4) (2002)
4. DiMaggio, P., et al.: Digital inequality: from unequal access to differentiated use. Soc. Inequal., 355–400 (2004)
5. Hargittai, E., et al.: Black box measures? How to study people's algorithm skills. Inf. Commun. Soc. **23**(5), 764–775 (2020)
6. Hargittai, E., Micheli, M.: Internet skills and why they matte. Society and the Internet: how networks of information and communication are changing our lives, pp. 109–124. Oxford University Press, Oxford (2019)
7. Gran, A.-B., Booth, P., Bucher, T.: To be or not to be algorithm aware: a question of a new digital divide? Inf. Commun. Soc. **24**(12), 1779–1796 (2021)
8. Yu, L.: How poor informationally are the information poor? J. Doc. **66**(6), 906–933 (2010)
9. Yan, P., Schroeder, R.: Grassroots information divides in China: theorising everyday information practices in the Global South. Telemat. Inform. **63**, 101665 (2021)
10. Yu, L., Zhou, W.: Information inequality in contemporary Chinese urban society: the results of a cluster analysis. J. Assoc. Inf. Sci. Technol. **67**(9), 2246–2262 (2016)
11. Hargittai, E., Walejko, G.: The participation divide: content creation and sharing in the digital age. Inf. Commun. Soc. **11**(2), 239–256 (2008)
12. Beer, D.: Power through the algorithm? Participatory web cultures and the technological unconscious. New Media Soc. **11**(6), 985–1002 (2009)
13. Eslami, M., et al.: I always assumed that I wasn't really that close to [her]: reasoning about invisible algorithms in news feeds. In: Proceedings of the 33rd Annual ACM Conference on Human Factors in Computing Systems, Seoul, Republic of Korea, pp. 153–162. (2015). Association for Computing Machinery
14. Huang, X.: A research on the attitudes of individuals towards recommendation algorithm: based on 1075 users of news apps applied recommendation algorithm in China. Editor. Friend **06**, 63–68 (2019)
15. Zarouali, B., Boerman, S.C., de Vreese, C.H.: Is this recommended by an algorithm? The development and validation of the algorithmic media content awareness scale (AMCA-scale). Telemat. Inform. **62**, 101607 (2021)
16. Tichenor, P.J., Donohue, G.A., Olien, C.N.: Mass media flow and differential growth in knowledge. Publ. Opin. Quart. **34**(2), 159–170 (1970)
17. Cotter, K., Reisdorf, B.C.: Algorithmic knowledge gaps: a new dimension of (digital) inequality (2020)
18. Napoli, P.M., Obar, J.A.: The emerging mobile internet underclass: a critique of mobile internet access. Inf. Soc. **30**(5), 323–334 (2014)

19. Eshet, Y.: Digital literacy: a conceptual framework for survival skills in the digital era. J. Educ. Multimedia Hypermedia **13**(1), 93–106 (2004)
20. Zhu, H., Jiang, X.: A review of domestic digital literacy research. Libr. Work Study (08), 52–59 (2019)
21. Shin, D., Kee, K.F., Shin, E.Y.: Algorithm awareness: why user awareness is critical for personal privacy in the adoption of algorithmic platforms? Int. J. Inf. Manag. **65**, 102494 (2022)
22. DeVito, M.A., Gergle, D., Birnholtz, J.: Algorithms ruin everything: #RIPTwitter, folk theories, and resistance to algorithmic change in social media. In: Proceedings of the 2017 CHI Conference on Human Factors in Computing Systems, Denver, Colorado, USA, pp. 3163–3174. Association for Computing Machinery (2017)
23. Bostandjiev, S., O'Donovan, J., Höllerer, T.: TasteWeights: a visual interactive hybrid recommender system. In: Proceedings of the Sixth ACM Conference on Recommender Systems (2012)
24. Herlocker, J.L., Konstan, J.A., Riedl, J.: Explaining collaborative filtering recommendations. In: Proceedings of the 2000 ACM Conference on Computer Supported Cooperative Work (2000)
25. Yang, G., She, J.: News visibility, user activeness and echo chamber effect on news algorithmic recommendation: a perspective of the interaction of algorithm and users. Journal. Res. (02), 102–118+123 (2020)
26. Peng, L.: Illusion, prisoner of algorithm, and transfer of rights: the new risks in the age of data and algorithm. J. Northwest Norm. Univ. (Soc. Sci.) **55**(05), 20–29 (2018)
27. Mayer-SchÖNberger, V.: Delete: The Virtue of Forgetting in the Digital Age. Princeton University Press (2009)
28. Beer, D.: The social power of algorithms. Inf. Commun. Soc. **20**(1), 1–13 (2017)
29. Van Deursen, A.J., Van Dijk, J.A.: The digital divide shifts to differences in usage **16**(3), 507–526 (2014)
30. Bourdieu, P.: Distinction: A Social Critique of the Judgement of Taste. Routledge, London (2010)
31. Li, Q.: A brief analysis of bourdieu's field. Theory J. Yantai Univ. (Philos. Soc. Sci. Ed.) (02), 146–150 (2002)
32. Peng, L.: How to achieve "living with algorithms": algorithmic literacy and its two main directions in the algorithmic society. Explor. Free Views (03), 13–15+2 (2021)
33. Peng, L.: The multiple factors that lead to the infor-mation cocoon and the path of "breaking the cocoon". Press Circ. (01), 30–38+73 (2020)
34. Shen, W.: The myth of the principle of algorithmic transparency: a critique of the theory of algorithmic regulation global. Law Rev. **41**(06), 20–39 (2019)

Investigating Factors Influencing Open Government from a Country's Perspective

Lateef Ayinde[1(✉)], Hanim Maria Astuti[1,2], Shezin Hussain[1], and Anisah Herdiyanti[1,2]

[1] Florida State University, Tallahassee, FL 32306, USA
{layinde,hastuti,swh20t,aherdiyanti}@fsu.edu, {hanim, anisah}@is.its.ac.id

[2] Institut Teknologi Sepuluh Nopember, Sukolilo, Surabaya 60111, Indonesia

Abstract. Open government (OG) has been seen as the act of government facilitating transparency and accommodating citizen and stakeholder engagement for public decision-making. Despite the widespread implementation of open government initiatives, what factors influence open government from a country's perspective remained unclear. This article investigated socio-technical aspects of open government by looking at five factors: e-government development, freedom of press, innovation capabilities, digital skills, and legal adaptability. This study used secondary data from 137 countries to measure the factors influencing OG globally, employing a multiple regression model. Only digital skills are considered less influential in open government initiatives among all the five factors.

Keywords: Open government · Factors · Country

1 Introduction

Practitioners and academics are increasingly concerned about government transparency and disclosure of data and information due to the development of information technology and the Internet [94]. Globally, countries are facing a number of complex issues, including inefficient and ineffective governance, legal barriers, slow economic recovery, corruption, aging technological infrastructure, and a reduction in freedom of the press [58, 77]. Those issues are considered the causes of the declining trend in trust in government, which some scholars classify as national economic [13, 21, 32, 53], socio-cultural [47, 70], and politics [66] causing factors. A great deal of research efforts has been done to find strategies for tackling challenges and reversing the loss of faith in government. One of the remedies is to have an open and transparent government [67, 71].

Open government is defined "as the extent to which a government shares information, empowers people with tools to hold the government accountable, and fosters citizen participation in public policy deliberations" [91]. Based on that definition, OG encompasses various mechanisms to ensure that the government fulfills the functions of transparency, accountability, and citizen participation. Since the first movement in

© The Author(s), under exclusive license to Springer Nature Switzerland AG 2023
I. Sserwanga et al. (Eds.): iConference 2023, LNCS 13971, pp. 221–241, 2023.
https://doi.org/10.1007/978-3-031-28035-1_16

the 1990s, more and more countries and jurisdictions have participated in open government initiatives and transformed their government sectors to be more transparent and accountable for citizens, increase citizen-government engagement, and reap the benefits for all stakeholders [1, 31, 41, 89]. Currently, the global and largest OG partnership called Open Government Partnership notes that 77 countries and 106 local governments have joined the partnership, ranging from low-income to high-income countries [64].

1.1 Problem Statement and Research Question

Many countries worldwide have devoted their resources to transforming their government into open governments [27, 31]. Several studies have investigated, initiated, and advocated for open government initiatives to understand government actions better. For instance, some scholars concentrate on one of the OGD initiatives, i.e., open government data (OGD). These scholars investigate the benefits of OGD [60–62], potential barriers to its adoption [35, 48, 55, 68], and the public sector and open data [29, 38]. Previous studies have also discussed factors influencing government institutions' adoption of open government-related data at the institution and a specific country level [23, 52, 80, 81]. These existing studies highly focus on examining open government at the institution level or in a particular country.

As more and more countries and jurisdictions have committed to an open government, there is a need to understand this phenomenon at the global level. Few attempts have been made to investigate factors influencing the adoption and implementation of OG at the country level. These existing studies highly focus on examining open government at the institution level or in a specific country. This study examines the socio-technical factors that influence the implementation of open government from the perspective of countries globally. We aim to answer the following research question: "What factors influence the implementation of OG globally?".

A conceptual model is proposed to explain how these factors influence OG implementation at the country level. Using secondary data from 137 countries taken from several international, recognized, and reputable sources. This study makes a valuable contribution to filling the gap in current literature and practice regarding OG factors as seen from a global perspective by providing a holistic understanding of the factors that contribute to the successful implementation of OG initiatives by taking an in-depth look at these factors. It also helps researchers establish evidence-based theoretical models for implementing OG based on the findings. As a result of the study, government managers, policymakers, and practitioners can formulate more effective strategies for managing OG initiatives and prioritizing the factors contributing to building an open, transparent, and collaborative government.

2 Literature and Hypotheses

2.1 Open Government: Definition, Benefits, and Challenges

Open government is not universally defined despite the adoption and implementation of OG in various countries [89]. According to the Organization for Economic Cooperation and Development, openness and responsiveness are attributes of an effective government [25]. Open government also refers to transparent, participatory, and collaborative government activities concerning citizens or businesses [26]. Furthermore, OG has been defined from the citizens' perspective, who have access to government information and decision-making, which involves monitoring and influencing government policy [51]. OG also integrates external knowledge into political and administrative processes through information and communication technologies [78].

Another study demonstrated that ICT could be a tool for promoting government transparency through citizen participation and collaboration [19]. ICT enables open government initiatives such as e-government and open data to make government more accessible, transparent, and service-oriented [30].

The definition of open government accentuates its three core values, transparency, collaboration, and public participation. Recent studies have explored the values or benefits of OG. Scholars such as [35, 54] categorized the benefits of OG based on political, social, and economic benefits. Other literature also coined OG to reduce corruption, generate economic growth and innovation, improve the public sector's responsiveness to citizens and businesses [25, 50, 83], and increase engagement between government, community, and citizens [41, 74]. OG is also believed to increase government accountability as a decisionmaker, as opening government data to the public will force the government to be more aware of its decision-making process [44].

Meanwhile, Schnell and Jo [79] state that political factors such as transparency and government openness are fundamental democratic values. Both are the demands or expectations of citizens of their government. In addition, both values also function as a check on executive power.

OG also increase the knowledge of citizens regarding what their government is doing. As a result, it can reduce information asymmetries between government and citizens and monitoring costs [49]. Furthermore, open government has been seen as an evolving and important topic for government practice and research, within which five dimensions are intertwined: information availability, transparency, participation, collaboration, and information technology [27].

Implementing OG is not without a challenge. Ubaldi [83] discussed six key dimensions for OGD initiatives among OECD members. These dimensions, which were referred to as "challenges," include a) policy challenges, b) technical challenges, c) economic and financial challenges, d) organizational challenges, e) cultural challenges, and f) legal challenges. In addition to presenting the challenges, the paper also discussed several examples of how the OECD member countries had encountered the challenges. For instance, policy challenges were discussed with the example from the UK Cabinet Office that published the Open Data White paper in June 2012, followed by the first Open Data Strategy in each government department. The "Regulations.gov" case study was mentioned to give an idea of the technical challenges in the US government. Due to its exclusivity rule with a limited search engine capability, the "OpenRegulations.org" was created to compete with the "Regulations.gov," where simple-to-navigate listings and a more sensible set of RSS feeds were offered, one for each department agency.

2.2 Implementation of OG Across Countries

Many countries have taken open government initiatives. The Open Government Partnership (OGP)—the most prominent international initiative promoting open government—stated that a growing number of countries and jurisdictions have participated in that partnership since its first initiation in 2011. Currently, their members comprise 77 countries and 106 local governments [64] around the world.

The government takes many initiatives to implement OG. One can be seen by looking at its open government policies, programs, and structural organizations. A previous study analyzed policy documents that include relevant policies and open government-related action plans in seven OGP members: Azerbaijan, Brazil, Canada, Kenya, Netherlands, the UK, and the US [14]. OECD mentioned some relevant policies for open government, such as the law on privacy and data protection, e-government policies, public interest disclosure policies, the law on access to information, et cetera [25]. Additionally, the presence of OG initiatives can also be seen by investigating common objectives and difficulties across OGP countries when implementing their open government action plans. For example, a previous study investigated the common objectives among three OGP countries, Brazil, France, and the US, and found out that the main objective of open government plans was to restore confidence in governments [7]. The study also revealed common difficulties, such as the ability to resist political changes and low public participation.

Another essential initiative is the publication of government data to the public. Not only at the national level, many government institutions at state and local levels also have data portals as the repository of government data accessible and available to the public [22]. Global Open Data Index presents the benchmark of 94 countries regarding the publication of government data on their portals, ranging from the government budget and procurement to land ownership data [37]. An independent organization also releases a WJP Rule of Law Index of 139 countries based on the indices of eight measurements, one of which is the open government index [91]. OG index measures the degree of government openness. Based on that index, Norway is the highest rank in open government index, followed by Denmark, Finland, Sweden, and the Netherlands in the second, third, fourth, and fifth ranks. Republic or Iran, Cambodia, and Egypt are countries with the lowest open government index.

Furthermore, a previous study [4] examined government websites in the Middle East to see if open government principles are being implemented. Among the 13 Middle Eastern countries under study, only three have made government-owned data public, Bahrain, United Arab Emirates (UAE), and Saudi Arabia promoting government transparency through open data and facilitating public engagement. Meanwhile, in the United States, open government data is primarily addressed through laws in Paperwork Reduction Act 1980, which primarily sought to reduce the federal paperwork burden for individuals, small businesses, and local and state governments. Minimizing the cost, maximizing the usefulness of the information collected, coordinating, integrating, and ensuring automatic data collection, processing, use, and dissemination is achieved.

Although OG initiatives have been implemented in many countries, there have been variations in evaluating their effectiveness. Evaluating ongoing OG initiatives can consider some technical, organizational, and regulation criteria. However, it is important to note that there is still little discussion on what factors are important to consider when designing and implementing global OG initiatives. A study pointed out that open government data research, as part of open government, typically undergoes four main phases, including a) OGD launch, b) evaluation and learning, c) OGD adoption and use, and d) implementation and comparison among countries [24]. Thus, studying influential factors affecting OG implementation can help the government manage OG initiatives, from planning to evaluation.

2.3 E-Government Development and Open Government

A technological revolution has forced the government to develop citizen services and digital government operations [42]. Many have noted that ICT is the key to promoting open government [19]. ICT enables the government to implement various initiatives to create a more open, accessible, transparent, and service-oriented government for the public [30]. As many scholars have paid attention to strategies in increasing trust in government, open government is believed to be the remedy for losing faith in government [59]. A government reform to be more open and transparent through the help of ICT and especially e-government is the solution. Through various e-government initiatives, citizens can access and receive government services effectively and efficiently [16], control and monitor government programs and activities, and other types of participation, including e-voting [2, 15]. E-government is associated with open government as it creates a massive amount of government data and thus triggers the government to publish its data to the public. The availability of government data in a massive number also stipulates that citizens push the government to be more open regarding their data and activities. Open government data (OGD) implementation is a global focus of government institutions.

However, a previous study [6] investigated the challenges of open government data. Most are related to technical challenges, such as data formats, ambiguity, quality, et cetera. In the literature on information systems, successful information systems, including e-government systems, are seen from the quality of their systems, services, and data/information [17, 18]. E-government is the key to open government [1, 43]. Therefore, we argue that e-government plays a vital role in achieving full openness in government. The better the e-government development in a country, the better the implementation of its open government is.

Hypothesis 1:
E-government development positively influences the implementation of OG.

2.4 Freedom of Press and Open Government

One of the core components of open government is transparency, defined as "the extent to which government makes available the data and documents the public needs in order to assess government action and exercise voice in decision-making" (p. 87) [31]. Transparency also enables government-citizen engagement. Citizens are not only allowed to access government data but also the freedom to monitor what the government is doing and report government performance to the public. Open government is often associated with freedom of press and freedom of information.

The Reporters Without Borders (RSF) defines press freedom as "the right for journalists to select, produce, and disseminate news in the public interest without political, economic, legal, or social interference and without threats to their physical and mental well-being." Press freedom includes freedom of expression, opinion, and information [76] which can be linked to the Freedom of Information Act. An individual's right to freedom of expression occurs when there are no restrictions in the media.

Despite some arguments against FOI, a previous study [9] mentioned five strong arguments favoring FOI. First, information should be used for public interests because the existence of government is to protect public interests. Second, to be accountable, the government needs to reveal what they are doing. So, information is the key to accountability. Third, a good government requires reliable and available information. Forth, it is the right to citizenship. In the US, for example, Article 19 of the Universal Declaration of Human Rights states that everyone has a right to access information, including "freedom of expression, opinion, and search, receive, and impart information and ideas regardless of frontiers." According to Article 19 of the 1966 International Covenant on Civil and Political Rights, freedom of expression includes the right to seek, receive, and impart information, ideas, and opinions of any kind, whether it is written, spoken, or otherwise [65]. Fifth, the exclusivity to possess information harms democracy and can lead to corruption and other abuse of power.

Both movements—the freedom of press and freedom of information—have forced governments to release data and make it easily accessible [19]. The movements also emphasize accountability and transparency, improve citizen preferences [40, 86], and amend previous data policies [8]. It involves media independence and citizens having access to the media. Having free media can help facilitate informed public debate, provide a forum for citizen perspectives, and limit government power and corruption. Press freedom helps to reduce corruption and bring about accountability [11]. Open government and press freedom are interconnected [63]. Thus, open government leads to greater press freedom.

Hypothesis 2:
Freedom of press positively influences the implementation of OG.

2.5 Country's Innovation and Open Government

Innovation is the heart of economic growth and social development. Porter (2001) mentioned that to be an innovative country, private sectors, including firms, are the engines. However, these private sectors depend on national policies to be innovative. Porter concluded that the strength of innovation in a country requires a good collaboration between private and public sectors [72]. Moreover, Porter highlighted that innovation resulting in competitive advantage and economic development could only be achieved whenever a favorable and collaborative environment exists. Innovation is not only believed to tackle economic challenges but also other wicked problems such as aging societies, climate changes, political instability, and other social and human issues [69].

The degree of innovativeness of a country is different from one another. Porter and Scott (2001) explained the aspects of innovative national capacity that shape a nation's innovation capability. One of the elements is the nation's common innovation infrastructure which encompasses "the set of cross-cutting investments and policies supporting innovation through an entire economy" (p. 5) [73]. Moreover, they mentioned that a fundamental of a strong innovation infrastructure is the government's support in building excellent research so that scientists and engineers can contribute to innovation. A country with good innovation capacity is committed to economic openness, including openness in trade and investment.

An open government environment emphasizes collaboration and participation, two elements that a country requires to be an innovative country. A country that emphasizes openness tends to be more flexible in organizing the collaboration and participation among the public, private sectors, and citizens. For example, some countries with high innovativeness, such as the United States, provide incentives for private investment in broadband infrastructure and liberalization in telecommunication networks to encourage more industry competition [12, 20]. However, the same policies could not be applied in other countries because various issues, such as the government's ideology, can influence a country's degree of innovativeness [87].

In addition, the open government also aims to create a more accountable government. A previous study [45] argued that innovation and economic development are related to good governance or how well the quality of government is defined by three basic elements, i.e., accountability, transparency, and justice. An innovative environment requires accountability marked by the absence of the abuse of power, "democracy and political pluralism," and participatory development (p. 9) [45]. They also mentioned the importance of freedom and the need for government to be open so that citizens can trust more in government, which eventually will reinforce positive development.

Therefore, we hypothesize that the degree of innovation in a country influences the implementation of open government. The more innovative a country is, the more it needs a government that supports an open, transparent, collaborative, and participative environment.

Hypothesis 3:
Innovation capabilities positively influence the implementation of OG.

2.6 Digital Skills

Open government facilitates government administration and provides better services to citizens and businesses. It facilitates the participation of citizens in democratic institutions and political processes. With the spread and adoption of technology, digital and technology-related skills are becoming increasingly crucial.

Digital skills are important in realizing open government, as one of the goals of open government is to be more engaged with citizens. Without these skills, citizens may not be able to access e-government services and government data [28]. There are two crucial aspects of digital skills, online information, and services [85]. Furthermore, Van Deursen and Van Dijk (2009) classified digital skills into operational skills (digital media skills), formal skills (internet skills), information skills (search, select and evaluate e-information), and strategic skills (e-skills attached to a goal). Citizens need to have these skills in order to access government data and services.

Moreover, by nurturing their digital skills, citizens are forced to interact with the government using different applications [5, 10, 33], such as e-government. A previous study noted an association between e-government and digital skills [75]. Following the same logic, we assume that digital skills positively influence the realization of open government initiatives.Hypothesis 4:

Hypothesis 4:
Digital skill positively influences the implementation of OG.

2.7 Adaptive Regulation and Open Government

An open government is functional when it is transparent, accountable, participatory, and collaborative. However, laws are also a vital component of open government. Citizens have the right to access information on public issues, public utilities, and decision-making processes through laws on the right to access information.

Learning from the United States, some policies, regulations, and laws are enacted, revised, and reenacted to facilitate government transparency. According to Article 19 of the Universal Declaration of Human Rights, everyone has a right to access information. According to Article 19 of the 1966 International Covenant on Civil and Political Rights, freedom of expression includes the right to seek, receive, and impart information, ideas, and opinions of any kind, whether it is written, spoken, or otherwise. Moreover, the Paperwork Reduction Act (PRA) was revised in 1995 to emphasize enhancing the quality and use of federal information, disseminating public information, and ensuring its integrity. Alongside the PRA, McDermott (2010) highlighted 1985 Circular A-130, which essentially states that government information is government information, and that the public has no right to access it. In addition, his study also pointed out that the E-Government Act of 2001 is the only legislation focusing on the government's management of its information content for access and accountability (p. 406) [50]. In 2002, the E-Government Act was rewritten and codified by the Federal Chief Information Officer (CIO) Council, whose activities have largely been unaccountable. The ability of a country to adapt to the required regulation is thus necessary for creating an open government. We hypothesize that the legal adaptability of a country influences the implementation of open government.

Hypothesis 5:
Legal adaptability positively influences the implementation of OG.

3 Conceptual Model

This paper investigates factors that influence a country's realization of open government. The five hypotheses emphasize the role of e-government development, freedom of press, innovation capabilities, digital skills, and legal adaptability of a nation to influence open government. In other words, open government implementation in a nation is a function of e-government development, freedom of press, innovation capabilities, digital skills, and legal adaptability. We depict the proposed relationship using Fig. 1.

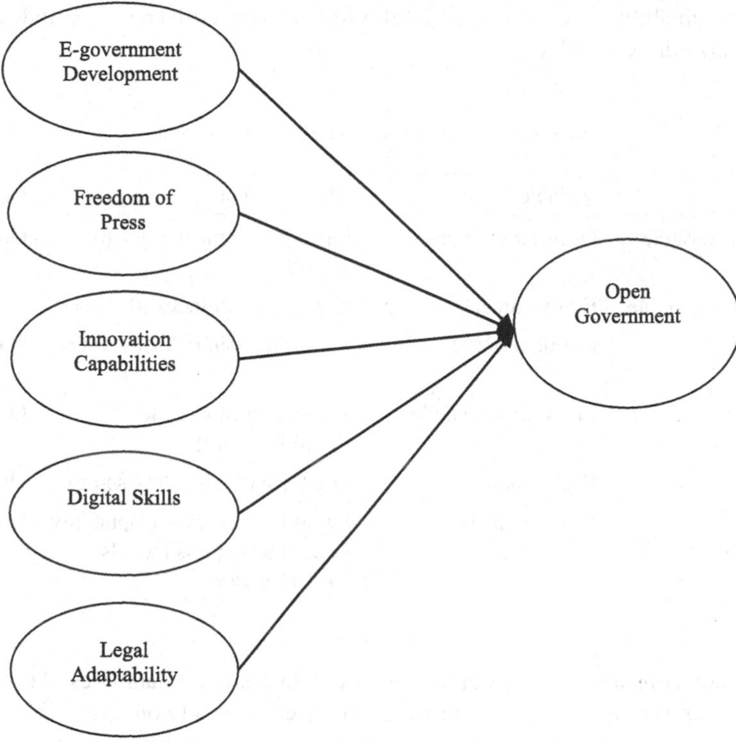

Fig. 1. The conceptual model

4 Methods

Based on the research model (Table 1), our study consists of six variables: open government, e-government development, freedom of press, digital skills, innovation capabilities, and legal adaptability to digital innovations. This study investigates the determinants of OG implementation using the data of 137 countries. The variables used in this study were taken from different data sources, i.e., World Bank Global Competitiveness 4.0 Index in 2019 [93], United Nations E-Government Survey for 2020 data [84], and World Justice Project Index in 2020 [90].

To test the hypotheses in our study, we used variables as depicted in Table 1. As we investigate the factors influencing open government, the dependent variable in the model is Open Government. We use the Open Government Index obtained from the World Justice Project Rule of Law Index [92] to measure this dependent variable.

The first factor we predict to influence is e-government development. We use the e-Government index, obtained from United Nations E-Government Survey to measure this factor, followed by an independent variable freedom of press. This variable is measured using the Press Freedom Index from World Bank Global Competitiveness 4.0 Index [93]. We also use innovation capabilities, which relies on the innovation capabilities indicator from World Bank Global Competitiveness 4.0 Index as the measurement. Digital skills and legal adaptability, we use World Bank Global Competitiveness 4.0 Index data to operationalize these variables.

Table 1. The variables and their measurements

Type	Variable name	Measurement	Data type
Dependent variable	Open government	Open government index (0–1 scale)	Ordinal
Independent variable	E-government	E-government index (0–1 scale)	Ordinal
	Freedom of press	Press Freedom index (0–100% score)	Ordinal
	Innovation capabilities	Innovation capabilities (0–100% score)	Ordinal
	Digital skills	Digital skills (0–100% score)	Ordinal
	Legal adaptability	Legal framework's adaptability to digital business models (0–100% score)	Ordinal

The study considered only countries whose data are in all databases. At first, there were 139 countries; however, we omitted 2 countries (Sierra Leone and Liberia) due to significant missing data. However, we still experienced some missing data. We use the simplest mechanism to address this by imputing the missing data by their means [34]. We imputed 15% (22 records) of Open Government Index data and 2% (3 records) of the legal adaptability variable. We realized that imputation by means could lead to bias. Thus, we discussed this issue in our future recommendation.

We analyze our data using multiple regression. To conduct the regression analysis, we ensure the three assumptions are met, i.e., linearity, normality, and homoscedasticity. We use the scatter plots and correlation matrix to ensure that each independent variable as a predictor has a linear relationship with the outcome or the dependent variable. In addition, the scatterplots and correlation matrix are also used to check the presence of multicollinearity issues among the independent variables. Descriptive analysis and histogram are used to describe the normality. Next, a residual plot is used to check the homoscedasticity.

5 Results and Findings

We check the three assumptions before conducting the analysis using multiple regression. We use scatterplots, correlation tables, and VIF values to check the first assumption, i.e., the linearity (Appendix). The scatterplots show a positive linear relationship between each pair of independent variables and the dependent variable. The correlation matrix also confirms the scatterplots, indicating strong linear relationships, as the values range between .568 and .679. We also check the multicollinearity issues using correlation tables and the Variance Inflation Factors (VIF) values. The correlation table shows no multicollinearity issue since the highest correlation value among two independent variables is below the cutoff value of .8. The VIF values of all predictors are far below the cutoff value of 10; therefore, there is no issue with multicollinearity. Therefore, the linearity assumption is met. The dependent variable is normally distributed over the independent variable. The third assumption is homoscedasticity which aims to check the homogeneity of the variance of the residuals. The scatterplot in the appendix, which describes the data point patterns between the standardized predicted value and the residuals, indicates that the plot is homoscedastic. As all three assumptions are met, we continue to conduct the regression analysis.

Subsequently, we run the data using multiple regression in SPSS to answer which predictors significantly predict open government implementation. Table 2 presents the summary of the regression analysis. The findings show that among the five independent variables, four of them are found to be significant predictors to open government. The digital skills variable is the only insignificant predictor to open government.

Based on the standardized coefficients, freedom of press is the most important predictor to open government as it has the highest value of standardized coefficients. This predictor also has a positive relationship with open government; an increase of 1 standard deviation of freedom of press will result in an increase of .295 standard deviations of open government. Other important predictors are e-government development and innovation capabilities, which indicate a positive relationship to open government. An increase of 1 standard deviation of e-government will cause an increase of about .298 standard deviations of open government. Similarly, increasing 1 standard deviation of innovation will improve the index of open government by about .298 standard deviations.

Legal adaptability also positively influences the open government index. However, this predictor is considered a weaker predictor to open government. An increase of 1 standard deviation of legal adaptability will likely increase .179 standard deviation of open government.

The digital skills variable, on the contrary, is insignificant as the significance value of this variable is higher than the p-value. Even though it is indicated in the table that this predictor has a negative influence on open government, however, this predictor is not important to explain open government at a global level.

Regarding the goodness of fit, the R-square value is 64.9%. It means that the independent variables in the model explained 64.9% of the variation in the open government index. However, we aim to understand the association between the dependent and independent variables. Therefore, we do not focus on the R-squared value.

Table 2. The summary of regression analysis.

Independent variables	Unstandardized coefficients	Standardized coefficients	Sig
E-government development	.218***	.298***	<.001
Freedom of press	.004***	.392***	<.001
Innovation capabilities	.002**	.261**	.006
Digital skills	−.001	−.101	.299
Legal adaptability	.002*	.179*	.037

R-squared: .649.
Dependent variable: Open Government.
*** $p < .001$, ** $p < .01$, *$p < .05$.

6 Discussion

This article addressed the question, "What factors influence the adoption and implementation of OG at the country level?" As part of its contribution to the empirical literature on open government, the study examines the factors influencing OG implementation at the country level. The multiple regression analysis shows that all factors significantly and positively influence open government, except digital skills. Among the four significant factors, freedom of press and e-government development are the strongest predictors of government openness. Innovation capabilities and legal adaptability are the least strong predictors. Therefore, this result implies that freedom of press, e-government development, innovation capabilities, and legal adaptability are more important for government openness than digital skills.

This study highlights the importance of freedom of press, including freedom of information, transparency, and open government. Our findings strengthen the argument of those who support the role of FOI as an integral component of open government [9]. Our results also support the statement made by the Open Government Partnership [63], which mentioned that access to information and media freedom is essential in open government reforms. Our study implies that a country that aims to achieve open government reforms should address issues that inhibit citizens from freely accessing, consuming, and sharing information. Furthermore, this study also underlines the roles of journalists and media in an open government environment.

The study also supports the notion that ICT is the key to open government [19, 30, 1, 43]. The results demonstrate the significance of e-government development in creating a more open and transparent government for the public. The study proves the existence of path dependence [82] between e-government and open government. A country with progressive e-government development will be most likely to have better open government implementation. Referring to the technical challenges of open government [6], a country with good e-government development could experience fewer technical challenges due to progressive development in e-government. The implication of our study suggests that nations should prioritize e-government development as part of their open government initiatives. E-government development such as improving data and systems integration, the quality of information and data, system usability, and e-customer services.

The study also helps to explain how legal adaptability is important to open government. For a country to have a more open and transparent government, its regulations need to be adaptive to follow the changes in society, including the needs of citizens. For example, in the open government environment, citizens function as service consumers [81], and thus, the government needs to be adaptive in regulations to protect citizens through privacy protection laws and regulations [3]. The study implies the need for government to be adaptive in meeting the rights of citizens to have access to information, including information related to public issues, public utilities, and decision-making processes through laws on the right to access information.

Regarding innovation, our findings complement the existing literature, which stresses that open government has a role in boosting innovation and a nation's competitive advantage [36, 39, 46]. However, the study reveals that the innovation capability of a nation also influences the progress of open government. The findings have two implications. First, a country that demands a transparent and open government should precede firms and private sectors. The government should also emphasize building excellent research. Second, we create a contribution to enrich the literature on innovation and OG. All this time, no study discusses the direct influence of innovation on open government. Our study reveals that innovation can have a direct influence on OG and a direct influence of OG on innovation. To conclude, there is a two-way direction between innovation and open government.

However, we are surprised that this study contradicts previous findings on the importance of digital skills to digital government. A previous study confirmed the relationship between digital skills and citizen involvement in e-government as part of the open government initiative in the European Union. Their study found that digital skills are critical to e-government [75] in a way that differs from ours. Another study also noted the relationship between digital skills and service consumers of government services [57]. Even though we find that e-government development is imperative in open government, our result does not see digital skills as a significant factor for open government. According to our study, no guarantee being digitally literate will lead to open data, services, or engagement on the part of the government. This argument works under the assumption that digital skills may not be the principal driver of a country of open government. In spite of the fact that citizens require literacy, numeracy, and analytical skills, the theoretical reasons for believing that openness leads to education are weaker [79]. The government should encourage the development of critical thinking, problem-solving, and productive, cognitive, and ethical skills among citizens and public officials so that government information can be shared, produced, and consumed.

7 Conclusion, Limitations, and Future Work

In open government literature, most academic interests focused on the formation, evolution, and institution of open government. Little attention is paid to factors influencing the adoption and implementation of open government globally, with a unique dataset from different universal and reputable world databases. We studied factors that influence open government globally within 137 countries. The paper examines the socio-technical factors that affect open government. The factors are e-government development, freedom of press, innovation capability, digital skills, and legal adaptability. The result confirms that four factors (*e-government development, freedom of the press, and innovation capability*) influenced open government except for digital skills. Past studies have identified digital skills as a barometer for government transparency, data sharing, and citizen engagement. However, this study suggests that digital skills might not be the most influential factor contributing to government openness. In other words, the more citizens and public office holders understand and use digital skills does not determine the level of openness of government in terms of data, services, and citizen engagement. Therefore, we argued that governments worldwide should identify other factors in this study (*e-government development, freedom of press, innovation capabilities, digital skills,* and *legal adaptability*) and use them to drive their openness to data, services, and citizen engagement.

Our research is limited in terms of our ability to disentangle causality; however, our findings offer plausible hypotheses and suggest avenues for further research. Additionally, they give practitioners some insight into how to advance OG globally. As a result of this study, there are two limitations; first, secondary data were collected, which can be analyzed quantitatively or qualitatively in future studies. A total of 137 countries were analyzed, which could be further categorized into developed, developing, and underdeveloped countries. Cities, counties, and states have developed open government initiatives over the past decade. Despite this, there is a lack of empirical research on the factors that affect the implementation of open government at the local and state levels. To understand how state and local governments implement open government initiatives, further research is needed. Further studies can look at these limitations and use them to guide their studies.

In addition, another limitation is related to handling the missing data. Some papers suggest avoiding missing data imputation using their mean because of bias issues [56, 88]. However, we handle our missing data by imputing them with their means. Therefore, further studies need to be done to find ways to handle missing data using other techniques.

Appendix

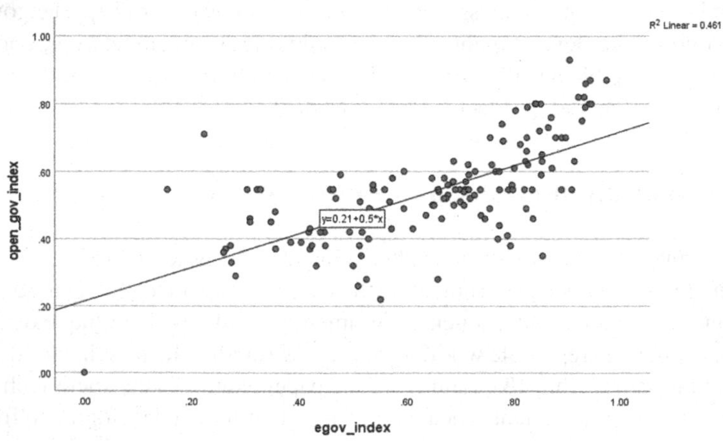

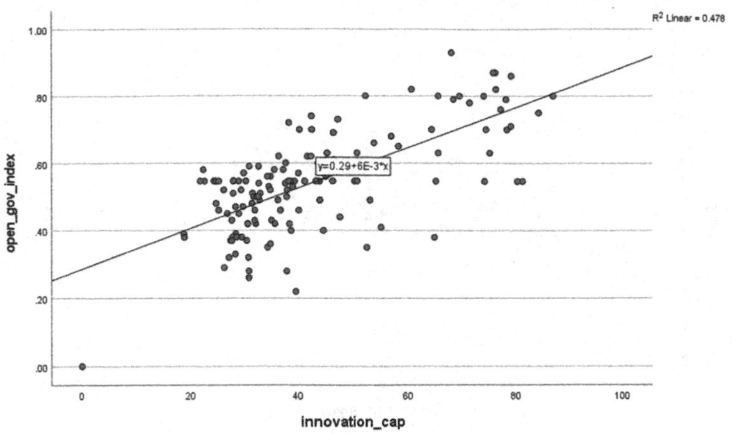
R² Linear = 0.478
y=0.29+6E-3*x
open_gov_index
innovation_cap

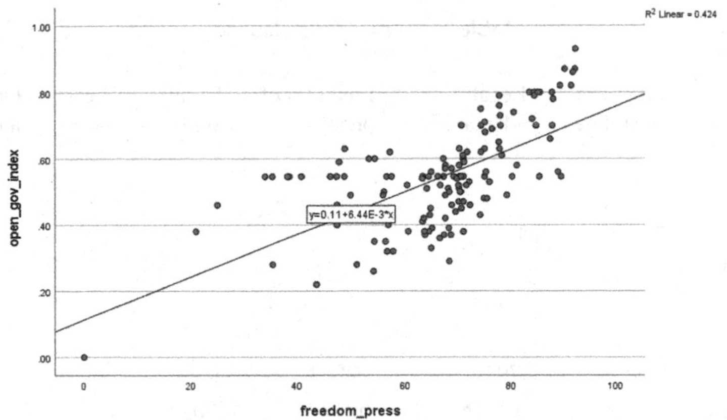
R² Linear = 0.424
y=0.11+6.44E-3*x
open_gov_index
freedom_press

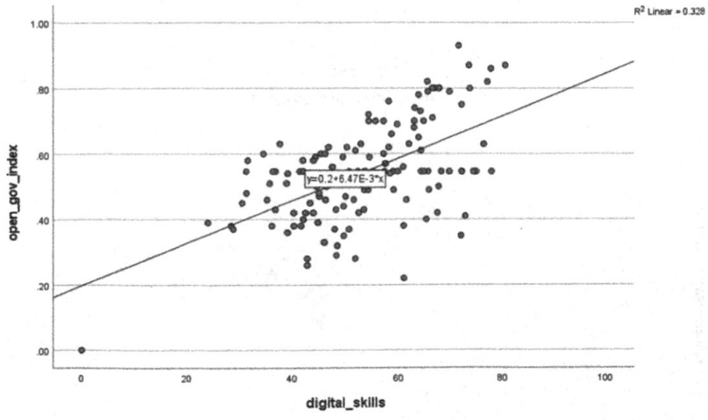
R² Linear = 0.328
y=0.2+6.47E-3*x
open_gov_index
digital_skills

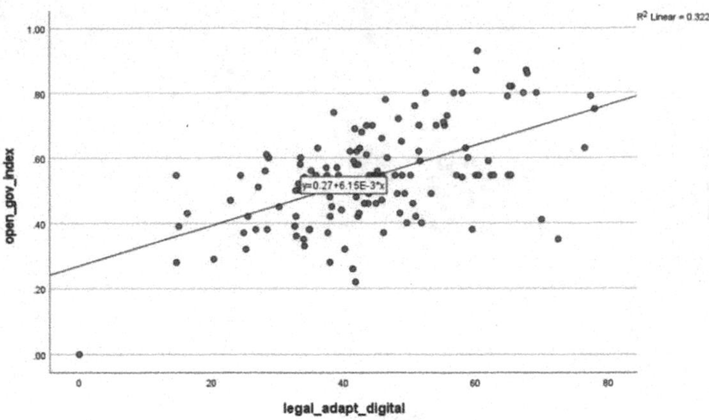

See Table 3.

Table 3. Pairwise correlations

	Innovation capabilities	Legal adaptability	Freedom of press	Digital skills	E-gov index	Open gov index
Innovation capabilities	1					
Legal adaptability	.716**	1				
Freedom of press	.440**	.440**	1			
Digital skills	.769**	.792**	.320**	1		
E-gov index	.711**	.616**	.405**	.702**	1	

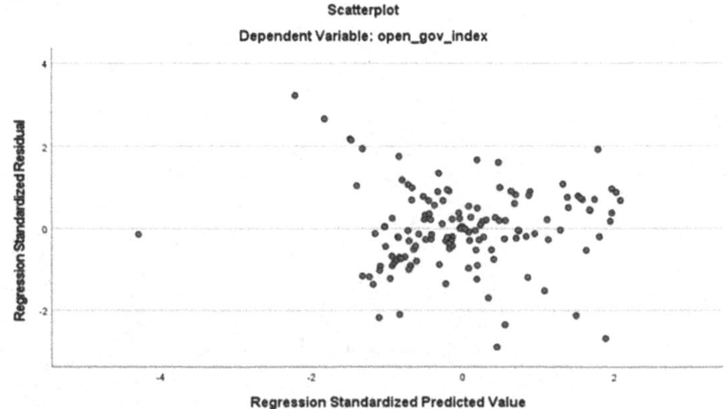

References

1. Abu-Shanab, E.A.: Reengineering the open government concept: an empirical support for a proposed model. Gov. Inf. Q. **32**, 453–463 (2015)
2. Adeshina, S.A., Ojo, A.: Factors for e-voting adoption - analysis of general elections in Nigeria. Gov. Inf. Q. **37**, 101257 (2020)
3. Al-Jamal, M., Abu-Shanab, E.: Open government: the line between privacy and transparency. Int. J. Public Adm. Digit. Age **5**, 64–75 (2018)
4. Alanazi, J., Chatfield, A.: Sharing government-owned data with the public: a cross-country analysis of open data practice in the Middle East. In: Americas Conference on Information Systems (AMCIS) 2012. AIS (2012)
5. Alkraiji, A.I.: Citizen satisfaction with mandatory E-government services: a conceptual framework and an empirical validation. IEEE Access **8**, 117253–117265 (2020)
6. Attard, J., Orlandi, F., Scerri, S., Auer, S.: A systematic review of open government data initiatives. Gov. Inf. Q. **32**, 399–418 (2015)
7. Bartoli, A., Blatrix, C.: Toward a transparent and responsible public action? The case of open government partnership. Revue française d'administration publique **166**, 275–292 (2018)
8. Bates, J.: The domestication of open government data advocacy in the United Kingdom: a neo-gramscian analysis. Policy Internet **5**, 118–137 (2013)
9. Birkinshaw, P.: Freedom of information and open government: the European community/union dimension. Gov. Inf. Q. **14**, 27–49 (1997)
10. Boughzala, I., Janssen, M., Assar, S. (eds.): Case Studies in e-Government 2.0: Changing Citizen Relationships. Springer Cham (2015). https://doi.org/10.1007/978-3-319-08081-9
11. Camaj, L.: The media's role in fighting corruption: media effects on governmental accountability. Int. J. Press Politics **18**, 21–42 (2012)
12. Choemprayong, S.: Closing digital divides: the United States' policies. Libri **56** (2006)
13. Citrin, J., Green, D.P.: Presidential leadership and the resurgence of trust in government. Br. J. Polit. Sci. **16**, 431–453 (1986)
14. Clarke, A., Francoli, M.: What's in a name? A comparison of 'open government' definitions across seven open government partnership members. JeDEM eJournal eDemocracy Open Gov. **6**, 248–266 (2014)
15. Darmawan, I.: E-voting adoption in many countries: a literature review. Asian J. Comp. Polit. **6**, 482–504 (2021)
16. Dawes, S.S., Helbig, N.: Information strategies for open government: challenges and prospects for deriving public value from government transparency. Electron. Gov. **6228**, 50–60 (2010)
17. DeLone, W.H., McLean, E.R.: Information systems success: the quest for the dependent variable. Inf. Syst. Res. **3**, 60–95 (1992)
18. DeLone, W.H., McLean, E.R.: The DeLone and McLean model of information systems success: a ten-year update. J. Manag. Inf. Syst. **19**, 9–30 (2003)
19. Evans, A.M., Campos, A.: Open government initiatives: challenges of citizen participation. J. Policy Anal. Manag. **32**, 172–185 (2013)
20. FCC: Connecting America: The National Broadband Plan. Federal Communications Commission (FCC) (2010)
21. Feldman, S.: Structure and consistency in public opinion: the role of core beliefs and values. Am. J. Polit. Sc. **32**, 416–440 (1988)
22. Foulonneau, M., Martin, S., Turki, S.: How open data are turned into services? In: Snene, M., Leonard, M. (eds.) IESS 2014. LNBIP, vol. 169, pp. 31–39. Springer, Cham (2014). https://doi.org/10.1007/978-3-319-04810-9_3
23. Gao, X., Lee, J.: E-government services and social media adoption: experience of small local governments in Nebraska state. Gov. Inf. Q. **34**, 627–634 (2017)

24. Gao, Y., Janssen, M., Zhang, C.: Understanding the evolution of open government data research: towards open data sustainability and smartness. Int. Rev. Adm. Sci., 002085232110099 (2021)
25. Gavelin, K., Burall, S., Wilson, R.: Open Government: Beyond Static Measures. OECD (2009)
26. Geiger, C.P., Von Lucke, J.: Open Government and (linked) (open) (government) (data). JeDEM eJournal eDemocracy Open Gov. **4**, 265–278 (2012)
27. Gil-Garcia, J.R., Gasco-Hernandez, M., Pardo, T.A.: Beyond transparency, participation, and collaboration? A reflection on the dimensions of open government. Public Perform. Manag. Rev. **43**, 483–502 (2020)
28. Goulding, A.: Information poverty or overload? J. Librariansh. Inf. Sci. **33**, 109–111 (2001)
29. Haini, S.I., Ab. Rahim, N.Z., Mohd. Zainuddin, N.M., Ibrahim, R.: Factors influencing the adoption of open government data in the public sector: a systematic literature review. Int. J. Adv. Sci. Eng. Inf. Technol. **10**, 611–617 (2020)
30. Hansson, K., Belkacem, K., Ekenberg, L.: Open government and democracy. Soc. Sci. Comput. Rev. **33**, 540–555 (2015)
31. Harrison, T.M., Pardo, T.A., Cook, M.: Creating open government ecosystems: a research and development agenda. Future Internet **4**, 900–928 (2012)
32. Hetherington, M.J.: The political relevance of political trust. Am. Polit. Sci. Rev. **92**, 791–808 (1998)
33. Irani, Z., et al.: An analysis of methodologies utilised in e-government research. J. Enterp. Inf. Manag. **25**, 298–313 (2012)
34. Jakobsen, J.C., Gluud, C., Wetterslev, J., Winkel, P.: When and how should multiple imputation be used for handling missing data in randomised clinical trials – a practical guide with flowcharts. BMC Med. Res. Methodol. **17** (2017)
35. Janssen, M., Charalabidis, Y., Zuiderwijk, A.: Benefits, adoption barriers and myths of open data and open government. Inf. Syst. Manag. **29**, 258–268 (2012)
36. Jetzek, T., Avital, M., Bjorn-Andersen, N.: Data-driven innovation through open government data. J. Theor. Appl. Electron. Commer. Res. **9**, 15–16 (2014)
37. Kassen, M.: Open data and e-government – related or competing ecosystems: a paradox of open government and promise of civic engagement in Estonia. Inf. Technol. Dev. **25**, 552–578 (2019)
38. Khurshid, M.M., Zakaria, N.H., Rashid, A., Ahmad, M.N., Arfeen, M.I., Faisal Shehzad, H.M.: Modeling of open government data for public sector organizations using the potential theories and determinants—a systematic review. Informatics **7**, 24 (2020)
39. Lakomaa, E., Kallberg, J.: Open data as a foundation for innovation: the enabling effect of free public sector information for entrepreneurs. IEEE Access **1**, 558–563 (2013)
40. Lau, R.R., Patel, P., Fahmy, D.F., Kaufman, R.R.: Correct voting across thirty-three democracies: a preliminary analysis. Br. J. Polit. Sci. **44**, 239–259 (2014)
41. Lee, G., Kwak, Y.H.: An open government maturity model for social media-based public engagement. Gov. Inf. Q. **29**, 492–503 (2012)
42. Lee, J., Kim, J.: Grounded theory analysis of e-government initiatives: exploring perceptions of government authorities. Gov. Inf. Q. **24**, 135–147 (2007)
43. Linders, D.: From e-government to we-government: defining a typology for citizen coproduction in the age of social media. Gov. Inf. Q. **29**, 446–454 (2012)
44. Linders, D., Wilson, S.C.: What is open government? One year after the directive. In: Proceedings of the 12th Annual International Digital Government Research Conference: Digital Government Innovation in Challenging Times, pp. 262–271
45. Lopez-Claros, A., Mata, Y.N.: The innovation capacity index: factors, policies, and institutions driving country innovation. In: The Innovation for Development Report 2009–2010, pp. 3–65. Palgrave Macmillan, London (2010)

46. Luo, Y., Tang, Z., Fan, P.: Could government data openness enhance urban innovation capability? An evaluation based on multistage DID method. Sustainability **13**, 13495 (2021)
47. Mansbridge, J.: Social and cultural causes of dissatisfaction with U.S. Government. In: Nye, J.S., Zelikow, P.D., King, D.C. (eds.) Why People Don't Trust Government, pp. 113–154. Harvard University Press, Cambridge (1997)
48. Martin, C.: Barriers to the open government data agenda: taking a multi-level perspective. Policy Internet **6**, 217–240 (2014)
49. Matheus, R., Janssen, M.: A systematic literature study to unravel transparency enabled by open government data: the window theory. Public Perform. Manag. Rev. **43**, 503–534 (2020)
50. McDermott, P.: Building open government. Gov. Inf. Q. **27**, 401–413 (2010)
51. Meijer, A.J., Curtin, D., Hillebrandt, M.: Open government: connecting vision and voice. Int. Rev. Adm. Sci. **78**, 10–29 (2012)
52. Mergel, I.: Open innovation in the public sector: drivers and barriers for the adoption of Challenge.gov. Public Manag. Rev. **20**, 726–745 (2018)
53. Miller, A.H., Borrelli, S.A.: Confidence in government during the 1980s. Am. Polit. Q. **19**, 147–173 (1991)
54. Mokobombang, N., Gutierrez, J., Petrova, K.: The benefits of open government data use: a crosscountry comparison. In: International Conference on Information Resources Management (CONF-IRM). Association for Information Systems (AIS)
55. Moore, M.: The limits of transparency. Polit. Q. **82**, 506–508 (2011)
56. Moore, R.A., et al.: Estimate at your peril: Imputation methods for patient withdrawal can bias efficacy outcomes in chronic pain trials using responder analyses. Pain **153**, 265–268 (2012)
57. Morte-Nadal, T., Esteban-Navarro, M.A.: Digital competences for improving digital Inclusion in e-Government services: a mixed-methods systematic review protocol. Int. J. Qual. Methods **21**, 160940692110709 (2022)
58. Nam, T.: Challenges and concerns of open government: a case of government 3.0 in Korea. Soc. Sci. Comput. Rev. **33**, 556–570 (2015)
59. Norris, P.: Digital Divide: Civic Engagement, Information Poverty, and the Internet Worldwide. Cambridge University Press, Cambridge (2001)
60. Noveck, B.S.: WIKI government: a public sector innovation. In: Proceedings of the 10th Annual International Conference on Digital Government Research: Social Networks: Making Connections between Citizens, Data and Government, p. 1. Digital Government Society of North America, Puebla, Mexico (2009)
61. Noveck, B.S.: Rights-based and tech-driven: open data, freedom of information, and the future of government transparency. Yale Hum. Rights Dev. Law J. **19** (2017)
62. Noveck, B.S.: 10. Open data: the future of transparency in the age of big data. In: Pozen, D.E., Schudson, M. (eds.) Troubling Transparency: The History and Future of Freedom of Information, pp. 206–225. Columbia University Press, New York (2018)
63. OGP: Media freedom and the Open Government Partnership (OGP). Open Government Partnership (OGP) (2019)
64. Open Government Partnership. https://www.opengovpartnership.org/our-members/
65. OHCHR: International covenant on civil and political rights. In: Nations, U. (ed.) General Assembly resolution 2200A (XXI) (1966)
66. Orren, G.: Fall from grace: the public's loss of faith in government. In: Nye, J.S., Zelikow, P.D., King, D.C. (eds.) Why people don't trust government, pp. 77–108. Harvard University Press, Cambridge, Mass (1997)
67. Park, C.H., Kim, K.: E-government as an anti-corruption tool: panel data analysis across countries. Int. Rev. Adm. Sci. **86**, 691–707 (2020)

68. Parycek, P., Schöllhammer, R., Schossböck, J.: 'Each in their own garden': obstacles for the implementation of open government in the public sector of the German-speaking region. In: Proceedings of the 9th International Conference on Theory and Practice of Electronic Governance. ACM (2016)
69. Pedersen, K.: What can open innovation be used for and how does it create value? Gov. Inf. Q. **37**, 101459 (2020)
70. PewResearch: How Americans view government. Pew Research Center (1998)
71. Piotrowski, S.J.: The "open government reform" movement: the case of the open government partnership and U.S. transparency policies. Am. Rev. Public Adm. **47**, 155–171 (2017)
72. Porter, M.E.: Regions and the new economics of competition. In: Scott, A.J. (ed.) Global City-Regions. Oxford University Press, Oxford (2001)
73. Porter, M.E., Stern, S.: National innovative capacity. In: The Global Competitiveness Report 2001–2002, vol. 2002, pp. 102–118. Oxford University Press, New York (2001)
74. Reddick, C., Ganapati, S.: Open government achievement and satisfaction in US federal agencies: survey evidence for the three pillars. J. E-Gov. **34**, 193–202 (2011)
75. Rodriguez-Hevía, L.F., Navío-Marco, J., Ruiz-Gómez, L.M.: Citizens' involvement in e-government in the European Union: the rising importance of the digital skills. Sustainability **12**, 6807 (2020)
76. Reporters Without Borders. https://rsf.org/en/index-methodologie-2022?year=2022&data_type=general
77. Sandoval-Almazan, R., Gil-Garcia, J.R.: Toward an integrative assessment of open government: proposing conceptual lenses and practical components. J. Organ. Comput. Electron. Commer. **26**, 170–192 (2016)
78. Schmidthuber, L., Krabina, B., Hilgers, D.: Local open government: empirical evidence from austrian municipalities. In: Parycek, P., et al. (eds.) EGOV 2018. LNCS, vol. 11020, pp. 110–119. Springer, Cham (2018). https://doi.org/10.1007/978-3-319-98690-6_10
79. Schnell, S., Jo, S.: Which countries have more open governments? Assessing structural determinants of openness. Am. Rev. Public Adm. **49**, 944–956 (2019)
80. Simonofski, A., Fink, J., Burnay, C.: Supporting policy-making with social media and e-participation platforms data: a policy analytics framework. Gov. Inf. Q. **38**, 101590 (2021)
81. Stratu-Strelet, D., Gil-Gómez, H., Oltra-Badenes, R., Oltra-Gutierrez, J.V.: Critical factors in the institutionalization of e-participation in e-government in Europe: technology or leadership? Technol. Forecast. Soc. Change **164**, 120489 (2021)
82. Tang, T., Ho, A.T.-K.: A path-dependence perspective on the adoption of Internet of Things: evidence from early adopters of smart and connected sensors in the United States. Gov. Inf. Q. **36**, 321–332 (2019)
83. Ubaldi, B.: Open government data: Towards empirical analysis of open government data initiatives. In: OECD Working Papers on Public Governance. OECD Publishing, Paris (2013)
84. UN: UN e-government survey 2020. In: Affairs, D.o.E.a.S. (ed.) United Nations, New York (2020)
85. van Deursen, A., van Dijk, J.: Improving digital skills for the use of online public information and services. Gov. Inf. Q. **26**, 333–340 (2009)
86. Van Dooren, W., Bouckaert, G., Halligan, J.: Performance Management in the Public Sector. Routledge (2015)
87. Wang, Q.-J., Feng, G.-F., Chen, Y.E., Wen, J., Chang, C.-P.: The impacts of government ideology on innovation: what are the main implications? Res. Policy **48**, 1232–1247 (2019)
88. White, I.R., Daniel, R., Royston, P.: Avoiding bias due to perfect prediction in multiple imputation of incomplete categorical variables. Comput. Stat. Data Anal. **54**, 2267–2275 (2010)
89. Wirtz, B.W., Birkmeyer, S.: Open government: origin, development, and conceptual perspectives. Int. J. Public Adm. **38**, 381–396 (2015)

90. https://worldjusticeproject.org/rule-of-law-index/factors/2021/Afghanistan/Open%20Government/
91. https://worldjusticeproject.org/rule-of-law-index/factors/2021/Open%20Government
92. World Justice Project (WJP). https://worldjusticeproject.org/our-work/research-and-data/wjp-rule-law-index-2021
93. The World Bank. https://tcdata360.worldbank.org/indicators/h9de5a263?country=BRA&indicator=41472&viz=line_chart&years=2017,2019
94. Zhang, N., Zhao, X., Zhang, Z., Meng, Q., Tan, H.: What factors drive open innovation in China's public sector? A case study of official document exchange via microblogging (ODEM) in Haining. Gov. Inf. Q. **34**, 126–133 (2017)

Lex Informatica and Freedom of Expression: Reflections on the Regulation of Internet Trolling Behaviors

David McMenemy(✉)

Information Studies, University of Glasgow, Glasgow, Scotland
david.mcmenemy@glasgow.ac.uk

Abstract. This paper revisits the concepts of *lex informatica* (Reidenberg) and *code is law* (Lessig), both early theories related to how regulation of behaviors on the internet might be managed, By focusing on the context of internet trolling in the United Kingdom, we consider the nature of trolling, how it has manifested in the UK in terms of actual notable incidences, and reflect on whether the law of the state within the regulatory regimes envisioned by Reidenberg and Lessig are in fact the best fit for managing these behaviors. Abusive behavior online can have profound impacts on people, causing significant fear and leading to an impact on private and family life. In balancing the qualified nature of freedom of expression rights versus other human rights we consider whether the laws of peoples, the regulatory capabilities of social media companies, and the wider culture of digital society are best placed collectively to create respectful norms on the Internet.

Keywords: Trolling · Freedom of expression · Harassment · Law · Social Media

1 Introduction

This paper explores a subset of Internet regulation by investigating practice with regards to the extent of trolling/offensive behaviors on Twitter, with emphasis on the United Kingdom.

As early as 1999, Lawrence Lessig claimed that the regulation of the Internet could be relatively straightforward, and although involving differences to regulation in the real world, could in essence be even *more* effective and potentially regressive than regulation in the real world. Lessig argued that what would emerge would be, "an architecture that will perfect control and make highly efficient regulation possible" spurred on by both governments and corporations [1]. Lessig's work was inspired by the earlier work of Reidenberg, who stated in a 1997 piece that, "the set of rules for information flows imposed by technology and communication networks form a "Lex Informatica" that policymakers must understand, consciously recognize, and encourage" [2].

What we have then is a digital domain where the laws of society have their place, but ultimately that is also controlled by the systems and architectures, rules, and norms of behaviors in the digital spaces we occupy. For Lessig these constraints on the digital

© The Author(s), under exclusive license to Springer Nature Switzerland AG 2023
I. Sserwanga et al. (Eds.): iConference 2023, LNCS 13971, pp. 242–255, 2023.
https://doi.org/10.1007/978-3-031-28035-1_17

world could be classified under four modalities of control: laws, norms, markets, and code (or architecture) [1]. We can see the viability of Lessig's four modalities clearly as still being of significant relevance. On the one hand social media companies demand all users sign up to a set of terms and conditions (T and Cs) before they are given an account, and these invariably include elements of regulation of behavior related to trolling and harassment. This is the element of regulation that is applied by the *market* itself, in the hope of encouraging acceptable *norms*. In addition, the system *architecture* itself can be utilized to control trolling behaviors by analyzing words and tone of posts and blocking content and/or restrict access to users who breach norms. On the other hand, the *law* also takes an interest in trolling activity, with the Crown Prosecution Service (CPS) in England and Wales producing clear guidelines and a typography for prosecutors on how to deal with alleged trolling behavior from a legal standpoint [3].

2 Social Media Trolling: An Ever-Growing Problem?

Social media trolling and bullying affects one in four young people, with targets disproportionately coming from disabled groups and ethnic minorities [4]. In recent years leading Members of Parliament (MPs) in the UK such as Jess Philips [5] and Yvette Cooper have also been victims of the activity, with Cooper calling for action to specifically prevent the abuse of women on social media [6]. In terms of creating a safe and welcoming space, "trolling has been framed as a major, if not the major, impediment to online community formation" [7]. In terms of Twitter trolling activity can quickly become a major news story, notwithstanding any legal implications which may follow. There have increasingly been incidents whereby public figures have been exposed to significant amounts of abuse online. MP Stella Creasy reportedly installed a panic button in her home after death threats on Twitter, and Caroline Criado-Perez reported impacts on her wellbeing and state of mind as a result of messages received. At the height of the abuse, Criado-Perez was receiving up to 50 offensive tweets per hour [8].

In 2017 a campaign utilizing the hashtag #ReclaimTheInternet was backed by MPs Yvette Cooper and Maria Miller. The campaign aimed to counter sexist trolling of women on social media and was launched by both MPs to significant publicity. Cooper raised the issue that much activity identified as trolling is not necessarily illegal:

> ..in most cases, online abuse isn't a crime. So, the question is what responsibility all of us have - as individuals, through campaigns, through schools, workplaces, unions, and through publishing platforms and social media - to challenge it and change attitudes [9].

In the words from Yvette Cooper, we can see reflected Lessig's modalities, with a call for better norms through individual behaviors, but also the responsibilities of the markets themselves to build better platforms. There is a crucial need, then, when discussing the regulation of trolling to consider both the potentially illegal elements of the behaviors, alongside the kinds of behaviors that, though not illegal, may be able to be dealt with by social media companies T and Cs.

2.1 Free Speech and Trolling: The Liberal Dilemma

A key aspect of the freedom desired by many on the Internet is that related to free speech, or freedom of expression. From an American perspective the cherished First Amendment to the Constitution has meant that free speech rights are guarded, and the emphasis falls most often on the right of the speaker unless they are defaming a person, breaching their target's intellectual property rights, or otherwise injuring them via some form of *fighting words* (words designed to provoke or incite violence).

The United Kingdom has no written constitution to protect free speech, however a rich tradition has evolved related to the utility of free speech for society, and the introduction of the European Convention on Human Rights via the 1998 *Human Rights Act* enshrined a *qualified* legal right to freedom of expression, balanced against other rights. The balancing of freedom of expression versus other human rights remains the crucial qualification. As Nussbaum argues, "none of the major philosophical theories gives us reason to think that repeated slurs, or cyber bullying, are high-value speech" [10]. The qualification stated in Article 10 is, "since [freedom of expression] carries with it duties and responsibilities, [it] may be subject to such formalities, conditions, restrictions or penalties as are prescribed by law and are necessary in a democratic society" [11].

2.1.1 The Nature of Communication on the Internet

Spinello has observed, "democratization of speech and information may well be the greatest legacy of the … Internet era" [12]. However, "unencumbered by generally accepted social norms [people] are more prone to say and do things that they perhaps would not under their real identities" [13]. McGoldrick suggests that "the empowerment provided by the internet has proved intoxicating and led individuals to issue communications as though they were within a 'Wild West' type, law-free, zone in Cyberspace" [14].

2.2 Arguments for and Against Free Speech in the Online Space

Barlow's "Internet Manifesto" declaration laid down a bold vision for free speech on the Internet, one that was grounded in a libertarian adherence to First Amendment principles. Barlow's cyberspace was "a world where anyone, anywhere may express his or her beliefs, no matter how singular, without fear of being coerced into silence or conformity" [15]. As Danielle Citron has observed, however: "The Internet is a double-edged sword. While it can facilitate the empowerment of people who often face discrimination, it can also be exploited to disenfranchise those very same individuals" [16]. It is an obvious assertion, but the Internet as it was envisioned by Barlow and the early pioneers did not foresee dilemmas such as online trolls, threats of physical violence, and death threats, and the types of discriminatory interactions as alluded to by Citron. With the distance of time passed since Barlow, there is an argument that could be posited that the free speech values of 1996 cyberspace are not readily applicable to 2022, assuming they ever were.

The 1997 Supreme Court decision in *Reno v ACLU* offered that the Internet enabled anyone to become "a pamphleteer…a town crier with a voice that resonates farther than it could from any soapbox" [17]. Important in the decision of the court was that levels of protection appropriate for children should not be the norm for adults using the Internet, and that while protections must rightly extend in the areas of obscenity or child pornography, free speech was too important a right to be toyed with. As was acknowledged, however, there are forms of expression that pose challenges to the notion of free speech on the Internet, and this poses "a contentious moral problem" [12].

Reno v ACLU encapsulated much of what is at stake in the free speech debate with regards to the Internet. A contemporary reflection on the case by Lipschultz offered that the decision of the court represented an adherence to the marketplace of ideas approach to free speech [18]. Within this philosophical approach to free speech the notion is that all ideas should be expressible, and the market (or the community) will decide which have efficacy or not, allowing all ideas to be tested. Critics of the marketplace of ideas approach to free speech would argue that some people have more access to distribute their ideas than others. As Barendt suggests, "the marketplace is not in practice open to everyone who wants to communicate his ideas……Differences in the availability of ideas have little to do with their truth" [19]. Others have posited that often what is expressed when hate speech is the topic are not ideas but merely passions that should not be supported in a civilized society [20].

The marketplace of ideas does not take into account that the expression of some types of view actually may work in such a way that those ideas drive others away through fear. Again, in the context of online trolling, Citron argues that:

> When individuals go offline or assume pseudonyms to avoid bigoted cyber-attacks, they miss innumerable economic and social opportunities. They suffer feelings of shame and isolation. Cyber mobs effectively deny people the right to participate in online life as equals [16].

Abah reiterates this view, stating: "the marketplace stops functioning as a marketplace of different ideas and becomes a monopoly if certain people are driven off from the center to the periphery, or chased completely off by intimidation and threats, not because their ideas and contributions are bad, but because their ideas contradict and challenge the status quo or are contrary to the presumed mainstream ideas" [21]. Free speech proponents might counter that the people who feel driven away by trolls have a right of reply, but this does not take into account where the victims may experience fear or harassment to such an extent that they feel a need to withdraw themselves or restrict their online interactions [22]. Such withdrawal has consequences for victims over and above any fear or harassment felt in terms of missed opportunities.

2.3 The Concept of Trolling

The Dictionary of Contemporary Slang defines troll as: "a malicious, anonymous online presence" [23]. As the Guardian newspaper commented in September 2011, '…technically speaking, a troll isn't someone who is merely offensive…They're people who purposefully drag an online conversation off-topic – often by being offensive, but sometimes just by being needlessly pedantic or bizarre' [24]. At the heart of the traditional meaning of troll, as it is applied to the Internet, is related to a sub-culture who sought to gain social capital among members by disrupting message board threads. This was seen as a challenge, and the more disruptive a troll could be, the more they earned respect in the eyes of the sub-culture. In this early phase of the Internet trolls were just that, a sub-culture, that might have a nuisance value to users of forums they had disrupted, but they were not in any way a societal problem. As Lovink highlights, "the problem of trolling can easily be isolated to individual cases. Trolls are figures of exception" [25].

Increasingly in the modern era, the term troll has been used extensively for a range of behaviors on the Internet, including significant incidences of harassment. In her research on the trolling phenomena, Whitney Phillips found significant frustration amongst those who identify as trolls in the "traditional" sense with the "increasingly fuzzy popular definition of trolling, which in mainstream media circles has been attributed to such a wide variety of behaviors that it has been rendered almost meaningless" [7, p. 158].

2.4 The Culture of Trolling in the Modern Era

There is little doubt that the idea of the Internet troll has transcended its sub-culture boundaries and become a staple of popular culture. In many ways this provides a cachet the perpetrator does not deserve. Another emerging element of trolling and online harassment in recent years has been its identification with the political movement known as the Alt-Right. This rise has been mapped by Angela Nagle in a recent book, and she suggests the link between trolling of vulnerable groups and the alt-right community is a significant one:

> One of the things that linked the often nihilistic and ironic chan culture to a wider culture of the alt-right orbit was their opposition to political correctness, feminism, multiculturalism, etc., and its encroachment into their freewheeling world of anonymity and tech [26].

While on one hand the troll subculture might argue their activities do not constitute genuine threats, the merging of elements of that subculture with the alt-right, and the white supremacist elements within it, suggest that trolling and politics have become more integrated. It therefore asks a lot for a victim of trolling to be able to make the distinction between the high jinks of "legitimate" trolls versus the received message that may constitute a significant threat. As Diaz has offered:

> Detecting when one is being "trolled" on the Internet is often an impossible task considering the anonymity of the speaker, and the ambiguity of text.' A jest may appear as a threat, sarcasm as defamation, or criticism as bullying [27].

It is unreasonable to ask digital citizens who are not part of a sub-culture to respect abuse and/or harassment as a joke when it appears to be identical to the real thing. The reality of the troll on social media is that they are often merely bullies, often targeting vulnerable groups and causing them distress at worst, and nuisance value at best:

> Anonymous mobs employ collaborative technologies to terrorize and silence women, people of color, and other minorities. The harassment typically includes threats of sexual violence, postings of individuals' home addresses alongside the

suggestion that they should be raped, and technological attacks that shut down blogs and websites. Cyber mobs brand targeted individuals as inferior beings and as sexual objects [16, Kindle Locations 379-381].

The anonymity element of cyberbullying/trolling cannot be underestimated. In research undertaken in 2015 by the Pew Research Center, the statistics on this were stark, highlighting the extent of anonymous harassment received:

> [O]f those who have experienced online harassment 38%, said a stranger was responsible for their most recent incident and another 26% said they did not know the real identity of the person or people involved. Taken together, this means half of those who have experienced online harassment did not know the person involved in their most recent incident [28].

The impact of trolling or cyberbullying can be significant on a victim. As Rosewarne has argued, "in the context of cyberbullying, a single electronic attack can in fact have recurrent and repetitious effects" [29]. The ubiquity of words on the Internet means that the victim may feel there is no escape from the repeatedly experiencing the bullying, since anyone with a computer can see it, and unless deleted or the perpetrator blocked, the victim may always see it in their timeline or on their account. The act of retweeting, a technique which forwards an initial tweet, means that the followers of the person retweeting will also then be aware of the initial act. Compounding this is the belief that perhaps the offending tweet will always be there, with the use of search engines to archive twitter data it may well always be on the Internet, following the victim and forever reminding them of the interaction. As Carrabis and Haimovitch argue, in the "new online world, victims have no safe haven to retreat from these public malicious acts of cyberbullying" [30]. As Delgado and Stefancic offer:

> [M]uch material posted on the Internet will remain there indefinitely, becoming "a permanent or semi-permanent part of the visible environment in which our lives, and the lives of vulnerable minorities, have to be lived." If the hate message "goes viral," it may attract millions of viewers and remain in cyberspace, perhaps forever [31].

Notwithstanding the ability of the victim to remove themselves from the perpetrator via blocking mechanisms and the like, the impact of trolling or cyberbullying can have profound effects on the person on the receiving end.

We will explore this further when we discuss the criminalization of trolling, but examples that challenge the victim/perpetrator narrative from the point of view of desert can also be regularly found and are of vital importance in considering the complexity of Internet culture. In Ronson's *So you've been publicly shamed*, the author explores the mass shaming on the Internet of people who have been believed to have transcended a norm. Such shaming exercises follow remarkably similar patterns as other cyberbullying and trolling examples. X says something that Y or Group Y on the Internet believes to be wrong, and the responses in opposition then are sent. Interestingly in Ronson's exploration, the group shaming was seen to be virtuous by those taking part in it. He highlights the case of Justine Sacco who tweeted a tasteless joke before boarding a flight to South Africa: 'Going to Africa. Hope I don't get AIDS. Just kidding. I'm white!' [32, p. 64]. Sacco arrived at the other side completely oblivious to the reality that her tweet had gone viral. Most of the tweets were genuine shock and outrage at something they deemed to be racist, however many of the tweets did seem to be akin to the type one would associate with trolling/cyberbullying. There is a sense in some of the public shaming that if people are so sure about their world view, they do not tend to see that what they are doing might constitute trolling or bullying. The notion that the victim *deserves* the treatment is one that all bullies may allow themselves to be justified by. Commenting on Ronson's work on public shaming, Peter Bradshaw of *The Guardian* suggested: "Twitter-shaming allows people who complacently think of themselves as basically nice to indulge in the dark thrill of bullying – in a righteous cause. Perhaps Ronson's article will cause a questioning of Twitter's instant-Salem culture of shame" [33].

A final point related to online harassment/trolling is the gendered elements that relate to it. While the Pew study found that men receive more harassment related to public embarrassment and the calling of offensive names, it also highlighted that females, and young females 18–24 especially, receive the most severe forms of online harassment, such as stalking, physical threats, and sustained harassment [28]. Clearly these more severe forms of harassment move beyond a simple freedom of expression justification into areas of wrongdoing that have genuine implications for women's safety online. In this context it is important to highlight that while harassment online is meted out to all, concern must be expressed at the types aimed primarily at women. Vitak et al. undertook a study of undergraduate women across US universities related to their experiences of online harassment, and a key finding suggested that women were becoming almost resigned to abuse being part of the online experience if they want to remain a part of it: "Even when women do not retreat from online spaces, a disheartening trend exposed in both anecdotal work and this study is the general sense that women are tolerant of these behaviors because they have become part and parcel of interacting online" [34].

3 Criminality of Trolling.

Social media is at its root an example of electronic communication, and the law is quite clear that electronic communications technology "can be used to incite, encourage or assist another in the commission of an offence, or to form a conspiracy" [35]. Jones organizes his treatment of the topic under four categories of offence, which closely relate to the CPS guidelines on prosecuting social media offences, as we will see further below:

- Threats of violence or damage to property.
- Harassment of an individual.
- Breaches of court orders.
- Communications that are grossly offensive, indecent, or obscene.

Jones points out that a threat to kill someone is unlawful under s.16 of the *Offences against the Person Act 1861* regardless of the medium from which that threat is received, and anyone doing so shall be guilty of an offence and liable on conviction on indictment to imprisonment for a term not exceeding ten years." Importantly, Jones points out that the *mens rea* (guilty mind) must be clear and that a threat delivered as a joke would not succeed: the intent must be to make the victim fear that the threat would be carried out. In an online scenario where over 50% of trolling behavior comes from an unknown person, how is one to tell a joke from the real thing?

General threats that might cause distress to a victim are an offence in England and Wales under s.1 of the *Malicious Communications Act* 1988 and s127 of the *Communications Act 2003*. s1 of the *Malicious Communications Act* states that a person may be guilty if they send "a letter or other article" which conveys a threat, and he is guilty of an offence if "distress or anxiety to the recipient or to any other person to whom he intends that it or its contents or nature should be communicated." Importantly there is a defense available which states that a person is not guilty if the threat was used to reinforce a demand, or he believed the threat was a legitimate means of doing so.

In *DPP v Collins* the network utilized for transmitting offensive content was the telephone network, with the defendant leaving a series of offensive telephone messages on the answering service of his MP [36]. The messages used several extremely strong racial epithets which were said to have extremely offended the MP's staff, none of whom were from the ethnic minorities targeted by the insults. The defendant was initially acquitted on the basis that his messages were offensive, but not grossly so. This was held on appeal initially; however, he was finally convicted on subsequent appeal when the Law Lords decided that the offensive messages would grossly offend a reasonable person in a multicultural society, and he should have been convicted under s127 of the *Communications Act 2003*. The *actus reus* (guilty act), then, was deemed to be sufficient to warrant conviction under s127, and the defendant should have been aware that his messages may offend, whether he intended them to or not.

Perhaps the most influential case related to social media behavior in UK law date has been *Chambers v DPP* [36] in which the key legal question related to the intention of the tweeter, and therefore the *mens rea*. In this case, which the defendant won on appeal, the defendant sent out a now infamous tweet to his followers about Robin Hood Airport in England, where he was due to leave for a trip with a love interest, and the fact that it was closed for snow. The tweet said:

> *Crap! Robin Hood Airport is closed! You've got a week and a bit to get your shit together otherwise I am blowing the airport sky high!!*

On viewing the tweet later, an airport employee informed the police and Chambers was arrested and charged under s127(1)(a) of the *Communications Act 2003* with sending a message of "a menacing character" on a public electronic communications network. Chambers was convicted at the original trial, despite him claiming that the tweet was an obvious joke and that no *mens rea* existed. Nevertheless, the court took the stance that s127(1)(a) was a strict liability offence, and that sending the tweet was sufficient to convict [36].

An initial appeal was lost by the defendant, but a later Divisional Court found in his favor, with the court taking the stance that the legislation was not designed to chill freedom of expression. The judgement summarized that: "We would merely emphasize that even expressed in these terms, the mental element of the offence is directed exclusively to the state of the mind of the offender, and that if he may have intended the message as a joke, even if a poor joke in bad taste, it is unlikely that the *mens rea* required before conviction for the offence of sending a message of a menacing character will be established" [36].

Chambers v DPP has provided a high threshold for prosecutions under s127, erring on the side of freedom of expression over offense. Convictions are still clearly possible and probable under the statute, but the dangers of a chilling wind of jokes being perceived as threats receded somewhat with the decision. Murray suggests that the case provided a rap on the knuckles for lower courts in England and Wales who failed to consider both the *actus reus* and *mens rea* of the offence [37]. The case arguably highlights a double-edged issue, in that technology is feared as a mechanism for delivering offensive content, but also that content related to terrorism, even bad jokes, is treated with little patience by some courts. Judge Bennett in the original appeal classified the tweet as being "being of a menacing nature in the context of the times in which we live" which suggests there was as much about fear of terrorism in the original decision as there was in a reasonable approach to s127 of the *Communications Act* [38]. The Chambers case led to the development of guidelines by the CPS for prosecuting social media cases, which we cited earlier.

R v Stacey was another case where the *Public Order Act 1988* was used to prosecute a Twitter troll [39]. In this case the defendant posted an offensive tweet with regards to a footballer, Fabrice Muamba, who had collapsed on the pitch gravely ill during a match. When taken to task by other Twitter users on the offending post, Stacey replied with further tweets that were racially offensive. Stacey was charged and convicted under elements of the *Public Order Act* related to racially offensive speech, rather than any of the legislation related to the online elements. This case reinforced that while the medium of the message may be at the heart of the ability to commit the crime, crimes that have real-world equivalences can be charged under existing legislation where it is deemed to be fit to do so.

A final important case to discuss is *R v Nimmo and Sorley* [40]. In this case Caroline Criado Perez and Stella Creasy MP were on the receiving end of harassing tweets from both defendants related to a campaign they had been involved in to have Jane Austen appear on a bank note. Tweets traced to an account operated by Sorley were summarized in the sentencing report as:

> "F*** off and die...you should have jumped in front of horses, go die; I will find you and you don't want to know what I will do when I do... Kill yourself before I do; r*** is the last of your worries; I've just got out of prison and would happily do more time to see you berried; seriously go kill yourself! I will get less time for that; r***?! I'd do a lot worse things than r*** you" [40].

Nimmo's tweets were in a similar vein, threatening, and coming from several accounts all linked to the defendant. The sentencing comments feature a victim report, and it makes for stark reading. Miss Criado-Perez stated that the tweets received had been life-changing in terms of putting her in fear. The report goes on to state:

> She feared the abusers would find her and carry out the threats. She felt hunted. She remembers feeling terror every time the doorbell rang. She has had to spend substantial time and money ensuring she is as untrackable as possible [40].

Creasy informed the court of the impact on her life, including installing a panic button at her home, as well as the fear it instilled in both her family and her staff.

R v Nimmo and Sorley brought the topic of Twitter abuse into the public consciousness even more strongly, especially around the gendered elements of the abuse. Despite one of the defendants in the case being female, the anonymity offered by Twitter accounts meant that the victims had no idea who made the threats, or where they were. This uncertainty and trepidation were clear in the comments made in the sentencing report, and mirrors the research discussed above by Citron. The fear instilled by harassment on social media is real, and notwithstanding times when the purpose is to trick or joke, the impact on victims is clearly stark in many circumstances. In *R v Nimmo and Sorley* an element of the case highlighted that both defendants were to some extent social misfits, and the technology allowed them to vent in what they perceived to be anonymity and without repercussions. This belief that such behavior on social media is unlikely to be traced back might explain some of the worst of the incidences, however as discussed earlier, the troll subculture may also mean that for some, trolling brings some kind of social benefit or kudos from within specific sub-communities that makes it worth the risk.

Harassment of an individual: Under s.2 and/or s.2A *Protection from Harassment Act 1997* two or more messages sent to a victim can constitute an offence. Citing *Majrowski v Guy's and St Thomas's NHS Trust* we are reminded by the courts that day to day life involves a range of situations where we will come across annoyances:

> Courts are well able to recognize the boundary between conduct which is unattractive, even unreasonable, and conduct which is oppressive and unacceptable. To cross the boundary from the regrettable to the unacceptable the gravity of the misconduct must be of an order which would sustain criminal liability [41].

In terms of social media, then, the messages received by the victim would need to meet this threshold to be liable to prosecution under the *Protection from Harassment Act*. In all of the potential prosecutions of social media interactions, the courts are reminded that the need to balance free speech with the rights of victims is paramount. Courts are especially reminded of the chilling effect on free speech of criminalizing behaviors that may well be unsavory but may well have to be permitted to occur in a free society. However, in the cases cited it is difficult to see how the laws passed by the state should not take a role in trying to punish such behaviors.

Can this be left simply to the *market*? It must be noted that the difficulty of regulating social media from the point of view of trolling and freedom of expression is a challenging task, given freedom of expression is such a culturally located value. Social media companies based in the USA and built on First Amendment values are essentially offering to the world a service that transcends the rights and values of even some liberal democracies in Europe. *Law* within a jurisdiction can attempt to address this, but the *code or architecture* of the social media companies may well be best placed to do so.

4 Regulation by Social Media

Outwith the differing legal systems in which companies such as Twitter and Facebook operate, there is also increasing pressure for the companies to be effective regulators of their own services, with a great deal of this work undertaken by code applied to the content setting standards, or norms, of behavior expected.

The relationship between the social media platform and the user forms a contract between them: the user agrees to adhere to behavioral norms, the social media company punishes anyone who deviates from these norms. Both sides living up to their side of the bargain ultimately would make regulation straightforward. Nevertheless, even if social media companies were successful in regulating most offensive content, some people would likely still be on the receiving end of content that could be deemed illegal.

In February/March 2017 Twitter introduced new initiatives to attempt to reduce the incidences of harassment some members were receiving. Included was the ability to ignore unverified accounts, set up safer searching, and provide more control over who can contact you (i.e., limiting access to you from people you do not follow, or new accounts) [42]. More recently, additions have included the ability to set who can respond to a tweet you send, as well as the ability to create a curated set of followers within your overall number. In addition, functions like blocking users who you may not wish to interact with, and reporting activity you feel breaks Twitter rules are open to anyone receiving (or seeing) abusive content.

Reidenberg highlighted that the regulation of content is a basic dilemma of policy, and that it "poses intricate philosophical, practical, and political complications" [2]. As social media companies operate in a global marketplace, the pressure on them to censor within specific jurisdictions and not others has become a pressing one. As Reidenberg summarizes, "network service providers may opt for the overly cautious route of self-censorship and opt policies of 'when in doubt, take it out'" [2].

The *Twitter Rules* document contains the regulatory information with regards to behaviors on the platform. At the preamble to the document, it is stated clearly that Twitter stresses the important of the user experience and the safety of its users. It requires all members to adhere to the rules, which include provisions related to abuse of copyright as well as specific behaviors related to harassment. The main elements that relate to the regulation of trolling behaviors (there are nine Twitter Rules in total) are:

- Violence
- Abuse/Harassment
- Hateful Conduct [43]

All the functionality in the world will not stop trolls from harassing victims when they simply need to create new accounts to perpetuate the attacks (such as in *R v Nimmo and Sorley*) if they are blocked and/or banned by the victim. Indeed, the increasing volumes of abuse received because of the use of multiple accounts is likely to make the victim feel even more vulnerable, since it is not clear if the harassment is coming from the same original troller, or if multiple others are joining the attacks. This enhanced fear is not something that is immediately within the power of the social media companies to prevent, unless the victim removes themselves from social media, and thus the obvious remedy does seem to necessitate recourse to the law.

5 Conclusions

This paper has sought to explore some legal and regulatory issues of Internet trolling and offensive behavior from a UK perspective. While there are calls on social media companies to do more to prevent abuse and harassment online, ultimately the UK state is of a mind to step in to regulate trolling via both new laws and existing laws, all the while being mindful of the clear potential for impacting on freedom of expression rights. At the time of writing in the UK, the government has introduced the *Online Safety Bill* which seems to place more onus on social media companies to regulate the content that is hosted by them [41]. The key emphasis in the bill is on companies to improve their architecture and procedures to limit exposure to harmful content, empowering users to be able to place more and easier limitations on what they are exposed to.

In closing, Lessig's four modalities remain a key paradigm of how trolling and abusive behaviors can be managed: the Internet can be regulated via the traditional justice system (law), which can be supported via the algorithms that govern usage of the services provided (code) leading to the third modality (markets) setting the parameters for the fourth (norms). Lovink suggests, the extent of how the modalities can deal with the problem is not straightforward and will say a lot about the society we live in: "Editors, programmers and, eventually, the Law will deal with the unstoppable deviant Other.... The way society deals with those who cross invisible lines tells us a lot about the limits of the rhetoric of tolerance, openness, and freedom" [25, p. 163].

References

1. Lessig, L.: Code: and Other Laws of Cyberspace (Basic Books 1999), p. 4 (1999)
2. Reidenberg, J.R.: Lex informatica: the formulation of information policy rules through technology. Texas Law Rev. **76**, 553 (1997–1998). https://ir.lawnet.fordham.edu/faculty_scholarship/42
3. Crown Prosecution Service: Guidelines on prosecuting cases involving communications sent via social media (2018). https://www.cps.gov.uk/legal-guidance/social-media-guidelines-prosecuting-cases-involving-communications-sent-social-media
4. Gani, A.: Internet trolling: quarter of teenagers suffered online abuse last year. The Guard. (2016). https://www.theguardian.com/uk-news/2016/feb/09/internet-trolling-teenagers-online-abuse-hate-cyberbullying
5. Allegretti, A.: Jess Phillips responds to trolls who sent her rape threats on Twitter. Huffington Post. http://www.huffingtonpost.co.uk/entry/jess-phillips-rape-threats-twitter_uk_574d95c6e4b03e9b9ed6262c
6. Labour's Yvette Cooper explores trolling aimed at women. BBC News, 17 December 2015. http://www.bbc.co.uk/news/av/uk-politics-35120551/labour-s-yvette-cooper-explores-trolling-aimed-at-women
7. Phillips, W.: This is Why We Can't Have Nice Things: Mapping the Relationship Between Online Trolling and Mainstream Culture, p. 16. MIT Press, Cambridge (2015)

8. Carter, C.: Twitter troll jailed for ‘campaign of hatred’ against Stella Creasy. Dly. Telegr. (2014). http://www.telegraph.co.uk/news/uknews/crime/11127808/Twitter-troll-jailed-for-campaign-of-hatred-against-Stella-Creasy.html
9. Cooper, Y.: Why I'm campaigning to reclaim the internet from sexist trolls. Telegraph (2017). http://www.telegraph.co.uk/women/politics/why-im-campaigning-to-reclaim-the-internet-from-sexist-trolls/
10. Levmore, S.X., Nussbaum, M.C.: The Offensive Internet: speech, Privacy, and Reputation. Harvard University Press (2010)
11. Council of Europe: European Convention on Human Rights (1950). https://www.echr.coe.int/documents/convention_eng.pdf
12. Spinello, R.A.: Regulating cyberspace: the policies and technologies of control, p. 109 (2002)
13. Gaus, A.: Trolling attacks and the need for new approaches to privacy torts. USFL Rev. **47**, 353 (2012)
14. McGoldrick, D.: The limits of freedom of expression on facebook and social networking sites: a UK perspective. Hum. Rights Law Rev. **13**, 125, 130 (2013)
15. Barlow, J.P.: A declaration of the independence of cyberspace (1996)
16. Citron. In: Levmore, S.X., Nussbaum, M.C. (eds.) The Offensive Internet: Speech, Privacy, and Reputation, pp. 378–379 (2010)
17. Reno Vs ACLU 521 U.S. 844 (1997)
18. Lipschultz, J.H.: Free expression in the age of the Internet: social and legal boundaries, p. 127 (1999)
19. Barendt, E.M.: Freedom of Speech, p. 12. Oxford (1985)
20. Group Vilification Reconsidered. Yale L.J. **89**, 308, 332 (1979)
21. Abah: Legal regulation of CSR: the case of social media and gender-based harassment. U. Balt. J. Media L. Ethics **5**, 38, 55 (2016)
22. Marshak, E.: Online harassment: a legislative solution. Harv. J. Legis. **54**, 501, 515–17 (2017)
23. troll2. In: Thorne, T. (ed.) Dictionary of Contemporary Slang, 4th edn. Bloomsbury, London (2014). http://search.credoreference.com/content/entry/acbslang/troll2/0?institutionId=396
24. Trolls – pass notes No 3,268. The Guardian, 22 October 2012. https://www.theguardian.com/technology/shortcuts/2012/oct/22/pass-notes-trolls
25. Lovink, G.: Social Media Abyss: Critical Internet Cultures and the Force of Negation, p. 163. Wiley, New York (2016)
26. Nagle, A.: Kill All Normies: Online Culture Wars From 4Chan and Tumblr to Trump and the Alt-Right Zero Books, p. 16 (2017)
27. Diaz, F.L.: Trolling and the First Amendment: Protecting Internet Speech in the Era of Cyber Bullies and Internet Defamation. U. Ill. J.L. Tech. Pol'y 135, 160, p. 137 (2016)
28. Pew Research Center, October 2014, Online Harassment. http://www.pewinternet.org/2014/10/22/online-harassment/
29. Rosewarne, L.: Cyberbullies, Cyberactivists, Cyberpredators: Film, TV, and Internet Stereotypes, p. 83 (2016)
30. Carrabis, A.B., Haimovitch, S.D.: Cyberbullying: adaptation from the old school sandlot to the 21st century world wide web—the court system and technology law's race to keep pace. J. Tech. L. Pol'y **16**, 143, 173 (2011)
31. Delgado, R., Stefancic, J.: Four observations about hate speech. Wake Forest L. Rev. **49**, 319, 344 (2014)
32. Ronson, J.: So You've Been Publicly Shamed. Pan Macmillan (2015)
33. Bradshaw, P.: Here come the Oscars: still a cruel joke in a cruel town. The Guardian, 18 February 2015. https://www.theguardian.com/commentisfree/2015/feb/18/oscars-awards-night-winner-tv

34. Vitak, J., et al.: Identifying women's experiences with and strategies for mitigating negative effects of online harassment. In: Proceedings of the 2017 ACM Conference on Computer Supported Cooperative Work and Social Computing, p. 1239 (2017)
35. DPP v Collins [2006] UKHL 40
36. Chambers v DPP [2012] EWHC 2157
37. Murray, I.: Information technology law: the law and society, 8th edition, p. 151 (2017)
38. Allen Green, D.: The high court is unable to agree on twitter joke trial appeal. New Statesman (2012)
39. R v Stacey Appeal No: A20120033
40. https://www.judiciary.gov.uk/judgments/r-v-nimmo-and-sorley-judgment/
41. [2006] UKHL 34; [2007] 1 A.C. 224
42. Constine, J.: Twitter lets you avoid trolls by muting new users and strangers. Tech Crunch (2017). https://techcrunch.com/2017/07/10/twitter-mute/
43. Twitter Rules. https://help.twitter.com/en/rules-and-policies/twitter-rules
44. Department for Culture, Media, and Sport. Online Safety Bill: Factsheet (2022). https://www.gov.uk/government/publications/online-safety-bill-supporting-documents/online-safety-bill-factsheet

AI and Machine Learning

"That's Not Damning with Faint Praise": Understanding the Adoption of Artificial Intelligence for Digital Preservation Tasks

Giulia Osti(✉) and Amber Cushing

University College Dublin, Dublin, Ireland
giulia.osti@ucdconnect.ie, amber.cushing@ucd.ie

Abstract. Memory organisations need to constantly address the adoption of digital technology to remain relevant in light of recent innovations that constitute the so-called fourth technological revolution. This study aims to expand the understanding of the current adoption of Artificial Intelligence for digital preservation tasks by investigating it through the lenses of the Diffusion of Innovations theory in relation to disruptive innovations. The analysis takes the form of an exploratory qualitative inquiry, performed on the transcripts of four focus groups presenting opinions on specific applications of Artificial Intelligence systems, mostly related to Computer Vision, expressed by professionals engaged in digital preservation. The study results indicate that there is strong interest in adopting these innovations. However, further research and the development of a dialogue among the involved communities of practice are necessary to determine the implications and potential outcomes of this technological advancement in the context of digital preservation.

Keywords: Artificial intelligence · Digital preservation · Focus groups · Abductive analysis · Qualitative methods · Diffusion of innovations theory

1 Introduction

GLAMs – Galleries, Libraries, Archives, and Museums, eventually cited as LAMs – is an umbrella term referring to organisations that are dedicated to memory-keeping, and therefore perform digital preservation, although following largely distinct curatorial practices. What these organisations have in common is the aim of collecting, documenting, preserving, and organising different kinds of documents [30]; the professionals within this diverse community provide information services in a wide variety of formats.

Fast-paced evolution and heightened access to Information and Communication Technologies (ICTs) have prompted GLAMs to explore new and dedicated methods for content publishing, access, indexing, and management, eventually including some Artificial Intelligence (AI) applications. Although the topic has

© The Author(s), under exclusive license to Springer Nature Switzerland AG 2023
I. Sserwanga et al. (Eds.): iConference 2023, LNCS 13971, pp. 259–276, 2023.
https://doi.org/10.1007/978-3-031-28035-1_18

a certain level of representation in the literature, the effective implementation of these technologies is challenging to evaluate. This is due to the lack of characterising settings and of a common understanding of the very concept of AI across GLAMs.

In our study, we offer a snapshot of the opinions expressed by GLAM professionals about the adoption of AI technologies. The analysis takes the form of a qualitative inquiry, performed on the transcripts of four focus groups discussing the adoption of AI systems through specific prompts – mostly related to the area of Computer Vision. We investigated the elements comprising the "perceived characteristics of innovation", one of the core aspects of the Diffusion of Innovation (DoI) theory in order to broaden our understanding of the variables related to this phenomenon.

The background section introduces the theoretical framework – the DoI theory and related concepts – as well as gives an essential overview of current AI applications in GLAMs. Following, methods, sample size and features are introduced and explained in detail; the analytic framework, which draws upon the most recent developments in the abductive analysis, is then explored. The results are presented in the form of a multi-level thematic analysis based on the final code equations, discussed and contextualised within the DoI theory. Last, the conclusions wrap up the major findings and highlight potential further research opportunities.

2 Background

2.1 Adoption and Diffusion of Technologies: An Overview

Recently, the adoption of technological innovations has become a vast and articulate research topic, with a wide-ranging representation and application in diverse fields, such as e-governance [18,43], healthcare [9,16,20] and more rarely in the context of heritage [3,4,26]. As emerging from a recent analysis [34], at least 21 theoretical frameworks have been developed to investigate the variables and dynamics characterising this phenomenon. The review identifies the Technology Acceptance Model (TAM) as the most popular framework used to explain Information Technology (IT) adoption, which closely focuses on users' behaviour and attitude towards the use of technology [8]. Following TAM, the second-ranking among the most frequently occurring theories in literature is the Diffusion of Innovations (DoI), originally introduced by Rogers [31]. Differently from TAM, DoI focuses on the processes of adoption and diffusion of innovations under different scenarios, characterising the adopters based on their innovativeness, either approaching them as individuals or organisations. Uncertainty, or the lack of predictability which triggers the information-seeking process, is at the core of the DoI theory. Rogers observed that even "knowing of a technological innovation creates uncertainty about its consequences in the mind of potential adopters [32]." Therefore, the reduction of uncertainty about the advantages/disadvantages of innovation is what drives the decision made about its adoption – whether it might result in acceptance or rejection.

The full dynamics of this event and its variables are illustrated in the five-stages innovation decision-process, presented in Fig. 1. To conceptualise his model, Rogers built upon the work of Ryan and Gross [33] which describes "the process through which an individual (or another decision-making unit) passes from gaining initial knowledge of an innovation to forming an attitude toward the innovation, to making a decision, to adopt or reject, to implementation of the new idea, and to confirmation of this decision [32]".

As summarised by Dearing and Cox [9], there are three sets of variables that can be analysed to explain the success (or the failure) of the diffusion of an innovation: the balance between the innovation's pros and cons, the characteristics of adopters and the larger socio-political context. By understanding the structural position of each adopter within the investigated context, it is possible to deduce motivation and time of adoption; Rogers individuated five different categories of adopters (innovators, early adopters, early majority, late majority and laggards) depending on their innovativeness, which reflects the (pro)activity towards the adoption of new ideas in comparison with other units of adoption part of the same system [32].

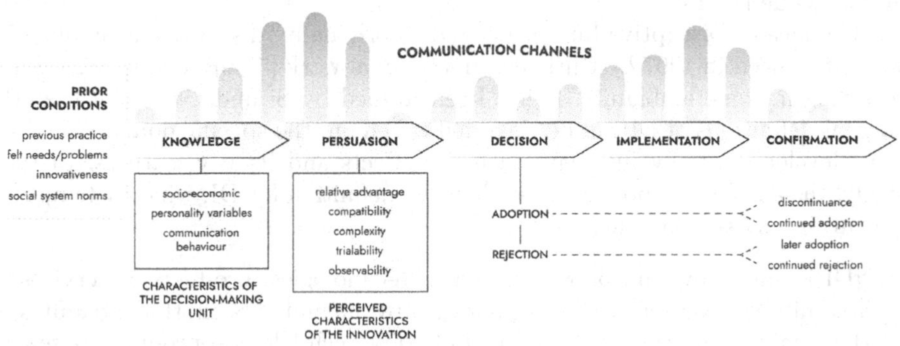

Fig. 1. The innovation-decision process from [32], re-designed by G. Osti.

As with other frameworks, Rogers' proposal has undergone a number of expansions and criticisms over the years. Kee [19] in the chapter written for the *Encyclopaedia of Organisational Communication* argues that the main criticisms moved to the DoI theory are the following:

- The pro-innovation bias, or the perception of the introduction of innovation as necessarily positive, which leads to overlooking the foreseen and unforeseen effects happening once reached the confirmation stage [15].
- The individual blame bias, highlighting the incorrect adoption and implementation of a piece of technology performed by an individual, instead of considering the context in which the failure happens [23].
- The knowledge gap bias, or the uneven distribution of knowledge causes the early adopters to have a higher socio-economic status [17].

Nevertheless, the nature of the innovation and the adoption domain have a central role in shaping the diffusion dynamics. Innovation can be something tangible or intangible which is receipted as "new" by the adopters no matter to its objective "newness" – which often develops along the axes of knowledge, persuasion or decision [32]. Hence, cutting-edge and (apparently) advantageous innovations might not be rapidly adopted as expected.

2.2 Towards the Adoption of Artificial Intelligence in GLAMs

Recognised as a research field in 1956 [22], Artificial Intelligence (AI) has no universally accepted definition but it is generally understood as "the capacity of computers or other machines to exhibit or simulate intelligent behaviour" [27]. AI has become a label for a wide-ranging set of methods and techniques applicable to any domain; the conversation around their adoption has never been so intense and ubiquitary as the accessibility threshold (intellectual, economical and practical) has been sensibly become more permeable in the recent years. AI, block-chain and more generally ICT, have been pointed at as a disruptive innovations, capable of re-shaping every sector of the economy and even our everyday life [12,14].

The idea of Disruptive Innovation (DI) – originally "disruptive technology" – was introduced in 1997 by Christensen's seminal work [5] and further expanded, resulting in some ambiguity. It has been argued by Si and Chen [36] that the current definitions of DI can be classified based on: the specific domain in which it is developed, its evolutionary trail, its effects and its key features. In their study, the authors propose a comprehensive definition for DI, which attempts at capturing its essential features:

> "[DI is an] innovation process in which technologies, products or services are initially inferior to those provided by incumbents in the attributes that mainstream consumers value, but these technologies, products or services can attract and satisfy the consumers in low-end or new markets with advantages in performance attributes (such as being cheap, simple, or convenient) that these consumers value but which at the same time are neglected by mainstream markets."

Within the context of GLAMs, AI is often used as a synonym of Machine Learning (ML), a subset of AI methods using experience to enhance performance or to allow making predictions [24], generally branched in supervised learning, unsupervised learning, and reinforcement learning. Among GLAMs, libraries have been proactively developing the discussion about AI adoption as testified by the increasing number of studies and reports available in literature [28,41,42]. The report on Machine Learning + Libraries commissioned by the Library of Congress Labs in 2020 gathers extensive documentation on the topic, proposing an overview of current applications of ML in libraries and other cultural heritage organisations, exploring extant criticalities and best practices [6].

Four main areas proposing a review of several promising ML applications are featured in the report:

1. Crowdsourcing, or the public participation in annotating collections.
2. Discoverability within and among collections, which application features: clustering and classification; pre-processing; Optical Character Recognition (OCR); Handwritten Text Recognition (HTR); metadata and historical tabular data extraction; non-textual data annotation and linking data.
3. Library administration and outreach including: collection management; preservation and conservation; ML literacy, education and support to patrons' ML experiments.
4. Creative and archivist interventions, exploiting ML's potential for expressive, artistic, and activist projects.

As emerging from this report, a certain and prolonged effort has been invested so far in experimenting with ML in the libraries. However, the section dedicated to the integration – the effective implementation – of these systems into libraries reveals a theoretical rather than practical nature. As suggested by the authors, "the ML and libraries field must develop means to bridge a world that prioritizes expert data and metadata, created slowly, and a set of methods that generate useful but flawed data and metadata, more quickly and at a larger scale [6]."

In 2020 a dedicated task force of Europeana Network Association experts realised a survey for environmental scanning purposes [21] or to assess the progress being made with AI in cultural heritage management and preservation. The survey included 56 memory institutions from 20 different (mostly EU) countries, which described 36 use cases featuring AI applications. The analysis revealed that memory institutions' interest in AI has mainly to do with facilitating the exploitation and eventually the production of their digitised collections. Most of the projects were text-based, in some cases making use of OCR and HTR for digitisation purposes; however, the sample was highly diversified in the approach and in terms of targeted contents. This variability was referenced to the experimental nature and high threshold for AI work, or due to the wide array of available applications and frameworks within AI. Nevertheless, the impacts of the use cases were described as still in an early stage, having their goals ranging from the improvement of production workflows to deepening knowledge about AI integration.

While not constituting more than a small benchmark providing us with the essential traits to evaluate the state of AI adoption in GLAMs, the aforementioned reports are symptomatic of a fuzzy situation. If we were to name a stage of the DoI innovation-decision process to explain what we observe, we might cautiously say between the persuasion and the implementation stage. Fear of redundancy/job loss, algorithmic discrimination and the eventual loss of institutional credibility are only some of the potential threats which seem to counterbalance the benefits that might be generated through AI adoption in GLAMs, which are currently hindering other sectors of application [11]. The reason these concerns – or better uncertainties – are globally shared, is AI's main strength and weakness: its universal applicability. The data used to feed the machine determine the goodness (or the badness) of the outputs, alongside theoretical and interpretive choices and frameworks [13]. As consequence, the forms of AI adoption in any field tend to be highly specific. The authors of a very recent review on teaching and learning AI resources for GLAMs agree on seeing the emergence of challenges unique to the GLAMs context [7]. Additionally, they observe that if professionals do not commit to develop the expertise to deal with AI within their domain, the benefits deriving from the adoption of this technology might not be fully exploited. Similarly, Strien et al. [37] argue that, independently of the extent and nature of involvement of GLAMs professionals into computational methods, having at least a basic understanding of AI methods will be pivotal, since many of those will be embedded to future technologies.

3 Materials and Methods

3.1 Focus Groups

This analysis is built upon a series of four focus groups, originally aimed at collecting the opinions on the adoption of AI systems for digital curation tasks expressed by professionals engaging with digital preservation. The focus groups were conducted between 2020 (FG1) and 2021 (FG2-4) by master students, as part of the module on digital curation run by A. Cushing; G. Osti participated in the original data analysis session for FG2-4.

In FG1 four professionals from an important library volunteered to discuss the outputs of the application of Computer Vision (CV) to some photographs of one of the library's collections. The CV task consisted of the generation of tags and descriptive titles for four of the historical photographs part of the collection; it was performed in Python, using Microsoft Azure Cognitive Services for Computer Vision.

FG2-4 were informed by the issues and themes emerging from FG1, and designed to extensively further inquiry theoretical and practical AI implementation aspects. The focus groups featured three to five practitioners in digital curation working for different institutions around the globe, recruited through word of mouth, social networks and mailing lists. Table 1 provides the demographics for the participants (n = 16); further details on the focus groups will be disclosed contextually with the results, in Sect. 4. Provenance, role and affiliation of the participants were coded to general categories, ensuring anonymisation.

3.2 Research Design

Abduction, a pragmatic qualitative method aiming at theory-making, was initially introduced by Peirce [29] as an alternative to purely inductive or deductive approaches in natural sciences, and later expanded by several scholars engaging with qualitative approaches. The abductive analysis is characterised by the research orientation, which is set to identify unexpected findings or exceptions violating a set of theoretical constructs, to be understood by analysing variation in order to expand the violated assumptions. The approach combines induction and deduction in various phases of the research process in an iterative fashion.

Table 1. Participants demographics

Focus group	Participant	Provenance	Role	Affiliation	Gender identity
FG1(2020)	PD101	Ireland	Digital Preservation Manager	Public GLAM	M
	PD102	Ireland	Digitisation Programme Manager	Public GLAM	M
	PD103	Ireland	Assistant Keeper	Public GLAM	F
	PD104	Ireland	Assistant Keeper	Public GLAM	F
FG2(2021)	PD201	Ireland	Researcher	Higher Education	F
	PD202	Ireland	Archivist	Higher Education	F
	PD203	Ireland	Digital Curator	Private GLAM	F
	PD204	Denmark	Librarian	Public GLAM	F
	PD205	UK	Archives Manager	Public GLAM	M
FG3(2021)	PD301	US	Digital Humanities Librarian	Higher Education	F
	PD302	China	User Manager Assistant	Private GLAM	F
	PD303	China	User Services Assistant	Private GLAM	F
FG4(2021)	PD401	Ireland	Project Manager	Higher Education	M
	PD402	UK	Digital curator	Public GLAM	F
	PD403	China	Digital curator	Public GLAM	M
	PD404	US	Library & Digitisation Manager	Public GLAM	F

This study aligns with the approach to abductive analysis described by Tavory [38] and Timmermans [39]. The coding process was built upon the methodology proposed by Vila-Henninger et al. [40], articulated in the following steps:

1. *Generation of the abductive codebook.* A deductive theory-based codebook was initially drafted, broadly based on the core elements mentioned in the innovation-decision process (Fig. 1). A second round of inductive coding to refine the codebook was performed to identify the unexpected findings, or anomalies violating the theoretical framework until reaching saturation.
2. *Abductive data reduction through code equations.* Code equations were created by collating codes from the original codebook to reach a higher degree of specificity. Several code equations were created and explored through queries and validated in a single round, which led to keeping only a subset.
3. *In-depth abductive analysis.* A final inductive coding step was performed on the validated code equations, in order to understand their relationship with the theoretical framework.

Multiple coding styles (structural, axial, and magnitude coding) were adopted at various stages [35]. The data analysis was performed in NVivo 12 Plus for Mac.

3.3 Limitations and Justifications of the Study

The study is not generalised based on several aspects. Recruitment was performed on a voluntary basis; the provenance and gender of the participants resulted unevenly distributed: 50%(8) worked in Ireland and the other remaining half in various EU and non-EU countries; 68.7%(11) identified their gender as female. 56.2%(9) of the participants were affiliated with a public GLAM, while the remaining 43.8%(7) were working for a private GLAM or in the higher education sector.

As a result of the small sample size, focus groups are not expected to rely on probability sampling, but rather to replicate the process of formulating and articulating complex concepts [10]. This study has a qualitative design, different from most of the studies undertaken to investigate the adoption of innovations which attempt to quantify some specific aspects of the phenomenon [1,4]. We chose this strategy to acquire in-depth information and capture group-thinking dynamics, which are crucial to tracking how a hardly-definable concept as AI is devised by members of different GLAMs.

4 Results and Analysis

4.1 Abductive Codebook and Final Code Equations

The abductive process allowed us to refine the research question from the conclusion of step one. The obtained abductive codebook included a reworked set of the concepts occurring in Fig. 1; its final version is presented in Table 2.

The "unexpected findings" were mostly concentrated in the fragments corresponding to Prompt 1 from FG2-4, which continuity with FG1 led to a structure-based re-coding of the focus groups; the presentation of the results has been influenced by this structural aspect. The emerging affinities and contrasts allowed the formulation of the code equations during step two; the validation, facilitated by the formulation of contextual queries in Nvivo, confirmed their consistency. The validated code equations are the following:

- AI potential adoption scenarios envisioned by participants are variable, eventually driven by the *technology cluster*.
- There are no clear *mitigation strategies* in response to the expressed *concerns and consequences*.
- The *technology cluster* to which AI is compared is still AI.

4.2 Adoption Scenarios

Prompt 1 required the participants to FG2-4 to delve into a realistic decision-making situation: they had to rely on their professional background and experience to discuss their choice. The task consisted in deciding among three different potential applications of AI which could help manage an extensive, unpublished and partially digitised collection of historical photographs from the first quarter of the 1900s. The available options were:

- automating the generation of descriptive metadata;
- automating the appraisal of the photographs;
- clustering and discovering hidden patterns in the photographs.

Table 2. The final abductive codebook.

Code	Description	Sub-codes
Use cases	Any real-world application of AI mentioned by the participants	*Prompt-based*, examples aligned with the discussion of the prompt given to the participants
		Off-prompt, any example provided which has no direct relationship with the discussed prompt
Perceived attributes	DoI theory-based categories related to the persuasion stage	*Relative advantage*, any aspect of the use of AI constituting an improvement for the participants
		Compatibility, consistency of AI application with the extant curatorial measures, values or practices
		Test/consumption balance, aspects connected with the usability, understandability and the observability of AI application
Uncertainties	Hardly rulable variables, which handling might determine the acceptance or the rejection of AI	*Mitigation strategies*, grounded actions proposed to reduce uncertainties
		Concerns and consequences, anxieties of the participants towards these variables, either based on observed outcomes or on personal opinions
Technology cluster	Distinguishable elements of technology perceived as closely interrelated to AI systems	

FG1 can be intended as an experimental real-world application of option one, since it demanded the participants to comment on the CV-based generation of descriptive metadata (titles and tags) performed on four historical photographs picked from a well-known collection from the institution of which the participants were working for. They were asked to build upon the outputs and discuss the potential of the tool in facilitating them to catalog photographs or in any other task.

Opt. 1: Automating the Generation of Descriptive Metadata. Almost the entirety of the participants to FG2-4 voted for option one, which was defined the "most useful" (PD201), "accurate" and "valuable" (PD203), or even "less harmful" (PD202); PD204 understood the automated generation of a baseline description as a relative advantage, potentially enhancing the accessibility of the collection.

The participants from FG1 were tendentially positive to the outputs although skeptical towards the further steps – two high and two low accuracy outputs were shown, to avoid the pro-innovation bias. PD104 questioned the full implementation of a similar system, acknowledging that:

> "[...] a relatively homogeneous group of photographs or something like that, then there's definitely potential. How realistic that is, or how practical that is, I'm not sure... that actually exists with every collection, because what you find with every collection is every collection is different."

PD103 was not satisfied with the specificity of the application "from what we seen, it's not doesn't seem to me to be particularly useful"; PD102 outlined the limits of the current level of the application: "I mean, as we say, it may not be that useful, but it's identified quite a lot there, that's, you know, it's part of the way there towards being something that might be useful. You know, that's not damning with faint praise."

Opt. 2: Automating the Appraisal. Option two was considered the most controversial, defined "too risky" (PD402) or facing a straightforward rejection "I am not trusting AI to make curatorial decisions" (PD404); PD303 simply deemed AI incapable to run the task. PD301 considered option two from the perspective of the end-user:

> "Yeah, number two isn't something I would do um. Like if I'm putting something into a repository, I would keep everything. Like you know if I'm putting a collection online. You know I don't know what's going to be valuable to the researchers, so I'd put everything."

PD403 was the only one choosing appraisal as their first option:

> "And I would choose two, it could be the most risky here, but I would say it probably depends on a different work, you know, work methods here, for

example, for me, [uh], from like my working perspective, how-how do you choose keep or not keep it's-it's depends on some technical(?) metadata here."

In FG1, either PD101 and PD102 recognised the relative advantage of facilitating appraisal, however not through a full automation process. PD101 recalled a situation in which AI application could have been strategic, applying it to manage born-digital collection featuring sequential shoots, a so characterised by a high redundancy of the same subjects and angles:

"And so we're, you know, we're kind of trying to get a sense of, of these, you know, let's say 100 photographs, how many kind of unique situations are there, people, location, camera angle; and it would be amazing, if there could be some way where it could at least do some sort of grouping, which would say, okay, in this sub folder, it looks like there's maybe eight unique moments. And here are the groupings. And then that could give you a sense of well, do we actually want to appraise and maybe dispose of all of these not duplicates, but similar images? And it would, it would kind of, it could aid in that very manual process of grouping them. And that, and then you can maybe have a single description for those groups, as opposed to trying to do an item level description. So that kind of sense of similarities and groupings with a lovely user interface around it, could be really helpful, I think, for my day to day work."

PD102 added to the observation by extending this AI application perspective towards what happens before appraisal:

"[...] but one area that I've had experience with previously and possibly seen some things here, is where no information or useful information exists already, because that does affect our workflows in terms of what images we keep, and what images we don't after we digitise. So, being able to supply information where it doesn't already exist to create a kind of baseline for description to be supplemented afterwards might be beneficial."

Opt. 3: Clustering and Discovering Hidden Patterns. Option three was eventually pointed as a potential follow-up to option one (PD203, PD204), but others addressed it as the hardest thing to do (PD401, PD404), being still in an early development stage (PD202) or eventually "unnecessary" (PD301). Almost none of the participants took a clear position in regards to this option and, to a certain extent, they expressed a different interpretation. While PD403 envisioned is as a sort of standalone knowledge systems "or the third one it's kind of, uh, it's not based on the item itself, but it's based on a whole system, like a whole database, and you need to uh, like make review if it's in the right position this database", PD301 compared it to the Semantic Web:

"[option] three is sort of like to me it sounds like a semantic web kind of thing. Which is interesting, but again, it would require some kind of [inaudible segment] expertise like to be able to make for an intelligent look over the AI, what the AI does. And also, it's not like entirely necessary for me to put out the collection, I just really need metadata."

PD101 from FG1 reported about a scenario in which AI adoption could provide an interesting application:

"[...] I wish that we could have had some sort of an AI project. And it was where there was a filmmaker who wanted to do a project using archival footage purely of the moon. And now, I thought that this was a perfect example because in the cataloguing, the descriptive cataloguing that we would be doing, you would never mention the existence of a moon and at any stage right? That's never the subject of any kind. It's just happens to be in the background. But it was the focus of what he wanted. And so our descriptions were actually quite useless to him. And it was purely going on the memory of people saying, 'Oh, I'm pretty sure there's a moon...appears in this particular film.' And so it would be amazing if you could, if you had access to a bunch of like access copies, like mp4 or something like that, and you could just run this. And like if it was 'moon', or if it was 'sun,' or you know, horse and carts."

Further Applications. The participants to FG1 deemed the presented CV application as "a way in, a low-level way in"(PD205) or "not alternative to cataloguing"(PD102) but something that has "a distinct role to play"(PD102) as, eventually noted by PD101 "there are certain times when there's an access case, or research case, where a traditional archival description or whatever just, just doesn't fit the bill." PD204 suggested looking at AI as a potential partner in digital transactions:

"Yeah my perspective on AI is that it should be used to improve services and I'd like to see a human-centred approach where humans learn from the computers machines, just like machines learn from the humans, humans. And in that way we can solve the main problems together, more like a partnership."

In the same fragment PD201 follows remarking the limits of current AI systems based on their experience:

"I suppose I work in a field quite close to AI, I work in national language processing, so for me AI is a very general term for, yeah, like what other people have said, that idea of trying to solve problems computationally, that are quite difficult for humans but may be trivial for machines that have these huge computing process power. But then I have, you know, applied that to my own field which is language, and so how can you understand and use language using computers, which obviously don't understand the language, it's just symbols to them."

4.3 Broadening Knowledge as a Mitigation Strategy

As anticipated by the validated code equation, there are no case-specific mitigation strategies, as most of the emerging uncertainties stem from the applications on AI in other domains. However, the observations made by the participants on the whole innovation-decision process provide us with a consistent answer: more knowledge and training are needed to start addressing some of the existing concerns. PD401 developed on the significance of training and the development of a skill set relevant with AI and the context in which it is applied, to avoid time-wasting:

> "So the type of job that we're doing has changed. And if you don't know how to build a ground truth you're wasting your time. If you buy an AI that hasn't got a ground truth built in with it that does what you want you've wasted your money. So it's not like these things are just out of the box solutions that will be put into a cultural heritage situation and work. I would imagine that you have things in the [library institution], that you could make your AI work on it, to say recognise pictures or drawings or maps, but they won't work in [country]. They'll have to create their own ground truth, so, it's not a universal solution, and it is a different set of skills that need to be learned before you're going to get anything out of it. So I think the whole thing comes down to training."

The need for a deeper understanding of the potential of AI in relation to big data is expressed by PD205, "it's a question of kind of human aspirations being matched to what's possible with technology to create something at a much larger scale than we could manage in the same space of time, just by doing it manually or analog, in analog ways", and also implicitly by PD202, which advocates for the awareness of the whole process and what to expect from it:

> "[...] I think it can be very easy to, to think of AI as solving problems and saving money and saving time, am, but in actual fact, if you don't resource it properly (cause more?) problems em, and, and, that needs to be put in place as well, making sure that the time is spent on it and making sure that you don't end up halfway through a project and realize, you have to cut corners and it makes the whole thing kind of null and void."

4.4 AI as a Technology Cluster

One of the most particular outstanding features from the transcripts is the way in which the participants refer to AI coeval technologies; in several cases the participants fail to define boundaries between AI and other technologies or in providing a clean cut definition, although all of them display a very good understanding of its functioning and its practical application:

> "AI always sort of speaks to a sort of a digitisation of a previously analog or manual process, so whether that's a simple code that's written to look

through a few documents for, to find terms or, or, or if it's something much more large scale, whether it's like running a factory through mainly computerised processes, it's, it's any level of that." (PD203)

Supporting the effective expertise of the participants, additional direct and indirect experience-based opinions on AI adoption occur in other fragments of the transcripts. The application areas mentioned in the examples mostly relate to text processing, featuring OCR and other technologies. PD401 mentions working with HTR on historical manuscripts and, according to their opinion "it's really good at it, and it is doing things that would frequently require human interaction and it does give good answers based on probabilities and so on, but I would make the point that I'm in Humanities because I'm really bad at maths [laughs]." Other AI applications like text extraction via ML (PD101) or text classification tasks performed in the context of literature/systematic reviews (PD203, PD204) are mentioned. Yet, is surprising to find observation like the following from PD301:

"Yeah I mean, I guess I wouldn't see OCR as AI. Um I don't know what you think but like we- I work pretty closely with our- we um, we have [a colleague with archiving position]. And we're looking at like you know, getting OCR because our main archive- online archives of theses [inaudible segment]. I don't know, I mean, I guess to me why OCR has been around for so long and why artificial intelligence implies like more to me – more like intelligence than is in OCR, but maybe I'm wrong."

Another interesting remark is made by PD101 that, while knowing the limits of application of the CV model outputs showed to them called in another method, arguing: "but my immediate question is like, why hasn't it just done the optical character recognition? Like the title is there in the photograph on the subject", defining it as "an obvious thing to do."

5 Discussion

Here we summarise our main findings:

- *AI adoption scenarios.* Despite some reservations, generating descriptive metadata through automation (opt. 1) was well received. Appraisal automation (option 2) was mostly viewed negatively: the process of determining the value of records in a specified context (e.g. collection, single item, file, etc.), is one of the pivotal functions of archival professionals, which is mostly empirical and so difficult to transfer to a machine. There was a suspension of judgement for clustering and hidden patterns discovery (opt. 3) since no participant took a position and different understandings of the task emerged from the discussion. Further applications envisioned for AI are built upon its current limits, providing a deeper snapshot of either the level of technology understanding on the participants and of the ongoing negotiation of the work relationship between humans and machines.

- *Knowledge as a mitigation strategy.* In contrast with the variable perspectives around the practical applications of AI, the participants showed a certain agreement on the need for developing a better understanding of the implied technologies and the for a strong vertical (context-based) specialisation.
- *AI as technology cluster.* Some participants mention other AI applications as coevals to AI, but do not necessarily recognize them as such. Most of the participants have a basic understanding of computational methods; image-based techniques are mostly discussed as part of the prompts while they tend to recall and build upon text-based techniques.

Re-invention, or "the degree to which an innovation is changed or modified by a user in the process of its adoption and implementation" [32] can be pivotal in mitigating uncertainties. It is essential to review the roles and tasks to be performed by humans and machines, since their eventual overlap has emerged as a strong source of uncertainty. It is not a coincidence that the concept of "human-in-the-loop" recently entered the academic debate: this umbrella term refers to the design of interactions between humans and ML algorithms that emphasise human involvement [25]. Therefore, identifying complementary spaces for algorithms and human-made decisions can be considered a high priority task in the AI adoption agenda of memory organisations.

The different opinions on the relative advantages of AI applications highlighted in this study might either reflect the diverging interests and work practices characterising the organisations part of the "GLAMs umbrella", or be the result of a lack of knowledge about the limitations and opportunities that AI applications provide. This is consistent with the need for a better understanding of AI expressed by the participants collected under the second code equation and with the extant literature [6,7,28,37].

Last, in the DoI framework the technology cluster comprises "one or more distinguishable elements of technology that are perceived as being closely interrelated" [32]. AI applications are interdependent and the fruit of an intense research layering, which for GLAMs is largely documented in the field of Digital Humanities, having a strong historicality on text-based applications [2,13]. Applications to non-textual media had a more recent development due to technology infrastructure and computing power constraints, which might explain why the participants were mostly presenting text-based examples.

6 Conclusions

This study attempted to explore and investigate the opinions of GLAMs professionals about AI in the context of digital preservation. The results suggest that AI adoption in memory organisations is still in an early stage. To better understand AI applications' advantages and disadvantages, GLAM professionals need to engage in a healthy dialogue and further experimentation to better understand their implications within digital preservation. These preliminary results can inform further mixed-methods inquiries, which might provide a detailed picture of the innovation-decision process for specific organisations or communities of practice.

Acknowledgements. This work was conducted with the financial support of the Science Foundation Ireland Centre for Research Training in Digitally-Enhanced Reality (d-real) under Grant No. 18/CRT/6224.

The authors would also like to thank Stephen Howell of Microsoft Ireland for his support with using Microsoft Azure to request tags and descriptions for the phase one focus group prompts. In addition, the authors would like to thank the following students who assisted with data collection in the study: Rachael Agnew, MacKenzie Barry, Nancy Bruseker, Sinead Carey, Emma, Carroll, Lauren Caravati, Na Chen, Caroline Crowther, Aoife Cummins Georghiou, Marc Dagohoy, Desree Efamaui, Haichuan Feng, Laura Finucane, Nathan Fitzmaurice, Conor Greene, Yazhou He, Yuhan Jiang, Joang, Zhou, Grainne Kavanagh, Kate Keane, Mark Keleghan, Miao Li, Danyang Liu, Xijia Liu, Siqi Liu, Hannah Lynch, Conor Murphy, Niamh Elizabeth Murphy, Rebecca Murphy, Kyanna Murray, Kayse Nation, Blaithin NiChathain, Roisin O'Brien, Niall O'Flynn, Abigail Raebig, Bernadette Ryan, Emma Rothwell, John Francis Sharpe, Lin Shuhua, Zhongqian Wang, Robin Wharton, Zhillin Wei, India Wood, Bingye Wu, Deyan Zhang, Zhongwen Zheng and Zheyuan Zhang.

References

1. Aizstrauta, D., Ginters, E., Eroles, M.A.P.: Applying theory of diffusion of innovations to evaluate technology acceptance and sustainability. Procedia Comput. Sci. **43**, 69–77 (2015)
2. Balkun, M.M., Deyrup, M.M.: Transformative Digital Humanities: Challenges and Opportunities. Routledge, Abingdon (2020)
3. Borowiecki, K.J., Navarrete, T.: Digitization of heritage collections as indicator of innovation. Econ. Innov. New Technol. **26**(3), 227–246 (2017). https://doi.org/10.1080/10438599.2016.1164488
4. Ch'ng, E., Cai, S.: Methods for evaluating the adoption and use of digital technologies in glams. MethodsX **7**, 100559 (2020)
5. Christensen, C.M.: The Innovator's Dilemma: When New Technologies Cause Great Firms to Fail. Harvard Business School Press, Boston (1997)
6. Cordell, R.: Machine Learning + Libraries. A Report on the State of the Art of the Field. Technical report, Library of Congress (2020)
7. Darby, A., Coleman, C.N., Engel, C., van Strien, D., Trizna, M., Painter, Z.W.: AI training resources for GLAM: a snapshot. Technical report. arXiv:2205.04738, arXiv (2022)
8. Davis, F.D., Bagozzi, R.P., Warshaw, P.R.: User acceptance of computer technology: a comparison of two theoretical models. Manag. Sci. **35**(8), 982–1003 (1989)
9. Dearing, J.W., Cox, J.G.: Diffusion of innovations theory, principles, and practice. Health Aff. **37**(2), 183–190 (2018). https://doi.org/10.1377/hlthaff.2017.1104
10. Farnsworth, J., Boon, B.: Analysing group dynamics within the focus group. Qual. Res. **10**(5), 605–624 (2010)
11. Fast, E., Horvitz, E.: Long-term trends in the public perception of artificial intelligence. In: Proceedings of the AAAI Conference on Artificial Intelligence, vol. 31 (2017)

12. Ford, M.: Could artificial intelligence create an unemployment crisis? Commun. ACM **56**(7), 37–39 (2013)
13. Gefen, A., Saint-Raymond, L., Venturini, T.: AI for digital humanities and computational social sciences. In: Braunschweig, B., Ghallab, M. (eds.) Reflections on Artificial Intelligence for Humanity. LNCS (LNAI), vol. 12600, pp. 191–202. Springer, Cham (2021). https://doi.org/10.1007/978-3-030-69128-8_12
14. Girasa, R.: Artificial Intelligence as a Disruptive Technology. Springer, Cham (2020). https://doi.org/10.1007/978-3-030-35975-1
15. Godin, B., Vinck, D.: Critical Studies of Innovation: Alternative Approaches to the Pro-innovation Bias. Edward Elgar Publishing, Cheltenham (2017)
16. Haider, M., Kreps, G.L.: Forty years of diffusion of innovations: utility and value in public health. J. Health Commun. **9**(S1), 3–11 (2004)
17. Hwang, Y., Jeong, S.H.: Revisiting the knowledge gap hypothesis: a meta-analysis of thirty-five years of research. Journal. Mass Commun. Q. **86**(3), 513–532 (2009)
18. Jun, K.N., Weare, C.: Institutional motivations in the adoption of innovations: the case of e-government. J. Public Adm. Res. Theory **21**(3), 495–519 (2011)
19. Kee, K.F.: Adoption and diffusion. Int. Encycl. Organ. Commun. **1**, 41–54 (2017)
20. Makowsky, M.J., Guirguis, L.M., Hughes, C.A., Sadowski, C.A., Yuksel, N.: Factors influencing pharmacists' adoption of prescribing: qualitative application of the diffusion of innovations theory. Implement. Sci. **8**(1), 1–11 (2013). https://doi.org/10.1186/1748-5908-8-109
21. Markus, G., et al.: AI in relation to GLAMs Task Force. Report and recommendations. Technical report, Europeana Network Association (2021). https://pro.europeana.eu/project/ai-in-relation-to-glams
22. McCarthy, J., Minsky, M.L., Rochester, N., Shannon, C.E.: A proposal for the dartmouth summer research project on artificial intelligence, august 31, 1955. AI Mag. **27**(4), 12–12 (2006)
23. Meyer, G.: Diffusion methodology: time to innovate? J. Health Commun. **9**(S1), 59–69 (2004)
24. Mohri, M., Rostamizadeh, A., Talwalkar, A.: Foundations of Machine Learning. MIT Press, Cambridge (2018)
25. Monarch, R.M.: Human-in-the-loop machine learning: active learning and annotation for human-centered AI. Simon Schuster (2021)
26. Navarrete, T.: Digital heritage tourism: innovations in museums. World Leisure J. **61**(3), 200–214 (2019). https://doi.org/10.1080/16078055.2019.1639920
27. Artificial Intelligence: Oxford English dictionary (2021). https://www.oed.com/view/Entry/271625?
28. Padilla, T.: Responsible operations: data science, machine learning, and AI in libraries (Dublin, Oh: OCLC Research, 2019) (2019)
29. Peirce, C.S.: Collected Papers of Charles Sanders Peirce, vol. 5. Harvard University Press, Cambridge (1974)
30. Rasmussen, C.H., Hjorland, B.: Libraries, archives and museums (LAM): conceptual issues with focus on their convergence (2021). https://www.isko.org/cyclo/lam
31. Rogers, E.M.: Diffusion of Innovations. The Free Press of Glencoe (1962)
32. Rogers, E.M.: Diffusion of Innovations, 5th edn. Free Press, New York (2003)
33. Ryan, B., Gross, N.C., et al.: Acceptance and diffusion of hybrid corn seed in two Iowa communities, vol. 372. Agricultural Experiment Station, Iowa State College of Agriculture and Mechanic Arts (1950)

34. Salahshour Rad, M., Nilashi, M., Mohamed Dahlan, H.: Information technology adoption: a review of the literature and classification. Univ. Access Inf. Soc. **17**(2), 361–390 (2018). https://doi.org/10.1007/s10209-017-0534-z
35. Saldaña, J.: The Coding Manual for Qualitative Researchers. SAGE Publications Ltd., Thousand Oaks (2021)
36. Si, S., Chen, H.: A literature review of disruptive innovation: what it is, how it works and where it goes. J. Eng. Tech. Manag. **56**, 101568 (2020). https://doi.org/10.1016/j.jengtecman.2020.101568
37. Strien, D.V., Bell, M., McGregor, N.R., Trizna, M.: An introduction to AI for GLAM. In: Proceedings of the Second Teaching Machine Learning and Artificial Intelligence Workshop, pp. 20–24. PMLR (2022). https://proceedings.mlr.press/v170/strien22a.html. ISSN 2640-3498
38. Tavory, I., Timmermans, S.: Abductive Analysis: Theorizing Qualitative Research. University of Chicago Press, Chicago (2014)
39. Timmermans, S., Tavory, I.: Theory construction in qualitative research: from grounded theory to abductive analysis. Sociol Theory **30**(3), 167–186 (2012). https://doi.org/10.1177/0735275112457914
40. Vila-Henninger, L., et al.: Abductive coding: theory building and qualitative (re) analysis. Sociol. Methods Res. 00491241211067508 (2022). https://doi.org/10.1177/00491241211067508
41. Wood, B.A., Evans, D.: Librarians' perceptions of artificial intelligence and its potential impact on the profession. Comput. Libr. **38**(1) (2018)
42. Yoon, J., Andrews, J.E., Ward, H.L.: Perceptions on adopting artificial intelligence and related technologies in libraries: public and academic librarians in north America. Library Hi Tech (2021)
43. Zhang, H., Xu, X., Xiao, J.: Diffusion of e-government: a literature review and directions for future directions. Gov. Inf. Q. **31**(4), 631–636 (2014)

Effects of Increasing Working Opportunity on Result Quality in Labor-Intensive Crowdsourcing

Kanta Negishi[1(✉)], Hiroyoshi Ito[2], Masaki Matsubara[2], and Atsuyuki Morishima[2]

[1] Graduate School of Comprehensive Human Sciences, University of Tsukuba, 1-2 Kasuga, Tsukuba-shi, Ibaraki 305-8550, Japan
negishi.kanta.sw@alumni.tsukuba.ac.jp

[2] Faculty of Library, Information and Media Science, University of Tsukuba, 1-2 Kasuga, Tsukuba-shi, Ibaraki 305-8550, Japan
{ito,masaki,mori}@slis.tsukuba.ac.jp

Abstract. When selecting workers in microtask crowdsourcing platforms, a common practice of requesters is to select qualified workers by looking at the evaluation results for the tasks in the past or by conducting qualifying tests for the tasks. This sometimes misses workers who may be able to complete some of the tasks. Increasing working opportunities for such workers has advantages not only for the workers but also for requesters because they obtain labor resources for faster completion of tasks. However, in general, an increase in the working opportunity and obtaining high-quality task results is a trade-off; if they choose workers whose skill levels are above a lower threshold to increase the number of workers, the quality of the task will be undermined. In this paper, we address the problem of improving the trade-off in labor-intensive crowdsourcing by exploring different task assignment strategies. For that purpose, we apply Item Response Theory to evaluate the skills of workers and the difficulty of tasks and devise an algorithm for assigning tasks in such a way that the variance in the number of tasks assigned among workers is minimized trying to take advantage of the potential parallelism of crowdsourcing. Second, we address the problem that the difficulty of the tasks is unknown in advance. We explore an approach that uses ML outputs for difficulty estimation. This paper reports on our experimental result, which shows the potential of this approach, and discusses when this approach is effective.

Keywords: Crowdsourcing · Task assignment · Human factor

1 Introduction

Crowdsourcing services serve as one of the important platforms for supplying tasks to people. Selecting workers to perform the task is important to keep the results of the task of good quality.

In the assignment of micro-tasks, where sufficient information about the worker is not always available, it is a common practice for requesters to select appropriate workers by referring to tasks that workers have worked on in the past and the percentage of

© The Author(s), under exclusive license to Springer Nature Switzerland AG 2023
I. Sserwanga et al. (Eds.): iConference 2023, LNCS 13971, pp. 277–293, 2023.
https://doi.org/10.1007/978-3-031-28035-1_19

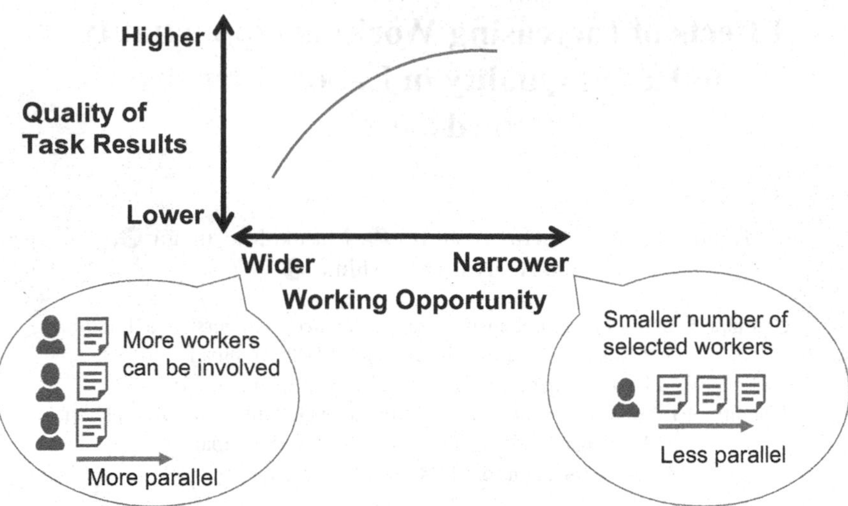

Fig. 1. The trade-off between working opportunity and task result quality. An increase in working opportunities has advantages for both workers and requesters. However, it results in lower-quality of task results in general. As shown in Sect. 5, we discuss how the trade-off line changes with different task assignment methods.

correct answers in ability tests, etc. Then, requesters select workers whose ability level is higher than the threshold. For example, Amazon Mechanical Turk allows requesters to assign tasks only to workers whose past task approval rates are higher than a threshold. This feature enables the requester to obtain high-quality task results.

However, selecting workers based solely on the average quality of task result quality in the past limits the number of candidate workers for the task, which can have a negative impact on both the requester and workers (Fig. 1). From the requester's perspective, they will encounter labor shortages and delays in task completion occur; from the worker's perspective, workers with sufficient skills to tackle some of the tasks may be excluded and may not be given a chance because their past task performance is not above the threshold. On the other hand, if we were to open our tasks to all workers, we would lose the quality of the task results.

The purpose of this study is to pursue a better trade-off between the increase in working opportunities and the quality of task results in labor-intensive crowdsourcing. Here, we define the quality of a task result as the percentage of correct answers. The working opportunity is the number of workers to whom tasks are assigned, and a worker's skill is their ability to answer a task correctly.

We compare several strategies for the trade-off. Our assumption is that considering the difficulty of tasks and the skills of workers in task assignments will give a better trade-off. To see whether the assumption is correct or not, we developed a strategy that applies *Item Response Theory (IRT)* [1] to evaluate the skills of workers and the difficulty of tasks. IRT is a theory for determining the distribution of task difficulty and worker ability when we are given a set of tasks *without known difficulty*, a set of results of the tasks *without known skills*, and the set of workers who completed the tasks. IRT has been widely used to create standardized tests such as TOEFL. IRT uses a parameter θ to denote the ability of the worker. In the IRT model, the obtained task difficulty maps the skill levels to the probability of giving the correct answer o the task (We will explain the detail with Fig. 2 in Sect. 3). Namely, given a worker with skill θ and a task with known difficulty, we can compute the probability of the worker's giving a correct result for the task.

The simplicity is the main reason we chose IRT.

Our research questions are as follows.

RQ1: Given a set of workers with known skills and a set of tasks with known difficulties based on IRT, is there a practical algorithm to assign the tasks that effectively exploits the available workers?

RQ2: Does the framework considering both task difficulty and worker skills give a better trade-off between the size of the working opportunity and the task quality results?

Then, assuming that we find that the framework is promising, an obstacle to the deployment of the framework is that we have a set of tasks whose difficulties are *unknown*. Therefore, the last but important question is as follows.

RQ3: In what situation the task assignment considering the worker's skills and task difficulties is effective?

Contributions and Key Findings. The contributions of this article are as follows. **(Algorithm)** We show that there is a polynomial-time algorithm that takes as inputs the task difficulties and worker skills based on IRT, and assigns the tasks to the workers considering the task quality and balanced assignment to exploit the size of working opportunities for parallel executions. **(Effects)** Through the experiment, we found that the IRT-based framework shows a better trade-off between the quality of the task and the size of working opportunities. **(Deployment)** We show a deployment framework of the approach and identify the situation in which the framework is effective; (1) there must be some overlap between worker skills and task difficulties, and (2) we need task features that correlate to the task difficulty in terms of IRT. We can check whether the conditions hold before adopting the task assignment strategy.

Limitation. Our result applies to classification tasks only. Other types of tasks, such as generation tasks and free-keyword tasks, are out of the scope of this paper. The result appears when some conditions are satisfied, which is explained in the discussion section.

2 Related Work

To the best of our knowledge, this work is the first that explores the better trade-off between the increase in working opportunity and task quality results. However, there are many studies that are related to our problem.

Involving More Workers in Task Assignment. Hashimoto et al. [8] addresses the task assignment problem considering both the requester perspectives, such as productivity and throughput, and working opportunities such as task participation rate and standard deviation of the number of tasks, for a given complex workflow consisting of various tasks. They have shown that an assignment strategy that prioritizes worker participation rate and standard deviation of the number of tasks among workers can be effective. The method is based on a simple assumption that we know the required skills for each task and the skills of workers, and the workers can always complete tasks correctly when they match.

Huang et al. [11] proposed a method for involving workers with different language skills in decomposed microtasks as much as possible in a video subtitling workflow and showed that it is possible to include workers with relatively low skills in some parts of the tasks. Again, this study assumes that the skills possessed by workers and the skills required by tasks are given as input in advance.

In contrast to these studies, we do not start with the assumption that the skills and required skills (difficulty for our case) are given. We need to estimate them.

In the context of spatial crowdsourcing, methods aimed at minimizing the workload distribution among workers as social fairness [14] and sharing rewards equally among workers [3] have been proposed. However, these methods do not take into account the skill of the worker, which is a factor that greatly affects the quality of the results of the task. We propose a method for estimating worker skill by IRT, in which the worker's skill has a significant impact on the quality of the results.

Task Assignment Considering Worker Skills. The idea of evaluating worker's skills towards the tasks to improve overall quality is discussed for both online task assignment [7,9,10,12,13], and batch-based assignment. [5,6,15]. Fan et al [7] proposed an online task assignment framework for estimating a worker's ability to answer correctly on tasks that the worker has not yet performed, based on the similarity between tasks and the worker's past performance. Specifically, a similarity graph between tasks is created based on the task content, and a personalized PageRank is calculated using the worker's performance on the test task as a profile. This method has been shown to improve the accuracy rate and throughput of assignment results. Hettiachchi et al. [9] used a method to estimate worker performance on various tasks using a cognitive ability test to estimate worker skills in tasks such as classification, counting, transcription, and sentiment analysis, and then assigned these tasks to workers. These studies have been successful in improving the worker's accuracy rate. The above studies share similarities with our method in that they estimate the skills possessed by workers and the knowledge and abilities required for the tasks before task assignment. Mavridis et al. [15] and Duan et al. [6] propose a batch assignment algorithm leveraging the structure of task sets and then assigning tasks such that the workers are good at. Also, the multiskill-based assignment algorithm in spatial crowdsourcing has been developed by [5]. In their work, they consider the constraints of time, budget, and skills required for the tasks. However, the objective functions of these works are mainly the quality and efficiency of the assignment results and do not address the problem of increasing working opportunities.

3 IRT-Based Framework

In this section, we first introduce Item Response Theory. Next, we show a polynomial-time algorithm that takes a set $\mathcal{W}$ of workers with known skills, a set $\mathcal{T}$ of tasks with known difficulties, and a quality target Th and assigns tasks in such a way that the variance in the number of tasks assigned among the workers is minimized trying to take

Table 1. Symbol definitions

Symbols	Definition
$\mathcal{W} = \{w_1, \cdots, w_n\}$	Set of workers
$\mathcal{T} = \{t_1, \cdots, t_m\}$	Set of tasks
$t_j = (j, d_j)$	A task (j = task id, d_j = Feature value of t_j)
$\mathcal{A}_k \subset \mathcal{W} \times \mathcal{T}$	Set of Assignment
$assigned(w_i) \subseteq \mathcal{T}$	Set of tasks assigned to w_i
Th	Threshold of required result quality
$d(\mathcal{A}_k)$	Variance of number of assigned tasks among workers
$ans(w_{k_i}, t_{k_i})$	Answer of workerw_{k_i} to taskt_{k_j}
$\hat{ans}_{k_j}$	Ground truth of task t_{k_j}
$\delta(\cdot)$	A function returns 1 if argument is true
$f(d_j)$	A function returns the answer of task t_j
$g(f(d_j))$	A function returns difficulty of task t_j

advantage of the increased working opportunity in terms of the parallelism of labor-intensive crowdsourcing. Finally, we show a deployment strategy for the situation in which we have tasks whose difficulties are unknown. The notations used here are summarized in Table 1.

3.1 Item Response Theory

Item Response Theory [1] is a theory for determining the distribution of task difficulty and worker ability when we are given a set of tasks without known difficulty, a set of results of the tasks without known skills, and the set of workers who completed the tasks. In IRT, the skill of each worker in the set $\mathcal{W}$ of workers is represented as a scalar value θ in a dimension named the *ability scale*. In the IRT model, the obtained task difficulty maps the skill levels to the probability of giving the correct answer o the task.

Here, people who have higher skills can answer more difficult questions (tasks) correctly. IRT helps us to develop a good ability test in a domain as follows: given the set of answers of workers to the set of candidate questions in the domain, IRT first produces the estimated ability of each worker and the description of each question that shows the difficulty of question (tasks), which is called *item Characteristic Curve (ICC)* (Fig. 2). The ICC of each question shows the probability that workers with different skill levels provide the correct answer to the question.

Therefore, given the ICCs for a set of candidate questions, we can choose good questions for an ability test, based on the ICC of each candidate question, to estimate the skill level of workers.

There are several variations of IRT and we adopt the 1-parameter logistic model [1] to represent the ICC here. Let θ_i be a skill parameter that represents the skill of a worker $w_i \in \mathcal{W}$. Then, the probability of correctly answering the task j (called an item in IRT) is expressed by the following equation.

$$P(ans(w_i, t_j) = \hat{ans}_j \mid \theta_i, b_j) = \frac{1}{1 + exp(-D(\theta_i - b_j))}, \quad (1)$$

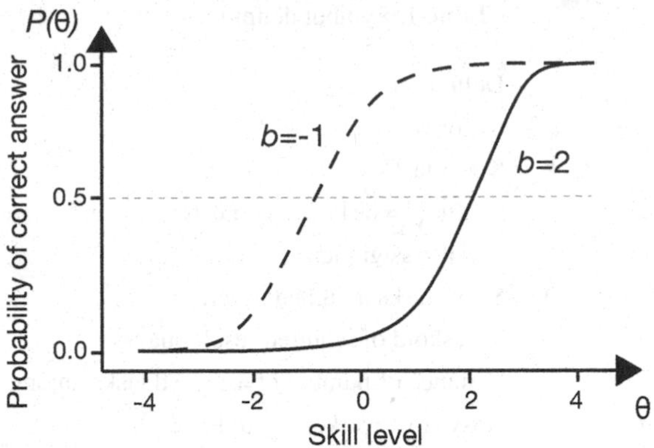

Fig. 2. Item Characteristic Curve in IRT. In the one-parameter model, the difficulty of a task is represented by b, which is the skill level for giving the correct answer with a probability of 0.5. IRT computes the CCI for each task.

where b_j is a difficulty parameter of a task t_j that represents the skill level for the worker returns the correct answer with a probability of 0.5 for the task t_j. D is a constant value called the "scale factor", and set at 1.7 for the model [1].

Given a set $\mathcal{T}$ of tasks (questions) and the answers to them by a set $\mathcal{W}$ of workers, IRT outputs the worker skills θ_{w_i} for $w_i \in \mathcal{W}$ and the ICC of each $t \in \mathcal{T}$[1].

3.2 Assignment Algorithm

Problem Formulation. Given a set $\mathcal{W}$ of workers, a set $\mathcal{T}$ of tasks and a quality threshold of the assignment result in Th, we seek a set $\mathcal{A}_k$ of tuples of worker and task assignments that satisfy the following requirements (1) and (2).

(1) Keep the quality above the threshold:

$$\frac{1}{|\mathcal{A}_k|} \sum_{(w_{k_i}, t_{k_i}) \in \mathcal{A}_k} \delta(ans(w_{k_i}, t_{k_i}) = an\hat{s}_{k_i}) \geq Th, \tag{2}$$

where $ans(w_{k_i}, t_{k_i})$ is the answer of w_{k_i} to t_{k_j} and $an\hat{s}_{k_j}$ is the ground truth for t_{k_j}.

(2) Minimize the variance of task assignments among workers:

$$\min_{\mathcal{A}_k \subset \mathcal{W} \times \mathcal{T}} d(\mathcal{A}_k), \tag{3}$$

where

$$d(A_k) = \frac{1}{|\mathcal{W}|} \sum_{i=1}^{|\mathcal{W}|} (|assigned(w_i)| - \overline{|assigned(w)|})^2. \tag{4}$$

[1] In our paper we use one parameter model of IRT. Therefore, each ICC is represented by θ_{w_i} difficulty b_j.

Algorithm 1. Assignment Algorithm

Input: $\mathcal{T}$ and $\mathcal{W}$, each are sorted by θ
Output: $\mathcal{A}_k$

$\mathcal{A}_k = \emptyset$
for $w_i \in \mathcal{W}$ **do**
  $assigned(w_i) \leftarrow \{t_j \in \mathcal{T} \mid good(w_i, t_j, Th)\}$
  $\mathcal{T} \leftarrow \mathcal{T} \backslash \{t_j\}$
  $flatten(i)$
end for

Algorithm 2. *flatten(i)*

Input: $\mathcal{A}_k$ and worker index i
Output: $\mathcal{A}'_k$

while $|assigned(w_{i-1})| > |assigned(w_i)|$ **do**
  move a task from $assigned(w_{i-1})$ to $assigned(w_i)$
  $flatten(i-1)$
end while

In this equation, $assigned(w_i) = \{t_{k_j} | (w_i, t_{k_j}) \in \mathcal{A}_k\}$ and $\overline{|assigned(w)|} = \frac{1}{|\mathcal{W}|} \sum_{i=1}^{|\mathcal{W}|} |assigned(w_i)|$, which are the set of tasks assigned to a worker w_{k_i} and the average number of tasks assigned to workers, respectively. Given the skills of the workers and the difficulties of the task, we need an assignment algorithm to solve our problem explained at the beginning of the section. Here RQ2 arises: whether there is a polynomial time algorithm exists or not. We positively answer the question by constructing such an algorithm. Let $good(w_i, t_j, Th) = true$ if $P(ans(w_i, t_j) = \hat{ans}_j \mid \theta_i, b_j) \geq Th\}$, which means that it holds if w_i completes t_j correctly at a greater probability than Th.

Before proceeding with the algorithm, we start with the following theorem.

Theorem 1. *Assume that $\theta_{w_j} \leq \theta_{w_i}$ if $j < i$. Let $assigned(w_i)$ be a set of tasks assigned to the worker w_i. Then, the assignment is optimal in terms two objective functions (1) and (2), if the following condition holds:*

$$\begin{aligned} &\forall\, w_i \in \mathcal{W},\ if\ \exists t \in assigned(w_i)\ s.t.\ good(w_{i-1}, t, Th) = true \\ &then\ \forall k\ s.t.\ good(w_k, t, Th) = true\ and\ k < i, \\ &\qquad |assigned(w_k)| = |assigned(w_i)| \end{aligned} \tag{5}$$

which means that if a worker w_i is assigned to a task that the other workers with less skills can complete, the workers with fewer skills have already been assigned the same number of tasks as w_i.

Proof. Any other assignment will increase the variance of task assignment or violates condition (1).

Next, we give another theorem on Algorithm 1.

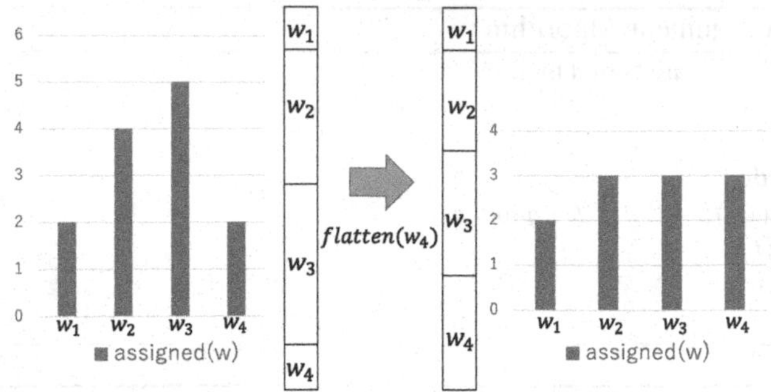

Fig. 3. How Algorithm 1 works.

Algorithm 3. Pseudo code for the deployment framework

Require: $\mathcal{W}, \mathcal{T}, \mathcal{T}', Th$, and the AI model $f : \mathcal{D} \rightarrow \mathcal{V}$
Ensure: $\mathcal{A}_k$

Apply IRT to $\mathcal{T}'$ and $\mathcal{W}$ to compute the skills of $\mathcal{W}$ and difficulties of $\mathcal{T}'$.
Find $g(d_j, f(d_j))$ that correlate with the IRT's difficulty values for $\mathcal{T}'$.
Apply the Task Assignment Algorithm 1 to $\mathcal{W}$ and $\mathcal{T} - \mathcal{T}'$, using $\{\theta_i\}$ for w_i and estimated $\{b_j\}$ for $t_j \in \mathcal{T} - \mathcal{T}'$ based on the regressions from $\{g(f(d_j))\}$.

Theorem 2. *Algorithm 1 guarantees that the condition (5) holds after it halts.*

Proof. The iteration (Line 2–5) proceeds with workers with incremental i (Line 2). We assume that all tasks and workers are classified by their skills and difficulties, *i.e.*, $\theta_{w_{i-1}} \leq \theta_{w_i}$ and $b_{j-1} \leq b_j$ for all i and j. Therefore, the iteration starts with w_1 who has the lowest skill. In each iteration, we assign w_i to all available tasks t_j if $good(w_i, t_j, Th)$ holds (i.e., w_i can complete the task with a probability greater than Th). Note that in this iteration i we have already assigned workers $w_1, \ldots, w_{i-1}$ to all tasks that they can complete with a probability greater than Th. Then, we we look at the assignments to previous workers to check whether there are workers w_j $(j < i)$ s.t. $|assigned(w_j)| > |assigned(w_i)|$.

If there exists (e.g., the left part of Fig. 3), we *flatten* the task assignment (Line 5, Algorithm 2, the middle part in Fig. 3) so that the consequence of the theorem holds (the right part in Fig. 3 at the end of each iteration for w_1, ... ,w_i.)

3.3 A Deployment Scenario

The previous section showed that if we know all of the worker skills and task difficulties for all tasks *in advance*, there is a task assignment algorithm to solve our problem. However, we will not know the difficulty of the tasks until we have completed the tasks. Therefore, we cannot directly apply the idea in practice.

This section explores a scenario where the approach can be used and a potential deployment framework for it. Through exploration, we try to find answers to **RQ3**: Are there any practical deployment frameworks for this approach?

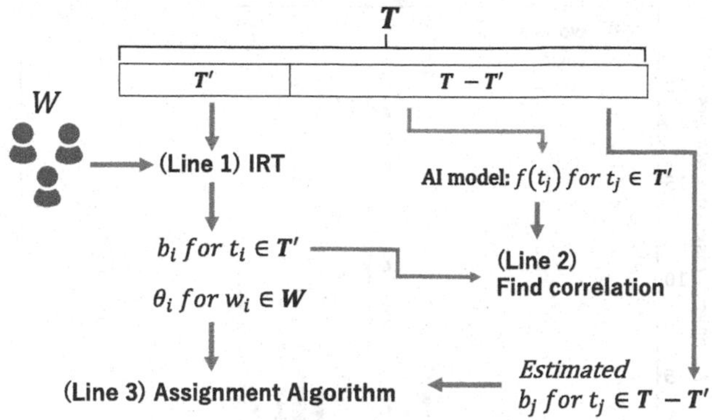

Fig. 4. A deployment framework

In this scenario, we assume that the task is an AI-result correction task, which asks workers to correct the AI's output shown in each task. This kind of task is ubiquitous in a variety of areas, such as translation [2, 16, 17], labeling [18, 20], object recognition [4, 19]. The idea behind the deployment framework is to use the ML outputs for the difficulty estimation.

In the framework, we do the following two things: (1) We assume an AI model[2] that returns the AI's results and its confidence level for tasks $\mathcal{T}$. (2) We prepare gold standard data for a small subset $\mathcal{T}'$ of $\mathcal{T}$. We can obtain the data by asking experts to complete the tasks.

The framework is illustrated in Fig. 4 and its pseudo-code is given in Algorithm 3. The inputs of the framework are $\mathcal{W}$ of workers, a set $\mathcal{T}$ of tasks, a small subset $\mathcal{T}' \subset \mathcal{T}$ that has gold standard data, a quality threshold Th, and the AI model to be used in the tasks, represented by a function $f : \mathcal{D} \rightarrow \mathcal{V}$. Here, given a task feature $d_i \in \mathcal{D}$ for a task $t_i \in \mathcal{T}$, $f(d_i)$ returns some output $v_i \in \mathcal{V}$, which is the task result, potentially with an associated information such as its confidence value.

First, we ask all workers in $\mathcal{W}$ to complete tasks in $\mathcal{T}'$ and apply IRT to the results to obtain b_i for $t_i \in \mathcal{T}'$ and θ_{w_i} for $w_i \in \mathcal{W}$ (Line 1). Then we compare the task difficulty values in IRT for $\mathcal{T}'$ and the tasks and their outputs $\{d_i, f(d_i)\}$ for $\mathcal{T}'$ to find $g(d_i, f(d_i))$ that correlates with the difficulty values of the IRT for $\mathcal{T}'$ (line 2). Then we perform a regression on the values to estimate b_j for $\mathcal{T} - \mathcal{T}'$ and apply the task assignment algorithm (Algorithm 1) to $\mathcal{W}$ and $\mathcal{T} - \mathcal{T}'$ using the estimated values (Line 3).

This deployment framework suggests that there are some prerequisites for it to work. First, we need gold standard data for at least a small set of tasks in $\mathcal{T}$. Second, there must be some correlation between b_j and the task features d_j and the task's output $f(d_j)$. As shown in the experiment, we found that there is a case where a weak correlation works.

[2] The AI model can be the result of a multi-model ensembles.

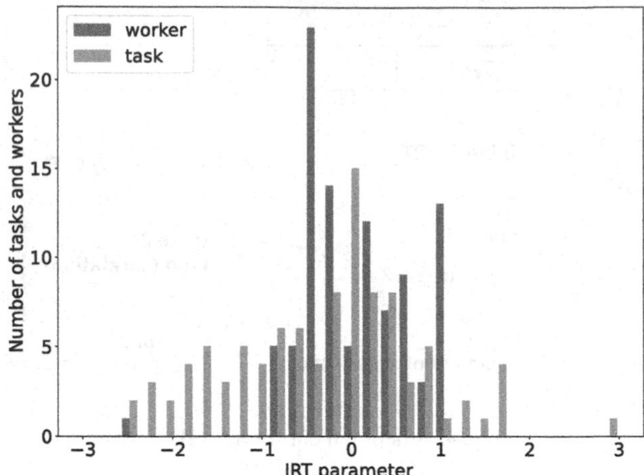

Fig. 5. Distributions of worker skills (Blue) and task difficulties (Orange). There is an overlap between them. Note that w_i is expected to give a correct task result at 50% probability when $\theta_i = b_j$. (Color figure online)

4 Experiment

We conducted an experiment to address **RQ2:** whether task assignment considering worker skills and task difficulty provides a better trade-off between task result quality and increasing task opportunity for balanced task assignment in labor-intensive crowdsourcing, and **RQ3:** in what situation this framework is effective. For the former, we applied IRT to a set of tasks and workers and executed the assignment algorithm shown in Algorithm 1. For the latter, we applied the deployment framework for a scenario and conducted a detailed analysis.

4.1 Settings and Statistics

(1) Tasks. In this experiment, we designed 100 tasks using news-aggregator-dataset[3] ($|T| = 100$). Each task displays the text of a news article title taken from the dataset and the result of the AI model's classification of the text into one of the following categories: Economy, Business, Technology&Science, or Health. The worker is asked to choose between two options to answer whether the result of the classification by the AI model is correct or not. In this experiment, a Naive Bayes model was used as the AI model, and the correct classification rate by the AI model was 92.8%.

Figures 6 and 7 show examples of easy and difficult tasks in the task set, respectively, according to the IRT result in our experiment.

[3] https://archive.ics.uci.edu/ml/datasets/News+Aggregator.

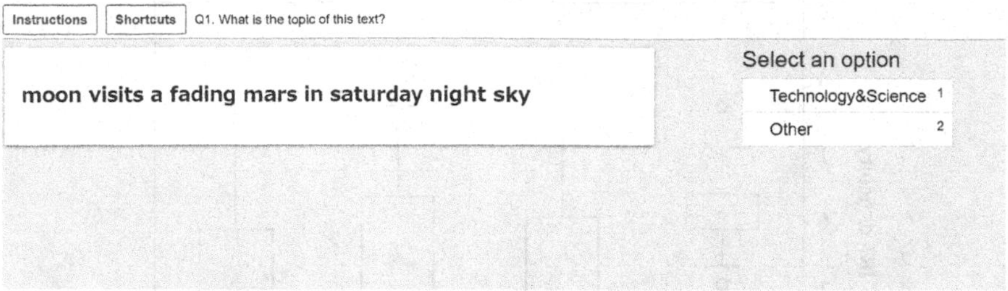

Instructions Shortcuts Q1. What is the topic of this text?

moon visits a fading mars in saturday night sky

Select an option

Technology&Science 1

Other 2

Fig. 6. One of the easiest tasks. The correct answer is 'Technology&Science' (option1)

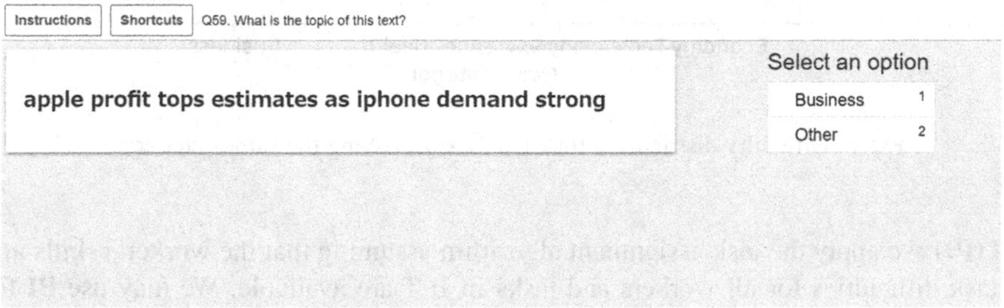

Instructions Shortcuts Q59. What is the topic of this text?

apple profit tops estimates as iphone demand strong

Select an option

Business 1

Other 2

Fig. 7. One of the most difficult tasks. The correct answer is 'Other' (option2)

(2) Platform and Workers. We recruited 100 workers on Amazon Mechanical Turk and collected task results asking them to complete all tasks in $\mathcal{T}$. We paid 0.70 USD to each worker. Then we removed two workers who did not give complete answers. Therefore, $|W| = 98$. The overall average (all workers and all tasks) of the accuracy of task results was 0.577.

(3) Worker Skills and Task Difficulty Distributions. Figure 5 shows the distributions of worker skills and task difficulties obtained by applying IRT to $\mathcal{W}$ and $\mathcal{T}$ based on the task results. In the setting of this experiment, we assume that there is substantial overlap between the two distributions.

(4) Assignment Strategies. We compare four strategies: Top, Random, Average Accuracy (AA), Perfect Information (PI) with IRT, and Difficulty Inference (DI) with IRT, with a variety of Ths.

Random This assigns a randomly chosen worker to each task. In the assignment strategy, each worker has an equal chance of being assigned a task, sacrificing the quality of the result.

Top This assigns tasks only to the top N workers ($N = 5$) in terms of the worker skills, i.e., the number of correct answers for task T'.

AA We choose workers whose accuracy of the task results for T' are greater than Th and assign them to tasks. This is a popular strategy in practice and therefore serves as an important baseline.

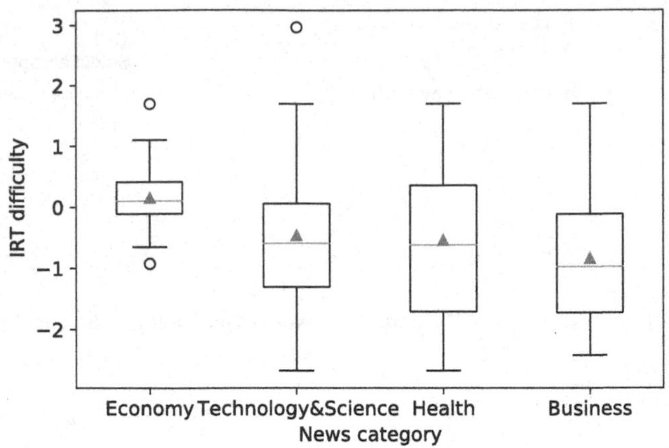

Fig. 8. Difficulty distribution for each task set having the same category

IRT(PI) We apply the task assignment algorithm assuming that the worker's skills and task difficulties for all workers and tasks in IRT are available. We may use **PI** for short.

IRT(DI) We apply the task assignment algorithm in the deployment framework for an example scenario where we have AI-result correction tasks. We may use **DI** for short.

For DI, we chose 40 qualification tasks for $\mathcal{T}'$ from $\mathcal{T}$. The result of each assignment strategy will be the average of 200 trials with different $\mathcal{T}'$ randomly chosen from $\mathcal{T}$. For AA, IRT(PI), and IRT(DI), if there is no qualified worker for a task, the task is assigned to one of the top 5 workers based on their respective skill estimation methods.

(5) Correlation between task difficulties and the feature of tasks. For DI, we need to find $g(d_j, f(d_j))$ that correlate with the IRT's difficulty values for $\mathcal{T}'$, so that we can estimate the difficulty of the task $\mathcal{T} - \mathcal{T}'$, based on the regression from $g(d_j, f(d_j))$. In our experiment, we found that there is some correlation between the difficulty and the label for each task (Fig. 8). Therefore, we computed the difficulty of a task in $\mathcal{T} - \mathcal{T}'$ by taking the mean value of the difficulty parameters of tasks in $\mathcal{T}'$ (i.e., the averages shown in Fig. 8), based on the labels estimated by the AI model for the task.

4.2 Result

Working Opportunity. Before we discuss the trade-off between the quality of the task result and the size of working opportunity, we show the effect of our framework on working opportunity. Figure 9 shows the number of workers assigned to at least one task) with $Th = \{0.5, 0.6, 0.7, 0.8\}$. The result shows that PI and DI can assign more workers to tasks than AA.

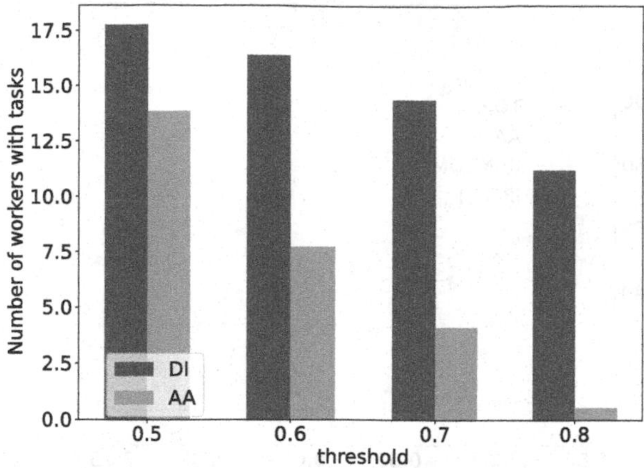

Fig. 9. Average number of workers who can perform at least one task (Blue: IRT(DI), Orange: AA). (Color figure online)

Theoretically, as the threshold Th increases, the number of assigned workers decreases, and thus the variance of the number of task assignments increases. Figure 10 shows the trend of a variety of strategies. Except for the random strategy of sacrificing the quality of the result of the task, PI and DI keep the variance low.

Trade-off between quality of task result and the size of working opportunity in terms of the maximum number of assigned tasks for workers. Figure 11 shows the trade-off between the accuracy of the results of the tasks and the number of tasks assigned to each worker which becomes smaller when the number of workers increases. The result clearly shows that IRT-based task assignment strategies (PI and DI) give better trade-offs.

We test whether there is a statistically significant difference in the accuracy between DI and the baseline method AA at two thresholds of 0.5 and 0.8. Here, we apply the independent Welch's t-test to the accuracies of the results by DI and AA to examine the difference between them. There is a statistically significant difference when the threshold is 0.5 ($p = 0.001$), and there is no significant difference when the threshold is 0.8 ($p = 0.41$). The above results indicate that DI has significantly higher accuracy than AA when Th = 0.5. Even when a high threshold $Th = 0.8$ is given, DI can maintain accuracy so high that there is no significant difference with AA.

Estimated Task Difficulty. Figure 12 shows the mean ratio of successful assignments made by DI when $Th = \{0.5, 0.6, 0.7, 0.8\}$. It shows that task assignments are generally good, although estimated difficulties are not necessarily correct. One of the reasons is that the error causes problems only if the difficulty is estimated to be higher than the correct one. Otherwise, the assignment of tasks remains good, as the assigned worker gives the correct result of the task at a probability greater than Th.

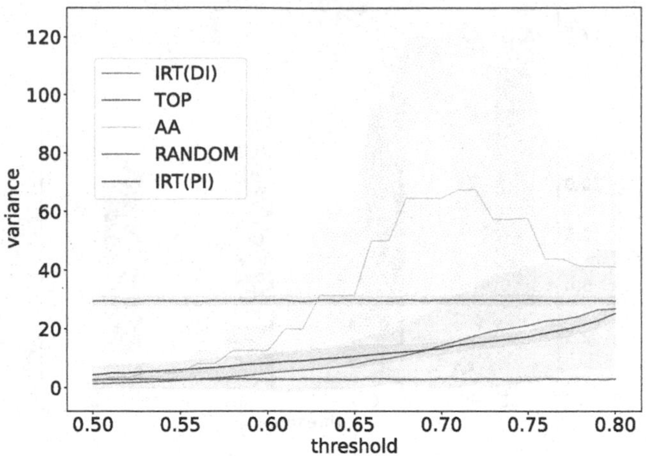

Fig. 10. The variance of a number of assigned tasks among workers with a variety of task assignment strategies, varying the threshold: Random, IRT(PI), and IRT(DI) can reduce the variance. TOP and AA are inferior because they only consider the required threshold.

5 Discussions

Our experimental results showed that the IRT-based assignment provides better trade-offs (answer to **RQ2**), and it does so when the following conditions hold (answer to **RQ3**):

(1) There is a substantial overlap between the distributions of task difficulties and the skills of the workers. If there are no overlaps or only a little overlap, we will have a trivial assignment or no assignment to guarantee the required data quality. For example, if only a few workers have the skills to produce the correct results for the tasks, we must assign them to all the tasks. If all tasks are easy enough for any worker to complete, we can assign any worker to each task.

(2) There must be a certain amount of correlation between the task difficulty and the features of the task and AI's output for it. If there is no correlation, it would be impossible to estimate the difficulty of the tasks. However, our experimental result suggests that the correlation does not need to be very high because the estimation error matters on only one side; if the skill is estimated to be less than the correct one, the task assignment's result will be correct. Given the above observation, there is a practical approach to adopting the framework. First, we choose $\mathcal{T}'$ and ask all workers to complete the qualification test. Then, we apply IRT to obtain the distributions, worker skills, and task difficulties. Then, if there is a substantial overlap between the two distributions, we look at whether there exist features of tasks and task results that are correlated to the task difficulties. If they exist, we apply the task assignment algorithm. Otherwise, we will take other strategies such as AA.

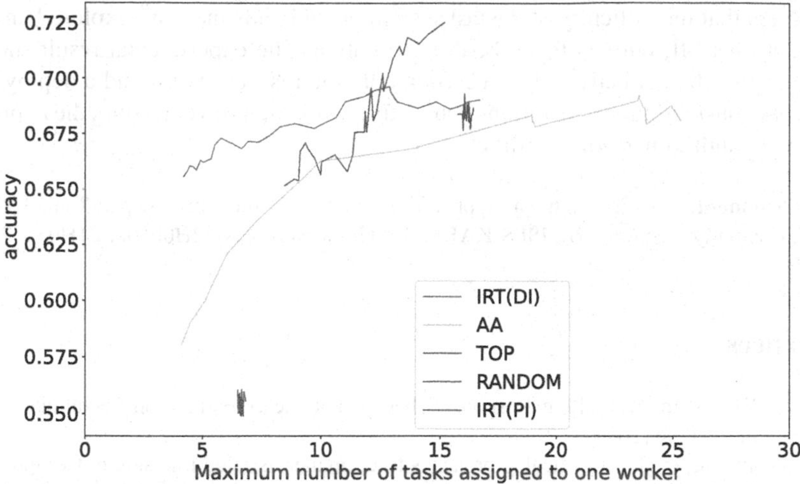

Fig. 11. The trade-off between the task result quality and the size of the working opportunity in terms of the maximum number of assigned tasks for workers. The number of tasks assigned to each worker becomes smaller when the number of workers increases. This clearly shows that IRT-based assignments (DI, PI) gives a better trade-off.

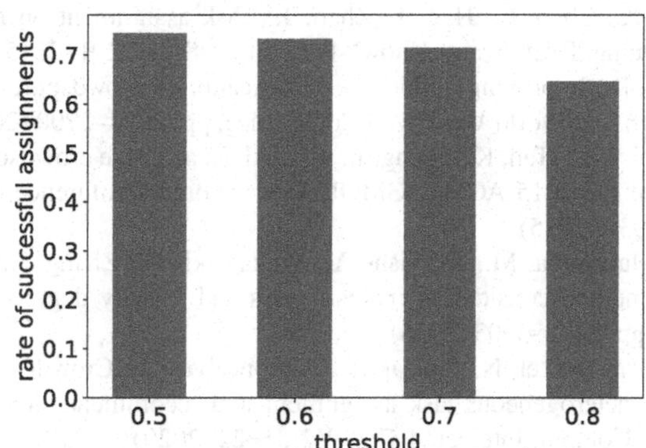

Fig. 12. Ratio of good assignments by DI at different thresholds.

6 Conclusion

This paper explored the trade-off between the increase of task opportunity and the task result quality in labor-intensive microtask-based crowdsourcing, with a hypothesis that considering the workers' skill levels and the task's difficulty in task assignment will be effective. For this purpose, we applied IRT to evaluate the skills of workers and the difficulty of tasks. We devised a principled algorithm for assigning tasks so that the variance in the number of tasks assigned among workers is minimized, trying to take advantage of the increase of working opportunity in terms of the parallelism of crowdsourcing while considering the worker skills and task difficulties. Second, we addressed the problem that the difficulty of the tasks is unknown in advance. We explored an approach that uses ML outputs for difficulty estimation. The experimental result showed that the approach is effective when a certain condition is met. We found a deployment framework considering the conditions. Our future work includes extending the approach to deal with multidimensional abilities.

Acknowledgment. This research was approved by the IRB of the University of Tsukuba. This work was partially supported by JSPS KAKENHI Grant Numbers 22H00508, 21H03552, and 22K17944.

References

1. Baker, F.B., Kim, S.H.: Item Response Theory: Parameter Estimation Techniques. CRC Press, Boca Raton (2004)
2. Barrachina, S., et al.: Statistical approaches to computer-assisted translation. Comput. Linguist. **35**(1), 3–28 (2009)
3. Basık, F., Gedik, B., Ferhatosmanoğlu, H., Wu, K.L.: Fair task allocation in crowdsourced delivery. IEEE Trans. Serv. Comput. **14**(4), 1040–1053 (2018)
4. Branson, S., et al.: Visual recognition with humans in the loop. In: Daniilidis, K., Maragos, P., Paragios, N. (eds.) ECCV 2010. LNCS, vol. 6314, pp. 438–451. Springer, Heidelberg (2010). https://doi.org/10.1007/978-3-642-15561-1_32
5. Cheng, P., Lian, X., Chen, L., Han, J., Zhao, J.: Task assignment on multi-skill oriented spatial crowdsourcing. IEEE Trans. Knowl. Data Eng. **28**(8), 2201–2215 (2016)
6. Duan, X., Tajima, K.: Improving multiclass classification in crowdsourcing by using hierarchical schemes. In: The World Wide Web Conference, pp. 2694–2700 (2019)
7. Fan, J., Li, G., Ooi, B.C., Tan, K.l., Feng, J.: iCrowd: an adaptive crowdsourcing framework. In: Proceedings of the 2015 ACM SIGMOD International Conference on Management of Data, pp. 1015–1030 (2015)
8. Hashimoto, H., Matsubara, M., Shiraishi, Y., Wakatsuki, D., Zhang, J., Morishima, A.: A task assignment method considering inclusiveness and activity degree. In: IEEE BigData 2018 (HMData), pp. 3498–3503 (2018)
9. Hettiachchi, D., Van Berkel, N., Kostakos, V., Goncalves, J.: CrowdCog: a cognitive skill based system for heterogeneous task assignment and recommendation in crowdsourcing. Proc. ACM Hum.-Comput. Interact. **4**(CSCW2), 1–22 (2020)
10. Ho, C.J., Vaughan, J.: Online task assignment in crowdsourcing markets. In: Proceedings of the AAAI Conference on Artificial Intelligence, vol. 26, pp. 45–51 (2012)
11. Huang, Y., Huang, Y., Xue, N., Bigham, J.P.: Leveraging complementary contributions of different workers for efficient crowdsourcing of video captions. In: Proceedings of the 2017 CHI Conference on Human Factors in Computing Systems, pp. 4617–4626 (2017)
12. Khan, A.R., Garcia-Molina, H.: CrowdDQS: dynamic question selection in crowdsourcing systems. In: Proceedings of the 2017 ACM International Conference on Management of Data, pp. 1447–1462 (2017)
13. Kurve, A., Miller, D.J., Kesidis, G.: Multicategory crowdsourcing accounting for variable task difficulty, worker skill, and worker intention. IEEE Trans. Knowl. Data Eng. **27**(3), 794–809 (2014)
14. Liu, Q., Abdessalem, T., Wu, H., Yuan, Z., Bressan, S.: Cost minimization and social fairness for spatial crowdsourcing tasks. In: Navathe, S.B., Wu, W., Shekhar, S., Du, X., Wang, X.S., Xiong, H. (eds.) DASFAA 2016. LNCS, vol. 9642, pp. 3–17. Springer, Cham (2016). https://doi.org/10.1007/978-3-319-32025-0_1

15. Mavridis, P., Gross-Amblard, D., Miklós, Z.: Using hierarchical skills for optimized task assignment in knowledge-intensive crowdsourcing. In: Proceedings of the 25th International Conference on World Wide Web, pp. 843–853 (2016)
16. Ortiz-Martínez, D.: Online learning for statistical machine translation. Comput. Linguist. **42**(1), 121–161 (2016). https://app.dimensions.ai/details/publication/pub.1032814773
17. Peris, l., Domingo, M., Casacuberta, F.: Interactive neural machine translation. Comput. Speech Lang. **45**, 201–220 (2017). https://app.dimensions.ai/details/publication/pub.1011205507
18. Shin, I., Kim, D.J., Cho, J.W., Woo, S., Park, K., Kweon, I.S.: Labor: labeling only if required for domain adaptive semantic segmentation. In: Proceedings of the IEEE/CVF International Conference on Computer Vision, pp. 8588–8598 (2021)
19. Wah, C., Branson, S., Perona, P., Belongie, S.: Multiclass recognition and part localization with humans in the loop. In: 2011 International Conference on Computer Vision, pp. 2524–2531. IEEE (2011)
20. Yu, F., Seff, A., Zhang, Y., Song, S., Funkhouser, T., Xiao, J.: LSUN: construction of a large-scale image dataset using deep learning with humans in the loop. arXiv preprint arXiv:1506.03365 (2015)

Aligning Visual and Lexical Semantics

Fausto Giunchiglia, Mayukh Bagchi(✉), and Xiaolei Diao

Department of Information Engineering and Computer Science (DISI), University of Trento, Trento, Italy
{fausto.giunchiglia,mayukh.bagchi,xiaolei.diao}@unitn.it

Abstract. We discuss two kinds of semantics relevant to Computer Vision (CV) systems - *Visual Semantics* and *Lexical Semantics.* While visual semantics focus on how humans build concepts when using vision to perceive a target reality, lexical semantics focus on how humans build concepts of the same target reality through the use of language. The lack of coincidence between visual and lexical semantics, in turn, has a major impact on CV systems in the form of the Semantic Gap Problem (SGP). The paper, while extensively exemplifying the lack of coincidence as above, introduces a general, domain-agnostic methodology to enforce alignment between visual and lexical semantics.

Keywords: Visual semantics · Lexical semantics · Computer vision · Knowledge representation · Semantic gap problem

1 Introduction

Let us begin with a motivating example from the domain of musical instruments. The musical instrument *Koto*, for instance, can be visually perceived in potentially an infinite number of ways. It can be, for example, perceived as a generic *musical instrument* or as a *stringed musical instrument* by someone who is not familiar with Japanese music. It can also be (mis)perceived as a Chinese *Zheng* or a Mongolian *Yatga* or a Kazakhstani *Jetigen* by individuals closer to Chinese, Mongolian or Kazakhstani culture. Those who are experts in Japanese music can perceive it as a *Gakuso, Chikuso, Zokuso* or *Tagenso* (types of *Koto*). Finally, the *Koto* can also be *Koto#2010*, a specific *Koto* which my music academy bought in 2010. However, the interesting observation is the fact that each of the above (visual) perceptions can subsequently be encoded linguistically in, again, potentially an infinite number of ways. Thus, for example, a *Koto* can be linguistically encoded as a *Koto* or as a *Kin* or as a *Jusangen* (all of them being synonyms) in Japanese [12]. The same *Koto*, however, being a *lexical gap* [8] in any of the Indian languages can only be defined as a board zither with 13 strings and movable bridges, without any assignment of a linguistic *label.*

We observe from the above motivating example that given any target reality, there is a clear and *unavoidable* lack of alignment between how humans visually perceive the target reality and how they linguistically interpret it for communication and reasoning [9,11]. In fact, the aforementioned lack of alignment is

© The Author(s), under exclusive license to Springer Nature Switzerland AG 2023
I. Sserwanga et al. (Eds.): iConference 2023, LNCS 13971, pp. 294–302, 2023.
https://doi.org/10.1007/978-3-031-28035-1_20

pervasive in Computer Vision (CV) systems and has been crystallized as the *Semantic Gap Problem* (SGP) [17], *viz.* the lack of coincidence between a visual data (such as object(s) in an *image*) and its user linguistic interpretation in a specific context. Thus, for instance, given the perceived visual data as an image of a *Koto*, it is not necessarily the case that its linguistic interpretation is codified as exactly that of a *Koto* in a particular context.

We recast the SGP to be essentially the problem of a many-to-many mapping between *Visual Semantics* (encoding the visual data as in SGP) and *Lexical Semantics* (encoding the user linguistic interpretation as in SGP) which generates the lack of alignment [4]. While visual semantics concentrate on how humans recognize and mentally internalize concepts via visually perceiving a target reality, lexical semantics is instead focused on how concepts are constructed by humans via linguistically encoding mental representations of a target reality in the form of words and word meanings in a particular language [7,8]. For instance, given the target reality of a specific instance of *Koto*, the visual semantics of a CV system (such as a *smartglass*) can perceive and encode the *Koto* at different levels of abstraction corresponding to different *partial views*, each of which can further be linguistically codified in different ways in different languages.

Towards resolving such misalignment, the goal of this paper is to *introduce a general, domain-agnostic methodology which enforces the alignment between visual and lexical semantics.* The key *novelty* of the methodology lies in the fact that, differently from mainstream CV approaches (see, for example, [16,18]), the very basis of computing visual semantics (via *visual properties*) [9] is independent from that of computing lexical semantics (via *linguistically grounded properties*), while still being functionally linked and aligned.

The remainder of the paper is organized as follows. Section 2 discusses and exemplifies the notions of visual semantics and lexical semantics. Section 3 details the SGP in terms of the misalignment of visual and lexical semantics. Section 4 illustrates the proposed methodology to align visual and lexical semantics and thus resolve the SGP. Section 5 concludes the paper.

2 Visual and Lexical Semantics

We assume that reality is composed of *substances*, where substances are things *"about which you can learn from one encounter something of what to expect on other encounters, where this is no accident but the result of a real connection"* [15]. Grounded in the above assumption, visual semantics focus on how *"humans build concepts when using vision"* [9] to perceive a target reality of substances. Such concepts generated from visual experientiality [4,5], are termed *Substance Concepts* (see [10]). Notice that substance concepts are always formed from *partial views* of a substance, such partiality arising from factors such as different focus or different confounding variables such as occlusion, clutter etc. For example, let us continue with the motivating case of a *Koto* which, in our terms, is a substance. Further, according to the theory above, the same substance *Koto* can generate different substance concepts depending on the different partial views.

For a member in the audience of a concert where the *Koto* is played, the substance concept can be just a *stringed musical instrument* because he/she recognizes that, differently from a keyboard, the *Koto* is played via taut strings. For the concertmaster, the same instrument can generate the substance concept of a *Koto* because he/she recognizes that a *Koto* has thirteen taut strings. For the musician playing the *Koto*, instead, the substance concept generated can be *my koto* which he/she bought in early 2021.

There are three characteristics of visual semantics, as exemplified above, which are of key significance to CV systems. Firstly, the fact that visual semantics is computed over the partially viewable *visual properties* [9] (e.g., thirteen taut strings) of a substance and not over linguistically grounded properties as is standard in mainstream CV benchmarks (see, for instance, [2,13]). Secondly, the computation of visual semantics is *hierarchical* by nature, i.e., it *implies* the continuous construction of a *visual subsumption hierarchy* [9] which taxonomically interrelates, over several levels, general and specific substance concepts. For example, the same *Koto* can generate a visual subsumption hierarchy where the most general substance concept is *stringed musical instrument*, the intermediate substance concept is *Koto* and the most specific substance concept is *Tagenso*. Thirdly and finally, the important observation that the visual subsumption hierarchy is constructed by exploiting *visual genus-differentiae* [9] over visual properties. For example, while a *stringed musical instrument* is recognized via its visual genus of *taut strings*, the visual differentia of *number of taut strings* taxonomically differentiates a *stringed musical instrument* into a *guitar* (six taut strings) or a *koto* (thirteen taut strings).

Lexical semantics, on the other hand, focus on how humans build concepts through the use of language (termed *Classification Concepts* as from [10]) for a particular target reality. It does so by constructing and exploiting large-scale (multilingual) lexical resources which are general (see, for instance, Princeton WordNet (PWN) [14]) or domain-specific [1] in scope. The fundamental language constructs which model the classification concepts composing such resources include word, word sense (encoding a specific meaning of a word), *synsets* (a set of synonyms having same word sense), *glosses* (a natural language definition encoding the meaning of a synset) and examples (exemplifying a gloss). For example, in the musical instrument domain hierarchy of a lexical resource, the word *Koto* can be the preferred term of a synset comprising of the synonyms - *Koto*, *Kin* and *Jusangen*. The synset *Koto* can be defined as *"a Japanese stringed instrument, consisting of a rectangular wooden body over which are stretched silk strings, which are plucked with plectrums or a nail-like device"*[1].

In sync with visual semantics, there are three key characteristics of lexical semantics which are noteworthy. Firstly, the fact that lexical semantics is computed over *linguistically grounded properties* of a substance which might not necessarily be visually perceptible. For example, the property of a *Koto* being made of a specific kind of Paulownia wood is *extravisual* in nature, the details of which can only be defined linguistically. Secondly, *lexical subsumption hierarchies*

[1] https://www.collinsdictionary.com/dictionary/english/koto.

[7] are computed based on linguistically grounded properties, which interrelates, over levels, generic classification concepts with their more specific counterparts. For instance, a lexical subsumption hierarchy about *Koto* can related the generic classification concept of *Koto* with *kotos* made of different grades of Paulownia wood, each of which is a distinct, more specific classification concept with respect to *Koto.* Last but not the least, the lexical subsumption hierarchy is constructed by modelling *lexical genus-differentiae* [8] out of linguistically grounded properties of classification concepts encoded in their glosses. To take an example, while the lexical genus of the classification concept *Koto* is *"made of wood"*, the lexical differentia *"type of wood"* helps differentiate (the classification concept of) *kotos* made of Paulownia wood from (the classification concept of) *kotos* made of other woods in the lexical subsumption hierarchy.

3 Visual Semantics $\neq$ Lexical Semantics

The root of the (in)correspondence between visual and lexical semantics lies in the Semantic Gap Problem (SGP) which has been formally defined as *"the lack of coincidence between the information that one can extract from the visual data* [encoded by visual semantics] *and the interpretation that the same data have for a user* [encoded by lexical semantics] *in a given situation"* [17].

There are three key dimensions (the combinations of) which result in the lack of coincidence as mentioned above. Firstly, given a target reality (such as an image of a musical instrument), the fact that its visual properties doesn't necessarily coincide with its linguistic properties as defined in a standard gloss. This generates different non-coinciding substance and classification concepts for the same image. Secondly, as a consequence of the above, the visual subsumption hierarchy of substance concepts doesn't necessarily coincide with the lexical subsumption hierarchy of classification concepts formed from the target reality in different languages. Thirdly, the differences in the choice of visual genus-differentiae and of lexical genus-differentiae with respect to the target reality results in potentially many visual subsumption hierarchies, each of which doesn't necessarily coincide with the potentially many lexical subsumption hierarchies. We briefly exemplify below some cases of incorrespondence between visual and lexical semantics (see Fig. 1) in the musical instruments hierarchy of ImageNet [2] as detailed in [6].

Let us concentrate on image (1) in Fig. 1. Though the image is classified as a good image in ImageNet [18] with a one-to-one correspondence between its visual and lexical semantics, it isn't necessarily the case. Depending on the focus of the visual properties of the image, it can be visually classified as different substance concepts such as *stringed instrument* (presence of taut strings), *guitar* (presence of six taut strings) and *acoustic guitar* (absence of output jack). Out of the three cases above, only *stringed instrument* respects a one-to-one alignment between visual and lexical semantics with respect to the ImageNet label. Further, for the same image, there can be different visual differentiae such as *number of strings*, *body shape* or *colour* which can, in turn, generate mutually incompatible

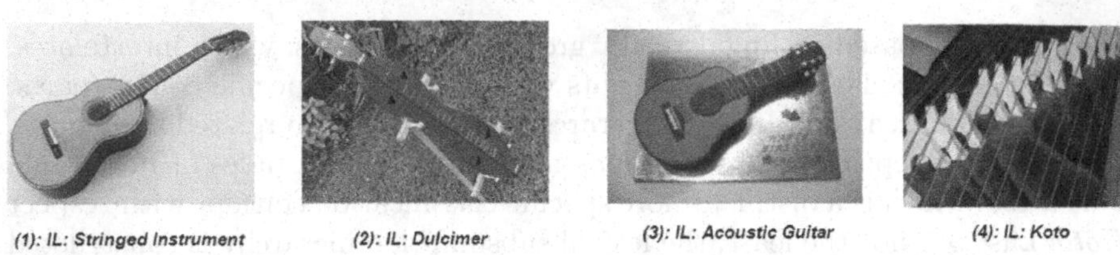

Fig. 1. Samples from ImageNet Musical Instrument Hierarchy (IL: *ImageNet Label)*

visual and lexical subsumption hierarchies. Similarly, image (2) can be visually classified as *stringed instrument* (presence of taut strings), *dulcimer* (presence of four taut strings) and *Apalachian dulcimer* (unique body shape), out of which only *dulcimer* respects the alignment between visual and lexical semantics with respect to the ImageNet label.

The image (3) in Fig. 1 is an example of mislabelled images in the musical instrument hierarchy of the ImageNet. It is clear from the image that it is of a birthday cake shaped in the form of a guitar (and thus should ideally be encoded as a *birthday cake*) at the visual semantic level. However, we notice a direct incorrespondence between its visual and lexical semantics in the form of a wrong (ImageNet) label titled *Acoustic Guitar*. Image (4), on the other hand, is a rather ambiguous image in the ImageNet. It can be visually classified on the basis of at least two visual property - *number of strings* and *number of movable bridges.* Each of the above properties would, in turn, generate a visual subsumption hierarchy of substance concepts inconsistent with the other and with lexical subsumption hierarchies in different languages.

4 Aligning Visual and Lexical Semantics

Given the exemplification of the misalignment between visual semantics and lexical semantics in CV systems, we now introduce a *general, domain-agnostic methodology* to enforce alignment between the two aforementioned semantics in such systems. The methodology is organized into four ordered steps:

1. *Step (1): Substance Concept Recognition.* Identify the relevant substance concepts in the visual data (such as in an image) by determining their relevant *visual properties.*
2. *Step (2): Visual Classification.* Organize the recognized substance concepts into a visual subsumption hierarchy by determining visual genus-differentia.
3. *Step (3): Linguistic classification.* Choose the language labels for each concept in the visual subsumption hierarchy, thus transforming each such substance concept into a classification concept.
4. *Step (4): Conceptual Classification.* Choose an *alinguistic* identifier to uniquely disambiguate each classification concept denoted by the selected label.

We now elaborate and exemplify each of the above steps one by one.

Step (1): Substance Concept Recognition. This step is focused on recognizing substance concepts from substances. Visual perception, which is the reference of a percept to the substance outside the mind [5], is incrementally facilitated by pure percepts and compound percepts [5]. Given an encounter with a substance from a particular partial view, pure percepts are meaningful impressions (i.e., visual properties) of the substance generated by a single primary sense (vision) and deposited in a memory. Pure percepts, over several sets of encounters, aggregate to form compound percepts. Compound percepts, being agglomerated (meaningful) impressions generated by the association of several pure percepts, are essentially the substance concepts. Such evolving assimilation of newly perceived percepts with pre-existing concepts in the memory is stored and updated in a continuously evolving *cumulative memory* [9].

Let us exemplify the above step with case of three stringed musical instruments - *Guitar*, *Flute* and *Koto* (see Fig. 1 for reference). From a certain distance, all the three can be definitively visually recognized as the substance concept *musical instruments* given their visual property of *means of producing music*. From a nearer distance, though, *Guitar* and *Koto* can be recognized as the substance concept *stringed musical instrument* and *Flute* as the substance concept *wind musical instrument* (the visual property being the different means of producing sound). Finally, from an even closer examination, even the substance concepts *Guitar* and *Koto* can be visually differentiated (the visual property being the number of taut strings). Notice that the substance concept *Guitar* and *Koto* are aggregations of several pure percepts perceived from different partial views deposited in the cumulative memory.

Step (2): Visual Classification. The visual classification step, instead, is focused on the modelling of the substance concepts recognized in the previous step into a visual subsumption hierarchy. Such a hierarchy is constructed by organizing substance concepts as a function of their visual properties via exploiting visual genus-differentiae. Let us continue with the previous example of a *Guitar*, *Flute* and *Koto*. The root of the visual subsumption hierarchy will be the substance concept *musical instruments*. On applying the visual differentia *means of sound production* to the visual genus *musical instruments*, the children substance concepts would then be *stringed musical instrument* (the means being *taut strings*) and *wind musical instrument* (the means being *sound pipe*). Further on, the visual genus *stringed musical instrument* can have children substance concepts - *Guitar* (six taut strings) and *Koto* (thirteen taut strings) based on the visual differentia - *the number of taut strings*. Notice that visual genus-differentia in this step is mapped one-to-one with the visual properties considered in the previous step.

Step (3): Linguistic Classification. The focus of the linguistic classification step is to exploit language labels, *viz.* words from an appropriate natural language or domain language to annotate the visual subsumption hierarchy as constructed above. This generates what we model as the lexical subsumption hierarchy composed of classification concepts at each level of the hierarchy. For example, the labelling of previous visual subsumption hierarchy of musical instruments in the Italian language will generate its Italian lexical subsumption hierarchy. The labelling of the same visual subsumption hierarchy in Japanese will, instead, generate its Japanese lexical subsumption hierarchy. It is worth noting that the lexical subsumption hierarchies are distinct for each language due to lexical gaps (as studied in [7,8]), but can also be highly *egocentric* depending on one single individual's purpose [3]. Further, the classification concepts and the lexical subsumption hierarchy *definitionally* correspond one-to-one to the substance concepts and visual subsumption hierarchy from the previous step.

Step (4): Conceptual Classification. The conceptual classification step formally identifies each concept in the lexical subsumption hierarchy with unique *alinguistic or language independent identifiers*, thus mitigating any remaining linguistic phenomena such as polysemy, homonymy and synonymy [8]. In the process, this step also facilitates disambiguation of classification concepts from language labels to uniquely machine-identifiable classification concepts for computational reasoning, analytics and communication purposes. For example, the classification concept *Guitar* and *Koto* can be assigned the unique identifers `1278956` and `9998705` respectively to computationally disambiguate them.

There are three crucial observations. Firstly, the fact that the four steps (individually and in unison) of the methodology enforce a one-to-one alignment between visual and lexical semantics, thus eliminating the many-to-many mapping between them existing in a particular context. The experiment design and execution reported in [6] for (a subset of) the musical instruments hierarchy of the ImageNet elucidates how such an alignment is enforced in practice. Secondly, notice that the algorithmic implementation of the methodology (see [6,9] for implementation and preliminary results) as described above is *continual* and *domain-agnostic* in nature. A CV system grounded in the methodology would thus be able to, for any domain, continually recognize substance concepts and incrementally generate, refine and disambiguate substance and classification concept hierarchies. Recent efforts in the direction include the ongoing project *Media UKC* [5], a multimedia extension of the multilingual lexical semantic resource *Universal Knowledge Core (UKC)* [7,8]. Finally, as reported in the experiments performed in [6], there is a *considerable improvement* in (image) classification accuracy when state-of-the-art (CV) neural network models are trained on *ground truth* generated following the proposed methodology above.

5 Conclusion

The paper introduced *Visual Semantics* and *Lexical Semantics* in the context of CV systems and exhaustively exemplified the misalignment between them. As a solution to such misalignment, the paper introduced a general, domain-agnostic methodology over four ordered steps to enforce alignment between the two kinds of semantics in a particular context.

Acknowledgement. The research conducted by Fausto Giunchiglia, Mayukh Bagchi and Xiaolei Diao has received funding from the *"DELPhi - DiscovEring Life Patterns"* project supported by the MIUR (PRIN) 2017.

References

1. Bentivogli, L., Forner, P., Magnini, B., Pianta, E.: Revising the wordnet domains hierarchy: semantics, coverage and balancing. In: Proceedings of the Workshop on Multilingual Linguistic Resources, pp. 94–101 (2004)
2. Deng, J., Dong, W., Socher, R., Li, L.J., Li, K., Fei-Fei, L.: Imagenet: a large-scale hierarchical image database. In: 2009 IEEE Conference on Computer Vision and Pattern Recognition, pp. 248–255 (2009)
3. Erculiani, L., Giunchiglia, F., Passerini, A.: Continual egocentric object recognition. In: ECAI 2020, pp. 1127–1134. IOS Press (2020)
4. Giunchiglia, F., Bagchi, M.: Millikan + ranganathan - from perception to classification. In: 5th Cognition and OntologieS (CAOS) Workshop, Co-located with the 12th International Conference on Formal Ontology in Information Systems (FOIS) (2021)
5. Giunchiglia, F., Bagchi, M.: Object recognition as classification via visual properties. In: 17th International ISKO Conference and Advances in Knowledge Organization, Aalborg, Denmark (2022)
6. Giunchiglia, F., Bagchi, M., Diao, X.: Visual ground truth construction as faceted classification. arXiv preprint arXiv:2202.08512 (2022)
7. Giunchiglia, F., Batsuren, K., Bella, G.: Understanding and exploiting language diversity. In: IJCAI, pp. 4009–4017 (2017)
8. Giunchiglia, F., Batsuren, K., Freihat, A.A.: One world-seven thousand languages. In: Proceedings 19th International Conference on Computational Linguistics and Intelligent Text Processing, CiCling2018, 18–24 March 2018 (2018)
9. Giunchiglia, F., Erculiani, L., Passerini, A.: Towards Visual Semantics. SN Comput. Sci. **2**(6), 1–17 (2021). https://doi.org/10.1007/s42979-021-00839-7
10. Giunchiglia, F., Fumagalli, M.: Concepts as (recognition) abilities. In: Formal Ontology in Information Systems (FOIS), pp. 153–166 (2016)
11. Giunchiglia, F., Fumagalli, M.: Teleologies: objects, actions and *functions*. In: Mayr, H.C., Guizzardi, G., Ma, H., Pastor, O. (eds.) ER 2017. LNCS, vol. 10650, pp. 520–534. Springer, Cham (2017). https://doi.org/10.1007/978-3-319-69904-2_39
12. Johnson, H.M.: A "Koto" by any other name: exploring Japanese systems of musical instrument classification. Asian Music **28**(1), 43–59 (1996)
13. Lin, T.-Y., et al.: Microsoft COCO: common objects in context. In: Fleet, D., Pajdla, T., Schiele, B., Tuytelaars, T. (eds.) ECCV 2014. LNCS, vol. 8693, pp. 740–755. Springer, Cham (2014). https://doi.org/10.1007/978-3-319-10602-1_48
14. Miller, G.A.: Wordnet: a lexical database for English. Commun. ACM **38**(11), 39–41 (1995)
15. Millikan, R.G.: On Clear and Confused Ideas: An Essay About Substance Concepts. Cambridge University Press, Cambridge (2000)
16. Porello, D., Cristani, M., Ferrario, R.: Integrating ontologies and computer vision for classification of objects in images. In: Proceedings of the Workshop on Neural-Cognitive Integration in German Conference on Artificial Intelligence, pp. 1–15 (2013)

17. Smeulders, A.W., Worring, M., Santini, S., Gupta, A., Jain, R.: Content-based image retrieval at the end of the early years. IEEE Trans. Pattern Anal. Mach. Intell. **12**, 1349–1380 (2000)
18. Tsipras, D., Santurkar, S., Engstrom, L., Ilyas, A., Madry, A.: From imagenet to image classification: contextualizing progress on benchmarks. In: International Conference on Machine Learning, pp. 9625–9635. PMLR (2020)

An Analysis of Classification Approaches for Hit Song Prediction Using Engineered Metadata Features with Lyrics and Audio Features

Mengyisong Zhao[1(✉)], Morgan Harvey[1], David Cameron[1], Frank Hopfgartner[2], and Valerie J. Gillet[1]

[1] The University of Sheffield, Sheffield S10 2TN, UK
{mzhao18,m.harvey,d.s.cameron,v.gillet}@sheffield.ac.uk
[2] Universität Koblenz, 56072 Koblenz, Germany
hopfgartner@uni-koblenz.de

Abstract. Hit song prediction, one of the emerging fields in music information retrieval (MIR), remains a considerable challenge. Being able to understand what makes a given song a hit is clearly beneficial to the whole music industry. Previous approaches to hit song prediction have focused on using audio features of a record. This study aims to improve the prediction result of the top 10 hits among Billboard Hot 100 songs using more alternative metadata, including song audio features provided by Spotify, song lyrics, and novel metadata-based features (title topic, popularity continuity and genre class). Five machine learning approaches are applied, including: k-nearest neighbours, Naïve Bayes, Random Forest, Logistic Regression and Multilayer Perceptron. Our results show that Random Forest (RF) and Logistic Regression (LR) with all features (including novel features, song audio features and lyrics features) outperforms other models, achieving 89.1% and 87.2% accuracy, and 0.91 and 0.93 AUC, respectively. Our findings also demonstrate the utility of our novel music metadata features, which contributed most to the models' discriminative performance.

Keywords: Hit song prediction · Music information retrieval · Machine learning · Text processing

1 Introduction

Music labels spend more than $4.5 billion every year discovering new talented artists and producing popular songs [1]. Precipitated by the growing importance of online digital music platforms and recent advancements in machine learning and big data technologies, a new research area called hit song science has attracted increasing attention [2]. A successful hit song prediction approach could bring considerable benefits to many music lifecycle stakeholders. Early hit song prediction studies illustrate the complexity of this problem, delivering only weak

© The Author(s), under exclusive license to Springer Nature Switzerland AG 2023
I. Sserwanga et al. (Eds.): iConference 2023, LNCS 13971, pp. 303–311, 2023.
https://doi.org/10.1007/978-3-031-28035-1_21

classification results [3–6]. In recent years, more advanced approaches have been able to accurately predict hits and non-hits using audio features [7–13]; however, many other potentially useful sources of information about the songs are also available. In this study, we employ 12 Spotify audio features (energy, liveness, tempo, speechiness, acousticness, time_signature, key, duration_ms, loudness, valence, mode and danceability), these features are drawn directly from Spotify, together with *novel features* based on Billboard music metadata (popularity continuity, genre class and title topic), as well as the topics extracted from the songs' lyrics to identify Top 10 hits among Top 100 hits. To our knowledge, this work is the first attempt to improve hit song prediction by extracting features from the topic of song titles and by using a song's prior popularity information. We examine the effectiveness of these novel features together with song audio and lyrics features for hit song prediction using a variety of machine learning approaches, including k-nearest neighbours (kNN), Naïve Bayes (NB), Random Forest (RF), Logistic Regression (LR) and Multilayer Perceptron (MLP). Our findings demonstrate the utility of the new features and provide state-of-the-art prediction performance, as well as providing promising avenues for future work in this area.

2 Related Work

Hit song prediction (HSP) has been investigated frequently in recent decades. Much seminal work failed to accurately predict hit songs, with some work even suggesting that popularity was not predictable [4,5]. An early approach by Dhanaraj and Logan [3] achieved promising results by using a SVM model to classify top 1 songs through acoustic and lyrics data. However, they provided only scant details about their data gathering, feature engineering, model training and parameter optimization procedure and found textual features to be more predictive than audio analysis. Salganik et al. [4], and Pachet and Roy [5] attempted to reproduce Dhanaraj and Logan's work but failed to achieve a similar level of accuracy.

Various algorithms have been applied to tackle this task, among them: Logistic Regression (LR), Support Vector Machine (SVM) and Neural Networks (NN) are commonly used [3,6,8,11]. Ni et al. [7] gained promising results in predicting UK Top 5 hits on the Top 40 single song charts, but again little implementation detail was provided. Fan and Casey [11] used LR and SVM models to predict British and Chinese hit songs but found that audio features worked better for predicting Chinese hits than British ones, and that textual features worked best overall.

Herremans et al. [6] focussed particularly on dance songs and classified hits using five machine learning models. Their research affirmed the importance of audio features; however, they achieved relatively poor accuracy results, perhaps due to their use of a large number of features without performing any feature selection. Georgieva et al. [8] compared six machine-learning algorithms when conducting Billboard hit song prediction; the most successful algorithms were LR and a

NN with a single hidden layer. Their work also demonstrated the utility of Spotify's audio features for this task. Nasreldin [12] did similar research but identified XGBoost as the top performing classifier; in their study the SVM model performed the worst. As they only use the raw data without any feature selection, they only achieved accuracy results similar to those of Herremans et al. [6]

Recently, Zangerle et al. [15] adopted deep neural networks and treat HSP as a regression task, and their experimental results show that the wide and deep neural network-based approach performed best, achieving 72.04% accuracy. However, the common problem with deep neural networks is that their results are hard to interpret. Essa et al. [16] tried to solve the HIS task by using both classification and regression models. They considered audio features alone and, through adopting seven machine learning models, they achieved results suggesting that both machine learning approaches (classification and regression) can be used for HSP.

Although previous studies have made a large contribution to this topic, it is still unclear which features can be used to successfully classify hit songs when including audio features, music metadata and song lyrics, and in what combination. Audio features have shown promise, but only raw terms have been used to construct features to date [5–7]. Textual features have rarely been adopted in hit song prediction tasks and, although Singhi and Brown [17] did attempt to extract 31 song lyrics features and build SVM model to predict hit songs, the performance achieved was not inspiring.

3 Data and Methodology

3.1 Data Collection and Preprocessing

To investigate hit song prediction, we obtained Billboard hot 100 songs data from the open-source platform *data.world* named "*Billboard Hot-100 Songs 2000-2018 w/Spotify Data+Lyric*"[1]. The dataset includes all songs in the Billboard hot 100 weekly charts from 2007 to 2017, as well as audio features, metadata and lyrics of each song provided by Spotify. The raw dataset includes 33 attributes in total. We firstly remove the irrelevant features (e.g., spotify_link, video_link, analysis_url). Then, we define "hits" in this context to be songs whose highest position in the Billboard Hot 100 list was at rank 10 or above to produce a binary classification of "hit" (1) that at some point reached the Top 10 or "not-hit" (0) that never reached the Top 10. The features used in this study include those engineered based on metadata (e.g., weeks, song title, music genre), 12 Spotify audio features, as well as lyrics of each song. 273 songs had missing audio features data and/or lyrics, and were subsequently removed as it would not be possible to extrapolate or estimate such features. This left 3581 unique songs in the final data set: 507 hits and 3074 non-hits.

[1] data.world/typhon/billboard-hot-100-songs-2000-2018-w-spotify-data-lyrics.

3.2 Feature Engineering

We engineered several additional features to augment the existing metadata features from the original Billboard data and the Spotify audio features. *Popularity continuity* was created to represent the sum of each song's popular duration (i.e., how many weeks it had already been listed in the hot 100 chart prior to the week of interest). Songs already present in the chart for more than 50 weeks were assigned a 3; those present for between 20 and 50 were assigned to 2; those between 10 and 20 were assigned 1; otherwise, a song was assigned 0. Unlike classical music, popular music has relatively rapid iterations [19]. The majority of songs only remain in the chart for a short period, typically less than 20 weeks. Therefore, we assign a number based on 3 duration splits where the assigned numbers are only based on weekly duration data. The *song title topic* feature was created based on the song title. We removed symbols, punctuation, short terms (i.e., fewer than 4 chars) and stopwords from the data, then, inspired by [3], used a bagofwords representation with Latent Dirichlet Allocation (LDA) to extract topics from the song titles. In total, ten topics were extracted, and each song was assigned to the topic number with the highest probability for that song in θ. The numerical variable named *genre class* was created to replace the existing string variable *broad_genre* in which each genre was assigned a numerical value: 1 to 6 representing country, electronic dance music (edm), pop, r&b, rock and rap music respectively. We treat song lyrics similar to how we treat song titles, the only difference being the number of topics: 20 topics were extracted from the lyrics. This is because lyrics are far longer than titles, thus providing sufficient data to extract a larger number of more meaningful topics. Each song was assigned to the topic number with the highest probability for that song in θ.

3.3 Training Environment

Min-max normalization method was applied to accelerate the algorithm convergence speed [16]. After preprocessing and feature engineering, a total of 16 features were used for model building. We treat each song as an individual, temporal factors were not considered in our experiment, the data were split into training and testing sets using a ratio of 80:20 and, due to the relatively small size of the overall data set, 5-fold cross validation was applied instead of an individual validation set. Due to the highly imbalanced classes (i.e., most songs are not top-10 hits), Synthetic Minority Over-Sampling (SMOTE) was adopted inspired by Chawla et al. [18], which could effectively increase the accuracy of minority class (hit song) prediction. In this paper, 5 nearest neighbours have currently used to over-sampling the minority class (hit songs). resulting in a final training set of 4918 songs (including hits 2459 and 2459 non-hits). Forward feature selection was carried out. All models were trained and tested using KNIME 4.4.0[2].

[2] https://www.knime.com/.

3.4 Model Setup and Optimisation

This study examined five commonly-used machine learning approaches from the prior literature, and all the model parameter tuning has been using 5-fold cross validation. The model hyperparameter and their optimum values are shown in Table 1.

k-Nearest Neighbour (kNN). We tested values of k between 1 to 20 to seek for more appropriate neighborhood distance when predicting hit songs, and when we tuned the hyperparameter to k = 1 has achieved most effective accuracy.

Naïve Bayes (NB). We tested the default probability from 0.001 to 1 every 0.01, the best setting was default probability = 0.031.

Random Forest (RF). When using RF to train our model, the different split criterion algorithm provides varied performance, which includes information gain, information gain ratio, and Gini index. We tested the number of models of all algorithms from 50 to 1000 every 50, and the Gini index achieved best performance at 600 numbers of models.

Logistic Regression (LR). We tested four ways to solve the equation, iteratively reweighted least squares with Gauss, iteratively reweighted least squares with Laplace, stochastic average gradient with Gauss, stochastic average gradient with Laplace. We find out using iteratively reweighted least squares with Laplace regularization to solve the equation is more effective. The Laplace equals to 3 has been accepted as best performance.

Neural Network (NN). Multilayer perceptron (MLP) model consisting of an input layer, a hidden layer, and an output layer has been conducted in this study. We tested the Maximum number of iterations from 500 to 5000 with 500 stop sizes, Number of hidden layers and Number of hidden neurons per layer from 1 to 25 was measured every 3. The best parameter tuning result is 4500, 4, 22, respectively.

Table 1. All model hyperparameter tuning optimization value.

Classifier	Hyperparameter	Value
kNN	K value	1
NB	Default probability	0.031
RF	Gini index: number of models	600
LR	Laplace	3
NN	Maximum number of iterations	4500
	Number of hidden layers	4
	Number of hidden neurons per layer	22

4 Findings, Results and Limitations

Our results include an analysis of accuracy, as well as AUC and the number of features used as a measure of parsimony (see Table 2 and Table 3). We compare models trained using all features, including our novel engineered ones, audio features and lyrics features together, against three "baseline" models, audio features alone, audio features and original metadata features, as well as novel features and audio features model. It is notable that Random Forest (Accuracy = 89.1%, AUC = 0.91) and Logistic Regression (Accuracy = 87.2%, AUC = 0.93) with all features performed best according to both metrics. Logistic Regression with Laplace regularisation achieves the best AUC score while only using 4 features. According to Han et al. [20], the reason L1 regularisation is more appropriate to this task could be it capable of reduce the coefficients of some features to zero and generate a spare solution. Random Forest achieved the best accuracy result, but required seven features to train the model, which leads to longer training times, and poorer explainability. MLP shows average performance in this task; this model requires a maximum number of features according to Table 2, and longest training time to achieve the best result, perhaps because the volume of the data available is insufficient to train the network well. Naïve Bayes performs worst on accuracy, but better on AUC score, which means this model has great ability on identifying hits but weak on identifying non-hits.

Table 2. Features selected for each model.

Classifier	Accepted feature combination
kNN	*popularity continuity*[a], *song title topic, genre class*, energy, liveness, key, **lyrics topic**[b]
NB	*popularity continuity, genre class*, key, loudness
RF	*popularity continuity, genre class, song title topic*, key, valence, energy, **lyrics topic**
LR	*popularity continuity, genre class*, **lyrics topic**, danceability
NN	*popularity continuity, genre class*, key, *song title topic*, **lyrics topic**, acousticness, liveness, tempo, danceability

[a] Novel features are marked in italics.

[b] Lyrics feature is marked in bold.

Table 3. All model training and test results summarisation and comparison.

	5-fold CV accuracy	5-fold CV AUC	Model test accuracy	Model test AUC
KNN (Audio)	83.98%	0.847	79.92%	0.530
KNN (Metadata+audio)	90.85%	0.917	82.08%	0.748
KNN (NFE[a] +audio)	93.79%	0.930	86.05%	**0.775**[b]
KNN (NFE+audio+lyrics)	**94.31%**	**0.937**	**86.38%**	0.745
NB (Audio)	62.71%	0.697	42.82%	0.609
NB (Metadata+audio)	82.78%	0.915	71.13%	0.899
NB (NFE+audio)	**86.26%**	0.924	74.76%	**0.922**
NB (NFE+audio+lyrics)	86.23%	**0.931**	**78.52%**	0.900
RF (Audio)	79.22%	0.876	71.13%	0.629
RF (Metadata+audio)	91.62%	0.977	74.76%	0.869
RF (NFE+audio)	93.84%	0.980	87.59%	0.908
RF (NFE+audio+lyrics)	**95.1%**	**0.989**	**89.12%**	**0.912**
LR (Audio)	61.26%	0.649	57.88%	0.603
LR (Metadata+audio)	84.83%	0.917	83.54%	0.927
LR (NFE+audio)	86.15%	0.928	86.47%	0.923
LR (NFE+audio+lyrics)	**87.07%**	**0.933**	**87.17%**	**0.927**
MLP (Audio)	68.20%	0.756	63.60%	0.563
MLP (Metadata+audio)	87.48%	0.923	76.85%	**0.847**
MLP (NFE+audio)	88.0%	0.929	79.36%	0.734
MLP (NFE+audio+lyrics)	**90.04%**	**0.931**	**84.66%**	0.808

[a] NFE stands for abbreviation of novel feature engineering.
[b] The best preformance has been marked in **bold**.

Compared to the baseline method, all the model test accuracy results with our novel metadata features provided significant performance improvement seen in Table 3, which proved our novel metadata features have contributed impact to HSP task. When adding *song lyrics topic* features, the accuracy score of all models are slightly increased, the AUC score of kNN and NB are decreased for .030 and .022 respectively, probably because the lyrics topic increase the complexity of features, which might be hard for both algorithm to classify the patterns of hits and non-hits. The novel variables almost frequently in the list of automatically selected features as shown in Table 2, demonstrating their discriminative power. The utility of *popularity continuity* indicates that the longer a song in a particular genre can maintain a position in the charts, the more likely it is to become a hit song. Certain topically-coherent sets of terms, such as *love, girls, life*, and *hearts* are more likely to appear in the hits than non-hits, as captured in the *song title topic* and *lyrics topic* feature. Based on the ablation studies, some of the Spotify audio features such as *key, liveness, energy*, and *danceability* are also important when classifying hit songs but less consistently so than our *novel features* and *song lyrics feature*. The contributed features are varied between each model. Compared to *song title topic*, *song lyrics feature* shows more contribution when using these two features together to identify hit songs.

The result of this study supports the findings of [6,8,13,14] that music metadata, audio features and lyrics can be used to classify hit songs through machine learning approaches. Adding all features together has achieved the best performance of all models. Moreover, we have been able to outperform the baseline results of [8–10], as their work achieved an accuracy score around 60% to 87% compared to our work, which gave accuracy scores around 79% to 89%.

As future work, we intend to further enrich our models by developing more features based on, for example, music reviews and social tags. More complex and granular genre classifications such as different types of music from various cultures, like Latin music or dance songs from India could be used to extend our model. Furthermore, a larger dataset covering a longer period will be examined. As the hit songs identified in our study can be defined as extremely popular songs (top 10 among100), the model generalisation ability may need more tests, particularly adding songs never achieved in billboard top 100. The substance of a hit song may change over time, and we will consider more complex models that include temporal aspects to model changes in genres and topical popularity over time. Other audio-based features could also be considered, such as Mel-frequency Cepstral Coefficients (MFCC) and compared with the Spotify audio features.

References

1. IFPI Global Music Report Homepage. http://www.ifpicr.cz/ifpi-global-music-report-2016/. Accessed 21 Nov 2022
2. Greenberg, D.M., Rentfrow, P.J.: Music and big data: a new frontier. Curr. Opin. Behav. Sci. **18**, 50–56 (2017)
3. Dhanaraj, R, and Logan, B.: Automatic prediction of hit songs. In: ISMIR, pp. 488–491 (2005)
4. Salganik, M.J., Dodds, P.S., Watts, J.D.: Experimental study of inequality and unpredictability in an artificial cultural market. Science **311**(5762), 854–856 (2006)
5. Pachet, F., Roy, P.: Hit song science is not yet a science. In: ISMIR, pp. 355–360 (2008)
6. Herremans, D., Martens, D., Sörensen, K.: Dance hit song prediction. J. New Music Res. **43**(3), 291–302 (2014)
7. Ni, Y., Santos-Rodriguez, R., Mcvicar, R., De Bie, T.: Hit song science once again a science. In: 4th International Workshop on Machine Learning and Music (2011)
8. Georgieva, E., Marcella S., Nicholas, B.: Hitpredict: predicting hit songs using Spotify data. Stanford Computer Science 229: Machine Learning (2018)
9. Middlebrook, K., Sheik, K.: Song hit prediction: predicting billboard hits using spotify data. arXiv preprint arXiv:1908.08609 (2019)
10. Kim, S.T., Oh, J.H.: Music intelligence: granular data and prediction of top ten hit songs. Decis. Support Syst. **145**, 113535 (2021)
11. Fan, J., Casey, M.: Study of Chinese and UK hit songs prediction. In: Proceedings of the International Symposium on Computer Music Multidisciplinary Research, pp. 640–652 (2013)
12. Song Popularity Predictor Homepage. https://towardsdatascience.com/song-popularity-predictor-1ef69735e380. Accessed 17 Oct 2021
13. Kawawa-Beaudan, J., Garza, G.: Predicting Billboard Top 100 Songs (2015)

14. Borg, N., Hokkanen, G.: What makes for a hit pop song? What makes for a pop song. Unpublished thesis, Stanford University, California, USA (2011)
15. Zangerle, E., Vötter, M., Huber, R., Yang, Y.H.: Hit song prediction: leveraging low-and high-level audio features. In: ISMIR, pp. 319–326 (2019)
16. Essa, Y., Usman, A., Garg, T., Singh, M.K.: Predicting the Song Popularity Using Machine Learning Algorithm (2022)
17. Singhi, A., Brown, D.G.: Can song lyrics predict hits. In: Proceedings of the 11th International Symposium on Computer Music Multidisciplinary Research, pp. 457–471 (2015)
18. Chawla, N.V., Bowyer, K.W., Hall, L.O., Kegelmeyer, W.P.: SMOTE: synthetic minority over-sampling technique. J. Artif. Intell. Res. **16**, 321–357 (2002)
19. Kinga, S.: The attributes and values of folk and popular songs. J. Bhutan Stud. (2001)
20. Han, J., Kamber, M., Pei, J.: Data Mining: Concepts and Techniques, 3rd edn. Elsevier, Amsterdam (2012)

How Many Features Do We Need to Identify Bots on Twitter?

Fatima Tabassum(✉), Sameera Mubarak, Lin Liu, and Jia Tina Du

STEM, University of South Australia, Mawson Lakes, SA 5095, Australia
Fatima.Tabassum@mymail.unisa.edu.au,
{Sameera.Mubarak,Lin.Liu,Tina.Du}@unisa.edu.au

Abstract. The number of malicious bots is increasing rapidly with the growing popularity of social media. We evaluate the importance of 19 commonly used features for Twitter bot detection. Our goal is to propose a set of minimal user-specific features for developing scalable Twitter bot detection systems. To identify the most important features, we apply three model inspection methods - Permutation Importance (PI), SHapely Additive exPlanation (SHAP), and Local Interpretable Model-agnostic Explanations (LIME). We find that the number of followers, friends, and favourites, and the rate of Tweets, making friends and liking Tweets are the most important user-specific features for Twitter bot detection. We apply the Wilcoxon signed rank test to compare the performance of the models trained using all features, using the important features and the features not found as important in our evaluation, respectively. We observe that there are no significant differences between the performance of the models trained using all features and the models trained using the important features. On the other hand, the models using the unimportant features by our evaluation show statistically significant poor performance. We demonstrate that the above six features are sufficient to identify Twitter bots.

Keywords: Social bot · Feature evaluation · Model inspection · Scalable twitter bot detection

1 Introduction

Twitter has become a popular publishing media for anyone to create and disseminate contents to a large online population. While social media platforms have many benefits to offer, their adversarial use is not uncommon. For instance, malicious actors exploited social media to spread deceptive and malicious contents to create social and political upheaval [13] and health hazards [23]. Malicious bot detection is an important task for preventing the ill affects of social media.

Researchers have proposed innovative solutions based on machine learning (ML) models to detect malicious bots on the Twitter platform. These ML models are trained using features extracted from contents (e.g., Tweets) and user profiles. Popular users' features include the number of friends, followers, the number

© The Author(s), under exclusive license to Springer Nature Switzerland AG 2023
I. Sserwanga et al. (Eds.): iConference 2023, LNCS 13971, pp. 312–327, 2023.
https://doi.org/10.1007/978-3-031-28035-1_22

of interactions, the rate of making friends, and followers [8,24,29,32]. Popular ML classifiers used for Twitter bot detection include Random Forest (RF), AdaBoost (AB), Logistic Regression (LR), and Decision Trees (DT) [27]. RF is a tree-based ensemble classifier and found to be the best performing classifier for Twitter data analysis [27,31]. In this work, we apply advanced tree-based ensemble classifiers such as Light Gradient Boosted Machines (LGBM), XGBoost and Extra Trees and find that these classifiers perform better than RF for bot detection.

A recent study by Cresci [4] highlights that due to the evolving nature of the bots existing bot detectors can detect a very few of the recent bots. Consequently, only 5% of the recent bots are being removed [6] from the social media platforms. There is a need for bot detection methods which can be adapted to recent bots easily. This can be achieved by careful selection of features.

The number of features used by the bot detectors varies in the literature. Varol et al. [27] used 1150 features. On similar datasets, Yang et al. [31] and Gilani et al. [14] achieved similar performance using 20 and 21 features respectively. To detect a different type of bot, Cresci et al. [5] used 19 features. The type of features mostly depends on the availability of the annotated data. However, it is essential to find an optimal set of features to develop bot detection models since the volume of Twitter data is huge and scalability is important for recent bot detection.

Some features are more important than others. For example, the number of characters in Tweets posted by bots will be similar to human users since the malicious bot will try to mimic non-malicious posts to maximize likes and shares to increase visibility and reliability (as non-malicious users). Thus, the number of characters in Tweets is not an important feature whereas the number of likes and shares are important.

Interpretable classifiers provide mechanisms to retrieve feature importance from the structure of the classifiers. For example, the variable importance in RF [2] or coefficients in logistic regression classifiers [3]. For non-interpretable classifiers, we need to use model agonistic measures such as Permutation Importance (PI) [1], SHapely Additive exPlanation (SHAP) [18] and Local Interpretable Model-agnostic Explanation (LIME) [22]. In this paper, we refer to these model agonistic measures as model inspection approaches as these measures work on trained classifiers and inspect the differences between the performance of the classifiers to estimate feature importance [3].

Scalability and dynamic contents are two major research challenges involving Twitter data analytics. Twitter is evolving every day, providing a huge amount of "user" and "content" data [31]. The large volume of Twitter data processing is very resource-intensive. Dynamic content refers to the evolving contemporary subjects discussed on Twitter. For example, COVID-19 related information, as well as misinformation, has been dominating Twitter for the past two years, and now the "Russia-Ukraine war" is taking over COVID-19 related tweets. Due to the changing nature of Twitter contents, analytics tasks, such as bot detection using content information will not perform well on future data streams.

In addition to ever-changing contents, bot creators change strategies to make bots invisible to existing detection methods. Therefore, more research is needed to develop methods that do not rely on content information i.e., methods leveraging information that are similar in characteristics among different types of bots across various datasets (e.g., user information).

The specific contributions of this paper are:

1. We combine three state-of-the-art model inspection approaches - Permutation Importance [1], SHAP [18], and LIME [22] to identify six most important features for Twitter bot detection. Using three importance measures makes the results more reliable than previous approaches. To the best of our knowledge, we are the first to use multiple feature inspection approaches to identify important features for bot detection.
2. We evaluated ten classifiers on ten Twitter datasets. Our evaluation includes both traditional classifiers such as RF, DT, LR, etc., and advanced classifiers such as Gradient Boosting. We found that advanced classifiers outperform currently preferred RF classifier on Twitter datasets [27,31].
3. Our comprehensive evaluation showed that six features - number of followers, friends, and favourites and frequencies of Tweets, making friends and liking Tweets are the most important features for developing bot detection systems. This result is important as using only six features will increase scalability, one of the existing problems in large Twitter analytics datasets.

2 Do All the Features Equally Contribute to Bot Detection?

In Sect. 1 we argue that all features do not contribute equally to bot detection. To see it concretely, we use predictive power score (pps) which is a measure of arbitrary predictive relationships (both linear and non-linear) between two variables [9,28]. Given two variables x and y, pps score is calculated by building a predictive model e.g., decision tree using x as feature and y as the target. A pps score 0 implies x cannot predict y better than a naïve baseline model and a score 1 implies the perfect predictability.

In this section, we demonstrate that not all features are useful or equally important for bot detection. There are mainly two types of features in Twitter datasets, they are *content features* and *user features*. Features related to Twitter contents or Tweets vary in different datasets according to the trending discussions at the time of data collections. The user features are extracted from the user profiles of Twitter users and do not depend on trending topics i.e., they do not change according to the discussions.

Table 1 shows the 19 user features we used in our empirical study. These features are the user features commonly used in literature on bot detection [30, 31]. In our experiments, we do not use the 'verified' feature, as it is already declared to be authentic or non-malicious users by Twitter. User age (u_{age}) is used to derive features f_8, f_9, f_{10}, f_{11} and f_{13}. User age is defined as the

Table 1. Twitter features used for bot detection.

ID	Feature	Type	ID	Feature	Type
f_1	Whether the user has a default profile	Binary	f_{11}	The ratio of favourites and user age $\frac{f_6}{u_{age}}$	Real
f_2	Whether the user has a background image	Binary	f_{12}	The ratio of followers and friends $\frac{f_4}{f_5}$	Real
f_3	Number of statuses posted by the user	Integer	f_{13}	The ratio of user's list growth $\frac{f_7}{u_{age}}$	Real
f_4	Number of followers	Integer	f_{14}	Number of characters in the screen name	Integer
f_5	Number of friends	Integer	f_{15}	Number of digits in the screen name	Integer
f_6	Number of favourite Tweets	Integer	f_{16}	Name length	Integer
f_7	Number of lists the user belongs to	Integer	f_{17}	Number of digits in the name	Integer
f_8	The ratio of status during user's age $\frac{f_3}{u_{age}}$	Real	f_{18}	Length of user's profile bio	Integer
f_9	The ratio of followers obtained $\frac{f_4}{u_{age}}$	Real	f_{19}	Likelihood of the screen name	Real
f_{10}	The ratio of friends made in user's age $\frac{f_5}{u_{age}}$	Real		(e.g., random, or authentic)	

difference between the time the data was collected and the time the account was created.

We hypothesize that if the features $f_1, f_2, \cdots, f_{19}$ equally contribute to bot detection, they will have similar pps scores i.e., $\text{pps}(f_1, \text{bot}) = \text{pps}(f_2, \text{bot}) = \cdots = \text{pps}(f_{19}, \text{bot})$. Here, the target 'bot' indicates human or bot accounts. We also hypothesize that if $\text{pps}(f_i, f_j)$ is high, then f_j should not be used in model building as f_j is highly correlated to f_i and f_i accurately predicts f_j.

We use pps scores in two ways. Firstly, we compute pps scores between each feature and target 'bot or human' which indicates contributions of features to bot detection. Secondly, we compute pairwise pps scores between all features which reveals if there is any highly correlated feature. We use all ten datasets shown in Table 2 and take the average pps scores for comparisons. The pps scores of the features on the ten datasets are illustrated in Fig. 1a.

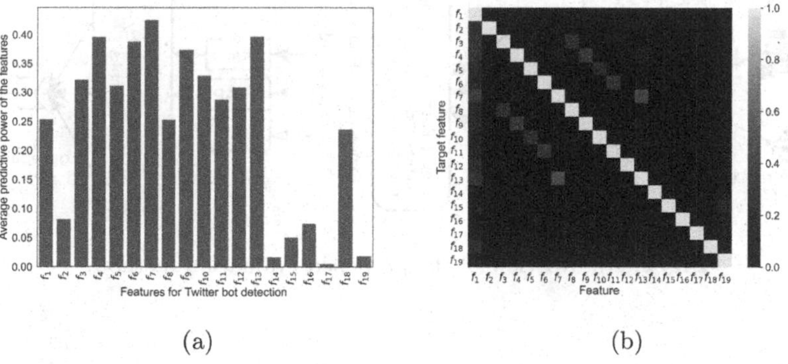

(a) (b)

Fig. 1. (a) Predictive power of the features to detect bots. (b) Predictive power of the features in the x axis to predict the features in the y axis

Figure 1a depicts the contribution of features for bot detection. The figures shows that all features do not contribute equally to bot detection task. Moreover, the predictive power of an individual feature is not very high (less than 0.40) which means none of the features can detect bots independently. Figure 1b shows that feature f_3 can predict f_8 to some degrees. Similarly, f_4 predicts f_9, f_5 predicts f_{10} and so on. We can interpret some of the correlations in Fig. 1b. For example, from Table 1, we see that f_8 and f_9 are computed using f_3 and f_4 respectively. Hence, these predictability scores are not arbitrary. However, we do not use pps score for evaluating feature importance as pps works only on individual features. A high value of $\text{pps}(f_i, \text{bot}), 1 \leq i \leq 19$ indicates that f_i is important for bot detection, but f_i may not contribute highly in presence of other features. Hence in the next section, we proposed a new method which uses three model inspection methods to identify most important features for bot detection. The identified important features should be used for developing scalable bot detection systems.

3 Proposed Feature Evaluation and Identification Method

An overview of our evaluation method is illustrated in Fig. 2. There are three main steps in our evaluation. Firstly, we identified the best performing classifiers from ten classifiers trained on each of the ten datasets. Secondly, we applied three model inspection methods on each best classifier corresponding to each dataset to identify the most important features according to the contribution of the features for Twitter bot detection. Then, we rank the features according to their contributions computed by each model inspection method. Finally, we identify the minimal feature set $\mathcal{F}'$ by aggregating the ranks of the features on all the datasets.

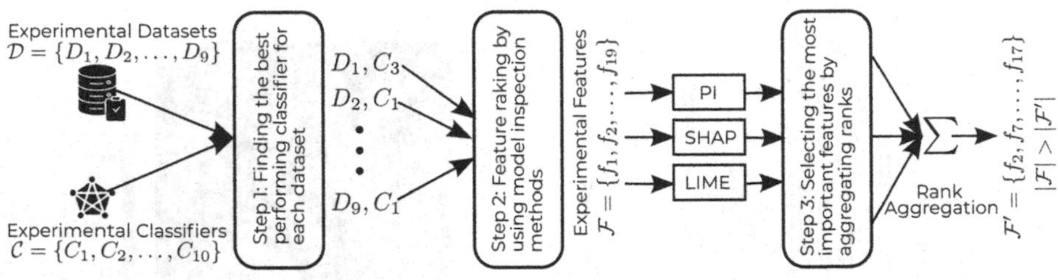

Fig. 2. An overview of the proposed evaluation method.

3.1 Identifying the Best Performing Classifiers

We cast the bot detection problem as a binary classification problem with the target class representing bot and benign human users. Let a set of Twitter datasets be $\mathcal{D} = \{D_1, D_2, \cdots, D_n\}$ and a set of classifiers $\mathcal{C} = \{C_1, C_2, \cdots, C_m\}$. To identify, which classifier C_i performs best on a dataset D_j, we train all the classifiers in $\mathcal{C}$ on all the datasets in $\mathcal{D}$ and C_i performs best on D_j if

$\text{per}(C_i, D_j) = \max_{1 \le i \le m} \text{per}(C_i, D_j), 1 \le i \le m \wedge 1 \le j \le n$. Here, $\text{per}(C_i, D_j)$ is the performance of C_i on D_j according to some performance metric such as accuracy or F1 score.

A summary of the ten datasets in our evaluation is given in Table 2. For each dataset, Table 2 shows the Dataset name, the research introducing the dataset (Source), the number of users in each class (Bot and Human), and a short description of the dataset. These datasets have different characteristics and have been used for malicious bot detection. We followed [30, 31] to prepare the datasets. In the original sources, some datasets included only human accounts or only bot accounts [30]. We combine the single-class datasets to prepare the training set. For example, the `pron-celebrity` dataset is formed by combining two single class datasets `pronbots` and `celebrity`. Another single class dataset `verified` is randomly sampled and combined with `vendor-purchased` and `botwiki` to form `vendor-verified` and `botwiki-verif- ied` datasets respectively. Similarly, `political-botometer` is a combination of `botometer-feedback` and `political-bots`.

Table 2. Summary of the evaluation datasets.

Dataset	Source	Bot	Human	Description
caverlee	[17]	22223	19276	Bot accounts and legitimate human accounts
cresci-rtbust	[19]	353	340	Bots and humans accounts sharing Italian retweets
cresci-stock	[7]	7102	6174	Humans and bots sharing malicious financial tweets
gilani	[14]	1090	1413	Manually labelled bots and humans accounts
midterm	[31]	42446	8092	Human and bot accounts discussing politics during 2018 U.S. midterm election
botwiki-verified	[30,31]	698	994	Bots from botwiki.org archive and verified human accounts
political-botometer	[30]	201	380	Political Twitter bots, human and bot accounts reported by Botometer users
pron-celebrity	[30]	17882	5918	Bots involving Twitter scams and verified celebrity accounts
vendor-verified	[30,31]	1087	993	Vendor purchased fake follower accounts and verified human accounts
Twibot-20	[11]	6589	5237	Human accounts are verified accounts and bots are annotated manually

The ten classifiers considered in our study are k-Nearest Neighbor (KNN), Decision Tree (DT), Logistic Regression (LR), Support Vector Machines (SVM), AdaBoost (Ada), Gradient Boosting (XGB), Random Forest (RF), Extra Trees (ET) and Light Gradient Boosting (LGBM). Among these classifiers, RF is the most popular one [31]. Similar to RF, Ada, XGB, ET, and LGBM use decision trees as base classifiers. However, they use different strategies to build the trees. These tree-based ensemble classifiers perform better on traditional non-social media datasets.

As for estimating the performance of the classifiers, we used cross-validation (CV). For datasets having less than 1000 samples, we used 3 folds CV and for the other datasets, we use 5 folds CV.

We evaluated our proposed approach using the macro averaged F1-score obtained by computing the harmonic mean of Precision and Recall. F1-score is a better choice than precision or recall for accessing classifiers' performance on imbalanced datasets. Macro averaging calculates F1-score for each class individually and then computes the unweighted average. Therefore, all target classes have the same influence on the performance despite an inequal number of samples per class. Note that some of our datasets are imbalanced i.e., have an unequal number of human and bot accounts.

3.2 Feature Ranking by Model Inspection Approaches

Each dataset $D_i \in \mathcal{D}$ is a collection of Twitter users described by a set of features $\mathcal{F} = \{f_1, f_2, \cdots, f_{19}\}$. The details of the features are introduced in Sect. 2. We trained the classifiers $\mathcal{C}$ using features $\mathcal{F}$. For the `caverlee` dataset (see Table 2) all the 19 features shown in Table 1 are not available in the original source. We used the available features - $f_3, f_4, f_5, f_8, f_9, f_{10}, f_{12}$, and f_{18} for `caverlee` dataset. The goal of this work is to identify a small number of features for malicious bot detection. That is, from the features $\mathcal{F} = \{f_1, f_2, \cdots, f_{19}\}$ we want to select a subset $\mathcal{F}' = f_1, f_2, \cdots, f_p$ such that $p < 19$ and $\mathcal{F}'$ only includes the most important features for the malicious bot detection task. We call a feature $f_i \in \mathcal{F}$ important if removing f_i i.e., $\mathcal{F} - f_i$ significantly affects the classification performance of a classifier. We estimate the contributions of features using model inspection approaches [1,18,22].

Instead of using feature importance provided by interpretable algorithms such as DT and LR, we are using model agonistic approaches such as Permutation Importance (PI) [1], Shapely Additive explanation (SHAP) [18], and Local Interpretable Model-agnostic Explanation (LIME) [22]. Interpretable algorithms are useful for small problems with very few variables. They become uninterpretable with the increasing complexity of the classification tasks. For example, a 20 level DT is hard to interpret. A previous study [25] showed that RF importance is biased towards the variables selected for tree construction. This bias also exists in other tree-based methods such as ADA, XGB, and LGBM. Another study [16] shows that linear models and RF generated inconsistent importance. Moreover, our results in Table 3 indicates that DT and LR did not achieve the best performance on any of the datasets.

Given a trained classifier and training data, the model inspection methods i.e., PI, SHAP, and LIME provide a list of features with the contributions of the features towards the classification task. Higher contribution means higher importance. We used this feature contribution list to rank the features in ascending order where the smallest rank represents the most important feature. We use ranks as the results produced by the three methods are not comparable.

To obtain a reliable estimate of feature importance, we aggregated the ranks from the three model inspection methods. These methods can produce inconsistent results due to the different approaches used for computing contributions of the features [20]. Furthermore, none of the model inspection methods is reliable alone. PI does not perform well in the presence of correlated features [1], LIME sometimes performs poorly on tabular data [22] and SHAP can produce misleading results [18].

Another important distinction among the model inspection methods lies in the number of instances used by the methods for computing feature importance. PI is a global approach i.e., the feature importance is computed on all the instances in the test set. On the other hand, SHAP and LIME are local approaches i.e., they provide feature importance for a single instance. We applied SHAP and LIME to each instance of a dataset using cross-validation and averaged the results to get the global importance of the features.

3.3 Identifying the Optimal Feature Set

It is important to aggregate feature ranks from the three methods to select most important features. We assumed that a feature ranked higher (i.e., important) by all the model inspection approaches must be included for malicious Twitter bot detection. Let the output of the previous step be a rank matrix $\mathcal{R} \in {Z^+}^{3*n \times p}$ where n is the number of experimental datasets and p is the number of experimental features. As we have three feature ranking methods, for each dataset and feature we have three ranks i.e., for n datasets we have $3 * n$ rows in $\mathcal{R}$. As discussed earlier a model inspection method will generate zero or very low importance for some features. We ignored such low importance. As a result, $\mathcal{R}$ is a sparse matrix i.e., for a particular dataset a feature may have less than three ranks.

To select the most important features, we needed to consider both the average rank of a feature and how many times the feature has been ranked. Let, $\mathrm{NC}^{1 \times p} = \mathrm{count\_nz}(r_{i*}), 1 \leq i \leq p$ be a vector of p elements where an element $\mathrm{nc_i}$ represent how many times feature f_i (represented in the ith column r_{i*} in $\mathcal{R}$) is ranked. Also let $S^{1 \times p} = \sum_{j=1}^{3*n} r_{ij}, 1 \leq i \leq p$ be a vector of sum of the ranks of all features.

We performed an element wise operation $\mathcal{R}'^{1 \times p} = \mathrm{NC}^{1 \times p} \div S^{1 \times p}$ to obtain the average ranks of each feature. For p experimental features, $\mathcal{R}'$ is a vector of size p where each element is the average rank of the corresponding feature. We selected the minimal feature set $\mathcal{F}'$ considering both $\mathcal{R}'^{1 \times p}$ and $\mathrm{NC}^{1 \times p}$.

3.4 Method Implementation

We utilized various Python libraries for implementing our experiments. More specifically, we used pandas for data processing and sklearn for building most of the experimental classifiers. Additionally, we employed Microsoft's LightGBM[1] and dmlc XGBoost[2] packages for building the LGBM and XGB classifiers. For all implementations, we used the default hyperparameters provided by the corresponding libraries. The permutation importance is available in the sklearn library. The python implementations of SHAP and LIME are freely available in GitHub[3,4].

---

1 https://github.com/Microsoft/LightGBM/.
2 https://xgboost.ai/.
3 https://github.com/slundberg/shap.
4 https://github.com/marcotcr/lime.

4 Results and Discussion

4.1 Best Performing Classifier on Each Dataset

We used macro F1 scores to select the best performing classifier for each dataset. Our experimental results are shown in Table 3. Each cell in the table shows the macro F1 score achieved by a classifier specified in the column header on the dataset specified in the corresponding row header. The best scores are highlighted using boldface texts.

Table 3. Macro averaged F1 scores of the classifiers on the experimental dataset.

SL	Dataset	DT	ADA	ET	KNN	LGBM	LR	NB	RF	SVM	XGB
1	botwiki-verified	0.9688	**0.9853**	0.9761	0.8588	0.9841	0.9405	0.8381	0.9805	0.9125	0.9762
2	caverlee	0.8590	0.8992	0.9045	0.8872	0.9061	0.8377	0.7527	**0.9063**	0.8626	0.9029
3	cresci-rtbust	0.6854	0.7545	0.7805	0.7024	0.7733	0.7226	0.6942	**0.7936**	0.7553	0.7778
4	cresci-stock	0.8125	0.8381	0.8498	0.6649	**0.8716**	0.6494	0.6556	0.8691	0.6843	0.8564
5	gilani	0.6798	0.7293	0.7368	0.6387	0.7510	0.7133	0.6966	**0.7550**	0.6932	0.7541
6	midterm	0.9740	0.9803	0.9810	0.9210	**0.9858**	0.9520	0.9223	0.9854	0.9436	0.9812
7	political-botometer	0.7389	0.7700	0.7713	0.6689	**0.8072**	0.6794	0.6018	0.8049	0.7085	0.7758
8	pron-celebrity	0.9996	0.9997	0.9968	0.9494	0.9994	0.9732	0.9658	0.9997	0.9749	**0.9999**
9	vendor-verified	0.9735	0.9793	0.9701	0.8288	**0.9802**	0.8850	0.8533	0.9793	0.8749	0.9749
10	Twibot-20	0.6653	0.7392	0.7361	0.6180	**0.7435**	0.6846	0.6487	0.7419	0.6575	0.7401

Though RF is shown to achieve the best performance on similar datasets in [27,31], we found LGBM, XGB, and ADA perform better than RF on some datasets. Our results show that the XGB obtained the highest F1 score on the `pron-celebrity` dataset which is nearly 1 (0.9999).

LGBM performs the best on majority of the datasets. LGBM gained F1 scores of 0.9858, 0.9802, 0.8716, 0.8072 and 0.7435 on the `midterm`, `vendor-purchased`, `cresci-stock`, `political-botometer` and `Twibot-20` datasets respectively. Similarly, ADA performs better than RF with F1 score of 0.9853 for the `botwiki-verified` dataset. The highest F1-score is achieved by RF is 0.9063 on the `caverlee` dataset, followed by 0.7936 and 0.7550 for the `cresci-rtbust` and `gilani` datasets respectively. Expectedly the non-ensemble methods such as DT, LR, and NB did not perform well.

4.2 Feature Importance

As discussed earlier, we ran our experiments with 3 different model inspection methods - PI, SHAP, and LIME on the best performing classifier for each corresponding dataset. The low-performing features return very low scores in all feature importance methods. Therefore, for each method, we showed 10 top-ranked features. Our experimental result showing feature ranks for the ten datasets is presented in Table 4. Each row represents a feature importance method and dataset, and each column represents a feature. A cell represents the rank of a feature on a particular dataset using a feature importance method.

The last two rows of Table 4 show the average ranks and the number of times a feature is ranked (Count) by the importance measures. We observe that some features such as f_2, f_{14} and f_{17} are not ranked by any methods i.e., they are not important for malicious user identification. From Table 1, we see that these features are whether the user has default profile image and the number of characters and digits in username. We also observe that f_4 (number of followers) and f_6 (number of favorite Tweets) are ranked as the most important having average ranks 3.3 and 3.5. Features f_4 and f_6 have 22 and 23 non-zero ranks respectively. Thus, considering both average ranks and the number of times a feature is ranked we select $\mathcal{F}' = \{f_4, f_5, f_6, f_8, f_{10}, f_{11}\}$ to be the minimal feature set for malicious Twitter bot detection. From the traditional 19 features, our comprehensive evaluation showed that six features i.e.,number of followers, friends, and favourites and frequencies of Tweets, making friends and liking Tweets are sufficient for developing machine learning-based effective malicious bot detection systems. number of followers, friends, and favourites and frequencies of Tweets, making friends and liking Tweets

4.3 Effectiveness of the Selected Features

Accuracy of the models are also as important as using the important features. To compare the performance of the models using only the selected features, we retrain our experimental models using the selected features $\mathcal{F}'$. We also compare the performance of the models with the features those are not selected by our inspection-based selection method i.e., features in $\mathcal{F} - \mathcal{F}'$. The results of the experiments are shown in Table 5 where column $\mathcal{F}$ shows the best performance without feature selection, column $\mathcal{F}'$ with feature selection and column $\mathcal{F} - \mathcal{F}'$ features those are not selected by our method on the corresponding datasets.

We observe that, feature selection achieves almost similar performance to the models without feature selection and the models with unimportant features perform poorly as expected. To confirm the statistical significance of the results, we perform the Wilcoxon signed rank test [21] on the results in Table 5. Specifically, we compare column $\mathcal{F}'$ with $\mathcal{F}$ and $\mathcal{F} - \mathcal{F}'$ with $\mathcal{F}$. The result of the significance test show that there is no significant difference in performance of the models with and without feature selection and models with unimportant features performance is significantly different than model with all features. The result of the significance test is given in Table 6. We use 95% significance level in our test.

4.4 Scalability Using Selected Features

To evaluate the scalability gained by our method, we conduct an experiment with a moderately large Twitter bot dataset i.e., `Twibot-22` [10] consisting of 1M labeled Twitter accounts. For this experiment, we took 200000 random samples (12764 bot and 187236 human) from the dataset. When working with Twitter data a lot of computation time is required by feature extraction. We observed

Table 4. Feature ranking from model inspection approaches.

		f_1	f_2	f_3	f_4	f_5	f_6	f_7	f_8	f_9	f_{10}	f_{11}	f_{12}	f_{13}	f_{14}	f_{15}	f_{16}	f_{17}	f_{18}	f_{19}
botwiki-verified	PI				1	3	2	4	5	6	7		10	8						9
	SHAP				1	3	2	4	5	7	9		6	10						8
	LIME				1	5	3	2	4	7	9		6	10						8
caverlee	PI			5	6	1			4	1	2	3							7	
	SHAP			4	6	1			5	7	2	3							8	
	LIME			4	8	1			5	6	2 .	3							7	
cresci-rtbust	PI					5	3		6		10	2	4	8			9		1	
	SHAP					8	2		6	4	9	3	5	7					1	
	LIME				7	3	1	7		10	2	4	9	6			8			
cresci-stock	PI			3	2	6	1	10	5	9	7	4							8	
	SHAP			4	1	5	2	9	6	10	7	3							8	
	LIME			9	1	3	4	7	5	10	6	2	8							
gilani	PI			2	5		3	10	1	7	9	4	6				8			
	SHAP			2	6		4	10	1	8	7	3	5	9						
	LIME			2	10	7	4	9	1			3	5	6					8	
midterm	PI			9	3	6	1	8	4	5	2			10					7	
	SHAP	10		4	1	5	2	7	6	1	3			9						
	LIME	10		4	1	7	3	6	2 ·	9	5								8	
political-botometer	PI			8		1	6	4	3	5	2	9		10					7	
	SHAP			9		2	4	3	7	5	1	6					10			8
	LIME					4	3	1	2	7	5	10	9				8		6	
pron-celebrity	PI																			
	SHAP																			
	LIME			7	1	9	8	2	6		4						5			3
vendor-verified	PI			8	3		5	2		6	1	9	4	7		10				
	SHAP			8	3	10	5	1		7	2		4	6					9	
	LIME			7	3	10	6	2	9	8	1		4	5						
Twibot-20	PI			6	1	5		3		4	7	10	2	8			9			
	SHAP			10	1	9	8			7		3	2	5					4	6
	LIME	8		2		6			1	9			5	3		10	7		4	
Average ranks		9.3		5.6	**3.3**	**5**	**3.6**	5.3	**4.3**	7.2	**4.8**	**4.7**	5.5	7.5		10	8		6.2	7
Count		3	0	21	**22**	**25**	**23**	21	**23**	25	**25**	**18**	17	17	0	2	8	0	15	6

Table 5. Comparison of performance with the selected and unselected features.

SL	Dataset	Model	$\mathcal{F}$	Model	$\mathcal{F}'$	Model	$\mathcal{F} - \mathcal{F}'$
1	botwiki-verified	Ada	0.9853	Ada	0.9823	LGBM	0.9731
2	caverlee	RF	0.9063	LGBM	0.8871	LGBM	0.8734
3	cresci-rtbust	RF	0.7936	ET	0.7470	Ada	0.7656
4	cresci-stock	LGBM	0.8716	LGBM	0.8665	LGBM	0.8052
5	gilani	RF	0.7550	XGB	0.7486	LGBM	0.7168
6	midterm	LGBM	0.9858	ET	0.9850	LGBM	0.9779
7	political-botometer	LGBM	0.8072	ET	0.8184	XGB	0.7591
8	pron-celebrity	XGB	0.9999	XGB	0.9999	LGBM	0.9988
9	vendor-verified	LGBM	0.9802	Ada	0.9706	Ada	0.9798
10	Twibot-20	LGBM	0.7435	XGB	0.7430	LGBM	0.7362
	Avg		0.8828		0.8895		0.8585

Table 6. Result of wilcoxon signed rank test.

Test	Test statistics **W**	p
$\mathcal{F}$ vs. $\mathcal{F}$'	7	0.066
$\mathcal{F}$ vs. $\mathcal{F} - \mathcal{F}'$	0	0.002

that for the 200000 samples, it requires approximately 15000 s to extract features $\mathcal{F}$ and 9800 s to extract $\mathcal{F}'$. In other words, it takes 0.0750 and 0.0488 s to extract 19 and 6 features respectively from each user metadata.

We train the RF model using 70% of the data ten times with features $\mathcal{F}$ and ten times with $\mathcal{F}'$ to observe the time required for model constructions from the extracted features. The sklearn RF library is quite efficient and the average time require by features $\mathcal{F}$ model is 56 s and by $\mathcal{F}'$ is 39 s approximately. Clearly, $\mathcal{F}'$ require less time for both feature extraction and model construction.

The procedures for feature extraction and classifier training are implemented on a personal computer (PC) with an Intel Core i7-7600U CPU (2.80 GHz) and 16 GB RAM. On this PC, it takes approximately 0.0753 (using features $\mathcal{F}$) and 0.0489 s (using features $\mathcal{F}'$) including feature generation and modelling to evaluate an account for bot detection.

We can obtain metadata about 8.6M accounts per day with a user API key from Twitter firehose [31]. According to our reported rate above, generating features $\mathcal{F}$ from the entire firehose data will require $\approx$ 7.5 days and for generating features $\mathcal{F}'$ will require $\approx$ 4.8 days. Once the features are extracted, building models will require $\approx$ 40 mins and $\approx$ 28 mins using $\mathcal{F}$ and $\mathcal{F}'$ respectively. In real-world applications often high performing computing resources are used for processing large volume of data. In such cases the data processing time will reduce significantly for both sets of features.

5 Related Works

Researchers have applied supervised machine learning (ML) methods to detect malicious Twitter users. In supervised ML methods, labelled datasets are used to train the classifiers. A wide range of social media features is used by researchers to train ML classifiers. For instance, Varol et al. [27] used 1150 features to train various ML classifiers including Random Forest (RF), AdaBoost, Logistic Regression, and Decision trees. Though RF showed the best performance, training with so many features require huge computational time. Yang et al. [31] showed that similar performance can be achieved using fewer features (specifically, they used 20 features). Gilani et al. [15] experimented with 21 features and developed an RF classifier to classify non-malicious (human) and malicious (bot) users.

Classifiers trained with lots of features are not easily scalable. It is essential to find task-specific important features and use them to improve the classifiers' performance [2]. Feature selection is important on both social media and non-social media datasets. A few examples of this type of feature selection task are - emotion classification [26], industrial recommendation system [33], and human activity recognition [2]. The existing feature importance analysis research greatly varies in measuring the feature importance for selecting the most important features. Chen et al. [2] used variable importance of RF algorithm and Recursive Feature Elimination methods. Gilani et al. [15] also used Recursive Feature Elimination. RF algorithm provides feature importance scores by considering the features appearing at the roots or upper levels in the base trees. As we mentioned earlier, RF generates biased results when less important features get selected for base tree constructions [25]. Feature importance measures are also inconsistent [20] i.e., multiple methods can produce different importance for the same features and classifier. We cannot rely on a single measure. Instead of selecting features, Yang et al. [31] selected training data for scalability. Social media datasets are increasing in numbers and volume rapidly. Therefore, selecting a subset of existing datasets as Yang et al. [31] may not be effective in the future. To address the above issues in existing research, we propose to use multiple feature importance measures on a large number of datasets and classifiers. Our approach combines multiple methods to get a more reliable estimate of feature importance and reduce inconsistencies of a single approach.

6 Conclusion

In this paper, we have demonstrated that six features are as effective as 19 commonly used features for bot detection. Scalable bot detection methods can be developed using six features. We proposed a framework for selecting features for malicious Twitter user detection. We used three model inspection approaches to reduce the inconsistencies in the importance generated by an individual approach. Our evaluation includes ten classifiers and 19 features from ten publicly available Twitter datasets. Previous works in social media bot detection found RF as an effective classifier. However, our empirical results suggest that more advanced tree-based ensemble classifiers such as XGB and LGBM perform better than RF. Most importantly, our findings show that only six features are sufficient and require less time for malicious bot detection. In the future, we will study the cross-domain performance of bot detectors using a minimal set of features.

This work contributes to a promising direction in developing scalable approaches for Twitter bot detection. Scalable methods for Twitter data analysis are in demand as the volume of data is increasing every day.

References

1. Breiman, L.: Random forests. Mach. Learn. **45**, 5–32 (2001)
2. Chen, R.-C., Dewi, C., Huang, S.-W., Caraka, R.E.: Selecting critical features for data classification based on machine learning methods. J. Big Data **7**(1), 1–26 (2020). https://doi.org/10.1186/s40537-020-00327-4
3. Christoph, M.: Interpretable Machine Learning. A Guide for Making Black Box Models Explainable, Creative Commons Attribution, 2 edn (2022). https://christophm.github.io/interpretable-ml-book/
4. Cresci, S.: A decade of social bot detection. Commun. ACM **63**(10), 72–83 (2020)
5. Cresci, S., Di Pietro, R., Petrocchi, M., Spognardi, A., Tesconi, M.: Fame for sale: efficient detection of fake twitter followers. Decis. Support Syst. **80**, 56–71 (2015)
6. Cresci, S., Di Pietro, R., Petrocchi, M., Spognardi, A., Tesconi, M.: The paradigm-shift of social spambots: evidence, theories, and tools for the arms race. In: Proceedings of the 26th International Conference on World Wide Web Companion, WWW 2017 Companion, pp. 963–972 (2017)
7. Cresci, S., Lillo, F., Regoli, D., Tardelli, S., Tesconi, M.: Cashtag piggybacking: uncovering spam and bot activity in stock microblogs on twitter. ACM Trans. Web (TWEB) **13**, 1–27 (2019)
8. Davis, C.A., Varol, O., Ferrara, E., Flammini, A., Menczer, F.: Botornot: a system to evaluate social bots (2016)
9. Engin, A.: The cognitive ability and working memory framework: interpreting cognitive reflection test results in the domain of the cognitive experiential theory. CEJOR **29**(1), 227–245 (2021)
10. Feng, S., et al.: Twibot-22: towards graph-based twitter bot detection. arXiv preprint arXiv:2206.04564 (2022)
11. Feng, S., Wan, H., Wang, N., Li, J., Luo, M.: Twibot-20: a comprehensive twitter bot detection benchmark. In: Proceedings of the 30th ACM International Conference on Information & Knowledge Management (2021)
12. Fisher, A., Rudin, C., Dominici, F.: All models are wrong, but many are useful: learning a variable's importance by studying an entire class of prediction models simultaneously. J. Mach. Learn. Res. **20**, 1–81 (2019)
13. Fisher, M., Cox, J.W., Hermann, P.: Pizzagate: from rumor, to hashtag, to gunfire in D.C. (2016). https://www.washingtonpost.com/local/pizzagate-from-rumor-to-hashtag-to-gunfire-in-dc/2016/12/06/4c7def50-bbd4-11e6-94ac-3d324840106c_story.html
14. Gilani, Z., Farahbakhsh, R., Tyson, G., Wang, L., Crowcroft, J.: Of bots and humans (on twitter). In: ASONAM 2017: Advances in Social Networks Analysis and Mining 2017, pp. 349–354. Association for Computing Machinery (2017)
15. Gilani, Z., Kochmar, E., Crowcroft, J.: Classification of twitter accounts into automated agents and human users. In: Diesner, J., Ferrari, E., Xu, G. (eds.) Advances in Social Networks Analysis and Mining 2017, pp. 489–496. Association for Computing Machinery (2017)

16. Grömping, U.: Variable importance assessment in regression: linear regression versus random forest. Am. Stat. 308–319 (2009)
17. Lee, K., Eoff, B., Caverlee, J.: Seven months with the devils: a long-term study of content polluters on twitter. In: Proceedings of the International AAAI Conference on Web and Social Media, vol. 5, no. 1, pp. 185–192 (2021)
18. Lundberg, S.M., Lee, S.I.: A unified approach to interpreting model predictions. In: Advances in Neural Information Processing Systems, vol. 30 (2017)
19. Mazza, M., Cresci, S., Avvenuti, M., Quattrociocchi, W., Tesconi, M.: Rtbust: exploiting temporal patterns for botnet detection on twitter. In: Proceedings of the 10th ACM Conference on Web Science, pp. 183–192 (2019)
20. Parr, T., Wilson, J.D., Hamrick, J.: Nonparametric feature impact and importance. arXiv preprint arXiv:2006.04750 1 (2020)
21. Rey, D., Neuhäuser, M.: Wilcoxon-Signed-Rank Test, pp. 1658–1659 (2011)
22. Ribeiro, M.T., Singh, S., Guestrin, C.: "Why should i trust you?" explaining the predictions of any classifier. In: KDD 2016: The 22nd ACM SIGKDD International Conference on Knowledge Discovery and Data Mining, pp. 1135–1144. ACM, New York (2016)
23. Samuels, E., Kelly, M.: How false hope spread about hydroxychloroquine to treat COVID-19 - and the consequences that followed (2020). https://www.washingtonpost.com/politics/2020/04/13/how-false-hope-spread-about-hydroxychloroquine-its-consequences/
24. Shao, C., Ciampaglia, G.L., Flammini, A., Menczer, F.: Hoaxy: a platform for tracking online misinformation. In: WWW 2016: 25th International World Wide Web Conference, pp. 745–750. International Conference Companion on World Wide Web (2016)
25. Strobl, C., Boulesteix, A.L., Zeileis, A., Hothorn, T.: Bias in random forest variable importance measures: illustrations, sources and a solution. BMC Bioinform. **8**, 1–21 (2007)
26. Tao, J., Kang, Y.: Features importance analysis for emotional speech classification. In: Tao, J., Tan, T., Picard, R.W. (eds.) ACII 2005. LNCS, vol. 3784, pp. 449–457. Springer, Heidelberg (2005). https://doi.org/10.1007/11573548_58
27. Varol, O., Ferrara, E., Davis, C., Menczer, F., Flammini, A.: Online human-bot interactions: detection, estimation, and characterization. In: Proceedings of the International AAAI Conference on Web and Social Media, vol. 11. AAAI (2017)
28. Wetschoreck, F., Krabel, T., Krishnamurthy, S.: 8080labs/ppscore: zenodo release (2020). https://doi.org/10.5281/zenodo.4091345
29. Wu, Y., Ngai, E.W., Wu, P., Wu, C.: Fake online reviews: literature review, synthesis, and directions for future research. Decis. Support Syst. 132 (2020)
30. Yang, K.C., Varol, O., Davis, C.A., Ferrara, E., Flammini, A., Menczer, F.: Arming the public with artificial intelligence to counter social bots. Hum. Behav. Emerg. Technol. **1**, 48–61 (2019)
31. Yang, K.C., Varol, O., Hui, P.M., Menczer, F.: Scalable and generalizable social bot detection through data selection. In: Conference on Artificial Intelligence, vol. 34, pp. 1096–1103. AAAI (2020)

32. Zhou, X., Zafarani, R.: A survey of fake news: fundamental theories, detection methods, and opportunities. ACM Comput. Surv. (CSUR) **53**, 1–40 (2020)
33. Zhu, F., Jiang, M., Qiu, Y., Sun, C., Wang, M.: RSLIME: an efficient feature importance analysis approach for industrial recommendation systems. In: International Joint Conference on Neural Networks (IJCNN), pp. 1–6. IEEE (2019)

Data Science

Disparity in the Evolving COVID-19 Collaboration Network

Huimin Xu[1], Redoan Rahman[1], Ajay Jaiswal[1], Julia Fensel[2], Abhinav Peri[2], Kamesh Peri[3], Griffin M. Weber[4], and Ying Ding[1(✉)]

[1] School of Information, University of Texas at Austin, Austin, TX 78701, USA
{huiminxu,redoan.rahman,ajayjaiswal,ying.ding}@utexas.edu
[2] Westlake High School, Austin, TX 78746, USA
Julia.smag1@gmail.com, abhinavperi16@gmail.com
[3] Katana Graph, Austin, TX 78701, USA
kamesh.peri@katanagraph.com
[4] Harvard Medical School, Boston, MA 02115, USA
griffin_weber@hms.harvard.edu

Abstract. COVID-19 pandemic has paused many ongoing research projects and unified researchers' attention to focus on COVID-19 related issues. Our project traces 712,294 scientists' publications related to COVID-19 for two years, from January 2020 to December 2021, in order to detect the dynamic evolution patterns of COVID-19 collaboration network over time. By studying the collaboration network of COVID-19 scientists, we observe how a new scientific community has been built in preparation for a sudden shock. The number of newcomers grows incrementally, and the connectivity of the collaboration network shifts from loose to tight promptly. Even though every scientist has an equal opportunity to start a study, collaboration disparity still exists. Following the scale-free distribution, only a few top authors are highly connected with other authors. These top authors are more likely to attract newcomers and work with each other. As the collaboration network evolves, the increase rate in the probability of attracting newcomers for authors with higher degree increases, whereas the increase rates in the probability of forming new links among authors with higher degree decreases. This highlights the interesting trend that COVID pandemic alters the research collaboration trends that star scientists are starting to collaborate more with newcomers, but less with existing collaborators, which, in certain way, reduces the collaboration disparity.

Keywords: COVID-19 Publications · Collaboration disparity · Collaboration network · Dynamic evolution · Degree centrality

1 Introduction

The science of science is a field to study the structure and evolution of science, which has offered rich quantitative and qualitative methods to uncover hindsight about creativity, collaboration, and impact in scientific endeavors. Despite the prominent contributions of science of science researchers, which are deeply rooted in normal science including

© The Author(s), under exclusive license to Springer Nature Switzerland AG 2023
I. Sserwanga et al. (Eds.): iConference 2023, LNCS 13971, pp. 331–339, 2023.
https://doi.org/10.1007/978-3-031-28035-1_23

scientific collaboration [11], team composition [14], novelty [13], and funding allocation [9], studies about scientific activities in abnormal conditions are largely overlooked. However, patterns or findings from studies on normal science cannot be applied to abnormal conditions. Normal science was coined by Thomas Samuel Kuhn [10] as a phase of science during which the scientific community has confidence in what the world is like. Normal science often suppresses fundamental differences/novelties because it favors fitting phenomena into the widely accepted conceptual theories/boxes [7]. So, when a novel pandemic occurs, we need to understand how scientists collaborate and what the team dynamics are, whether out-of-the-box thinking can be supported by scientific communities. This paper studies the scientific collaboration of COVID-19 authors from the perspective of evolving networks.

The ongoing COVID-19 pandemic certainly not only disturbed the normal routines of scientific activities, but also demanded solutions from science to resolve the spread. Understanding scientific activities in abnormal times are urgent and imperative [8]. Studying the patterns of scholarly communications during pandemic times can help us understand how science can bend the trajectories of pandemic spreading and provide implications for science policy makers to have a better risk management plan for future unexpected disasters.

2 Related Work

Barabasi et al. [4] explored the evolving collaboration networks in mathematics and neuro-science disciplines covering eight years. They found that the average degree (i.e., degree centrality) increases and the node separation (i.e., the average distances of all shortest paths between two given nodes) decreases. In addition to uncovering the power law distribution of networks [3], he also revealed two mechanisms to explain the preferential attachment phenomenon – "the richer get richer". In the research, [4] found that a new author is more likely to work with authors who already have many coauthors. Also, authors who already have many authors are more likely to build more links as the network evolves. Azondekon et al. [2] analyzed the connectedness of researchers in malaria research by building a co-authorship network from papers collected by Web of Science. They found that prolific authors have higher probabilities of collaborating with more authors and the giant component covers 94% of all the vertices to confirm a small-world network. Furthermore, Uddin et al. [12] extended the relationship between network centrality measures with the impact and productivity of authors. They established the regression model and revealed that degree centrality and betweenness centrality of authors are positively correlated with the strength of their scientific collaborators (i.e., number of coauthors of a given author) and impact (i.e., the citation count of a research article authored by a given author). In our project, we want to apply the network science measures into the COVID-19 collaboration network to detect the collaboration disparity during the pandemic.

3 Methodology

Data

We use the LitCOVID dataset[1] as our source of COVID-19 publications. LitCOVID collects COVID-19 publications from PubMed dataset[2] through searching relevant keywords, such as "coronavirus", "ncov", and "2019-nCoV" [5, 6]. The results are updated daily and reviewed by human and machine learning algorithms. By December 23rd in 2021, there are 205,476 COVID-19 papers, including specific PubMed id and title information. By tracing the PubMed id in the PubMed dataset, we can get author lists and publication time of each paper. We deal with the author name disambiguation problem with the assistance of Semantic Scholar dataset[3] [1]. Xu et al. [15] evaluated the effect of author name disambiguation in the Semantic Scholar, which reaches 96.94% in F1 score. LitCOVID and Semantic Scholar both keep the PubMed id, thus we can match author names in LitCOVID with unique author ids in Semantic Scholar through the common PubMed id. Finally, we get 186,046 COVID-19 related papers, with complete publication time, author names, and author ids from 2020 January to 2021 December. Among these papers, there are 712,294 unique authors. A majority of 89% papers (166,126) papers have more than one author and 99% (704,164) authors have collaborators. In order to observe the evolution of the collaboration network, we document eight quarters based on publication time. Table 1 and Fig. 1 describe the cumulative nodes and links added into the network over time. We can see that the node increase rate appears to be stable, whereas the link grows suddenly at the first and second quarter in 2021 and then keeps stable.

Table 1. Cumulative number of nodes and links for the COVID-19 collaboration network up to a given time.

Date	N of nodes	N of links
2020_Q1	13,062	139,562
2020_Q2	128,589	2,223,421
2020_Q3	245,330	11,310,419
2020_Q4	349,479	16,507,786
2021_Q1	469,920	85,371,561
2021_Q2	573,649	146,582,029
2021_Q3	658,173	162,823,954
2021_Q4	712,294	177,493,364

[1] https://www.ncbi.nlm.nih.gov/research/coronavirus/.

[2] https://pubmed.ncbi.nlm.nih.gov/download/.

[3] https://api.semanticscholar.org/corpus/download/.

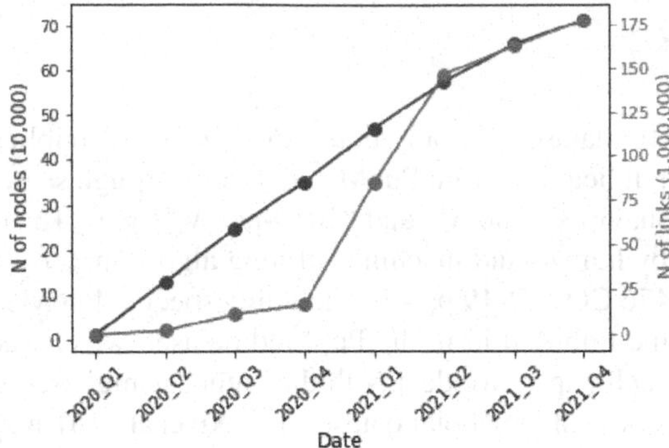

Fig. 1. Cumulative number of nodes (left indicating Authors) and links (right: indicating co-authorship) for the COVID-19 collaboration network up to a given time.

Measures

Authors have formed the collaboration network if any given two authors have co-authored at least one paper, there is an edge to connect these two nodes. Degree centrality for an author i can be defined as: $DegreeCentrality(a) = \frac{k}{n-1}$, where k is the degree of author a (represents the number of authors with whom author a is directly connected in the co-authorship network), n represents the number of authors in the network.

Figure 2 shows how to calculate the probability of attracting external new nodes and forming new internal links. Probability of attracting new authors for an old node with degree k_i: $P(k_i) = \frac{V(k_i)}{N(k_i)}$, where $V(k_i)$ means the number of newcomers that authors with degree k_i attract, $N(k_i)$ means the number of authors with degree k_i. Probability of forming new links among old nodes with degree k_i and k_j: $P(k_i, k_j) = \frac{L(k_i,k_j)}{N(k_i)*N(k_j)}$, $L(k_i, k_j)$ means the number of new links between authors with degree k_i and k_j, $N(k_i)*N(k_j)$ means the number of combination pairs between authors with degree k_i and k_j.

4 Results

We observe the evolution of the collaboration network at eight different stages, from the first quarter of 2020 to the fourth quarter of 2021. Firstly, we found the degree distributions of networks up to the indicated time all follow scale-free power law distribution (Fig. 3). We can see most of the authors have a relatively small number of collaborations, but a few authors have the ability to connect with many partners. This result is consistent in these eight networks. The degree distributions gradually shift upward as more new authors join the community, and meanwhile move rightward as existing authors enhance their collaboration ties.

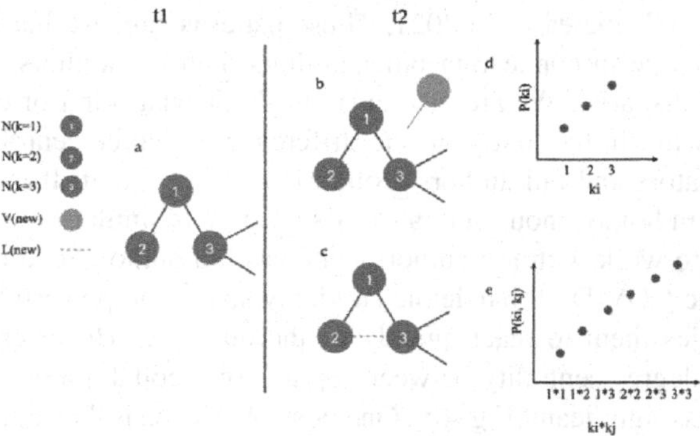

Fig. 2. The illustration of calculating probability of attracting new nodes and forming new links among old nodes. a. At the time t1, there are three kinds of nodes with different degrees (green) in the network. We calculate the number of these nodes, like, N(k = 1) means the number of nodes with degree 1. At the next time t2, new nodes (orange) join in (b) and new links (orange) among old nodes appear (c). V(new) represents the number of new nodes, and L(new) represents the number of new links. d. We calculate the probability of attracting new nodes for an old node with degree k_i. f. We calculate the probability of forming a new link for an old node with degree k_i and an old node with degree k_j.

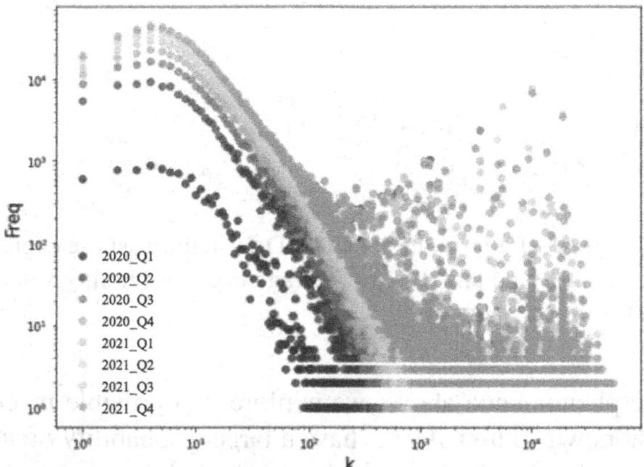

Fig. 3. Degree distribution for COVID-19 authors, showing the cumulative results up to a given time. The plot is drew using a logarithmic scale for both the x-axis and the y-axis. X axis k represents the number of collaborators an author has, whereas y-axis frequency shows the number of authors in the network with degree k.

Given the scale-free distribution, we choose to separately observe the top and tail authors' degree centrality. The tail 20% authors' average degree centrality values have trivial changes over time (Fig. 4a). At the very beginning (2020_Q1), the degree centrality is relatively large for top 10% and top 20% authors as the network has a few nodes. We also need to note that one year later (2021_Q1), there is an apparent increase in degree centrality for top authors. Meanwhile, the gap in degree centrality between top 10%, top 20% and tail 20% increases in 2021. These patterns suggest that top authors play a more important role in connecting other authors than tail authors, which increases the collaboration disparity. We are also curious about what kind of collaborators top authors connect with. In the first year, the difference in degree centrality between top authors' collaborators and tail authors' collaborators is evident. It indicates that they prefer to work with homogenous authors whose degree is similar to them. Specifically, top authors tend to work with top authors, whereas tail authors tend to work with tail authors. When the COVID-19 pandemic suddenly starts, the powerful alliance among top authors enables them to react quickly to the outbreak. However, one year later, the difference in degree centrality between top authors' collaborators and tail authors' collaborators is less significant (Fig. 4b). One possible reason is that although top authors still work with each other, they attract more newcomers as more people pay attention to the COVID-19 pandemic and join the community. Thus, high degree centrality and low degree centrality cancel out each other.

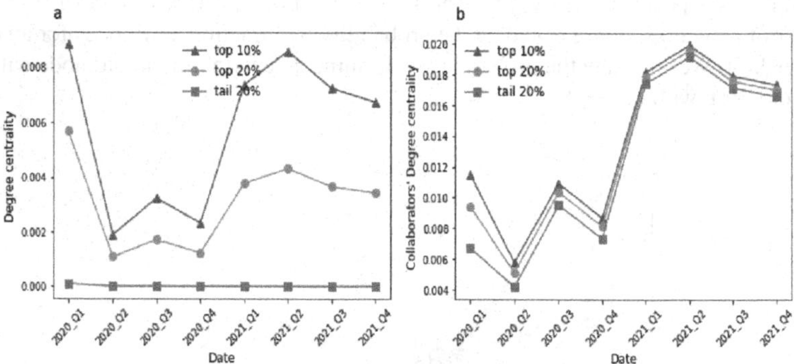

Fig. 4. a) Average degree centrality values of COVID-19 authors whose degree centrality values are in the top 10%, top 20% and tail 20%. b) Average degree centrality values of top 10%, top 20% and tail 20% authors' collaborators.

To explain the phenomenon above, we explore two possible mechanisms. On the one hand, old authors with a high degree have a larger probability of attracting external new authors. On the other hand, old authors with a high degree have a larger probability of forming internal new collaborations. In Fig. 5 and Fig. 6, we calculate the probability of collaborating with external new authors and forming new internal links among old authors. The slope of the dashed line corresponds to the exponent of power law distribution. The slope values are positive, which signifies that authors with larger k are more likely to connect with new authors (Fig. 5). From 2020 to 2021, the increase rates in the probability of attracting newcomers increases for top authors with more collaborators, indicated by the slope changes. In the first quarter of 2021, the second quarter of 2021 and the fourth quarter of 2021, the slopes are above 1. On the whole, the inequality of newcomer distribution is aggravated until 2021. Similarly, the slope values are positive in Fig. 6, which indicates that authors with larger k are more likely to publish COVID-19 papers together. But the difference is the increase rate in the probability of building new connections among old nodes with high degree decreases from 2020 to 2021. In the second quarter of 2020, the third quarter of 2020 and the fourth quarter of 2020, the slopes are above 1.

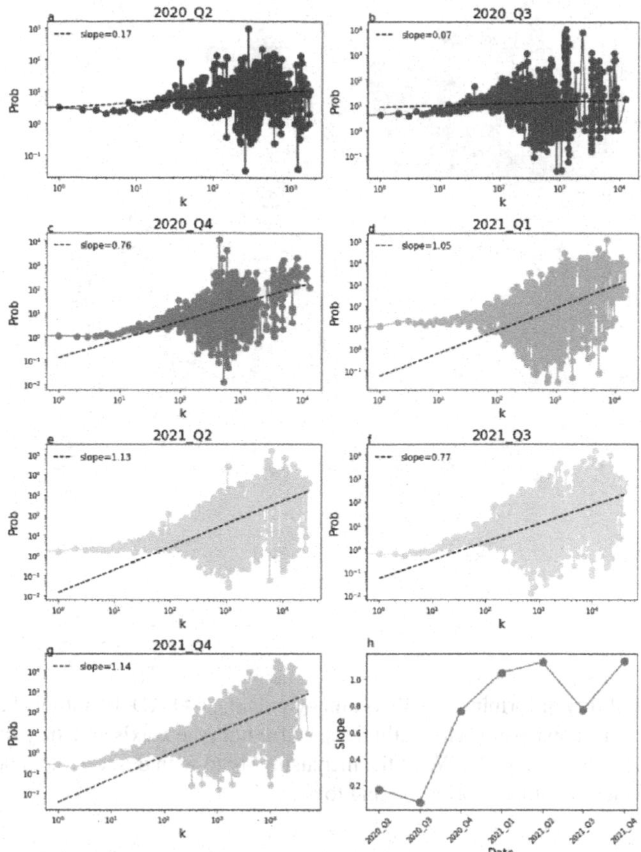

Fig. 5. The probability of attracting newcomers for existing COVID-19 authors before the given time. a-g. The plot is drew using a logarithmic scale for both the x-axis and the y-axis. The x-axis and y-axis are calculated as Fig. 2d. We fit the increasing trend with dashed lines and calculate the slope. h. The changes of slopes corresponding to a-g.

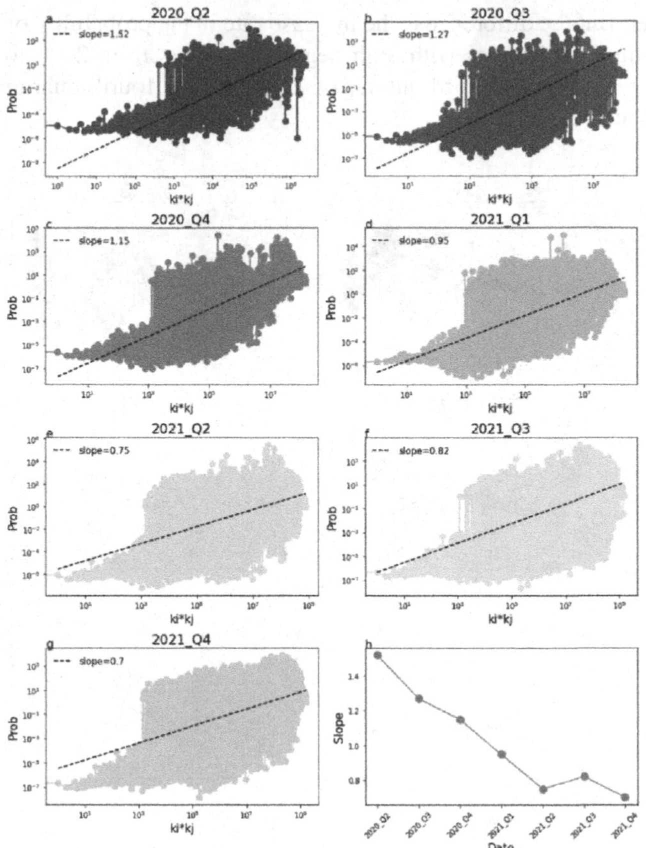

Fig. 6. The probability of forming new links among existing COVID-19 authors before the given time. a-g. The plot is drawn using a logarithmic scale for both the x-axis and the y-axis. The x-axis and y-axis is calculated as Fig. 2e. We fit the increasing trend with dashed lines and calculate the slope. h. The changes of slopes corresponding to a-g.

5 Conclusion

The current COVID-19 pandemic has caused a huge economic loss with the record high unemployment, the collapse of industry giants (e.g., large retails), the bankruptcy of small and medium-sized businesses, and spiral decline in spending, traveling, producing, and servicing. The whole world is on the pause button, and the world economy is on a spiral downturn. Uncertainty lies ahead of us. With our ever-growing highly connected world, simple infectious diseases can rapidly transform into pandemics, the threat and damage of future infectious diseases can be immense. Understanding scientific activities in the current and past pandemics/epidemics can help us identify patterns and pinpoint wrongdoings. This paper conducts preliminary research about the connectivity of scientific activities of COVID-19 authors who are working at the frontlines to fight against COVID-19. In addition to describing the static topology of the COVID-19 collaboration network, we also reveal the dynamic evolution of the network. We found that COVID pandemic alters the research collaboration trends that star scientists are starting to collaborate more with newcomers, but less with their peers, which, in certain way, reduces the collaboration disparity.

References

1. Ammar, W., et al.: Construction of the literature graph in semantic scholar (2018). arXiv preprint arXiv:1805.02262
2. Azondekon, R., Harper, Z.J., Agossa, F.R., Welzig, C.M., McRoy, S.: Scientific authorship and collaboration network analysis on malaria research in Benin: Papers indexed in the Web of Science (1996–2016). Global Health Research and Policy **3**, 11 (2018)
3. Barabási, A.L., Albert, R.: Emergence of scaling in random networks. Science **286**(5439), 509–512 (1999)
4. Barabási, A.L., Jeong, H., Néda, Z., Ravasz, E., Schubert, A., Vicsek, T.: Evolution of the social network of scientific collaborations. Physica A **311**(3–4), 590–614 (2002)
5. Chen, Q., Allot, A., Lu, Z. Keep up with the latest coronavirus research. Nature **579**(7798), 193–194 (2020)
6. Chen, Q., Allot, A., Lu, Z.: LitCovid: an open database of COVID-19 literature. Nucleic Acids Res. **49**(D1), D1534–D1540 (2021)
7. Collins, R.: Why the social sciences won't become high-consensus, rapid-discovery science. Sociol. Forum **9**(2), 155–177 (1994)
8. Fry, C.V., Cai, X., Zhang, Y., Wagner, C.S.: Consolidation in a crisis: Patterns of international collaboration in early COVID-19 research. PLoS ONE **15**(7), e0236307 (2020)
9. Jacob, B., Lefgren, L.: The impact of research grant funding on scientific productivity. J. Public Econ. **95**(9–10), 1168–1177 (2011)
10. Kuhn, T.: The structure of scientific revolutions. University of Chicago Press (1962)
11. Leahey, E.: From sole investigator to team scientist: Trends in the practice and study of research collaboration. Ann. Rev. Sociol. **42**, 81–100 (2016)
12. Uddin, S., Hossain, L., Rasmussen, K.: Network effects on scientific collaborations. PLoS ONE **8**(2), e57546 (2013). https://doi.org/10.1371/journal.pone.0057546
13. Uzzi, B., Mukherjee, S., Stringer, M., Jones, B.: Atypical combinations and scientific impact. Science **342**(6157), 468–472 (2013)
14. Wu, L., Wang, D., Evans, J.A.: Large teams develop and small teams disrupt science and technology. Nature **566**, 378–382 (2019)
15. Xu, J., et al.: Building a PubMed knowledge graph. Scientific Data **7**(1), 205 (2020). https://doi.org/10.1038/s41597-020-0543-2

Text Mining and Visualization of Political Party Programs Using Keyword Extraction Methods: The Case of Portuguese Legislative Elections

Ricardo Campos[1,2(✉)], Adam Jatowt[3], and Alípio Jorge[1,4]

[1] LIAAD – INESCTEC, Porto, Portugal
ricardo.campos@ipt.pt
[2] Polytechnic Institute of Tomar, Ci2 - Smart Cities Research Center, Tomar, Portugal
[3] University of Innsbruck, Innsbruck, Austria
adam.jatowt@uibk.ac.at
[4] FCUP, University of Porto, Porto, Portugal

Abstract. Extracting keywords from textual data is a crucial step for text analysis. One such process may involve a considerable amount of time when done manually. In this paper, we show how keyword extraction techniques can be used to untap texts of political nature. To accomplish this objective, we conduct a case-study on top of 16 Portuguese (PT) political party programs made available in the context of the legislative elections that took place in 30th of January 2022. Our contributions are two-fold. At the level of resources, we make available a curated dataset and a python notebook that systematizes the process of transforming text into quantitative data and into visual aspects. At the methodological level, we propose to extend the keyword extraction algorithm used in this study to extract the most relevant keywords, not only from individual political party programs, but also across the entire collection of documents. A further contribution is the case-study itself, which calls attention to the fact that such solutions may be of interest not only to common people, but also to journalists or politicians alike. Broadly, we demonstrate how the discussion and the analysis that stems from the results obtained may foster the political science research by making available large-scale processing of documents with marginal costs.

Keywords: Text Mining · Text Visualization · Keyword Extraction · Political Texts

1 Introduction

Text Mining refers to the use of natural language processing techniques to automatically mine text from unstructured data making it suitable for text analysis, visualization, or machine learning. It is widely used in social media networks to analyze the sentiment of Twitter posts [19], in clinical records to understand the clinical history of a patient [13] or in general documents to extract narratives from texts [21]. It has also been an important technique in political science [15] and a valuable resource for researchers

© The Author(s), under exclusive license to Springer Nature Switzerland AG 2023
I. Sserwanga et al. (Eds.): iConference 2023, LNCS 13971, pp. 340–349, 2023.
https://doi.org/10.1007/978-3-031-28035-1_24

interested in getting insights from texts of political nature. The adoption of these techniques by the political science community dates back to over twenty years ago [10]. The last decade, however, has seen a dramatic increase in the number of research works using computational methods for political text analysis. Loris et al. [17], for example, proposed a methodology to discover the polarization of social media users during election campaigns. Kokil et al. [16] evaluated the effectiveness of different methods on predicting election results from Twitter posts in three Asian countries. Kall et al. [4] addressed cross-disciplinary innovation in political text analysis for party positioning. Stefano and Sara [24] devised a model to classify agreement and disagreement between points of view in the political domain. Text as visualization approaches [2] also became mainstream in political science allowing researchers to get insights from texts, discover news trends, correlations, and associations which in the past were only possible through manual techniques.

Much of this work on political computational analysis, has only be made possible by the efforts carried out by dedicated projects focused on collecting and making available data to track public policies, such as The Comparative Agendas Project [9] whose purpose is to collect and organize data from archived sources to track policy outcomes across countries. Another important resource in this context is web archives [5] which give historians, political and computer scientists a valuable resource to explore information from the past that is no longer available on the conventional web. Further initiatives involve making political data, freely available for anyone to access, use and share under the paradigm of open data [3]. Another important dataset, widely used by political scientists is the Manifesto Corpus [25], a free, digital, multilingual, and annotated collection of electoral programs from more than 50 different countries in almost 40 languages.

Although extracting policy positions from political texts using words is not a new application [18] at the crosslinks between political science and NLP, few has been done to perform comparative policy analysis [8]. In this paper, we apply an existing keyword extraction method to perform political and comparative text analysis and show how this methodology can be used to uncover texts of political nature. We envision that one such solution may be an important contribution for increasing the transparency in the political sphere and in reducing the gap between citizens and political parties. It may also be of interest to journalists looking for a tool that enables fast access and digestion of large portions of texts. A recent example of the use of this kind of tools within news outlets can be found in "Journal Público"[1], a Portuguese reference newspaper, which, during the course of the Legislative Portuguese 2022 elections conducted a word cloud analysis of the programs of the two biggest political parties. In our paper, we make use of proper keyword extraction algorithms to obtain the most relevant keywords (not necessarily the most frequent) from the programs of the 16 political party candidates to the Portuguese (PT) legislative elections held on January 30th, 2022. The conducted analysis reveals how to transform text into quantitative knowledge, while discarding information that will likely be not helpful for the common reader. A curated dataset and the procedure to pre-process the documents, extract relevant keywords and generate the plots, is made

[1] https://www.publico.pt/2022/01/18/politica/noticia/peso-empresas-justica-programas-ps-psd-1992182.

available in this github[2] repository as a contribution to the research community. Such code can also be easily adapted in the future to further political text scenarios sharply decreasing the costs of applying it to large collections of text. Although automated content analysis will probably never replace careful and close reading of texts [14] it certainly helps reducing the effort and the labor of manually processing these documents one by one. It also opens up the possibility to be applied in a vast array of applications going from text visualization to multilingual text collections and social media texts.

2 Text-as-Data Through Keyword Extraction

Extracting keywords from textual data is a crucial step for text analysis. One such process may involve a considerable amount of time when done manually and does not scale well upon large or huge number of documents. Recent advances in NLP help to overcome this problem by offering users the chance to resort to automatic methods. Multiple algorithms have been proposed over the years from unsupervised methods to supervised ones. A review of key phrase extraction can be found in the work of Eirini and Grigorios [7]. A recent tutorial [20] in this topic has also been conducted in ECIR'22 conference showing the importance of this subject. In this article, we will be applying YAKE! [22], keyword extraction Python package[3] to extract relevant keywords from political texts. We follow the same approach as that followed by the General Index[4], which has used this method to extract over 19 billion keywords from 107 million scientific articles. Alternative approaches such as topic rank [1], key2vec [6], kea [11] or kp-miner [23] could have been used instead or in parallel. Note however, that the aim of this work is not to compare the behavior of the different keyword extraction methodologies, but to highlight how this kind of tools can be used to reduce the gap between citizens and political parties by making the documents transparent via text visualization and by increasing the text processing speed. YAKE's plug-and-play nature, availability through a python package and adaptability to different domains and languages, plus a good compromise between effectiveness and efficiency, make it a good solution for this use-case scenario. Other solutions such as Voyant Tools[5], a web-based text analysis, reading and visualization environment, have been considered, however the fact that their code is not available as a python package impedes large-scale analysis. Scattertext[6], A tool for finding distinguishing terms in corpora and displaying them in an interactive HTML scatter plot, was also considered to a certain extent, however it is not comparable to YAKE! as it only allows for a text scatter comparison between two texts. A recent paper closely aligned with our work is that of Dilay and Dilai [13] who focused on the detection of keywords in political speeches, particularly those of the American Senator John McCain. In this paper, the authors have compared the keywords at the beginning and at the end of his political career and linked them with the values promoted by the politician. In contrast to this work, we focus on political party programs rather than on

[2] https://github.com/rncampos/PT-LegislativeElections2022.

[3] https://github.com/LIAAD/yake.

[4] https://archive.org/details/GeneralIndex.

[5] https://voyant-tools.org.

[6] https://github.com/JasonKessler/scattertext.

political speeches. As a basis to our study, we opt to make use of 16 recent political party programs as opposed to the well-known Manifesto corpus [25], which gathers a set of political curated texts from different countries. With this, we aim to showcase how to get raw texts as an input stream and from there how to perform a comparative visual analysis of the different party programs.

3 Dataset

In this paper, we will be using the electoral programs of the 16 political party candidates to the PT legislative elections held on January 30th, 2022. We refer to 9 political parties with parliamentary representation in the last legislature (2019–2021): Partido Socialista (PS); Partido Social Democrata (PSD); Bloco de Esquerda (BE); Coligação Democrática Unitária PCP-PEV (CDU); Partido do Centro Democrático e Social (CDS-PP); Partido Pessoas-Animais-Natureza (PAN); Chega; Iniciativa Liberal (IL); Livre; and to 7 political parties which did not have a representation in the parliament. We refer to: ADN; Ergue-te; MAS; MPT; Nós Cidadãos; RIR; Volt Portugal. Four other political parties, PTP; PCTP/MRPP; JPP; Aliança, ran in the elections but did not make their programme available online. The parsed dataset and a python notebook is available in Google Colab[7]. The text files went through a data acquisition (from pdf files, using pdfminer package) and a pre-processing stage (with the help of clean-text and self-developed functions) to cope with noisy text (e.g., roman numerals - I.I.- were discarded, among other functions that are described and used in the notebook). Stopwords were not removed as these are handled by YAKE! Linguistic features such as stemming were also not employed as YAKE is language agnostic. Each electoral programme has on average a total of 33,284 tokens. The smallest one (MAS) contains 1,558 tokens. The largest one (IL) has 175,272 tokens.

4 Text Analysis

To start with our analysis, we begin by running YAKE! keyword extraction algorithm on each text considered and we set the system to retrieve the top-200 most relevant keywords from each of the 16 texts as the electoral programs are quite large and embody much information. However, any other number of keywords may be considered by the users depending on their specific scenario. In addition to this, we also set the *max_ngram_size* parameter set to 3, meaning that the returned keywords may have from 1 up to 3 terms. Below, we list one characteristic keyword from each of the political party programs[8] obtained within the list of top-200 keywords. Naturally, the process of selecting keywords is prone to subjectiveness and may differ from person to person. In this case, we wanted to highlight (grounded on our knowledge of the Portuguese political spectrum) a few keywords that we know characterize the thoughts and the ideologic nature of each

[7] https://drive.google.com/file/d/1X3UEGoPl9WZb2I2JXAoDhihE6l79pkFn/view?usp=sharing.

[8] For a matter of comprehensiveness, we have translated the keywords from Portuguese to English, meaning that some of the keywords may end up being formed by more than 3 terms.

of political parties analyzed. PS: "national rail plan"; PSD: "national maritime space"; BE: "essential public services"; CDU: "capital"; CDS-PP: "Jewish-Christian ethics"; PAN: "intersex genital mutilation"; Chega: "social parasitism"; IL: "TAP - flag carrier airline of Portugal"; Livre: "nature conservation"; ADN: "political freedom"; Ergue-te: "Compulsory military service"; MAS: "miserable wages"; MPT: "designed nuclear power plant"; Nós Cidadãos: "we want equal pay"; RIR: "guarantee salary conditions"; Volt: "mental health". An interesting note here, is the use of keywords of a protest nature ("miserable wages" to "political freedom") from those political parties which are not in the parliament. Others, refer to military services or nuclear power plants, two important issues discussed by these days, due to the war in Ukraine, but that were not discussed in January. Another interesting remark comes from "Chega", an extreme right-wing political party that makes a reference to "social parasitism", in CDU – the communist political party" with a reference to "capital" or in CDS-PP, a political party that has a religious matrix and that makes a reference to "Jewish-Christian ethics". Figure 1 shows how to move from text to visualization by making available a word cloud for the 9 political parties with parliamentary representation in the last legislature (2019–2021). The remaining 7-word clouds pertaining to political parties without parliamentary representation can be found in the notebook. The figures follow the shape and the colors of the Portuguese flag. Several keywords stand-out here. From left to right word-clouds: "national strategy"; "public administration"; "public services"; "freedom"; "state"; "public transportation"; "national production"; "national identity"; "ONU ODS"; "agriculture"; "teaching"; "youth"; "health care"; "higher education"; and "European union".

Further to this analysis, we compared the differences between keywords used by left-wing ("BE", "Livre", "PAN", "PCP", "PS") and right-wing ("CDS", "Chega", "IL", "PSD") political parties. To do so, we began by doing an intersection (a more relaxed approach, such as union, can be used instead) of all the relevant keywords retrieved by left-wing parties and did the same for the right-wing ones, before determining a difference between the two sets. As a matter of comparability, we also used scattertext as it fits this problem of comparing two different sides of the story. Figure 2 shows (top-left hand side, red circle) words that tend to appear only at the left-hand side, which are very infrequent at the right. These are the cases of 3 political parties ("pan", "bloco de esquerda" and "pcp") and a few other interesting words, such as "fishing", "deficiency", "planet", "eradicate", "evasion" and "workers". Instead, doing a left difference in YAKE returned keywords such as "public administration" or "housing", "culture", "justice", "development", "resources", "public services" or "national territory" without references to the names of the political parties. Such keywords were deemed as relevant in all of the electoral programs of the left-wing political spectrum, but not, on all the right-wing parties.

Likewise, keywords such "bureaucracy", "subsystems", "liberal" or "chega" (the latter, again, are the names of political parties) were found by scattertext in the right-wing side, while "citizens", "Europe", "quality" or "security" were found by YAKE. What this anecdotal example shows is that both systems are able to capture characteristic keywords (except for the names of the political party programmes). A major difference between them, however, is that, unlike YAKE!, scattertext is limited to perform analysis

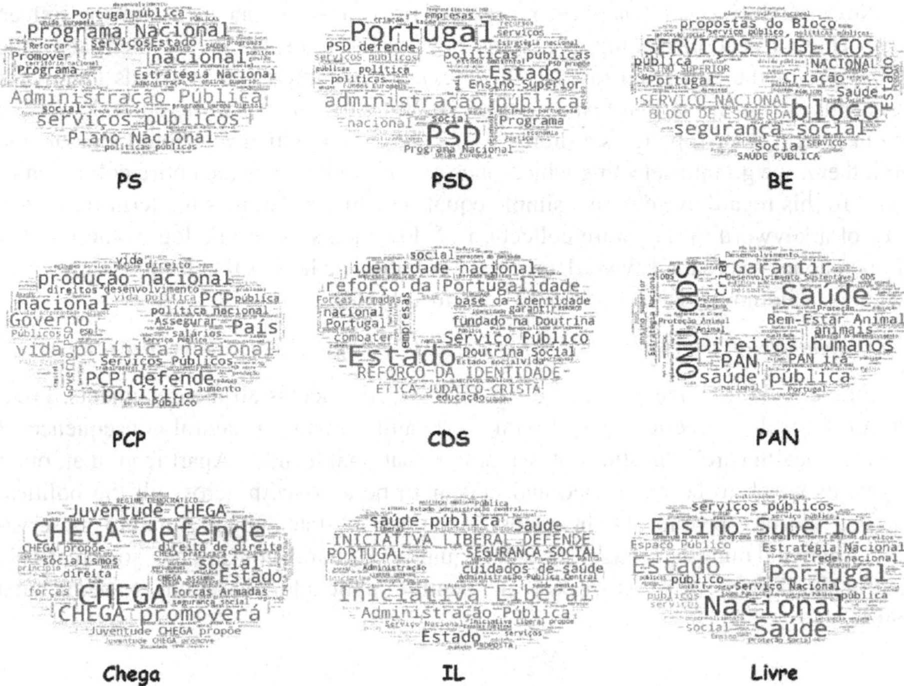

Fig. 1. Word cloud for the nine political parties with parliamentary representation

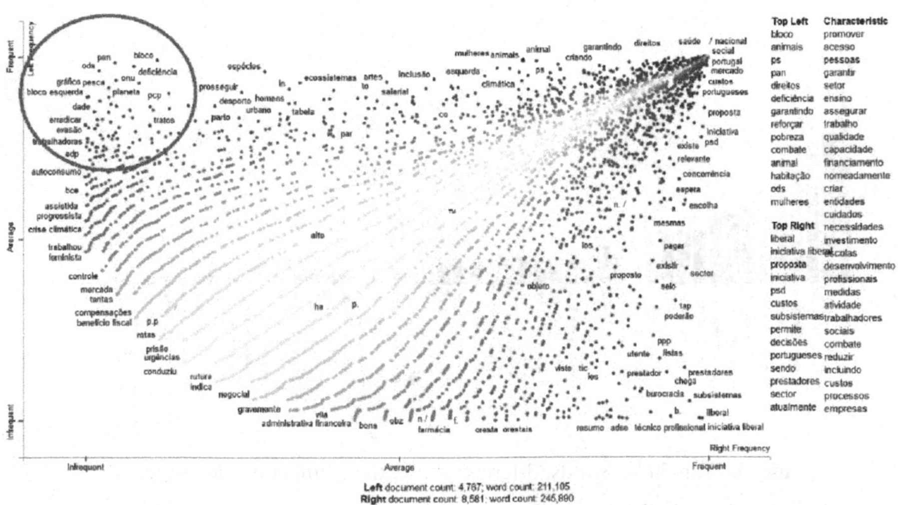

Fig. 2. ScatterText. Comparing left-wing and right-wing parties

in scenarios with two documents, while YAKE! can perform the analysis of individual texts.

Next, we decided to look at the number of times a word appears across the sixteen texts. Thus, instead of picking words that occur a lot in a specific document and little in the rest of the collection (as TF.IDF does), we are interested in words that occur frequently across the various texts considered. We assume, as a starting point, YAKE! to be our filtering step, giving us a short list of keywords to which we should look at, and from there, we go into selecting which ones are relevant across the entire collection of texts. To this regard, we devise a simple equation which multiplies the term frequency (TF) of a keyword in the entire collection of documents D, by the log of the number of documents where the keyword appears. The rationale here is that frequent keywords that appear in more documents should be valued higher.

$$GlobalWeight(keyword) = TF(keyword, D) * \log(|\{d \in D : keyword \in d\}|)$$

Figure 3 shows a bar plot of the top-50 keywords across all the documents. From the top-4 results, three are related with the health domain (a natural consequence of Covid): "health care", "health professionals", "national health". Apart from that, other keywords worth to be mentioned and appear to be a concern across all the political parties: "disabled people", "fight against corruption", "state budget", "nature conservation", "national minimum wage", "gender equality", "quality education", "job creation", "national rail plan", "Lisbon Airport" or "central public administration", to name but a few.

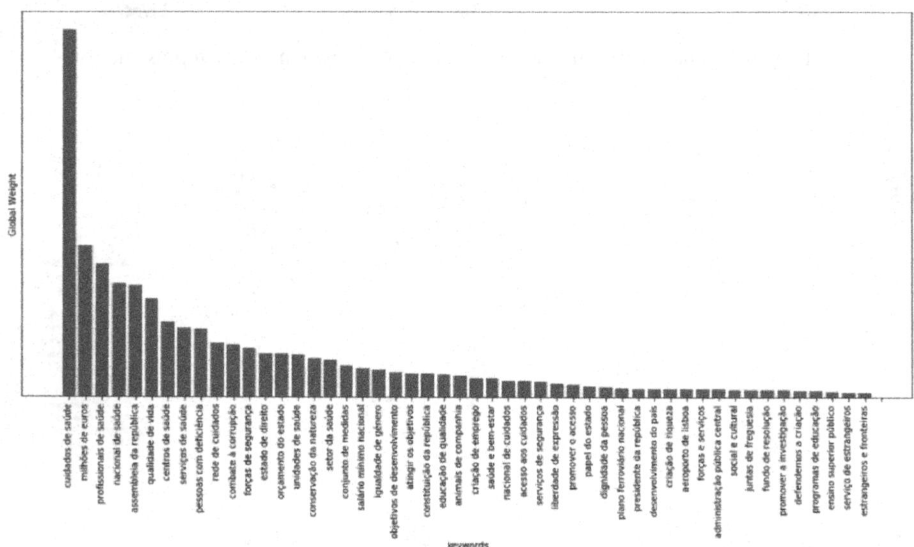

Fig. 3. Top-50 keywords (3-terms) across the entire collection of texts

5 Conclusion

In this paper, we describe a simple but effective approach to demonstrate how keyword extraction systems can be of help for those interested and in need of digesting large portions of text, such as political programs. This can be of interest for different profile of users, including citizens, journalists, or politicians alike. One such solution should be faced not as a replacement of the human understanding and comprehension, but rather as a complement of knowledge. The contribution of this paper is twofold. First, we release a curated dataset from 16 Portuguese political party programs along with a python notebook which will guide users to the practical issues related to extracting keywords from political texts and transforming text into visual aspects. Second, we show how such a tool can be used to unlock political texts and become an important platform for political science research. Parallel to this, we came up with a global weight measure to value words that occur frequently across the various texts considered to understand common topics discussed. In the future, we plan to make a comparative analysis of the political party programs overtime to see how language evolves. In addition, we aim to develop an online demo which will allow users to generate this kind of analysis and plots without the need to resort to a python notebook.

Acknowledgments. Ricardo Campos and Alípio Jorge were financed by the ERDF - European Regional Development Fund through the North Portugal Regional Operational Programme (NORTE 2020), under the PORTUGAL 2020 and by National Funds through the Portuguese funding agency, FCT - Fundação para a Ciência e a Tecnologia within project PTDC/CCI-COM/31857/2017 (NORTE-01–0145-FEDER-03185). This funding fits under the research line of the Text2Story project.

References

1. Bougouin, A., Boudin, F., Daille, B.: TopicRank: Graph-Based Topic Ranking for Keyphrase Extraction. In: Proceedings of the Sixth International Joint Conference on Natural Language Processing (IJCNLP'13), pp. 443–551 (2013). https://aclanthology.org/I13-1062
2. Britzolakis, A., Kondylakis, H., Papadakis, N.: AthPPA: A Data Visualization Tool for Identifying Political Popularity over Twitter. Information **12**, 8 (July 2021). https://doi.org/10.3390/info12080312
3. van Aggelen, A., Hollink, L., Kemman, M., Kleppe, M., Beunders, H.: The debates of the European Parliament as Linked Open Data. Semantic Web – Interoperability, Usability, Applicability **8**(2), 271–281 (December 2016). https://doi.org/10.3233/SW-160227
4. Kaal, A.R., Maks, I., van Elfrinkhof, A.M.E.: From Text to Political Positions: Text analysis across disciplines. John Benjamins, Amsterdam (2014)
5. Gomes, D., Cruz, D., Miranda, J., Costa, M., Fontes, S.: Search the Past with the Portuguese Web Archive. In: Proceedings of the 22nd International Conference on World Wide Web (WWW'13), pp. 321–324. ACM, Rio de Janeiro, Brazil (2013). https://doi.org/10.1145/2487788.2487934
6. Mahata, D., Kuriakose, J., Shah, R.R., Zimmermann, R.: Key2Vec: Automatic Ranked Keyphrase Extraction from Scientific Articles using Phrase Embeddings. In: Proceedings of the 2018 Conference of the North American Chapter of the Association for Computational Linguistics: Human Language Technologies, (NAACL-HLT'18), pp. 634–639. ACL (2018). https://aclanthology.org/N18-2100
7. Papagiannopoulou, E., Tsoumakas, G.: A Review of Keyphrase Extraction. Wiley Interdisciplinary Reviews: Data Mining and Knowledge Discovery **20**(2), e1339 (2020). https://doi.org/10.1002/widm.1339

8. Gilardi, F., Wüest, B.: Using Text-as-Data Methods in Comparative Policy Analysis. In: Guy Peters, B., Fontaine, G. (eds.) Handbook of Research Methods and Applications in Comparative Policy Analysis, pp. 203–217. Edward Elgar Publishing, Cheltenham (April 2020). https://doi.org/10.4337/9781788111195.00019
9. Baumgartner, F.R., Breunig, C., Grossman, E.: Comparative Policy Agendas: Theory, Tools. Data. Oxford University Press, USA (2019)
10. Glavas, G., Nanni, F., Ponzetto, S.: Computational Analysis of Political Texts: Bridging Research Efforts Across Communities. In: Proceedings of the 57th Annual Meeting of the Association for Computational Linguistics: Tutorial Abstracts, pp. 18–23. ACL, Florence, Italy (2019). https://doi.org/10.18653/v1/P19-4004
11. Witten, I.H., Paynter, G.W., Frank, E., Gutwin, C., Nevill-Manning, C.G.: KEA: practical automatic keyphrase extraction. In: Proceedings of the fourth ACM conference on Digital Libraries, pp. 254–255 (August 1999). https://doi.org/10.1145/313238.313437
12. Spasic, I., Nenadic, G. Clinical Text Data in Machine Learning: Systematic Review. JMIR Med Inform **8**(3), e17984 (March 2020). https://doi.org/10.2196/17984
13. Dilay, I., Dilai, M.: Automatic Extraction of Keywords in Political Speeches. In: Proceedings of the IEEE 15th International Conference on Computer Sciences and Information Technologies (CSIT'20), pp. 291–294 (2020). https://doi.org/10.1109/CSIT49958.2020.9322011
14. Grimmer, J., Stewart, B.M:. Text as Data: The Promise and Pitfalls of Automatic Content Analysis Methods for Political Texts. Political Analysis **21**(3), 267–297 (2013). Cambridge University Press. https://doi.org/10.1093/pan/mps028
15. Wilkerson, J., Casas, A.: Large-Scale Computerized Text Analysis in Political Science: Opportunities and Challenges. Annual Review of Political Science **20**(1), 529–544 (May 2017). https://doi.org/10.1146/annurev-polisci-052615-025542
16. Jaidka, K., Ahmed, S., Skoric, M., Hilbert, M.: Predicting elections from social media: a three-country, three-method comparative study. Asian Journal of Communication **29**(3), 252–273 (March 2018). https://doi.org/10.1080/01292986.2018.1453849
17. Belcastro, L., Cantini, R., Marozzo, F., Talia, D., Trunfio, P.: Learning Political Polarization on Social Media Using Neural Networks. IEEE Access **8**, 47177–47187 (March 2020). https://doi.org/10.1109/ACCESS.2020.2978950
18. Laver, M., Benoit, K., Garry, J.: Extracting Policy Positions from Political Texts Using Words as Data. American Political Science Review **97**(2), 311–331 (August 2003). https://doi.org/10.1017/S0003055403000698
19. Öztürk, N., Ayvaz, S.: Sentiment analysis on Twitter: A text mining approach to the Syrian refugee crisis. Telematics and Informatics **35**(1), 136–147 (April 2018). https://doi.org/10.1016/j.tele.2017.10.006
20. Meng, R., Mahata, D., Boudin, F.: From Fundamentals to Recent Advances: A Tutorial on Keyphrasification. 2022. In: Hagen, M., et al. (eds.) Advances in Information Retrieval. ECIR'22, Stavanger, Norway. April 10 - 14). Lecture Notes in Computer Science, vol 13186, pp. 582–588. Springer (2022)
21. Campos, R., Jorge, A., Jatowt, A., Bhatia, S., Litvak, M.: The 5th International Workshop on Narrative Extraction from Texts: Text2Story 2022. In: Hagen, M., et al. (eds.) ECIR 2022. LNCS, vol. 13186, pp. 552–556. Springer, Cham (2022). https://doi.org/10.1007/978-3-030-99739-7_68
22. Campos, R., Mangaravite, V., Pasquali, A., Jorge, A., Nunes, C., Jatowt, A.: YAKE! Keyword extraction from single documents using multiple local features. Information Sciences **509**, 257–289 (January 2020). https://doi.org/10.1016/j.ins.2019.09.013
23. El-Beltagy, S.R., Rafea, A.: KP-Miner: A keyphrase extraction system for English and Arabic documents. Information Systems **34**(1), 132–144 (March 2009). https://doi.org/10.1016/j.is.2008.05.002

24. Menini, S., Tonelli, S.: Agreement and Disagreement: Comparison of Points of View in the Political Domain. In: Proceedings of the the 26th International Conference on Computational Linguistics: Technical Papers (Coling'16). Osaka, Japan, pp. 2461–270 (2016). https://aclanthology.org/C16-1232
25. Burst, T., et al.: Manifesto Corpus. Version: 2021-1. WZB Berlin Social Science Center, Berlin (2021). Retrieved 21 March 2022 from https://manifesto-project.wzb.eu/information/documents/corpus

Exploring the Impact of the Quality of Social Media Early Adopters on Vaccine Adoption

Ran Sun[1], Lu An[1,2(✉)], and Gang Li[1,2]

[1] School of Information Management, Wuhan University, Wuhan 430072, China
anlu97@163.com

[2] Center for Studies of Information Resources, Wuhan University, Wuhan 430072, China

Abstract. As social media such as Twitter has become an important medium for disseminating information, it is essential to understand how the information diffusion on social media influences public adoption of vaccines. Based on the innovation diffusion theory, we construct a user and information quality indicator system for early adopters of COVID-19 vaccination by identifying their creation of user-generated content on social media. Machine learning approaches and text analysis methods are used to perform topic clustering and sentiment analysis on vaccination-related tweets on Twitter. Based on each country's vaccination data in January 2021, the study examines the relationship between the quality of social media early adopters, and the quality of the information they publish with vaccine adoption by using the OSL regression model. The empirical results show that the total number of tests, the number of new COVID-19 cases, and the human development index have a significantly positive influence on vaccine adoption. Neutral emotions and offensive language of early adopters on social media have a significantly negative relationship with vaccine adoption. These interesting findings can help governments and public health officials understand early adopters' perceptions of vaccines and play an important role in targeted policy interventions.

Keywords: Vaccine Adoption · Information Quality · Early Adopters

1 Introduction

On January 11, 2021, the World Health Organization announced that more than 40 countries have started vaccination against COVID-19[1]. Some research has been carried out on identifying factors that influence vaccine adoption, such as vaccine confidence, collective responsibility, anxiety, religious leadership, government intervention, and fear of side effects [13, 26]. Most scholars have used questionnaires, user interviews, and other methods to analyze public attitudes and willingness to get vaccinated [11]. However, there are still limitations related to the small sample size and the granularity of limited time and space [12]. Social media can provide the public with the functions of generating, sharing, commenting, and accepting multimedia social content among multiple

[1] http://news.cnr.cn/native/gd/20210112/t20210112_525389026.shtml.

© The Author(s), under exclusive license to Springer Nature Switzerland AG 2023
I. Sserwanga et al. (Eds.): iConference 2023, LNCS 13971, pp. 350–358, 2023.
https://doi.org/10.1007/978-3-031-28035-1_25

users [22]. It shortens the social distance between users and has a major impact on the way users discuss and communicate various products and services. Extensive research has shown that more than half of the world's population are active social media users [7]. MOORE [21] holds the view that successful market adaptation of an innovative product requires the support of enough early adopters in the early stages of dissemination. The same applies to innovative vaccine products that use social norms to overcome vaccination hesitancy. It is crucial to attracting early adopters of Covid-19 vaccines to demonstrate their vaccination intentions [4, 27]. Previous studies have widely explored the information quality of online users, while there are few explorations on whether users' posts on social media affect vaccine adoption during COVID-19. Thus, we intend to solve the question that how the quality of early adopters on social media and the quality of information they post affect vaccine adoption from a novel perspective.

Based on the innovation diffusion theory, the term 'early adopter' on social media is used here to refer to users who have posted on Twitter that they or their loved ones (parents, grandparents, etc.) have made an appointment or have been vaccinated. We group these users by their vaccination date and location. We analyze the views and influence of early adopters on social media when COVID-19 vaccines enter the international market. We also adopt an Ordinary Least Squares (OLS) regression to identify the relationship between the quality of early adopters on social media, and the quality of the information they post with vaccine adoption. The specific objective of this study is to study the behavior of vaccine adoption and provide decision support for government departments to close the gap and promote the new vaccine.

2 Related Research

Recent studies have attempted to discuss the dissemination and diffusion of innovative products and innovative knowledge information from multiple dimensions through qualitative analysis and theoretical modeling. According to Rogers's innovation diffusion theory in communication studies [24], adopters of new technologies are classified as innovators (2.5%), early adopters (13.5%), early majority (34%), late majority (34%), and laggards (16%). Early adopters of social media tend to exert influence on specific topics related while their influence is not significantly different from other users [19]. While early adopters are usually willing to recommend innovations to late adopters, early adopters with a high need for uniqueness can also spread dissuasive word of mouth on social media [20].

Previous studies use qualitative interviews or online questionnaires to analyze the factors of early adopters [15, 17, 31]. Sociodemographic characteristics, personality characteristics, behavioral characteristics, and resource characteristics are commonly used to identify early adopters. Early adopters are characterized by youth, high activity, high socioeconomic status, high education level, and high personal income. While there are also studies showing older adults are more likely to adopt new ideas [23]. Chen and Lu [3] exploited the temporal and topological features of early adopters to effectively predict the popularity of messages on social media. In addition, social relationships and topic diversity of early adopters can predict topical popularity [25, 28]. Most studies have used the community characteristics of early adopters as an indicator to evaluate the intensity of information diffusion [16, 18]. Extroversion, openness, and conscientiousness have significant positive effects on information sharing among early adopters, while negative effects on rumor spreading [19]. Harris et al. [11] compared local health department social media accounts across adoption categories. They found that the frequency of tweets was independent of the adopter category, while varied across geographic regions.

Age, gender, education level, concerns about vaccine safety and efficacy, and psychosocial factors significantly predict vaccine acceptance [9, 14]. Lazarus et al. [14] adopt logistic regression to assess the associations of age, gender, and level of education with vaccine acceptance. They found higher education levels were associated with lower vaccination acceptance in Canada, Spain, and the UK. Chia et al. [5] examined how perceptions and acceptance of the COVID-19 vaccine among low-income elderly people were influenced by social media misinformation. In addition to the characteristics of population statistics, messages released by social media users can also influence public opinion. In the process of emotional diffusion, tweets published by the Centers for Disease Control and Prevention and the Food and Drug Administration of the United States during COVID-19 have a wide impact on public emotions [29]. Users with different occupations pay different attention to different topics [30]. Few researchers examine how the diffusion of vaccine information on social media impact vaccine decision-making. In this paper, we focus on the characteristics of early adopters on social media and explored the impact of the quality of early adopters and the quality of their user-generated content on vaccine adoption.

3 Research Methods

3.1 Data Sources and Sample Selection

As shown in Fig. 1, the curve of cumulative vaccination[2] is an S-shaped diffusion curve that conforms to the law of Roger's innovation diffusion curve. In the early stage, the spread of vaccine adoption is very slow. After a period of time, the accumulation of users of a certain scale accelerates the spread of the vaccine. We chose to collect social media data during January 2020, which is consistent with the proportion of early adopters of vaccines (15%).

The sample dataset consists of two parts: (1) 852, 805 vaccine-related COVID-19 tweets including replies, quotes, and retweets are collected from Twitter from January 4 to January 31, 2021. We identify the early adopters of vaccines by analyzing the text of tweets such as "Got my second dose of the vaccine," and "My dad got his COVID vaccine!" We finally select 17,189 early adopters and their behavioral data including 107, 227 tweets. Useful metadata such as user description, user geographic location, user creation date, text, links, etc. is also extracted for the following investigation. (2) The total number of vaccinations per country per day between January 5 and February 1, 2021[3].

[2] https://ourworldindata.org/covid-vaccinations?country=OWID_WRL.

[3] https://github.com/owid/covid-19-data.

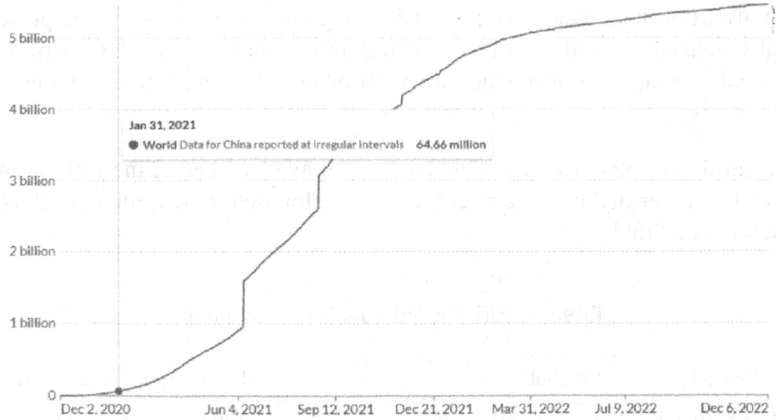

Fig. 1. Number of people vaccinated (cumulative) around the world between December 2, 2020, and December 6, 2022.

3.2 Variable Definition and Measurement

This article measures vaccine adoption using daily updated vaccination data for each country worldwide. The explanatory variables include the quality of the early adopters, and the quality of information published by the early adopters as follows. The early adopter on social media in this paper refers to users who have posted on Twitter between January 4 and January 31, 2021, that they or their loved ones (parents, grandparents, etc.) have made an appointment or have been vaccinated.

The Quality of Early Adopters. The quality of early adopters is categorized into authority, activity, and topic richness. a. User authority includes the level of personal information disclosure (geographical location, personal description, link in personal description or not), authentication, number of followers, number of friends, number of tweets, and user registration age. b. User activity is the number of vaccine-related tweets posted by early adopters during the data collection period (January 4 to January 31, 2021). c. The topic richness of early adopters is the number of different topic categories to which early adopters' tweets belonged during the data collection period. Topics of COVID-19 vaccine-related tweets are generated by the BERTopic topic modeling algorithm [10]. The coherence score (C_V coherence) in the Gensim package is calculated to measure the performance of the topic model. The higher the coherence score, the better the topic model [6].

The Quality of Information Published by Early Adopters. The quality of information published by early adopters is categorized into readability, objectivity, media richness, and reliability [8]. a. There is a correlation between lexical, and syntactic features with text quality [1]. We measure the complexity of the tweets by the comprehensive evaluation of the Automated Readability Index (ARI), Flesch-Kincaid, Coleman-Liau Index (CLI), and other readability indexes. b. We adopt the TweetEval evaluation framework [2] based on the pre-trained model BERTweet to perform sentiment analysis on the text of tweets. The framework includes sentiment classification (positive, negative, and neutral), irony, hate speech, and offensive language recognition. c. The presence of hyperlinks, images, and videos is incorporated into media richness. d. Reliability is the comprehensive evaluation of interactions with other users (@user) and the number of retweets and likes.

As control variables, we consider the total number of cases, the total number of tests, population density, positive rate, human development index, life expectancy, and reproduction rate (Table 1).

Table 1. Variable definition and description

Variable Category	Symbol	Description / Measurement
Dependent Variable	Vaccine Adoption	Total number of COVID-19 vaccination per country per day
Explanatory Variables	Quality of Early Adopters	Authority, Activity, Topic Richness
	Quality of Information Published by Early Adopters	Readability, Objectivity, Media Richness, Reliability
Control Variable	Total Cases	Total cases for COVID-19 per country per day
	Total Tests	Total tests for COVID-19 per country per day
	Positive Rate	The share of COVID-19 tests that are positive per country per day
	Population Density	Number of people divided by land area, measured in square kilometers
	Human Development Index (HDI)	A composite index measuring average achievement in three basic dimensions of human development (life, knowledge, living)
	Life Expectancy	Life expectancy at birth in 2019
	Reproduction rate	The effective reproduction rate of COVID-19

4 Empirical Analysis and Results

The descriptive statistics of this study are shown in Table 2. For data processing, we use the mean normalization method and dimensionless processing. The entropy weight method (EWM) is applied to determine the weight of each indicator. We first remove some highly correlated variables such as activity. The variance inflation factors (VIF) are commonly calculated as part of regression analysis to measure how much the variance is inflated. The results showed that the VIF values for each variable are all less than 5, indicating that all variables are uncorrelated with other variables.

Table 2. Descriptive statistics of explanatory variables

Variables	N	MIN	MAX	AVG	Std	Median
Authority	2206	0.021	43.537	0.585	1.38	0.585
Activity	2206	1	364.5	6.648	15.189	6.648
Topic Richness	2206	1	10	2.115	1.095	2.115
Reliability	2206	0.01	29.287	0.725	1.509	0.268
Media Richness	2206	0	2	0.304	0.353	0.229
Readability	2206	0.076	2.297	0.965	0.271	0.976
offensive	2206	0.035	0.909	0.176	0.13	0.138
hate	2206	0.031	0.885	0.052	0.038	0.044
irony	2206	0.045	0.942	0.417	0.189	0.388
Negative	2206	0.004	0.952	0.297	0.232	0.281
Neutral	2206	0.017	0.946	0.472	0.212	0.474
Positive	2206	0.009	0.976	0.231	0.217	0.18

This paper uses the OLS regression model to test whether the quality of early adopters and the quality of variance-related information they publish on Twitter can affect vaccination adaptation. Model 1 contains 7 control variables, and Model 2 includes 10 more independent variables on the basis of Model 1. The results of both the White and BP heteroskedasticity tests reject the null hypothesis ($p < 0.05$), indicating the occurrence of heteroscedasticity between random interference items. Robust standard errors are computed to eliminate the heteroscedasticity between the data.

As shown in Table 3, the results of regression Model 1 show the effect of control variables on explanatory variables. The results show that the total number of tests, the total number of new cases, and the human development index are significantly positively related to vaccine adoption. We observe a significant negative relationship between life expectancy, reproduction rate, and the rate of people testing positive for COVID-19 with vaccine adoption. While population density shows no significant effect on vaccine adoption.

Model 2 includes explanatory variables in addition to model 1, and the significance of the model is $p < 0.001$. Results reveal that neutral emotion and offensive language have a significant negative relationship with vaccine adoption. This indicates that users on social media can influence vaccination adoption through specific emotions conveyed by user-generated content. While readability, irony, hate speech, positive emotion, reliability, topic richness, media richness, and authority show no significant effect on vaccine adoption. This suggests that vaccine adoption does not differ significantly based on the authority and activity levels of early adopters on social media.

Table 3. Results of the OLS regression analysis

Symbol	Model 1	Model 2
Authority		0.007 (1.889)
Neutral emotion		−0.349* (−2.544)
Positive emotion		−0.248 (−1.919)
Offensive language		−0.541* (−2.340)
Media Richness		0.006 (0.086)
Trustworthiness		−0.003 (−0.283)
Topic Richness		−0.022 (−1.052)
Readability		0.011 (0.123)
Irony		0.004 (0.028)
Hate speech		0.061 (0.122)
Life expectancy	−1.637** (−4.756)	−1.656** (−4.614)
Log10 (total tests)	0.538** (11.462)	0.528** (11.352)
Log10 (population density)	0.022 (0.651)	0.018 (0.535)
Log10 (total cases)	0.546** (12.819)	0.551** (12.782)
Reproduction rate	−0.332* (−2.185)	−0.290 (−1.908)
Positive rate	−1.111** (−3.575)	−1.181** (−3.648)
Human development index	4.179** (6.398)	4.191** (6.141)
Constant	−3.393** (−6.816)	−3.039** (−5.860)
F value	F (7, 821) = 377.082, $p = 0.000$	F (17, 811) = 178.398, $p = 0.000$

* $p < 0.05$ ** $p < 0.01$

5 Conclusion

This paper attempts to show whether the diffusion of vaccine information on social media impact vaccine adoption. We find that neutral emotion and offensive language have a significant negative relationship with vaccine adoption. While the quality of early adopters shows no significant effect on vaccine adoption. A possible explanation for this might be that there is a lag in the impact of social media users, and users in certain countries have limited access to Twitter. In addition, the effects of high-influence users and low-influence users in the same country are offset, making the average effect insignificant. In the future, we will consider the influence of early adopters' opinions on other users on social media as a mediating variable to analyze the influence factors of vaccine adoption. Findings can help public health authorities target vaccine promotion messages more effectively.

Acknowledgements. This research was funded by the National Natural Science Foundation of China (grant nos 71921002, 72174153, 71790612, and 71974202).

References

1. Al Qundus, J., Paschke, A., Gupta, S., Alzouby, A.M., Yousef, M.: Exploring the impact of short-text complexity and structure on its quality in social media. J. Enterp. Inf. Manag. **33**(6), 1443–1466 (2020)
2. Barbieri, F., Camacho-Collados, J., Neves, L., Espinosa-Anke, L.: Tweeteval: Unified benchmark and comparative evaluation for tweet classification (2020). arXiv preprint arXiv:2010.12421
3. Chen, X., Lu, Z.M.: A real-time method to predict social media popularity. Int. J. Mod. Phys. C **28**(12), 1750144 (2017)
4. Chevallier, C., Hacquin, A.S., Mercier, H.: COVID-19 vaccine hesitancy: Shortening the last mile. Trends Cogn. Sci. **25**(5), 331–333 (2021)
5. Chia, S.C., Lu, F., Sun, Y.: Tracking the influence of misinformation on elderly people's perceptions and intention to accept COVID-19 vaccines. Health Communication, 1–11 (2021)
6. Chong, M., Chen, H.: Racist Framing through Stigmatized Naming: A Topical and Geo-locational Analysis of# Chinavirus and# Chinesevirus on Twitter. Proceedings of the association for information science and technology **58**(1), 70–79 (2021)
7. Cillóniz, C., Greenslade, L., Dominedò, C., Garcia-Vidal, C.: Promoting the use of social networks in pneumonia. Pneumonia **12**(1), 1–7 (2020)
8. Clerwall, C.: Enter the robot journalist: Users' perceptions of automated content. Journal. Pract. **8**(5), 519–531 (2014)
9. Fadhel, F.H.: Vaccine hesitancy and acceptance: An examination of predictive factors in COVID-19 vaccination in Saudi Arabia. Health Promotion International (2021)
10. Grootendorst, M.: BERTopic: Neural topic modeling with a class-based TF-IDF procedure (2022). arXiv preprint arXiv:2203.05794
11. Harris, J.K., Mueller, N.L., Snider, D.: Social media adoption in local health departments nationwide. Am. J. Public Health **103**(9), 1700–1707 (2013)
12. Hussain, A., et al.: Artificial intelligence–enabled analysis of public attitudes on facebook and twitter toward covid-19 vaccines in the United Kingdom and the United States: Observational study. Journal of medical Internet research **23**(4), e26627 (2021)
13. Kwok, K.O., et al.: Psychobehavioral responses and likelihood of receiving COVID-19 vaccines during the pandemic, Hong Kong. Emerging infectious diseases **27**(7), 1802 (2021)
14. Lazarus, J.V., et al.: Hesitant or not? The association of age, gender, and education with potential acceptance of a COVID-19 vaccine: a country-level analysis. Journal of Health Communication **25**(10), 799–807 (2020)
15. Lee, S.Y.: Examining the factors that influence early adopters' smartphone adoption: The case of college students. Telematics Inform. **31**(2), 308–318 (2014)
16. Li, C.T., Lin, Y.J., Yeh, M.Y.: Forecasting participants of information diffusion on social networks with its applications. Inf. Sci. **422**, 432–446 (2018)
17. Li, S.C.S., Huang, W.C.: Lifestyles, innovation attributes, and teachers' adoption of game-based learning: Comparing non-adopters with early adopters, adopters, and likely adopters in Taiwan. Comput. Educ. **96**, 29–41 (2016)

18. Lu, X., Szymanski, B.K.: Scalable prediction of global online media news virality. IEEE Trans. Computat. Soci. Sys. **5**(3), 858–870 (2018)
19. Lynn, T., Muzellec, L., Caemmerer, B., Turley, D.: Social network sites: early adopters' personality and influence. J. Prod. Brand Manage. **26**(1), 42–51 (2017)
20. Moldovan, S., Steinhart, Y., Ofen, S.: Share and scare: Solving the communication dilemma of early adopters with a high need for uniqueness. J. Consum. Psychol. **25**(1), 1–14 (2015)
21. Moore, G.A., McKenna, R.: Crossing the chasm (1999)
22. Moorhead, S.A., Hazlett, D.E., Harrison, L., Carroll, J.K., Irwin, A., Hoving, C.: A new dimension of health care: systematic review of the uses, benefits, and limitations of social media for health communication. J. medi. Inter. Res. **15**(4), e1933 (2013)
23. Planing, P.: Innovation acceptance: the case of advanced driver-assistance systems. Springer Science & Business Media (2014)
24. Rogers, E.M.: Diffusion of innovations, 5th edn. Free Press, New York (2003)
25. Romero, D., Tan, C., Ugander, J.: On the interplay between social and topical structure. Proceedings of the international AAAI conference on web and social media **7**(1), 516–525 (2013)
26. Tolia, V., Renin Singh, R., Deshpande, S., Dave, A., Rathod, R.M.: Understanding factors to COVID-19 vaccine adoption in Gujarat, India. Int. J. Environm. Res. Public Health **19**(5), 2707 (2022)
27. Ueda, Y., Katayama, K., Yagi, A., Kimura, T.: The chasm we must cross in Japan for re-promotion of the HPV vaccine. Cancer Prev. Res. **14**(7), 683–686 (2021)
28. Weng, L., Menczer, F.: Topicality and impact in social media: diverse messages, focused messengers. PLoS ONE **10**(2), e0118410 (2015)
29. Xi, H., Zhang, C., Zhao, Y., He, S.: Public Emotional Diffusion over COVID-19 Related Tweets Posted by Major Public Health Agencies in the United States. Data Intelligence **4**(1), 66–87 (2022)
30. Zhao, Y., Xi, H., Zhang, C.: Exploring occupation differences in reactions to COVID-19 pandemic on twitter. Data and Information Management **5**(1), 110–118 (2021)
31. Zijlstra, T., Durand, A., Hoogendoorn-Lanser, S., Harms, L.: Early adopters of Mobility-as-a-Service in the Netherlands. Transp. Policy **97**, 197–209 (2020)

Characterizing Data Practices in Research Papers Across Four Disciplines

Sanwoo Lee[1], Wenqi Li[2(✉)], Pengyi Zhang[2], and Jun Wang[2]

[1] School of Computer Science, Peking University, Beijing 100871, China
shanyu2325@pku.edu.cn

[2] Department of Information Management, Peking University, Beijing 100871, China
{wenqili,pengyi,junwang}@pku.edu.cn

Abstract. Research Data Practices (RDP) refer to research activities conducted across the lifespan of data. Characterizing RDP in disciplinary contexts is beneficial for providing data stakeholders with practical understanding of RDP necessary to design data curation services which are tailored to researchers' need. In this paper, we focus on the five most common types of RDP – collecting data, processing data, analyzing data, representing data, and publishing or citing data. First, we compared the distributions of the five types of RDP across disciplines and observed noticeable differences between disciplines. In addition, we examined the characteristics of each type of RDP under different disciplinary contexts, by developing discipline-specific RDP vocabulary employing the tf-idf approach. Based on the common terms as well as the discipline-specific ones, we found that the five types of RDP can be distinctly conceptualized, while each type of RDP varies by disciplines in terms of their action, object, and instrument.

Keywords: Research data practices · Data activities · Data curation · Scholarly communication · Digital scholarship

1 Introduction

Research Data Practices (RDP) refers to a series of research activities conducted across the lifespan of data. RDP include activities like collecting data, processing data, analyzing data, managing data, representing data and sharing data [1]. As data-driven scientific discovery becomes more widespread across many research areas [2, 3], researchers, libraries and funding agencies are more aware of the importance of understanding RDP in order to meet data curation responsibilities, design data related tools, and construct research infrastructure [4, 5].

RDP vary by disciplines, and these differences should be considered attend to specific requirements and provide more tailored digital scholarship supports [1]. Studies investigating RDP in various disciplines have emerged in recent years [6–11]. Most of the empirical studies focused on researchers' perspectives, process behaviors and articulated experience gathered by questionnaires, observations, and interviews. Yet another way to examine their RDP is through the artifacts researchers created – their scholarly

© The Author(s), under exclusive license to Springer Nature Switzerland AG 2023
I. Sserwanga et al. (Eds.): iConference 2023, LNCS 13971, pp. 359–368, 2023.
https://doi.org/10.1007/978-3-031-28035-1_26

publications, where they are usually required to rigorously document the process and details of how they work with their data.

In this paper, we focus on five RDP types that commonly appear in research papers – collecting data, processing data, analyzing data, representing data, and publishing and citing data. We aim to explore the following research questions by analyzing the texts describing data activities in research papers:

1. How does the distribution of different types of data practices differ across disciplines?
2. What are the characteristics of different types of RDP activities across disciplines?

2 Related Works

As RDP are influenced by researchers' disciplines [4], most of the empirical RDP studies focused on a specific discipline. Borgman conducted interviews and ethnographic studies to investigate RDP in habitat ecology, including data sharing, data collection and data analysis [8]. Rolland and Lee explored data sharing and reuse practices in collaborative cancer epidemiology research by interviews [10]. Yoon and Kim examined data reuse practices of social scientists by conducting surveys [12]. Thoegersen interviewed humanities researchers on their data management practices [7]. Ma and Xiao explored the RDP in digital history on how researchers collect, process, analyze and present their data [9]. Differences can be revealed by comparing the results from these studies. For example, while data sharing and reusing practices is more mature in science disciplines, social scientists are more concerned with data reuse. Meanwhile, the notion of data is still obscure to some humanities scholars.

Borgman compared the RDP in science, social science and humanities disciplines with case studies as well as the disciplinary requirements on data curation and knowledge infrastructure [13]. But the RDP and differences are narrated in a macroscopic way. By contrast, Chao et al. constructed a vocabulary of data practices and curation by interviewing researchers in earth and life sciences. Though derived from a specific discipline, the vocabulary depicts the RDP in fine granularity and can be expanded to accommodate other disciplines [1]. Referring to this work, a vocabulary with broader coverage can be generated from research papers quantitatively.

Research papers are major venues to communicate research results [14], thus are used for analyzing scientific discourse and argumentation structures in many studies. Wang et al. annotated 40 research papers in LIS and biomedical to analyze and compare the argumentation structure in these two disciplines [15]. These manual annotations can further contribute to automatic recognition of specified entities or semantics [16, 17]. Yet few research has adopted this approach to study RDP. In-discipline and cross-discipline RDP have largely been characterized with qualitative data analysis. On the contrary, this paper utilizes text mining to identify the keywords descriptive of RDP and reveal the variance of disciplines. This approach adds to the previous studies from a quantitative perspective.

3 Methods

3.1 Data Collection and Preprocessing

We chose two journals each in four disciplines including sociology, economics, physics, and biology (see Table 1) and selected 15 papers published between 2020 and 2021 from each journal, resulting in 120 papers in total. We only included empirical studies that involve substantial RDP. Theoretical papers and literature reviews were not used.

We selected paragraphs in the papers to build a corpus of content potentially relevant to RDP. All the paragraphs in "methods/methodology," "data," and "abstracts" were included as they usually contain dense descriptions of RDP. Paragraphs in "related literature," "previous research" and "research background" were eliminated as they are not likely to describe data activities pertinent to that study. In other sections, we selected all the paragraphs that contain the keyword "data." The selection process yielded 3075 candidate paragraphs in the corpus.

Table 1. Overview of source journals

Discipline	Journal	Number of candidate paragraphs
Sociology	Sociology	198
	The british journal of sociology	138
Economics	The quarterly journal of economics	412
	Journal of financial economics	342
Biology	Cell	901
	Nature cell biology	589
Physics	The astrophysical journal	198
	Nature physics	297
Total		3075

3.2 Annotation of Research Data Practices

To identify the RDP appeared in research papers, we proposed an annotation scheme referring to the DPCVocab [18]. Five most representative RDP types were included in the annotation scheme - collecting, processing, analyzing, representing, and publishing or citing data, all of which were listed with definition and examples (Table 2).

Next, the corpus was annotated by annotators trained through a guideline. We recruited 14 undergraduate and graduate students and assigned them to label the journals corresponding to their specialized discipline.

We asked nine annotators to assign one or more RDP types to each sentence in a given paragraph and highlight the words, phrases, or clauses which had the most impact on that decision. If there is no RDP type applicable, the sentence was labeled "non-data

Table 2. Annotation Scheme for research data practices

Type of RDP	Definition	Examples
Collecting data	Collecting or generating data, as well as selecting and searching for data	• Questionnaires • Interviews • Generating data through experiments • Reusing existing data or code
Processing data	Processing the collected data to have them fit for the purpose of data analysis	• Preprocessing • Cleaning • Transforming • Aggregating data from different sources
Analyzing data	Analyzing, interpreting, and summarizing data, which often entails certain data analysis skills and technologies	• Classifying • Comparing • Testing hypothesis • Mining data • Developing software or scripts
Representing data	Describing the external and internal features of data to organize, manage and display data without changing the original content or shape of data	• Using metadata • Presenting data in the form of table or figure • Assigning data identifier
Publishing or citing data	Publishing and sharing data, as well as citing others' data	• Publishing or sharing data • Citing others' data

practice." When it is ambiguous to pick up such words, phrases, or clauses, they were asked to highlight the whole sentence. The labels are reviewed by the first author and then used to compare the distribution of RDP and generate the vocabulary.

3.3 Development of the RDP Vocabulary

We built the RDP vocabulary for each discipline to identify similarities and differences of activities in the same type of RDP across disciplines. Specifically, we collected all highlighted words, phrases, and clauses (the "spans") along with its label. The spans were split into smaller segments based on their source discipline and label, yielding 20 segments (4 discipline $\times$ 5 categories). The keywords from the segments were simply extracted through tf-idf term weighting scheme [19], with each segment being a "document" when calculating tf-idf weights.

Prior to the step above, stop words, punctuation, numbers, and words other than noun and verb were excluded from the spans. In addition, all nouns and verbs were lemmatized for better estimation of tf-idf weights. We listed 100 highest weighted terms of each RDP type of each discipline to develop the vocabulary.

4 Findings

4.1 Differences of Distribution of RDP Types Across Disciplines

The proportion of each RDP type in the four disciplines were calculated based on sentence-level label assignments. As shown in Fig. 1, biology has the highest percentage of "processing" among the disciplines. In biological experiments, there could be a large gap between organisms as data source and the structured data which is ready to be digested by data analysis instruments, thus requiring a lot of efforts to clean and transform the data. Economics had the largest percentage of "analyzing" among disciplines, implying that economic research may need to elaborate on sophisticated analytic methods. However, economics had the least percentage of "processing," which might suggest that the original data is usually in a structured or semi-structured format in economic research, such as statistical reports. The percentage of "publishing or citing" in physics exceeded other disciplines by a wide margin. It confirms that the practice of data sharing is more established in physics. "Collecting" data accounted for a half in sociology, which might be caused by detailed descriptions on questionnaire design or interviewing process.

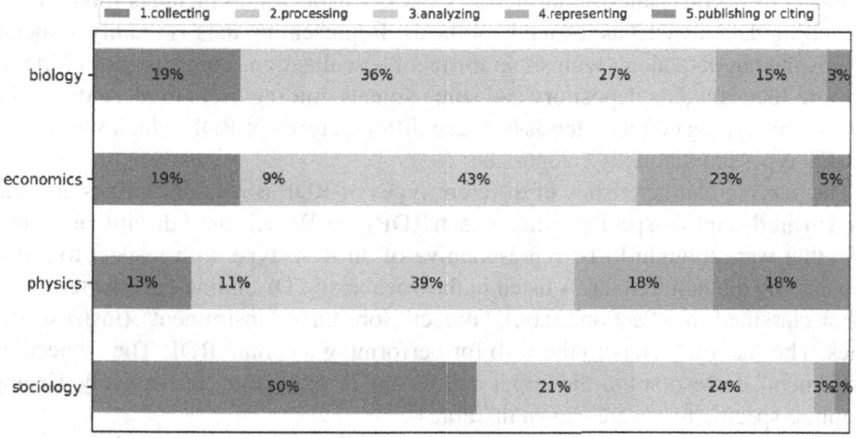

Fig. 1. Comparison of proportion distributions of RDP categories between disciplines

4.2 Characteristics of Different Types of RDP Across Disciplines

Based on the RDP vocabulary, we further examined the common RDP characteristics across disciplines as well as those unique to a discipline. Terms are considered to represent common characteristics of an RDP type ("common terms") if they are within the k highest weighted terms at least n times out of 4 disciplines with respect to a type of RDP. Since the annotated corpus for "publishing or citing data" is small, we set k = 50 and n = 2 for this type. Otherwise, we set k = 100 and n = 3.

Table 3. Common terms of different types of RDP

Type of RDP	Common terms
Collecting data	Collect, record, obtain, provide, include, take, sample, observation, survey, base
Processing data	Exclude, apply, combine, remove, normalize, compute, process, record, value, sample
Analyzing data	Examine, test, estimate, compare, compute, construct, define, follow, show, present, sample, value, parameter, method
Representing data	Show, display, present, illustrate, describe, plot, map, represent, provide, see, data, result, detail, figure, table, statistic, panel, line
Publishing or citing data	Study, paper, database, source, see, code, find, support, https, obtain

As shown in Table 3, core concepts of the RDP type can be seen in the common terms. Collecting data involves generating and selecting data. Processing data is primarily concerned with cleaning, normalizing, and integrating the raw data. Analyzing data is about discovering patterns and trends from the data, which includes modeling and interpreting data, as well as testing hypothesis. Representing data is mainly associated with displaying data along with some forms of visualization. Publishing or citing data has more focus on data depository and some signals guiding users to reuse data. There are few overlapping common terms between different types of RDP, which suggests that the RDP types are distinctly categorized.

The varying characteristics of different types of RDP across disciplines are manifested in the discipline-specific terms of each RDP type. We selected "discipline-specific" terms that were thought to be representative of an RDP type with respect to a discipline, among the hundred terms listed in the vocabulary. Discipline-specific terms were further classified into "action" (act.), "object" (obj.) and "instrument" (inst.) subcategories. The "action" refers to the verb for performing a certain RDP. The "object" and "instrument" correspond to the target and means of the action, respectively. Example discipline-specific terms are shown in Table 4.

Overall, the most distinct differences across disciplines exist in the object terms. For example, the objects of data processing are demographic characteristics in sociology, whereas physical quantities are the main target of processing in physics. Collecting data is the one that differed in instrument across disciplines, where the report and database are retrieved in economics and the questionnaire is distributed in sociology. Biology has distinctive discipline-specific action terms both for collecting and processing data, which illustrates complicated experiment operations. Biology also shows rich terms in its instruments of representing data, in which a variety of visualization elements were introduced. For publishing or citing data, although the disciplines use different action terms, many of these terms could be used interchangeably. Yet in sociology, there's lack of terms in this RDP types, which would suggest relatively less data sharing and citing RDP in sociology.

Table 4. Example discipline-specific terms of different types of RDP

		Sociology	Economics	Biology	Physics
Collecting data	*Act.*	Interview Recruit Invite Guide	Gather Retrieve	Harvest Image Clone Inoculate Infect Inject	Define Observe Detect
	Obj.	Participant interviewee Respondent community Group Variable	Firm Bond Borrower Holding Loan Transaction Credit Subsidy	Sequence Mouse Cell Tissue Gene Dna	State Degree Rotation Cluster Space Energy Momentum Torsion
	Inst.	Questionnaire ethnography fieldnote	Database Report	Centrifuge microscopy	Qubit Tensor
Processing data	*Act.*	Code Transcribe operationalize categorize anonymize	Digitize Aggregate	Wash Purify Isolate Quantify Trim	Fit Catalog Derive characterize Train
	Obj.	Parent Earning Gender Student Item	Outlier Maturity Security Equity Loan	Cell Tissue	Granule Flux Field Parameter
	Inst.	Transcript Memo Tape	Indicator	Centrifuge Plate	Algorithm simulation
Analyzing data	*Act.*	Code conceptualize	Regress Predict	Detect Visualize	Obtain Implement Satisfy
	Obj.	Theme Factor Hypothesis	Effect Investment Price Return Debt Leverage	Assay Cell Gene Genotype Antibody Tissue	Circuit Band Network Density Eigenstate

(*continued*)

Table 4. (*continued*)

		Sociology	Economics	Biology	Physics
	Inst.	–	Series	Library Cytometry chromatography	Equation Function
Representing data	*Act.*	Highlight	Summarize	Overlay Tabulate	Define
	Obj.	Factor Variable Structure	Increase Year Baseline Rate Effect	Cell	Parameter State Density Curvature emission
	Inst.	Appendix	Column	Heatmap Scatterplot Box	Measurement
Publishing or Citing data	*Act.*	–	Replicate Extend	Publish Download Modeling	Request correspond provide Find
	Obj.	–	Statistic	Sequence Virus Protein	Finding Theory Algorithm
	Inst.	–	–	–	–

5 Conclusion and Discussion

In this paper, we compared the distributions of the five types of research data practices (RDP) across four disciplines and observed noticeable differences across disciplines. In addition, we examined the characteristics of each type of RDP under different disciplinary contexts by developing discipline-specific RDP vocabulary. Based on the common terms as well as the discipline-specific ones, we found that the five types of RDP as recognized in [1] can be distinctly conceptualized, while each type of RDP varies by disciplines in terms of their action, object, and instrument. These distribution and characteristics can inform researchers, librarians, funders, and other data stakeholders to understand the RDP in disciplinary contexts and provide tailored data services to meet disciplinary needs.

Yet limitations exist in current research approach. First, the paragraphs were not randomly sampled, hence it was impossible to test whether the four disciplines had a significant difference in their distributions of RDP. In the future, we can improve the research design to support statistical testing. Second, the descriptions of different types of RDP are often intertwined, making it difficult for annotators to decide on the specific RDP type to label. On the one hand, this suggests that more detailed guidelines and training for the annotators are needed. On the other hand, there might be a need for more structured descriptions about the RDP in research papers, similar to research method descriptions commonly adopted by certain disciplines. Third, adopting the tf-idf approach to build the vocabulary is just a preliminary step. In the future, we can leverage more sophisticated methods such as topic modeling for identifying the keywords or cluster analysis for exploring which documents are similar than others. The initial vocabulary we developed can be further refined and expanded to provide a shared terminology for researchers, curators, tool developers and other stakeholders to describe and characterize RDP.

Acknowledgments. This work is supported by the National Natural Science Foundation of China (Grant No. 72174014 and Grant No. 72010107003).

References

1. Chao, T.C., Cragin, M.H., Palmer, C.L.: Data practices and curation vocabulary (DPCVocab): an empirically derived framework of scientific data practices and curatorial processes. J. Am. Soc. Inf. Sci. **66**, 616–633 (2015)
2. Gray, J., Liu, D.T., Nieto-Santisteban, M., Szalay, A., DeWitt, D.J., Heber, G.: Scientific data management in the coming decade. SIGMOD Rec. **34**, 34–41 (2005)
3. Schroeder, R.: Big data: towards a more scientific social science and humanities?. In: Society and the Internet. Oxford University Press, Oxford (2014)
4. Palmer, C.L., Teffeau, L.C., Pirmann, C.M.: Scholarly information practices in the online environment: themes from the literature and implications for library service development. OCLC Research (2009)
5. Hey, T., Trefethen, A.: The data deluge: an e-science perspective. In: Grid Computing: Making the Global Infrastructure a Reality, pp. 809–824. Wiley Online Library (2003)
6. Weller, T., Monroe-Gulick, A.: Understanding methodological and disciplinary differences in the data practices of academic researchers. Libr. Hi Tech. **32**, 467–482 (2014)
7. Thoegersen, J.L.: "Yeah, I Guess That's Data": data practices and conceptions among humanities faculty. Portal-Libr. Acad. **18**, 491–504 (2018)
8. Borgman, C., Wallis, J.C., Enyedy, N.: Building digital libraries for scientific data: an exploratory study of data practices in habitat ecology. In: Gonzalo, J., Thanos, C., Verdejo, M.F., Carrasco, R.C. (eds.) ECDL 2006. LNCS, vol. 4172, pp. 170–183. Springer, Heidelberg (2006). https://doi.org/10.1007/11863878_15
9. Ma, R., Xiao, F.: Data practices in digital history. Int. J. Digit. Curation **15**, 21 (2020)
10. Rolland, B., Lee, C.P.: Beyond trust and reliability: reusing data in collaborative cancer epidemiology research. In: Proceedings of the 2013 Conference on Computer Supported Cooperative Work - CSCW '13, pp. 435. ACM Press, San Antonio, Texas, USA (2013)
11. Yoon, A.: "Making a square fit into a circle": researchers' experiences reusing qualitative data: "Making a Square Fit into a Circle": researchers' experiences reusing qualitative data. Proc. Am. Soc. Info. Sci. Tech. **51**, 1–4 (2014)
12. Yoon, A., Kim, Y.: Social scientists' data reuse behaviors: exploring the roles of attitudinal beliefs, attitudes, norms, and data repositories. Libr. Inf. Sci. Res. **39**, 224–233 (2017)
13. Borgman, C.L.: Big Data, Little Data, No Data: Scholarship in the Networked World. MIT Press (2015)
14. Walton, D., Zhang, N.: The epistemology of scientific evidence. Artif. Intell. Law. **21**, 173–219 (2013). https://doi.org/10.1007/s10506-012-9132-9

15. Wang, X., Song, N., Zhou, H., Cheng, H.: The representation of argumentation in scientific papers: a comparative analysis of two research areas. J. Assoc. Inf. Sci. Technol. **73**(6), 863–878 (2021). https://doi.org/10.1002/asi.24590
16. Blake, C.: Beyond genes, proteins, and abstracts: Identifying scientific claims from full-text biomedical articles. J. Biomed. Inform. **43**, 173–189 (2010). https://doi.org/10.1016/j.jbi.2009.11.001
17. Liakata, M., Saha, S., Dobnik, S., Batchelor, C., Rebholz-Schuhmann, D.: Automatic recognition of conceptualization zones in scientific articles and two life science applications. Bioinformatics **28**, 991–1000 (2012). https://doi.org/10.1093/bioinformatics/bts071
18. Chao, T.C., Cragin, M.H., Palmer, C.L.: Data practices and curation vocabulary (DPCVocab). http://hdl.handle.net/2142/44032. Last Accessed 12 Nov 2021
19. Manning, C.D., Raghavan, P., Schutze, H.S.: Term weighting, and the vector space model. Int. Inf. Retr. 109–133 (2008)

Information and Digital Literacy

Fighting Misinformation: Where Are We and Where to Go?

Huyen Nguyen, Lydia Ogbadu-Oladapo, Irhamni Ali, Haihua Chen, and Jiangping Chen(✉)

University of North Texas, Denton, TX 76203, USA
Jiangping.chen@unt.edu

Abstract. This study reviews existing studies on misinformation. Our purposes are to understand the major research topics that have been investigated by researchers from a variety of disciplines, and to identify important areas for further exploration for library and information science scholars. We conducted automatic descriptive analysis and manual content analysis after selecting journal articles from 4 major databases. The automatic analysis of 5,586 journal articles demonstrated that misinformation has been an increasingly popular research area in recent 12 years, and scholars in more than 1,200 fields of study have published related articles in more than 2,400 journals. Topics explored include misinformation environments, impact of misinformation, users/victims, types of misinformation, misinformation detection & correction, and others; The content analysis of 151 articles published in library and information studies journals found that more than 40 different theories/models/frameworks have been applied to understand or fight misinformation. Furthermore, information scholars have suggested that the research of misinformation could be explored further in 5 categories, including further understanding misinformation, its spread, and impacts; misinformation detection and correction, Policy and education to fight misinformation, more case studies, and more theory and model development. This study provides a broad picture of misinformation research, which allows researchers and practitioners to better plan and develop their projects and strategies for fighting misinformation. It also provides evidence to information schools to enhance curriculum development for educating the next generation of information professionals.

Keywords: Misinformation · Systematic literature review · Topic analysis

1 Introduction

Misinformation has been a challenge for the public, the social media industry, and the academia, especially with the advancement of the Internet, social media, and other information technologies. The wrong messages submitted or posted on social media might lead to incorrect understanding and even harmful behavior by individuals. The negative impact of misinformation might be tremendous and cause huge damage to the human society; Social media platforms must spend time and effort to detect misinformation and seek balance between free speech and misleading messages; And scholars in multiple

© The Author(s), under exclusive license to Springer Nature Switzerland AG 2023
I. Sserwanga et al. (Eds.): iConference 2023, LNCS 13971, pp. 371–394, 2023.
https://doi.org/10.1007/978-3-031-28035-1_27

disciplines, such as medicine, computer science, communication, political science are actively exploring theories, methods, and technologies to explain, detect, and correct misinformation.

As information professionals, we are at the forefront of helping information users fight misinformation [1, 2]. Although extensive research has been conducted, systematic understanding of such effort is not performed. There is no big picture on what disciplines are active, what have been explored, and especially, what information scientists have performed in this area. We believe information scientists could do much more to help the general public, to educate modern information professionals, and also to provide insights on future solutions to misinformation. However, the basis of further exploration needs to be a good understanding of what have been done ever since.

The purposes of this study are to understand the major research topics investigated by researchers from a variety disciplines, and to examine the important areas for further exploration for information scientists. Specifically, we would like to answer the following questions:

- RQ1: What are the characteristics of existing literature (2010–2022) on misinformation?
- RQ2: What are the major topics explored by researchers from different disciplines?
- RQ3: What are the theories that information scientists have applied to misinformation research?
- RQ4: What are considered important future research topics or directions?

The rest of the paper is organized as follows. Section 2 reviews the definition of misinformation and a few literature reviews we could find that are related to this study; Sect. 3 describes our research design, including literature selection and data analysis approaches. Section 4 presents our analytical results on the selected papers' metadata, and manual library and information science articles. Next, we discuss our results and concluded the paper.

2 Related Review Studies

2.1 Misinformation Defined

Earlier authors portray misinformation and disinformation as false information [3], inaccurate information [4], as a virus [5, 6], and as "articles that are intentionally and verifiably false and could mislead readers" [7].

Contemporary authors, however, present misinformation as the umbrella term that includes all inaccurate or false information or reports spreading on social media [8, 9]. However, misinformation, disinformation, fake news, rumor, spam, troll, and urban legend all share the wrong message(s) as a common characteristic that can lead to distress or adverse effects via social media if not curbed [9, 10]. This effect explains why false information and fake news are confused with various other terms associated with inaccurate information. Lazer and colleagues [11] argue that fake news is the most challenging to define as they are fabricated stories that mimic news media content and sometimes intend to accomplish a political goal.

Our study applies a broad definition of misinformation to include most of the aspects being specified by other researchers - as misinformation refers to articles, posts, messages, and other representations that are intentionally fabricated and verifiably false to mislead people.

2.2 Literature Analysis of Misinformation Research

There are very few review studies that have been found in this area. Revez and Corujo [2] conducted a systematic literature review on librarians against fake news. They reviewed 27 articles from 2018–2020 and concluded that a librarian could develop formal instruction, apply a framework and use checklists or learner-centred approaches. Librarians may also produce campaigns through social media or library guides through audio-visual activities.

Another study by E, Sakura, and Li [12] reviewed 135 papers published before 2020 on misinformation correction and its effects. Their review tried to answer questions including characteristics of the literature, psychological and behavioral outcomes, and theories used to explain or predict the performance of misinformation correction. Their research found that there have been consistent interests on information correction topics over the past four decades with a sharp increase in the topic relevance in the last ten years. However, most research conducted in misinformation correction has been built using psychological perspectives with quantitative methodologies. They concluded that misinformation treatment is a complex process that sometimes generates unwanted outcomes.

Both reviews have presented a systematic process of selecting relevant articles from literature databases for review, which is very similar to what we have used for this study. Specifically, E, Sakura, and Li [12] used Preferred Reporting Items for Systematic review and Meta-Analysis (PRISMA) approach to analyze articles collected from google scholar, EBSCO academic, and Web of Science.

3 Research Design

We used a systematic review approach in order to answer the research questions. A systematic review was defined as: "a review of a clearly formulated question that uses systematic and explicit methods to identify, select and critically appraise relevant research and to collect and analyze data from the studies that are included in the review" [13]. Automatic analysis and manual content analysis were combined in this study. The whole research process involves the following steps: 1) relevant literature identification, or data collection; 2) article selection and verification, and (3) automatic and manual analysis. Our study starts with retrieving metadata from well-known large scholarly databases. The collected data were then filtered using the inclusive and exclusive criteria we predefined for automatic and manual analysis. After that, the selected data sets were analyzed automatically or manually to answer the research questions (Fig. 1).

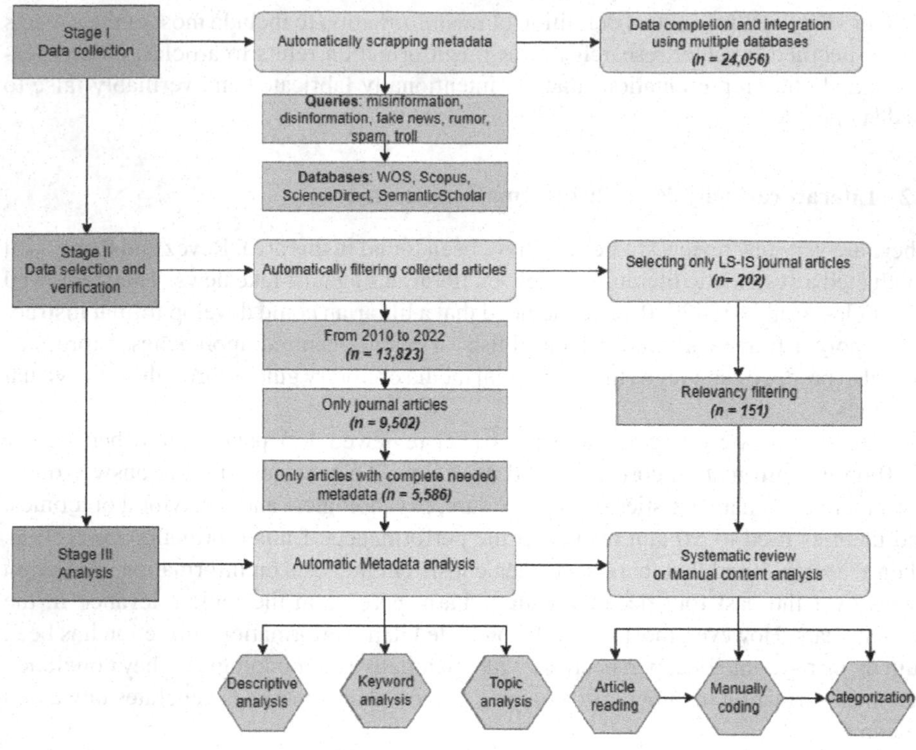

Fig. 1. Research design: Semi-automatic systematic review workflow

3.1 Data Collection

As misinformation covers many related terms such as "disinformation", "fake news", "rumors", "spams", and "troll". [9, 14, 15]. They are often used interchangeably. Therefore, together with "misinformation", we included the above terms as queries to retrieve "misinformation" articles from the following four well-known databases: Web of Science, Scopus, ScienceDirect, and Semantic Scholar. Furthermore, we set the publication year filter from 2010 to 2022. In other words, we tried to retrieve misinformation-related articles in the past 12 years as the scope of this study.

Most databases do not have complete metadata attributes, which are helpful for our data filtering strategy. Therefore, we merged metadata from different databases using DOI (if available) and titles. Web scraping and APIs given by Scopus, ScienceDirect, and Semantic Scholar were used to scrap and integrate data from the four sources automatically. As a result, we obtained metadata records of 24,056 articles. Each metadata record may include the following fields: title, authors, venue, publication year, citation count, fields of study, abstract, DOI, query, and database.

3.2 Data Selection and Verification

Data selection and verification, or data cleaning, are necessary to ensure the quality of the data for analysis. Our data selection process includes duplicates removal, journal article identification, and Library and Information Science (LIS) journal article identification.

Because the data collected from different sources contained many duplicate records, we normalized the titles by lowercasing and removing punctuations. Then we removed 8,449 duplicated records by comparing them with each other using a Python program. After this process, 15,607 unique articles were kept. Then we removed 1,780 articles that were published before 2010.

The remaining 13,823 records contain journal articles, conference proceedings, books, and other types of publications. The quality of these articles varies and is challenging to control. We made a difficult decision that our analysis would focus on journal articles. To verify that a paper is a journal article, we gathered the publication type attributes from Semantic Scholar and compared them with our data set. None of the other databases offer more complete information on publication type than Semantic Scholar. Still, we manually evaluated about 1,200 records that could not be verified automatically. After dropping papers with other publication types, 9,502 journal articles remained. Then we kept the articles that included necessary metadata fields for our analysis. Specifically, we filtered out articles missing values on DOI, abstract, and field of study. We finally selected metadata records of 5,586 articles for our automatic analysis.

To answer research questions 3 and 4, we selected articles that were published in LIS journals for manual analysis. Based on the LIS journal list provided by SCImago JR, we found 202 LIS journal articles in the 5,586 records, and 151 of them were kept for manual content analysis.

3.3 Automatic Metadata Analysis

Our automatic analysis of the metadata of 5,586 articles was conducted using the pipeline suggested by Chen, Chen, and Hguyen [16]. First, the analysis explores the metadata features using simple descriptive statistics. Then we conducted keyword and topic analysis using statistical models to gain more insights into the topics of the articles. Finally, statistical models were used to extract the keywords and topics as they are corpus-independent and do not require training data as supervised learning models.

Descriptive Analysis. The descriptive analysis aims to identify high-level bibliometric characteristics of literature about misinformation. For our purposes, we aim to identify distributions of articles regarding publication years, disciplines, and venues of the 5,586 records.

Keyword Analysis. Keyword analysis extracts the most important and representative keywords from a large corpus. Statistical and unsupervised-learning models are preferred as they are efficiently computed and do not depend on any corpus or domain. YAKE! outperformed among those models (i.e., TF.IDF, KP-Miner, RAKE, TextRank, SingleRank, ExpandRank, TopicRank, TopicalPageRank, PositionRank and MultipartiteRank) on over twenty datasets [17]. YAKE! takes into account features of casing, position, frequency, context relevancy, and term dispersion, returning a ranking score for each keyword extracted by the algorithm [17]. We concatenated titles and abstracts to input into YAKE! as they contain the most concise information of the articles. The most common lengths of word phrases are from one to three tokens, so we set up a maximum n-gram of three.

Topic Analysis. Topic analysis, also called topic modeling, is preferred to use to gain more insight into a large text dataset as it clusters the most representative information into word categories. Latent Semantic Analysis (LSA) and Latent Dirichlet Allocation (LDA) are the two most widely-used algorithms for topic modeling based on mathematical techniques [18]. LSA looks at the whole corpus as a whole matrix. It attempts to find the latent relationships within texts by first computing similarity among document vector representations, then using Singular Value Decomposition (SVD) to reduce the matrix dimension. On the other hand, LDA assumes that each document contains a mixture of topics described by a multinomial distribution over a word vocabulary [18]. Using Umass topic coherence as an evaluation metric, Bellaouar, Bellaouar, and Ghada [19] empirically proved that LDA provided better-quality topics with higher coherence scores than LSA on a scientific publication dataset. Therefore, LDA was chosen to extract the latent topics from the misinformation publications we selected. To choose an optimal number of topics, we based on *cv topic coherence* scores. We investigated the coherence of a range of topic numbers between 20 and 40; this range is proper to balance the topic's interpretability and specificity. With the highest coherence scores (0.485) for 30 topics, we chose to cluster the dataset into 30 topics.

3.4 Manual Content Analysis

As aforementioned, we selected 202 LIS journal articles for our systematic review. To ensure that those articles are research publications with regard to misinformation, we manually verified them and kept 151 articles for the systematic review. For the purpose of this study, we manually analyzed the full texts of these articles to: identify theories or frameworks used in misinformation research (RQ3), and to extract and summarize future research directions (RQ4) by the authors of these articles.

Coding Process and Codes. We applied an inductive approach to conducting a coding process to answer RQ3 and RQ4. In other words, the coding process aims to identify theories (RQ3) and future directions (RQ4) from the 151 library and information science articles. Because there is no coding scheme available, we identified the theories and future directions of the articles and then summarized them to form appropriate categories. The two-level codes: theories or future directions, and their categories, are presented in the Results Section. In Sect. 4.3, Table 4 lists the categories of theories in the first column, the frequency count and percentage, and the examples of existing theories/models/frameworks in the last column. In Sect. 4.4, Table 5 lists the categories of future directions in the first column, and actual future directions in the second column. One of the authors did the coding for each table, and another author reverified the coding results.

4 Results

This section reports the results of our automatic analysis and manual content analysis.

4.1 General Characteristics of Misinformation Literature

We automatically analyzed the following features: Distribution of Publication, Publication Fields, and Publication Venues.

Distribution of Publication. Figure 2 depicts the distribution of 5,586 journal articles published in 2010–2022 related to misinformation. It indicated that research on misinformation had become an upward trend between 2010 and 2021. Evidently, the number of publications has doubled each year since 2019. Although we do not have complete data for 2022, with this tendency, it can be forecasted to grow higher at the end of this year.

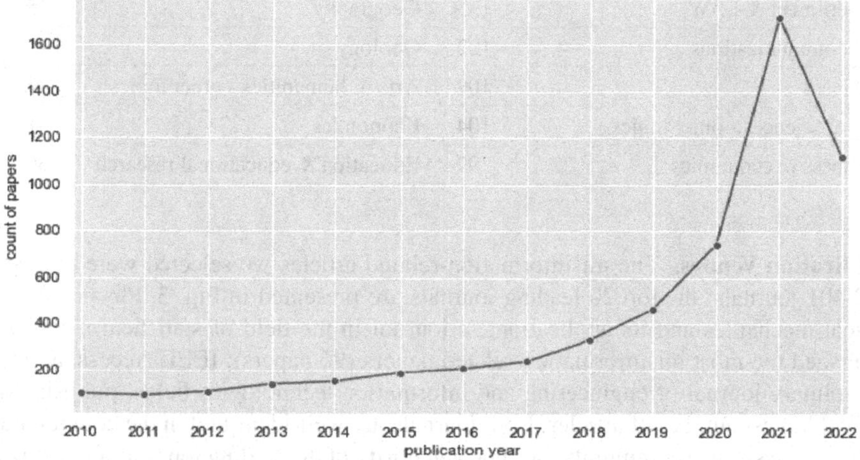

Fig. 2. Distribution of publications 2010–2022

Publication Fields. Scrapping the field-of-study metadata from Semantic Scholar to merge with our collected data allows us to understand the interdisciplinary nature of the misinformation research. We found 1,278 disciplines that have contributed to this research area. Table 1 lists the top 30 fields of study that have published the greatest number of articles. Medicine, followed by Computer science, has the most publications about misinformation, accounting for 27% and 24% respectively of the whole data set (n = 5,586). Psychology takes up the third largest portion (10%). Among the misinformation publications we selected, the Information science & Library science field also contributes 182 articles, making it the eighth largest field.

Table 1. Top 30 disciplines studying misinformation.

Field of study	Count	Field of study	Count
Medicine	1508	Science & technology - other topics	99
Computer science	1321	History	93
Psychology	546	Environmental sciences & ecology	83
Communication	419	Public	71
Engineering	250	Environmental & occupational health	71
Political science	226	Chemistry	51
Sociology	186	International relations	50
Information science & library science	182	Operations research & management science	50
Physics	170	Linguistics	46
Mathematics	138	Materials science	45
Government & LAW	135	Geography	45
Telecommunications	122	Geology	45
Business	109	Arts & humanities - other topics	44
Social sciences - other topics	104	Economics	41
Business & economics	99	Education & educational research	36

Publication Venues. The misinformation-related articles we selected were published in 2,401 journals; the top 20 leading journals are presented in Fig. 3. Physica A: Statistical mechanics and its applications, a journal in the field of statistical mechanics, published the most misinformation-related papers (96 papers); IEEE Access, an interdisciplinary journal of engineering and information technologies fields, published the second largest number of articles. Both journals are well-identified in the computer and information science community. Further, a majority of the leading journals are computer and information science (about eight journals) and medicine and health science (about seven journals), affirming the incredible growth of this topic in those two areas.

Based on the journal list given by SCImago JR[1], we found that 62 out of 2,401 journals in our selected misinformation literature are of Library and Information Science. Table 2 shows the top 20 LIS journals leading in misinformation research. The Publications journal ranks first with 16 articles, followed by Government Information Quarterly, Journal of Information Science, International Journal of Information Management, and JASIST, almost half of that number.

[1] https://www.scimagojr.com/.

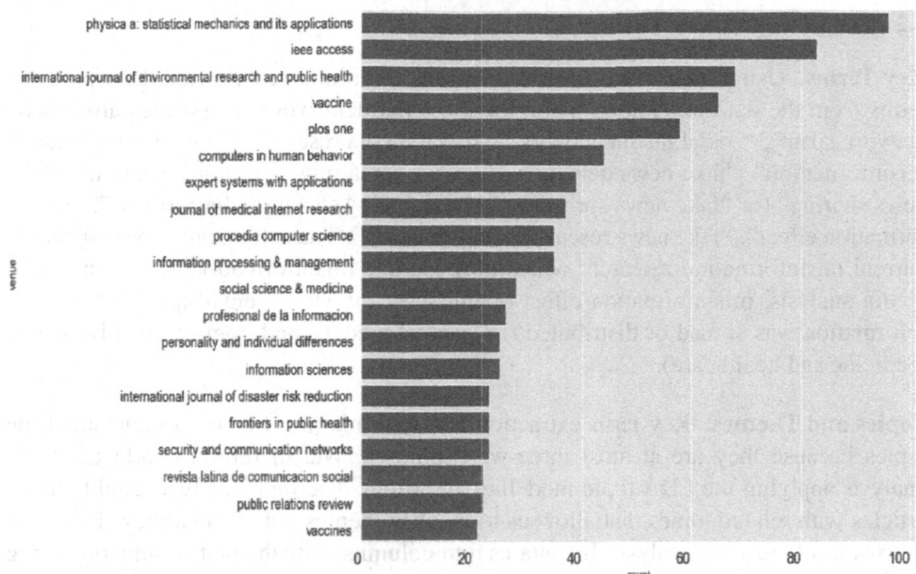

Fig. 3. Top 20 journals publishing misinformation-related research.

Table 2. Top 20 leading library and information science journals

LIS journal	Frequency
Publications	16
Government information quarterly	9
Journal of information science	8
International journal of information management	8
Journal of the association for information science and technology (JASIST)	8
Online information review	7
Profesional de la informacion	6
Library & information science research	5
IEEE transactions on information forensics and security	4
Social science computer review	4
Electronic library	4
Journal of health communication	4
Information communication and society	3
Journal of documentation	3
Reference services review	3
Communications in information literacy	3

4.2 Major Topics and Themes

Key Terms. Using YAKE! Keyword extraction algorithm, we extracted the top 50 key terms from the dataset. Among them, the most frequent words or phrases are "social network spam", "social media network", "social media research", "fake news", "health misinformation", "fake news detection", "rumor spreading", "rumor detection", "fake news sharing" (or "fake news spreading"), "vaccine", "social media analysis", "misinformation effect", "fake news research", and "rumors". These terms indicate aspects of current misinformation research, which may include misinformation detection, social media analysis, misinformation effect or impact, contexts, or environments that misinformation was spread or distributed (i.e., social media), and domains involved (i.e., medicine and healthcare).

Topics and Themes. Key term extraction has its limitation for us to understand the topics because they are at most three-word phrases. We, therefore, conducted topic analysis applying the LDA topic modeling algorithm. The topic analysis could cluster articles with related topics that allow us to identify themes out of the topics. Table 3 is the results of the topic analysis. It contains four columns, with the first column providing an ID for each topic identified by the system. The second column lists the 10 terms that represent each topic. These terms are extracted from the title and abstract of the 5,583 records; the third column is topics annotated by the authors based on the terms, which was challenging because annotation is subjective and could be wrong, even though we have 10 terms for each topic. The last column lists themes that we identified based on the terms and topics. We identified 6 themes, including Environment of rising misinformation, Impact of misinformation, User research, Domain-specific misinformation research, types of misinformation, and fighting misinformation. Several topics detected by the system are labeled as "Unknow topic" because we failed to assign an appropriate label to it. We assigned them into a category called "Other."

Even though it is sometimes challenging to accurately interpret the results of the topic analysis, most misinformation is created and spread on Internet environments, including social media such as Facebook, Twitter, Instagram, and emails. Noticeably, misinformation also exists in the form of visual advertisements on Instagram. Additionally, we found that Cybercrime contributed to misinformation creation and growth.

Spam, fake news, and rumors are found to be major types of misinformation, which is consistent with the aforementioned misinformation definition by Wu and others [9]. Misinformation especially involves various domains, from controversial social issues, environment, and medicine to the political dilemma; specifically, some popular topics of misinformation found are scandal, medical treatment, sexual misconduct, COVID-19 pandemic, abortion, political issues in the election, and vaccination concerns in community. Also, approaches to fight misinformation, including educating, managing healthcare risks, making scientific evidence visible, and using algorithms to automatically detect misinformation, are explored in the literature. Furthermore, we found that misinformation literature also focused on studying the impact of misinformation on human memory and stock trading market, while behavior studies and online review studies are significant research in this area. However, as a tradeoff of automatic content analysis methods, some word clusters (i.e., Topics 25–30) are not easily interpretable, so we named them unknown topics.

Table 3. Topics and themes of LIS misinformation research.

Topic ID	Word cluster	Annotated topic	Themes
1	Social, media, inform, misinformation, twitter, content, user, platform, tweet, analysis	Misinformation on social media (Twitter)	A. Environment of rising misinformation
2	Model, network, spread, rumor, inform, propagation, social, dynamic, control, node	Rumor spreading through social network	
3	Cyber, youth, cyberbullying, aggressive, self, trait, person, relationship, answer, dark	Cybercrime	
4	Image, visual, Instagram, panic, advertise, buy, project, forest, density, tag	Visual advertisements on Instagram	
5	Rumor, market, food, consume, product, stock, cost, price, trade, impact	Rumor impacts on the stock trading market	B. Impact of Misinformation
6	Misinformation, effect, memory, participate, correct, false, inform, test, study, belief	Effect of misinformation on memory	
7	Troll, study, online, use, bully, behavior, measure, analysis, data, indicate	Behavior study about online bullying and troll	C. User research
8	Review, user, research, use, base, data, inform, online, develop, paper	Research on online users' reviews	
9	Couple, lie, pathway, poison, tolerate, pseudo, scandal, gate, hotspot, beij	Scandal	D. Domain Specific misinformation research
10	Patient, medical, treatment, publish, clinical, case, report, disorder, article, journal	Medical treatment publications	
11	Video, women, adolescent, victim, YouTube, gender, school, score, sexual, year	Victims of sexual abuse	

(continued)

Table 3. (*continued*)

Topic ID	Word cluster	Annotated topic	Themes
12	Covid, health, pandemic, study, public, inform, misinformation, prevent, people, risk	Misinformation in COVID-19 pandemic	
13	Politics, media, election, ideology, right, Russian, campaign, social, speech, online	Russian-related political issues in election	
14	Fish, surface, environment, estimate, field, water, area, land, catch, region	Environment	
15	Vaccine, hesitate, accept, barrier, community, uptake, health, immune, concern, including	Vaccination concerns in community	
16	Disinformation, article, community, public, digital, govern, research, case, state, politics	Political disinformation	
17	Rumor, social, abort, event, attention, inform, Weibo, microblog, model, refute	Rumor of abortion	
18	Spam, mail, attack, message, email, system, page, secure, mobile, rate	Email spam	E. Types of misinformation
19	News, fake, media, inform, credible, social, share, fact, study, trust	Fake news on social media	
20	Inform, student, study, research, educate, literacy, university, participate, social, find	Educating	F. Fighting misinformation
21	Inform, community, manage, risk, care, health, provide, need, use, response	Heathcare risk management	

(*continued*)

Table 3. (*continued*)

Topic ID	Word cluster	Annotated topic	Themes
22	Detect, spam, propose, method, base, feature, model, learn, use, algorithm	Spam detection algorithm	
23	Children, parent, cell, interview, child, family, mother, report, study, trial	Interviewing family	
24	Science, scientific, knowledge, policy, climate, public, evidence, expert, access, scientist	Scientific evidence	
25	Contracept, random, formula, graph, call, station, time, nuclear, protocol, accident	Unknown topic	G. Other
26	Game, level, interact, echo, book, chamber, liquid, dietary, micro, smoke	Unknown topic	
27	Particle, source, mass, species, size, single, aerosol, concentration, period, observe	Unknown topic	
28	Energy, sensor, island, rout, flood, Christian, renew, entropy, cryptocurrency, protocol	Unknown topic	
29	Perpetrate, urban, fatal, Taiwan, domestic, middle, diplomacy, opioid, Asian, entry	Unknown topic	
30	Comment, signal, blog, emission, linguistic, film, coal, humor, annual, biomass	Unknown topic	

4.3 Theories Applied by Library and Information Science Scholars

Our manual content analysis identified more than 40 different theories, models, or perspectives that library and information science scholars have applied to research misinformation. Table 4 lists the categories of major theories from the 151 articles.

Table 4. Theories, models, or perspectives applied to misinformation research[2]

Category	Frequency (percentage)	Description or sample theories
No theory	59 (39.1%)	No specific theories identified. Even though papers provide literature for concepts being explored
Computational algorithms/models	38 (25.2%)	BERT, deep learning models, different types of classifiers, supervised and non-supervised machine learning models
Information credibility	9 (6.0%)	Information credibility theory
Information literacy frameworks/models	6 (4.0%)	Media literacy key elements, ACRL information literacy framework
Other theories	42 (27.8%)	Theories in information seeking, behavior, cognition, social diffusion, deterrence theory, uses and gratification

No Theory. Fifty-nine or 39.1% of the papers does not mention specific theories applied, even though they have reviewed concepts or certain perspectives in the literature for their research purposes. Among them, 3 papers are on bibliometrics and 8 are literature review papers. Some papers have applied a grounded theory approach [20, 21], which aims to discover or construct theory from data that is systematically obtained and analyzed using comparative analysis [22]. Some of the papers focused on understanding misinformation impact on different user groups, or fake news spread at different media platforms [23–26]. Legal perspective was also used to guide the discussion of misinformation [27–30]. Other theories or perspectives to understand misinformation include systematic review and bibliometric [2, 31–35].

Computational Algorithms and Models. Computational methods, such as deep learning and machine learning models have been used in 38 studies. These studies explored the use of machine learning methods [36–51], deep learning methods [52–63], and other computation models or theories [64–66] to analyze social media, email, or other data. Studies aimed to experiment or identify most effective models or algorithms for misinformation detection, information classification, or impact understanding. Many of the studies experimented multiple algorithms for evaluation purposes. It is sometimes challenging to differentiate different types of computational models.

Information Credibility. There are 9 papers that are related to information credibility [67–75]. Information credibility theories define related concepts, such as credible information, trust, belief, and provide approaches to assessing credibility of information in various format [73].

[2] A complete table of theories/models is available in our GitHub site.

Information Literacy Frameworks/Models. Authors of 6 articles considered that information literacy was the key to deter and correct misinformation, and have applied existing information literacy framework to guide their research [76–81]. The information literacy framework from the Association of College and Research Libraries (ACRL: https://www.ala.org/acrl/standards/ilframework) has been applied by multiple studies.

Other Theories. Forty-two studies applied theories or models in business, human behavioral research, Psychology, political science, policy, and information seeking. Here are a few examples: uses and gratification theory [82, 83], fact checking [84], elaboration likelihood model [85], Kuhlthau's information seeking behavior and process [86], technology adoption model [87], themes of misinformation [88], Longo health information model [89], Heuristic system model [90], and integrated behavioral model [91].

4.4 Important Future Research Directions

We are interested in what scholars consider important future research on misinformation. Table 5 lists the important future research directors identified by information science scholars. These directions can be categorized into the following areas:

Further Understanding Misinformation, its Spread, and its Impacts: About 29 authors would be conducting studies in this category. Examples include longitudinal studies [24] and expanding library intervention [20, 50]. While others include exploring the extent of the spread of misinformation on social networks [15, 41, 43, 66, 92, 93], sentiments or reason behind the spread [52, 94], relationships between variables [44, 95, 96], and predicting virality [97]. Other authors propose to explore misinformation spread in other languages [47, 98], in other countries [90, 99], investigating public relations and crises intervention [35, 100], entrepreneurial space [101], perception [71, 75, 102] and addressing structural inequalities [103].

Misinformation Detection and Correction. Authors of about 20 articles proposed to work toward improving misinformation detection, including spam detection [54, 55, 61]; using natural language processing [48], using the bot [104], applying machine learning [46], probability sampling [77]; text extraction [59, 105], and modified label training [106]. Moreover, other future works relate to refining previous analysis [57], exploring systematic modeling and theorization effort [107], employing classifiers [108], and more exploration of effective rumorr extraction [70, 85, 109–111].

Policy and Education to Fight Misinformation. Authors of 50 articles would be developing policies and procedures for emergency responses [79, 87, 100, 112, 113], professional neutrality [114], privacy [42], promotion of awareness [115], exploring ways of exposing players of misinformation [29, 60, 116–118] and tracking blogs [119]. More studies are need on understanding information behavior and limitations of participants [120, 121], exploring instructional methods [14, 26, 28, 31, 80, 122, 123], and staff development [124, 125].

Conducting more Case Analyses and Studies. Authors of about 23 articles suggested more case analyses and studies being conducted for various purposes [2, 24, 36, 44, 53, 126–130]. Here we mention just a few.

Theory and Model Development. Authors of about 21 articles proposed that new models be applied or developed in this area. A few examples include the architecture model [56], exploring patterns [67], interactivity [72], cross-linkability between biometric templates in different databases [62], and models for controlling misinformation [131].

Table 5. Future research directions identified[3]

Category	Major topics	Number of articles
Further understanding misinformation, spread, and its impacts	Health related Media, youths, information literacy, & others Spread: Extent, form, sentiments, & perception	7 8 15
Misinformation detection and correction	Text & rumor extraction Misinformation correction with AI/machine learning	8 12
Policy and education to fight misinformation	Developing policies and educational guidelines Intervention: library & crises Information behavior to overcome limitation of participants	31 12 7
Conducting more case analysis and studies	Empirical, mixed methods, longitudinal & heuristic study	23
Theory and model development	Proposing new models related to architecture, patterns, interactivity Enhancing generalizability: update, scope, reliability	8 13
Not stated		13

5 Discussions

5.1 Answers to Research Questions

Characteristics of Existing Literature (2010–2022). We explored the literature from three perspectives: distribution of publication over time, disciplines involved, and publication venues. Our automatic analysis found that misinformation research has gained

[3] A complete table of future research directions is available in our GitHub.

popularity since 2017, with more than 200 journal articles published in this area. Moreover, the number of publications has doubled each year since 2019. In 2021, we found more than 1,600 journal articles on misinformation; The fields that have studied misinformation are numerous, spanning from medicine, computer science, and psychology to political science, information science, and economics; More than 2,400 journals have published articles on misinformation.

Major Topics Explored by Researchers from Different Disciplines. Our key term analysis and topic analysis of the 5,586 journal articles indicated that extensive research had been conducted to understand misinformation on social media, misinformation spreading, user behavior as related to misinformation, and misinformation in different areas and their impact on different types of people. As a result, six categories of misinformation research with about 24 topics were identified and listed in Table 2.

Theories that Information Scientists Have Applied to Misinformation Research. Our content analysis of the 151 journal articles in Library and Information Studies (LIS) identified more than 40 theories or models that have been applied by information scholars. These theories were used to guide the development of new theories/algorithms for misinformation understanding/detection, to explore misinformation spread, to assess misinformation impact on people, or to improve people's capabilities of evaluating information.

Important Future Research Topics or Directions. We also analyzed the future research direction proposed or suggested by the authors of the 151 LIS journal articles. Five themes or categories were identified for future research in misinformation: Further understanding of misinformation, spread, and its impacts, Misinformation detection, and correction, Policy and education to fight misinformation, Conducting more case analysis and studies, and theory and model development.

5.2 Significance and Limitations of the Study

This study provides a broad picture of misinformation research. Focusing on understanding the current status of this field, including characteristics of existing literature, topics explored by scholars, theories being applied, and suggestions from authors on future directions. As fighting misinformation is an ongoing topic in information studies, results from this study help researchers develop and plan their research ideas and projects. Also, this study provides evidence to inform schools that we need to develop related curricula on understanding and fighting misinformation to educate future information professionals.

This study has several limitations: we had to limit our data set to journal articles in the recent 12 years to complete the study in a manageable timeframe. Many papers related to misinformation may be published in other venues, such as books and conference proceedings. However, as shown in the initial exploratory data analysis of Stage II, the number of journal articles accounts for nearly 70%, compared to that of conference, books, and others, proving a reasonable data sample. Another limitation is due to the data incompleteness in the existing databases: we had to drop a significant number of data (almost 41% of 9,502 journal articles) which metadata needed for our meta-analysis are missing. Therefore, our driven implications and conclusions might not be scalable for the whole science community; The third limitation is, due to time constraints, our content analysis had only focused on theories and future directions in LIS; the two areas that most interest the authors. The investigation could be more extensive and deeper, for example, to summarize different research designs, or identify new theories or models originally targeting and curbing misinformation.

6 Summary and Future Research

This study conducts systematic literature review to understand misinformation research topics, theories applied, and future directions as proposed by information scholars. Through a systematic approach, we selected 5,586 articles for automatic analysis and 151 articles in library and information science for manual content analysis. Our analysis discovered that misinformation research had attracted broad interests from many disciplines and extensive research has been conducted in LIS.

To address the limitations of this study, we plan to continue our analysis using the same dataset to build an ontology of misinformation, then extend the dataset to expand the ontology. Finally, guided by ontology, we will explore specific topics, such as developing models, strategies, curricula, and guidelines to help organizations and the public fight misinformation. Python codes and our analysis results are publicly available on our GitHub.[4]

References

1. Lim, S.: Academic library guides for tackling fake news: a content analysis. J. Acad. Librariansh. **46**(5), 102195 (2020)
2. Revez, J., Corujo, L.: Librarians against fake news: a systematic literature review of library practices (Jan 2018–Sept 2020). J. Acad. Librariansh. **47**(2), 102304 (2021). https://doi.org/10.1016/j.acalib.2020.102304
3. Fetzer, J.H.: Information, misinformation, and disinformation. Minds Mach. **14**(2) (2004)
4. Karlova, N.A., Lee, J.H.: Notes from the underground city of disinformation: a conceptual investigation. Proc. Am. Soc. Inf. Sci. Technol. **48**(1), 1–9 (2011)
5. Spinney, L.: In Congo, fighting a virus and a groundswell of fake news. Science **363**(6424), 213–214 (2019). https://doi.org/10.1126/science.363.6424.213
6. Smith, J.H., Bastian, N.D.: A ranked solution for social media fact checking using epidemic spread modeling. Inf. Sci. **589**, 550–563 (2022)
7. Allcott, H., Gentzkow, M.: Social media and fake news in the 2016 election. J. Econ. Perspect. **31**(2), 211–236 (2017)
8. Wang, Y., McKee, M., Torbica, A., Stuckler, D.: Systematic literature review on the spread of health-related misinformation on social media. Soc. Sci. Med. **240**, 112552 (2019)
9. Wu, L., Morstatter, F., Carley, K.M., Liu, H.: Misinformation in social media: definition, manipulation, and detection. ACM SIGKDD Explor. Newsl. **21**(2), 80–90 (2019)
10. Zrnec, A., Poˇzenel, M., Lavbiˇc, D.: Users' ability to perceive misinformation: an information quality assessment approach. Inf. Process. Manage. **59**(1), 102739 (2022)

[4] https://github.com/HuyenNguyenHelen/Misinformation.

11. Lazer, D.M., et al.: The science of fake news. Science **359**(6380), 1094–1096 (2018)
12. Qinyu, E., Sakura, O., Li, G.: Mapping the field of misinformation correction and its effects: a review of four decades of research. Soc. Sci. Inf. **60**(4), 522–547 (2021). https://doi.org/10.1177/05390184211053759
13. Gough, D., Thomas, J.: Systematic reviews of research in education: aims, myths and multiple methods. Rev. Educ. **4**(1), 84–102 (2016)
14. Rubin, V.L.: Disinformation and misinformation triangle: a conceptual model for "fake news" epidemic, causal factors and interventions. J. Doc. **75**(5), 1013–1034 (2019)
15. Hopp, T.: Fake news self-efficacy, fake news identification, and content sharing on Facebook. J. Inform. Tech. Polit. **19**(2), 229–252 (2022)
16. Chen, H., Chen, J., Nguyen, H.: Demystifying covid-19 publications: institutions, journals, concepts, and topics. J. Med. Libr. Assoc.: JMLA **109**(3), 395 (2021)
17. Campos, R., Mangaravite, V., Pasquali, A., Jorge, A., Nunes, C., Jatowt, A.: Yake! keyword extraction from single documents using multiple local features. Inf. Sci. **509**, 257–289 (2020)
18. Alghamdi, R., Alfalqi, K.: A survey of topic modeling in text mining. Int. J. Adv. Comput. Sci. Appl. (IJACSA) **6**(1) (2015)
19. Bellaouar, S., Bellaouar, M.M., Ghada, I.E.: Topic modeling: comparison of LSA and LDA on scientific publications. In: 2021 4th International Conference on Data Storage and Data Engineering, pp. 59–64 (2021)
20. Young, J.C., Boyd, B., Yefimova, K., Wedlake, S., Coward, C., Hapel, R.: The role of libraries in misinformation programming: a research agenda. J. Librariansh. Inf. Sci. **53**(4), 539–550 (2021)
21. Paris, B., Carmien, K., Marshall, M.: "We want to do more, but…": new jersey public library approaches to misinformation. Libr. Inf. Sci. Res. **44**(2), 101157 (2022)
22. Chun Tie, Y., Birks, M., Francis, K.: Grounded theory research: a design framework for novice researchers. SAGE Open Med. **7**, 2050312118822927 (2019)
23. Bianchini, C., Truccolo, I., Bidoli, E., Group, C.I.Q.A., Mazzocut, M.: Avoiding misleading information: a study of complementary medicine online information for cancer patients. Libr. Inf. Sci. Res. **41**(1), 67–77 (2019)
24. Blanco-Herrero, D., Amores, J.J., Sánchez-Holgado, P.: Citizen perceptions of fake news in Spain: socioeconomic, demographic, and ideological differences. Publications **9**(3), 35 (2021)
25. El Rayess, M., Chebl, C., Mhanna, J., Hage, R.-M.: Fake news judgement: the case of undergraduate students at Notre Dame University-Louaize, Lebanon. Ref. Serv. Rev. **46**(1), 146–149 (2018)
26. Johnston, N.: Living in the world of fake news: High school students' evaluation of information from social media sites. J. Aust. Libr. Inf. Assoc. **69**(4), 430–450 (2020)
27. Shankar, R., Ahmad, T.: Information technology laws: mapping the evolution and impact of social media regulation in India. DESIDOC J. Libr. Inf. Technol. **41**(4) (2021)
28. Christensen, B.: Cyber state capacity: A model of authoritarian durability, ICTs, and emerging media. Gov. Inf. Q. **36**(3), 460–468 (2019)
29. Kigerl, A.C.: Evaluation of the can spam act: testing deterrence and other influences of e-mail spammer legal compliance over time. Soc. Sci. Comput. Rev. **33**(4), 440–458 (2015)
30. Gaozhao, D.: Flagging fake news on social media: an experimental study of media consumers' identification of fake news. Gov. Inf. Q. **38**(3), 101591 (2021)
31. Baber, H., Fanea-Ivanovici, M., Lee, Y.-T., Tinmaz, H.: A bibliometric analysis of digital literacy research and emerging themes pre-during covid-19 pandemic. Inf. Learn. Sci. **123**(3/4), 214–232 (2022). https://doi.org/10.1108/ILS-10-2021-0090
32. Patra, R.K., Pandey, N., Sudarsan, D.: Bibliometric analysis of fake news indexed in web of science and scopus (2001–2020). Global Knowledge, Memory and Communication (ahead-of-print) (2022)

33. Adams, J.: Information and misinformation in bibliometric time-trend analysis. J. Informet. **12**(4), 1063–1071 (2018)
34. Janmohamed, K., et al.: Interventions to mitigate covid-19 misinformation: a systematic review and meta-analysis. J. Health Commun. **26**(12), 846–857 (2021)
35. Awan, T.M., Aziz, M., Sharif, A., Ch, T.R., Jasam, T., Alvi, Y.: Fake news during the pandemic times: a systematic literature review using prisma. Open Inf. Sci. **6**(1), 49–60 (2022)
36. Yılmazel, I.B., Arslan, A.: An intrinsic evaluation of the waterloo spam rankings of the clueweb09 and clueweb12 datasets. J. Inf. Sci. **47**(1), 41–57 (2021)
37. Sedhai, S., Sun, A.: An analysis of 14 million tweets on hashtagoriented spamming. J. Am. Soc. Inf. Sci. **68**(7), 1638–1651 (2017)
38. Zamir, A., Khan, H.U., Mehmood, W., Iqbal, T., Akram, A.U.: A feature-centric spam email detection model using diverse supervised machine learning algorithms. Electron. Libr. **38**(3), 633–657 (2020). https://doi.org/10.1108/EL-07-2019-0181
39. Trivedi, S.K., Dey, S.: A novel committee selection mechanism for combining classifiers to detect unsolicited emails. VINE J. Inf. Knowl. Manag. Syst. **46**(4), 524–548 (2016)
40. Choi, E.B., Kim, J., Jeong, D., Park, E., del Pobil, A.P.: Detecting agro: korean trolling and clickbaiting behaviour in online environments. J. Inf. Sci. 01655515221074325 (2022)
41. Shrivas, A.K., Dewangan, A.K., Ghosh, S., Singh, D.: Development of proposed ensemble model for spam e-mail classification. Inf. Technol. Control **50**(3) (2021)
42. Resende, A., Railsback, D., Dowsley, R., Nascimento, A.C., Aranha, D.F.: Fast privacy-preserving text classification based on secure multiparty computation. IEEE Trans. Inf. Forensics Secur. **17**, 428–442 (2022)
43. Del-Fresno-García, Mi., Manfredi-Sánchez, J.-L.: Politics, hackers and partisan networking. misinformation, national utility and free election in the Catalan independence movement. Prof. Inf. **27**(6), 1225 (2018). https://doi.org/10.3145/epi.2018.nov.06
44. Al-Zaman, M.S.: A thematic analysis of misinformation in India during the covid-19 pandemic. Int. Inf. Libr. Rev. **54**(2), 128–138 (2022)
45. Velichety, S., Shrivastava, U.: Quantifying the impacts of online fake news on the equity value of social media platforms–evidence from twitter. Int. J. Inf. Manage. **64**, 102474 (2022)
46. Lim, L.P., Singh, M.M.: Resolving the imbalance issue in short messaging service spam dataset using cost-sensitive techniques. J. Inf. Secur. Appl. **54**, 102558 (2020)
47. Al-Zoubi, A., Alqatawna, J., Faris, H., Hassonah, M.A.: Spam profiles detection on social networks using computational intelligence methods: the effect of the lingual context. J. Inf. Sci. **47**(1), 58–81 (2021)
48. Ma, J., Luo, Y.: The classification of rumour standpoints in online social network based on combinatorial classifiers. J. Inf. Sci. **46**(2), 191–204 (2020)
49. Kerr, E., Lee, C.A.L.: Trolls maintained: baiting technological infrastructures of informational justice. Inf. Commun. Soc. **24**(1), 1–18 (2021)
50. Bringula, R.P., Catacutan-Bangit, A.E., Garcia, M.B., Gonzales, J.P.S., Valderama, A.M.C.: "Who is gullible to political disinformation?": predicting susceptibility of university students to fake news. J. Inform. Tech. Polit. **19**(2), 165–179 (2022)
51. Shan, G., Zhao, B., Clavin, J.R., Zhang, H., Duan, S.: Poligraph: intrusion-tolerant and distributed fake news detection system. IEEE Trans. Inf. Forensics Secur. **17**, 28–41 (2021)
52. Antenore, M., Camacho Rodriguez, J.M., Panizzi, E.: A comparative study of bot detection techniques with an application in twitter covid-19 discourse. Soc. Sci. Comput. Rev. 08944393211073733 (2022)
53. Zeng, J., Chan, C.-h.: A cross-national diagnosis of infodemics: comparing the topical and temporal features of misinformation around covid-19 in China, India, the US, Germany and France. Online Inf. Rev. (2021)

54. Lu, H.-Y., Yang, J., Fang, W., Song, X., Wang, C.: A deep neural networks-based fusion model for covid-19 rumor detection from online social media. Data Technol. Appl. **56**(5), 806–824 (2022). https://doi.org/10.1108/DTA-06-2021-0160
55. Rastogi, A., Mehrotra, M., Ali, S.S.: Effective opinion spam detection: a study on review metadata versus content. J. Data Inf. Sci. **5**(2), 76–110 (2020)
56. Luo, Y., Ma, J., Yeo, C.K.: Exploiting user network topology and comment semantic for accurate rumour stance recognition on social media. J. Inf. Sci. **48**(5), 660–675 (2022)
57. Chen, X.K., Na, J.-C., Tan, L.K.-W., Chong, M., Choy, M.: Exploring how online responses change in response to debunking messages about covid-19 on WhatsApp. Online Inf. Rev. **46**(6), 1184–1204 (2022). https://doi.org/10.1108/OIR-08-2021-0422
58. Aiwan, F., Zhaofeng, Y.: Image spam filtering using convolutional neural networks. Pers. Ubiquit. Comput. **22**(5–6), 1029–1037 (2018). https://doi.org/10.1007/s00779-018-1168-8
59. Imam, N.H., Vassilakis, V.G., Kolovos, D.: Ocr post-correction for detecting adversarial text images. J. Inf. Secur. Appl. **66**, 103170 (2022)
60. Wu, H., Zhou, J., Tian, J., Liu, J., Qiao, Y.: Robust image forgery detection against transmission over online social networks. IEEE Trans. Inf. Forensics Secur. **17**, 443–456 (2022)
61. Wang, H.C., Chiang, Y.H., Lin, S.T.: Spam detection and high-quality features to analyse question–answer pairs. Electron. Libr. **38**(5/6), 1013–1033 (2020). https://doi.org/10.1108/EL-05-2020-0120
62. Skoric, B., de Vreede, N.: The spammed code offset method. IEEE Trans. Inf. Forensics Secur. **9**(5), 875–884 (2014)
63. Bunker, D.: Who do you trust? the digital destruction of shared situational awareness and the covid-19 infodemic. Int. J. Inf. Manage. **55**, 102201 (2020)
64. Zhuang, X., Zhu, Y., Chang, C.-C., Peng, Q., Khurshid, F.: A unified score propagation model for web spam demotion algorithm. Inf. Retr. J. **20**(6), 547–574 (2017). https://doi.org/10.1007/s10791-017-9307-9
65. Kiwi, M., Caro, C.T.: Fifo queues are bad for rumor spreading. IEEE Trans. Inf. Theory **63**(2), 1159–1166 (2016)
66. Colladon, A.F., Gloor, P.A.: Measuring the impact of spammers on e-mail and twitter networks. Int. J. Inf. Manage. **48**, 254–262 (2019)
67. Giachanou, A., Rosso, P., Crestani, F.: The impact of emotional signals on credibility assessment. J. Am. Soc. Inf. Sci. **72**(9), 1117–1132 (2021)
68. Masip, P., Suau, J., Ruiz-Caballero, C.: Perceptions on media and disinformation: Ideology and polarization in the Spanish media system. Prof. Inf. **29**(5) (2020)
69. Zhang, Z., Zhang, Z., Li, H.: Predictors of the authenticity of internet health rumours. Health Info. Libr. J. **32**(3), 195–205 (2015)
70. Herrero-Gutiérrez, F.-J., Urchaga-Litago, J.-D.: The importance of rumors in the Spanish sports press: an analysis of news about signings appearing in the newspapers Marca, As. Mundo Deportivo And Sport. Publications **9**(1), 9 (2021)
71. Baptista, J.P., Correia, E., Gradim, A., Piñeiro-Naval, V.: The influence of political ideology on fake news belief: the Portuguese case. Publications **9**(2), 23 (2021). https://doi.org/10.3390/publications9020023
72. Montesi, M.: Understanding fake news during the covid-19 health crisis from the perspective of information behaviour: The case of Spain. J. Librariansh. Inf. Sci. **53**(3), 454–465 (2021)
73. Savolainen, R.: Assessing the credibility of covid-19 vaccine mis/disinformation in online discussion. J. Inf. Sci. 01655515211040653 (2021)
74. Charbonneau, D.H., Vardell, E.: The impact of covid-19 on reference services: a national survey of academic health sciences librarians. J. Med. Libr. Assoc.: JMLA **110**(1), 56 (2022)
75. Moreno, A., Tench, R., Verhoeven, P.: Trust in public relations in the age of mitrusted media: a European perspective. Publication **9**(1) (2021)

76. Faix, A.., Fyn, A..: Framing fake news: Misinformation and the ACRL framework. portal: Libraries and the Academy **20**(3), 495–508 (2020). https://doi.org/10.1353/pla.2020.0027
77. Igbinovia, M.O., Okuonghae, O., Adebayo, J.O.: Information literacy competence in curtailing fake news about the covid-19 pandemic among undergraduates in Nigeria. Ref. Serv. Rev. **49**(1), 3–18 (2020). https://doi.org/10.1108/RSR-06-2020-0037
78. Perry, H.B.: Understanding financial conflict of interest: implications for information literacy instruction. Commun. Inf. Lit. **12**(2), 215–225 (2018)
79. Haggar, E.: Fighting fake news: exploring George Orwell's relationship to information literacy. J. Doc. **76**(5), 961–979 (2020)
80. Krutkowski, S., Taylor-Harman, S., Gupta, K.: De-biasing on university campuses in the age of misinformation. Ref. Serv. Rev. **48**(1), 113–128 (2019). https://doi.org/10.1108/RSR-10-2019-0075
81. Pérez-Escoda, A., Pedrero-Esteban, L.M., Rubio-Romero, J., Jiménez-Narros, C.: Fake news reaching young people on social networks: distrust challenging media literacy. Publications **9**(2), 24 (2021)
82. Lin, T.-C., Huang, S.-L., Liao, W.-X.: Examining the antecedents of everyday rumor retransmission. Inf. Technol. People (2021)
83. Sampat, B., Raj, S.: Fake or real news? understanding the gratifications and personality traits of individuals sharing fake news on social media platforms. Aslib J. Inf. Manag. (2022)
84. Juneström, A.: An emerging genre of contemporary fact-checking. J. Doc. (2020)
85. Pal, A., Banerjee, S.: Internet users beware, you follow online health rumors (more than counter-rumors) irrespective of risk propensity and prior endorsement. Inf. Technol. People (2020)
86. Evanson, C., Sponsel, J.: From syndication to misinformation: how undergraduate students engage with and evaluate digital news. Commun. Inf. Lit. **13**(2), 228–250 (2019)
87. Simon, T., Goldberg, A., Adini, B.: Socializing in emergencies—a review of the use of social media in emergency situations. Int. J. Inf. Manage. **35**(5), 609–619 (2015)
88. Al-Zaman, M.S.: Prevalence and source analysis of covid-19 misinformation in 138 countries. IFLA J. **48**(1), 189–204 (2022)
89. Ahmadinia, H., Eriksson-Backa, K., Nikou, S.: Health information seeking behaviour during exceptional times: a case study of Persian-speaking minorities in Finland. Libr. Inf. Sci. Res. **44**(2), 101156 (2022)
90. Sharma, A., Kapoor, P.S.: Message sharing and verification behaviour on social media during the covid-19 pandemic: a study in the context of India and the USA. Online Inf. Rev. **46**(1), 22–39 (2021)
91. Dhawan, D., Bekalu, M., Pinnamaneni, R., McCloud, R., Viswanath, K.: Covid-19 news and misinformation: do they matter for public health prevention? J. Health Commun. **26**(11), 799–808 (2021)
92. Fichman, P., Sanfilippo, M.R.: The bad boys and girls of cyberspace: how gender and context impact perception of and reaction to trolling. Soc. Sci. Comput. Rev. **33**(2), 163–180 (2015)
93. Wang, X., Zhang, M., Fan, W., Zhao, K.: Understanding the spread of covid-19 misinformation on social media: the effects of topics and a political leader's nudge. J. Am. Soc. Inf. Sci. **73**(5), 726–737 (2022)
94. López-Marcos, C., Vicente-Fernández, P.: Fact checkers facing fake news and disinformation in the digital age: a comparative analysis between Spain and United Kingdom. Publications **9**(3), 36 (2021). https://doi.org/10.3390/publications9030036
95. Oliphant, T.: Emerging (information) realities and epistemic injustice. J. Am. Soc. Inf. Sci. **72**(8), 951–962 (2021)
96. Sanfilippo, M., Yang, S., Fichman, P.: Trolling here, there, and everywhere: perceptions of trolling behaviors in context. J. Am. Soc. Inf. Sci. **68**(10), 2313–2327 (2017)

97. King, K.K., Wang, B.: Diffusion of real versus misinformation during a crisis event: a big data-driven approach. Int. J. Inf. Manage. 102390 (2021)
98. Barakat, K.A., Dabbous, A., Tarhini, A.: An empirical approach to understanding users' fake news identification on social media. Online Inf. Rev. (2021)
99. Stone, M., Aravopoulou, E., Evans, G., Aldhaen, E., Parnell, B.D.: From information mismanagement to misinformation–the dark side of information management. Bottom Line (2018)
100. Yu, W., Chen, N., Chen, J.: Characterizing Chinese online public opinions towards the covid-19 recovery policy. Electron. Libr. (2022)
101. Radu, R., Kettemann, M.C., Meyer, T., Shahin, J.: Normfare: norm entrepreneurship in internet governance. Telecommun. Policy **45**(6), 102148 (2021)
102. Tan, W.-K., Hsu, C.Y.: The application of emotions, sharing motivations, and psychological distance in examining the intention to share covid-19-related fake news. Online Inf. Rev. (ahead-of-print) (2022)
103. Soler, J., Cooper, A.: Unexpected emails to submit your work: spam or legitimate offers? the implications for novice English l2 writers. Publications **7**(1), 7 (2019)
104. Nonnecke, B., et al.: Harass, mislead, & polarize: an analysis of twitter political bots' tactics in targeting the immigration debate before the 2018 us midterm election. J. Inf. Technol. Politics 1–12 (2021)
105. Esteban-Navarro, M.-Á., Nogales-Bocio, A.-I., García-Madurga, M.-Á., Morte-Nadal, T.: Spanish fact-checking services: an approach to their business models. Publications **9**(3), 38 (2021). https://doi.org/10.3390/publications9030038
106. Mertoğlu, U., Genç, B.: Automated fake news detection in the age of digital libraries. Inf. Techno. Libr. **39**(4) (2020)
107. Kwon, K.H., Rao, H.R.: Cyber-rumor sharing under a homeland security threat in the context of government internet surveillance: the case of south-north Korea conflict. Gov. Inf. Q. **34**(2), 307–316 (2017)
108. Lyu, H.-S.: Internet policy in Korea: A preliminary framework for assigning moral and legal responsibility to agents in internet activities. Gov. Inf. Q. **29**(3), 394–402 (2012)
109. Deng, S., Fu, S., Liu, Y., Li, H.: Modelling users' trust in online health rumours: an experiment-based study in China (2021)
110. Luo, Y., Ma, J., Yeo, C.K.: Identification of rumour stances by considering network topology and social media comments. J. Inf. Sci. **48**(1), 118–130 (2022)
111. Wang, P., Yixia, H., Li, Q., Yang, H.: Trust mechanisms underlying the self-efficacy-rumour use relationship. Electron. Libr. **39**(2), 373–387 (2021). https://doi.org/10.1108/EL-12-2020-0332
112. Elbanna, A., Bunker, D., Levine, L., Sleigh, A.: Emergency management in the changing world of social media: framing the research agenda with the stakeholders through engaged scholarship. Int. J. Inf. Manage. **47**, 112–120 (2019)
113. Lor, P., Wiles, B., Britz, J.: Re-thinking information ethics: truth, conspiracy theories, and librarians in the covid-19 era. Libri **71**(1), 1–14 (2021)
114. Froehlich, T.: Some thoughts evoked by Peter Lor, Bradley Wiles, and Johannes Britz, "re-thinking information ethics: Truth, conspiracy theories, and librarians in the covid-19 era", in Libri, March 2021. Libri **71**(3), 219–225 (2021)
115. Farfán, J., Mazo, M.E.: Disinformation and responsibility in young people in Spain during the covid-19 era. Publications **9**(3), 40 (2021). https://doi.org/10.3390/publications9030040
116. Cheng, J.W., Mitomo, H., Kamplean, A., Seo, Y.: Lesser evil? public opinion on regulating fake news in Japan, South Korea, and Thailand– a three-country comparison. Telecommun. Policy **45**(9), 102185 (2021)

117. Herasimenka, A., Bright, J., Knuutila, A., Howard, P.N.: Misinformation and professional news on largely unmoderated platforms: the case of telegram. J. Inf. Technol. Politics 1–15 (2022)
118. Xiao, X., Su, Y.: Integrating reasoned action approach and message sidedness in the era of misinformation: the case of HPV vaccination promotion. J. Health Commun. **26**(6), 371–380 (2021)
119. Oguz, F., Holt, M.: Library blogs and user participation: a survey about comment spam in library blogs. Library Hi Tech **29**(1), 173–188 (2011)
120. Flores-Saviaga, C., Savage, S.: Fighting disaster misinformation in Latin America: the# 19s Mexican earthquake case study. Pers. Ubiquit. Comput. **25**(2), 353–373 (2021)
121. Muriel-Torrado, E., Pereira, D.B.: Correlations between the concepts of disinformation and Fogg's behavior model. Transinformaciao **32** (2020)
122. Elmwood, V.: The journalistic approach: evaluating web sources in an age of mass disinformation. Commun. Inf. Lit. **14**(2), 269–286 (2020)
123. Vamanu, I., Zak, E.: Information source and content: articulating two key concepts for information evaluation. Inf. Learn. Sci. (2022)
124. LaPierre, S.S., Kitzie, V.: "lots of questions about 'fake news'": How public libraries have addressed media literacy, 2016–2018. Public Libr. Q. **38**(4), 428–452 (2019)
125. de Vicente Domínguez, A.M., Beriain Bañares, A., Sierra Sánchez, J.: Young Spanish adults and disinformation: do they identify and spread fake news and are they literate in it? Publications **9**(1), 2 (2021)
126. Agarwal, N.K., Alsaeedi, F.: Creation, dissemination and mitigation: toward a disinformation behavior framework and model. Aslib J. Inf. Manag. (2021)
127. Cano-Orón, L., Calvo, D., Llorca-Abad, G., Mestre-Pérez, R.: Media crisis and disinformation: the participation of digital newspapers in the dissemination of a denialist hoax. Prof. Inf. **30**(4) (2021)
128. Jane, E.A.: Flaming? what flaming? the pitfalls and potentials of researching online hostility. Ethics Inf. Technol. **17**(1), 65–87 (2015)
129. Patra, R.K., Pandey, N.: Disinformation on novel coronavirus (covid19): a content analysis of news published on fact-checking sites in India. DESIDOC J. Libr. Inf. Technol. **41**(4) (2021)
130. Sun, L.H., Fichman, P.: The collective trolling lifecycle. J. Am. Soc. Inf. Sci. **71**(7), 770–783 (2020)
131. Chipidza, W., Krewson, C., Gatto, N., Akbaripourdibazar, E., Gwanzura, T.: Ideological variation in preferred content and source credibility on reddit during the covid-19 pandemic. Big Data Soc. **9**(1), 20539517221076490 (2022)

The Potential of Digital Literacy to Curb Problematic Information: An Integrative Literature Review

Stacey Wedlake(✉) and Charles Bugre

University of Washington Information School, Seattle, WA 98115, USA
staceyaw@uw.edu

Abstract. In this integrative literature review, we examine how digital literacy can help adults identify problematic information (misinformation, disinformation, etc.). We found that some studies do indicate that digital literacy can help address problematic information, but how digital literacy is conceptualized and operationalized needs to change. Digital literacy approaches need to incorporate lateral reading skills and how structural factors influence how information is presented and consumed online. Additionally, incorporating games into instructional practices may help diffuse the political implications of teaching about problematic information. However, digital literacy instruction cannot cure the global problem of problematic information and more community-based, rigorous research needs to explore the effectiveness of instruction.

Keywords: Digital literacy · Media literacy · Information literacy · Misinformation · Disinformation

1 Introduction

The 2016 election and COVID-19 pandemic brought a renewed focus to online problematic information which is "inaccurate, misleading, inappropriately attributed, or all together fabricated" [1]. This umbrella term includes misinformation, disinformation, fake news, information disorder, or conspiracy theories; all of which can lead to physical or emotional harm and interfere with proper functioning of public institutions [1]. A subject of much discussion in academia and popular press has focused on improving individual skills for identifying online problematic information [2–4]. The kinds of literacies, competencies, and skills people need to navigate our current online information environment are categorized under a broad set of categories such as "digital literacy," "media literacy," "information literacy," "news literacy," "critical literacy," "civic online reasoning," multi-literacy," and "metaliteracy" [3, 4]. These frameworks overlap and complement each other and are more of a reflection of their disciplinary background than mutually exclusive approaches [5].

"Digital literacy" as defined by the American Library Association's Digital Literacy Taskforce and the National Digital Inclusion Alliance (NDIA) is "the ability to use information and communication technologies to find, evaluate, create, and communicate

© The Author(s), under exclusive license to Springer Nature Switzerland AG 2023
I. Sserwanga et al. (Eds.): iConference 2023, LNCS 13971, pp. 395–404, 2023.
https://doi.org/10.1007/978-3-031-28035-1_28

information, requiring both cognitive and technical skills" [6]. In recent years, academic research has recognized digital literacy as "far broader than specific tasks, englobing the entire sphere of computer operation and media use in a cultural context" including identifying problematic information [7]. However, much of research on the use of digital literacy to curb problematic information focuses on K-12 and higher education students, but all adults need to know how to verify online information [4, 8–10]. After exiting formal education, adults learn additional digital literacy skills on their own from people in their personal networks and from such as public libraries, nonprofits, and community organizations [11]. These digital literacy educators teach people how to use information and communication tools through a variety of formats such as a classroom setting with an instructor, one-on-one, appointment-based assistance, or ad hoc help from a case manager [12]. The subjects taught by these classes can be far ranging and include getting online for the first time, navigating the internet, using common workplace software, and creating multimedia [13]. We recently conducted an analysis of recommended digital literacy resources and found a mixture of approaches to teaching about problematic information and some resources did not cover the topic at all [14].

To have a more complete understanding of how digital literacy intersects with discerning online problematic information, we conducted an integrative literature review to understand the following:

1. How does digital literacy help adults identify online problematic information?
2. What are the evidence-based practices for teaching digital literacy to adults for problematic information identification?

2 Methodology

To answer our research questions, we conducted an integrative literature review of publications from 2009–July 31, 2022. We began our search with the year 2009 because the United States Broadband and Telecommunications Opportunity Program (BTOP) began that year and provided $4.7 billion for broadband adoption, including digital literacy programs [15]. The purpose of an integrative literature review is to review, critique, and synthesize literature "in an integrated way such that new frameworks and perspectives on the topic are generated" [16]. One of the reasons we chose this approach is because it has the opportunity to "combine perspectives and insights from different fields or research traditions" [17]. The academic literature concerning problematic information and digital literacy spans many fields such as information science, education, and communication. Because of the dispersed nature of our topic, we searched the databases with the commonly used terms (misinformation OR disinformation OR "fake news") and then paired each one with the terms "digital literacy," "media literacy," and "information literacy." We expanded our search to include media and information literacy to capture the full range of literature across academic disciplines [5].

We searched the following databases: Library Information Science Source, Library & Information Science Abstracts (LISA), Communication Source, Web of Science, Academic Search Complete, ScienceDirect, Google Scholar, and ERIC. We also examined relevant citations from the selected literature. Our inclusion criteria included at least one of the following: a) examination of how digital literacy can or cannot be used to help people identify online problematic information, b) empirical research into the effects of digital literacy programs, and c) available in English. Our exclusion criteria included a) descriptions of programs without any empirical evaluation or assessment, b) only brief mentions of digital literacy and/or problematic information and not focused on how the two may intersect, c) focus on non-digital media literacy, d) focus on academic-related information skills (such as searching academic databases). We did not restrict the review to any particular country or region. Although our research questions focused on adults, we kept our search broader to identify best practices that may span age groups. After we applied the inclusion and exclusion criteria, we conducted a staged reviewed of all the literature collected (an initial review of the abstracts followed by an in-depth review) [18]. After completing this process, we had 39 papers included in our review and conducted a document analysis framed by our research questions [19].

3 Results

Only four papers were published before 2018: the earliest published in 2010. Almost half (19) were published in either 2021 or 2022. Despite not restricting the search geographically, most of the papers were focused on the United States or Western Europe.

3.1 Digital LITEracy's Ability to Help Adults Identify Online Problematic Information

In answering our first research question, how does digital literacy help adults identify online problematic information, we grouped our findings into three sub-categories:

- Digital literacy can improve problematic information identification.
- Digital literacy needs a new conceptualization.
- Digital literacy cannot be the only solution to problematic information.

Digital Literacy Can Improve Problematic Information Identification. Six studies attempted to quantitively measure whether digital literacy had an impact on someone's ability to identify problematic information. All six found that digital literacy increased the ability to identify problematic information across different geographies – United States [20–22], Indonesia [23], Ghana [24], and Nigeria [25]. However, one study found that despite an increase in identification ability, digital literacy skills did not prevent people from sharing problematic information [20]. The studies measured digital literacy skills using self-assessments (such as rating oneself on a Likert-scale), but each study used different question sets. One subset of these studies attempted to measure someone's existing digital literacy skills and compared individuals of different skill sets with their ability to identify problematic information [20, 22, 23]. In the other subset, the studies set up an experiment that had treatment and control groups to measure the success of a specific digital literacy intervention [21, 24, 25]. The interventions tested varied from watching videos and memes [21], to unspecified training [24], to an eight week course [25]. The interventions' effectiveness was tested shortly or immediately after receiving the treatment. Due to a lack of longer-term testing, it is unclear on whether the effectiveness will wear off over time.

Digital Literacy Can Help But Needs a New Conceptualization. Overall, the papers had broad agreement that a more traditional approach to digital literacy that focuses solely on skills was not sufficient to learn how to identify problematic information. For example, American students have been receiving information evaluation instruction for decades but it "hasn't prevented a significant portion of the population from fervidly embracing an elaborately populated world of disinformation while rejecting 'mainstream media'" [4]. In a review of library information literacy practices, Revez and Corujo identified librarian taught methods of information evaluation as two pronged: 1) task-oriented strategies and 2) critical thinking approaches; sometimes these approaches are taught concurrently but most often "critical thinking" is an advanced step beyond the task-based strategies [26]. Additionally, even though librarians recognize the emotional and cognitive-based aspect of problematic information, it is largely absent from their practices [26]. The papers divide up into two sets of arguments to improve digital literacy instruction: 1) reframe digital literacy as metaliteracy 2) teach skills in context.

Reframe Digital Literacy as Metaliteracy. Several authors recommend shifting from a conceptualization of digital literacy to *metaliteracy*, "an overarching, self-referential, and comprehensive framework…a shift in emphasis from discrete skills to collaborative production and sharing of information using participatory interactive technologies" [27]. Adopting *metaliteracy* across disciplines "should decrease theoretical discrepancies, connect practical applications and strengthen central lifelong learning goals across literacy types" [28]. Cooke advocates for *metaliteracy* for teaching about problematic information because "*metaliteracy* asks us to understand the format type and delivery mode of information; evaluate dynamic content critically; evaluate user feedback of information; produce original content in multiple media formats; create a context for user-generated information; understand personal privacy, information ethics, and intellectual property issues; and share information in participatory environments" [3]. A variety of educators can implement metaliteracy (college instructors, public and academic librarians, community educators) in their instruction due to its adaptability in "different formats and within both scholarly and non-scholarly environments" and create a shared understanding of learning goals [29].

Teach Skills in Context. A set of papers advocate for teaching digital literacy skills in context of the emotional, sociocultural, psychological, interpersonal, structural, and historical factors that play a role in information evaluation [30–32]. Caulfield writes "most literacies are heavily domain-dependent and based not on skills, but on a body of knowledge that comes from mindful immersion in a context" [33]. For example, if students understand how a website makes money they "could understand the incentives for lies and spin, and how these incentives differ from site to site" [33]. Tagg and Sergeant advocate for "social digital literacies" which build upon individual capabilities "but also situates both within a broader awareness of how the flow of information in society as a whole is managed in the era of social media, and the implications this can have for the maintenance of an effective society" [31].

Digital literacy instruction should not simply include skills to identify discrete pieces of information as true or false "but of identifying the forms of bias that are present in all sources of information more broadly" [34]. One example, from Tynes et al., argues for "critical race digital literacy" because "young people will need to able to identify race-related messaging" and "learn the ability to unmask hidden white supremacist narratives in online information" [35]. Educators should "frame discussions of knowledge through the lens of democracy rather than through partisan political positions…including clearly reject the notion that truth is simply a matter of political allegiance or personal choice" [4]. Sulzer uses three framing ideas in her instruction to encourage students to explore the interplay of power and digital tools: 1) Representation (How do digital technologies present the world to its users? Who is missing and why?), 2) Access (How is information made available? Who has access and why?), and 3) Contestation (How are meanings contested within digital environments? Who is involved and why?) [36]. Nichols and LeBlanc argue an adoption of an ecological orientation over literacy– "how users produce, share, access, and interpret messages, but tracing the wider relations of human and non-human activities that condition such practices in a given environment" [37]. However, most of these authors do not address the potential political threat that some public educators could face addressing these topics and what approaches could help them minimize risk [30].

Digital Literacy Cannot be the Only Solution to Problematic Information. No matter the approach or framework, several authors had doubts that digital literacy instruction could have a meaningful impact on problematic information. An ongoing challenge toward effective instruction is that this type of learning has no particular place in the curriculum and "the people who care about it the most have had their jobs felled by the austerity axe" [4]. Additionally, it is a challenge to develop comprehensive measures for the more complex conceptual frameworks to understand effectiveness [28]. Digital literacy can also be leaned on as an ineffective cure all – asking educators to fix structural problems of "digital capitalism" through instructional methods [34]. Thus, problematic information needs "global level" solutions through technological methods [2].

3.2 Teaching Digital Literacy for Problematic Information

Despite some authors' doubts of the effectiveness of digital literacy interventions, to answer our question regarding what are the evidence-based practices for teaching digital literacy to adults for problematic information identification, we identified empirical studies that examined what content to include and by what method. [38]. As previous research has shown [26], only a subset of studies empirically measured the effectiveness of methods or content approaches. In those that did measure effectiveness, papers found teaching lateral reading an important skill and using games as a promising pedagogical methodology.

Important Skill: Lateral Reading. Problematic information can often pass checklists used by common digital literacy frameworks [33, 39]. These checklists use "vertical reading," staying on the webpage to assess credibility, but this method has proven less effective in helping people identify problematic information [11, 33, 38–40]. As a contrast, journalists and professional fact-checkers do not use checklists but read laterally, using the web to verify information found on the webpage, and thus more successfully identify problematic information [38, 41]. Lateral reading refers to the strategy of scanning multiple web search results to get a sense of what others say about a piece of information or an information source of interest before deciding to read the content itself [38, 41–44]. One author was skeptical that people would maintain these approaches outside of the classroom [34]. However, a study of a lateral reading education intervention of 2,324 Canadian students in grades 7–12 found that lateral reading instruction improved their ability to accurately assess the credibility of sources and claims as compared to a control group and found no erosion in those strategies six weeks later [43]. However, as pointed out in the earlier critique of skills without context, lateral reading alone does not unearth the "material technical, and economic currents that underwrite" problematic information [37].

Teaching Methodologies: Games. Two studies identified games as an effective way to teach digital literacy skills to curb problematic information. Games can combine fun and apolitical strategies (such as fictional characters) to inoculate learners against the risk of problematic information "without the distraction of political stances and divisions" [45, 46]. The games took two different approaches. For instance, LAMBOOZLED! is a deck-building card game where players use a set of cards called "evidence" and "context" cards to justify if a fictional "news card" is real or fake [45]. Trustme is an online game-like quiz aimed at testing the impact of digital game-based learning to curb problematic information; players are given points and feedback on each quiz item [46]. The fictional nature of games is relevant since one of the obstacles in teaching digital literacy for problematic information identification is to not be seen by learners as advocating a certain political agenda [47]. However, the studies that demonstrated the effectiveness of games did not list all the skill sets in the games that participants were tested on or used a variety of different approaches. While Chang et al., in their game included teaching skepticism (making learners aware that both factual claims and opinions can be illustrated with evidence that looks convincing), it is difficult to determine how much skepticism readers should have [45]. Walsh captures the dangers of teaching skepticism vividly as follows: "want the users to be skeptical enough to investigate for evidence to verify the information, but not so skeptical that they would ignore accurate information in their quest for verification" [48]. Thus, while games may be promising and remove the instructor from any suspicion of partiality, the longer-term effects and the learning outcomes need more study.

4 Conclusion

Our review found that digital literacy has the potential to help adults identify problematic information, but more research is needed to understand the longer-term effectiveness of skills, conceptualization, teaching approaches, and instructor types. Due to the unreliability of self-assessments, future research should move away from relying on self-reporting to testing actual digital literacy knowledge and skills [23]. More accurate and unified digital literacy measures would give more confidence and clarity to what knowledge and skills help with problematic information identification. Although the need for digital literacy applies to all, how instruction is operationalized can differ across groups, and we need more understanding how digital literacy can support older adults [10], different racial and political groups [21, 35], and in communities outside of the United States and Europe. As for the skills taught, lateral reading appears a promising skill, but more investigation into its use with adults is needed. At the same time, more exploration is needed into how to incorporate skills with the emotion and cognitive-based aspects of problematic information and lessons on the broader ecosystem that influences information creation and dissemination [4, 26, 39]. Researchers can build relationships with public libraries, community organizations, and senior centers to design, implement, and evaluate effective programming [8, 10, 30, 49]. Instructors in these organizations have the community-level trust needed to educate about politically sensitive topics [31, 37, 50–53]. However, these educators need professional development and support to create effective interventions that are grounded in community-needs – including local political realities.

References

1. Jack, C.: Lexicon of Lies: Terms for Problematic Information. Data & Society (2017)
2. Sullivan, M.C.: Why librarians can't fight fake news. J. Librariansh. Inf. Sci. **51**, 1146–1156 (2019). https://doi.org/10.1177/0961000618764258
3. Cooke, N.A.: Fake News and Alternative Facts: Information Literacy in a Post-Truth Era. American Library Association, Chicago, United States (2018)
4. Fister, B.: Lizard people in the library. PIL Provocation Series, vol. 1, no. 1. Project Information Literacy (2021)
5. Hobbs, R.: Digital and Media Literacy: A Plan of Action. Aspen Institute, Washington, D.C. (2010)
6. NDIA: Definitions. https://www.digitalinclusion.org/definitions/
7. Tinmaz, H., Lee, Y.-T., Fanea-Ivanovici, M., Baber, H.: A systematic review on digital literacy. Smart Learn. Environ. **9**, 21 (2022). https://doi.org/10.1186/s40561-022-00204-y
8. Seo, H., Erba, J., Altschwager, D., Geana, M.: Evidence-based digital literacy class for older, low-income African-American adults. J. Appl. Commun. Res. **47**, 130–152 (2019). https://doi.org/10.1080/00909882.2019.1587176
9. Rasi, P., Vuojärvi, H., Rivinen, S.: Promoting media literacy among older people: a systematic review. Adult Educ. Q. **71**, 37–54 (2021). https://doi.org/10.1177/0741713620923755
10. Lee, N.M.: Fake news, phishing, and fraud: a call for research on digital media literacy education beyond the classroom. Commun. Educ. **67**, 460–466 (2018). https://doi.org/10.1080/03634523.2018.1503313
11. Rhinesmith, C., Kennedy, S.: Growing Healthy Digital Ecosystems During COVID-19 and Beyond. Benton Institute for Broadband & Society, Evanston, IL (2020)
12. Dahya, N., Garrido, M., Yefimova, K., Wedlake, S.: Technology access & education for refugee women in Seattle & king county. Technology & Social Change Group (2020)
13. Wedlake, S., Lothian, K., Keyes, D., Coward, C.: Digital Skill Sets for Diverse Users: A Comparison Framework for Curriculum and Competencies. Technology & Social Change Group. University of Washington Information School, Seattle (2019)
14. Bugre, C., Wedlake, S.: How do adult digital literacy curricula address problematic information? Proc. Assoc. Inf. Sci. Technol. **59**, 627–629 (2022). https://doi.org/10.1002/pra2.671

15. Hauge, J.A., Prieger, J.E.: Evaluating the impact of the American recovery and reinvestment act's BTOP on broadband adoption. Appl. Econ. **47**, 6553–6579 (2015). https://doi.org/10.1080/00036846.2015.1080810
16. Torraco, R.J.: Writing integrative literature reviews: using the past and present to explore the future. Hum. Resour. Dev. Rev. **15**, 404–428 (2016). https://doi.org/10.1177/1534484316671606
17. Snyder, H.: Literature review as a research methodology: an overview and guidelines. J. Bus. Res. **104**, 333–339 (2019). https://doi.org/10.1016/j.jbusres.2019.07.039
18. Torraco, R.J.: Writing integrative literature reviews: guidelines and examples. Hum. Resour. Dev. Rev. **4**, 356–367 (2005). https://doi.org/10.1177/1534484305278283
19. Bowen, G.A.: Document analysis as a qualitative research method. Qual. Res. J. **9**, 27–40 (2009). https://doi.org/10.3316/QRJ0902027
20. Sirlin, N., Epstein, Z., Arechar, A.A., Rand, D.G.: Digital literacy is associated with more discerning accuracy judgments but not sharing intentions. Harvard Kennedy School Misinformation Review (2021). https://doi.org/10.37016/mr-2020-83
21. Helmus, T.C., Marrone, J.V., Posard, M.N., Schlang, D.: Russian Propaganda Hits Its Mark: Experimentally Testing the Impact of Russian Propaganda and Counter-Interventions. RAND Corporation, Santa Monica, CA (2020)
22. Kahne, J., Bowyer, B.: Educating for democracy in a partisan age: confronting the challenges of motivated reasoning and misinformation. Am. Educ. Res. J. **54**, 3–34 (2017). https://doi.org/10.3102/0002831216679817
23. Khan, M.L., Idris, I.K.: Recognise misinformation and verify before sharing: a reasoned action and information literacy perspective. Behav. Inf. Technol. **38**, 1194–1212 (2019). https://doi.org/10.1080/0144929X.2019.1578828
24. Dame Adjin-Tettey, T.: Combating fake news, disinformation, and misinformation: experimental evidence for media literacy education. Cogent Arts Humanit. **9**, 2037229 (2022). https://doi.org/10.1080/23311983.2022.2037229
25. Apuke, O.D., Omar, B., unca, E. A.: Literacy concepts as an intervention strategy for improving fake news knowledge, detection skills, and curtailing the tendency to share fake news in Nigeria. Child Youth Serv. 1–16 (2022). https://doi.org/10.1080/0145935X.2021.2024758
26. Revez, J., Corujo, L.: Librarians against fake news: A systematic literature review of library practices (Jan. 2018–Sept. 2020). J. Acad. Librariansh. **47**, 102304 (2021). https://doi.org/10.1016/j.acalib.2020.102304
27. Mackey, T.P., Jacobson, T.E.: Reframing information literacy as a Metaliteracy | Mackey | college & research libraries. Coll. Res. Libr. **72**, 62–78 (2011). https://doi-org.offcampus.lib.washington.edu/10.5860/crl-76r1
28. Jones-Jang, S.M., Mortensen, T., Liu, J.: Does media literacy help identification of fake news? information literacy helps, but other literacies don't. Am. Behav. Sci. **65**, 371–388 (2021). https://doi.org/10.1177/0002764219869406
29. De Paor, S., Heravi, B.: Information literacy and fake news: How the field of librarianship can help combat the epidemic of fake news. J. Acad. Librariansh. **46**, 102218 (2020). https://doi.org/10.1016/j.acalib.2020.102218
30. Young, J.C., Boyd, B., Yefimova, K., Wedlake, S., Coward, C., Hapel, R.: The role of libraries in misinformation programming: a research agenda. J. Librariansh. Inf. Sci. **53**, 539–550 (2020). https://doi.org/10.1177/0961000620966650
31. Tagg, C., Seargeant, P.: Context design and critical language/media awareness: implications for a social digital literacies education. Linguist. Educ. **62**, 100776 (2021). https://doi.org/10.1016/j.linged.2019.100776
32. Lim, S.: Academic library guides for tackling fake news: a content analysis. J. Acad. Librariansh. **46**, 102195 (2020). https://doi.org/10.1016/j.acalib.2020.102195

33. Caulfield, M.: Yes, digital literacy. But Which One?. https://hapgood.us/2016/12/19/yes-digital-literacy-but-which-one/ (2016)
34. Buckingham, D.: Teaching media in a 'post-truth' age: fake news, media bias and the challenge for media/digital literacy education/La enseñanza mediática en la era de la posverdad: fake news, sesgo mediático y el reto para la educación en materia de alfabetización mediática y digital. Cult. Educ. **31**, 213–231 (2019). https://doi.org/10.1080/11356405.2019.1603814
35. Tynes, B.M., Stewart, A., Hamilton, M., Willis, H.A.: From google searches to Russian disinformation adolescent critical race digital literacy needs and skills. Int. J. Multicult. Educ. **23**(12), 110–130 (2021). https://doi.org/10.18251/ijme.v23i1.2463
36. Sulzer, M.A.: (Re)conceptualizing digital literacies before and after the election of Trump. Engl. Teach. Pract. Crit. **17**, 58–71 (2018). https://doi.org/10.1108/ETPC-06-2017-0098
37. Nichols, T.P., LeBlanc, R.J.: Media education and the limits of "literacy": ecological orientations to performative platforms. Curric. Inq. **51**, 389–412 (2021). https://doi.org/10.1080/03626784.2020.1865104
38. Wineburg, S., McGrew, S.: Lateral reading and the nature of expertise: reading less and learning more when evaluating digital information. Teach. Coll. Rec. **121**, 1–40 (2019). https://doi.org/10.1177/016146811912101102
39. Breakstone, J., McGrew, S., Smith, M., Ortega, T., Wineburg, S.: Why we need a new approach to teaching digital literacy. Phi Delta Kappan **99**, 27–32 (2018). https://doi.org/10.1177/0031721718762419
40. Hanz, K., Kingsland, E.S.: Fake or for real? a fake news workshop. Ref. Serv. Rev. **48**, 91–112 (2020). https://doi.org/10.1108/RSR-09-2019-0064
41. Wineburg, S., McGrew, S.: Lateral Reading: Reading Less and Learning More When Evaluating Digital Information. Social Science Research Network, Rochester, NY (2017)
42. Addy, J.M.: The art of the real: fact checking as information literacy instruction. Ref. Serv. Rev. **48**, 19–31 (2020). https://doi.org/10.1108/RSR-09-2019-0067
43. Pavlounis, D., Johnston, J., Brodsky, J., Brooks, P.: The Digital Media Literacy Gap: How to Build Widespread Resilience to False and Misleading Information Using Evidence-Based Classroom Tools. CIVIX Canada (2021)
44. Warner, J.: Getting Beyond the CRAAP Test: A Conversation with Mike Caulfield | Inside Higher Ed. https://www.insidehighered.com/blogs/just-visiting/getting-beyond-craap-test-conversation-mike-caulfield
45. Chang, Y.K., et al.: News literacy education in a polarized political climate: how games can teach youth to spot misinformation. Harvard Kennedy School Misinformation Review (2020). https://doi.org/10.37016/mr-2020-020
46. Yang, S., Lee, J.W., Kim, H.-J., Kang, M., Chong, E., Kim, E.: Can an online educational game contribute to developing information literate citizens? Comput. Educ. **161**, 104057 (2021). https://doi.org/10.1016/j.compedu.2020.104057
47. Pappas, S.: Fighting fake news in the classroom. https://www.apa.org/monitor/2022/01/career-fake-news
48. Walsh, J.: Librarians and controlling disinformation: is multi-literacy instruction the answer? Libr. Rev. **59**, 498–511 (2010). https://doi.org/10.1108/00242531011065091
49. Seo, H., Blomberg, M., Altschwager, D., Vu, H.T.: Vulnerable populations and misinformation: a mixed-methods approach to underserved older adults' online information assessment. New Media Soc. **23**, 2012–2033 (2021). https://doi.org/10.1177/1461444820925041
50. Guess, A.M., et al.: A digital media literacy intervention increases discernment between mainstream and false news in the United States and India. Proc. Natl. Acad. Sci. U.S.A. **117**, 15536–15545 (2020). https://doi.org/10.1073/pnas.1920498117
51. Johnston, B., Webber, S.: Information literacy in higher education: a review and case study. Stud. High. Educ. **28**, 335–352 (2003). https://doi.org/10.1080/03075070309295

52. Lim, S.S., Tan, K.R.: Front liners fighting fake news: global perspectives on mobilising young people as media literacy advocates. J. Child. Media **14**, 529–535 (2020). https://doi.org/10.1080/17482798.2020.1827817
53. Moore, R.C., Hancock, J.T.: A digital media literacy intervention for older adults improves resilience to fake news. Sci. Rep. **12**, 6008 (2022). https://doi.org/10.1038/s41598-022-08437-0

Coding Funds of Knowledge in the iVoices Media Lab: Student Stories About Technologies

Diana Daly(✉) and Anna R. Leach

University of Arizona, Tucson, AZ 85721, USA
didaly@arizona.edu

Abstract. This paper reports on an in-progress study analyzing youth technology experiences through a collection of stories created and openly licensed by students. We analyzed the transcripts of student-created animated video stories for a student media lab-based project in a social media studies course in spring 2021. Open coding of 44 transcripts found that students reflect on their past social media experiences through key thematic heuristics, such as contexts of adoption including grade level, mood, and influence; and dimensions of growing self-awareness around use including influences of others, changes in popular platforms like Instagram, and changes from playful to curated self-presentation. We present early analysis of code co-occurrences including emotion and influence, grade level and influence, and emotional weight specifically around Instagram. We end with plans for further research on this and related datasets, including audiovisual data and analysis through the lens of media literacy, and implications for researchers and instructors in information, new media, and education.

Keywords: Digital storytelling · Higher education · Social media · Instagram · Media production

1 Introduction

"As I recall my first encounter with social media, I now look back and realize that my entry into the online world may have been too early. It all started on my 11th birthday, when I received my first iPod touch and downloaded an app, the little camera icon. That, to my knowledge, was just a picture editing app, also known as Instagram. As a kid, just excited to edit photos of flowers and puppies, purely for my own enjoyment, I was naively unaware that saving these images also meant posting them. Releasing them out into the world for other people's enjoyment as well, leaving strangers free to comment whatever they liked on my innocent images. I will never forget the first comment I received. Also, the moment I realized that picture editing app was not just for adding vibrance to my photos, but the start to my endeavors and exploring this new world at my fingertips. The comment read, "This picture sucks." Puzzled as to how that got there, my heart sunk in disappointment, that a picture that I was so proud to have [00:01:00] made, made me now feel ashamed and insecure. At first, I let it get the best of me and was discouraged from taking photos, despite the happiness it brought me. But eventually I came to the

© The Author(s), under exclusive license to Springer Nature Switzerland AG 2023
I. Sserwanga et al. (Eds.): iConference 2023, LNCS 13971, pp. 405–416, 2023.
https://doi.org/10.1007/978-3-031-28035-1_29

realization that it doesn't matter what other people think. If I like it and it makes me happy, that is the only opinion that matters." (From a student video from the iVoices CC BY Spring 2021 dataset [16])

Today's college students have moved through their lives with social and educational technologies as their constant companions, yet Institutions of Higher Education have few instruments in place to understand those companions' influence on their learning about such technologies. In 2020, a project was launched at an institution in the southwestern part of the United States that used media production training and digital storytelling to learn about students' experiences with technologies and integrate them into tech-focused teaching. One outcome of this project is the current study, involving analysis of students' digital stories about salient technology experiences. We wanted to understand, *what do college students' digital stories reveal about the educational roles digital technologies have played in their lives?*

While current curricula on social and instructional technologies are grounded in valuable theories and principles, a key ingredient missing is student perspectives on the technologies in which they are immersed. Social and instructional technologies factor heavily in students' college careers and retention rates [30], weaving through their experiences in ways ranging from supportive to problematic [8, 17, 23, 27]. Technologies affect users differently across even similar populations because users make sense of them through different personal, ideological, and cultural lenses [2, 11]. Ideally emerging from this sensemaking are individualized new media knowledge and literacy, which in tech-rich environments can be foundations for students' senses of self-efficacy and resulting persistence as learners [1]. On the other hand, disregarding students' distinct histories with technologies leaves out a vital component of research in the field of media use in education and a rich opportunity for student-centered learning [22]. Additionally, the need for a participatory model for the study of new media grows more crucial with the mass movement to online learning due to the COVID-19 pandemic.

1.1 Funds of Knowledge Accessed Through Digital Storytelling

A foundational objective of the iVoices project has been to integrate students' experiences with social and instructional technologies into our curricula through cultivation of digital stories, which are then shared in materials for future learners through open pedagogy or involving students in creation of course content [15]. The project was developed based on the principle that undergraduate students form critical "funds of knowledge" [12, 13, 20] around personal and group uses of technologies at home and among peers, knowledge we have invited them to share through stories they tell and creative work they produce. As educators and researchers at a Hispanic Serving Institution, we knew that students in tech classrooms at our institution might have knowledge about technological uses that were underrepresented in or even absent from new media curricula and scholarship [see 8].

Our cultivation of digital storytelling as a tool to access student knowledge has been designed to promote critical thinking and form connections between storyteller and listener, to promote additional stories as students interpret their own ideas from the previous stories told [26], and to enhance student engagement with the materials and each other [28]. Digital storytelling gives tellers opportunities to be creative and share their personal histories, thus deepening the connection with others in the course as well as their connection with the course materials.

In the iVoices project, student media lab workers helped create digital storytelling assignments, and then ran live online workshops in class to help students post their assignments in Pressbooks, an open-source Content Management System. Instructors then invited the storytellers to share their stories for reuse including integration in the curriculum through the course's open textbook, *Humans R Social Media* (HRSM) [7]. Sharing student-created content in course materials is a staple of open textbook development, within the broader praxis known as Open Educational Practices (OEP) [4, 10]. HRSM has been in development since 2017 and has included student content since the iVoices media lab project began in the 2020–2021 academic year.

Guided by the principles of OEP and the Rebus community [20] and the institution's Open Education Librarian, iVoices collected three datasets of stories openly licensed by students for inclusion in HRSM, representing three semesters of running the iVoices media lab project. The dataset collected at the end of the spring 2021 semester includes the collection of animated videos students created and then chose to give Creative Commons Attribution licenses, with the iVoices (so it reads "the iVoices team") team offering the additional option of full or partial anonymity for student privacy. These practices were used and the stories shared across semesters to build a community of learners and practitioners, collectively navigating the emergent ecology of social networking sites and its impacts on their lives.

2 Methods

2.1 iVoices Media Lab CC bY Collection as Dataset

iVoices was a student media lab project that produced a collection of reusable multimedia projects each semester. Data collected and analyzed in the media lab required student consent through a memorandum of understanding, following the conventions of Open Educational Practices [4]. Only data from consenting students was used from the collection for this study [5, 6].

The dataset that this in-progress study focused on contained 44 student-created animated videos produced in spring 2021. Videos were designed in response to the following prompt, created in conjunction with student media lab workers: *Make a 30-s to 2-min short animated story about one of your first encounters with some social media platform or tech device or system.* Student media lab instructors presented workshops on the use of Adobe Illustrator and Adobe Premiere Pro as well as online resources including the Noun Project site for reusable graphics. Students were required to score their videos with reusable music, for which they were offered a playlist of Creative Commons-licensed musical tracks created by a student media lab worker.

Open licensing was built into the video project in order to create a reusable collection and dataset of student work. Students were trained throughout the semester in the meaning and use of Creative Commons licenses and media. At the end of the semester, student creators were invited to openly license each of their projects produced in the course under the Creative Commons Attribution 2.0 license (CC BY). Of 130 students registered in the spring 2021 course, 44 (34%) elected to openly license their video projects. 25 chose to have their full name as their project attribution, 12 chose only their first name as their attribution, and 7 chose to only be identified as "iVoices Media Lab Student."

2.2 Open Coding Analysis

We were interested in understanding students' work through connections across their stories. Using a grounded theory approach [29] and deploying the principles of content analysis [25], our study began with the open coding of the spoken content of the 44 videos. All iVoices datasets with spoken aural content are transcribed, both to aid research analysis and to support Universal Design for Learning—specifically format flexibility—for learners interacting with these media in the future [14, 24]. To create the dataset, the key identifiers, transcripts, and links to videos were migrated into a shared spreadsheet document in Google Sheets. Columns were added to the sheet that allowed for the researchers to independently review the transcripts and begin the initial open coding process.

Through the open coding process performed iteratively, each of the two authors independently reviewed the text. After we each created an initial list of individual codes, we jointly reviewed and discussed them, forming tentative definitions [3]. Next, armed with our shared discussions, we did a second round of independent coding further narrowing focus, creating additional codes, and removing codes that no longer fit or could be absorbed into a larger code. Again, we met to discuss findings from our coding process, now noting similarities and discrepancies and discussing our individual thought processes. The culmination of our open coding was a codebook with definitions we shared and agreed upon [19].

Our research team then analyzed the transcripts through our final codebook in Dedoose. Dedoose is a web-based tool for analyzing qualitative and mixed method data [9]. The dataset consisting of transcripts and unique identifiers was loaded into the program. With the codebook in place, we reviewed the transcripts in Dedoose, and coded text based on analytical memos and notes in the spreadsheet document. We used this analytical software to enhance the trustworthiness of our coding process [18]. Once the dataset was fully coded in Dedoose, we used the analytical functions of the program to examine the data further.

Our goal in coding was to understand, through students' reflections on early experiences with technologies, their histories, and the knowledge these histories had given them. Funds of Knowledge is a methodology initially developed by and for educators working with students in Mexican American communities, to understand how students' cultural lives outside of school endow them with resources that can be represented in curricula and cultivated by educators [12, 13, 21]. The premise at the basis of Funds of Knowledge is that "people are competent and have knowledge, and their life experiences have given them that knowledge" [12, p. 625]. There seemed no better theory than this to enhance engagement in a class teaching tech-immersed students from diverse backgrounds about social media.

3 Preliminary Findings

Through analysis of transcripts, we have found that young people composed multimodal narratives about convergent stages of development related to technologies in youth school learning, tech development, and how they use applications. Throughout the corpus, students focused on specific technological affordances that they learned to deploy, to take photos, communicate, play games, listen to music, download and use applications, and read. These are themes we plan to explore more in the near future.

For early analysis, we were particularly interested in how students chose to reflect their uses, including their heuristics: what types of measures or categories were important to them to emphasize. Numerous themes emerged from our heuristic analysis of student reflections—how students gauge what type of information is important in their formative technological experiences.

3.1 Theme: Context of Adoption

Students frequently reflected on the contexts of their initial uses of specific technologies, including their educational levels at time of adoption, their remembered reasons for adopting, and how they felt or their moods at their first encounters with technologies they adopted. Contexts emphasized included stages of development connected with grade level (21 instances); identity realization beyond "likes" (14 instances); and mood of first encounter (16 instances). Reflecting upon the context in which they learned about technologies was evidently a useful heuristic for illustrating roles those technologies played in their lives (Table 1).

3.2 Theme: Growing Self-awareness of How They Use Technologies

Students often chose to reflect in their videos on a growing self-awareness of *how* they use technologies. This included becoming aware of their ability to reach others and consume information from others, and additional technological affordances. In these stories, awareness of the wider connection to others added a dimension to their reflections around how they connect through technology (Table 2). Students reflected on dimensions of growing self-awareness around technological use including influence of others (22 instances), Instagram uses and meanings (18 instances), playful to curated usage patterns (12 instances), apps as identity (10 instances), and connection (10 instances).

3.3 Code Co-occurences

We also examined co-occurrences of posts in Dedoose. The highest co-occurrences were between Mood of first encounter and Influence, Grade and Influence, and Instagram and Mood of first encounter, with nine instances where both codes were assigned to a transcript. These unique codes demonstrate meaning on their own but provide an additional layer of depth when exploring the instances where codes co-occur. The following section examines these co-occurrences and pulls direct quotes from student videos.

Table 1. Context of adoption emphasized, with descriptions and examples

Code	Descriptions	Example
Stages of development connected with grade level (21 instances)	Each of these students emphasized their grade level at the time of a first technological adoption or encounter. Students commonly associated their first encounters with technologies such as mobile devices generally or Instagram specifically with the grade they were in. 4th grade and 6th grade were common examples.	"…the first time that I wanted Snapchat back in middle school, all my friends had Snapchat, but I wasn't allowed to get it. So, I felt very out of place and really left out. And obviously I ended up getting it at some point. And I feel like my first experience with it was more like, oh my gosh, I'm finally included because everyone around me had Snapchat and I actually moved going into freshman year of high school. And it was really big then."
Identity realization beyond "likes" (14 instances)	Each of these students acknowledged a shift from posting for "likes", associated with feelings of anxiety or lack of confidence, to posting for oneself, associated with confidence.	"At first, I let it get the best of me and was discouraged from taking photos, despite the happiness it brought me, but eventually I came to the realization that it doesn't matter what other people think. If I like it and it makes me happy, that is the only opinion that matters."
Mood of first encounter (16 instances)	Mood of first encounter has to do with affect and the kind of emotion that is presented with a situation. Each of these students emphasized strong emotions or mood upon first encountering or adopting a technology, ranging from excited to threatened.	"The year was 2005 and as a kid in Africa, I spent most of my leisure outdoors, riding bikes and playing soccer. In fourth grade, my school had a contest that I quite can't remember what it was for, but the first prize was a brand-new Nokia phone. Phones were rare at the time, usually used by adults, and I wanted it. I entered the contest and to my surprise, I won. I have never won anything in my life, so I was pretty excited about it. I use the phone to take pictures, play games, and call my friends, but I never thought that technology and phones would get so advanced as to have a minicomputer in your hands. Looking forward to what the future holds."

Mood of First Encounter X Influence (9 Co-occurrences)
We interpret this co-occurrence to show that the affect students present in their stories is associated to them with those who influenced their adoption or uses of a technology. Influence was salient to students when students spoke about how they felt when first using a technology. In several of the videos, students referred to the influence as the reason for initially wanting to or starting to use a specific technology.

Table 2. Dimensions of growing awareness around technological use, with descriptions and examples.

Code	Description	Example
Influence of others (22 instances)	Each of these stories refers to a parent, friend, sibling, teacher, or online connection as a key influence in how the student used a given technology. This code connotes reference to people in the student's life or whom the students are exposed to who influence how they use technologies.	"I quickly learned my family weren't the only people I could talk to and follow online. There were amazing strangers and individuals I wanted to know. One of them being an incredibly talented artist who blew me away with his works. To say I flooded his DM with endless questions would be an understatement. He did try to get back to me in a timely manner, but ultimately couldn't keep up and an answer would turn into a follow-up question and so on and so forth. Finally, he simply sent me a link to a streaming platform and said he would show me real time how to do his fancy tricks and techniques."
Instagram uses and meanings (18 instances)	Instagram played an outsized role in the development of students according to these reflections. These stories included descriptions of the use or meaning of Instagram, which was mentioned 3 times more often than the next most commonly mentioned platform, Snapchat (6 stories).	"In 2013, I moved to America from the Dominican Republic. I made a new friend named Adam, and one day me and him were walking down the street to go to Speedway to get some slushies. And he told me about this brand-new app on your phone called Instagram. Later, in 2019, I proceeded to get over a thousand followers on Instagram, which I thought was a huge milestone for me. And finally, the last photo is a picture of me on vacation because that's all I use my Instagram for it. I use it to post pictures of me on vacation."
Playful to curated usage patterns (12 instances)	These stories demonstrated changes in how students post on Instagram over time personally as well as shifting trends, moving as they get older from playful to curated posts.	"When I first downloaded Instagram, I went pretty crazy with the posting. I posted literally everything. I posted pictures of my dog, pictures of my Starbucks, pictures of my outfits and pictures of my nails. There were quite a few other posts, but those are my favorite things to take pictures of. As I started to learn more about the app and interacted with it more, I realized people didn't need to be seeing my every move and it was better if some things were left a mystery."

(*continued*)

Table 2. (*continued*)

Code	Description	Example
App as Identity (10 instances)	In these stories students recounted their evolution toward a social media platform (usually Instagram) becoming a core part of their sense of self or how they are who they are today.	"I was just excited that I got to have a phone in the first place. But then I started hearing so many new things about phones. I heard things from all my friends and social media apps. Didn't really know what it was. Then I heard about Instagram. It was a social media app where you could share pictures, share your life, get followers and likes. I thought it was so exciting. I downloaded the app and started to figure out how to use it. This is my first real touch with social media. I started loving it and figuring out how likes worked. I started chatting with people and I finally started to learn different ways to use it. After posting and messaging lots of people, I figured out just how to use Instagram. Ever since, I love social media and been super excited about using the platform. Never have I stopped using Instagram."
Connection (10 instances)	Students in these stories emphasized connection, including feeling connected to others online, or desiring the feeling of being connected to others online.	"I decided I was going to do a story on my first experience with Snapchat. And I think that our generation was basically the first people to go through this app and have this app basically change our whole life. I didn't know that after Snapchat being created, that it was going to be one of the main ways that I contacted with friends and even people I don't know, like, I have been communicating through Snapchat with classmates, and I even have friends who they communicate with their parents through Snapchat. And I feel like it has grown even bigger, um, since it came out. But the first time that I wanted Snapchat back in middle school, all my friends had Snapchat, but I wasn't allowed to get it."

Some were excited about the prospect of using a specific technology due to the Influence of their peers. For example:

> "I remember my friends and classmates started to talk about [Instagram] all the time at school, and about what they were posting. I'm at home one day and begged my mom to let me make an account because I wanted to feel included in the excitement with all of my friends."

Other students presented fluctuation in the mood of their first encounter with a technology based around the influence of others. For example, "All of my friends had an Instagram, except for me. I was super sad about it … my mom finally let me download the app and I was thrilled." This story emphasized not only the influence friends had on their desire for Instagram, but also parental gatekeeping modifying influence.

Grade X Influence (9 Co-occurrences)

When students were asked to reflect on their first experience with technology, many shared both their grade level and those who influenced them to show initial interest in the technology at that age. Young people assiciated their education level and the progression of their education with learning about technology, even as this learning was informally acquired outside of school. We interpret this finding to show that young people recognize informal learning of technologies and gauge their readiness for them within grade-level peer groups. For example,

> "So, this story is about the time that I first downloaded Instagram. And I was about, I was in seventh grade, and it was pretty new, and everybody was just starting to get it. So, I first got the app… But then my mom found out I had an Instagram and previously she had expressed how she did not want me having an Instagram and said that I wasn't old enough yet, but I ended up going behind her back and creating one anyways because I really wanted to be a part of social media, but she ended up making me delete the app, but I later re-downloaded it and continued my Instagram career."

Parental influence is overridden in this student's story by the imperative to keep pace with peers.

Another student chose to share their grade and the pressure they felt from peers, in this case to download Snapchat. "All my friends back in middle school were telling me, 'Hey, download Snapchat, download Snapchat.' And I didn't know anything about this. I'd recently just gotten a phone from my parents, and I then decided to download Snapchat." Students a given social networking site it as a means to communicate, a necessary tool for social interaction.

Instagram X Mood of First Encounter (9 Co-occurrences)

Within this dataset, Instagram is mentioned more often than any other technology. Our interpretation of these stories finds that Instagram entered many young people's lives at highly impressionable stages of social development and connection formation.

One student noted that they did not recall having specific feelings about the platform itself, but instead were interested in the ability to connect with people. "My first experience with Instagram wasn't very exciting, but it was fun for me and helped me connect with my friends and find people that like the same things as I do."

In another example of this co-occurrence, a student shared an experience of excitement around the prospect of using the platform.

> "I will describe to you my first encounter with the app Instagram. I first discovered the social media platform when it was just released. I was in sixth grade. My friends and I quickly jumped onto this app because of its amazing features. At the time,

the ability to share pictures and communicate with friends online was new and very exciting."

Conversely, a different student shared a disdain for the technology and expounded their process and reasonings behind the eventual removal of the app from their life.

> "...once I got into sixth grade, I did get my first phone and one of the first apps which I downloaded was Instagram. I didn't really like Instagram. I felt that a lot of things people posted were fake or I just didn't really care for. So, I decided to delete it because I thought it would make me happier."

With more analysis, we hope to understand how this and other co-occurrences reveal cultural and generational understandings of students' informal learning around new media.

4 Conclusion

In this work, we offer early analysis of a collection and narrowed dataset developed through Open Educational Practices and grounded in the theory that students have rich Funds of Knowledge around technologies in their lives, which can be integrated into new media and technology research and curricula. In the animated video story transcripts we coded, collected through students' openly licensed personal stories, students examined the roles technologies played in their histories. Students recalled ranges of emotion, influences around adoption, and impacts of specific technologies. Here we have presented our early findings on the heuristics students used to represent these salient technological experiences.

Our ongoing and future research will expand on this preliminary analysis in numerous ways. We will drill down within the themes presented here, to learn what they reveal about technological evolution and generational use of social media, in general and around Instagram specifically. Through exploring the evolution of Instagram and comparing the student experiences with Instagram, we wonder if it is possible to find areas where trust is gained and lost with the use of these technologies with respect to what the platform is doing. For example, student say throughout their reflections that Instagram changed. What does this mean to the student? What ways did it change and how may that have impacted the student's use or trust in the platform?

Further, we will add analysis of the images, sounds, and audio the students selected for their digital storytelling by looking at the diverse ways that students express themselves in video imagery. What images did they choose? What music? And how does it compare to what they say? Are there other themes that begin to surface as we investigate students' expression around technologies?

The iVoices media lab is an Open Educational Collection "What Do We Do with the Fruits of Open Educational Practices? A Case for Open Educational Collections" by Daly, Collection containing many other stories and student perspectives. Using the codes that have developed from this analysis, we will examine other data sets within iVoices, not only to validate the themes from this work, but also to remain open to other codes that may reveal themselves from other questions and perspectives.

Finally, we have also begun to analyze these video stories and other stories in the larger iVoices datasets through the lens of media literacy. Here, we will analyze how students think about and make connections to media they consume and its impact on their early and current uses of technology. What media and in what modes do students consume information? How do they interact with these modes and how do they interpret their meaning and experiences through these media?

By continually and repeatedly looking at this corpus of student-centered data through different lenses, we can gain a valuable insight to student thoughts and evolution of technology incorporation. These insights will help us to keep the student in the center of learning as well as ask them to reflect on their own uses of technology and consumption of media. Our hope is that these works will help students to think critically about technology use and help curriculum designers to consider the student's pasts as an impact on their technology use. We forward this work to advance the fields of STEM education and new media studies, by inviting the distinct cultural knowledge of those traditionally characterized as learners into Information curricula and scholarship.

References

1. Bandura, A., Freeman, W.H., Lightsey, R.: Self-efficacy: the exercise of control. J. Cogn. Psychother. **13**(2), 158–166 (1999). https://doi.org/10.1891/0889-8391.13.2.158
2. Boyd, D.: It's Complicated: The Social Lives of Networked teens. Yale University Press (2014)
3. Charmaz, K.: Constructing Grounded Theory, 2nd edn. Sage, London (2014)
4. Bali, M., Catherine, C., Rajiv, S.J.: Framing Open Educational Practices from a Social Justice Perspective. J. Interact. Media Educ. **2020**(1) (2020). Harvard
5. Cuillier, C.A., Daly, D.P.: Open pedagogy: independence and interdependence in teaching about new media. In: Association of Internet Researchers 2021 Virtual Conference (2021)
6. Daly, D.: What do we do with the fruits of Open Educational Practices? A Case for Open Educational Collections. Paper accepted for iConference 2023, annual meeting of the iSchools consortium, Barcelona, Spain, 27–29 Mar 2023 (2022)
7. Daly, D., students.: Humans R Social Media (Winter 2022 Open Textbook Edition). iVoices Media Lab at the University of Arizona. https://ivoices.ischool.arizona.edu/humans-r-social-media
8. Daniels, J.: Race and racism in internet studies: a review and critique. New Media Soc. **15**(5), 695–719 (2013)
9. Dedoose: https://www.dedoose.com/ (2022). Retrieved 16 Sep 2022
10. Ehlers, U.-D.: Extending the territory: from open educational resources to open educational practices. J. Open, Flex. Distance Learn. **15**(2), 1–10 (2011)
11. Gershon, I.: Media ideologies: an introduction. J. Linguist. Anthropol. **20**(2), 283–293 (2010)
12. González, N., Moll, L.: Cruzando el Puente: building bridges to funds of knowledge. Educ. Policy **16**, 623–641 (2002)
13. González, N., Moll, L.C., Amanti, C.: Funds of knowledge: Theorizing practices in households, communities and classrooms. Erlbaum, Mahwah, NJ (2005)
14. Hitchcock, C., Meyer, A., Rose, D., Jackson, R.: Providing new access to the general curriculum: universal design for learning. Teach. Except. Child. **35**(2), 8–17 (2002)
15. Tietjen, P., Asino, T.I.: What is open pedagogy? Identifying commonalities. Int. Rev. Res. Open Distrib. Learn. **22**(2), 185–204 (2021)

16. iVoices Media Lab: The iVoices Media Lab 2021 CC BY Dataset (2021). Retrieved from https://iVoices.ischool.arizona.edu/research
17. Lau, L.K.: Institutional factors affecting student retention. Education **124**(1), 126–136 (2003)
18. Lemon, L.L., Hayes, J.: Enhancing trustworthiness of qualitative findings: using Leximancer for qualitative data analysis triangulation. The Qual. Report **25**(3), 604–614 (2020)
19. MacQueen, K.M., McLellan, E., Kay, K., Milstein, B.: Codebook development for team-based qualitative analysis. CAM J. **10**(2), 31–36 (1998)
20. Mays, E., et al.: A Guide to Making Open Textbooks with Students. Pressbooks, Montreal, Canada (2017)
21. Moll, L.C., Amanti, C., Neff, D., Gonzalez, N.: Funds of knowledge for teaching: using a qualitative approach to connect homes and classrooms. Theory Pract. **31**(2), 132–141 (1992)
22. Motschnig-Pitrik, R., Holzinger, A.: Student-centered teaching meets new media: concept and case study. Educ. Technol. Soc. **5**(4), 160–172 (2002)
23. Purvis, A.J., Rodger, H.M., Beckingham, S.: Experiences and perspectives of social media in learning and teaching in higher education. Int. J. Educ. Res. Open **1** (2020). 100018
24. Rose, D.H., Meyer, A.: Teaching Every Student in the Digital Age: Universal Design for Learning. ERIC (2002)
25. Saldaña, J.: Fundamentals of Qualitative Research. Oxford University Press, New York (2011)
26. Sarris, G.: Storytelling in the classroom: crossing vexed chasms. Coll. Engl. **52**(2), 169–185 (1990). https://doi.org/10.2307/377449
27. Selwyn, N.: Education and technology: Key issues and debates, 2nd edn. Bloomsbury Academic, London, New York (2017)
28. Spanjaard, D., Garlin, F., Mohammed, H.: Tell me a story! blending digital storytelling into marketing higher education for student engagement.J. Mark. Educ. (2022). https://doi.org/10.1177/02734753221090419
29. Strauss, A., Corbin, J.M.: Grounded Theory in Practice. Sage, London (1997)
30. Tawfik, A.A., Reeves, T.D., Stich, A.: Intended and unintended consequences of educational technology on social inequality. TechTrends **60**(6), 598–605 (2016). https://doi.org/10.1007/s11528-016-0109-5

An Exploratory Study of Intergenerational Technical Help from the Youth's Perspective

Manyu Sheng, Jun Wang, Xixi Zhu, and Pengyi Zhang(✉)

Department of Information Management, Peking University, Beijing 100871, China
{1900016610,wgjun,xixi,pengyi}@pku.edu.cn

Abstract. It becomes increasingly common for youth to help their parents use digital technology; a phenomenon called "intergenerational technical help" (ITH). This article aims to explore ITH in the family. We interviewed 20 college students who have experiences proving ITH to their parents. We used the grounded theory to analyze ITH from its triggering mechanism, specific behaviors, and outcomes. The main conclusion is that information and communication technology (ICT) usage level, facilitating conditions, and willingness to help are direct factors that impact ITH behavior, while parents' age, occupation, cognitive level, performance expectancy, family relationship, technical dependence to youth, and self-efficacy also relate to how ITH takes place. We find that successful ITH helps parents to solve technical problems, bridge the digital divide, and improve intergenerational relationships. But interruptions or failures can significantly discourage the willingness of further ITH from both generations.

Keywords: Intergenerational technical help · Digital divide · Grounded theory

1 Introduction

Information and communication technology (ICT) is deeply integrated with our lives. The youth growing up with new technology, surrounded by smartphones, computers, and other tools of the digital age, are called "digital natives." In contrast, their parents, and grandparents, as "digital migrants," are not born in the digital age to begin with, but passively adapted to technological developments [1]. Although studies have shown that many factors can lead to different ICT usage levels, such as cognitive level, technical participation and media use habits, the technological gap created by age and growing environment between generations still exists [2]. Prensky suggested that digital natives' brains, thinking patterns and cognitive skills are likely to be physically different as a result of the digital input they received when growing up [3]. It is this intergenerational digital divide that has had a profound impact on the values, attitudes, life horizons and participation capabilities of two generations, and has thus become an important social motivator for ITH [4]. Parents need to be taught more skills to adapt to information society, known as "Intergenerational technical help." The ability of youth to give ITH to their parents is due to their high sensitivity and receptivity to new things, and they are less bound by old values and behavioral patterns [5]. The essence of this unique phenomenon

© The Author(s), under exclusive license to Springer Nature Switzerland AG 2023
I. Sserwanga et al. (Eds.): iConference 2023, LNCS 13971, pp. 417–425, 2023.
https://doi.org/10.1007/978-3-031-28035-1_30

is the process of "reverse socialization," which is passing on the informative culture from the younger generation to their predecessors [6]. The reverse socialization is the beginning of social change, and the cultural rupture formed by the change greatly creates the ability of young people to give ITH and is the driving force for social modernization [7]. Gittell and Vidal divide social capital into "bonding social capital" and "bridging social capital." Family relationship is a kind of bonding social capital, which forms the closest type of social network [8]. The social capital of the youth as a strong relationship can provide the parents with the motivation and competitiveness to digitally alleviate poverty through technical support, emotional reinforcement, and expectation [9]. Many scholars are interested in the factors that influence the ITH, but few have explored the process of it and the mechanism among the factors involved in.

This study is carried out in the context of the deep binding of people and media, the emergence of the intergenerational digital divide, and the wave of reverse socialization, and is committed to exploring the mechanism of ITH of the family. The "mechanism" includes the structural relationship between the elements and how they operate. Therefore, this study explores the connections between the various aspects and makes suggestions for bridging the digital divide.

2 Related Research

We are inspired by the research on "informatics moment," "reverse cultural teaching" and "intergenerational technical help."

The "informatics moment" is an important concept that focuses on how to bridge the digital divide. Williams first proposed the "informatics moment" when exploring the technical help of libraries, referring to "the interaction of readers and libraries in the process of seeking help when using computers or the Internet [10]." The concept of "informatics moment" was limited to the library at that time. Then Williams expanded it into a variety of fields, namely "the moment when a person asks for help when they encounter difficulties in using digital technologies [11]." This term has led scholars to focus more on the process of bridging the digital divide and emphasizing the role of social capital [12]. The youth, as the bonding social capital of their parents [13], will play an important role in bridging their digital divide.

In 1968, the Western anthropologist Bell proposed "reverse socialization", arguing that children would impact the socialization process of parents. Then Margaret Mead proposed "post-metaphorical culture" in 1970, which means the older generation learns from the younger generation [14]. The younger generation is more skilled in using new media and acquiring information more efficiently, and this gap makes the older generation learn from them. [14, 15]. The Chinese scholar Zhou proposed the concept of "reverse cultural teaching," that is, "the process of cultural assimilation from the older generation to the younger generation during rapid cultural change [16]." Zhou demonstrated the existence of a digital divide between different age groups through quantitative research, consider the digital divide in the family, and put forward the concept of the "digital generation gap," referring to the gap between generations in the adoption of new media and technology [17]. And Zhou pointed out that the way for families to cross the "digital generation gap" is for children to teach their parents to use new media and technologies such as computers and mobile phones, and the process of reverse cultural teaching on the Internet and digital technology is called "intergenerational technical help [5]." The levels of ITH include accessible technical help, skilled technical help, and literate technical help. The ITH is the embodiment of "reverse cultural teaching" in the use of digital technology and new media [18].

We find that the research of ITH is mainly based on communication and sociological perspectives, primarily focusing on the influencing factors of ITH, or limited to specific media such as WeChat or short-video apps. For example, the wider the knowledge generation gap is found to be associated with the more frequent the ITH [19]. Liang summarized the characteristics of the objects of ITH and analyzed the methods of ITH by investigating the use of WeChat in rural China [20]. Venkatesh put forward the "Unified Theory of Acceptance and Use of Technology model," pointing out that behavioral intention and use behavior is affected by performance expectancy, effort expectancy, social influences, and facilitating conditions [21]. Thus, previous research did not explore the mechanism of ITH in the family from a more abstract and condensed perspective, did not explain the influencing mechanism of various elements in the process of ITH, and did not explain the specific obstacles and solutions of ITH. This study is not limited to a specific media and is committed to exploring the process of ITH and the influence mechanism of various elements, explaining the difficulties and solutions that may be encountered in the process of ITH, and finally providing some suggestions for bridging the digital divide.

3 Method

This study used the grounded theory approach, which is commonly used in qualitative research to conduct exploratory analysis, the phenomenon was analyzed by an inductive method, and the results were excavated through systematic data collection [22–24]. We followed the procedure below (see Fig. 1) to establish connections from the source data, using a grounded theory approach to explain the mechanism of ITH and the connections between elements.

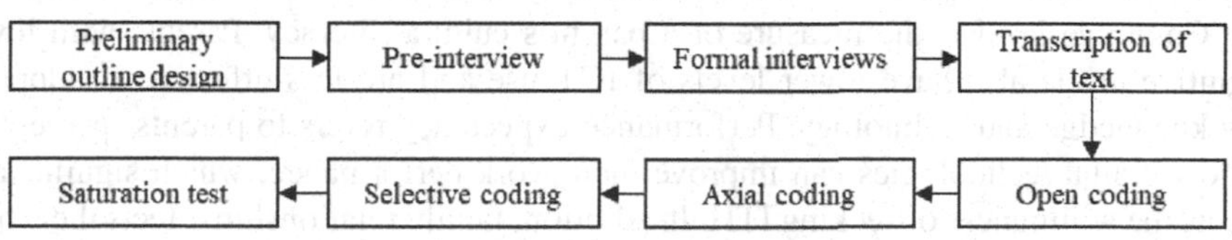

Fig. 1. The main process of grounded theory

The young generation was the focus of our study. This study designed the outline of interviews on the causes, processes, and outcomes of ITH [25]. We recruited participants who are college students from different regions in China, who are capable of implementing ITH. In addition, the ICT usage level of their parents was quite diverse. The semi-structured interviews were conducted between December 2021 and February 2022. These interviewees included undergraduate and graduate students, whose parents come from both urban and rural areas with diverse socioeconomic backgrounds. The interview questions were about the process of providing technical assistance to parents and its impact. A total of 20 interviews were conducted (numbered A-T). Data collection was completed when we reached saturation point during the analysis.

4 Findings

4.1 Triggering Mechanism of Intergenerational Technical Help

This study found ten factors that impact ITH behavior: ICT usage level, facilitating conditions, and subjective willingness are direct factors, while parents' age, occupation, cognitive level, performance expectancy, family relationship, technical dependence to youth, and self-efficacy are indirect factors. Generally speaking, the lower the level of ICT usage of parents, the more technical difficulties they will encounter, and the more likely it will lead to ITH. Facilitating conditions refer to the physical distance between parents and youth and the convenience of technical help tools. When parents and youth can talk face to face, or communication tools are efficient, it is easier to induce ITH, and the effect of it will be better, but if they communicate through text messages, it will significantly reduce the technical help efficiency, as the respondent H says, "my parents often ask me at home instead of at school." The willingness to implement ITH includes the intention of parents to inquire and learn deeply, and youth's initiative to implement technical help, which is an essential factor in improving the efficiency of ITH. We find that the motives of parents are complicated. Some parents can open their hearts. For example, respondent F's parents always ask him when they encounter problems. However, respondent A's parents worry that they may cause some trouble to her. At the same time, the parents will have different degrees of willingness to learn. If the parents' learning willingness is low, the youth's initiative will be frustrated, as the respondent G says, "in the face of many problems, my parents don't think about why, and I also don't want to talk more."

Parents' age, occupation, and cognitive level affect ITH behavior indirectly. In general, the older the parents are, the lower the ICT usage level is, and the more likely that ITH will occur. And parents' occupation directly determines the demand for ICT use. The Cognitive level is the measure of a parent's cultural literacy. Parents with lower cognitive levels also have lower levels of ICT use and are less effective at adopting new knowledge and technology. Performance expectancy refers to parents' perception of how digital technologies can improve their work performance, which significantly affects the willingness of seeking ITH. In addition, family relationship affects the whole process of ITH behavior. The higher the intimacy between the two generations, the more likely that the ITH will occur. Technical dependence refers to the degree that which parents are inherently dependent on the youth in learning digital technologies. When the youth's cognitive level and information literacy gradually surpass that of the parents, the parents will develop technical dependence on them. This is determined by the parents' personality and is a certain tendency of the parents to learn new technology. For example, respondent P thinks that although he is close to his parents, and they often encounter technical problems, his parents do not rely on him and first try to solve the problem in other ways. Self-efficacy refers to parents' judgment on whether they can master new technologies and the difficulty of learning, which can greatly stimulate or hinder parental willingness to seek ITH.

4.2 Intergenerational Technical Help Behavior

We reveal the main characteristics of ITH from six aspects: subject, media, frequency, scene, pattern, and level of ITH. The subject of ITH is extensive, including social, entertainment, work and shopping, and other situations that may occur in daily life. And the ITH behavior can be carried out for many media, such as mobile phones, computers, TV, game consoles, and other digital devices. The frequency of ITH is mainly 0–4 times per month. The ITH can be carried out face-to-face or with the help of communication tools when parents and youth are separated. According to parents' involvement, ITH can be divided into surrogate, injunctive, and heuristic. Surrogate ITH refers to the operation performed by the youth directly instead of the parents. As the respondent I says, "I always finish it all for my parents." In injunctive ITH, parents follow youth's instructions without thinking, which is most common. For example, as the respondent A says, "I tell them where to click, and they do it." Parents have the highest degree of autonomy in heuristic ITH, and the youth provide specific guidance. In this situation, the parents complete the particular operation and expanded learning independently. The levels of ITH include accessible technical help, skilled technical help, and literate technical help. Most cases are skilled technical help, with literate technical help coming second, mainly reflected in the youth helping their parents cultivate the awareness of using network safely, identifying the value of information, and using data efficiently. And accessible technical help is the least.

4.3 Intergenerational Technical Help Outcomes

ITH can succeed or fail. Successful ITH can help parents solve technical problems efficiently, facilitate their better integration into the technological environment, and help improve their digital literacy. For example, respondent G believes that "my parents gradually care about design idea and operation logic of some software." At the same time, ITH can also help the youth improve their information literacy. In addition, ITH provides a bridge for communication between parents and youth. For example, respondent F believes that his family is closer. We also found that in the process of ITH, there is a phenomenon that seems to "put the cart before the horse." Respondent I believe that her parents will ask questions more frequently after receiving positive incentives, and even the technical problems are no longer important. They just want to communicate with youth.

And part of ITH will be interrupted or does not produce the benefits that the youth expect. Nelissen's study indicates that when children teach their parents more about digital media, there appears to be more media conflict between them [26]. We also find that these obstacles mainly include parents adopting new technology inefficiently (C, J), repeated teaching for many times (I), parents being less willing to learn (G), communication tools being inconvenient to use (F), the youth may be impatient (O), and parents fear that new technology is difficult to learn (I). Many respondents mentioned these problems. They said that "it takes several times to teach my parents how to collect emojis, and they will soon forget and continue to ask me," "we cannot describe it clearly on the WeChat." When encountering these obstacles, both generations can calm down, practice many times, seek efficient ITH methods, such as screen recording, start with techniques that are easy to learn, and youth could consciously recommend efficient learning ways for parents and cultivate their' self-learning consciousness.

If ITH can be successfully implemented, it can solve the technical problems for parents, improve their digital literacy, and make the family relationship closer. But if they give up without trying, it will hurt the next ITH behavior, which will reduce the parents' self-efficacy and willingness to inquire.

4.4 Analysis of Intergenerational Technical Help Mechanism

According to the trigger mechanism of ITH, various elements involved in the process of technical help, and the ITH mechanism model is finally constructed, as shown in Fig. 2. First, the ICT usage level will affect the level, pattern, and frequency of ITH. Parents with a higher level of ICT use will foster heuristic ITH and literate ITH. Parents' age, occupation, and cognitive level affect their ICT usage level. Second, facilitating conditions directly affect the scene and frequency of ITH. Third, the willingness of ITH directly affects the frequency, pattern, and level of ITH. Parents are more willing to learn, and more heuristic ITH and literate ITH will occur. Performance expectancy, family relationship, technical dependence, and parents' self-efficacy have indirect effects on ITH behavior through Subjective willingness. In addition, the level, pattern, scene, frequency, subject, and media of ITH also directly impact the effect of improving the digital divide. Implementing a higher level of technical help, heuristic technical help, a higher frequency, and face-to-face technical help are more conducive to bridging the digital divide.

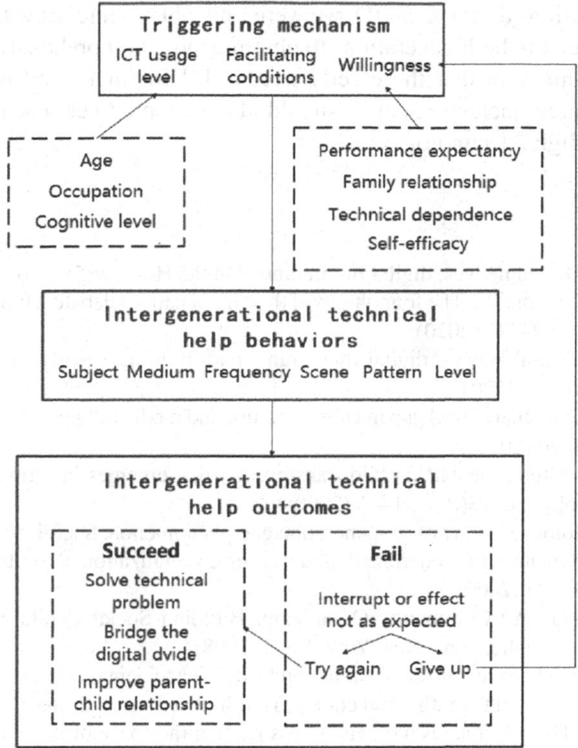

Fig. 2. Intergenerational technical help model

5 Conclusion and Discussion

This study analyzed intergenerational technical help (ITH) from three aspects: trigger mechanism, specific behavior, and outcomes, and identifies obstacles to ITH and their solutions. We identified 10 factors that affected ITH behavior among youth and elder generations. The gap in ICT use between parents and youth is the basis of ITH, the willingness is the driving force, and facilitating conditions are the guarantee of ITH. Among all the indirect factors, parents' technical dependence on the youth directly impacts whether they are willing to ask for help. Successful ITH can help solve technical problems, bridge the digital divide, and make family relationships closer, while the interruption of ITH will reduce the willingness of both generations.

We also find some different characteristics of ITH and general technical help. First, family relationship plays a vital role in the whole process of ITH, which can be both beginning and destination. Second, parents' willingness is more complex. Meanwhile, the repeated technical help phenomenon occurs frequently and may increase the degree of technological dependence. As the bonding social capital of the parents, the youth play a very important role in bridging the digital divide, especially for parents with a low level of ICT use.

Due to restrictions during COVID, we were only able to interview the youth. Future research should talk to both generations to obtain a more comprehensive understanding of ITH. The assumption that the elderly needs ITH for their well-being needs care examination. A more inclusive society should allow people to choose to live their lives with or without digital technology.

References

1. Prensky, M.: Digital natives, digital immigrants. On the Horiz. **9**(5), 1–6 (2001)
2. Evans, C., Robertson, W.: The four phases of the digital natives debate. Human Behav. Emerg. Technol. **2**(3), 269–277 (2020)
3. Prensky, M.: Digital natives, digital immigrants part 2: do they really think differently? On the Horiz. **9**(6), 1–6 (2001)
4. Zhou, X.H.: Intergenerational gap in cultural return and media influence. The J. Jiangsu Adm. Inst. **16**(2), 63–70 (2016)
5. Zhou, X.H.: Cultural feedback: child transmission that emerges in a time of drastic social changes. Sociol. Stud. **15**(02), 51–66 (2000)
6. Zhou, Y.: Sociological study of the generation gap phenomenon. Sociol. Stud. **9**(4), 13 (1994)
7. Wei, B.: The dynamics of modernization: the reverse socialization of youth. Contemp. Youth Res. **18**(04), 31–34 (2000)
8. Gittell, R., Vidal, A.: Community Organizing: Building Social Capital as a Development Strategy. SAGE Publications, New York, USA (1998)
9. Wang, M., Yan, H.: Value of social capital on bridging accidental digital di-vide among rural residents: a field report from Jing Hai county, Tianjin. J. Libr. Sci. China **39**(05), 39–49 (2013)
10. Williams, K.: The informatics moment: Grass rooting the space of flows in an urban branch library. In: iConference 2010, Springer, Champaign, IL, USA (2010)
11. Williams, K.: Informatics moments: digital literacy and social capital in civil society and people's everyday lives. Publ. Libr. Q. **29**, 47–73 (2012)
12. Qian, Z.C., Jang, X., Su, Y., Zhang, P.Y., Han, S.L.: Analysis on the influencing factors of tech help from the perspective of information stratification theory. J. Libr. Data **3**(3), 17 (2021)
13. Putnam, R.D.: Bowling Alone: The Collapse and Revival of American Community. Simon and Schuster, New York, USA (2000)
14. Reich, C.A.: The Greening of America: How the Youth Revolution is Trying to Make America Livable. Random House, New York, USA (1970)
15. Li, L.L., Guo, C.: Post-metaphorical culture: cultural feedback in the information age. J. Lover **31**(01), 37–41 (2016)
16. Zhou, X.H.: On the significance of the cultural back-feeding of contemporary Chinese youth. Youth Stud. **11**(11), 22–26 (1988)
17. Zhou, Y.Q.: The digital generation gap and cultural feedback: a quantitative examination of the "quiet revolution" within the family. Pattern Commun. (J. Commun. Univ. Chin.) **36**(2), 117–123 (2014)
18. Wang, Q.: The digital gap and the digital feedback: an empirical research on the relationship of the use of new media and parent-child relationship, M.A. Thesis. Chongqing: Chongqing University (2017)
19. Wan, L.H., Liu, J., Wen, X.: Cultural feedback among adolescents: re-examining communications and education in a family setting-A quantitative study on the digital divide and cultural feedback of adolescents in a family setting. Future Commun. **25**(3), 45–52 (2018)
20. Liang, F.: Generational differences in the use of WeChat in rural households and digital back-feeding: Based on an interview in Longxia Village, Wanzhou, Chongqing. J. News Res. **12**(09), 29–31 (2021)

21. Venkatesh, V., Morris, M.G., Davis, G.B., Davis, F.D.: User acceptance of information technology: toward a unified view. MIS Q. JSTOR **27**, 425–478 (2003)
22. Chen, X.M.: Exploration of the application of grounded theory in Chinese social-cultural research. Peking Univ. Educ. Rev. **13**(1), 2–15 (2015)
23. Strauss, A.L., Corbin, J.M.: Basics of Qualitative Research: Grounded Theory Procedures and techniques, 4th edn. SAGE Publications, New York, USA (2014)
24. Glaser, B.G., Strauss, A.L.: The Discovery of Grounded Theory: Strategies for Qualitative Research, 3rd edn. Routledge, London, UK (2017)
25. Zheng, C.Y., Xu, X.J.: Research on the mechanism of digital feedback: taking the use of short videos by post-95s and their parents as an example. Chin. Youth Study **31**(03), 12–17 (2019)
26. Nelissen, S., Van den Bulck, J.: When digital natives instruct digital immigrants: active guidance of parental media use by children and conflict in the family. Inf. Commun. Soc. **21**(3), 375–387 (2018)

Exploring the Association Between Multiple Classifications and Journal Rankings

Shir Aviv-Reuven(✉) and Ariel Rosenfeld

Department of Information Sciences, Bar-Ilan University, Ramat Gan, Israel
{avivres,ariel.rosenfeld}@biu.ac.il

Abstract. Journal classification systems use a variety of (partially) overlapping and non-exhaustive subject categories which results in many journals being classified into more than a single subject category. Given a subject category, respective journals are often ranked based on a common metric such as the Journal Impact Factor or SCImago Journal Rank. However, given a specific journal, it might be ranked very differently across its associated subject categories. In this study, we set to explore the possible association between the number of categories a journal is classified to and its associated rankings using the two most widely used indexing systems - Web Of Science and Scopus. Using known distance measures, our results show that a higher number of classified categories per journal is associated with an increased range and variance of the associated rankings within them. Findings and possible implications are discussed.

Keywords: Scientometrics · Journal subject classification · Journal ranking

1 Introduction

Evaluating and assessing the value of a scholarly journal is often pursued by one of a set of scientometric measures, such as the well established Journal Impact Factor (JIF) or SCimago Journal Rank (SJR) [5,7]. These scores are commonly used to induce a *ranking* of journals classified to the same category. In fact, researchers are often evaluated based on the articles they published in high ranking journals (e.g., top 25% of the journals in a subject category) [4,9,13].

Unfortunately, classifying journals into subject categories is an ill-defined problem since the delineation of a scientific field of research is, itself, unclear and journals' boundaries need not necessarily align with those of any given field of study [1,18]. The two most prominent scholarly indexing services – Web of Science (WoS) and Scopus – have developed their own unique journal subject classification systems which use a variety of (partially) overlapping subject categories. Since many journals are classified into more than a single category in

© The Author(s), under exclusive license to Springer Nature Switzerland AG 2023
I. Sserwanga et al. (Eds.): iConference 2023, LNCS 13971, pp. 426–435, 2023.
https://doi.org/10.1007/978-3-031-28035-1_31

these subject classification systems, they need not necessarily be ranked in the same way across their respective categories. In this work, we focus on the two leading journal subject classification systems (i.e., WoS and Scopus) and examine the potential relation between the number of categories a journal is classified to and that journal's metrics and rankings.

It is hard to intuitively speculate if and what is the nature of the relationship between the multi-labeling of a journal and its associated metrics and rankings. Presumably, one could argue that assigning multiple categories to a given journal is indicative of its multidisciplinarity. If that is the case, it is reasonable to expect a larger audience (both authorship and readership) for that journal which, in turn, is likely to bring about higher citation metrics and rankings across its assigned categories. Conversely, another could argue that such multi-labeling is, in fact, indicative of a journal's crude definition of its scope of interest or, alternatively, indication of a "niche journal" which focuses on a narrow field of research at the intersection of several other fields. If that is the case, such a multi-labeled journal is likely to have a smaller audience and thus may be associated with lower metrics and rankings. Previous research regarding multidisciplinary and interdisciplinary categories observed these and similar problems associated with using scientometrics to evaluate such journals (e.g., [6]).

In this work, we explore this possible relation by following two research questions: First, how is the number of categories a journal is classified to associated with that journal's impact metrics and rankings? Second, what is the relation between the number of categories a journal is classified to and the statistical range & variation in its associated rankings. To the best of our knowledge, this is the first work to examine this possible relation in the literature.

2 Background

WoS and Scopus are the two most influential scholarly indexing services. Countries and institutions often require authors to publish almost exclusively in journals which are indexed in either of the systems [10]. Many studies have compared the two systems along with other indexing databases. The main focus of these studies were the coverage and accuracy of these databases [2,14,16]. These studies identified that both systems suffer from incompleteness and inaccuracy of citation links and incorrect transcription of author names and/or title and showed that WoS was the most selective with respect to the number of journals indexed. Our work focuses on the journal subject classification systems of these two systems. Previous work brought to attention some of the issues related to these classification systems. Wang et al. [17] performed a detailed comparison of the classification systems of WoS and Scopus based on citation relations where they measured the "connectedness" of a journal in respect to its assigned category and to other categories based on the citation percentage. They observed that, on average, journals have significantly more categories assignments in Scopus than in WoS. Furthermore, in Scopus, journals are assigned to categories with which they are only weakly connected much more frequently than in WoS.

They conclude that WoS and especially Scopus tend to be too lenient in assigning journals to categories. These findings were corroborated in a recent longitudinal analysis by [3] where the authors observed the changes over time in number of categories per journal and number of journals per category in Scopus. They showed an increase on average in both aspects and concluded that newly added sources have been assigned to more fields and sub-fields on average than those indexed before the time period examined. A recent logical set theory based study by Aviv and Rosenfeld [1] showed that both system display unusually sized categories, high overlap and incohesiveness between categories and that across the two systems, journals are systematically classified to a different number of categories and most categories in either system are not adequately represented in the other system. The focus of the above studies was related to the journals classified within the indexing systems categories and their relation to their assigned categories.

Several studies have also focused on the bibliometric values and respective rankings of journals in the categories they are assigned to. Leydesdorff and Bornmann [8] showed that WoS subject categories are insufficient for performing bibliometric normalization due to "indexer effects". They focused on the two fields- "Library and Information Science" (LIS), which has a WoS subject category and "Science and Technology Studies" (STS) which does not, and performed a mapping of citation behavior for journals in these fields. Their results showed that normalization using these categories might seriously harm the quality of the evaluation. Subochev et al. [15] proposed ranking journals using methods from social choice and set theories to define aggregation methods of existing metrics. In a study related to ours, Pajić [12] analysed the stability of journals ranking across various metrics in respect to their assigned categories and over a specified time period. Their results show that the stability of journal rankings differs significantly among indicators and among subject areas.

In this work we follow the same line of research. Specifically, our work complements these and similar previous findings by examining the possible association between the number of categories and the ranking of any journal across its assigned categories. To the best of our knowledge, this possible association has yet to be examined.

2.1 Mathematical Definitions

In this work, we use the following mathematical definitions and notations. A journal subject classification system assigns each journal $j_i \in J$ possibly more than a single category from the set C. We denote the set of categories associated with journal j_i as $C_i = \{c_k\}$.

For each of the assigned categories c_k, j may be ranked differently based on its impact measure – Journal Impact Factor (JIF, in WoS) or SCImago Journal Rank (SJR, in Scopus). We denote this ranking as $j_i^{c_k}$ reading as journal j_i's ranking in category c_k. For our analysis, we consider the ranking as the journal's percentile ranking in each of its classified categories. Thus, for each journal, we have a set of percentiles corresponding to its set of classified categories.

In order to evaluate possible differences in rankings across categories, we adopt two standard distance measures: Min-Max (MM) and Variance (VAR). The Min-Max of journal j_i is defined as follows:

$$MM(j_i) = \max_{C_i}(j_i^{c_k}) - \min_{C_i}(j_i^{c_k}) \tag{1}$$

In words, $MM(j_i)$ is the difference between the highest and lowest percentile journal j_i is ranked to in any of its assigned categories. This measure captures the "range" of rankings associated with a specific journals. The variance is defined as follows:

$$VAR(j_i) = \frac{1}{|C|}\sum_{C_i}(j_i^{c_k} - \mu)^2 \tag{2}$$

In words, $VAR(j_i)$ is the sum of squared distances from the mean of all percentiles journal j_i is ranked in all of its assigned categories, divided by the number of categories it is assigned to. This measure captures the variation in rankings associated with a specific journal- that is, how "noisy" are the rankings of a journal across its assigned categories.

3 Data Collection

Our study focused on WoS and Scopus indexing systems. From each of these systems, we downloaded the complete set of the indexed journals and their associated categories and metrics as of end of 2020. Overall, 21,424 journals were extracted from WoS and 40,804 journals were extracted from Scopus. All associated metrics reflect the 2019 scores. We excluded journals which were designated as "Discontinued" or "Inactive" from Scopus (WoS does not contain such a designation), resulting in 25,751 journals. Journals which did not have a scientometric score assigned to them in one of the systems were excluded from further analysis as well. The final set of journals for our analysis comprised of 12,094 journals with 244 categories in WoS and 17,046 journals with 328 categories in Scopus.

Table 1 summarizes the descriptive statistics for each of these systems and of the data used in the following analysis. The descriptive statistics of mean,

Table 1. Descriptive statistics of the data

Descriptive statistics	WoS	Scopus
Number of categories	244	328
Total number of journals	21,424	40,804
Number of journals analysed	12,094	17,046
Mean number of subject categories assigned to each journal	1.62	2.32
SD number of subject categories assigned to each journal	0.8	1.27
Median number of subject categories assigned to each journal	1	2

standard deviation (SD) and median in Table 1 were calculated based on the sets of journals and categories under analysis.

All data and code are available in GitHub under Journals Subject Classificationand ranking.

4 Data Analysis

In order to examine our hypotheses, we analyse each of the two systems separately and begin by examining the number of categories each journal was classified to. As can be seen in Figs. 1a and 1b, in WoS, the number of categories each journal is classified to decreases quickly, with most journals being classified to a single category and the highest number of classifications for a single journal is 6 (i.e., 9 journals are classified to 6 categories). In Scopus, however, the majority of journals are classified in to two or more categories (approximately 70% of all journals under analysis), with a single journal being classified to 11 different categories (i.e, "Latin America research review").

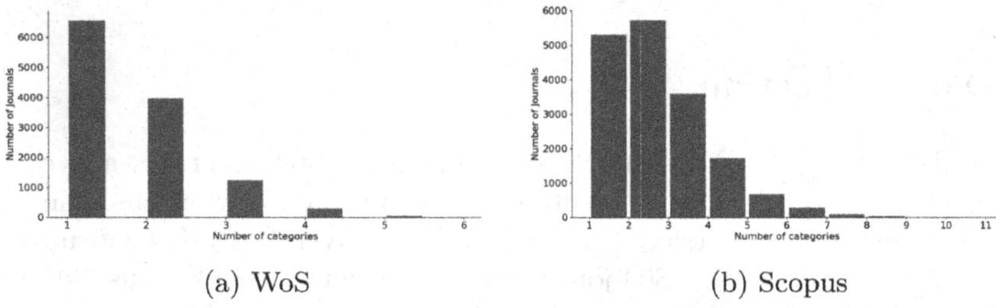

(a) WoS (b) Scopus

Fig. 1. Number of categories assigned to each journal.

Categories and Journals' Metrics. In order to understand how the scientometric scores of journals are related to the journals subject classifications in each system, we extract the JIF score for every journal in WoS and the SJR score for every journal in Scopus, respectively. We then analyse these values in respect to the number of categories each journal is classified to. The results are displayed in Fig. 2 and show the scientometric statistics by the number of assigned categories. Specifically, the top part of the figure display the highest score by any journal classified to a given number of categories. The box plots in the bottom part of the figure show the quartile values of the scientometric measure, extending from Q1 to Q3, with a horizontal line at the median (Q2). The whiskers extend from the edges of the box to show the range of the data up to 1.5 times the inter quartile range. The $\triangle$ shows the mean of the scientometric measure. In WoS, the highest JIF ranking decreases with the number of categories assigned to a journal, while all other statistics display an opposite trend, increasing with the number of categories a journal is classified to. In Scopus, only a single journal is classified into 11 categories and no journal is classified into 10 categories, thus we omit this journal in this analysis. Observing the classification of up to 9 categories, the highest SJR score shows a similar behaviour to that observed in WoS, namely decreasing with the number of categories. However, all other metrics displayed do not show any clear upward or downward trend. Thus, while for both WoS and Scopus a lower number of categories is positively associated with the highest score, the other statistics present a different picture. On average, in WoS, a higher number of categories is indicative of a higher metric score. This is not the case for Scopus in which the number of categories does not seem to be associated with the scientometric score.

Categories and Journals' Ranking. We further analyse the possible relation between the number of categories a journal is classified to and the differences in rankings among these categories. To that end, we adopt the MM and VAR measures (see Sect. 2) as functions of the number of classified categories. Figs. 3 and 4 display the results. The box plots in the figures extend from Q1 to Q3 quartile values for the MM and VAR of the percentile rankings, with a horizontal line

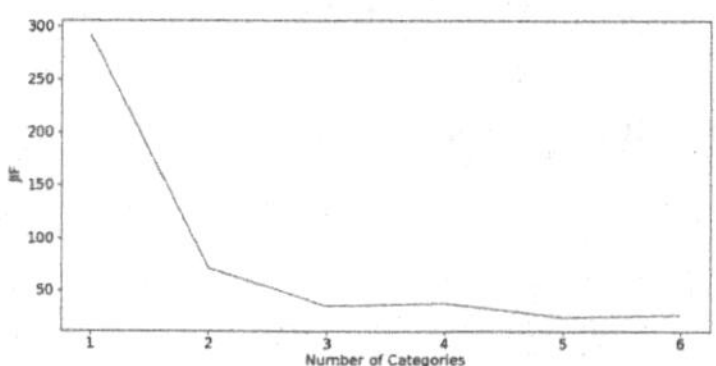

(a) WoS - Highest JIF by number of categories

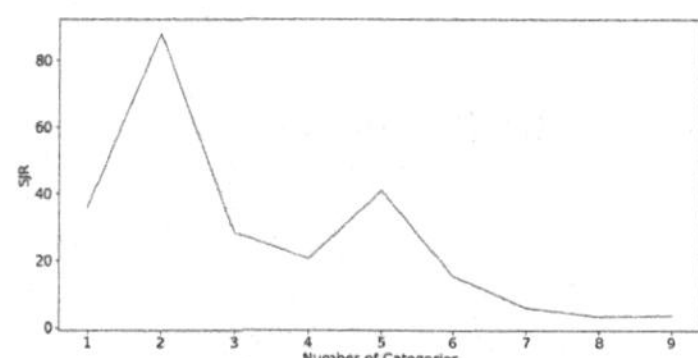

(b) Scopus - Highest SJR by number of categories

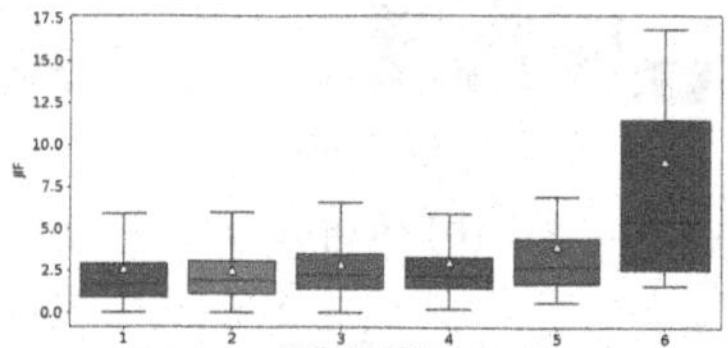

(c) WoS - JIF statistics by number of categories

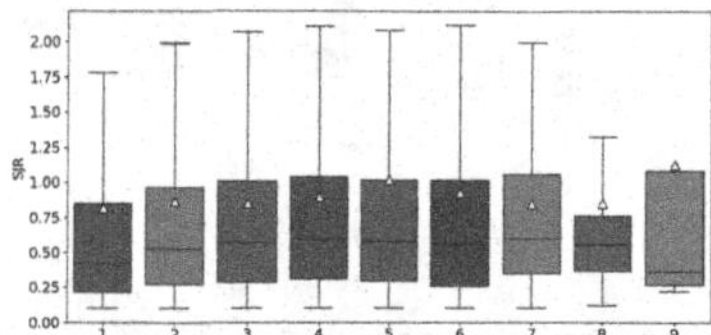

(d) Scopus - SJR statistics by number of categories

Fig. 2. highest scientometric score and q1–q3 range of scientometric scores

at the median (Q2). The whiskers extend from the edges of the box to show the range of the data up to 1.5 times the inter quartile range. The $\triangle$ shows the mean of the respective MM and VAR functions. As can be seen, WoS shows an increase in the mean and median of both the MM and VAR as the number of categories increases up to five categories and a decrease for 6 categories classification. Note, however that only 9 journals are classified to 6 categories (~0.16% of all multi-labeled journals in WoS). Hence, this observed decrease could be associated with the low number of journals rather than a meaningful change in pattern. Scopus shows a small yet consistent increase in the mean and median of both the MM and VAR as the number of classified categories increases. This means that, as the number of categories any single journal is classified to increases, its range of rankings as well as the variance within this range tend to increase as well. To verify our observations, we calculate the Pearson's correlation on both the MM and VAR measures with respect to the number of classified categories, for WoS and Scopus. For both indexing systems results were weakly positive yet statistically significant; for the MM (WoS: $r = 0.26, p < 0.001$; Scopus: $r = 0.31, p < 0.001$) and for the VAR (WoS: $r = 0.08, p < 0.001$; Scopus: $r = 0.08, p < 0.001$).

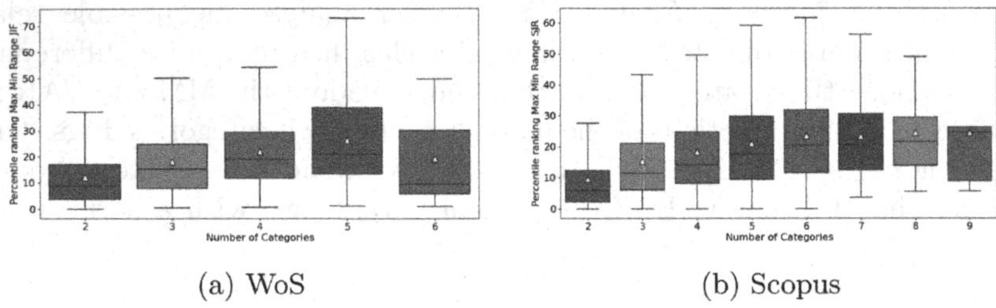

(a) WoS (b) Scopus

Fig. 3. MM of percentile rankings per number of categories

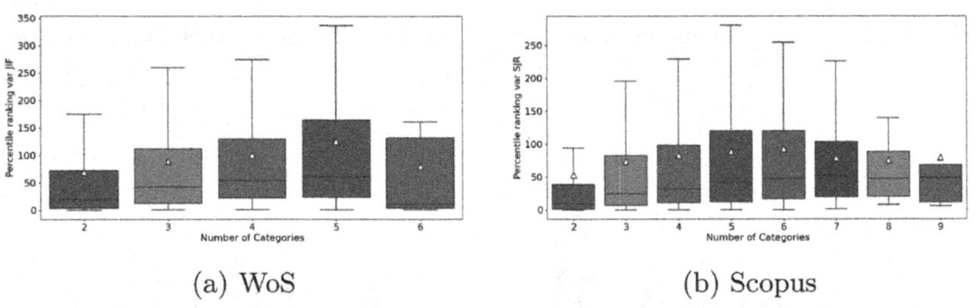

(a) WoS (b) Scopus

Fig. 4. Variance of percentile rankings per number of categories

5 Conclusion and Discussion

In this work, we explored the relation between the number of categories a journal is classified to and its scientometric scores (i.e., the JIF and SJR) and the rankings they induce within each category. We find that in WoS, a journal which is classified to several categories is likely to receive higher scholarly attention from the various disciplines associated with it. Our results further suggest that for both WoS and Scopus, as the number of categories a journal is classified to increases, both the range of the ranking and the variance within the range increase.

Our results, and especially the high variation in rankings across categories, suggest that there is an apparent inflation in high ranking of journals. Specifically, multi-labeled journals can highly bias any ranking which considers the "best ranking" any journal received in any of its categories. This inflation could be exploited by different actors to "pick and choose" the "best" ranking among the assigned categories. On the other hand, considering the ranking of a multi-labeled journal within a given (single) category could also lead to unwarranted insights or assumptions regarding its quality due to this high variation in ranking. Specifically, a journal may be ranked poorly in one category but ranked well in another, so considering only one of these rankings jeopardize the validity of the evaluation. For example, in Scopus, the journals are displayed according to the highest ranking they have in **any** category they are assigned to. This may be highly misleading. Since journal rankings play a pivotal role both in the selection of a venue to publish in and when evaluating researchers, departments and institutions [10, 11] recognising and addressing the aforementioned limitations of the current journal classification systems is crucial.

We plan to further explore, both quantitatively and qualitatively, the causes for these variations in rankings and examine different potential implications such as the "pick and choose" phenomena to better understand if these phenomena are indeed being exploited and if so, how. In future studies we also aim to explore possible solutions for the identified variations in ranking.

We recognize that this study is limited in several respects. While our study was comprised of a very large set of journals, encompassing an extensive variety of research fields, it contained only the subset of journals for which we have the metrics under analysis. The metrics used in our analysis were the JIF and SJR. These two metrics are calculated differently and could be a confounding factor in our ranking analysis and comparison. However, previous studies have shown the correlation of these metrics [15], somewhat mitigating this concern. Additionally, our analysis did not consider additional metrics such as those which apply normalization techniques. These metrics may induce different rankings which may or may not present similar patterns.

References

1. Aviv-Reuven, S., Rosenfeld, A.: A logical set theory approach to journal subject classification analysis: intra-system irregularities and inter-system discrepancies in web of science and Scopus. Scientometrics, 1–19 (2022)
2. Bar-Ilan, J., Levene, M., Lin, A.: Some measures for comparing citation databases. J. Informetr. **1**(1), 26–34 (2007)
3. Bordignon, F.: Tracking content updates in Scopus (2011–2018): a quantitative analysis of journals per subject category and subject categories per journal. In: ISSI, pp. 1630–1640 (2019)
4. Dennis, A.R., Valacich, J.S., Fuller, M.A., Schneider, C.: Research standards for promotion and tenure in information systems. Mis Q., 1–12 (2006)
5. González-Pereira, B., Guerrero-Bote, V.P., Moya-Anegón, F.: A new approach to the metric of journals' scientific prestige: the SJR indicator. J. Informetr. **4**(3), 379–391 (2010)
6. Haustein, S.: Multidimensional journal evaluation: analyzing scientific periodicals beyond the impact factor. Walter de Gruyter (2012). https://doi.org/10.1515/9783110255553
7. Larivière, V., Sugimoto, C.R.: The journal impact factor: a brief history, critique, and discussion of adverse effects. In: Glänzel, W., Moed, H.F., Schmoch, U., Thelwall, M. (eds.) Springer Handbook of Science and Technology Indicators. SH, pp. 3–24. Springer, Cham (2019). https://doi.org/10.1007/978-3-030-02511-3_1
8. Leydesdorff, L., Bornmann, L.: The operationalization of"fields" as WoS subject categories (WC s) in evaluative bibliometrics: the cases of "library and information science" and "science & technology studies". J. Assoc. Inf. Sci. Technol. **67**(3), 707–714 (2016)
9. McKiernan, E.C., Schimanski, L.A., Nieves, C.M., Matthias, L., Niles, M.T., Alperin, J.P.: Meta-research: use of the journal impact factor in academic review, promotion, and tenure evaluations. Elife **8**, e47338 (2019)
10. Nicholas, D., et al.: Choosing the 'right' journal for publication: perceptions and practices of pandemic-era early career researchers. Learned Publ. (2022)
11. Niles, M.T., Schimanski, L.A., McKiernan, E.C., Alperin, J.P.: Why we publish where we do: faculty publishing values and their relationship to review, promotion and tenure expectations. PLoS ONE **15**(3), e0228914 (2020)
12. Pajić, D.: On the stability of citation-based journal rankings. J. Informetr. **9**(4), 990–1006 (2015)
13. Rice, D.B., Raffoul, H., Ioannidis, J.P., Moher, D.: Academic criteria for promotion and tenure in biomedical sciences faculties: cross sectional analysis of international sample of universities. Bmj, 369 (2020)
14. Singh, V.K., Singh, P., Karmakar, M., Leta, J., Mayr, P.: The journal coverage of web of science, Scopus and dimensions: a comparative analysis. Scientometrics **126**(6), 5113–5142 (2021)
15. Subochev, A., Aleskerov, F., Pislyakov, V.: Ranking journals using social choice theory methods: a novel approach in bibliometrics. J. Informetr. **12**(2), 416–429 (2018)
16. Visser, M., van Eck, N.J., Waltman, L.: Large-scale comparison of bibliographic data sources: Scopus, Web of science, dimensions, crossref, and Microsoft academic. Quant. Sci. Stud. **2**(1), 20–41 (2021)

17. Wang, Q., Waltman, L.: Large-scale comparison of bibliographic data sources: Scopus, Web of science, dimensions, crossref, and Microsoft academic. J. Informetr. **10**(2), 347–364 (2016)
18. Zitt, M., Lelu, A., Cadot, M., Cabanac, G.: Bibliometric delineation of scientific fields. In: Glänzel, W., Moed, H.F., Schmoch, U., Thelwall, M. (eds.) Springer Handbook of Science and Technology Indicators. SH, pp. 25–68. Springer, Cham (2019). https://doi.org/10.1007/978-3-030-02511-3_2

The Design, Development, and Implementation of an LIS General Education Course for Non-LIS University Students in the Philippines

Elijah John F. Dar Juan(✉)

School of Library and Information Studies, University of the Philippines Diliman, Quezon City, Philippines
efdarjuan@up.edu.ph

Abstract. This paper presents information on LIS 10 Information and Society, a general education course offered by the School of Library and Information Studies (SLIS), University of the Philippines Diliman. LIS 10 is the first course of its kind in the Philippines. This narrative establishes the motivations that led to the course's development and gives pertinent information, including its description, expected student outcomes, and an enumeration of course topics. It also presents qualitative feedback received from students who took the course. As the pioneering instructor of the course, the author employs the autoethnographic method to narrate his personal experience and perspective on the collective conduct of UP SLIS faculty members on the design and development of the GE course.

Keywords: LIS education · Undergraduate general education · Social aspects of information · Information society · Information issues

1 Introduction

It is undeniable that the developments in information and communications technologies (ICTs) in the past decades have immensely affected the way humans create, disseminate, access, and use information. The WWW and social media enhanced access to information creation, processing, and dissemination tools, and people are now empowered to contribute to the societal knowledge pool. This empowerment has also led to issues and concerns about the state of the information environment, the disruption of information infrastructures [1], and the questionable quality of circulating information.

The growth and development of information and ICTs are a worldwide phenomenon, and the Philippines is not spared from these post-truth-era issues and concerns. In response to these growing concerns, the University of the Philippines Diliman (UP Diliman) School of Library and Information Studies (SLIS) took the opportunity to offer a general education course in library and information science (LIS) that is focused on recognizing information issues and encouraging a critical response. The course was envisioned to become a venue for undergraduate students to discuss prevailing information-related issues that concern everyone and not just those specializing in LIS.

© The Author(s), under exclusive license to Springer Nature Switzerland AG 2023
I. Sserwanga et al. (Eds.): iConference 2023, LNCS 13971, pp. 436–444, 2023.
https://doi.org/10.1007/978-3-031-28035-1_32

This paper presents information on LIS 10 Information and Society, a course designed and offered by UP SLIS for non-LIS students. The ensuing narrative establishes the motivations that led to the course's development and gives pertinent information, including its description, expected student outcomes, and an enumeration of course topics. As the pioneering instructor of the course, the author employed the autoethnographic method to narrate his personal experience and perspective on the collective conduct of UP SLIS faculty members on the design and development of the GE course.

2 Motivations

Based on initial research, there are LIS departments in US universities that offer general education (GE) courses. The University of Arizona School of Information offers ESOC 150 Social Media and Ourselves as part of its Tier 1 Individuals and Societies series of courses [2]. At the same time, the State University of New York at Albany has CINF 100X Information in the 21st Century, a course that equips students with ICT skills for study and research [3]. Florida State University has a selection of information courses under the Social Sciences and History area, specifically on information ethics, information literacy, IT, and technical communication [4].

As early as 2002, the window of opportunity was already open for academic degree-granting units in UP Diliman, including SLIS, to offer GE courses when the UP GE Framework was revised out of the reflection of philosophy, purpose and function, and rationalization toward more efficient use of resources. In the mid-2010s, under former Dean Prof. Kathleen Lourdes B. Obille, there was renewed interest in prospecting for a GE course in SLIS. In 2017, a proposal was submitted and discussed alongside working on the revisions of all undergraduate programs in UP due to the K-12 transition in Philippine basic education.

The idea of an information literacy skills course was brought to the table during the conceptualization of the overall course goal and approach. The course underwent the normal process of proposal submission and review. However, suggested revisions from curriculum committees and approving bodies shifted the focus away from information literacy skills development and onto student recognition and understanding of information issues. This significant revision also aligned with the mandate of the University Library to offer information literacy instruction [5].

The course was designed with the undergraduate UP Diliman student in mind. It was also aligned with the mandate of UP as the national university of the Philippines "to lead in setting academic standards and initiating innovations in teaching, research, and faculty development" [6]. It was also aligned with the School's responsibilities to LIS in the Philippines, the information professions, and broadly, as part of its public service to the country.

UP SLIS capitalized on proposing a GE course to enhance its image as an academic unit and increase its influence within the University community. In an interview, former SLIS College Secretary Prof. Benedict Salazar Olgado recalled his vigorous efforts in proposing a GE course. Driven by the desire to extend the reach and influence of the School, Prof. Olgado envisioned that the course should express the perspective and direction of SLIS as an information school. He visualized the course as a manifestation of the subject areas that are the specializations of UP SLIS, moving from traditional librarianship toward a broader appreciation of information and information studies.

Through a relatively expeditious yet arduous approval process, the latest version received approval from the review committees and University officials and was finally approved on June 25, 2018. LIS 10 Information and Society of UP SLIS is presumed to be the first course in LIS offered as part of the General Education program of a higher education institution (HEI) in the Philippines. At the time of writing, no other HEI in the Philippines offers a general education course on LIS.

3 Design

LIS 10 Information and Society was designed with the general undergraduate student in mind and amidst the contemporary social climate in the Philippines and worldwide. The course was created in response to this current technology-reliant, information-rich environment and the growing need for students to be aware of such an environment and better situate themselves, act appropriately, and contribute to positive societal change.

Based on a discussion with the SLIS Faculty members, the course evolved through several iterations. Draft course proposals situated information issues in different environmental contexts such as political, economic, cultural, and technological. Given that UP follows a standard process of instituting a course, approval is endorsed at various levels. During this process, the course was refined and refocused, with the most drastic change being the context of the discussion. From environmental contexts, the information issues were recontextualized within information processes, making them more grounded and easier to grasp. The five major information processes serving as anchors were creation, storage, dissemination, retrieval, and use [5].

The Course Description for LIS 10 was written to faithfully express the likeness of a GE course that would allow students to acknowledge information having an essential role in people's lives and framed in today's information-focused living. The approved Course Description reads, "Appreciation of the role of information in human endeavors in the context of its creation, management, dissemination, and use in an increasingly information-driven society" [7]. LIS 10 was designed with the awareness of the current social climate in the Philippines and around the world.

Due to the nature of GE courses in UP, the three-unit course has no prerequisites and was planned to be offered every semester, with three hours of contact time per week for a three-unit course. UP SLIS initially offered LIS 10 Information and Society in the First Semester of the Academic Year (AY) 2018–2019, the semester following its approval.

3.1 Course Goal and Outcomes

The goal of LIS 10 Information and Society is "to enable the students to explore and comprehend the complex nature of information and its processes for them to become responsible creators, disseminators, and users of information" [7]. The course aims to open a venue for students to discuss prevailing information issues in society and how they can appropriately respond to and act toward these issues. Aside from this, the course is facilitated in an explorative manner so that students can acquire knowledge of information concepts and how these concepts exist, affect, and shape our society. The Course Goal also expresses the aspiration of SLIS to influence undergraduate students of UP Diliman by educating them for a more morally upright and accountable citizenry with their information engagements.

The course outcomes of LIS 10 are restated with an emphasis on what the students can accomplish after completing the course:

- CO1: Explain the nature, history, and characteristics of information.
- CO2: Analyze the issues of information creation, organization, dissemination, retrieval, use, and preservation of [i.e., within] relevant societal issues across various disciplines.
- CO3: Appraise information authenticity, accuracy, and integrity and become responsible creators, disseminators, and users of information [7].

The course is designed for students to appreciate better and understand basic information concepts and the relevance of information in various sociohistorical contexts. Upon finishing the course, the students should also be capable of independently analyzing and evaluating common information issues that may affect them in their different disciplines and as citizens of society. Finally, as students will be exposed to information issues, the course is designed to develop their skills in evaluating information and being responsible and responsive in their information engagements, such as creation, dissemination, and use.

3.2 Coverage

In the first few versions of the course proposal, the course topics for LIS 10 were placed in the following contexts: health, economics, and technology, among others. However, feedback from reviewing and approving bodies refocused the course content to the five major information processes: creation, preservation, dissemination, retrieval, and use. The course also covers intellectual property, data privacy, the democratization of information, viral content, intellectual freedom, the digital divide, net neutrality, open movements, freedom of information, and information disorder. Almost all the SLIS faculty members were involved in developing content for the course, with each faculty member overseeing one or two topics related to their specialization.

Table 1 shows the course topics and their corresponding number of contact hours. After the introductory first meeting, Parts II and III acquaint students with basic information concepts and the historical contexts that led to the contemporary information environment. Students are first introduced to information issues in Part IV on Information Creation, where the democratization of information and intellectual property issues such as ownership, infringement, and plagiarism are discussed. Part V on Information Preservation discusses the importance of records and archives amid historical negationism and data privacy in securing personal information. The issues of Part VI on Information Dissemination tackle the credibility of media organizations and the value/insignificance of viral content.

The most extensive topic of the course, Part VII on Information Retrieval and Access, examines information issues concerning intellectual freedom and censorship, the digital divide, movements for free and open information sharing, and the demand for transparency and accountability in government through Freedom of Information. Part VIII on Information Use and Analysis discusses information disorder. The widespread concern about misinformation and disinformation is examined so that students are guided in responding to the harmful effects of false information.

Table 1. LIS 10 Information Society Course Coverage

Course topics	No. of hours
I. Introduction	1.5
II. From the Codex to the Codec: The History of Information A. Pre-Writing and Writing Era B. Print Era C. Information Explosion D. Digital Era	4.5
III. Information Demystified: Fundamental Concepts A. Contexts and Characteristics (as Energy, as Communication, as Fact, as Documentation, as Phenomenon) B. General Definition of Information (Floridi, 2010) C. The Information Cycle D. The Knowledge Spectrum	10.5
IV. Make iT! Information Creation and Resources A. The Process of Information Creation B. Democratization of Information: From One to Many C. Information as Property: Issues on Ownership of Information	6
V. Keep iT! Information Storage and Preservation A. The Ephemerality of Information and the Politics of Revisionism B. Information and the Archives C. We Are What We Keep: Archival Paradigms	6
VI. Share iT! Information Dissemination A. Key Players in Information Dissemination: Industries and Institutions B. Making Information Look Good: Information Design and Visualization	6
VII. Get iT! Information Retrieval Access A. Beyond Google: Varying Approaches to Information Search and Retrieval B. Talk Dewey to Me: Organization of Information and Its Implications on Retrieval C. Net Neutrality and the Digital Divide: The Right to Equal Information Access D. Holding Governments Accountable: The Fight for Freedom of Information	6
VIII. Use iT! Information Use and Analysis A. Information Literacy B. Critical Evaluation and Use of Information in Various Contexts: Economic, Political, Scientific, Health, etc C. The User's Response to Misinformation and Disinformation	7.5
	48

3.3 Pedagogy

LIS 10 Information and Society is a perfect opportunity to showcase the field and engage a vast audience in LIS discourse. Issues such as information disorder, information poverty, digital divide, intellectual freedom, open access, and mass media credibility are addressed by presenting basic information concepts, exposing current information issues, and engaging the exchange of viewpoints among students.

LIS 10 adopts a critical pedagogy to let learners analyze culture and society and challenge the power structures within. Emerging information issues from current events are examined using critical thinking questions, e.g., "Why is this happening?" and "What is our response? What can we do about it?".

Outcomes of the course are achieved through activities that let students explore the intricacies of information issues and, by doing so, form insights, perspectives, or responses on such issues. Since students do not have a significant background in LIS, course topics are introduced by definition and conceptualization. Class activities include teacher-led discussions that use probing questions, allowing students to dig deep into the information issue and formulate their opinions. Students are engaged to think and act within their means to inflict positive change in the current environment.

In the recent semesters before AY 2020–2021 (before COVID-19 and the shift to remote learning), the course follows a no-homework policy, given that it is a GE course and that it should not take too much time away from their 'majors' or their specialization. Activities such as games, short workshops, and student presentations were facilitated to provide variety during sessions. Specific examples include a debate on the ethics of websites that disseminate copyrighted content, content analysis of fake news, and the simple Pass the Message game to illustrate the difficulties in transferring information from person to person.

Guest lecturers were invited to enrich discussions and provide expert perspectives on issues. In this case, the faculty in charge of the course is responsible for contextualizing the discussion of course topics and providing a holistic view of the topic concerning LIS and society. Slide presentations and short video clips were shown in the class, with the latter as an alternative to teacher-delivered lectures. General assessment activities such as quizzes, minute papers, short take-home papers, and exams are used to grade students.

4 Student Feedback

In its first three semesters of implementation (from AY 2018–2019 to AY 2019–2020), SLIS saw batches of students from the different colleges and schools within UP Diliman, mostly coming from the College of Engineering and the College of Arts and Letters.

The objectives of LIS 10 were achieved. Overall, the course was found to be successful in its goal of leading the students to comprehend the nature of information and its processes. Based on the data gathered from the semestral Student Evaluation of Teaching (SET), an official survey for evaluating all courses offered at UP, the students found the course to be informative, relevant, and necessary. Table 2 shows the scores in the seven questions under Part 2A The Course of the Student Evaluation of Teaching, are all above 1.60 (scale of 1–5 with 1 as the highest).

In the question on critical thinking, "This course develops critical thinking," the course got 1.2889, while on creative thinking, 1.3313. The students expressed that topics were highly relevant in contemporary times. Being non-LIS majors, most students who took the course found a level of relatability with the course topics. Guest lectures were highly effective in providing accessible depth of knowledge and insight. They expressed satisfaction with the way the course was handled. Several students even suggested that LIS 10 should be a required GE course for all UP Diliman students. The course received a 1.2681 rating on the item "Even if this course were not required, it would still be worthwhile taking it." Table 3 shows selected open-ended responses of students about the course, the majority of which are consistent with the numerical scores. Students expressed one crucial factor for improvement: the inclusion of more varied activities to enhance teaching and learning.

Table 2. Student Evaluation of Teaching (SET) Scores for the Course

SET question	Weighted average
1. This course stimulates me to study beyond the lessons assigned	1.4077
2. This course has developed in me a greater sense of responsibility. (i.e., self-reliance, self-discipline, independent study)	1.3789
3. I have worked more conscientiously in this course than in most other courses	1.5976
4. Even if this course were not required, it would still be worthwhile taking it	1.2681
5. I am fully satisfied with the way this course was handled/conducted	1.2843
6. This course stimulates me to think creatively	1.3313
7. This course develops critical thinking	1.2889
Part 2. The Course (Overall Rating)	1.3653

5 Insights and Directions

The course was designed to respond to contemporary information issues plaguing the Philippines and the world. Since social problems and concerns evolve, the faculty in charge constantly reviews the LIS 10 Information and Society syllabus every semester. Evolving content such as viral content samples, data privacy cases, and technology trends in the Information Society are reviewed and revised as needed. Course subtopics are also modified to include crowdsourcing, data visualization, and intellectual property activism topics.

The COVID-19 pandemic and the shift to remote learning significantly influenced the course's coverage and delivery. Due to the modified Academic Calendar of UP Diliman, course topics were streamlined to fit a 12-week learning period. The faculty revised course materials for the content to be ready for asynchronous learning, while online class sessions facilitated probing questions and interaction among class members. A textbook made for the course is currently in production. At the same time, there are ongoing talks with the University television production unit TVUP about creating online educational resources (OERs) in streaming video format.

Research on LIS academic units offering GE courses may be undertaken in the future to determine the types of courses, topics covered, and pedagogy.

Table 3. SET responses of students about the course

Themes	Example Responses
Enlightening, educational, informative	"Learned so much in this class that goes beyond what I had expected from this discipline." "This course is fine for me the way it is, everything taught is useful or insightful information."
Valuable, timely, relevant	"The course itself is a great innovation. It is very needed in these times." "I think a lot [of objectives] have been covered already but are all useful in our daily lives not just as students but as people." "I'm very satisfied and think that the course is valuable for me."
Indispensable, vital, necessary	"All in all, this MST [Math, Science, and Technology course] is very different from all other MSTs in a very good way. It has a fresh take on how sciences can help and integrate with other sciences in solving problems. …" "His class is very informative and socially relevant that I think it should be taken by all UP students."

6 Conclusion

LIS 10 Information and Society is the first of several possible GE courses from UP SLIS. The course affirms and establishes the role of the School as the leader in LIS education in the Philippines. It is also a pivot to the direction of the School to embody the ideals of an iSchool [8]. More than the hopes and plans of UP SLIS, the offering of LIS 10 is a testament to the capability and resources of SLIS to educate and influence UP Diliman undergraduate students as the country's future leaders in becoming responsible information creators, disseminators, and users.

LIS is an ever-growing, constantly developing field. LIS and information schools should keep up with the changing times. It includes making information discourse relevant to university students. It is beneficial for LIS scholars and researchers to nurture the field by letting the academic community be aware of LIS as a field and the issues that it can influence. The course LIS 10 Information and Society is just one of many venues where information discourse can be conducted. LIS can become more influential to non-LIS students when framed in the appropriate contemporary context and delivered with a fundamental, issues-based approach. Through openness and determination, LIS academic units can garner increased interest in the field. Who better to spearhead the progress of information studies and champion social responsibility than the LIS practitioners, scholars, and researchers themselves?

References

1. Rubin, R.E., Rubin, R.: Foundations of Library and Information Science, 5th edn. ALA Neal-Schuman, Chicago (2020)
2. The University of Arizona School of Information. Degree Requirements – Information Science & eSociety. https://ischool.arizona.edu/ba-information-science-and-esociety/requirements. Last accessed 11 Dec 2022
3. University at Albany, State University of New York. Courses in Informatics. https://www.albany.edu/undergraduate_bulletin/87296.php. Last accessed 11 Dec 2022
4. Florida State University School of Information. Undergraduate Courses (both IT and ICT courses), https://ischool.cci.fsu.edu/academics/courses/undergrad. Last accessed 11 Dec 2022
5. Dar Juan, E.J.F.: The Design, Development, and Implementation of a General Education Course in Library and Information Science at the University of the Philippines Diliman. University of the Philippines Diliman, School of Library and Information Studies (2021)
6. The University of the Philippines Charter of 2008 (Republic Act No. 9500). http://officialgazette.gov.ph/2008/04/19/republic-act-no-9500. Last accessed 26 Feb 2022
7. ProposedGE from UP SLIS: LIS 10: Information and Society: Internal document: unpublished, School of Library and Information Studies, University of the Philippines Diliman, Quezon City (2017)
8. Dillon, A.: What it Means to be an iSchool. J. Educ. Libr. Inf. Sci. **53**(4), 267–273 (2012)

"It's Nice to Mix Up the Rhythm": Undergraduates' Experiences in a Large Blended Learning Course in Information Science in the Context of COVID-19

Lilach Alon(✉), SeoYoon Sung, and René F. Kizilcec

Cornell University, Ithaca, NY 14853, USA
la367@cornell.edu

Abstract. The abrupt transition to online instruction in the COVID-19 pandemic presented an opportunity for instructors in information science to engage with new teaching and learning modalities. After their online semester (i.e., Spring 2020), some decided to utilize the insights they gained and offer blended-learning courses in the post-pandemic semester. In this mixed-methods study, we surveyed a sample of 388 students in a large undergraduate information science course that transitioned from online to blended learning: 212 students in the online offering and 176 students in the blended offering of the course. We compared students' experiences in online and blended learning modalities and examined their perspectives on the blended learning component. Our quantitative and qualitative analyses yielded mixed results. Findings showed students preferred blended learning over online learning. They perceived it to be more engaging and active and reported that it allowed more peer interaction. Students had mostly positive perspectives of the blended learning components. However, some offered feedback on improving attendance requirements for the online component of the blended learning. Others reported online fatigue following online instruction during the pandemic. We discuss the findings and offer suggestions for effectively incorporating blended instruction in large information science courses.

Keywords: Blended learning · Online learning · Information science education · COVID-19 · Undergraduates

1 Introduction

1.1 Purpose

Disruptive innovation theory [1] frames a crisis, such as the COVID-19 pandemic, as a valuable opportunity to break common schemas and move towards more creative and innovative agendas. In a bottom-up process, a disruptive situation induces a new and creative category that gradually replaces the traditional one. In this process, a disruption might encourage a change in the long run. In this study, we frame the sudden transition to emergency online learning in higher education as a crisis event that could lead to

© The Author(s), under exclusive license to Springer Nature Switzerland AG 2023
I. Sserwanga et al. (Eds.): iConference 2023, LNCS 13971, pp. 445–460, 2023.
https://doi.org/10.1007/978-3-031-28035-1_33

sustainable instructional change in higher education [2, 3]. We rely on the disruptive innovation theory to frame and explain students' perceptions of transitioning from online learning to blended learning following the COVID-19 pandemic.

In this paper, we address the gaps in literature and examine the learning experiences of a sample of undergraduates in an information science course offered online during the pandemic (spring 2021 semester) and then transformed into a blended learning modality when the university returned to in-person instruction (fall 2022 semester). By drawing on disruptive innovation theory, we aim to shed light on the opportunities for pedagogical innovation that emerged from instructors' unique teaching experiences during the pandemic. We argue that learning from student experiences can expand our understanding of emerging pedagogical approaches in the post-pandemic era. Based on our findings, we suggest guidelines and principles for implementing well-designed blended instruction in information science courses in higher education.

1.2 Background

The pandemic caused a disruption in academic routines during the spring semester of 2020, forcing most higher education institutions to transition to online learning [4]. Despite the abrupt disruption, studies show that students mostly perceived the transition as a positive step towards improving their digital competencies [5, 6]. For example, a mixed-method study of faculty and students in three universities discovered students enjoyed the flexibility of online learning and felt the new learning experience contributed to their skills and knowledge [7]. Many higher education institutions continued the online instruction in subsequent semesters, allowing students and instructors to become familiar with learning and teaching online and appreciate its advantages. Following these teaching and learning experiences, course instruction in higher education has started to slowly change to include blended learning courses [8].

Blended learning is commonly defined as a flexible instructional method that combines several modalities of instruction (e.g., in-person and online) [9, 10]. Studies show that when designed well, blended learning can improve student learning experience, engagement, and achievements [11–14]. Integrating blended learning into large-scale courses might improve course interactivity and increase peer interaction via smaller group activities in an interactive online platform (e.g., in Zoom breakout rooms) [15]. The blended learning instructional method is also inclusive, as it offers more flexibility for learners (e.g., learning modality, course attendance), and enables personalized learning [15, 16]. To construct a sustainable, well-designed, blended learning course, instructors should consider the course structure (i.e., the balance of in-person and online instruction), the selection of activities within the course, and their own role in building relationships with the students [17]. Given these requirements, designing a blended course in higher education has remained a challenge for instructors [18].

Despite the challenges of constructing sustainable blended-learning courses, Porter and collogues [19] predict that in the future, 80–90% of courses will feature blended instruction. In fact, their prediction is already becoming a reality; Ma and Lee [8] argue that in the post-pandemic era, blended learning might become the *new normal* in higher education. A meta-analysis conducted before the pandemic challenges this notion, as it found students do not necessarily prefer blended learning. However, findings of a recent study examining student experiences in a sports and exercise program during the pandemic support Ma and Lee; in this case, students preferred blended learning over online learning [12].

Although instructional changes in higher education might be inevitable in the post-pandemic era [8, 19], little is known about the actual processes involved. For example, there is limited evidence so far on instructional changes in information science courses. Exploring how students' perspectives and instructors' experiences have changed might yield insights that are important for curriculum and course development.

1.3 Research Questions

In a mixed-methods study, we compared undergraduates' experiences of an information science course in two semesters that offered different learning modalities: an online learning modality (spring 2021 semester) and a blended learning modality (fall 2021 semester). We focused on the blended learning modality to understand how students perceived the course-related changes implemented by the instructor following the pandemic. We asked the following research questions:

RQ1. How did students' experiences change moving from online instruction to blended instruction?
RQ2. What were students' perspectives of the blended instruction?

2 Methods

2.1 Research Context

The study was conducted in the Department of Information Science at a large research university in North America. The course is a large-enrollment (200–250 students) mid-level course for undergraduates on web applications and data visualizations; it focuses on topics such as human-computer interaction, programming, and data science.

The course was offered pre-pandemic in a regular in-person modality. During the outbreak of COVID-19 in spring 2020, the course was transformed to an online learning modality and was reoffered in an online learning modality in spring 2021. Once COVID-19 restrictions were lifted, the course was offered in a blended learning modality in fall 2021. In this study, we focused on two offerings of the course: spring 2021 (online learning modality) and fall 2021 (blended learning modality). We chose the spring 2021 semester as an example of an online instruction modality, because the first online offering (spring 2020) was not planned, and the modality switched in the middle of the semester.

All the different modalities of the course (i.e., in-person, online, and blended) were taught by the same instructor following the same curriculum. The lectures in the online and blended instruction modalities were structured the same: three 50-min lectures every week; after each lecture, the instructor uploaded recorded lectures and notes to the course website. The course's content, projects, and assessment were the same for both modalities. The only difference between the two semesters was the instruction modality. The online semester offered three synchronous Zoom sessions per week. The blended semester included three weekly sessions, mainly in-person. During the blended learning semester, every three weeks the third weekly session on Friday was replaced by a 50-min synchronous Zoom meeting.

The transition to blended instruction was promoted by the instructor who wanted to implement several online components that he found useful for improving student engagement and learning during the pandemic. In particular, the instructor wanted to tackle some of the instructional challenges posed by the large scale of the course. The first challenge was encouraging peer interaction and group activities in a large course. This is important for information science students who will need collaborative skills in the workplace [26]. The second challenge was incorporating design critique activities. The instructor considered this important in a course focusing on developing design skills [27], such as data visualization. Design critique activities encourage students to evaluate their own and their peers' work, and in the process, they improve their data visualization skills. However, this type of activity is difficult to implement effectively in a large classroom setting.

To achieve these goals in the blended learning modality, the instructor incorporated two types of activities in the Zoom sessions throughout the semester: (1) group design activities; (2) group design critique activities. The design activity sessions focused on developing design skills by conducting mini projects in groups. The design critique sessions focused on developing critical thinking skills by evaluating peers' work. While the learning goals and nature of the activities for each type of session were different, all Zoom sessions had a similar structure, as described in Table 1.

Table 1. Structure of online sessions in the blended learning modality

Structure	Description	Practices
1. Introduction	- Instructor presented the session's topic, learning goals, and activities	- Instructor used Zoom chat to ask for students' questions and comments
2. Small-group activity in breakout rooms	- Students worked in groups of 5–6 - Design activity: students designed a mini group-project - Design critique: students evaluated peers' work	- Instructor gave prompts for the group activity - Instructor and TAs visited breakout rooms to facilitate group activity - Instructor sent notifications to facilitate the time management within the groups
3. Large-group discussion	- Large group discussion on the activity	- Design activities: students shared the mini-projects with the larger group - Design critique: students shared their experiences with the larger group - Instructor used Zoom chat to ask for students' questions and comments

2.2 Participants

Participants were 388 information science undergraduate students (59.3% female, 40.7% male) who completed a survey in one of the course offerings, either spring 2021 (online learning) or fall 2021 (blended learning). We collected 222 responses for spring 2021 and 188 responses for fall 2021. We removed 4 and 6 duplicate responses for spring 2021 and fall 2021, respectively, where students responded multiple times to the same survey, and 6 and 6 incomplete surveys, respectively, where students submitted an empty or an incomplete survey. This yielded 388 responses: 212 responses in spring 2021 (online learning) and 176 responses in fall 2021 (blended learning).

Table 2 summarizes the sociodemographic characteristics of the participants in each semester based on data provided by the university registrar.

Table 2. Participant demographics

		Online instruction Spring 2021 N = 212	Blended instruction Fall 2021 N = 176
Sex	Female	61.8%	56.3%
	Male	38.2%	43.8%
Race/ethnicity	Asian	40.6%	46.6%
	White	18.9%	13.6%
	Hispanic or Latino	0%	1.1%
	Black or African American	5.2%	2.8%
	Two or more races	9.4%	9.1%
	American Indian	0%	0.6%
	International/ Not specified	25.9%	26.1%

2.3 Measures

We collected data using self-reported surveys developed to measure student experiences in a course. Gathering quantitative and qualitative data through surveys is a common approach for studying phenomena related to disruptive innovation theory [e.g., 28, 29]. Our survey included nine statements that students rated on Likert scales, which examined the following aspects: overall learning experience in the course, course organization, difficulty level, perceived gained knowledge, perceived engagement, perceived activeness in the course, perceived collaboration with peers, the number of peers they collaborated with, and students' emotions during the course [20] (see Table 3).

For the semester of blended instruction in fall 2021, we added an additional statement and an open-ended question. The statement asked students to rate on a Likert scale the perceived benefits of two blended learning activities they had experienced on Zoom (i.e., group design critique, group design activity). The open-ended question asked them to describe their experiences in the online sessions as part of their blended learning experience. Table 3 summarizes all of the survey items and the response scales.

2.4 Procedure and Analysis

The study was conducted at the end of the spring 2021 semester (i.e., online instruction) and at the end of the fall 2021 semester (i.e., blended instruction) after receiving approval from the institutional review board. Surveys were distributed by the course instructor via a hyperlink to a Qualtrics survey, a web-based surveying platform. The survey was presented to students as part of a project to examine their learning experiences in the course. Students who completed the survey received extra credit and provided informed consent to use their responses.

For the quantitative data, we performed descriptive analysis and *t*-tests for independent samples, using IBM-SPSS statistical software. Qualitative data were analyzed by

Table 3. Survey items and response scale

Variables	Statements	Reference	Rating scale
Experience	How would you describe your experience in this course?	Alon et al. 2021	0 (poor) to 4 (excellent)
Organized	How well organized was this course?		0 (poor) to 4 (excellent)
Skills	Compared to how much you knew about the course topic at the start, how much new knowledge and skills have you learned by taking this course?		0 (not at all) to 4 (a great deal)
Engaged	How often did you synthesize ideas, think critically about the content, and apply the material to unfamiliar topics and problems?		0 (never) to 4 (always)
Difficulty	How easy or difficult is the course relative to other courses you have taken at Cornell?		−3 (difficult) to 3 (easy)
Active learning	How active or passive was the learning experience in this course?		−3 (passive) to 3 (active)
Active peers	How often during class time did you discuss course materials with fellow students?		0 (never) to 4 (always)
Number of peers	How many fellow students in this class do you feel comfortable asking for help with the course?		Integer input field
Concentration Frustration Confusion Anxiety	How often did you experience each of these emotions during the course?	Calvo and D'Mello 2010	0 (never) to 5 (always)
How much do you feel that this new activity helped you learn in the course?		Alon et al., 2021	1 (not at all) to 4 (a lot)
Tell us about your experience with the new activity (design activity; design critique)			Open-ended question – Coded

using bottom-up content analysis [21]. According to this method, content is analyzed into categories that are gradually developed into sub-categories. In this study, we identified three categories that reflected students' experiences in blended learning. These were gradually developed into eight sub-categories.

3 Findings

3.1 Student Experiences in Online Versus Blended Learning

We conducted *t*-tests for independent samples to compare student experiences in online learning and blended learning (Table 4).

Table 4. Mean scores, standard deviations (SD), and *t*-test statistics with *p*-values for independent samples of student experience in online and blended learning (N = 388).

Survey measure	Online learning M (SD); *N* = 212	Blended learning M (SD); *N* = 176	*t*-test	*p*-value
Experience	3.47 (0.63)	3.53 (0.57)	$t = 1.00$	$p = .319$
Organized	3.46 (0.61)	3.52 (0.59)	$t = 1.00$	$p = .327$
Skills	3.21 (0.92)	3.23 (0.85)	$t = 0.13$	$p = .828$
Engaged	2.71 (0.71)	2.88 (0.71)	$t = 2.32$	$p = .021$
Difficulty	0.41 (1.21)	0.49 (1.18)	$t = 0.65$	$p = .518$
Active learning	1.27 (1.42)	1.61 (1.18)	$t = 2.52$	$p = .012$
Active peers	1.72 (1.00)	1.95 (0.95)	$t = 2.26$	$p = .024$
No. of peers	2.73 (1.83)	3.48 (2.27)	$t = 3.62$	$p < .001$
Concentration	3.23 (0.90)	3.11 (0.96)	$t = -1.35$	$p = .178$
Frustration	1.65 (1.01)	1.43 (1.06)	$t = -2.12$	$p = .034$
Confusion	1.56 (0.83)	1.54 (0.88)	$t = -0.25$	$p = .805$
Anxiety	1.15 (1.02)	1.07 (1.01)	$t = -0.68$	$p = .486$

Results showed students' learning experiences were somewhat different in the two semesters (i.e., online learning and blended learning). They reported a similar satisfaction with the course, and their affective experience was similar in terms of concentration, confusion, and anxiety levels. However, in blended learning, students reported being more engaged and active in the course. They collaborated more with their peers, and the number of peers they felt comfortable approaching for help increased. They also reported less frustration during the blended learning than the online learning semester.

3.2 Students' Perspectives on Blended Learning

To answer the second research question, we examined students' perspectives on the blended learning semester. First, we calculated mean scores, SDs, and frequencies for student responses for the question: "How much do you feel that this new activity helped you learn in the course?" The distribution of responses is visualized in Fig. 1.

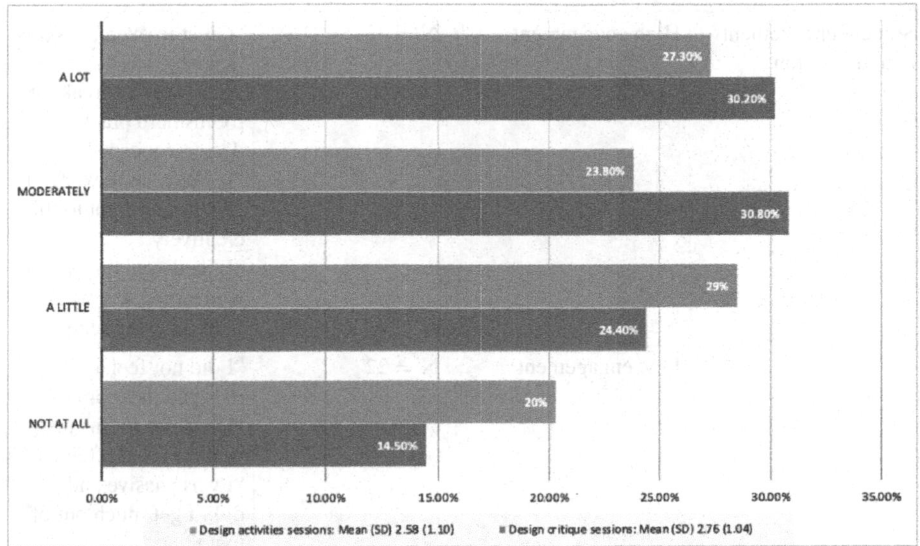

Fig. 1. Distribution of students' responses (N = 176) to the question "How much do you feel that this new activity helped you learn in the course?" for two blended learning activities: design activities (orange) and design critiques (blue).

On average, students perceived the blended instruction activities to be moderately beneficial for their learning. They reported more satisfaction with the group design critique sessions (*Mean* = 2.76, *SD* = 1.04) than the design activity sessions (*Mean* = 2.58, *SD* = 1.10).

To better understand why students favored or did not favor the blended learning experience, we analyzed 173 responses to an open-ended question that asked students to describe their overall experience during the online Zoom sessions (three students did not answer the question). The analysis revealed more than one comment for several students (i.e., they referred to multiple topics); this resulted in 212 student comments.

A conventional content analysis of the comments revealed three categories that described student experiences in blended learning: (1) student engagement and motivation; (2) perceived benefits of the blended learning modality; (3) balance between in-person and online instruction in blended learning. For each category, we then identified sub-categories according to student responses.

In Table 5, we summarize our findings for the three categories and eight sub-categories and offer examples of student comments.

Most reactions to the blended learning experience were positive. Out of 212 student comments, 145 comments (68.4%) reflected a good student experience with the blended learning, and 67 comments (31.6%) reflected a negative student experience.

Table 5. Content analysis of student perspectives on blended learning

Categories	Sub-categories	No. of comments	Examples of student comments
Student engagement and motivation	High engagement	N = 42	"Great to exercise skills in a new way" "Activities in breakout rooms help practice design concepts" "It was nice to work in groups and I got to think creatively" "I liked applying skills we learned and work with other students"
	Low engagement	N = 22	"I did not feel as engaged in Zoom" "Breakout rooms just were not that effective" "I was passive and didn't get much out of them" "It's frustrating to be in a group who doesn't care as much as you"
	Attendance policy as a motivator	N = 31	"Attendance being required could serve as an incentive to go" "These were optional, so many peers were not motivated to attend" "I felt less bad missing these because Zoom feels less formal"
Perceived benefits of blended learning modality	Peer interaction	N = 22	"Zoom provides an opportunity to really talk to our classmates" "It was nice to have an environment where you can freely talk to a small group of people, especially in a large class"

(*continued*)

Table 5. *(continued)*

Categories	Sub-categories	No. of comments	Examples of student comments
	Convenience	N = 33	"It removes the necessity of traveling to get to class" "Having some flexibility eases our stress" "Helps me get my schedule more flexible"
	Helpful during the pandemic	N = 3	"This helps a lot during covid time" "It was a nice option for students especially during the pandemic"
Balance of in-person and online instruction in blended learning	Good balance	N = 45	"They offered a good balance of online and in-person lectures" "It's nice to mix up the rhythm and attend in a different modality" "The Friday Zoom meeting was a change of pace" "Keep it! I am braver on Zoom"
	Do not like Zoom sessions	N = 14	"I personally don't like anything on Zoom" "After a year of Zoom learning, I am wholly Zoom-fatigued" "Zoom makes me easier to fall asleep"

For the student engagement and motivation category, findings showed most students perceived the blended learning experience to be engaging and helpful for their learning, as it enabled them "to exercise skills in a new way". However, several students reported they were not engaged in the online sessions, as they were frustrated with group work and engagement in breakout rooms. In addition, some students perceived the lack of mandatory attendance as a factor that reduced their motivation to attend the online sessions and harmed their engagement.

For the perceived benefits of the blended learning modality category, students mentioned the added value of peer interaction during online sessions. Their positive responses about peer interaction suggest the benefit of adding an online component in a large-scale course in which students have fewer opportunities to interact with peers and participate in interactive activities. Students also mentioned the convenience of having occasional remote sessions every once in a while. Finally, Zoom sessions were helpful for students who could not attend class because of limitations related to COVID-19 and other health-related concerns.

Overall, students felt that the blended instruction offered a good balance of the two instructional modalities (in-person instruction, online instruction). They expressed that the blended instruction was a "change of pace" and an opportunity to "mix up the rhythm" of the class. Nonetheless, other students complained about online fatigue after prolonged online instruction and stated that they preferred in-person instruction.

4 Discussion

Our study examined undergraduates' experiences in an information science course that was transformed into a blended learning modality following the COVID-19 pandemic. We wanted to compare students' experiences in the online learning modality with their experiences in the blended learning modality and examine their perspectives on the two blended learning activities. We aimed to identify the learning barriers and opportunities created by teaching changes during the pandemic, hoping to find ways to allow instruction in information science courses to evolve in the post-pandemic era.

Our first research question asked how students' experiences changed with the move from online instruction to blended instruction. We discovered students preferred the blended learning modality over the online modality [12]. They reported a good overall learning experience in both instances (online and blended) and perceived the course to be organized and clear in the two learning modalities. Their affective experiences were also alike in terms of their level of confusion, concertation, and anxiety. However, they said the blended learning modality offered more opportunities to be engaged with the course, and their learning was more active. Their social interactions also improved, as they collaborated with more peers and felt more comfortable asking for their help. They reported less frustration during blended learning as well.

These findings correspond with previous studies that suggest blended learning is more inclusive and accessible to students when it is carefully designed [11, 12, 16]. In large classes, such as the course we examined, blended learning offers more opportunities for social interaction and peer support [15, 17]. This can be done, for example, by incorporating features of online conferencing tools that allow students to break into smaller groups for class discussions and group work. Such smaller group practices are more difficult to implement in large classroom setups [26].

Taking into consideration that planning a blended learning course is both challenging and complicated [18], these are positive findings. Students' satisfaction with the course supported the instructor's efforts to create a sustainable and supportive learning environment. It also showed that a well-planned blended course might serve as an active learning method in large information science courses, bringing students together and increasing their engagement and interaction [15, 23].

Our findings for the second research question painted a more complicated picture of students' perspectives of the blended instruction. Overall, our quantitative and qualitative analysis yielded mixed findings. Students were somewhat satisfied with the online component of the course (i.e., Zoom sessions on Friday), but they also had constructive feedback for future offerings of the blended learning course. They mentioned multiple positive aspects of blended learning, including its engaging and interactive nature, its convenience and flexibility, and the opportunity to interact with peers in a large course. These findings are consistent with previous studies which found that blended learning could enhance student engagement and collaboration [15, 17], and improve instruction flexibility [16].

Particularly, students mentioned that one benefit of joining the online meetings was that it enabled them to interact with their peers. They appreciated this interaction which does not happen too often in a large, lecture-based classroom setting. Collaborating and interacting with peers could enhance students' sense of belonging in the classroom and help them to acquire collaborative skills [26]. Another positive aspect of blended learning that was mentioned by the students was the opportunity to exercise higher-order thinking skills during online activities. For example, being able to practice design critique skills teach students how to evaluate their own and their peers' work. Through this process, they can improve their data visualization skills and learn best practices [27]. These aspects of online meetings (e.g., collaborating with peers, exercising practical skillsets) indicate the opportunities that blended learning holds to encourage peer interaction and group activities in large information science courses [23].

Nonetheless, students' perspectives of the blended learning instruction also shed light on the aspects that should be improved. These included the students' lack of engagement with the online component of the course (i.e., Zoom meetings) and the optional attendance policy that harmed student motivation. Several students also reported online fatigue following the long period of online instruction during the pandemic [22].

Disruptive innovation theory [1] suggests disruptions and changes might not be adopted by all people immediately. It might take time for some people to adjust to changes and embrace novelty. Student resistance to change in course instruction might reflect a challenging transition after a few semesters of instable instruction [7]. After transitioning from in-person to online instruction during the pandemic, students might struggle as they navigate their way back onto campus [8]. Hence, students may have trouble adopting yet another new learning modality – blended learning.

Our study suggests that despite some difficulties during the transition, students are relatively open to trying a new learning modality and welcoming the opportunities it brings for enhancing their learning experience. We therefore recommend that instructors in information science incorporate blended learning components into their courses. This is particularly important in large in-person undergraduate courses, where it is difficult to engage students, promote peer interaction, and experience various types of activities that can promote students' skills (e.g., design critiques, group work).

That said, it is important to be aware of best practices when planning blended learning instruction with an online component. First, instructors should consider having synchronous sessions that enable more interaction and engagement than asynchronous online sessions [24]. As mentioned above, interactive online sessions have the potential to encourage more peer interaction and enable collaborative activities. Second, the balance between in-person and online sessions should be carefully planned, as students are still coping with online fatigue and their pandemic experiences [22]. Instructors should consider focusing on in-person instruction while adding the online component as an added bonus to their classes. Balancing in-person lectures with online activities can help instructors take advantage of the best parts of each learning method [12, 15]. It is also important to communicate to students the rational for choosing a blended learning method. Instructors should explain the reasons for incorporating online meetings and describe the expected benefits from students. Third, students' experiences during the course should be monitored (e.g., student evaluations or surveys) to see how they handle the change in instruction and how to support students who might struggle with blended instruction. This may be especially beneficial for supporting ethnic minority students, who have been found to be at a disadvantage in online instruction [25].

The current study has several limitations. First, we relied on students' self-reported surveys to examine their perceptions of online and blended learning. Future studies might examine students' behavior during blended learning by extracting and analyzing log data from learning systems and/or online platforms. This research path might reveal additional insights regarding students' learning and behavior in blended learning courses. Second, we examined students' experiences in one information science course, and did not explore the role of sociodemographic backgrounds in their perceptions of the blended learning experience. We recommend that future studies examine students' perspectives on blended instruction in a larger sample of students, in multiple courses, and focusing on the role of students' identity-based groups in their blended-learning experience. It is also important to explore if and how instructors in information science are willing to change instruction modalities following the experience gained during the pandemic. Future work can also examine how institutions can effectively support instructors in this transition to blended learning.

References

1. Christensen, C., Raynor, M.E., McDonald, R.: Disruptive Innovation. Harvard Business Review, Brighton, MA (2013)
2. Mali, D., Hyoungjoo, L.: How do students perceive face-to-face/blended learning as a result of the Covid-19 pandemic? The Int. J. Manage. Educ. **19**, 10052 (2021)
3. Yang, B., Huang, C.: Turn crisis into opportunity in response to COVID-19: experience from a Chinese university and future prospects. Stud. High. Educ. **46**(1), 121–132 (2021)
4. Trout, B.S.: The coronavirus-induced transition to online learning perceptions and intentions of first-time online students. Q. Rev. Distance Educ. **21**(1), 1–1 (2020)
5. Hajjej, F., Ayouni, S., Shaiba, H., Alluhaidan, A.S.: Student perspective-based evaluation of online transition during the COVID-19 outbreak: a case study of PNU Students. Int. J. Web-Based Learn. Teach. Technol. (IJWLTT) **16**(5), 21–38 (2021)
6. Tang, Y.M., et al.: Comparative analysis of Student's live online learning readiness during the coronavirus (COVID-19) pandemic in the higher education sector. Comput. Educ. **168**, 104211 (2021)
7. Benito, Á., et al.: Changes that should remain in higher education post COVID-19: a mixed-methods analysis of the experiences at three universities. High. Learn. Res. Commun. **11**, 51–75 (2021)
8. Ma, L., Lee, C.S.: Evaluating the effectiveness of blended learning using the ARCS model. J. Comput. Assist. Learn. **37**(5), 1397–1408 (2021)

9. Vo, H.M., Zhu, C., Diep, N.A.: The effect of blended learning on student performance at course-level in higher education: a meta-analysis. Stud. Educ. Eval. **53**, 17–28 (2017)
10. Owston, R., York, D., Murtha, S.: Student perceptions and achievement in a university blended learning strategic initiative. The Internet High. Educ. **18**, 38–46 (2013)
11. Güzer, B., Caner, H.: The past, present and future of blended learning: an in depth analysis of literature. Procedia Soc. Behav. Sci. **116**, 4596–4603 (2014)
12. Finlay, M.J., Tinnion, D.J., Simpson, T.: A virtual versus blended learning approach to higher education during the COVID-19 pandemic: the experiences of a sport and exercise science student cohort. J. Hospitality, Leisure, Sport Tourism Educ. **30**, 100363 (2022). https://doi.org/10.1016/j.jhlste.2021.100363
13. Jonker, H., März, V., Voogt, J.: Collaboration in teacher design teams: Untangling the relationship between experiences of the collaboration process and perceptions of the redesigned curriculum. Stud. Educ. Eval. **61**, 138–149 (2019)
14. López-Pérez, M.V., Pérez-López, M.C., Rodríguez-Ariza, L.: Blended learning in higher education: students' perceptions and their relation to outcomes. Comput. Educ. **56**(3), 818–826 (2011)
15. Singh, J., Steele, K., Singh, L.: Combining the best of online and face-to-face learning: Hybrid and blended learning approach for COVID-19, post vaccine, & post pandemic world. J. Educ. Technol. Syst. **50**(2), 140–171 (2021)
16. Bamoallem, B., Altarteer, S.: Remote emergency learning during COVID-19 and its impact on university students perception of blended learning in KSA. Educ. Inf. Technol. **27**(1), 157–179 (2021). https://doi.org/10.1007/s10639-021-10660-7
17. Heilporn, G., Lakhal, S., Bélisle, M.: An examination of teachers' strategies to foster student engagement in blended learning in higher education. Int. J. Educ. Technol. High. Educ. **18**(1), 1–25 (2021). https://doi.org/10.1186/s41239-021-00260-3
18. Bruggeman, B., Tondeur, J., Struyven, K., Pynoo, B., Garone, A., Vanslambrouck, S.: Experts speaking: crucial teacher attributes for implementing blended learning in higher education. The Internet Higher Educ. **48**, 100772 (2021). https://doi.org/10.1016/j.iheduc.2020.100772
19. Porter, W.W., Graham, C.R., Spring, K.A., Welch, K.R.: Blended learning in higher education: institutional adoption and implementation. Comput. Educ. **75**, 185–195 (2014)
20. Calvo, R.A., D'Mello, S.: Affect detection: an interdisciplinary review of models, methods, and their applications. IEEE Trans. Affect. Comput. **1**(1), 18–37 (2010)
21. Hsieh, H.F., Shannon, S.E.: Three approaches to qualitative content analysis. Qual. Health Res. **15**(9), 1277–1288 (2005)
22. Nesher Shoshan, H., Wehrt, W.: Understanding "Zoom fatigue": a mixed-method approach. Appl. Psychol. **71**(3), 827–852 (2022)
23. Alon, L., Sung, S., Kizilcec, R.F.: How does active learning change undergraduate learning experiences? A case of a large technology design course. In: Innovate Learning Summit, pp. 201–208. Association for the Advancement of Computing in Education (AACE) (2021)
24. Jaggars, S.S., Xu, D.: How do online course design features influence student performance? Comput. Educ. **95**, 270–284 (2016)
25. Lee, K., Fanguy, M., Bligh, B., Lu, X.S.: Adoption of online teaching during the COVID-19 Pandemic: a systematic analysis of changes in university teaching activity. Educ. Rev. **74**(3), 460–483 (2022)
26. Cartwright, N.M., Patil, P., Liddle, D.M., Newton, G., Monk, J.M.: Enhancement of professional behaviours and perceptions of critical skill job preparedness through the use of a group work contract in fourth-year nutritional science students. Int. J. Higher Educ. **10**(2), 27–41 (2021)
27. McDonald, J.K., Michela, E.: The design critique and the moral goods of studio pedagogy. Des. Stud. **62**, 1–35 (2019)

28. Guo, J., Pan, J., Guo, J., Gu, F., Kuusisto, J.: Measurement framework for assessing disruptive innovations. Technol. Forecast. Soc. Chang. **139**, 250–265 (2019)
29. Flavin, M.: A disruptive innovation perspective on students' opinions of online assessment. Res. Learn. Technol. **29**, 1–22 (2021)

Visual Information Processing in Virtual Reality: Merging Theory and Practice

Jack Clark(✉)

University of Arizona, Tucson, AZ 85721, USA
jaclarkent@arizona.edu

Abstract. Understanding visual information processing is becoming more important as technologies like virtual reality (VR) are being integrated into our training and learning experiences. A dissection between reception from perception is necessary to accommodate researching these visually intensive technologies. For instance, visual reception is the act of encoding information from the outside world, whereas perception is the act of interpreting that information internally. Theories regarding cue location, hierarchy of features, perceptional salience, postattentive amnesia, inattentional blindness, change blindness, and attentional blink will be discussed in this paper to focus on the separation of visual reception and perception. This paper will also highlight human thresholds of visual interpretations and the reliability of immersive technologies like VR for researching and understanding visual information processing. Concluding, this paper will discuss the need for iSchool communities to collaborate on this type of research. Specifically, educators, developers, and researchers working with VR contexts to better understand human behavior and software design.

Keywords: Virtual reality · Visual perception · Information processing

1 Introduction

Through our visual channel alone, we interpret information in several different modes: graphics, written text, movement, depth, spatial awareness of avatars in digital gaming experiences, etc. Each mode can be dissected to fundamental visual cues that trigger visual attention and cognitive recall [19]. For instance, color tends to trigger emotions and memories, that designates placement of categorical knowledge [19] and each person will interpret the color differently based on their various funds of knowledge [20]. These triggers change the way we interpret and interact with different experiences, especially in a visually intensive technology like virtual reality (VR). Additionally, many aspects of information processing are unconsciously occurring within milliseconds of reception, before altering perception, interpretation, and cognitive load on working memory [12]. This review will highlight important theories for understanding visual information processing and how it is affects our ability to thrive in an immersive environment like VR. Specifically, the dissection of reception from perception, and saliency of visual information.

© The Author(s), under exclusive license to Springer Nature Switzerland AG 2023
I. Sserwanga et al. (Eds.): iConference 2023, LNCS 13971, pp. 461–468, 2023.
https://doi.org/10.1007/978-3-031-28035-1_34

2 Visual Reception

Visual reception is the act of collecting information through our visual channel. This behavior is comprised of both automatic and controlled cognitive processes. These processes are happening in rapid succession as the eye is constantly fixating to different points of a visual scene. For example, imagine looking at a landscape painting of a beach with waves, some surrounding cliffs with trees, and both sail boats and barges are depicted along the horizon. To notice all aspects of the painting, one must first look at each part of the painting individually before bringing the information to a full image. The same is true at a more detailed level when defining a sailboat from a barge and organizing images from a pixel level. It is the combination of lines, colors, and textures that create knowledge of the visual scene, yet the process is not linear [23]. Furthermore, the limited shape of the eye's Field of View (FoV) and the rapidity of information reception are obstacles when encoding images through the human eye [11, 23].

2.1 Saccades and Blindness

Visual attention encompasses a trail of automatic processes that connect what the eye is seeing to what the brain is interpreting. The human eye's fixated FoV is limited; "about the size of a thumb nail at arms-length" [11]. This means that when we are interpreting visual information the eye is rapidly moving across different areas of the virtual stimulus, fixating at certain points to make an overall sense of the environment [11]. Consequently, each time the eye moves from place to place it is not collecting information, resulting in momentary blindness. This blindness is referred to as a saccade [11]. The transfer between fixation and saccade occurs 3–4 times per second of visual stimulus [11]. During each saccade, the brain is deciding the location of the next fixation based on contrasting features like color, orientation, luminance, etc., as well as the individual's intent, tasks, previous experiences, and mental state [11].

2.2 Visual Cue Location

In 1980, Posner and other psychologists began to establish an understanding of retinal position and how it affects fixation interpretation [23]. Fixation interpretation is the process of receiving visual information from a single saccade. Posner and colleagues first posed the concept that visual attention should be viewed as a spotlight to show there are varying degrees of fixation occurring at a given moment. From this concept, two types of spatial cues were created that dictate visual attention: central cues and peripheral cues [10, 29]. Central cues are designated by the direct fixation (e.g., center of the spotlight), whereas peripheral cues are past the margin of light and in the 'fringe' of the fixation (See Fig. 1) [10, 23, 29]. Peripheral cues are not usually in detail like central cues, nor do they derive accurate depictions of shape [10, 23, 29]. However, they do indicate spatial location in relation to the central cue or current fixation [10]. The knowledge from peripheral and central cues are collected and categorized internally for mental organization and meaning making [10, 23]. As each fixation is collected, it is grouped with other previous information and encoded in visual working memory to offer an encapsulation of an image (e.g., Feature Extraction) [10, 11, 17].

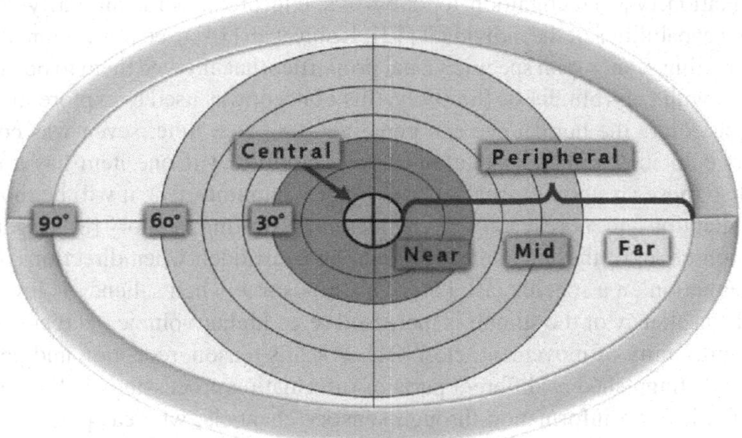

Fig. 1. This image depicts the FoV of human vision. It shows the varying types of cues involved in visual reception [22].

2.3 Hierarchy of Features

There are four main factors that affect involuntary visual attention and encoding to visual working memory: shape, color, proximity to focused visual location, and length of time allotted for searching [6, 18]. Color was discovered to be a more distinctive feature for manipulating involuntary attention than shape regardless of proximity to focused visual location [6, 7, 18]. Meaning, the proximity to visual location and presentation duration did not affect encoding for color yet did affect encoding for shape [6, 7, 18]. For instance, when viewing a set of 6 shapes with 6 different colors, shapes will be encoded depending on the fixation location, whereas the colors have equal opportunity to be encoded regardless of location (i.e., located in peripheral FoV) (See Fig. 1). Results suggest color is interpreted parallel to other colors regardless of fixation location. For shape, a bottleneck style filtration system is used based on proximity to the fixation location [7, 18]. The farther away from the fixation location the shape is, the more it will have to compete with other peripheral shapes for accurate encoding into visual working memory [6, 7, 18]. Additionally, results yielded a positive correlation with the increase of presentation duration for shape [7, 18]. This means that shape can affect involuntary visual attention when presentation time is increased, and the bottleneck filtration is overcome [7, 18].

3 Visual Perception

A main factor that alters the perception of received visual information is perceptual saliency. Perceptual salience refers to the degree in which a specific stimuli or feature is capturing attention and encoded into working memory [7, 11, 13, 17]. It is the overarching concept that drives preattentive processing theories and expands to other channels. The capturing effect could be due to the stimuli's properties like contrast, color, movement across a fixation, object recognition, loudness of sound, pitch, word familiarity, etc., or the processing capabilities of the individual [17]. Kuhn et al. [14] used this notion to develop ways of creating scenes with specific visual properties that allowed them to be viewed by individuals with colorblindness. Similarly, this concept was used to explore the number of different colors the human eye can perceive at a given time; seven was concluded [11]. This coincides with the isolation effect, stating that if one item has a different feature than those around it (visually) or in its group (auditorily), it will be more likely to direct attention and more readily be encoded into working memory [8]. Regardless of the isolation effect of these features, they can be overridden when directions are given to focus attention on a specific task [31]. This holds true when saliency is low yet may not be when saliency of the stimuli is increased (e.g., higher volume, increased contrast intensity, proximity of movement, etc.) [31]. For this reason, reception and perception need to be distinguished as different parts of information processing [14]. Reception is the act of collecting information through sensory channels, whereas perception is the combination of reception and meaning making "Perception is a higher-level process that combines information from the senses and filters, organizes, and interprets those sensations to give meaning and to create subjective, conscious experiences." [14].

3.1 Postattentive Amnesia and Inattentional Blindness

Postattentive Amnesia shows information is not readily transferred to long term memory during visual exploration activities. Details of a visual scene are not encoded into visual working memory when a separate scene is subsequently viewed [30]. The individual cannot remember the details of the previous scene, except when intentionally focused on that task specifically [30]. Inattentional blindness occurs when the individual is accidentally missing certain details of the scene [27]. The most often used example of this is from Simons & Chabris, who tested to see if individuals noticed a woman in a gorilla suit entering a scene while teams were passing a basketball [27]. The viewer's task was to 'press a key' each time their designated team (e.g., black or white shirts) passed the ball. The woman in the gorilla suit enters the scene from the left, does not interact with the ball, and exits to the right of the frame within 4 s. Once the 25 s clip was completed, very few participants stated noticing the gorilla walk by. To ensure this phenomenon was inattentional blindness, the researchers had participants view the same clip without the executive functioning task. 100% of the participants noticed the gorilla when free from the task orientation [27]. This further supports the weighted impact that intent and focused attention have on visual perception.

3.2 Change Blindness and Attentional Blink

Change Blindness occurs when information is being viewed in separate spatial locations, deliberately causing increased saccades (e.g., comic strips, 'find the difference' visual puzzles, etc.) [24]. Simons suggests that during each saccade the information previously encoded is lost, manipulated, or compared to new information before being stored in working memory [26]. Details can be overwritten by new information, overwrite new visual information (i.e., lasting first impressions), be deleted after the display is gone, stored yet require conscious focus to retrieve, or combined with new visual information (i.e., memory cannot recall where specific details are derived amongst multiple visual stimuli) [26]. Additionally, inattentional blindness can occur when information fails to be stored in visual working memory because of unfocused attention; it is focused attention that affords the opportunity for perception and efficient visual processing [24, 26].

More recently in 2005, Simons and Rensink described "Low-level object properties of the same kind (e.g., color or size) appear to compete for recognition in visual short-term memory, but different properties seem to be encoded separately and in parallel" [28]. Consequently, low-level object properties of visual stimulus like shape and color can affect what is encoded in visual working memory [6, 7, 28]. This research supports the idea that visual processing operates in a bottleneck style feature hierarchy [6, 7]. If the visual reception and information processing are overloaded, it will be difficult for the individual to focus on the task at hand [28]. More importantly, reception and attention are highly temporal; opening like a gate for a few moments then closing to consolidate what has been seen for categorization in working memory [11]. Each encapsulation of information received is labelled and organized to create a perception in working memory.

4 Thresholds of Visual Processing and Technology

The process of visual attention to cognitive interpretation is continually being researched as video games and virtual reality advance and integrate with modern society. For instance, Belchoir et al. (2013) found that visual attention can be learned and practiced for effectiveness and efficiency. The researchers discovered that individuals who have been playing video games long term were able to pay attention to 7–8 moving objects at once, compared to individuals with no digital gaming experience being able to focus on 2–3 moving objects. Following this discovery, they placed experimental groups through several weeks of video game or UFOV (useful field of view) training, resulting in an increase in information processing from 2–3 to 5–6 moving objects at once. This would support the idea that the ability to effectively pay attention to multiple moving elements can be both practiced and perfected through playing video games. Furthermore, there could be an increase in the average visual capabilities as digital technologies intertwine with everyday life [3].

4.1 Eye- Tacking

While it is possible to log cues, fixations, and spatial location through eye-trackers, it is difficult to analyze cognitive interpretation of each fixation and cue. In other words, reception (objective content being fixated on) does not automatically transfer to perception (subjective interpretation of fixated content). Due to this understanding of visual attention, eye trackers alone cannot depict what is seen versus what is encoded into memory. That being said, the pairing of eye-trackers with modern EEG technology can connect what is occurring internally with what is being seen externally. The combination of these devices will enable the measurement of different types of information stimuli and their effect on cognitive load.

4.2 Reliability of VR for Visual Processing Research

The reliability of the HTC Vive and other VR devices for analyzing aspects of the human visual processing capacity is increasing as developers create more intuitive and accessible technologies [4]. The separation of the virtual world from the real-world allows for constantly changing variables, like real-world lighting conditions, to be consistent between participants regardless of time. HMDs also increase participant accessibility by enabling individuals who previously could not engage to be testable (e.g., individuals who cannot sit up on their own, etc.) [9]. In 2016, Rebecca Foerster and colleagues compared the reliability of a standard Cathode Ray Tube (CRT) screen to the Oculus Rift for testing conscious perception thresholds, capacity of visual working memory, and visual processing speed [9]. It was found that the Oculus Rift is as reliable as CRT testing and the HMD enables full control over visual input [9]. In tandem to reliability, the breadth of existing research discusses limitations of VR, like motion-sickness, eyestrain, and hardware challenges, that have informed design guidelines [4, 13].

Most of the research surrounding this topic focuses on learning outcomes, such as retention, recall and transfer [15, 16, 21]. While this research is necessary, it lacks the moment to moment focus on the stimuli that is building knowledge. As designers continue to build these environments for research, training, and entertainment, it is important to understand the thresholds of our visual channel so we can draw attention to specific pieces of information at specific times. For instance, at what point does the user make a mistake in a visual-spatial problem-solving activity because there is too much distracting information in the virtual environment?

5 Conclusion

Overtime, researchers questioned the limitations of using HMDs and stereoscopic lenses, including when it may be unhelpful to the training process [4]. This paper discussed the relevancy of understanding the inner workings of visual reception and perception while in visually intensive immersive environments like VR. In the future, this dissection of reception and perception will drive research connecting what is occurring externally and internally during visual processing in technologies like VR, specifically during learning opportunities and training contexts [1, 5]. Although research has been done to understand aspects of immersive visual processing (e.g., clutter, motion, fidelity, etc.), there are still some gaps. One gap is in understanding how distinct visual disruptions affect cognitive load and what happens when refocusing from distracting stimuli in VR. To understand this phenomenon, recent researchers suggest electroencephalograms (EEGs) be used to measure unconscious cognitive reactions and temporal changes to attentional state alongside VR equipment [2]. Measuring mental activity through EEGs in VR environments would allow for the depiction of cognitive load at any stage of the designated event and the opportunity to understand the effect distracting visual stimuli has on the user [25].

This type of VR exploration is relevant for understanding the inner workings of distraction and refocusing of human cognition. It will provide insights for how people make meaning of information and how they balance cognitive overloading in new technologies like VR. The combination of equipment and theories proposed will allow for neuropsychological research on human behavior to be explored by the diverse communities of information science. This type of research will provide an arena for teachers and students of iSchools, immersive software developers, and learning specialists to collaborate on evolving technologies like VR. This research enables students to analyze the nuances of visual distractions while learning about 3D environment building, human computer interaction, and game creation. It could help university researchers and upcoming developers connect by highlighting various visual distractions embedded in software designs that inhibit focus and slow neural processing. It could also guide educators and developers towards creating efficient training and learning experiences that adhere to our cognitive thresholds. With the integration of video games and virtual reality into our training experiences, it is important to understand the thresholds of visual processing and work together to optimize the experience for the user.

References

1. Albus, P., Vogt, A., Seufert, T.: Signaling in virtual reality influences learning outcome and cognitive load. Comput. Educ. **166**, 104154 (2021). Hale, K.S., Stanney, K.M. (eds.) Handbook of Virtual Environments, 2nd ed., pp. 87–114. CRC Press, Boca Raton (2021)
2. Baceviciute, S., Mottelson, A., Terkildsen, T., Makransky, G.: Investigating representation of text and audio in educational VR using learning outcomes and EEG. In: Proceedings of the 2020 CHI Conference on Human Factors in Computing Systems, pp. 1–13 (2020)
3. Belchior, P., et al.: Video game training to improve selective visual attention in older adults. Comput. Hum. Behav. **29**(4), 1318–1324 (2013). https://doi.org/10.1016/j.chb.2013.01.034
4. Bowman, D.A., McMahan, R.P.: Virtual reality: how much immersion is enough? Computer **40**(7), 36–43 (2007)
5. Bozgeyikli, L., Raij, A., Katkoori, S., Alqasemi, R.: Effects of Environmental Clutter and Motion on User Performance in Virtual Reality Games. In: FGE@ CHI PLAY (2016)
6. Callaghan, T.C.: Dimensional interaction of hue and brightness in preattentive field segregation. Percept. Psychophys. **36**(1), 25–34 (1984)
7. Callaghan, T.C.: Interference and dominance in texture segregation: hue, geometric form, and line orientation. Percept. Psychophys. **46**(4), 299–311 (1989)
8. Dunlosky, J., Hunt, R.R., Clark, E.: Is perceptual salience needed in explanations of the isolation effect? J. Exp. Psychol. Learn. Mem. Cogn. **26**(3), 649 (2000)
9. Foerster, R.M., Poth, C.H., Behler, C., Botsch, M., Schneider, W.X.: Using the virtual reality device Oculus Rift for neuropsychological assessment of visual processing capabilities. Sci. Rep. **6**(1), 37016 (2016). https://doi.org/10.1038/srep37016
10. Golomb, J.D.: Remapping locations and features across saccades: a dual-spotlight theory of attentional updating. Curr. Opin. Psychol. **29**, 211–218 (2019)
11. Healey, C., Enns, J.: Attention and visual memory in visualization and computer graphics. IEEE Trans. Visual Comput. Graphics **18**(7), 1170–1188 (2011)
12. Hsia, H.J.: The information processing capacity of modality and channel performance. AV Commun. Rev. **19**(1), 51–75 (1971)
13. Jerald, J.: The VR book: Human-Centered Design for Virtual Reality. Morgan & Claypool (2015)
14. Kuhn, G.R., Oliveira, M.M., Fernandes, L.A.: An efficient naturalness-preserving image-recoloring method for dichromats. IEEE Trans. Visual Comput. Graphics **14**(6), 1747–1754 (2008)
15. Lowe, R.K.: Animation and learning: selective processing of information in dynamic graphics. Learn. Instr. **13**(2), 157–176 (2003)

16. Makransky, G., Terkildsen, T.S., Mayer, R.E.: Adding immersive virtual reality to a science lab simulation causes more presence but less learning. Learn. Instr. **60**, 225–236 (2019)
17. Mayer, R.E.: Cognitive theory of multimedia learning. The Cambridge Handbook Multimed. Learn. **41**, 31–48 (2005)
18. Ma, C., Huang, J.B., Yang, X., Yang, M.H.: Hierarchical convolutional features for visual tracking. In: Proceedings of the IEEE international conference on computer vision, pp. 3074–3082 (2015)
19. McCloud, S.: Understanding Comics: The Invisible Art. Northampton, Mass (1993)
20. Moll, L.C., Amanti, C., Neff, D., Gonzalez, N.: Funds of knowledge for teaching: using a qualitative approach to connect homes and classrooms. Theor. Pract. **31**(2), 132–141 (1992)
21. Park, W.D., Jang, S.W., Kim, Y.H., Kim, G.A., Son, W., Kim, Y.S.: A study on cyber sickness reduction by oculo-motor exercise performed immediately prior to viewing virtual reality (VR) content on head mounted display (HMD). Vib. Proced. **14**, 260–264 (2017)
22. Peddie, J.: Augmented Reality. Springer International Publishing, Cham (2017). https://doi.org/10.1007/978-3-319-54502-8
23. Posner, M.I., Snyder, C.R., Davidson, B.J.: Attention and the detection of signals. J. Exp. Psychol. Gen. **109**(2), 160 (1980)
24. Rensink, R.A., O'Regan, J.K., Clark, J.J.: To see or not to see: the need for attention to perceive changes in scenes. Psychol. Sci. **8**(5), 368–373 (1997)
25. Sanei, S., Chambers, J.A.: EEG Signal Processing. John Wiley & Sons (2013)
26. Simons, D.J.: Current approaches to change blindness. Vis. Cogn. **7**(1–3), 1–15 (2000)
27. Simons, D.J., Chabris, C.F.: Gorillas in our midst: sustained inattentional blindness for dynamic events. Perception **28**(9), 1059–1074 (1999). https://doi.org/10.1068/p281059
28. Simons, D.J., Rensink, R.A.: Change blindness: past, present, and future. Trends Cogn. Sci. **9**(1), 16–20 (2005)
29. Styles, E.A.: The Psychology of Attention. Taylor & Francis, Abingdon, UK (1997)
30. Wolfe, J.M., Klempen, N., Dahlen, K.: Postattentive vision. J. Exp. Psychol. Hum. Percept. Perform. **26**(2), 693 (2000)
31. Yantis, S., Jonides, J.: Abrupt visual onsets and selective attention: evidence from visual search. J. Exp. Psychol. Hum. Percept. Perform. **10**(5), 601 (1984)

From Noisy Data to Useful Color Palettes: One Step in Making Biodiversity Data FAIR

Hong Cui[1](✉), Noah Giebink[1], Julian Starr[2], Dylan Longert[2], Bruce Ford[3], and Étienne Léveillé-Bourret[4]

[1] University of Arizona, Tucson, AZ 85711, USA
hongcui@arizona.edu
[2] University of Ottawa, Ottawa, ON K1N 6N5, Canada
[3] University of Manitoba, Manitoba, MB R3T 2N2, Canada
[4] University of Montreal, Montreal, QC H3T 1J4, Canada

Abstract. Due to the differences in individual's color perception and the variations in color naming and color rendering under different settings, color has historically been a challenging trait in describing species for taxonomic and systematic research. Reusing a noisy color dataset collected from high-quality images of *Carex* specimens, we developed a data mining method (e.g., clustering and classification) for constructing domain-specific color palettes. Color palettes associated with color values measured in a color space help systematists record color data in a way that the differences in colors can be more accurately compared and computed, making color data interoperable and reusable. The *Carex* color palette was evaluated by *Carex* experts and the evaluation data showed that experts overwhelmingly preferred using color palette over color strings.

Keywords: Data mining · Color traits · Inconsistent color data · t-SNE · K-means · Support vector machines · L * a * b color space · sRGB color space · Automate color palette creation

1 Introduction

Plant color traits are important for a wide range of research due to their significance to the ecology and evolution of plants, from mediating pollinator interactions to thermoregulation [1, 2]. Recently they have become important for climate change studies, for example, [3]. Though strides have been made to encourage controlled vocabularies for plants which would drastically increase our ability to leverage computational analyses of taxonomic descriptions [4], the inconsistency and subjectivity of color description hinders progress, see examples in [5, 6]. In biodiversity, the key character that set two species apart can be the color, as in the case of *Carex* vulpinoidea (a common species) and *Carex* annectens (a very rare species in Québec). A confusion between the two can derail the conservation efforts for the latter.

In the context of a US-NSF funded project aiming to make biodiversity trait records FAIR (Findable, Accessible, Interoperable, and Reusable, [7]), this study utilized an

© The Author(s), under exclusive license to Springer Nature Switzerland AG 2023
I. Sserwanga et al. (Eds.): iConference 2023, LNCS 13971, pp. 469–481, 2023.
https://doi.org/10.1007/978-3-031-28035-1_35

unique dataset that has been built by a co-author's team over the years for climate research to develop an automated method for generating domain specific color palettes so future authors and citizen scientists can record color traits in an interoperable and reusable manner.

Research questions to be answered include: (1) Can the color labels used in FNA by authors be used to compute the similarities or differences among colors? In other words, will the colors with the same labels be grouped into the same clusters and the colors with different labels be grouped into different clusters? (2) Can clustering or classification methods of machine learning automatically select a small set of colors from thousands of measured colors and generate color palettes in a way that makes sense to domain experts (in this case, *Carex* systematists)? (3) 3. If (2) is successful, will domain experts be willing to use machine-generated color palettes when describing their specimens?

2 Method

2.1 Knowing the Data and Data Transformation

The color datasets collected by a co-author's team to study climate impact on *Carex* species were the primary data used in this study (Table 1, the first two datasets). This dataset includes 2883 sRGB values of various organs of 456 *Carex* species, measured from high-quality images using ImageJ (v. 1.50i; [8]) with color calibration against the reference colors included in the images. For about 1/3 of total data a written record can be located in Flora of North American (FNA), color labels (text string, e.g., "red") used by authors when describing the organs and species were also semi-automatically extracted and included in the dataset (see Fig. 1, left).

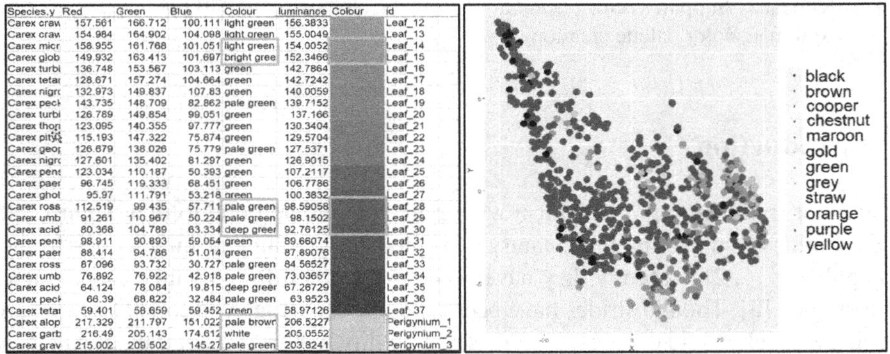

Species.y	Red	Green	Blue	Colour	luminance	Colour	id
Carex craw	157.561	166.712	100.111	light green	156.3833		Leaf_12
Carex craw	154.984	164.902	104.098	light green	155.0049		Leaf_13
Carex micr	158.955	161.768	101.051	light green	154.0052		Leaf_14
Carex glob	149.932	163.413	101.697	bright gree	152.3466		Leaf_15
Carex turbi	136.748	153.567	103.113	green	142.7864		Leaf_16
Carex tetar	128.671	157.274	104.664	green	142.7242		Leaf_17
Carex nigro	132.973	149.837	107.83	green	140.0059		Leaf_18
Carex peck	143.735	148.709	82.862	pale green	139.7152		Leaf_19
Carex turbi	126.789	149.854	99.051	green	137.166		Leaf_20
Carex thon	123.095	140.355	97.777	green	130.3404		Leaf_21
Carex pity	115.193	147.322	75.874	green	129.5704		Leaf_22
Carex geop	126.679	138.026	75.779	pale green	127.5371		Leaf_23
Carex nigro	127.601	135.402	81.297	green	126.9015		Leaf_24
Carex pens	123.034	110.187	50.393	green	107.2117		Leaf_25
Carex paer	96.745	119.333	68.451	green	106.7786		Leaf_26
Carex ghol	95.97	111.791	53.218	green	100.3832		Leaf_27
Carex ross	112.519	99.435	57.711	pale green	98.59058		Leaf_28
Carex umb	91.261	110.967	50.224	pale green	98.1502		Leaf_29
Carex acid	80.368	104.789	63.334	deep greer	92.76125		Leaf_30
Carex pens	98.911	90.893	59.054	green	89.66074		Leaf_31
Carex paer	88.414	94.786	51.014	green	87.89076		Leaf_32
Carex ross	87.096	93.732	30.727	pale green	84.56527		Leaf_33
Carex umb	76.892	76.922	42.918	pale green	73.03657		Leaf_34
Carex acid	64.124	78.084	19.815	deep greer	67.26729		Leaf_35
Carex peck	66.39	68.822	32.484	pale green	63.9523		Leaf_36
Carex tetar	59.401	58.659	59.452	green	58.97126		Leaf_37
Carex alop	217.329	211.797	151.022	pale browr	206.5227		Perigynium_1
Carex garb	216.49	205.143	174.612	white	205.0552		Perigynium_2
Carex grav	215.002	209.502	145.27	pale green	203.8241		Perigynium_3

Fig. 1. A portion of the original dataset. Includes measured RGB values and color labels used by authors. Color labels use in the literature are noisy. Left: A portion of the original datasheet. Highlighted color labels "light green" and "bright green" are different, but corresponding colors are very similar; the corresponding colors of the two "pale green" are more different than those of a "pale green" and a "deep green"; labels "pale brown", "white", and "pale green" sound so different but their colors are quite similar. Right: A t-SNE visualization of the colors containing the 12 color keywords in the dataset based on their R, G, B values. These visuals show color labels are not consistently applied and they cannot be used to compute the distance between colors.

Using RGB values as features, the clustering tendency of the dataset was first examined by ordered distance matrix and Silhouette width. Both suggested two clusters, which did not match the dataset as there were more colors in the dataset. To further visualize the data, a t-SNE [9] (Rtsne in R, perplexity = 10, Euclidean distance) plot based on color RGB values was generated (Fig. 1, right). T-SNE visualizes higher dimensional data in 2D spaces and preserve the relative distances amongst data points. The plot confirmed again the two clusters suggested by the other two methods (tip vs. base of the "cone" shape). When data points were colored with the simplified color presented in their label (e.g., light green became just green), we found that each of the two clusters contained a mix of different colors and both clusters were dominated by brown. This revealed that author color labels were not consistent with color RGB values or among different authors: similar colors (with smaller Euclidean distances) were labeled differently, while colors farther apart had similar labels. This answered the first research question.

Removing author color labels from the picture, Fig. 2 Left shows the same t-SNE plot except data points are now colored with the color rendered from their RGB values. This plot revealed that colors in this dataset were spread in a continuous spectrum, making finding definitive boundaries for different color clusters difficult even for a human expert. Additionally, although we couldn't find the purple, orange or yellow as an abstract color wheel would show, colors were less but still mixed to some extent in the t-SNE's 2D space (e.g., those data points at the tip of the cone shape contained what looked like black, grey, and brown to an author's eye). This made us wonder if RGB was the good feature space for this challenging task.

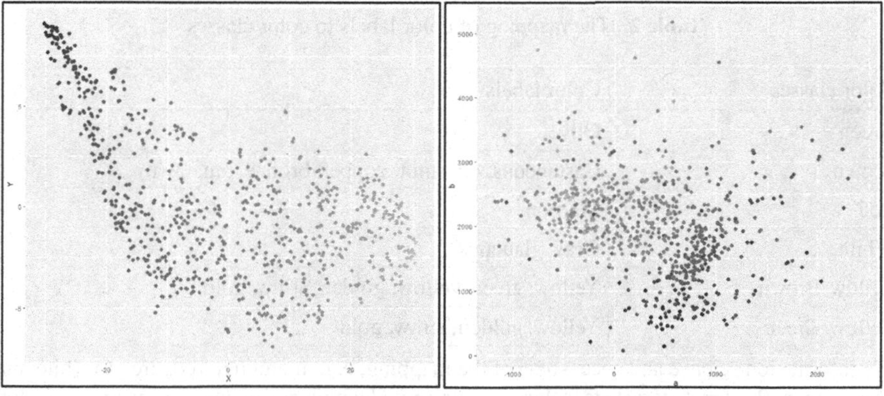

Fig. 2. Visualization of data points by their RGB colors. Left: t-SNE visualization of RGB colors in 2D space. Data points are colored with their RGB color. Right: Visualization of the same data in the a*b space. Data points are colored with their RGB color.

Since domain experts would like the final color palettes to group colors by their hue and saturation (i.e., perceived "color") and then by brightness (e.g., light, medium, and dark), CIE L * a * b color space emerged as a better feature space. It expresses colors along the three axes: the L axis expresses the lightness, the a axis expresses the proportion of green vs. red, and the b axis expresses the proportion of blue vs. yellow in a color. Using L * a * b color space allows for the separation of elements of hue and saturation from color brightness and in effect projects colors from the three-dimensional RGB space to the two-dimensional a * b space. The conversion of RGB values to L * a * b values were done using grDevices package in R. The transformed dataset is the "Color Measurements" dataset in Table 1.

Table 1. Datasets used in this study

Data Set	Columns/Features	Number of Rows
Original sRGB*	Species name, organ, R,G,B values	2883
Original Labels*	Species name, organ, color label from FNA	793
Color Measurements	Species name, organ, R,G,B values, L,a,b values	2883
Final Dataset	Species name, organ, R,G,B values, L,a,b values, color class	792
SVM Training Set	a, b values, color class	631
Test Set	a, b values, color class	161
SVM Training (down sampled)	a, b values, color class	215

* Original datasets received from the co-author's team.

Table 2. The mapping of color labels to color classes

Color classes	Color labels
Green	Olive
Brown	Castaneous, chestnut, copper, bronze, tan, tawny
Red	Maroon*
White	Gray, glaucous*
Yellow-Brown	Yellow, green-yellow, golden, straw, gold
Yellow-Green	Yellow, golden, straw, gold

* To information science audience, some of the mapping, e.g., maroon to red, grey to white, may seem strange. But for systematists, colors are interpreted within a context – a gray center can look white on a green leaf. Authors therefore can record either 'white' or 'gray' in their description of the leaf center. "Maroon" is a poorly defined color because a group of experts cannot agree on what kind of color is "maroon". For this reason, domain experts would like to limit the colors to the basic colors – colors with consistent interpretation across culture, gender, age, and left and right eye of any individual, etc.

The second major transformation was to map color labels extracted from FNA to a set of color classes. In most published plant descriptions, color labels/phrases used are not from a controlled vocabulary, resulting in a large variation of different color labels, for example, chestnut-dark brown, red-brown to dark maroon, golden brown, etc. As shown above, such labels are not consistently applied. To reduce variation and promote interoperability, *Carex* systematists would like to limit the color palettes to basic simple colors and the combinations amongst them (e.g., green, yellow, yellow-green). Using the tm package in R, the most frequent single-word color terms were first identified and after mapping expert-approved synonyms to their preferred classes (Table 2), six color classes were identified and other color labels in the original dataset were manually mapped to these classes based on their colors. After this mapping and a join on the species name and organ (leaf, perigynium, etc.) between the "original labels" and "color measurements" datasets, the clean, Final Dataset (Table 1) was obtained. This dataset was the base for subsequent analyses.

2.2 Methods for Creating the Color Palettes

Color palettes for biodiversity contain both a set of representative colors seen in the specimens and the recommended names for colors. Colors in the color palettes need to be selected from all 2883 colors, but only about 1/3 of the colors have a class name. Therefore, we needed to (1) group colors into classes (2) select representative colors from color classes and name them.

Methods for Grouping Colors. With the transformation of colors from the sRBG color space to L * a * b color space, the problem of grouping color hues and saturations had been simplified in the 2D space (i.e., a * b space). In this 2D space two methods were employed to group all colors in Color Measurements dataset into the six color classes:

1. Manual thresholds: Using Color Measurements, set manual a and b thresholds for different color classes by consecutively dividing colors along their distribution gaps in the a*b space into smaller and smaller groups so that the divisions resembled the six color classes. Since these thresholds were either vertical or horizontal lines, the resulting color groups may be less natural than ideal.
2. SVMs: First train a supervised machine learning model, i.e., Support Vector Machines (e1071 in R package), on the subset of data with color class labels, then use this model to predict their color class for records in the entire Color Measurements dataset using a and b values. SVMs was chosen for its well tested robustness and noise tolerance.

Due to the imbalanced distribution of different color classes, the initial 80–20 training/test split is further down sampled so each color class has the same number of instances in the final training set (Table 1 and Table 3). Note, White was essentially dropped due to lack of training examples. Linear and radial kernels with different cost parameters were evaluated to obtain the best performing model.

Table 3. Color class distribution in training and test dataset

	Brown	Green	Red	White	Yellow-Brown	Yellow-Green
Final dataset	431	133	65	12	97	54
Training	344	106	52	9	77	43
Training (down sampled)	43	43	43	NA	43	43
Test	87	27	13	3	20	11

Recall the color classes were derived from the labels extracted from FNA, and the latter was quite noisy (see Fig. 1). In other words, the training datasets for SVM were noisy. Because of this, we used a lower cost parameter (0.5) when training SVMs to penalize the model less for wrong predictions.

Using both the manual and machine learning approaches was to cross-validate the quality of final color palettes, since there is not a gold standard palette to quantitively evaluate either approach. While manual thresholds may result in good palettes, our goal was to develop a procedure that required as little human intervention as possible.

Method for Selecting and Naming the Colors for the Palettes.
Once the source 2883 colors were classified into the six color classes, the following procedures were taken to create the color palettes. One set of color palettes were created from the grouping result of the manual and the machine learning approach, respectively. One set of final color palettes consists of 15 or 30 different colors for each of the six color classes (see Results).

1. Apply K-means clustering method (k = 3) on the L value of the colors to create light, medium, and dark subgroups for each color class.
2. Sample n (n = 5 or 10) colors from each of the brightness subgroups of each color class. The sampling was based on the average distance of a color to its 3 nearest neighbors in the a * b space. The higher the distance the smaller the probability for the color to be sampled. This is to exclude very similar colors in the final color palettes.
3. Prefix light, medium, and dark in front of the class name of the selected colors (Fig. 3).

2.3 Color Palette Evaluation

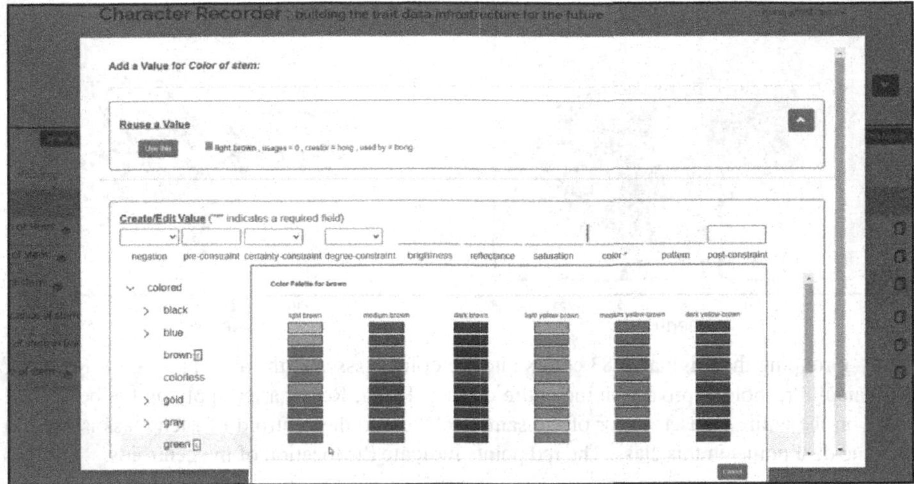

Fig. 3. Color input interface of Character Recorder. User is entering a color for "Color of stem". User clicking in 'color' blank triggers the display of a term tree for "colored" that holds all colors the user could use. Colors "brown" and "green" has color palettes and a click on the red C box next to "brown" brings up the color palette for brown.

3 Results

Table 4. Performance of the Best SVM models and Manual Thresholds on Test Data

	Linear SVMs			Manual thresholds		
	Precision	Recall	F1	Precision	Recall	F1
Brown	0.87	0.62	0.72	0.73	0.70	0.71
Green	0.55	0.41	0.47	0.43	0.33	0.38
Red	0.43	1	0.60	0.35	0.54	0.42
Yellow-Brown	0.23	0.25	0.24	0.29	0.19	0.23
Yellow-Green	0.25	0.55	0.34	0.20	0.36	0.26
White				0.33	0.33	0.33

Given the known noise in the training dataset, the performance of either methods was not expected to be high. Table 4 presents the performances of manual threshold method and SVMs on the same set of Test data. The classification of all colors in Color Measurements using SVMs and manual thresholds in the a*b color space is displayed in Fig. 4.

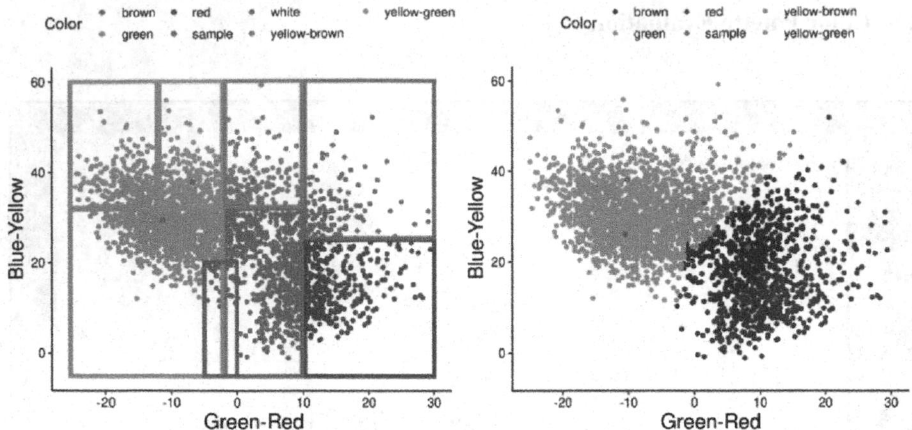

Fig. 4. Grouping the original 2883 colors into the color classes in the a*b space. Left: Result of the manual threshold approach on the entire dataset. Right: Result after applying the best SVM model on the entire dataset. Color of the sample closest to the centroid of each class is used to color the data points in this class. The red points indicate the location of the centroids.

Applying the methods of creating color palettes described above, the grouping produced by manual thresholds and SVMs resulted in color palettes shown in Fig. 5. To fit the palettes in one page, 15 instead of 30 colors are shown for each color class.

The above results suggest that resultant color grouping using SVMs is similar to that produced with manual threshold. Adopting SVMs approach helps automate the process for further expansion of this work and similar works.

Data obtained from *Carex* experts' evaluation of Character Recorder under the same setting (including light setting) a botanist would use when describing a specimen showed that among a total of 78 distinct color values for 15 characters recorded, 57 (57/78 = 66%) were covered by the color palettes implemented in Character Recorder (green, brown, red, and yellow) and 21 were not covered. These 21 colors were mostly white and transparent (hyaline) colors (20), with one instance of 'blue green'. Among the 57 covered colors, 48(48/57 = 84%) were recorded using the color palettes. Figure 6 shows color values recorded for character "Color of sheath". It is evident that the similarities among values recorded as colors can be easily computed and it is not the case for the colors recorded as color label strings.

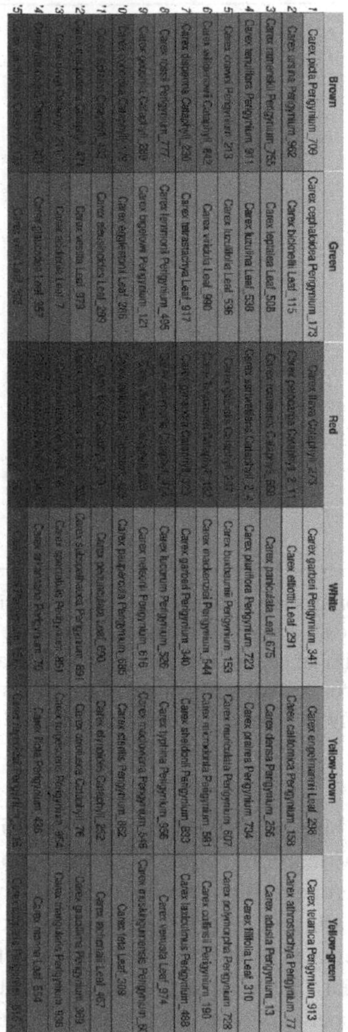

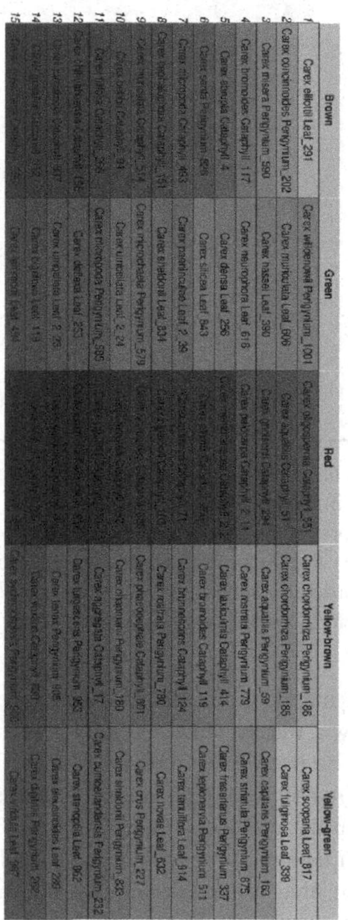

Fig. 5. Color palettes produced using manual thresholds (left) and SVMs (right). The label on a color is the id of the sample where the color was obtained. First 5 colors are light, the next 5 are median, and the last 5 are dark.

4 Related Work and Discussion

Color research has historically been focused on arts and design applications [10] which is very different from that of documenting biodiversity, as the latter is exclusively focused on recording the truth of the colors as the nature presents them. This difference makes some of the color research in arts and design not applicable to color management for documenting biodiversity. From the World Color Survey [11], however, we learned that the 11 basic color names that are consistently applied and recognized by different cultures

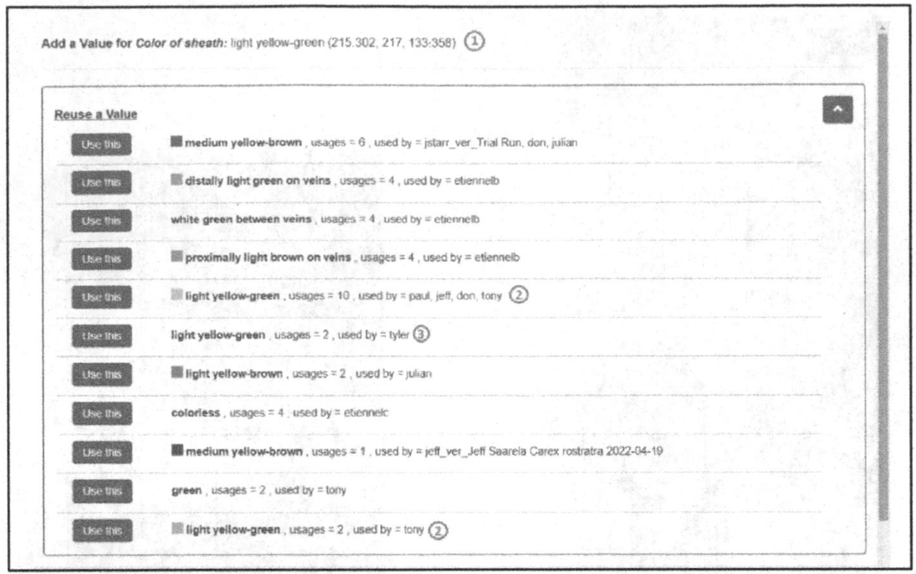

Fig. 6. Color values recorded by *Carex* experts at the usability study or Color of sheath for different specimens. Users were free to use color labels or select colors from available color palettes. (1) Colors/RGB values always accompany color labels. (2) Similar colors are represented by the same color label (e.g., "light yellow-green") for human users, but the real RGB values of the colors are recorded for subsequent computer analyses. (3) Similarity of colors recorded as string labels to other colors is difficult to define.

and mappable in different languages: red, green, blue, yellow, orange, purple, pink, brown, black, white and gray. Colors such as straw, maroon, chestnut, or olive should not be used if we aim for global biodiversity interoperability. We also learned from the massive color palette generations exercises for arts and design, using colors taking from the real world (e.g., photos of real objects) creates more effective color palettes than using abstract colors [12]. Techniques [10] that enable rapid collection of colors from images are also important to create domain specific color palettes from existing biodiversity specimen collections, e.g., SEINet (https://swbiodiversity.org/seinet) and iDigBio (https://www.idigbio.org/portal).

In biodiversity domain, a well-known effort to standardize colors and color nomenclature (i.e. color names) was dated 1912 by [13] and more efforts can be seen in [6], but (1) using standard color names is not a common practice in many biodiversity domains, and (2) not all biodiversity domains have a color name standard, for example, there is not a color name standard in botany. Even if a color name standard exists (e.g., Fig. 7) and standard color names are used in publications, they are often not connected directly back to their color values (e.g., RGB). When a downstream data integration project exacts color traits from the literature at large, the color names following different standards would be mixed and difficult, if not impossible, to map back to their color (RGB) values. This lack of color control in general has contributed to the wide use of author preferred color labels in published taxonomic works, such as Flora of North American (FNA) and Flora of China (FoC). A recent survey showed that ambiguities in phenotype traits (including colors) have made 73% of responders frustrated and 85% are eager to use a new authoring platform to produce FAIR data at the time of publishing their work [15].

This is the reason we strongly urge that phenotype data (or any scientific data) be connected to ontologies (color palettes may be seen as a kind of ontology) at the time of the publication by the authors, to avoid the costly and error prone third-party curation post-publication [14]. In terms of color traits, it is critically important that final publication includes not only color names, but also color values (e.g., RGB), because interoperability and reusability ultimately rely on accurate distance measures between colors, and the distance cannot be computed reliably between two text strings.

To our knowledge, usability of color palettes in biodiversity has not been formally examined, but such research is much needed. For example, is RGB the best color gamut For example, how to decide the number of color variations should be included in a color palette for a domain? FNQL color palette (Fig. 7) has one name for one color patch, but ours has 10 colors for one color name. One could argue that more variations increase selection difficulties, but on the other hand, fewer variations discourage users from using the color palette because their needed colors are not included. In our implementation, one color label covers 10 different color variations. This was done because too many color labels could create confusion for human users, but computerized analyses could handle color values at much higher precision levels. When Character Recorder generates a taxonomic description for human readers, it uses color labels, but when it outputs RDF graphs (Resource Description Framework) for data harvesters, it uses both color labels and color RGB values. The real-world benefit of this design is to be verified.

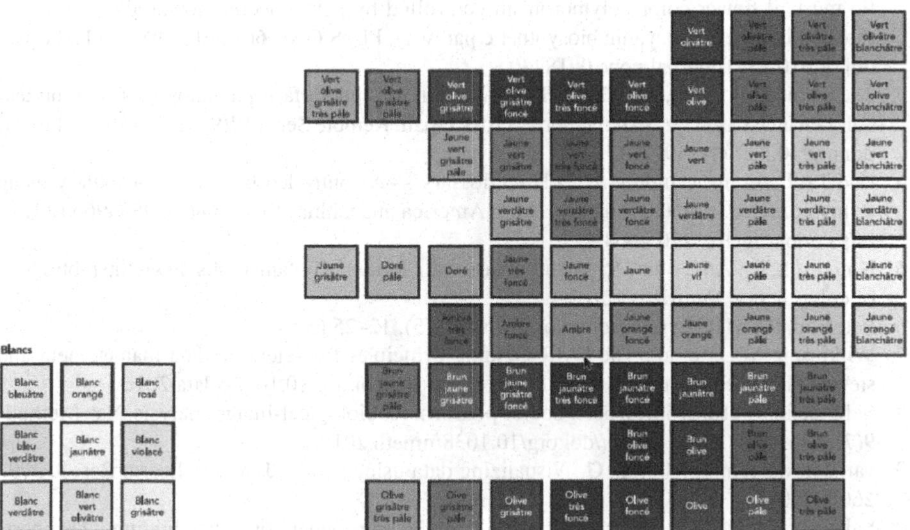

Fig. 7. About a quarter of the 278-color color palette recommended for use by Flore Nordique du Québec et du Labrador (FNQL). Color names are labeled on each color patch. RGB values not recorded.

5 Conclusion

Color remains a challenging trait for botany and many other biodiversity realms after over 200 years of documenting biodiversity since Carl Linnaeus. In this paper, we showed that color labels used by authors in publications such as FNA cannot be used to compute the distance between colors. Colors must be represented in a standard color space to support interoperability and reusability. We demonstrated a straightforward method of creating domain specific color palettes with colors measured from high-quality images and showed how it can be used by *Carex* experts to produce FAIR data for color traits. The effective size of the data needed to train SVM models were very small (<50 data points per color), but the result was quite effective: the color palette was used by the experts to record 84% of the 78 color values.

All code and results are publicly accessible at: https://github.com/biosemantics/Authors-Utilities/tree/master/color_processing.

Acknowledgements. The project was supported in part by NSF DBI-1661485. The authors thank anonymous Carex experts who participated in the color palette evaluation experiments.

References

1. Rosas-Guerrero, V., et al.: A quantitative review of pollination syndromes: do floral traits predict effective pollinators? Ecol. Lett. **17**(3), 388–400 (2014). https://doi.org/10.1111/ele.12224
2. Dick, C.A., Buenrostro, J., Butler, T., Carlson, M.L., Kliebenstein, D.J., Whittall, J.B.: Arctic mustard flower color polymorphism controlled by petal-specific downregulation at the threshold of the anthocyanin biosynthetic pathway. PLoS ONE **6**(4), e18230 (2011). https://doi.org/10.1371/journal.pone.0018230
3. Tsutsumida, N., Shin, N., Miura, T.: Evaluation of land surface phenology for autumn leaf color change based on citizen reports across Japan. Remote Sens. **14**(9), 2017 (2022). https://doi.org/10.3390/rs14092017
4. Endara, L., et al.: Building the 'Plant Glossary'—A controlled botanical vocabulary using terms extracted from the Floras of North America and China. Taxon **66**(4), 953–966 (2017). https://doi.org/10.12705/664.9
5. Nicholson, R.: Am I blue? In pursuit of an exotic bloom, a botanist falls down the rabbit hole of color theory. Nat. Hist. 121(5)
6. Peterson, R.: Making sense of color. FUNGI **8**(5), 12–25 (2016)
7. Wilkinson, M.D., et al.: The FAIR Guiding Principles for scientific data management and stewardship. Sci. Data **3**(1), 160018 (2016). https://doi.org/10.1038/sdata.2016.18
8. Schindelin, J., et al.: Fiji: an open-source platform for biological-image analysis. Nat. Methods **9**(7), 676–682 (2012). https://doi.org/10.1038/nmeth.2019
9. van der Maaten, L., Hinton, G.: Visualizing data using t-SNE. J. Mach. Learn. Res. **9**, 579–2605 (2008)
10. Salman, R.: Paletto: An Interactive Colour Palette Generator : Facilitating Designers' Colour Selection Processes. http://urn.kb.se/resolve?urn=urn:nbn:se:lnu:diva-115035 (2022). Accessed 10 Aug 2022
11. Kay, P., Cook, R.S.: World color survey. In: Luo, M.R. (ed.) Encyclopedia of Color Science and Technology, pp. 1265–1271. Springer New York, New York, NY (2016). https://doi.org/10.1007/978-1-4419-8071-7_113

12. Kojima, A., Ozeki, T.: Color palette generation for image classification by bag-of-colors. In: 2015 21st Korea-Japan Joint Workshop on Frontiers of Computer Vision (FCV), pp. 1–5 (2015). https://doi.org/10.1109/FCV.2015.7103734
13. Ridgway, R.: Color standards and color nomenclature, by Robert Ridgway, Curator of the Division of Birds, United States National Museum. With fifty-three colored plates and eleven hundred and fifteen named colors. The author, Washington, D.C. (1912)
14. Cui, H., et al.: Incentivising use of structured language in biological descriptions: author-driven phenotype data and ontology production. Biodivers. Data J. **6**, e29616 (2018). https://doi.org/10.3897/BDJ.6.e29616
15. Cui, H., Ford, B., Starr, J., Reznicek, A., Zhang, L., Macklin, J.A.: Authors' attitude toward adopting a new workflow to improve the computability of phenotype publications. Database **2022**, baac001 (2022). https://doi.org/10.1093/database/baac001
16. Dignard, N., et al.: Flore Nordique du Québec et du Labrador, vol. 1. PUL Diffusion (2013)

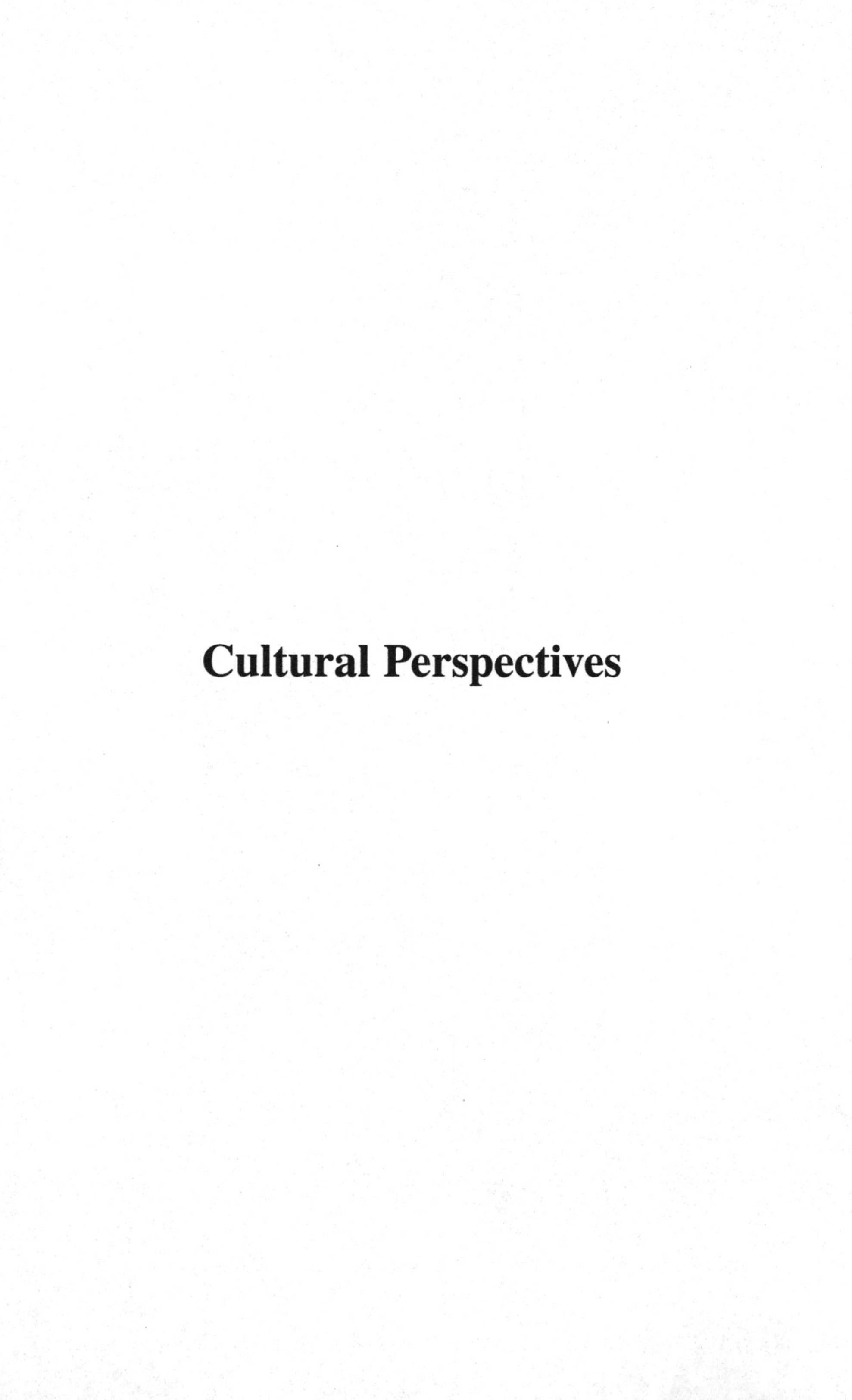

Cultural Perspectives

"Will the Day Ever Come When We Will Be Judged on Our Merit and not on Our Blackness?" The Black Caucus of the American Library Association and the Long Freedom Struggle in the United States, 1970–1975

Alex H. Poole(✉)

Drexel University, Philadelphia, PA 19104, USA
ahp56@drexel.edu

Abstract. This paper centers on the early years (1970–1975) of the Black Caucus of the American Library Association. The Caucus sought to combat structural, professional, and personal racism, to achieve equity in library employment, services, and materials, and to imbue Black librarians and Black library users at all types of libraries and in all geographic locations with a sense of dignity, pride, agency, and self-determination.

We engage with five literatures in this paper; each engagement shows the interpenetration of information and library science with larger currents of political, social, and cultural history. First, historian Stephen Tuck posits a "long freedom struggle" starting with Emancipation in 1863, not merely a narrow civil rights period embracing the late 1950s and first half of the 1960s. The Black Caucus's work comprised a crucial part of this broader, longer, multifaceted Black protest agenda. Second, like Tuck we embrace an ecumenical definition of Black activism: both building and resisting proved essential. We explore Black Caucus activism in four cases of resistance and four of building. Third, following historian Darlene Clark Hine, we argue that Black middle-class professionals, in this case librarians, played a vital role in the freedom struggle. Fourth, we complicate the conventional periodization narrative in library and information science history that ends with the desegregation of state associations and public libraries by the end of 1966. The struggle for racial equality and equity in librarianship remained far from complete. Fifth, scholars have paid considerable attention to the desegregation of public libraries but have neglected other aspects of the freedom struggle in LIS. This paper contributes robustly to the 2023 iConference theme of inclusivity.

Keywords: Diversity · Equity · And inclusion (DEI) · Social justice · Historical research

1 Introduction

On a frigid January day in Chicago, Illinois, the Council of the American Library Association (ALA) convened for its 1970 midwinter meeting. Amidst Council's prosaic business, eleven Black librarians—Thomas Alford, Willis Bolton, Emily Copeland, Audrey

© The Author(s), under exclusive license to Springer Nature Switzerland AG 2023
I. Sserwanga et al. (Eds.): iConference 2023, LNCS 13971, pp. 485–500, 2023.
https://doi.org/10.1007/978-3-031-28035-1_36

N. Jackson, Virginia Lacy Jones, E.J. Josey, Effie Lee Morris, Carrie Robinson, Edith Prunty Spencer, Binnie Tate, and James Welbourne, Jr.—took a momentous stand.

Introduced by Virginia Lacy Jones, Dean of Atlanta University's School of Library Service, Effie Lee Morris of the San Francisco Public Library read a "Statement of Concern." The statement underscored Black librarians' exigent concerns about institutional racism, poverty, and lack of educational, employment, and promotional opportunities [1].

Despite national political attention to these issues, Morris upbraided the library profession for its glacial response. Challenging ALA's passivity, a new Black Librarians' Caucus was formulating an agenda for action. The group, Morris stated, pledged not only to continue to meet at ALA conferences, but to monitor and ultimately to evaluate ALA's progress in "fulfilling its social and professional responsibilities to minority groups" [1].

This statement heralded the birth of the Black Caucus. According to its founder, E.J. Josey, the formation of the caucus represented a survival tactic: only through such a vehicle could Black librarians shatter their longstanding invisibility, demand respect from a white-dominated profession, increase their professional involvement, promote self-determination and empowerment, and grapple with ALA's onerous bureaucracy in service of social change [2–4]. Josey summed up, "if [B]lack people are to have justice and an effective response from American society, they must organize into enclaves of [B]lack strength" [5, p. 4].

This paper centers on the early years (1970–1975) of the Black Caucus. Established a year before the U.S. Congressional Black Caucus, the Black Caucus sought to combat structural, professional, and personal racism, to achieve equity in employment, service, and materials, and to imbue Black librarians and library users at all types of libraries, from public to academic to special, and in all geographic locations, with a sense of dignity, pride, and self-determination. As Fisk University's Ann Allen Shockley insisted, "The weapons of black librarians for instituting change are those of books and related services. These should be wielded with honor as goals are sought and changes are made. The time is now. The moment is here" [6, p. 1].

We contribute to five historiographical conversations in this paper, each of which imbricates political, social, and cultural history. First, historian Stephen Tuck posits a "long freedom struggle" starting with Emancipation in 1863, instead of a narrow civil rights period (i.e. the direct action phase) embracing the late 1950s and first half of the 1960s [7, p. 8]. The Black Caucus's work comprised an essential part of this broader, longer, and multifaceted Black protest agenda locally, nationally, and internationally.

In fact, the Caucus debuted at a peculiar moment in the long freedom struggle. On the one hand, President Lyndon Johnson's Great Society legislation, most notably the Civil Rights Act of 1964 and the Voting Rights Act of 1965, indicated great progress on civil rights, as did the appointment of the first Black person to the Supreme Court, the first appointment of a Black person to a presidential cabinet, and sundry affirmative action programs [8]. On the other hand, as historian Thomas Holt contends, the movement's tenuous consensus of the early 1960s frayed pursuant to the Voting Rights Act of 1965 [7, 9]. The second half of the 1960s saw profound unrest in Northern urban communities, the ascent of Black nationalism, Pan-Africanism, and postcolonialism, tensions between integration and separatism, and the questioning of nonviolence tactics [7, 9–11]. Moreover, the 1968 election of Richard Nixon brought together under the

GOP banner suburban whites, white southerners, and working class whites even as it furthered ongoing fragmentation among Black activists [9]. The Black Caucus therefore coalesced at a far from auspicious moment.

Second, like Tuck we embrace an ecumenical definition of Black activism: both building and resisting proved essential [7]. We explore Black Caucus activism in four cases of resistance and four of building. Third, following historian Darlene Clark Hine, we argue that Black middle-class professionals, in this case librarians *qua* grassroots information professionals, played a vital role in the long freedom struggle [11]. Fourth, we complicate the conventional narrative in library and information science history that culminates with the desegregation of state associations and public libraries by the end of 1966. The struggle for racial equity and equality in librarianship, however, remained far from complete [12]. Fifth, although scholars pay considerable attention to the desegregation of public libraries they neglect other aspects of the long freedom struggle in librarianship [13–20].

After setting forth our methodological approach, we first explore the gestation of the Black Caucus. Next, we discuss the broader political, social, and cultural contexts that presaged the Caucus's founding. Third, we broach the Caucus's goals and its membership. We then unpack key examples of Caucus activism between 1970 and 1975, highlighting both resistance and building. Finally, we discuss the Caucus's early achievements and its agenda for promoting diversity, equity, and inclusion in information and library science and in larger political, social, and cultural contexts.

2 Historical Method

As Zachary Schrag notes, "history is not about the past but rather about people: *history is the study of people and the choices they made*" [21, p. 9]. Historical writing therefore constitutes a constant interaction between facts and interpretation. It depends upon collecting, evaluating, prioritizing, and interpreting sources, and then upon transparently communicating that interpretation [22].

First, we identified and located sources. Relying upon multiple sources of documentary evidence in service of trustworthiness, we located documents through berrypicking: flexible, iterative searches involving, e.g., footnote chasing, citation searching, journal browsing, database searching and browsing (by subject, keyword, and author) [23, 24].[1] We vetted a wide variety of primary and secondary sources, published and unpublished, created by institutions and by extra-institutional actors. These sources ranged from journal articles to periodicals, books to reports, book chapters to archival manuscripts.

[1] Exemplary search terms included "Black Caucus," "Negro librar*," "Black librar*," "Afro-American librar*," "African-American librar*," and "African American librar*." Useful databases included Library Literature & Information Science Full-Text, Library Literature & Information Science Retrospective: 1905–1983, Library, Information Science & Technology Abstracts (LISTA), LISA: Library & Information Sciences Abstracts, JSTOR, Project Muse, ProQuest Central, ArchiveGrid, Historical Newspapers-Black Newspapers, HistoryMakers Digital Archive, New York Times 1851–3 years ago: ProQuest Historical Newspapers, Washington Post—ProQuest Historical Newspapers 1877–2001, and Reader's Guide to Periodical Literature.

Second, to assess our sources' nature and value we employed the critical method. We engaged both in external criticism, namely by establishing the authenticity and provenance of our sources, and in internal criticism, namely by interpreting the content of our sources. We asked questions such as: when was a given source produced? By whom? For what purpose(s)? Third, we interpreted our evidence, seeking to understand when, where, how, and why certain events occurred and to determine their consequences. Fourth, we sought to communicate that interpretation transparently [22].

U.S. library scholar Jesse Shera contends that historical writing should provide "a synthesis, a series of generalizations, that not only will give the past a living reality but will make of it a medium for the better understanding of the present" [25, p. 241]. This paper pursues Shera's noble goal.

3 Roots

The establishment of the Black Caucus was decades in the making. ALA historically remained aloof from or neglected racial equity issues [8, 12, 26]. An ALA "Work with Negroes" round table convened in 1922 and again in 1923, but friction among its members triggered its disbandment [27, 28].

Yet the 1936 annual meeting in Richmond, Virginia, proved a tipping point. A furor erupted because of segregated meeting facilities; this led to an ALA resolution mandating integration at such meetings [29]. The pallid 1936 resolution constituted the ALA's last word on the subject for more than a decade and a half, however [30]. The ALA's Bill of Rights (1939) and Code of Ethics (1939) ignored equal, much less equitable, collective treatment of Black librarians, dealing only with strictures on individual members at ALA conferences.

A 1952 constitutional change mandated only one ALA chapter per state instead of putatively separate but equal chapters, as had prevailed in North Carolina and a handful of other southern states [20]. White librarians grudgingly accepted integration, especially after *Brown v. Board of Education* (1954) [30]. Yet substantive change remained wanting; Black librarians could not but doubt the association's commitment to equality [31].

In response to ALA's longstanding recalcitrance, as early as the 1930s a handful of Black librarians convened at ALA meetings to share concerns at lunches or dinners. These gatherings gave way to similar meetings in hotel suites in the 1950s, and then to dinners sponsored by Atlanta University's School of Library Service where Black librarians "fellowshipped" [3, 8]. But the driver for the Caucus's creation was E.J. Josey, "the conscience of the American Library Association" [32, p. 13, 33].

Born in 1924, Josey grew up impoverished in segregated Portsmouth, Virginia. Not until his World War II service (1943–1945) was Josey permitted to use an integrated library. His wartime experiences in the U.S.'s Jim Crow army made him "an implacable foe of segregation and second class citizenship" [26, p. 300]. Josey fought for the "Double V": victory abroad over fascism, and victory at home over racism. To these commitments Josey added another—to overthrow colonialism worldwide.

In 1950, Josey began an illustrious six decades in librarianship when he matriculated as a graduate student at Columbia University. Joining the American Library Association two years later and attending his first ALA annual meeting in 1957, he found much to lament in the organization's stance on racial equality, which was at best one of benign neglect and at worst one of complicity [26].

An indefatigable civil rights activist both locally and nationally, Josey played a key role in the 1960 Savannah, Georgia, lunch counter sit-ins and subsequent local business boycotts. As Librarian and Assistant Professor at Savannah State College (1959–1966), he collaborated with the local National Association for the Advancement of Colored People (NAACP) chapter and served as student advisor to the protesting collegians. Josey also served on the Savannah NAACP's Executive Board, which in 1962 successfully persuaded the mayor not only to desegregate the main public library, but also to appoint two Blacks to the Library Board, including Josey [8, 26].

Like the 1952 constitutional change, ALA's 1962 "Statement on Individual Members, Chapter Status, and Institutional Membership" seemed propitious. It enjoined local associations to provide equal rights for individuals or risk losing their chapter status. Though the statement lacked enforcement measures, much to Josey's consternation, in a histrionic display of bigotry the state library associations of Louisiana, Georgia, Alabama, and Mississippi withdrew from ALA membership anyway [34].

In 1964, Josey vigorously protested the Association of College and Research Libraries bestowing a National Library Week award to the Mississippi Library Association. What was more, a 1964 meeting of the similarly secessionist Georgia Library Association featured an ALA staff member as a speaker. Josey successfully motioned that ALA proscribe its officers and staff from attending or speaking at state library association meetings that were not ALA chapters. A year later, Josey sponsored still another resolution; this one barred from ALA any institution that discriminated against library users based on race, religion, or personal belief. But ALA Council voted the resolution down. Despite these travails, segregation in librarianship soon faltered. In 1965 Josey became the first Black member of the Georgia Library Association. Moreover, in a remarkable turn of events all state library associations were integrated by the end of 1966 [26].

Overall, as historian Dennis Thomison suggests, rival constituencies cleaved ALA in the 1960s. Acting too slowly for activists and too quickly for traditionalists, the Association predictably pleased neither [34]. Many ALA members and leaders greeted the period's social ferment with indifference if not hostility; the shibboleth that social problems were beyond the purview of professional associations died hard [34]. For his part, Josey found professional discrimination practiced unabashedly and widely [35]. Black librarians remained effectively shut out of leadership positions and professional publication venues, and the profession refused to view Black librarians as legitimate [5, 36].

By 1970, however, some professional leadership gains were evident, as suggested by the elections of Joseph Reason (second vice president, ALA), A. P. Marshall (president, Missouri Library Association), Alma Jacobs (president, Montana Library Association), John E. Scott (president, West Virginia Library Association), and Milton Byam (vice president, New York Library Association) [4]. Further, a handful of Black librarians occupied upper-level positions in predominantly white institutions and Blacks such as Reason stood for ALA offices [37].

Reflecting on the 1960s, Fisk University's Ann Allen Shockley called the decade "the movement years—the years of change, years of confusion, and years of identity searching—all sparked by a new black assertiveness" [38, p. 182]. Even so, at the time of the Caucus's founding, only two Blacks had served as ALA division presidents (Charlemae Rollins and Augusta Baker). Los Angeles Public Library's James E. Crayton wondered poignantly, "Will the day ever come when we will be judged on our merit and not on our blackness?" [39, p. 204].

Josey ramped up his protest activities still further. Serving on the 1969–1970 ALA Nominating Committee, Josey, by this point Chief of New York State's Bureau of Academic and Research Libraries, determined to advance a Black candidate for president. To garner broad support, he asked fellow Black librarians to attend ALA's midwinter meeting in Chicago. The group decided to nominate A.P. Marshall of Eastern Michigan University for president (by petition) and to support other Blacks for Council. This channeled into the formal creation of the caucus, whose members unanimously elected Josey chair [3].

4 Overall Caucus Goals

After its foundational meeting in Chicago, the Caucus consolidated organizationally. Its 1970 constitution reiterated the group's raison d'être, stressing the egregious lag in librarianship opportunities for Blacks, the dearth of publications concentrating on social and economic issues disproportionately affecting Blacks, and ALA's and the profession's complacency [37]. Louise Giles of Macomb Community College trumpeted, "the winds of revolution (racial, social, and moral), which have been buffeting society for the last few years, have finally begun to be felt in the library profession" [40, p. 258]. The Caucus had these winds, however tenuous and however capricious, at their back.

The Caucus brought together diverse Black librarians. In some cases, tensions surfaced between those favoring integrationism and those favoring Black Power-based separatism, but all Black librarians could unite under an anti-racism banner. As inaugural Black Caucus *Newsletter* editor Jeanne English, librarian of Evanston Township (Illinois) High School, wrote, "members range from university librarians to children's librarians, from information science librarians to leaders of large urban public libraries, from far-out librarians to conservative[s]" [41, p. 2]. The Caucus's inaugural directory (1973) boasted 315 Black librarians who worked in eight types of venue [42].

In a flurry of activity, the Caucus pressed ALA to respond to Black members' needs in recruitment, training, employment conditions, representation, and promotion, to vet candidates for ALA offices, to scrutinize ALA planning and policy, to assess library materials and services, and to serve as an information clearinghouse [37, 43]. The Caucus thus represented a fruitful pressure group that sensitized other librarians to the needs of the Black community [44]. Despite rampant professional and social prejudice, Black librarians knew their worth. As Mohammed Aman of St. John's University put it, "Black librarians have encouraged the young to dream, to pursue excellence and to contribute to the history of the [B]lack man, and have worked diligently and consistently for the universal recognition of the identity, rights and talents of all men" [45, p. 155]. The Black Caucus built on this time-honored commitment.

5 Key Initiatives, 1970–1975

The Black Caucus's activities in the early 1970s included ALA annual meeting programs, a Distinguished Service Award (begun in 1970), a newsletter (begun in 1972), and a membership directory (first published in 1973). More broadly, it plunged into activism. On the one hand, the Caucus resisted. Its members worked to prevent public libraries from supplying segregated southern schools, to forestall the abolition of an innovative community-based librarianship program at the University of Maryland, and to combat employee discrimination both at the Library of Congress and in the Los Angeles County Public Library system. On the other hand, the Caucus built, notably in increasing Black representation in ALA and in encouraging members to run for ALA office, in building coalitions, in cultivating local chapters, and in establishing an African exchange program.

5.1 Resisting

Public School Desegregation and Public Library Service (1970–1971). At the Caucus's 1970 founding, Virginia Lacy Jones introduced a resolution. It targeted southern schools' stratagems to evade desegregation as ordered by the Supreme Court in *Brown v. Board of Education* (1954) and *Brown II* (1955) by establishing "segregation academies" [46]. The resolution proposed censure of such evaders of the law [47]. Although considerable procedural wrangling ensued, the Resolution on Library Service to Educational Institutions Established to Circumvent Desegregation Laws ultimately passed, earning the Caucus its first victory [48].

The NAACP summarily endorsed the Caucus's resolution. In tandem with NAACP officers from 42 chapters in 12 southern and three border states, Josey searched for evidence of "coddling segregation" [49]. Although southerners denied the charge, Josey and his NAACP allies documented segregationists transferring materials from public libraries and public schools to segregation academies [50].

Southerners responded with vitriol. Charged with receiving books from McGehee Public Library, the school board president of Arkansas's Bayou Park Academy wrote, "We were shocked to learn that such a person would be so small and petty as to file a complaint of this order, knowing it was untrue" [51]. Apropos of the resolution, an Atlanta school librarian rescinded her ALA membership. She dismissed the resolution as "a statement of the principle of a small misguided group" [52].

The ALA never censured a southern school, but by their vigorous action, the Caucus established a base for further resistance.

The University of Maryland's Urban Information Specialist program (1970–1971). Not only did the Caucus attack racism in school librarianship; it also confronted racism in graduate library education. In 1970, supported by U.S. Office of Education funding, the University of Maryland's School of Library and Information Services launched an Urban Information Specialist (UISP) program with Caucus founding member James Welbourne, Jr., as its director. Given the information crisis of the inner cities, librarianship demanded novel approaches [53]. UISP's approach, Welbourne reflected, "was both critical of the traditional role of libraries in urban communities and optimistic relative to the possibility of a more activist role for librarians as urban information specialists in economically depressed neighborhoods" [54, pp. 124–5]. These specialists would offer "critical life needs" services, including information on affordable housing, on health and welfare, on cultural awareness and racism, and on job and unemployment assistance [54, p. 125].

By promoting grassroots cultural self-determination and empowerment, UISP foregrounded social justice. It piloted a new work role for the librarian of the future: that of information interpreter, a community-information source liaison [55]. To develop these liaisons, the program recruited nontraditional students, many of whom lacked an undergraduate degree, from local communities who were familiar with those communities' social problems. Instead of a book-centric orientation, moreover, the program premised broader information skills given rapid socio-technological change, and experiential learning [55].

But the Office of Education elected not to fund the program for a second year, and Maryland's faculty and administrators refused to support it. Addressing the Caucus in 1970, Welbourne castigated such "manifest discriminatory behavior" [56, p. 8]. Outraged Caucus members wrote letters of support to the Office of Education. Jeanne English, for instance, pointed to the "great courage, insight, and particular education and experience [necessary] to translate information in its many forms into active aid for the impoverished, the intellectually and spiritually starved" [56, p. 75]. But their pleas were to no avail. Racism lived still as "an active, vital and institutionalized social force" [56, p. 1].

The death of UISP, Welbourne lamented, truncated librarians' efforts to engage urban communities economically and politically. Also sacrificed was the activist goal of preparing a new generation of socially responsible public librarians [54]. In this case, Caucus resistance fell short even though their emphasis on community-centered librarianship lived on.

Discrimination at the Library of Congress (1970–1974). Complementing its educational activism, the Caucus trained its sights on discrimination at the United States's citadel of librarianship, the Library of Congress (LC). In the spring of 1970, the Library of Congress compelled copyright examiner and leader of the Black Employees of the Library of Congress (BELC) Joselyn Williams to resign after he and other employees filed a lawsuit under Title VIII of the 1964 Civil Rights Act. The suit claimed LC failed to recruit qualified Blacks, relegated Black employees to "dead-end" positions, maintained policies that tamped down on Blacks' career advancement, and enlisted only whites as supervisors [57].

Workers conducted sit-ins in the spring of 1971 to protest these conditions and Williams appealed to the Caucus for support [37]. Spurred by the Caucus, ALA Council passed a resolution upbraiding LC for racially discriminatory employment practices. An ALA committee gathered evidence of rampant racial discrimination, namely in promotion and recruitment. The committee called upon LC to initiate an affirmative action program, human relations training for supervisors, and federally-funded job training to promote employees' upward mobility [58].

The Caucus honored Williams's efforts with a 1973 resolution. It characterized him as "a fearless leader of the Black Employees of the Library of Congress, who had the temerity and the courage to bring charges of racism and blatant discrimination in employment and promotion against [B]lacks to the attention of the American Library Association" [59, p. 7].

ALA subsequently reviewed LC's progress. It found reported grievances addressed begrudgingly if at all. Moreover, an atmosphere of "apathy, fear and mistrust," even the occasional specter of violence, curbed the potential of affirmative action policies [60, p. 199].

Despite its troubling findings, ALA suggested no immediate solution. Rejecting censure, it fell back on platitudes, urging LC staff and administrators to develop better mutual understanding. Yet undoubtably due to Caucus actions, subsequent years saw an increase in the employment of Blacks at higher levels [3].

In line with its advocacy for Williams and Black LC workers, the Caucus promulgated a resolution in support of Barbara Ringer's complaint that LC had denied her a register of copyrights position because of her gender and her support for Black LC workers [37, 61]. The hearing officer of the Equal Opportunity Employment Committee ruled in Ringer's favor. Faced with a legal battle, LC awarded her the job, one for which she showed exemplary credentials [62, p. 590]. The Caucus thus notched another victory, however modest, in the struggle for racial equity in librarianship.

Los Angeles County Public Library (LACPL) discrimination (1971–1974). In a final example of resistance, the Black Caucus leapt to the barricades on behalf of Los Angeles County Public Library (LACPL) librarians of color. In the spring of 1971, these workers charged LACPL with discriminating against minorities in its hiring, placement, and promotion practices and sought redress from the California Fair Employment Practices Commission (FEPC) [39].

The status of librarians of color was dire. Of more than 60 supervisory positions in the LACPL system, librarians of color filled not one, and of more than 230 professional librarians, only 16 were Black or Latinx. LACPL neither actively recruited workers of color nor gave them equitable promotional opportunities [63]. The FEPC substantiated these charges.

The FEPC ruling was soon put to the test. In August of 1972, the LACPL made two affirmative action appointments. But the seven librarians who scored higher than the appointees on the County Civil Service Test appealed to the Los Angeles Civil Service Commission, arguing reverse discrimination. The Commission found, however, that the two appointees' experience and professional abilities, if not their test scores, outweighed those of the petitioners.

Castigating administrators' "gross neglect, insensitivity, and conscious racism" [63, p. 386], James E. Crayton thundered, "We will protect our rights through the ballot, through organized State and Local caucuses, through strategy and tactics, through unity of action, and by all other necessary means," he promised [39, p. 206]. This activism funneled into the 1972 founding of the California Librarians Black Caucus (CLBC), discussed below.

Whether resisting segregation academies, institutional racism at LIS programs, or professional discrimination between 1970 and 1975, the Caucus mobilized passionately and effectively. In other cases, however, they built.

5.2 Building

Black representation in the American Library Association (1970–1975). From its 1876 founding, ALA leaders and members relegated Black librarians to nominal participation, much less leadership [8, 64]. In the 1960s, for example, ALA's eleven standing committees included 374 members, but Black librarians received only five of these appointments and served on only three of the committees. Over the same period, of the 542 nominees for ALA Council, only 18 were Black; membership elected nine.

Bolstered by Caucus efforts, Black representation increased over time [37]. In 1974 alone, five Blacks served on ALA standing committees. Moreover, the number of Black Council candidates between 1970 and 1974 doubled from 1960 to 1970—though merely a dozen succeeded. By 1974, Blacks consistently served on the Nominating Committee, the Appointments Committee, and the Committee on Professional Ethics. Most significant, the Caucus's efforts led to the 1975 election of Clara Stanton Jones, Director of the Detroit Public Library (the first woman and the first Black to hold this position), as ALA president.

Coalition-Building (1970–1975). The Caucus remained independent, but elected not to sever ties with ALA. Robert Wedgeworth, later to serve as ALA Executive Director and as the Dean of Columbia University's School of Library Service, underlined the need for a strategic balance between separatism and integration. He lobbied for fusing the Caucus's separate power base and its influence in various ALA decision-making units, a most delicate balance [64]. Neither integration and separatism nor local and global engagement were mutually exclusive.

The Caucus's efforts complemented the work of other social justice-oriented groups such as the Social Responsibilities Round Table (SRRT) (established in 1969), the Task Force on the Status of Women (TFSW) (1970), the Task Force on Gay Liberation (1971), and the National Association to Promote Library and Information Services to Latinos and the Spanish Speaking (REFORMA) (1971) [65–67].

Some coalition-building occurred. For instance, Josey coauthored a resolution to establish the Standing Committee on the Status of Women in Librarianship, the TFSW's precursor. He also consistently enjoined the ALA Executive Board to support the Equal Rights Amendment (ERA). Further, several Black librarians, Josey included, participated in the founding of SRRT [3]. The Caucus moreover endorsed the SRRT Task Force's 1971 resolution on the recruitment of minorities, "Action Now to Achieve Racial and Sexual Parity in Library Staffing." Also in league with SRRT, the Caucus proposed an alternative slate of candidates for ALA offices in 1975; this resulted in the election of Clara Stanton Jones [31]. Wedgeworth observed that on the one hand, alliance with SRRT potentially expanded the Black Caucus's power base to encourage social change. On the other hand, alliance likely meant compromising on priorities and commitments [64]. Testifying to this tension, Josey staunchly resisted suggestions for the Caucus to become part of SRRT; he wrote, "my reaction to the suggestion is that it is absurd!" [68, p. 347]. In many cases, then, alliances remained provisional and elusive.

Local Chapters (1970–1975). Encouraging further activism and coalition-building at the community level, the Black Caucus midwifed the birth of local chapters in Chicago,

New York, and California. The Chicago chapter came to life as the ad hoc Chicago Planning Committee at ALA's 1970 midwinter meeting. Its members then formed an ad hoc committee to plan a Black Caucus program and activities for ALA's 1972 annual meeting [69]. Two events galvanized the chapter. First, in late 1972 library school graduate student Voree Gordon applied to the Illinois Manpower Advisory Committee for a scholarship. Encountering peculiar obstacles, Gordon appealed to the Chicago chapter, whose protest to Advisory Committee proved successful. Second, in 1973 a vacant higher administrative position at the Chicago Public Library (CPL) was filled without sufficient advertising; the nascent Caucus successfully protested this oversight, and the search was reopened [70].

These dual crises aside, Chicago's Black librarians wanted systematically to address the local Black community's educational and intellectual needs [69]. As the Black Caucus of Librarians-Chicago Chapter, the group convened in October 1973.

The CBLC organized to aid the Black community educationally, politically, and professionally. It stimulated the Black community's interest in library services and programs, offered educational opportunities, recruited Blacks into the field, and augmented the community role of the Black librarian [69].

Another local caucus effloresced in New York. In Queens, communities of color received inequitable public library service. Meager collections, employment inequities, and lack of career development opportunities for Black librarians predominated [71, 72]. In the summer of 1970, Ernestine Washington, the first Black branch supervisor in Queens, and children's librarian Cynthia Jenkins established the Black Librarians Caucus of Queens.

The new Caucus's Statement of Concerns zeroed in on the system's lack of proportional representation: Blacks comprised 22% of Queens's population, but far fewer than 22% of the borough's public librarians [71]. Moreover, not one borough branch employed a Black person as principal librarian. The Caucus also supported the efforts of Black librarians to evaluate Black literature and to develop relevant spaces, programs, and collections. These material and personnel deficits unjustly hindered the educational development of Black children.

Still another local chapter, the California Librarians Black Caucus (CLBC), gelled in 1972. Two events animated its founding [73, 74]. First, James E. Crayton's activism in fair employment practices in 1970 and 1971 put him in frequent communication with the officers of the Black Caucus, including Effie Lee Morris. Second, in 1971 several California Library Association (CLA) Council members began conversations about discrimination against and proportionate representation of librarians of color. The next spring, Black librarians from both southern and northern California convened to form a statewide Black caucus.

The CLBC's goals mirrored those of other chapters and of the national Black Caucus [73]. Grounded in outreach and activism, CLBC strove to eradicate professional inequities by monitoring legislative activities, by supporting Black librarians for leadership positions, by participating on local and national committees, by giving scholarships to aspiring Black librarians, and by professional recruitment, mentoring, support, and recognition. Not to be overlooked, it sought to promote and evaluate Black literature and services to the Black community, to preserve Black culture, and to fight for community information equity.

The African Exchange (1972–1974). Invigorated by global postcolonial currents, the Caucus embarked upon international collaboration in the early 1970s. As Mohammed Aman exhorted, "The feeling of brotherhood among [B]lacks should be extended to mutual actions between [B]lacks in the United States and their brothers and sisters in Africa" [45, p. 159].

UNESCO proclaimed 1972 International Book Year (IBY), but ALA seemed blithely to ignore Africa in its programming [3]. Hence the Caucus passed a midwinter resolution in support of IBY that established an exchange program [75].

The exchange program promised information sharing and cultural understanding. Not only would American Black librarians offer training to African librarians, but the former would "learn from their African brothers and sisters the ways and means to involve the library and the cultural center in combating illiteracy and spreading reading and knowledge" [45, p. 160].

In the inaugural exchange, Thomas Battle of Howard University spent the 1972–1973 academic year in Sierra Leone while Harry Kamara of the Sierra Leone's National Library Board served on the Howard staff. In 1974, Wallace Van Jackson, Virginia State College librarian emeritus, served on the library faculty of the University of Botswana. Battle later reflected appreciatively, "This exchange initiated great possibilities for cooperation with our African colleagues" [76, p. 13].

In the first half of the 1970s, the Black Caucus joined the freedom struggle with gusto. Whether it was building or resisting, establishing an exchange program with African librarians or protesting public library service to segregation academies, the Caucus persistently and innovatively furthered the freedom struggle. In doing so, they established a beachhead for subsequent advances.

6 Conclusion

In their history of southern United States public library desegregation, Wayne and Shirley Wiegand emphasize librarians' tendency to invest in longstanding professional myths of opposing censorship, defending intellectual freedom, and providing unbiased service to all [13]. Just as their work explodes these myths, so too does the story of the Black Caucus; it underscores the gulf between librarianship's professional ideals and its practices in a previously unexplored way. The Black Caucus fought racism locally, nationally, and internationally, on political, social, and cultural fronts, at micro and macro levels, and in both de jure and de facto segregated spaces.

As the aforementioned examples of resistance and building indicate, this paper contributes to library and information science history by concentrating on previously overlooked actors, communities, and institutions. This focus expands our understanding beyond southern public libraries, which have drawn most scholarly attention. Using the Black Caucus as a lens, we also flesh out the larger social and cultural history of the Black freedom struggle in the United States. Though often overshadowed in recent historiography, Black middle class professionals such as librarians played a fundamental role in all phases of the freedom struggle.

The story of the Black Caucus also challenges conventional periodization. The fight for racial justice in libraries and librarianship as well as in American society continued even after the death of de jure desegregation. Moreover, the freedom struggle did not sink into declension after the mid-1960s; rather, members of the Black Caucus borrowed from numerous protest traditions, pursuing not only those of integration and separatism, but also local, national, and global engagement. The 1970s, argues historian Stephen Tuck, constituted a period in which Blacks tried to expand their rights, not merely to fight rearguard actions—and attained success in some areas despite formidable resistance [7]. The history of the Black Caucus supports these hypotheses.

This paper's scope remains necessarily selective given spatial constraints. The group would go on in the second half of the 1970s and for decades thereafter to entrench itself even more firmly as a vital force for social justice in both the ALA and the broader profession. Celebrating the Black Caucus's silver anniversary, ALA Executive Director Tracie D. Hall, herself a BCALA member, lauded its "unflagging commitment to equity." "I cannot help but think of how prescient its founding was," she celebrated [77, p. 34]. All the same, the imperative to promote social justice and decimate structural racism remains just as urgent in 2023 as in 1970, as does the need for recruiting, mentoring, and leadership development of Black librarians, providing relevant and current information services and resources, and engaging communities [77]. So long as racism exists, as Lisa Biblo prophetically argued, so too will there be a need for the Black Caucus [31]. The group remains a stalwart force fighting for diversity, equity, inclusion, and social justice.

References

1. Black Librarians: A Statement of Concern. 0601006a_040_BlackCaucus1970–71a, American Library Association Archives at the University of Illinois at Urbana–Champaign (1970)
2. Josey, E.J.: Black caucus. Libr. J. **95**(6), 531 (1970)
3. Josey, E.J.: Black caucus of the american library association: the early years. In: Josey, E.J., DeLoach, M.L. (eds.) Handbook of Black Librarianship, 2nd edn., pp. 83–97. Scarecrow Press, Lanham (2000)
4. Josey, E.J.: Introduction. In: Josey, E.J. (ed.) The Black Librarian in America, pp. vii–xvi. Scarecrow Press, Metuchen (1970)
5. Josey, E.J.: Introduction. In: Josey, E.J. (ed.) What Black Librarians Are Saying, pp. 1–9. Scarecrow Press, Metuchen (1972)
6. Shockley, A.A.: Message from the Editor. Black Caucus Newsl. 1(1), 1 (1972)
7. Tuck, S.G.N.: We Ain't What We Ought To Be: The Black Freedom Struggle from Emancipation to Obama. Harvard University Press, Cambridge (2011)
8. Josey, E.J.: The civil rights movement and american librarianship: the opening round. In: Bundy, M.L., Stielow, F.J. (eds.) Activism in American Librarianship, 1962–1973, pp. 13–20. Greenwood, Westport (1987)
9. Holt, T.C.: Children of Fire: A History of African Americans. Hill and Wang, New York (2011)
10. Hall, J.D.: The long civil rights movement and the political uses of the past. J. Am. Hist. **91**(4), 1233 (2005). https://doi.org/10.2307/3660172
11. Hine, D.C.: Black professionals and race consciousness: origins of the civil rights movement, 1890–1950. J. Am. Hist. **89**(4), 1279–1294 (2003). https://doi.org/10.2307/3092543
12. Wiegand, W.A.: 'Any Ideas?': the american library association and the desegregation of public libraries in the american south. Libr. Cult. Hist. Soc. **1**(1), 1–22 (2017). https://doi.org/10.5325/libraries.1.1.0001

13. Wiegand, W.A., Wiegand, S.A.: The Desegregation of Public Libraries in the Jim Crow South: Civil Rights and Local Activism. Louisiana State University Press, Baton Rouge (2018)
14. Knott, C.: Not Free, Not For All: Public Libraries in the Age of Jim Crow. University of Massachusetts Press, Amherst (2016)
15. Hanbury, D.: The Development of Southern Public Libraries and the African American Quest for Library Access, 1898–1963. Lexington Books, Lanham (2019)
16. Cresswell, S.: The last days of jim crow in southern libraries. Libr. Cult. **31**(3/4), 557–573 (1996)
17. Fultz, M.: Black public libraries in the south in the era of de jure segregation. Libr. Cult. Rec. **41**(3), 337–359 (2006). https://doi.org/10.1353/lac.2006.0042
18. Battles, D.M.: The History of Public Library Access for African Americans in the South, or, Leaving Behind the Plow. Scarecrow Press, Lanham (2009)
19. Tucker, J.M. (ed.): Untold Stories: Civil Rights, Libraries, and Black Librarianship. Publications Office, Graduate School of Library and Information Science, Champaign (1998)
20. Poole, A.H.: 'Could my dark hands break through the dark shadow?': gender, jim crow, and librarianship during the long freedom struggle, 1935–1955. Libr. Q. **88**(4), 348–374 (2018). https://doi.org/10.1086/699269
21. Schrag, Z.M.: The Princeton Guide to Historical Research. Princeton University Press, Princeton (2021)
22. Shep, S.: Historical investigation. In: Gorman, G.E., Clayton, P. (eds.) Qualitative Research for the Information Professional, pp. 160–181. Facet, London (2005)
23. Bates, M.J.: The design of browsing and berrypicking techniques for the online search interface. Online Rev. **13**(5), 407–424 (1989). https://doi.org/10.1108/eb024320
24. Poole, A.H.: Archival divides and foreign countries? historians, archivists, information-seeking, and technology: retrospect and prospect. Am. Arch. **78**(2), 375–433 (2015). https://doi.org/10.17723/0360-9081.78.2.375
25. Shera, J.H.: On the value of library history. Libr. Q. **22**(3), 240–251 (1952). https://doi.org/10.1086/617906
26. Josey, E.J.: A dreamer with a tiny spark. In: Josey, E.J. (ed.) The Black Librarian in America, pp. 297–323. Scarecrow Press, Metuchen, N.J (1970)
27. Rose, E.: Work with negroes round table. Bull. Am. Libr. Assoc. **16**(4), 361–366 (1922)
28. Settle, G.T.: Work with negroes round table. Bull. Am. Libr. Assoc. **17**(4), 274–279 (1923)
29. Roden, C.: Report of the committee on racial discrimination. Bull. Am. Libr. Assoc. **31**, 37–38 (1937)
30. Marshall, A.P.: The search for identity. In: Josey, E.J. (ed.) The Black Librarian in America, pp. 173–183. Scarecrow Press, Metuchen, N.J (1970)
31. Biblo, L.: Black caucus of the american library association: an organization of empowerment. In: Josey, E.J. (ed.) The Black Librarian in America Revisited, pp. 324–337. Scarecrow Press, Metuchen, NJ (1994)
32. Black Caucus of the American Library Association. Visionary Perspectives: Beyond the First Two Decades. Black Caucus (1990)
33. Chancellor, R., Josey, E.J.: Transformational Leader of the Modern Library Profession. Rowman & Littlefield, Lanham (2020)
34. Thomison, D.: A History of the American Library Association, 1876–1972. American Library Association, Chicago (1978)
35. Josey, E.J.: Black aspirations, white racism and libraries. Wilson Libr. Bull. **44**(1), 97–98 (1969)
36. Yates, E.G.: Community and outreach librarians: challenge and change. In: Josey, E.J. (ed.) What Black Librarians are Saying, pp. 241–248. Scarecrow Press, Metuchen, NJ (1972)

37. Cunningham, W.D.: The black caucus of the american library association: the first four years. In: Bundy, M.L., Stielow, F.J. (eds.) Activism in American Librarianship, 1962–1973, pp. 115–121. Greenwood, Westport (1987)
38. Shockley, A.A.: Establishing Afro-American collections. In: Josey, E.J., Shockley, A.A. (eds.) Handbook of Black Librarianship, pp. 182–192. Libraries Unlimited, Littleton (1977)
39. Crayton, J.E.: As a black librarian, i am asking, what's next? In: Josey, E.J. (ed.) What Black Librarians are Saying, pp. 202–207. Scarecrow Press, Metuchen (1972)
40. Giles, L.: The black librarian as change agent. In: Josey, E.J. (ed.) What Black Librarians are Saying, pp. 256–267. Scarecrow Press, Metuchen (1972)
41. English, J.: ALA black caucus. Black Caucus Newsl. **1**(1), 2 (1972)
42. ALA Black Caucus. ALA Black Caucus Membership Directory (1973)
43. ALA Black Caucus Program Action Committee Proposal. Black Caucus Newsl. **2**(1), 5–6 (1973)
44. Axam, J.A.: The black caucus: a meaningful source of action. In: Josey, E.J. (ed.) What Black Librarians are Saying, pp. 208–217. Scarecrow Press, Metuchen (1972)
45. Aman, M.M.: Against all odds, we have been believers. In: Josey, E.J. (ed.) What Black Librarians are Saying, pp. 150–162. Scarecrow Press, Metuchen (1972)
46. Cleghorn, R.: The old south tries again. In: Saturday Review, pp. 76–77, 88–90 (1970)
47. Resolution: Library Service to Educational Institutions Established to Circumvent Desegregation Laws (1970). 0601006a_040_BlackCaucus1970-71b, American Library Association Archives at the University of Illinois at Urbana–Champaign
48. Council Minutes, January 20–23 (1970). 0601006a_040_BlackCaucus1970-71b, American Library Association Archives at the University of Illinois at Urbana–Champaign
49. Josey, E.J.: Coddling segregation. School Libr. J., 40–1 (1971)
50. Josey, E.J.: Libraries Providing Service to Segregated Schools (1971). 0601006a_040_BlackCaucus1970-71b, American Library Association Archives at the University of Illinois at Urbana–Champaign
51. Turney, L.R.: 0601006a_040_BlackCaucus1970–71b, American Library Association Archives at the University of Illinois at Urbana–Champaign (1971)
52. Lewis, M.: 0601006a_040_BlackCaucus1970–71b, American Library Association Archives at the University of Illinois at Urbana–Champaign (1970)
53. Welbourne, J.C., Jr.: Black recruitment: the issue and an approach. In: Josey, E.J. (ed.) The Black Librarian in America, pp. 92–97. Scarecrow Press, Metuchen (1970)
54. Welbourne, J.C., Jr.: Achieving black economic self-reliance: the urban public library strengthens the economic base of its community. In: Josey, E.J. (ed.) The Black Librarian in America Revisited, pp. 122–132. Scarecrow Press, Metuchen (1994)
55. Bundy, M.L.: Crisis in library education. Libr. J. **96**, 797–800 (1971)
56. Bundy, M.L., Welbourne, J.C., Jr.: The Devil has a PhD: A Documentary Account of Racism, University Style. Urban Information Interpreters Inc., College Park (1974)
57. Durrett, D.: Library of Congress Workers File Employment Bias Suit. Afro-American, p. 19 (1970)
58. Three requests for action reports. Am. Libr. **3**(3), 277–284 (1972)
59. BCALA Steering Committee. Black Caucus Resolution in Support of Joslyn Williams. Black Caucus Newsl. **1**(2), 7–8 (1973). 5640010a_BlackCaucusNewsletter, American Library Association Archives at the University of Illinois at Urbana–Champaign
60. Memo. Am. Libr. **5**(4), 198–205 (1974)
61. Hearing officer tells LC to appoint ringer to copyright post. Libr. J., 2791–2 (1972)
62. News. Am. Libr. **4**(10), 590–4 (1973)
63. Crayton, J.E.: Overdue. Wilson Libr. Bull. **48**, 385–387 (1974)
64. Wedgeworth, R.: ALA and the black librarian: strategies for the '70s. In: Josey, E.J. (ed.) The Black Librarian in America, pp. 69–76. Scarecrow Press, Metuchen (1970)

65. Poole, A.H.: 'Tearing the shroud of invisibility': communities of protest information practices and the fight for LGBTQ rights in US librarianship. Libr. Q. **90**(4), 530–562 (2020). https://doi.org/10.1086/710255
66. Samek, T.: Intellectual Freedom and Social Responsibility in American Librarianship, 1967–1974. McFarland & Co, Jefferson (2001)
67. Cassell, K.A.: The Women's rights struggle in librarianship: the task force on women. In: Bundy, M.L., Stielow, F.J. (eds.) Activism in American Librarianship, 1962–1973, pp. 21–29. Greenwood Press (1987)
68. Josey, E.J.: More than two decades later. In: Josey, E.J. (ed.) The Black Librarian in America Revisited, pp. 345–361. Scarecrow Press, Metuchen (1994)
69. Woods, A.L.: Chicago black librarians caucus: the early years. In: Josey, E.J., DeLoach, M.L. (eds.) Handbook of Black Librarianship, 2nd edn., pp. 115–118. Scarecrow Press, Lanham, Md (2000)
70. Chicago Black Caucus Victory. Black Caucus Newsl. **2**(1), 8 (1973). 5640010a_BlackCaucusNewsletter, American Library Association Archives at the University of Illinois at Urbana–Champaign
71. Jenkins, C., Washington, E.: New York Black Librarians Caucus, Inc. In: Handbook of Black Librarianship, pp. 84–88. Libraries Unlimited, Littleton (1977)
72. Bennett, Y., Cole, J.E.: New York black librarians caucus revisited: the dream moves forward. In: Josey, E.J., DeLoach, M.L. (eds.) Handbook of Black Librarianship, 2nd edn., pp. 109–113. Scarecrow Press, Lanham (2000)
73. Jolivet, L.: California librarians black caucus. In: Josey, E.J., DeLoach, M.L. (eds.) Handbook of Black Librarianship, 2nd edn., pp. 119–126. Scarecrow Press, Lanham (2000)
74. Crayton, J.E.: Overdue. Wilson Libr. Bull. **48**(5), 385–387 (1974)
75. Resolution In Support of International Book Year. Black Caucus Newsl. **1**(1), 5–7 (1972). 5640010a_BlackCaucusNewsletter, American Library Association Archives at the University of Illinois at Urbana–Champaign
76. Notes and quotes: some reflections on the BCALA in the 70s. Black Caucus Newsl. **6**(4), 13 (1980). 5640010a_BlackCaucusNewsletter, American Library Association Archives at the University of Illinois at Urbana–Champaign
77. Marcotte, A.: Black caucus of the ALA celebrates 50 years. In: American Libraries, pp. 34–38 (2020)

How Inclusive Are the International Conferences? Attending Conferences in an Unequal World

Güleda Doğan[1(✉)], Zehra Taşkın[1,2], Emanuel Kulczycki[2], and Krystian Szadkowski[2]

[1] Hacettepe University, Ankara, Turkey
gduzyol@hacettepe.edu.tr
[2] Adam Mickiewicz University, Poznań, Poland

Abstract. Scientific conferences are essential venues where researchers present their preliminary research findings, establish new networks, and lay the groundwork for future collaborations. Geopolitical inequalities, however, overlaps with inequalities in academia and have effects on conference participation. These conferences, which are easily accessible for central countries and researchers from these countries, are often unaffordable for researchers from peripheral countries. The main aim of this study is to determine from which country researchers have an advantage in participating in scientific conferences. In this context, the iConference2023 to be held in Barcelona was taken as an example, and participation fees, accommodation, and transportation expenses were compared with the GDP per capita of 218 countries. Visa requirements were also evaluated. As a result of the research, while researchers from central countries with high-income levels can participate in conferences with very little expenditure, unaffordable costs often arise for researchers from regions with low-income levels. For this reason, sharp measures should be taken to ensure equal access opportunities for researchers.

Keywords: International conferences · Inclusivity in academia · Inequality in academia

1 Introduction

Scientific conferences are one of the most important information environments in academia, as they are the platforms where researchers present their new findings, discuss the results and exchange ideas. Sharing scientific research results and forming new networks are possible thanks to these events. However, like everything else, the structure of scientific conferences has also been greatly affected after the pandemic what, in the long term, can deepen the now severe geopolitical inequalities in academia.

It is known that conferences that can be held with a limited number of participants before the pandemic impose numerous problems on participants in terms of transportation to the conference venues, visa requirements, and extremely high fees [1, 2]. Although it is thought that these problems have decreased as the virtual conferences

© The Author(s), under exclusive license to Springer Nature Switzerland AG 2023
I. Sserwanga et al. (Eds.): iConference 2023, LNCS 13971, pp. 501–508, 2023.
https://doi.org/10.1007/978-3-031-28035-1_37

become widespread with the pandemic, the existing problems have transformed due to the differences between the responsibilities of researchers across genders [3], registration fees for virtual conferences [4], and the increasing inflation rates all over the world after the pandemic and the Russian invasion of Ukraine.

Although the conferences are slowly returning to "normal mode," the economic problems faced by the whole world also affect the conference participations. Participation in on-site international conferences, which are indispensable to developing collaborations, becomes unaffordable especially for many academics/researchers from peripheral countries. Even though the organizers try to arrange hybrid meetings to reach more researchers, the registration fees for virtual conferences are still unaffordable for academics working in peripheral countries. The support of the affiliated institutions in paying the fees is either greatly reduced or completely cut off [5]. Note that most institutions do not support paying the fees of online conferences. On the other hand, even if the institutions cover the expenses or researchers are invited as keynotes to the events, it is usually possible only on a refund basis. What is important, researchers very often have to buy at least plane tickets in advance, but the purchasing power of researchers from the center and the periphery differs substantially. This, in turn, affects researchers' decisions to attend conferences. Also, when several such events a year pile up, it is very difficult to sustain the flow of money. In view of these facts, the academia must work to make itself more inclusive, resilient, and sustainable than ever, as stated by Sharan Burrow in a report on life after Covid-19 [6].

This paper adds to a broader debate on the centers and peripheries in knowledge production [7, 8] and focuses on the inclusivity of scientific conferences and the inequalities in access that emerged between researchers from central and peripheral countries. We considered iConference2023 as a case and answered the following research questions.

- What are the average expenses of an international conference, and who can afford them? How does the affordability change when the conference is held online?
- Which countries have privileges to join the conferences in terms of visa requirements and transportation opportunities?

Having these questions answered in relation to the case selected, this paper engages into a discussion about what the feasible solutions to the problem of unequal access to scientific conferences are globally. While many research have dealt with the issue of existing barriers to access to scientific conferences [9–11], there are still few concrete proposals on what needs to be done to put an end to ongoing reproduction of the inequalities in the sphere of science communication [9]. This paper adds to the literature on designing the ways of providing equity in scholarly academic conferences.

2 Method

We created a dataset on the basis of data for 218 countries and classified these countries using The World Bank's country classification [12], in four groups by income (Low-Income, Lower-Middle, Upper-Middle, High-Income) and in seven groups by region (South Asia, Europe & Central Asia, Middle East & North Africa, East Asia & Pacific, Sub-Saharan Africa, Latin America & The Caribbean, North America).

The most basic expenses for a conference are registration fee, travel, and accommodation. If visa required for the host country (which is Barcelona, Spain for iConference2023), this will be an additional fee. Since visa costs vary and difficult to collect the data for it, it is not covered in this study. However, we collected data for visa requirements (except three countries) on a yes/no basis using Spainvisa.eu. The dataset includes two flight prices for each country, one is for best flight, the other is for an alternative cheap flight with a longer duration for most of the countries. Cost of the travel was calculated on 18 August 2022 using Skyscanner[1] for a round trip to Barcelona, Spain from the capital cities of each country (departure date: 26 March 2023, return date: 30 March 2023). Flight prices for 30 countries could not be determined.[2] Since there are two registration alternatives (physical and virtual) for iConference2023, we used early bird regular registration fees for physical event ($ 385) and virtual event ($ 265). We calculated the median accommodation price for four nights from March 26 to March 30 ($ 613) using data on Booking.com.[3] We considered all hotels/apartments within 1 km or less of the *Universitat Oberta de Catalunya.*

We calculated the cost of the iConference2023, consisting of registration, accommodation, and travel expenses, for each country and compared it with GDP of the relevant country. We used GDP per capita (2020) gathered from the World Bank.[4] All currencies are in USD.

We used Excel and JASP for data analysis, visualizations, and calculations.

3 Findings

Since 2005, 17 iConferences have been held, mostly in the USA. iConferences were held online during the pandemic period (2020–2022). So far, two iConferences have been held in Europe and one iConference in China. iConferences are organized by iSchools, the international organization of library and information science schools. Figure 1 shows the geographic distribution of 123 library and information science schools under iSchools as of the end of 2022 and the regions hosting iConferences. Most iSchools members are from North America (51 schools, 41%), followed by Asia (37 schools, 30%) and Europe (31 schools, 25%).

3.1 Conference Costs of Physical Event by GDP Per Capita

One way to understand what it would cost to attend the iConference 2023 for potential participants from different countries is to look at the ratio of the calculated conference

1 https://www.skyscanner.com/.

2 American Samoa, Andorra, Belize, Bhutan, British Virgin Islands, Channel Islands, Eswatini, Greenland, Honduras, Kiribati, Korea, Dem. People's Rep., Libya, Marshall Islands, Micronesia, Fed, Sts., Monaco, Nauru, New Caledonia, Northern Mariana Islands, Palau, Russian Federation, San Marino, St. Kitts and Nevis, St. Vincent and the Grenadines, Syrian Arab Republic, Timor-Leste, Tonga, Tuvalu, Virgin Islands (U.S.), West Bank and Gaza, Yemen, Rep.

3 https://booking.com/.

4 https://data.worldbank.org/indicator/NY.GDP.PCAP.PP.CD.

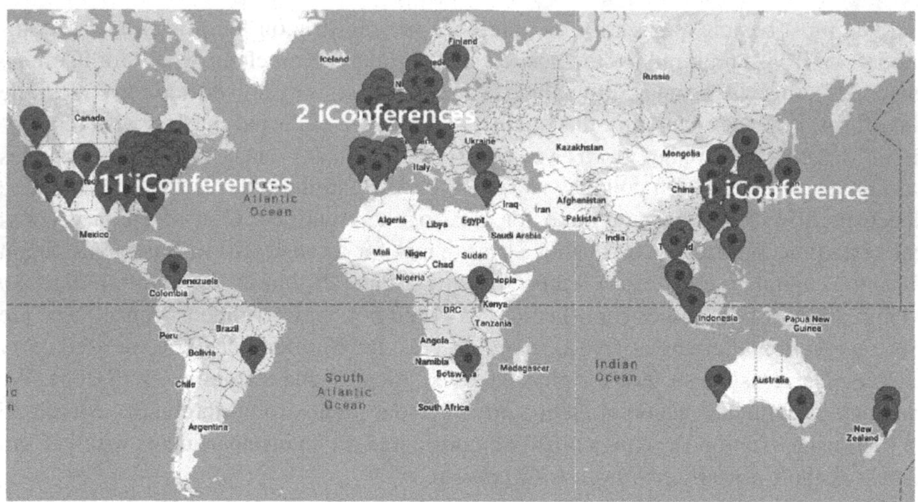

Fig. 1. Geographic distribution of iSchools and iConferences

costs to the GDP per capita of the respective countries. We calculated the ratio of conference costs to GDP per capita for both flight alternatives and found that they do not differ considerably. Therefore, the cost calculated with best flight is considered for further analysis. The conference costs are at least as much as GDP per capita for 40 countries. All these 40 countries are from Low or Lower-Middle income groups, and 30 of them are Sub-Saharan countries (three from each of South Asia, East Asia & Pacific and Europe & Central Asia regions, and one from Latin America & The Caribbean).

The conference cost for 24 countries is between half and all of GDP per capita, all but two of which are in the Lower-Middle income group. The other two countries, Fiji, and Suriname are in the Upper-Middle income group. East Asia & Pacific and Sub-Saharan Africa stands out as the region. For an affordable conference, the ratio of conference cost to GDP per capita is expected to be as low as possible. There are 33 countries for which iConference2023 costs less than 5% of GDP per capita. All except Nicaragua are High income countries, and 21 of them from Europe & Central Asia region (three from each North America and East Asia & Pacific, two from Latin America & The Caribbean, and four from Middle East & North Africa).

Figure 2 shows that the power to attend scholarly academic conferences to develop collaborations, networks, and future projects etc. by meeting the conference costs is directly related to the income level of the country. If researchers live in a High-income country, they are the luckiest ones, but unfortunately, researchers' chances in this sense decrease as their income decreases.

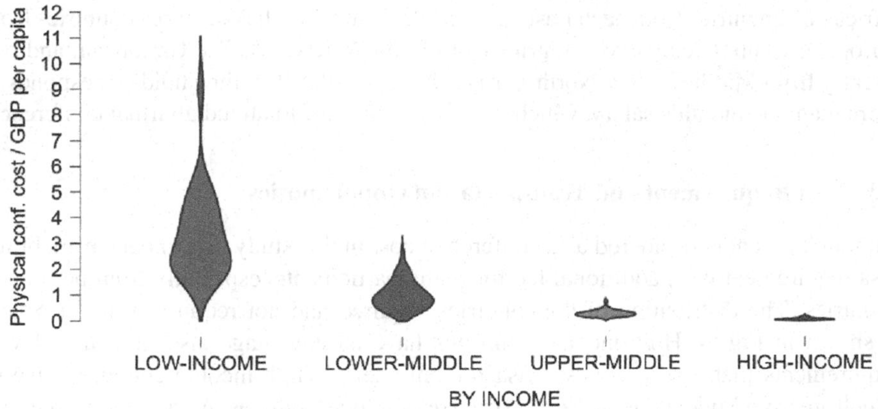

Fig. 2. The ratio of iConference2023 participation cost for physical event to GDP by country income groups.

3.2 Participation in the Virtual Event

Participating in virtual events can also be an option, although they do not offer as many opportunities as physical events in terms of communication and collaboration. Since the only fee to be paid for participation in the virtual event is the conference registration fee, virtual events are more affordable than physical events. However, they are still unaffordable for many countries as also presented in Fig. 3.

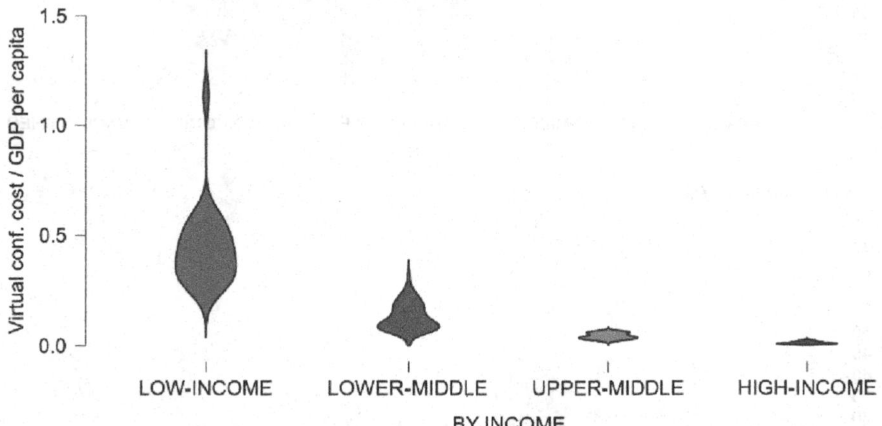

Fig. 3. The ratio of iConference2023 participation cost for virtual event to GDP by country income groups.

There is one country where this fee exceeds GDP and seven countries where GDP is more than half. Except for Pakistan, these countries are Sub-Saharan African countries. Virtual event participation fee is more than 10% of GDP per capita for 54 countries consists of Low and Lower-Middle income countries, 37 of which are from Sub-Saharan

Africa (six countries from each East Asia & Pacific and South Asia, three countries from Europe & Central Asia, two countries from Latin America & The Caribbean, and one country from Middle East & North Africa). Note that the 10% threshold corresponds to more than one month's salary, which is a very high price to attend a virtual conference.

3.3 Visa Requirement and Transportation Opportunities

Although it is not considered as a conference cost in this study due to data availability, visa requirement is an additional fee for many participants, especially from peripheral countries. The distribution of the countries required and not required visa for Spain, is shown in Fig. 4. High-income countries have an advantage also in terms of visa requirements that Spain requests visa for only seven High-income countries, five of which are from Middle East & North Africa region (two from East Asia & Pacific region).

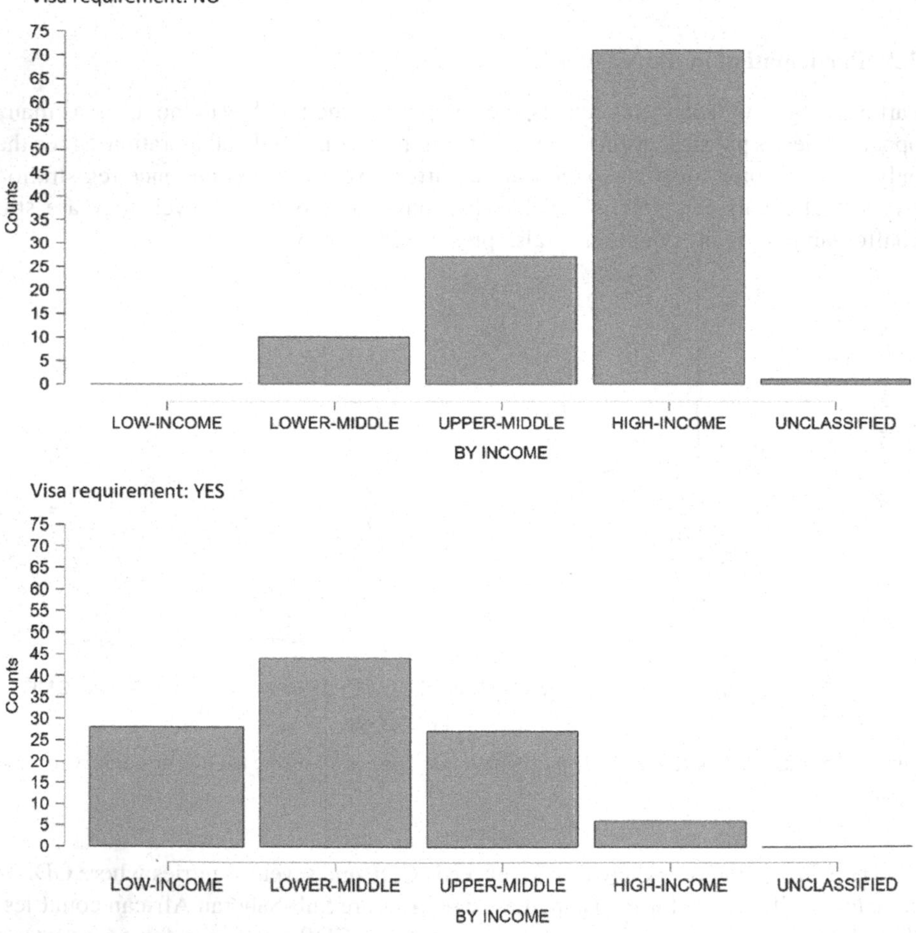

Fig. 4. Visa requirements for Barcelona, Spain by income groups of countries

All Low-income countries and many of the Lower-Middle income countries will have an additional conference expense to obtain a visa. Also, it is known that researchers from some peripheral countries such as Turkey have difficulties obtaining visa even if their papers are accepted to the conferences [13].

Only flight to Barcelona is more than the half of GDP per capita for four countries, and more than 10% of GDP for 35 countries, among which the countries from Latin America & The Caribbean region stands out. Note that, the flight is less than 10% percent of GDP per capita for 77% of countries from European & Central Asia region, and less than 5% percent of GDP per capita for 54%.

4 Discussion

This paper presents the preliminary results of an ongoing project on ways of providing equity in scholarly academic conferences. In their current form, conferences only serve researchers from central countries which already have enough research funds to join conferences. Researchers from the periphery—who already have disadvantages in networking and access to research funding—are missing out on potential collaboration opportunities by being unable to participate in such events. Considering our results, to avoid these inequalities:

- Conference fees should be affordable for researchers from the periphery. There should be various tariffs and waiver options for different country groups. In addition, scholarship opportunities should be provided for young researchers and students. Most importantly, the chance to virtual participation in the conferences should be offered and this should be provided free of charge to the researchers of the peripheral countries.
- Conferences should be organized in countries that have fewer visa requirements and are easy to access. Also, it is important to provide cheap accommodation opportunities to the researchers.

In addition to the inequalities, there are many concerns about environmental sustainability [1]. Hosting conferences means thousands of researchers' carbon footprints. For this reason, this issue should be addressed in all aspects of future studies and applications that will provide equal opportunities to all researchers and that will cause the least harm to nature should be started.

References

1. Sarabipour, S., et al.: Changing scientific meetings for the better. Nat. Hum. Behav. **5**, 296–300 (2021). https://doi.org/10.1038/s41562-021-01067-y
2. Rojo, L.M.: Hegemonies and inequalities in academia. Int. J. Sociol. Lang. **2021**, 169–192 (2021). https://doi.org/10.1515/ijsl-2020-0077
3. Górska, A.M., Kulicka, K., Staniszewska, Z., Dobija, D.: Deepening inequalities: what did COVID-19 reveal about the gendered nature of academic work? Gender Work Org. **28**, 1546–1561 (2021). https://doi.org/10.1111/gwao.12696
4. Gewin, V.: The career cost of COVID-19 to female researchers, and how science should respond. Nature **583**, 867–869 (2020). https://doi.org/10.1038/d41586-020-02183-x

5. Adolfo Neto [@adolfont]: Question for academics (professors and students): have you ever had to pay out of your own pocket, at least in part, to attend an academic event?. https://twitter.com/adolfont/status/1565768647976558592. Accessed 16 Sept 2022
6. Suskind, D., Mankiya, J., Saldanha, J., Burrow, S., Rebelo, S., Bremmer, I.: Life post-COVID-19. https://www.imf.org/en/Publications/fandd/issues/2020/06/how-will-the-world-be-different-after-COVID-19. Accessed 15 Sept 2022
7. Medina, L.R.: Centers and Peripheries in Knowledge Production. Routledge, Abingdon (2013)
8. Demeter, M.: Academic Knowledge Production and the Global South: Questioning Inequality and Under-Representation. Palgrave Macmillan, London (2020)
9. Nicolson, D.J.: Academic Conferences as Neoliberal Commodities. Palgrave Macmillan, Basingstoke (2017)
10. Hansen, T.T., Pedersen, D.B.: The impact of academic events—A literature review. Res. Eval. **27**(4), 358–366 (2018)
11. Momm, Ch.F., Jöns, H.: Decentralized concentration through cyclical events: the geographies of academic conferences in urban and regional development and planning in Brazil, 2004–2013. Geoforum **112**, 104–117 (2020)
12. World Bank Country and Lending Groups – World Bank Data Help Desk. https://datahelpdesk.worldbank.org/knowledgebase/articles/906519-world-bank-country-and-lending-groups. Accessed 24 Sept 2020
13. Yılmaz, T.: MP tables parliamentary motion on Turks' visa-related problems - Türkiye News (2022). https://www.hurriyetdailynews.com/mp-tables-parliamentary-motion-on-turks-visa-related-problems-176240

Locating Black Information Lives: "Scoping" the Literature on African American Genealogical Research

LaVerne Gray(✉), Jeongbae Choi, Shannon Crooks, and Ariana Cook

Syracuse University, Syracuse, NY 13244, USA
lgray01@syr.edu

Abstract. The genealogical path for African Americans is a distinct and intimate journey in the discovery of self-using personal artifacts, archives, and biological data. We view those that practice genealogy as information seekers utilizing information communities to uncover familial narratives and the ancestral line. As a part of a larger project, *Uncovering Black Lives*, we are comprehensively exploring the literature on African American genealogical researchers across disciplines. To accomplish this, we conducted a five round literature search using EBSCO Host, *ProQuest,* and *Web of Science* making iterative shifts in the search terms and fields to gather relevant materials. This paper details the scoping literature review as method for determining the size and nature of an under-researched multidisciplinary topic. Our process is explicated in first demonstrating the scoping process through research platform and database choice and searching, next we perform a pilot analysis by taking three disciplines (Sociology, Library and Information Science, and Familial Artifacts) looking at keywords, research methods, and publishing over time. Our initial analysis suggests a distinct gap in the literature across disciplines on African American Genealogy research, qualitative approaches including (orality, Black feminisms, and ethnography) are utilized, and research on African American familial artifacts is rare. Our hope is to move forward with a more comprehensive review and utilize results in support of determining approaches for a larger project.

Keywords: Black genealogy · Scoping review · Methodology · Libraries · Multidisciplinary

1 Introduction

This paper describes the approach we adopted during a literature search for African American genealogy studies. The main purpose of the paper is to provide enough information for the reader to replicate our literature search if needed. Our main research project ('Uncovering Black Lives'-UBL) aims to examine information behavior in genealogical studies, explore family artifacts, and support the more effective and diverse dissemination of previously overlooked histories of African Americans. The project illuminates how African American genealogical communities as sites are formed and cultivated

© The Author(s), under exclusive license to Springer Nature Switzerland AG 2023
I. Sserwanga et al. (Eds.): iConference 2023, LNCS 13971, pp. 509–522, 2023.
https://doi.org/10.1007/978-3-031-28035-1_38

through the collection, provision, and exchange of information among their members. The project builds upon decades of tradition exploring how marginalized communities use and search for information in support of diversity and inclusion.

African American genealogy became popularized in the 20th century with the publishing of Alex Haley's Roots: The Saga of an American Family. The revelatory narrative told both in the text and in the broadcast, introduced, many viewers to a historical tale centered on the saga of one American family. Alex Haley's family became an historical representation of what was both assumed and unknown of African American contributions to American History. As a result of Haley's groundbreaking work and with the advent of the internet and technological tools to research ancestors, genealogy is popularized in media. The UBL project aims to examine information behavior, explore familial collection building, and support dissemination of unearthed histories of African Americans through investigating genealogy work. This paper recounts the work-in-process of locating research on Black/African American genealogy in the literature. The work of African American genealogical researchers whether hobbyist or professional reflects the continuity of the struggles to resist placement of the Black experience at the margins—and functions as an integral part of the information community spectrum which needs further study. This works aims to tackle the 'multiplicity' issue in genealogy studies in terms of its different definitions as a discipline, history, literature, and so on.

Our exploratory literature search provides an informed 'scope' for our research. Scoping reviews aim to identify the potential size and nature of the literature on a broad topic area. This type of review tends to ask generic questions about research trends. The main goal of the scoping/mapping review is to conduct a comprehensive survey, but feasibility can be a point of consideration when doing so [1]. The overall questions of the scoping review are: What disciplines feature research on African American familial genealogy? and What methods and tools are utilized in research on African American familial genealogy?

Our search centered on the following objectives: (1) gaining a broader picture of genealogy studies which have been conducted in diverse disciplines such as biology, sociology, history, literature, and library and information science; (2) comparing generalized genealogy studies with specifically African American genealogy studies; (3) surveying the methodologies and methods adopted by genealogy researchers; and (4) exploring what "counts" as research on genealogy practices, particularly focusing on the locations of 'family history' and 'family artifacts' in genealogy studies.

2 'Scoping' Sources: Platforms, Databases, and Disciplines

Given the interdisciplinary characteristics of genealogy studies as a field, we did not initially impose any constraints on the sources of literature. We started using four principal scholarly platforms (i.e., *EBSCOhost*, *ProQuest*, *Web of Science*, and *JSTOR*). Based on the initial search results using the keyword 'genealogy' (using *"genealog*"*) in the full text (i.e., 'open field') and abstract fields from the platforms, we selected the following databases, which consider the number of retrieved items, research goals, and research areas. We decided to exclude *JSTOR* because it returned a relatively small number of results from the initial search attempt and does not provide a subject search function, which is a crucial requirement to meet the criteria for the robustness and comparability of the results.

In terms of other platforms (*EBSCOhost*, *ProQuest*, and *Web of Science*), we selected 13 databases potentially relevant to our research goals (see Table 1). For *EBSCOhost*, six databases in the humanities, (historical) education, and LIS were selected for our literature search. For *ProQuest*, we selected three databases from not only the humanities but also social sciences and sociology. By doing so, we expected to discover how social science researchers consider genealogical methodologies and methods and family artifacts. For *Web of Science*, we intended to focus on 'impactful' journals and articles in the domains of science (SCIE), the humanities (A&HCI), and social sciences (SSCI). The CPCI (Conference Proceedings Citation Index) was also included to compare publication trends for journals and conferences. To ensure efficiency in our comparison, we integrated CPCI-S (science) and CPCI-SSH (social science and humanities).

Table 1. Selected platforms and databases.

Platform (N)	Database
EBSCOhost (6)	Humanities International Index (HII)
	MLA International Bibliography (MLAIB)
	Education Source (ES)
	America: History & Life (AHL)
	Library, Information Science & Technology Abstracts (LISTA)
	Library Literature and Information Science (LLIS)
ProQuest (3)	Arts & Humanities Database (AH)
	Social Science Database (SS)
	Sociological Abstracts (SA)
Web of Science (4)	Science Citation Index Expanded (SCIE)
	Arts & Humanities Citation Index (A&HCI)
	Social Science Citation Index (SSCI)
	Conference Proceedings Citation Index (CPCI)

We only searched for literature dated up to June 30, 2022, as we conducted our literature search from July to August 2022. Given the historical aspects of the research topic, we did not designate the start date of our search. We implemented a five-round literature search and held meetings after finishing each round to review the results and refine our approach to the next round.

3 'Scoping' Search Process: Criteria and Attempts

3.1 Search Criteria

We searched the platforms using the following criteria: search keywords, search fields, and source types. These criteria were developed through iterative refinement based on discussions about the given search results. Additionally, we only searched for literature written in English. All those search criteria were simultaneously employed in each round, providing diverse sets of search results as described in the next section.

Search Keywords. We selected the following separate search keywords for our literature survey. These keywords essentially reflect the primary goals and scope of our research project. The keywords were used were based on capturing a broad view of the discipline to clarify the depth of research in the various fields. To simplify the process, more specific terminology was avoided.

- #1. genealog*;
- #2. genealog* AND method*
- #3. genealog* AND methodolog*
- #4. African American AND genealog*
- #5. African American AND (genealogy OR genealogical)
- #6. African American AND (family OR familial)
- #7. African American AND "family history"
- #8. African American AND "family artifact*"
- #9. Black AND genealogy*
- #10. Black AND (genealogy OR genealogical)
- #11. Black AND (family OR familial)
- #12. Black AND "family history"
- #13. Black AND "family artifact*".

Search Fields. At first, we searched the literature without designating specific field codes (i.e., 'open field'). However, in the latter rounds of our search attempts, we primarily searched the subjects and abstracts. The choice to limit search fields was made to increase the precision and feasibility of the search results. (For example, some articles simply contain the term 'genealogy of something,' which is irrelevant to genealogy studies, in their main text.) However, the fourth round was conducted in the 'open field' for the purpose of comparing the results with those of the fifth round, which limited the search fields to subject and abstract while using the same search keywords.

Source Types. We did not designate specific source types in the earlier search attempts. However, we included only 'academic journals' as our source type in the fourth and fifth attempts to enhance our efficiency and the feasibility of conducting a literature review.

Table 2. Literature search attempts and refinement (in total)

Round	Source types	Search keywords	Search fields	No. of publications*
1	Undesignated ('Open')	#5. African American AND (genealogy OR genealogical)	Open	13,827
		#6. African American AND (family OR familial)		192,964
		#10. Black AND (genealogy OR genealogical)		19,617
		#11. Black AND (family OR familial)		10,048,796
2	Academic journal, conference paper, magazine, biography, dissertation	#4. African American AND genealog*	Open	13,869
		#7. African American AND "family history"		108,218
		#9. Black AND genealogy*		19,794
		#12. Black AND "family history"		145,955
3		#4. African American AND genealog*	Subject, Abstract	774
		#7. African American AND "family history"		2,672
		#9. Black AND genealogy*		1,387
		#12. Black AND "family history"		2,227
		#8. African American AND "family artifact*"	Open	16
		#13. Black AND "family artifact*"		29
4	Academic journal	#1. genealog*	Open	61,607
		#2. genealog* AND method*		25,016
		#3. genealog* AND methodolog*		13,417
5		#1. genealog*	Subject, Abstract	44,014
		#2. genealog* AND method*		6,697
		#3. genealog* AND methodolog*		1,832

** Note. Duplicates are not excluded in this stage.*

3.2 Search Attempts

We conducted five attempts to glean and refine our search results from different combinations of search criteria. Tables 2 and 3 show the criteria that we adopted in each round of the five search attempts.

In the first search attempt, we intended to see how African American genealogy studies have been conducted in different disciplines. To this end, we used four search keywords (#5, #6, #10, #11) in the open search field and undesignated source types. Next, we narrowed down the source types to trace the research tendencies. Books, book reviews, commentaries, and editorials were excluded. Search keywords were slightly changed (#4, #7, #9, #12), given the broad first search results. In the third attempt, we adopted phrase searching using quotation marks (e.g., "family artifact*") (#8, #13). The field codes were changed to 'subject' and 'abstract' to gain more relevant results. Lastly, in the fourth and fifth attempts, we searched for literature on genealogical methodologies in general (#1, #2, #3), switching the search fields from 'open' to 'subject' and 'abstract.' We restricted the source type to 'academic journal' and 'conference paper' to trace the trends in academic research.

4 'Scoping' Analysis: Sociology, Libraries, and Artifacts

For the purposes of an exploratory literature search, we only removed duplicates from the search results within the same platform. Retracted articles were excluded. Therefore,

Table 3. Literature search attempts and refinement (by research platforms)

Round	Source types	Search keywords	Search fields	No. of publications* EBSCOhost	Proquest	Web of Science
1	Undesignated ('Open')	#5.	Open	673	12,971	183
		#6.		12,186	152,955	27,823
		#10.		984	18,268	365
		#11.		16,610	9,996,985	35,201
2	Academic journal, conference paper, magazine, biography, dissertation	#4.	Open	497	13,211	161
		#7.		514	104,334	3,370
		#9.		782	18,681	331
		#12.		674	141,591	3,690
3		#4.	Subject, Abstract	311	224	204
		#7.		142	108	2414
		#9.		427	412	535
		#12.		131	112	1,978
		#8.	Open	0	16	0
		#13.		0	29	0
4	Academic journal	#1.	Open	11,163	36,127	14,317
		#2.		1,169	20,717	3,130
		#3.		602	12,138	677
5		#1.	Subject, Abstract	11,532	7,731	24,571
		#2.		697	582	5,418
		#3.		290	362	1,180

* *Note. Duplicates are not excluded in this stage.*

the final numbers of the selected literature will differ from those in this document. Even though we conducted a more segmented literature search with the aforementioned criteria, only some of the significant figures are presented here due to space limitations.

After excluding duplicates, we read the abstracts of the surveyed articles to identify the literature more suitable for our main research projects. We had several discussions through which we decided on the relevance of the literature. Once an article was considered relevant and/or significant to our research, we read the main text of the article to gain more detailed knowledge into the methodologies, approaches, and findings at play (Fig. 1).

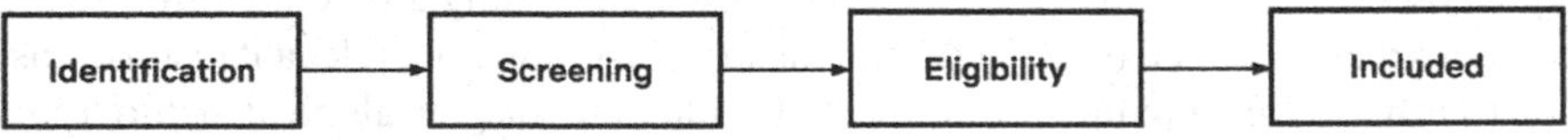

Fig. 1. Literature search process

4.1 Sociology

In round 3 there was an increase in academic scholarship contributions over time in genealogical research. There are 216 Sociology items between 1980–2022. We examined dissertations and non-dissertations using search keywords #4 ("African American AND genealog*") and #9 (Black AND genealog*) (Fig. 2, Table 4). Both publication types increased steadily from the 1990s to the 2010s. Notably 59 non-dissertation items were located using black and genealogy as keywords. Other keywords of note included 10 'colonialism' [2–11] and 'feminism/feminist' [12–21].

Colonialism in partnership with enslavement is shown in sociological research on African American genealogy. One of the articles explores internalized colonialism [8]. That theory explains racial poverty and isolation on indigenous communities and the effects of enslavement and military control [8]. This analysis reflects how colonial power supported and sustained oppression of black and indigenous people throughout history. German colonialism is also explored through the investigative genealogical analysis of race relations in German Southwest Africa [10]. Colonial powers have widened the inequality gap in black genealogical research.

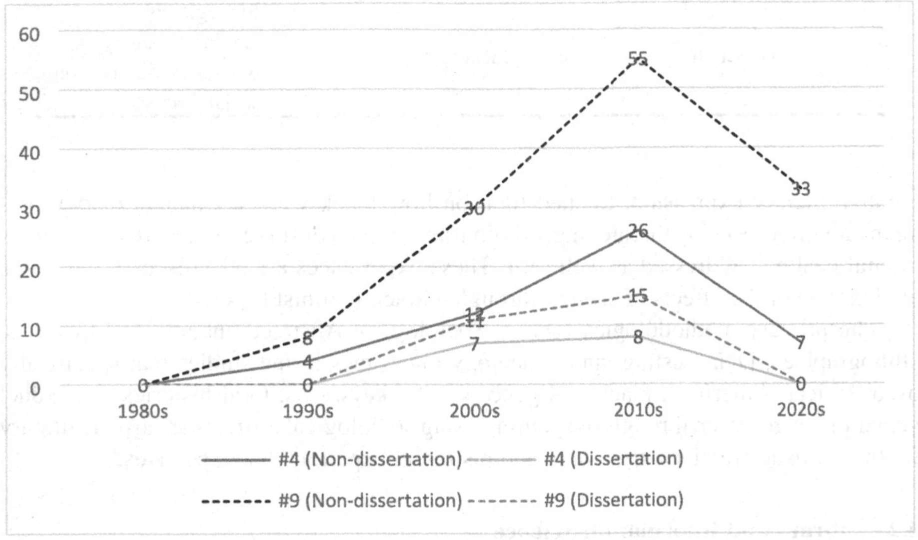

Fig. 2. Number of items in SA (*ProQuest*) (Round 3, Search keywords: #4, #9)

The black diaspora is featured in Sociological Abstracts results. In Cohen's article the word diaspora is analyzed from a its various meanings and its cultural political influence in Jewish and Black relations [22]. Adams [23] attempts to reveal the societal contributions of Afro-Latin Americans to American history and discusses how those contributions have been concealed from history through invisibility. The Black Diaspora illuminates black genealogy through black artists' international contributions of visual, literary and performing arts in the 1920s and 1930s [24]. This artistic expression provides insight into how black internationalism through artistic contributions tells the stories of how black people were impacted by racism universally [24].

Black genealogy from a black feminist perspective is also conceptualized in the articles. One article used intersectionality as a focal point for evaluation and analysis of black feminist storytelling [17]. Waggoner [20] analyzes white feminist twentieth

Table 4. Principal keywords and methods in SA (*ProQuest*) (Round 3, Search keywords: #4, #9)

Search keyword	Source type	Number of items	Keywords	Methods
#4	Non-dissertation	49	African diaspora, black feminist genealogy, black identity	DNA testing analysis, genetic testing, interviews, oral history, oral historical examination
	Dissertation	15	African American, child, history, memory, racial	Dissemination of photos, ethnography
#9	Non-dissertation	126	African diaspora, colonialism, culture, feminist, intersectionality	ethnography, genealogical interview, genetic testing, participant observation
	Dissertation	26	Identity, race	Ethnography, oral history analysis, participant observation, social analysis

creative literary expression, to shed light on how black women's mental distress has been racialized as being threatening, criminal and in need of surveillance. Black women's mental health is addressed as well [20]. These experiences are also discussed in Stitt's explanation of the effects of slavery through a black feminist lens [21].

The primary methodologies used in Sociological Abstracts include oral histories, ethnographies, DNA testing, and genealogy interviews in the studies that specifically used African American, black and genealogy as keywords. Oral histories to conduct genealogical research through storytelling using sociological artifacts are artistic literary writing, artistic creative expression, and historical experiential perspectives.

4.2 Library and Information Science

Keywords recognized the most were Genealogist, African American Research, African American History, Family Trees, Ancestry, Blackness, African American Funerals and death records, DNA analysis, Roots, and Black family (Fig. 3, Table 5).

Common methodologies included ethnological research, resources from archives such as photographs, documents, microfilms and text, review of genealogical research, ancestry research, and DNA analysis. The most prominent methodologies noticed in the text were oral histories, death records and funeral programs. Funeral programs provide a valuable documentation source [25]. Interviews with family members and relatives of frees people and former slaves were common as well as conversations with genealogists or specialists in library and research fields.

The review of birth and death records as well as obituaries and funerals are surprisingly popular items of interest for researchers. Funeral programs document the lived-life [26]. This documentation is unique in that it is not necessarily official government documents but rather self-documented by families and locals. Oral history in the form of

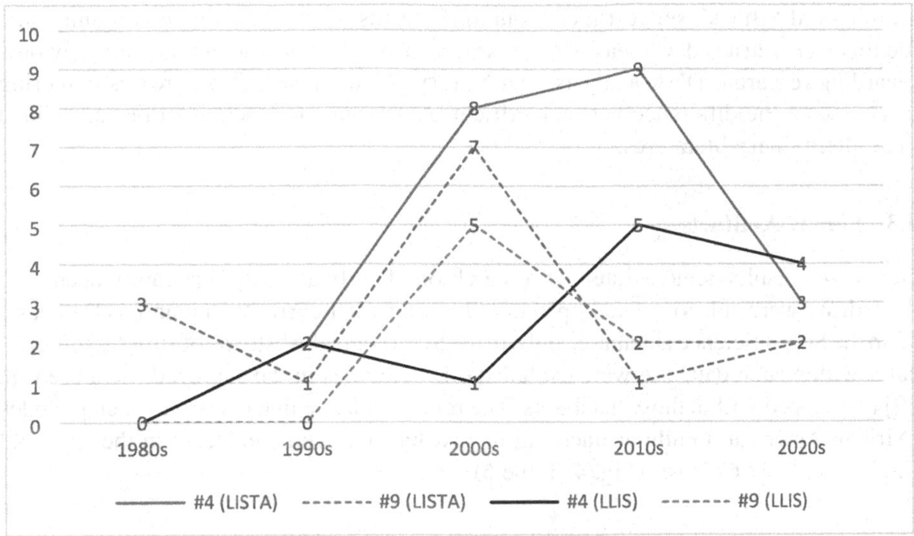

Fig. 3. Number of items in LISTA and LLIS (*ProQuest*) (Round 3, Search keywords: #4, #9)

Table 5. Principal keywords and methods in LISTA and LLIS (*EBSCOhost*) (Round 3)

Database	Search keyword	Keywords	Methods
LISTA	#4	African American funerals, African American heritage, archives, birth/death records, Blackness, descendants, DNA analysis, family trees, genealogy, local history	Archival research, ethnographic research, interviews
	#9	Genealogy, Faith, Black Family, Black, Blackness, Black people, Roots, Etymology	Archival research, bibliographical research, genealogical research, interviews, reviews of catalogs, archival research
LLIS	#4	African American funerals, African American heritage, ancestry, churches, communities, family history	
	#9	Ancestry, Black people, etymology, family history, family tree, roots	archival research, genealogical research,

interviews was the most prominent research method that appeared in the surveyed literature. This is most likely due to the importance and relevance of oral history in the African American communities. Interviewing friends and relatives fill an important gap [27].

Despite the seeming similarities of the search words "African American" and "Black" used in the literature review the search results had unique identifiers. When using the search word "Black" suggest a connotation towards ideas of family, community, and identity were retrieved whereas African American resulted in articles that with keywords regarding research, DNA analysis, and history. As the research progresses exploring discourse on the difference between African American and black identities as defined in all disciplinary literatures.

4.3 Family Artifacts

Our search results demonstrate that research on "family artifacts" has rarely been conducted. We were able to locate 11 pieces of literature in the Arts & Humanities Database, 13 in the Social Science Database, and 6 in the Sociological Abstracts of *ProQuest* (duplicates within each database were excluded). Two articles in the surveyed literature [28, 29] overlapped within those databases. The results indicate that research which includes 'African American family artifacts' in its text has not been conducted in the LIS field (included in *EBSCOhost*) (Fig. 4, Table 6).

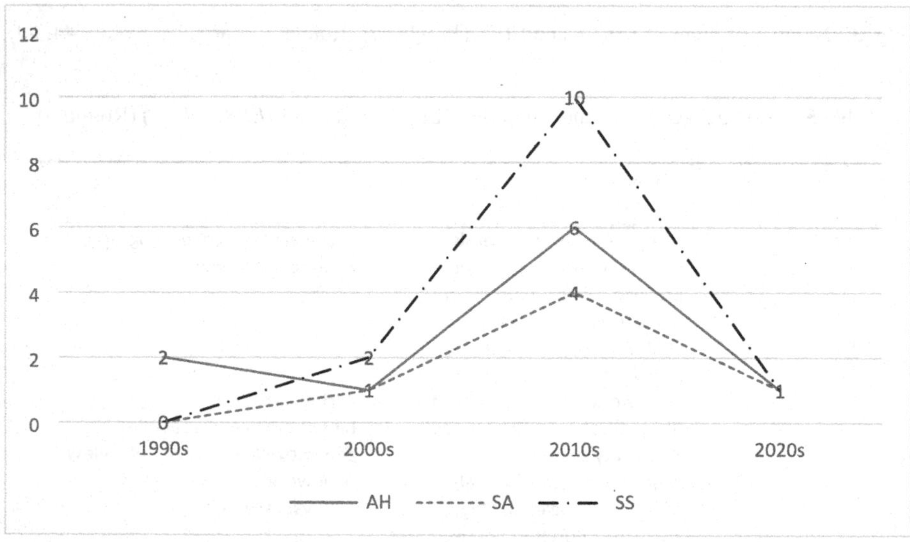

Fig. 4. Number of items in AH, SA, and SS (*ProQuest*) (Round 3, Search keywords: #8, #13)

Several tendencies were identified in the surveyed literature. First, most literature did not directly focus on 'family artifacts' or genealogy perspectives. The term "family artifacts" mostly appeared in the literature as a component of the empirical data for research in education/teaching [30–32], organizations [29, 33], media [34], and so on. 'Family artifacts' included in the publications in the Arts & Humanities Database were predominantly related to the usage of those artifacts in art forms such as poetry, plays, novels, and music.

Table 6. Principal keywords and methods for family artifacts (*ProQuest*) (Round 3, Search keywords: #8, #13)

Database	Number of items	Keywords	Methods
AH	10	**Artworks, curriculum, ethics, teaching**	**Feminist methodology/methods**
SA	6	**Culture, education, family, identity, race/racialization**	**Artifacts, ethnography, interviews, participant observation, qualitative content/data analysis**
SS	13	**Culture/cultural heritage, identity, gender, women**	**Interview, mixed-methods approach**

Second, despite the prevalence of 'non-genealogist' studies, some of the surveyed publications provide useful insights into African American genealogy studies. For example, Haynes et al. [35], in their ethnographic research of Black women doctoral students, employed various family artifacts such as report cards and photographs to triangulate their findings from the autobiographies of the participants. Fredlund [36] demonstrates the importance of artifacts ("objects of discourse and other material conditions") when contextualizing the historical practices of feminist women's clubs in the 19th century. In particular, this research includes as a crucial historical case the Woman's Era Club (WEC), which was founded in 1893 as a collaborative community for African American women activists. Bresnahan's [37] analysis of 'family photo-making rituals' broadens our understanding of photographs as not only symbolic artifacts but also communication processes and practices.

Third, some studies were found to be more directly related to genealogy and (family) artifacts than others. For example, Scodari [28] takes a critical view of television advertisements for commercialized genealogy services (23andMe and AncestryDNA) based on genetic essentialism, i.e., "fetishization" of ethnically associated objects, artifacts, and practices, which deprives them of their cultural contexts and turning them into superficial receptacles. By adopting cultural psychology perspectives, Cota [38] argues that culture consists of social practices including both material and symbolic tools such as physical objects [artifacts], abstract knowledge, beliefs, values, and observable patterns of behavior.

Finally, we found certain methodological tendencies regarding 'family artifacts' studies. As the family has been traditionally associated with feminity and motherhood, studies employing family artifacts often adopt feminist methodology/methods [33, 36, 39]. On the other hand, many studies that adopt qualitative mixed methods tend to underpin such approaches by adopting cognate philosophical foundations such as phenomenology, ground theory, critical theory, and social justice. Such similarities seem to reflect the characteristics of both the field (i.e., genealogy studies) and research topic (i.e., family artifacts).

5 Concluding Thoughts

In brief, scoping the literature provided us with a sense location African American genealogical research. In terms of research methods of genealogy studies, we discovered a few differences between LIS and non-LIS (social sciences) literature. LIS literature tends to adopt document-oriented methods employing archives, bibliographies, and catalogs, whereas social science literature was found to be more ethnography-oriented, involving participant observation, oral history, and interviews. We also found Research gap in genealogy studies employing family artifacts as named entity—but research in library and information science revealed the funeral program as a type of artifact. Early scoping of the literature provided the researchers with a path forward to further analysis of African American genealogical research. Although we also found substantive research in biology, literature, and history, we chose to examine smaller retrieved results to scope the dimensions of the topic. The preliminary findings indicate a way forward in understanding best methods used to examine the population we intend to for the larger UBL project will use more descriptive and narrative approaches to the further review of literature.

References

1. Paré, G., Trudel, M.-C., Jaana, M., Kitsiou, S.: Synthesizing information systems knowledge: a typology of literature reviews. Inf. Manag. **52**, 183–199 (2015). https://doi.org/10.1016/j.im.2014.08.008
2. Figueroa, Y.: After the hurricane: Afro-Latina decolonial feminisms and destierro. Hypatia **35**, 220–229 (2020). https://doi.org/10.1017/hyp.2019.12
3. Márquez, J.D., Rana, J.: Black radical possibility and the decolonial international. South Atl. Q. **116**, 505 (2017)
4. Fuste, J.I.: Colonial laboratories, irreparable subjects: the experiment of "(b)ordering" San Juan's public housing residents. Soc. Identities **16**, 41–59 (2010). https://doi.org/10.1080/13504630903465886
5. McCalman, J., Smith, L., Anderson, I., Morley, R., Mishra, G.: Colonialism and the health transition: aboriginal Australians and poor whites compared, Victoria, 1850–1985. Hist. Fam. **14**, 253–265 (2009). https://doi.org/10.1016/j.hisfam.2009.04.005
6. Numark, M.: Constructing a Jewish Nation in Colonial India: history, narratives of dissent, and the vocabulary of modernity. Jew. Soc. Stud. **7**, 89 (2001)
7. Ndlovu-Gatsheni, S.J.: Discourses of decolonization/decoloniality. Pap. Lang. Lit. **55**, 201–226, 300 (2019)
8. Gutierrez, R.A.: Internal colonialism: an American theory of race. Bois Rev. Soc. Sci. Res. Race **1**, 281–295 (2004). https://doi.org/10.1017/S1742058X04042043
9. Howell, A., Richter-Montpetit, M.: Racism in Foucauldian security studies: biopolitics, liberal war, and the whitewashing of colonial and racial violence. Int. Polit. Sociol. **13**, 2–19 (2019). https://doi.org/10.1093/ips/oly031
10. Fitzpatrick, M.P.: The threat of "woolly-haired grandchildren": race, the colonial family and German nationalism. Hist. Fam. **14**, 356–368 (2009). https://doi.org/10.1016/j.hisfam.2009.08.002
11. Mendieta, E.: What can Latinas/os learn from Cornel West? The Latino postcolonial intellectual in the age of the exhaustion of public spheres. Nepantla Views South **4**, 213–233 (2003)

12. Anim-addo, J.: Acrid text: memory and auto/biography of the "new human." Fem. Rev. **100**, 167–171 (2012). https://doi.org/10.1057/fr.2011.58
13. Anim-addo, J.: Activist-mothers maybe, sisters surely? Black British feminism, absence and transformation. Fem. Rev. **108**, 44–60 (2014). https://doi.org/10.1057/fr.2014.35
14. Randolph, S.M.: Evelyn Brooks Higginbotham, the metalanguage of race, and the genealogy of black feminist legal theory. Signs **42**, 621 (2017). https://doi.org/10.1086/689629
15. Jean-Thomas, T.: Feminist breathing. Differences **30**, 92–117 (2019). https://doi.org/10.1215/10407391-7974016
16. Ilmonen, K.: Feminist storytelling and narratives of intersectionality. Signs **45**, 347–371 (2020). https://doi.org/10.1086/704989
17. Lepinard, E.: Impossible intersectionality? French feminists and the struggle for inclusion. Polit. Gend. **10**, 124–130 (2014). https://doi.org/10.1017/S1743923X13000585
18. Thomas, A.: "Little boats" in the storm: racial ambiguity and gender in two postemancipation adoptions. Womens Stud. Q. **43**, 147 (2015)
19. Shorter-Bourhanou, J.I.: Maria W. Stewart, ethnologist and proto-black feminist. Hypatia **37**, 60–75 (2022). https://doi.org/10.1017/hyp.2021.75
20. Waggoner, J.: Race, gender, and sanism: remapping mad feminist genealogies. Signs **47**, 885–904 (2022). https://doi.org/10.1086/718867
21. Stitt, J.F.: The aftereffects of slavery: a black feminist genealogy: feminism, race, transnationalism. Meridians **17**, 150–162 (2018). https://doi.org/10.1215/15366936-6955120
22. Cohen, P.: Rethinking the diasporama. Patterns Prejudice **33**, 3–22 (1999)
23. Adams, R.L., Jr.: Rewriting the African Diaspora in the Caribbean and Latin America: beyond disciplinary and national boundaries. Afr. Black Diaspora **5**, 3–20 (2012). https://doi.org/10.1080/17528631.2012.629430
24. Baldwin, K.: Proximate practices?: Gender, Diaspora, and the rise of black internationalism. Diaspora **12**, 231–246 (2003). https://doi.org/10.1353/dsp.2011.0006
25. Mastrovita, M.L., Hakes, D.: Digital library of Georgia. Ga. Libr. Q. **57**, 1–5 (2020)
26. Peet, L.: Growing the family tree. Libr. J. **141**, 27–31 (2016)
27. Richey, N.: Genealogy gems: beginning African American research. Ky. Libr. **77**, 33–35 (2013)
28. Scodari, C.: When markers meet marketing: ethnicity, race, hybridity, and kinship in genetic genealogy television advertising. Genealogy **1**, 22 (2017). https://doi.org/10.3390/genealogy1040022
29. Islam, G.: Business ethics and quantification: towards an ethics of numbers: JBE. J. Bus. Ethics **176**, 195–211 (2022). https://doi.org/10.1007/s10551-020-04694-z
30. Erwin-Davidson, L.: How conceptual-relational words are taught, used, and learned: a cross-case analysis (2019). https://libezproxy.syr.edu/login?url=https://www.proquest.com/dissertations-theses/how-conceptual-relational-words-are-taught-used/docview/2236411199/se-2?accountid=14214
31. Kramer Santamaria, C.: Family voices in two-way dual language education (2020). https://libezproxy.syr.edu/login?url=https://www.proquest.com/dissertations-theses/family-voices-two-way-dual-language-education/docview/2543453483/se-2?accountid=14214
32. Buehl, J., Chute, T., Fields, A.: Training in the archives: archival research as professional development. Coll. Compos. Commun. **64**, 274–305 (2012)
33. Ammons, S.K.: Boundaries at work: a study of work-family boundary stability within a large organization (2008). https://libezproxy.syr.edu/login?url=https://www.proquest.com/dissertations-theses/boundaries-at-work-study-family-boundary/docview/304531733/se-2?accountid=14214

34. Reznik, D.: I usually know a Jew when I see one?: Race, American Jewish identity, and 21st century U.S. film (2010). https://libezproxy.syr.edu/login?url=https://www.proquest.com/dissertations-theses/i-usually-know-jew-when-see-one-race-american/docview/743815773/se-2?accountid=14214
35. Haynes, C., Stewart, S., Allen, E.: Three paths, one struggle: black women and girls battling invisibility in U.S. classrooms. J. Negro Educ. **85**, 380–391 (2016)
36. Fredlund, K.: Feminist CHAT: collaboration, nineteenth-century women's clubs, and activity theory. Coll. Engl. **78**, 470–495 (2016)
37. Bresnahan, K.M.: From portraits to selfies: family photo-making rituals (2016). https://libezproxy.syr.edu/login?url=https://www.proquest.com/dissertations-theses/portraits-selfies-family-photo-making-rituals/docview/1862126836/se-2?accountid=14214
38. Cota, C.P.: Representation of Iranian-American identity and finding the funds of knowledge in the resilience of cultural heritage (2018). https://libezproxy.syr.edu/login?url=https://www.proquest.com/dissertations-theses/representation-iranian-american-identity-finding/docview/2041881374/se-2
39. Faulkner, S.L.: Crank up the feminism: poetic inquiry as feminist methodology. Humanities **7**, 85 (2018). https://doi.org/10.3390/h7030085

Do You Speak Meme? A Dynamic Digital Language for the Information Society

Minhyung Jo(✉), Shuyuan Mary Ho, and Gary Burnett

School of Information, Florida State University, Tallahassee, FL 32306, USA
{mj20bh,smho,gburnett}@fsu.edu

Abstract. The popularity of social media has made meme culture more popular than ever. As a result, memes have become a digital language that extends beyond digital culture within information societies. Unfortunately, recent studies have not examined diverse factors of meme communication in interactive contexts. This study investigates how memes are used for interactive forum-based communication as cybersecurity groups interact in cyberspace. More specifically, we examine synchronous meme communication between hackers and cyber defender groups from the 2022 Southeast Collegiate Cyber Defense Qualification Competition. We adopt the theoretical lens of information domains to examine interactive meme communication scripts in forum-based interactions. Collective identity and characteristics representing each information society tend to appear in synchronous meme communication between these two groups. This study also identifies unique information representation systems endemic to cyber security society. Moreover, this study interestingly finds that memes describing individual participants' emotions and attitudes are actively used in synchronous communication. These memes reflect individuals' emotions, and also describe the attitudes of the participants such as looking down at the opposite team. This phenomenon has rarely been observed in previous studies about meme communication in asynchronous situations.

Keywords: Meme communication · Cyber security society · Information behavior · Forum-based social media · Computer-mediated communication

1 Introduction

With the popularity of social media, a new digital culture has appeared—meme culture arrived. Meme culture has begun to draw attention as a research topic, and many studies have paid attention to its communicational aspects [14, 30]. Generally, meme communication occurring on widely used social media platforms like Facebook and Instagram is static and asynchronous [3]. For example, social media users can post memes and other users can react to the content whenever they want to unless the meme is removed. It is ever more important to investigate other types of social media platforms to further our understanding of meme communication, however, because types of communication may differ by social media platforms.

© The Author(s), under exclusive license to Springer Nature Switzerland AG 2023
I. Sserwanga et al. (Eds.): iConference 2023, LNCS 13971, pp. 523–534, 2023.
https://doi.org/10.1007/978-3-031-28035-1_39

Forum-based social media platforms like Slack, or Discord, on the other hand, have a couple of unique characteristics for meme communication. First, meme communication occurs in a synchronous context frequently [2, 35]. Second, meme communication on forum-based social media platforms affords individuals opportunities to voice opinions not only on their own but also in groups during discussions.

In cyberspace, the interaction between hackers and cyber defenders who are major groups within a cyber security society is ever more dynamic [16, 17]. Their interaction clearly impacts the safety, privacy, and personal cybersecurity of individuals as well as the stability of society. This suggests the importance of understanding the interaction between hackers and cyber defenders and how their thoughts and ideas are exchanged.

This study aims to explore meme communication between hacker and cyber defender groups by examining their communication in the Southeast Collegiate Cyber Defense Qualification Competition (SECCDQC) held on February 12, 2022, as an example. All the participants used Slack—a forum-based social media platform—as a communication channel.

Participants' communication scripts are examined and analyzed to understand how memes are used in a cyber security society, particularly by hackers and cyber defender groups. Our investigation is driven by this research question: *What are the characteristics of memes as a digital language in a synchronous situation used by cybersecurity groups*? To answer this question, we adopt the information domains framework that provides a theoretical lens for understanding information behaviors [6]. This study seeks to illustrate the characteristics of meme communication in a cyber security society and compare them to other information societies. Furthermore, this study hopes to provide theoretical implications and constructive guidelines for future studies on diverse meme communication.

2 Theoretical Background

This section discusses the origin and definition of memes and how they began to be recognized as a digital language. We will also discuss the significance and literature of cyber defense and offense context, and the information domains framework.

2.1 Memes as a Digital Language

Dawkins coined the term *meme* in 1976 [9] to refer to cultural units of information such as arts, fashions, and learned skills. Memes are transferrable and can evolve as they spread to the public and are modified over time. Memes have been widely adopted and used in diverse areas. For example, Zhu and Liu [36] use memes to refer to the cultural heritage of a specific ethnic group. Blackmore [4] describes memes as an abstract and cultural concept that survives by being spread from person to person.

Among meme variations, the *internet meme* is the most well-known, and can be easily found in online communities. Internet memes are defined in a similar way as the original definition – "units of popular culture that are circulated, imitated, and transformed by individual Internet users, creating a shared cultural experience in the process" [31]. There is no fixed template for internet memes, but generally, they consist of multiple audiovisual components like images, videos, and text (See Fig. 1). With these components, internet users can express their opinions in funnier, more effective, and more efficient ways. Nowadays, there are meme generators like ImgFlip and online databases that share looping video clips like GIPHY. They are often embedded in online services including social media platforms as a function to search for memes and allow internet users to find and use memes easily. As a result, internet memes have become more popular and the most representative type of meme, and internet users use them as a language for diverse kinds of communication [10, 11, 14, 28, 29, 32].

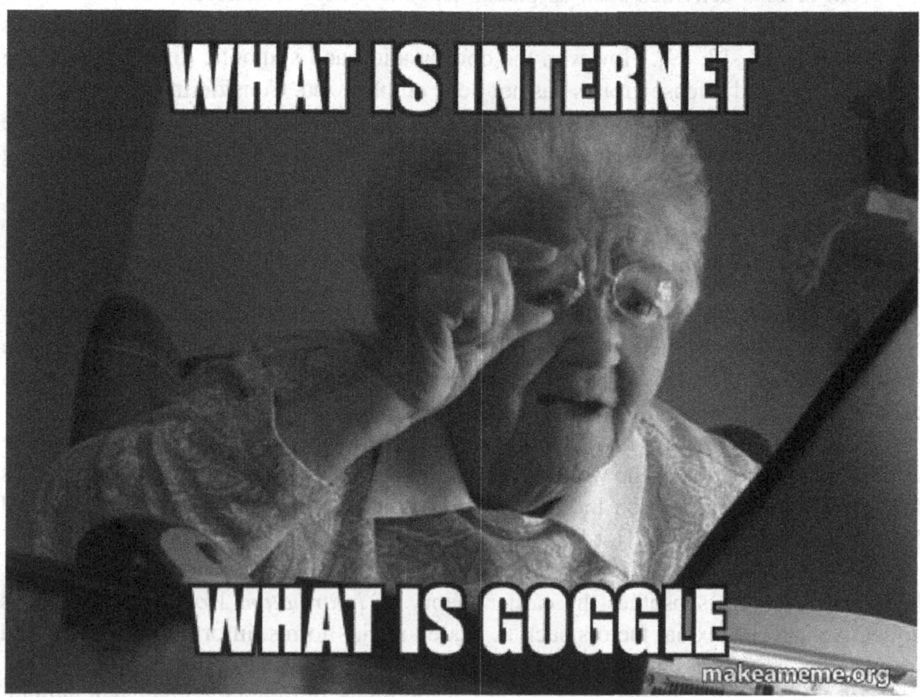

Fig. 1. An example of internet memes (Retrieved [34])

Meanwhile, "shared cultural experiences," as described in the definition of internet memes above, play an important role in meme communication [23, 26, 28, 31]. They are considered more significant in specific contexts such as politics or gender and are often described as creating "collective identities" that distinguish "insiders" from "outsiders" [12, 15, 20, 22, 33]. They are projected into memes, and readers are expected to know them in advance in order to understand the implications of the memes as the creator intended [1, 22, 24, 25]. In other words, insiders who belong to the same group as the creator can understand the meme as intended, while outsiders might not share this understanding, even though the meme looks familiar to them [27]. This indicates that internet memes play a role as a digital language among internet users who share the same "collective identities."

2.2 The Context of Cyber Security

Cyber security is increasingly important as information technology becomes more deeply entrenched in our lives. Moreover, as cyber threats become more sophisticated and serious, the necessity of enhancing cyber security also becomes even more important [13]. In this regard, there have been numerous efforts to investigate interaction and communication between cyber defenders and offenders (i.e., hackers) because this allows cyber defenders to improve their cyber defense consciousness [17]; it also provides practical implications for the best cyber security practice [16].

From diverse activities such as games and laboratory exercises, previous studies have found that interaction and communication between cyber defenders and hackers are dynamic [13, 18, 19]. However, the conversation and symbolic discussion among cyber defense and offense groups has not been emphasized. Considering the popularity of meme culture and the dynamic interaction between two groups, exploring the meme communication of those two groups can provide new insight and a deeper understanding of meme communication.

2.3 Information Domains

This study adopted the *Information domains* theory as a theoretical framework. This theory was outlined by Burnett [6] as a framework for understanding and examining human information behaviors [6]. There are three intertwined domains, and which interact with each other – the domains of the individual, the social, and signification.

The domain of the individual examines information behavior through the lens of the individual's perception of the world, information-seeking processes, and characteristics [6]. This domain focuses on the role of individual cognitive, affective, and physical factors in information behavior [8].

Second, *the domain of the social* examines information behavior from a broader level. This domain subsumes the earlier theory of *Information Worlds,* and includes collective and contextual factors such as shared social norms, information values, and information boundaries as influencing factors in information behavior [5, 6, 21].

Third, *the domain of signification* focuses on modes of interaction between individuals and social groups [6]. This domain examines the various systems – linguistic and otherwise – used to encode and represent information and to enable communications and information sharing [6, 7]. All interaction between individuals and other individuals, between individuals and social groups, and between different social groups depends on the tools and practices of the domain of signification.

As described above, this theory provides a theoretical lens for understanding information behaviors of diverse information societies. Therefore, it is used here to examine aspects of meme communication between cyber defenders and hackers across and between the three information domains.

3 Method

In the method section, we first introduce the detailed context of the SECCDQC. Then, we discuss how the dataset was collected, and describe its main characteristics.

3.1 The Context of Southeast Collegiate Cyber Defense Qualification (SECCDQC)

The Southeast Collegiate Cyber Defense Qualification Competition (SECCDQC) is an annual event held by the Center for Infrastructure Assurance and Security (CIAS) and the University of Texas San Antonio (UTSA) as a part of the ten regions of the National Collegiate Cyber Defense Competition (NCCDC). The pre-qualifier event lasts 6 h, with 27 competing teams from colleges and universities in the southeast region of the United States. Students—representing cyber defenders from 27 teams—are commissioned to defend their cyberinfrastructure (i.e., systems and networks) from hackers' attacks. Cyber defenders and hackers meet in cyberspace.

This study focuses on the latest SECCDQC pre-qualifier event, held on February 12, 2022. The entire pre-qualifier event was launched and conducted through Amazon's AWS cloud server, and a forum-based social media platform, Slack was used as a discussion channel through which participants communicate. There were three groups in the competition (See Table 1); this study looks at communications among the participant groups.

This competition is a good example of how memes are used as a digital language because the settings of this competition have great situational characteristics – there are two opposite groups, each with their own duties, and their communication occurs synchronously through Slack. These characteristics have not been actively explored in previous studies on meme communication. Therefore, through the analysis of meme communication between these two groups, this study hopes to gain new insight into memes and their communicational characteristics.

Table 1. Description of participant groups in SECCDQC

Team	Description
Blue	The cyber defender (students) group with the mission to defend—taking the charge to defend information and information systems
Red	The hacker group with the mission to attack
Gold	The organization (the organizer) group with the mission to provide products/services requiring information confidentiality, integrity, availability (CIA), and the continuity of operations

3.2 Data Collection

The dataset was directly collected from Slack and encoded as a Word document. It contains chat logs from the 6-h SECCDQC 2022 competition. The dataset includes user profiles, time stamps, modification status, profile pictures, and links to the source of the memes used. Private information such as the participants' names has been removed and is described as their role such as 'Blue Team Coach' or 'Blue Team Captain.' There are 54 memes, and detailed information about the characteristics of collected memes are below (See Table 2).

Table 2. General characteristics of the collected memes

Categories	Information	Values
Types of memes	Static Animated	29 19
Origination of memes	External resources (Outside of Slack) Internal resources (GIPHY* in Slack)	34 14
Invalid	Unknown, not displayed, or not available	6

* 'GIPHY' is an embedded function within Slack to search for memes.

4 Data Analysis and Discussion

The collected dataset has been analyzed qualitatively with an interpretivist focus based on the information domains theory. Firstly, we looked at the surface features of the memes as shown in Table 2. Then, we tried to identify the traits and attributes behind each meme such as emotions or hacking techniques. Based on the analysis, we below discuss the characteristics of the memes.

4.1 Data Analysis

In this section, we examine the collected memes based on the information domains framework and provide examples. Not all 54 memes are introduced here, but only the most representative memes for each domain.

The Domain of the Individual. In this domain, the most common factor in the dataset's memes was the individual's emotions and attitudes, such as boredom or supercilious-ness (See Fig. 2). Participants used memes from both inside and outside of Slack, but external resources were used more frequently. These memes were posted more actively by members of the red team (hackers) than the blue team (defenders).

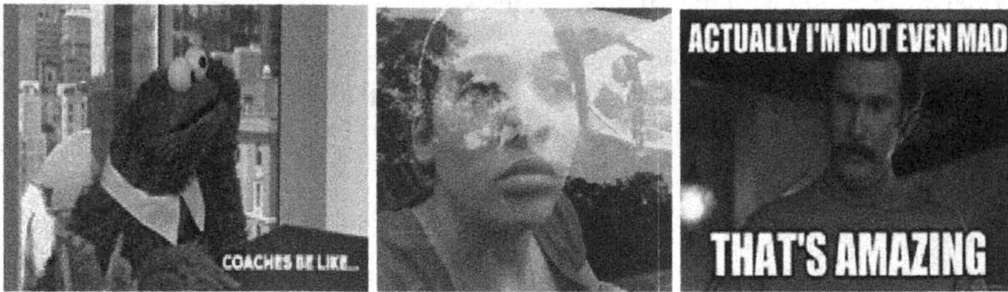

Fig. 2. The left and middle memes are animated-type and came from GIPHY. The right meme is a static type, and it was brought by an individual participant.

The Domain of the Social. As discussed before, this domain includes the characteris-tics of collective "information worlds." In this study, the three participant groups can be considered to be three different information worlds, and each group's characteristics can be seen in the memes that they use.

Each group's characteristics are related to its defined duty within the competition. The duty of the red team was to attack the cyber defenders' system successfully, and it was reflected in their use of memes including images of 'attacking' or the 'chaotic situation' of the opposing side (See Fig. 3). Conversely, the duty of the blue team was defending attacks from the red team. Likewise, this was projected into memes representing their successful or frustrating situation after the attack (See Fig. 4). Lastly, since the duty of the gold team was to facilitate the event rather than to participate in the competition, their memes tend to be neutral, containing only information related to the progress of the event (See Fig. 5).

Fig. 3. Memes posted by the red team The left meme is static and describes a chaotic situation that the blue team, the cyber defender group faced from the red team's attack. The right meme is animated-type and came from GIPHY. It describes the massive attack of the red team on the blue team.

Fig. 4. Memes posted by the blue team. The left meme is animated-type and describes the situation attacked by the red team. The right meme is static, and it describes the failure of the red team's attack.

The Domain of Signification. Our analysis indicates that the participant groups used memes to describe the hacking techniques that they used. They show the way of representing information of cyber security society. For example, the term "Shell" refers

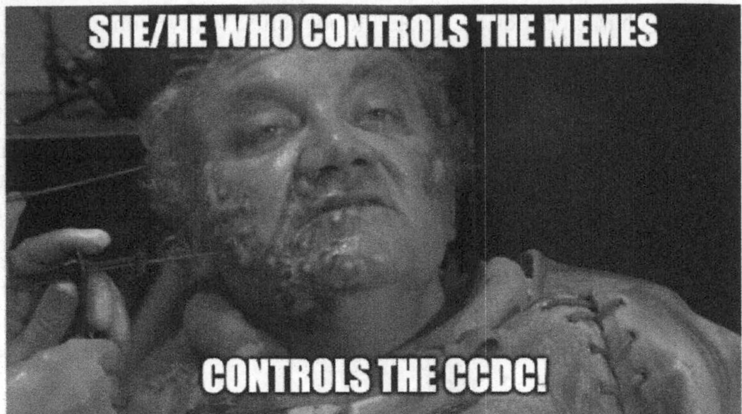

Fig. 5. Meme posted by the gold team This meme is a static type and it describes a welcoming greeting to the participant groups.

both to the hard outer casing of a certain kind of sea creature and, in the cyber security world, to a Unix shell script programming language. However, it is hard to describe the Unix shell script programming language through memes, so the image of shellfish is used as a metaphoric reference (See Fig. 6). Likewise, some terms like "log" or specific expressions within the cyber security world are implicitly represented through meme metaphors using familiar images (See Fig. 7).

Fig. 6. Memes that describe the hacking techniques used in the competition Both memes describe the hacking techniques used in the competition - Shell. The left meme is animated-type and came from GIPHY. The right meme is a static type and is brought by the individual participant.

Fig. 7. Memes that describe the specific situation and terminology The left meme describes the under-attack situation of Trojan hacking. The right meme describes the term "log" which means programming codes as food. Both memes adopted images from pop culture – anime.

4.2 Discussion

Through our analysis, based on the information domains framework, we found the following characteristics of memes as a digital language in the synchronous interactions among participant groups in the SECCDQC. First, at the individual level, memes usually represent individuals' emotions and attitudes as discussed in the theoretical framework section. Second, we found that memes reflected each group's characteristics (or defined duties, in the case of this study) via the images used in the memes, which are clearly related to each group's duty. This suggests that meme communication at the group level between hackers and cyber defender groups reflects not only individual characteristics, but also shared group norms and values, as the domain of the social discusses. Third, we also noticed that the collected memes use modes of signification and representation that reflect unique practices and terminologies of the cyber security society. Both hacker and cyber defender groups communicated with each other through such distinctive practices of representation. In other words, the memes in the dataset functioned as a digital language among the participant groups as suggested by the domain of signification. This further suggests that people outside of the cyber security community might not fully understand the memes as intended; the memes play a role as a kind of semiotic system among cyber security societies. Lastly, although the participants preferred to bring their memes outside of Slack, we found that GIPHY, an embedded function in Slack was used frequently at both individual and group levels. Except for the gold team, about a third of the memes in each group came from GIPHY. GIPHY was also frequently used to represent specific types of information like the example of 'Unix Shell.'

5 Conclusion

This exploration of meme communication among the participant groups in SECCDQC, suggests how memes can function as a part of the digital language among cyber security communities, particularly in a synchronous context. We also found several characteristics of meme communication at not only individual and group levels but also the whole cyber security society level through the information domains framework.

Our findings suggest that meme communication between hackers and cyber defenders also reflects each group's characteristics, along the lines of the "collective identity" discussed in the previous studies. We also found that there is a unique mode of representing information among this cyber security society group, and that this mode is reflected in the memes used by participants. And we could observe that memes were frequently used to simply express individual participants' personal emotions and attitudes like boredom or superciliousness in the synchronous group discussion. It is not observed frequently in asynchronous meme communication in previous studies. Lastly, the participants actively used GIPHY, which has not been highlighted in previous studies on meme communication, but it might be an important aspect of active meme communication at both individual and group levels, suggesting that the domain of signification may be influenced not only by individual choice or normative social behaviors, but also by the affordances of technological platforms and tools.

Meanwhile, this study examined meme communication in only one specific event. Therefore, there should be further studies with more in-depth consideration of diverse aspects such as synchronous communicational environments and meme communication among cyber security societies. It is also necessary to get a deeper understanding of meme communication in not only cyber security society but also in other information worlds. This paper hopes to provide a useful beginning point for such future studies.

References

1. Askanius, T.: On frogs, monkeys, and execution memes: exploring the humor-hate nexus at the intersection of neo-Nazi and alt-right movements in Sweden. Telev. New Med. **22**(2), 147–165 (2021). https://doi.org/10.1177/1527476420982234
2. Barnad, B.: Discord to support synchronous communication in distance learning. In: Proceeding of the 2nd Annual Conference on Blended Learning, Educational Technology and Innovation (ACBLETI 2020), vol. 560, pp. 34–38 (2021). https://doi.org/10.2991/assehr.k.210615.007
3. Benson, D.: The power of asynchronous communication. The Social Chic (2012). http://thesocialchic.com/2012/04/29/the-power-of-asynchronous-communication/
4. Blackmore, S.: The Meme Machine. Oxford University Press, Oxford (1999)
5. Burnett, G., Jaeger, P.T.: Small worlds, lifeworlds, and information: the ramifications of the information behaviors of social groups in public policy and the public sphere. Inf. Res. **13**(2), 346 (2008). http://informationr.net/ir/13-2/paper346.html
6. Burnett, G.: Information worlds and interpretive practices: toward an integration of domains. J. Inf. Sci. Theory Pract. **3**(3), 6–16 (2015). https://doi.org/10.1633/JISTaP.2015.3.3.1
7. Burnett, K., Burnett, G.: Information domains, information ethics. In: Proceedings of the Tenth International Conference on Conceptions of Library and Information Science. Information Research, vol. 24, no. 4, paper colis1942 (2019). http://informationr.net/ir/24-4/colis/colis1942.html
8. Burnett, K., Burnett, G.: Information domains and the analysis of distributed morality in "always onlife" information societies. In: 2020 Proceedings of the iConference. iConference (2020). http://hdl.handle.net/2142/106568
9. Dawkins, R.: The Selfish Gene. Oxford University Press, Oxford (1976)

10. Davison, P.: 9. The language of Internet memes. In: Mandiberg, M. (ed.) The Social Media Reader, pp. 120–134. New York University Press (2012). https://doi.org/10.18574/9780814763025-011
11. DeCook, J.R.: Memes and symbolic violence:# proudboys and the use of memes for propaganda and the construction of collective identity. Learn. Med. Technol. **43**(4), 485–504 (2018). https://doi.org/10.1080/17439884.2018.1544149
12. Gal, N., Shifman, L., Kampf, Z.: "It gets better": Internet memes and the construction of collective identity. New Med. Soc. **18**(8), 1698–1714 (2016). https://doi.org/10.1177/1461444814568784
13. Gross, M., Ho, S.M.: Collective learning for increasing cyber defense consciousness: an activity system analysis. J. Inf. Syst. Educ. **32**(1), 65–76 (2021)
14. Grundlingh, L.: Memes as speech acts. Soc. Semiot. **28**(2), 147–168 (2018). https://doi.org/10.1080/10350330.2017.1303020
15. Guenther, L., Ruhrmann, G., Bischoff, J., Penzel, T., Weber, A.: Strategic framing and social media engagement: analyzing memes posted by the German Identitarian Movement on Facebook. Soc. Media + Soc. **6**(1), 2056305119898777 (2020). https://doi.org/10.1177/2056305119898777
16. Ho, S.M., von Eberstein, A., Chatmon, C.: Expansive learning in cyber defense: transformation of organizational information security culture. In: The 12th Annual Symposium on Information Assurance (ASIA 2017), Albany, NY, 6–8 June 2017, pp. 23–28 (2017)
17. Ho, S.M., Gross, M.: Consciousness of cyber defense: a collective activity system for developing organizational cyber awareness. Comput. Secur. **108**, 102357 (2021). https://doi.org/10.1016/j.cose.2021.102357
18. Ho, S.M., Oliveira, D., Rathi, R.: Consciousness of cyber defense: boundary objects for expansive learning through creation of contradictions. In: Nah, F.-H., Siau, K. (eds.) HCII 2019. LNCS, vol. 11589, pp. 338–353. Springer, Cham (2019). https://doi.org/10.1007/978-3-030-22338-0_28
19. Ho, S.M., Oliveira, D., Rathi, R.: The shield and the sword: expanding learning in cyber defense through competition. In: Proceedings of the iConference 2019, Illinois Digital Environment for Access to Learning and Scholarship (IDEALS), Washington, DC., 31 March–3 April 2019, pp. 1–4 (2019). https://doi.org/10.21900/iconf.2019.103318
20. Ismangil, M.: Subversive nationalism through memes: a dota 2 case study. Stud. Ethn. Nationalism **19**(2), 227–245 (2019). https://doi.org/10.1111/sena.12298
21. Jaeger, P.T., Burnett, G.: Information Worlds: Social Context, Technology, & Information Behavior in the Age of the Internet. Routledge, New York (2010)
22. Kanai, A.: Sociality and classification: reading gender, race, and class in a humorous meme. Soc. Med. + Soc. **2**(4), 1–12 (2016). https://doi.org/10.1177/2056305116672884
23. Miltner, K.M.: Internet memes. SAGE Handb. Soc. Med. **55**, 412–428 (2018)
24. Mina, A.X.: Batman, pandaman and the blind man: a case study in social change memes and Internet censorship in China. J. Vis. Cult. **13**(3), 359–375 (2014). https://doi.org/10.1177/1470412914546576
25. Mortensen, M., Neumayer, C.: The playful politics of memes. Inf. Commun. Soc. **24**(16), 2367–2377 (2021). https://doi.org/10.1080/1369118X.2021.1979622
26. Papapicco, C., Mininni, G.: Impact memes: PhDs HuMor(e). Multimedia Tools and Applications **79**(47), 35973–35994 (2020). https://doi.org/10.1007/s11042-020-09166-0
27. Pelletier-Gagnon, J., Pérez Trujillo Diniz, A.: Colonizing Pepe: Internet memes as cyberplaces. Space Cult. **24**(1), 4–18 (2021). https://doi.org/10.1177/1206331218776188
28. Petrova, Y.: Meme language, its impact on digital culture and collective thinking. In: E3S Web of Conferences, vol. 273, no. 11026 (2021). https://doi.org/10.1051/e3sconf/202127311026
29. Procházka, O.: Internet memes–a new literacy? Ostrava J. Engl. Philol. **6**(1), 53–74 (2014)

30. Rashiti, V.: When did we become the meme generation? A walk through the origin of memes. Youth Time (2020). https://youth-time.eu/when-did-we-become-the-meme-generation-a-walk-through-the-origin-of-memes/
31. Shifman, L.: Memes in a digital world: reconciling with a conceptual troublemaker. J. Comput.-Mediat. Commun. **18**(3), 362–377 (2013). https://doi.org/10.1111/jcc4.12013
32. Styler, W.: The linguistics of memes. UCSD (n.d.). https://wstyler.ucsd.edu/talks/meme_linguistics.html/
33. Trillò, T., Shifman, L.: Memetic commemorations: remixing far-right values in digital spheres. Inf. Commun. Soc. **24**(16), 2482–2501 (2021). https://doi.org/10.1080/1369118X.2021.1974516
34. What is internet What is goggle [Online image]: Make a Meme (n.d.). https://makeameme.org/meme/what-is-internet-eacc79fbc6
35. White, K., Grierson, H., Wodehouse, A.: Using Slack for synchronous and asynchronous communication in a global design project. In: Proceedings of the 19th International Conference on Engineering and Product Design Education, pp. 346–351. Design Society (2017). ISBN 9781904670841
36. Zhu, W.S., Liu, X.: Vernacular landscapes building and protection of meme in the Dong ethnic minority regions. Soc. Sci. Q. **101**(2), 732–743 (2020). https://doi.org/10.1111/ssqu.12769

Author Index

© The Editor(s) (if applicable) and The Author(s), under exclusive license to Springer Nature Switzerland AG 2023

I. Sserwanga et al. (Eds.): iConference 2023, LNCS 13971, pp. 535–538, 2023.
https://doi.org/10.1007/978-3-031-28035-1

Printed in the United States
by Baker & Taylor Publisher Services